John Muir:
Nature Writings

Happy Hour Books

Published by:

HAPPY HOUR BOOKS

www.happyhoursbooks.com

email: happyhourbooks1@gmail.com

First published by Happy Hour Books 2024

Title : **John Muir : Nature Writings**

Paperback ISBN : 9789358480672

Hardback ISBN : 9789358480689

CONTENTS

THE STORY OF MY BOYHOOD AND YOUTH

CHAPTER I

THE SIERRA NEVADA

Go where you may within the bounds of California, mountains are ever in sight, charming and glorifying every landscape. Yet so simple and massive is the topography of the State in general views, that the main central portion displays only one valley, and two chains of mountains which seem almost perfectly regular in trend and height: the Coast Range on the west side, the Sierra Nevada on the east. These two ranges coming together in curves on the north and south inclose a magnificent basin, with a level floor more than 400 miles long, and from 35 to 60 miles wide. This is the grand Central Valley of California, the waters of which have only one outlet to the sea through the Golden Gate. But with this general simplicity of features there is great complexity of hidden detail. The Coast Range, rising as a grand green barrier against the ocean, from 2000 to 8000 feet high, is composed of innumerable forest-crowned spurs, ridges, and rolling hill-waves which inclose a multitude of smaller valleys; some looking out through long, forest-lined vistas to the sea; others, with but few trees, to the Central Valley; while a thousand others yet smaller are embosomed and concealed in mild, round-browed hills, each, with its own climate, soil, and productions.

Making your way through the mazes of the Coast Range to the summit of any of the inner peaks or passes opposite San Francisco, in the clear springtime, the grandest and most telling of all California landscapes is outspread before you. At your feet lies the great Central Valley glowing golden in the sunshine, extending north and south farther than the eye can reach, one smooth, flowery, lake-like bed of fertile soil. Along its eastern margin rises the mighty Sierra, miles in height, reposing like a smooth, cumulous cloud in the sunny sky, and so gloriously colored, and so luminous, it seems to be not clothed with light, but wholly composed of it, like the wall of some celestial city. Along the top, and extending a good way down, you see a pale, pearl-gray belt of snow; and below it a belt of blue and dark purple, marking the extension of the forests; and along the base of the range a broad belt of rose-purple and yellow, where lie the minor's gold-fields and the foot-hill gardens. All these colored belts blending smoothly make a wall of light ineffably fine, and as beautiful as a rainbow, yet firm as adamant.

When I first enjoyed this superb view, one glowing April day, from the summit of the Pacheco Pass, the Central Valley, but little trampled or plowed as yet, was one furred, rich sheet of golden compositae, and the luminous wall of the mountains shone in all its glory. Then it seemed to me the Sierra should be called not the Nevada, or Snowy Range, but the Range of Light. And after ten years spent in the heart of it, rejoicing and wondering, bathing in its glorious floods of light, seeing the sunbursts of morning among the icy peaks, the noonday radiance on the trees and rocks and snow, the flush of the alpenglow, and a thousand dashing waterfalls with their marvelous abundance of irised spray, it still seems to me above all others the Range of Light, the most divinely beautiful of all the mountain-chains I have ever seen.

The Sierra is about 500 miles long, 70 miles wide, and from 7000 to nearly 15,000 feet high. In general views no mark of man is visible on it, nor anything to suggest the richness of the life it cherishes, or the depth and grandeur of its sculpture. None of its magnificent forest-crowned ridges rises much above the general level to publish its wealth. No great valley or lake is seen, or river, or group of well-marked features of any kind, standing out in distinct pictures. Even the summit-peaks, so clear and high in the sky, seem comparatively smooth and featureless. Nevertheless, glaciers are still at work in the shadows of the peaks, and thousands of lakes and meadows shine and bloom beneath them, and the whole range is furrowed with cañons to a depth of from 2000 to 5000 feet, in which once flowed majestic glaciers, and in which now flow and sing a band of beautiful rivers.

Though of such stupendous depth, these famous cañons are not raw, gloomy, jagged-walled gorges, savage and inaccessible. With rough passages here and there they still make delightful pathways for the mountaineer, conducting from the fertile lowlands to the highest icy fountains, as a kind of mountain streets full of charming life and light, graded and sculptured by the ancient glaciers, and presenting, throughout all their courses, a rich variety of novel and attractive scenery, the most attractive that has yet been discovered in the mountain-ranges of the world.

In many places, especially in the middle region of the western flank of the range, the main cañons widen into spacious valleys or parks, diversified like artificial landscape-gardens, with charming groves and meadows, and thickets of blooming bushes, while the lofty, retiring walls, infinitely varied in form and sculpture, are fringed with ferns, flowering-plants of many species, oaks, and evergreens, which find anchorage on a thousand narrow steps and benches; while the whole is enlivened and made glorious with rejoicing streams that come dancing and foaming over the sunny brows of the cliffs to join the shining river that flows in tranquil beauty down the middle of each one of them.

The walls of these park valleys of the Yosemite kind are made up of rocks mountains in size, partly separated from each other by narrow gorges and side-cañons; and they are so sheer in front, and so compactly built together on a level floor, that, comprehensively seen, the parks they inclose look like immense halls or temples lighted from above. Every rock seems to glow with life. Some lean back in majestic repose; others, absolutely sheer, or nearly so, for thousands of feet, advance their brows in thoughtful attitudes beyond their companions, giving welcome to storms and calms alike, seemingly conscious yet heedless of everything going on about them, awful in stern majesty, types of permanence, yet associated with beauty of the frailest and most fleeting forms; their feet set in pine-groves and gay emerald meadows, their brows in the sky; bathed in light, bathed in floods of singing water, while snow-clouds, avalanches, and the winds shine and surge and wreathe about them as the years go by, as if into these mountain mansions Nature had taken pains to gather her choicest treasures to draw her lovers into close and confiding communion with her.

Here, too, in the middle region of deepest cañons are the grandest forest-trees, the Sequoia, king of conifers, the noble Sugar and Yellow Pines, Douglas Spruce, Libocedrus, and the Silver Firs, each a giant of its kind, assembled together in one and the same forest, surpassing all other coniferous forests in the world, both in the number of its species and in the size and beauty of its trees. The winds flow in melody through their colossal spires, and they are vocal everywhere with the songs of birds and running water. Miles of fragrant ceanothus and manzanita bushes bloom beneath them, and lily gardens and meadows, and damp, ferny glens in endless variety of fragrance and color, compelling the admiration of every observer. Sweeping on over ridge and valley, these noble trees extend a continuous belt from end to end of the range, only slightly interrupted by sheer-walled cañons at intervals of about fifteen and twenty miles. Here the great burly brown bears delight to roam, harmonizing with the brown boles of the trees beneath which they feed. Deer, also, dwell here, and find food and shelter in the ceanothus tangles, with a multitude of smaller people. Above this region of giants, the trees grow smaller until the utmost limit of the timber line is reached on the stormy mountain-slopes at a height of from ten to twelve thousand feet above the sea, where the Dwarf Pine is so lowly and hard beset by storms and heavy snow, it is pressed into flat tangles, over the tops of which we may easily walk. Below the main forest belt the trees likewise diminish in size, frost and burning drought repressing and blasting alike.

The rose-purple zone along the base of the range comprehends nearly all the famous gold region of California. And here it was that miners from every country under the sun assembled in a wild, torrent-like rush to seek their fortunes. On the banks of every river, ravine, and gully they have left their marks. Every gravel- and boulder-bed has been desperately riddled over and over again. But in this region the pick and shovel, once wielded with savage enthusiasm, have been laid away, and only quartz-mining is now being carried on to any considerable extent. The zone in general is made up of low, tawny, waving foot-hills, roughened here and there with brush and trees, and outcropping masses of slate, colored gray and red with lichens. The smaller masses of slate, rising abruptly from the dry, grassy sod in leaning slabs, look like ancient tombstones in a deserted burying-ground. In early spring, say from February to April, the whole of this foot-hill belt is a paradise of bees and flowers. Refreshing rains then fall freely, birds are busy building their nests, and the sunshine is balmy and delightful. But by the end of May the soil, plants, and sky seem to have been baked in an oven. Most of the plants crumble to dust beneath the foot, and the ground is full of cracks; while the thirsty traveler gazes with eager longing through the burning glare to the snowy summits looming like hazy clouds in the distance.

The trees, mostly Quercus Douglasii and Pinus Sabiniana, thirty to forty feet high, with thin, pale-green foliage, stand far apart and cast but little shade. Lizards glide about on the rocks enjoying a constitution that no drought can dry, and ants in amazing numbers, whose tiny sparks of life seem to burn the brighter with the increasing heat, ramble industriously in long trains in search of food. Crows, ravens, magpies—friends in distress—gather on the ground beneath the best shade-trees, panting with drooping wings and bills wide open, scarce a note from any of them during the midday hours. Quails, too, seek the shade during the heat of the day about tepid pools in the channels of the larger mid-river streams. Rabbits scurry from thicket to thicket among the ceanothus bushes, and occasionally a long-eared hare is seen cantering gracefully across the wider openings. The nights are calm and dewless during the summer, and a thousand voices proclaim the abundance of life, notwithstanding the desolating effect of dry sunshine on the plants and larger animals. The hylas make a delightfully pure and tranquil music after sunset; and coyotes, the little, despised dogs of the wilderness, brave, hardy fellows, looking like withered wisps of hay, bark in chorus for hours. Mining-towns, most of them dead, and a few living ones with bright bits of cultivation about them, occur at long intervals along the belt, and cottages covered with climbing roses, in the midst of orange and peach orchards, and sweet-scented hay-fields in fertile flats where water for irrigation may be had. But they are mostly far apart, and make scarce any mark in general views.

Every winter the High Sierra and the middle forest region get snow in glorious abundance, and even the foot-hills are at times whitened. Then all the range looks like a vast beveled wall of purest marble. The rough places are then made smooth, the death and decay of the year is covered gently and kindly, and the ground seems as clean as the sky. And though silent in its flight from the clouds, and when it is taking its place on rock, or tree, or grassy meadow, how soon the gentle snow finds a voice! Slipping from the heights, gathering in avalanches, it booms and roars like thunder, and makes a glorious show as it sweeps down the mountain-side, arrayed in long, silken streamers and wreathing, swirling films of crystal dust.

The north half of the range is mostly covered with floods of lava, and dotted with volcanoes and craters, some of them recent and perfect in form, others in various stages of decay. The south half is composed of granite nearly from base to summit, while a considerable number of peaks, in the middle of the range, are capped with metamorphic slates, among which are Mounts Dana and Gibbs to the east of Yosemite Valley. Mount Whitney, the culminating point of the range near its southern extremity, lifts its helmet-shaped crest to a height of nearly 14,700 feet. Mount Shasta, a colossal volcanic cone, rises to a height of 14,440 feet at the northern extremity, and forms a noble landmark for all the surrounding region within a radius of a hundred miles. Residual masses of volcanic rocks occur throughout most of the granitic southern portion also, and a considerable number of old volcanoes on the flanks, especially along the eastern base of the range near Mono Lake and southward. But it is only to the northward that the entire range, from base to summit, is covered with lava.

From the summit of Mount Whitney only granite is seen. Innumerable peaks and spires but little lower than its own storm-beaten crags rise in groups like forest-trees, in full view, segregated by cañons of tremendous depth and ruggedness. On Shasta nearly every feature in the vast view speaks of the old volcanic fires. Far to the northward, in Oregon, the icy volcanoes of Mount Pitt and the Three Sisters rise above the dark evergreen woods. Southward innumerable smaller craters and cones are distributed along the axis of the range and on each flank. Of these, Lassen's Butte is the highest, being nearly 11,000 feet above sea-level. Miles of its flanks are reeking and bubbling with hot springs, many of them so boisterous and sulphurous they seem over ready to become spouting geysers like those of the Yellowstone.

The Cinder Cone near marks the most recent volcanic eruption in the Sierra. It is a symmetrical truncated cone about 700 feet high, covered with gray cinders and ashes, and has a regular unchanged crater on its summit, in which a few small Two-leaved Pines are growing. These show that the age of the cone is not less than eighty years. It stands between two lakes, which a short time ago were one. Before the cone was built, a flood of rough vesicular lava was poured into the lake, cutting it in two, and, overflowing its banks, the fiery flood advanced into the pine-woods, overwhelming the trees in its way, the charred ends of some of which may still be seen projecting from beneath the snout of the lava-stream where it came to rest. Later still there was an eruption of ashes and loose obsidian cinders, probably from the same vent, which, besides forming the Cinder Cone, scattered a heavy shower over the surrounding woods for miles to a depth of from six inches to several feet.

The history of this last Sierra eruption is also preserved in the traditions of the Pitt River Indians. They tell of a fearful time of darkness, when the sky was black with ashes and smoke that threatened every living thing with death, and that when at length the sun appeared once more it was red like blood.

Less recent craters in great numbers roughen the adjacent region; some of them with lakes in their throats, others overgrown with trees and flowers, Nature in these old hearths and firesides having literally given beauty for ashes. On the northwest side of Mount Shasta there is a subordinate cone about 3000 feet below the summit, which, has been active subsequent to the breaking up of the main ice-cap that once covered the mountain, as is shown by its comparatively unwasted crater and the streams of unglaciated lava radiating from it. The main summit is about a mile and a half in diameter, bounded by small crumbling peaks and ridges, among which we seek in vain for the outlines of the ancient crater.

These ruinous masses, and the deep glacial grooves that flute the sides of the mountain, show that it has been considerably lowered and wasted by ice; how much we have no sure means of knowing. Just below the extreme summit hot sulphurous gases and vapor issue from irregular fissures, mixed with spray derived from melting snow, the last feeble expression of the mighty force that built the mountain. Not in one great convulsion was Shasta given birth. The crags of the summit and the sections exposed by the glaciers down the sides display enough of its internal framework to prove that comparatively long periods of quiescence intervened between many distinct eruptions, during which the cooling lavas ceased to flow, and became permanent additions to the bulk of the growing mountain. With alternate haste and deliberation eruption succeeded eruption till the old volcano surpassed even its present sublime height.

Standing on the icy top of this, the grandest of all the fire-mountains of the Sierra, we can hardly fail to look forward to its next eruption. Gardens, vineyards, homes have been planted confidingly on the flanks of volcanoes which, after remaining steadfast for ages, have suddenly blazed into violent action, and poured forth overwhelming floods of fire. It is known that more than a thousand years of cool calm have intervened between violent eruptions. Like gigantic geysers spouting molten rock instead of water, volcanoes work and rest, and we have no sure means of knowing whether they are dead when still, or only sleeping.

Along the western base of the range a telling series of sedimentary rocks containing the early history of the Sierra are now being studied. But leaving for the present these first chapters, we see that only a very short geological time ago, just before the coming on of that winter of winters called the glacial period, a vast deluge of molten rocks poured from many a chasm and crater on the flanks and summit of the range, filling lake basins and river channels, and obliterating nearly every existing feature on the northern portion. At length these all-destroying floods ceased to flow. But while the great volcanic cones built up along the axis still burned and smoked, the whole Sierra passed under the domain of ice and snow. Then over the bald, featureless, fire-blackened mountains, glaciers began to crawl, covering them from the summits to the sea with a mantle of ice; and then with infinite deliberation the work went on of sculpturing the range anew. These mighty agents of erosion, halting never through unnumbered centuries, crushed and ground the flinty lavas and granites beneath their crystal folds, wasting and building until in the fullness of time the Sierra was born again, brought to light nearly as we behold it today, with glaciers and snow-crushed pines at the top of the range, wheat-fields and orange-groves at the foot of it.

This change from icy darkness and death to life and beauty was slow, as we count time, and is still going on, north and south, over all the world wherever glaciers exist, whether in the form of distinct rivers, as in Switzerland, Norway, the mountains of Asia, and the Pacific Coast; or in continuous mantling folds, as in portions of Alaska, Greenland, Franz-Joseph-Land, Nova Zembla, Spitzbergen, and the lands about the South Pole. But in no country, as far as I know, may these majestic changes be studied to better advantage than in the plains and mountains of California.

Toward the close of the glacial period, when the snow-clouds became less fertile and the melting waste of sunshine became greater, the lower folds of the ice-sheet in California, discharging fleets of icebergs into the sea, began to shallow and recede from the lowlands, and then move slowly up the flanks of the Sierra in compliance with the changes of climate. The great white mantle on the mountains broke up into a series of glaciers more or less distinct and river-like, with many tributaries, and these again were melted and divided into still smaller glaciers, until now only a few of the smallest residual topmost branches of the grand system exist on the cool slopes of the summit peaks.

Plants and animals, biding their time, closely followed the retiring ice, bestowing quick and joyous animation on the new-born landscapes. Pine-trees marched up the sun-warmed moraines in long, hopeful files, taking the ground and establishing themselves as soon as it was ready for them; brown-spiked sedges fringed the shores of the newborn lakes; young rivers roared in the abandoned channels of the glaciers; flowers bloomed around the feet of the great burnished domes,—while with quick fertility mellow beds of soil, settling and warming, offered food to multitudes of Nature's waiting children, great and small, animals as well as plants; mice, squirrels, marmots, deer, bears, elephants, etc. The ground burst into bloom with magical rapidity, and the young forests into bird-song: life in every form warming and sweetening and growing richer as the years passed away over the mighty Sierra so lately suggestive of death and consummate desolation only.

It is hard without long and loving study to realize the magnitude of the work done on these mountains during the last glacial period by glaciers, which are only streams of closely compacted snow-crystals. Careful study of the phenomena presented goes to show that the pre-glacial condition of the range was comparatively simple: one vast wave of stone in which a thousand mountains, domes, cañons, ridges, etc., lay concealed. And in the development of these Nature chose for a tool not the earthquake or lightning to rend and split asunder, not the stormy torrent or eroding rain, but the tender snow-flowers noiselessly falling through unnumbered centuries, the offspring of the sun and sea. Laboring harmoniously in united strength they crushed and ground and wore away the rocks in their march, making vast beds of soil, and at the same time developed and fashioned the landscapes into the delightful variety of hill and dale and lordly mountain that mortals call beauty. Perhaps more than a mile in average depth has the range been thus degraded during the last glacial period,—a quantity of mechanical work almost inconceivably great. And our admiration must be excited again and again as we toil and study and learn that this vast job of rockwork, so far-reaching in its influences, was done by agents so fragile and small as are these flowers of the mountain clouds. Strong only by force of numbers, they carried away entire mountains, particle by particle, block by block, and cast them into the sea; sculptured, fashioned, modeled all the range, and developed its predestined beauty. All these new Sierra landscapes were evidently predestined, for the physical structure of the rocks on which the features of the scenery depend was acquired while they lay at least a mile deep below the pre-glacial surface. And it was while these features were taking form in the depths of the range, the particles of the rocks marching to their appointed places in the dark with reference to the coming beauty, that the particles of icy vapor in the sky marching to the same music assembled to bring them to the light. Then, after their grand task was done, these bands of snow-flowers, these mighty glaciers, were melted and removed as if of no more importance than dew destined to last but an hour. Few, however, of Nature's agents have left monuments so noble and enduring as they. The great granite domes a mile high, the cañons as deep, the noble peaks, the Yosemite valleys, these, and indeed nearly all other features of the Sierra scenery, are glacier monuments.

Contemplating the works of these flowers of the sky, one may easily fancy them endowed with life: messengers sent down to work in the mountain mines on errands of divine love. Silently flying through the darkened air, swirling, glinting, to their appointed places, they seem to have taken counsel together, saying, "Come, we are feeble; let us help one another. We are many, and together we will be strong. Marching in close, deep ranks, let us roll away the stones from these mountain sepulchers, and set the landscapes free. Let us uncover these clustering domes. Here let us carve a lake basin; there, a Yosemite Valley; here, a channel for a river with fluted steps and brows for the plunge of songful cataracts. Yonder let us spread broad sheets of soil, that man and beast may be fed; and here pile trains of boulders for pines and giant Sequoias. Here make ground for a meadow; there, for a garden and grove, making it smooth and fine for small daisies and violets and beds of heathy bryanthus, spicing it well with crystals, garnet feldspar, and zircon." Thus and so on it has oftentimes seemed to me sang and planned and labored the hearty snow-flower crusaders; and nothing that I can write can possibly exaggerate the grandeur and beauty of their work. Like morning mist they have vanished in sunshine, all save the few small companies that still linger on the coolest mountainsides, and, as residual glaciers, are still busily at work completing the last of the lake basins, the last beds of soil, and the sculpture of some of the highest peaks.

CHAPTER II

THE GLACIERS

Of the small residual glaciers mentioned in the preceding chapter, I have found sixty-five in that portion of the range lying between latitude 36° 30′ and 39°. They occur singly or in small groups on the north sides of the peaks of the High Sierra, sheltered beneath broad frosty shadows, in amphitheaters of their own making, where the snow, shooting down from the surrounding heights in avalanches, is most abundant. Over two thirds of the entire number lie between latitude 37° and 38°, and form the highest fountains of the San Joaquin, Merced, Tuolumne, and Owen's rivers.

The glaciers of Switzerland, like those of the Sierra, are mere wasting remnants of mighty ice-floods that once filled the great valleys and poured into the sea. So, also, are those of Norway, Asia, and South America. Even the grand continuous mantles of ice that still cover Greenland, Spitsbergen, Nova Zembla, Franz-Joseph-Land, parts of Alaska, and the south polar region are shallowing and shrinking. Every glacier in the world is smaller than it once was. All the world is growing warmer, or the crop of snow-flowers is diminishing. But in contemplating the condition of the glaciers of the world, we must bear in mind while trying to account for the changes going on that the same sunshine that wastes them builds them. Every glacier records the expenditure of an enormous amount of sun-heat in lifting the vapor for the snow of which it is made from the ocean to the mountains, as Tyndall strikingly shows.

The number of glaciers in the Alps, according to the Schlagintweit brothers, is 1100, of which 100 may be regarded as primary, and the total area of ice, snow, and névé is estimated at 1177 square miles, or an average for each glacier of little more than one square mile. On the same authority, the average height above sea-level at which they melt is about 7414 feet. The Grindelwald glacier descends below 4000 feet, and one of the Mont Blanc glaciers reaches nearly as low a point. One of the largest of the Himalaya glaciers on the head waters of the Ganges does not, according to Captain Hodgson, descend below 12,914 feet. The largest of the Sierra glaciers on Mount Shasta descends to within 9500 feet of the level of the sea, which, as far as I have observed, is the lowest point reached by any glacier within the bounds of California, the average height of all being not far from 11,000 feet.

The changes that have taken place in the glacial conditions of the Sierra from the time of greatest extension is well illustrated by the series of glaciers of every size and form extending along the mountains of the coast to Alaska. A general exploration of this instructive region shows that to the north of California, through Oregon and Washington, groups of active glaciers still exist on all the high volcanic cones of the Cascade Range,—Mount Pitt, the Three Sisters, Mounts Jefferson, Hood, St. Helens, Adams, Rainier, Baker, and others,—some of them of considerable size, though none of them approach the sea. Of these mountains Rainier, in Washington, is the highest and iciest. Its dome-like summit, between 14,000 and 15,000 feet high, is capped with ice, and eight glaciers, seven to twelve miles long, radiate from it as a center, and form the sources of the principal streams of the State. The lowest-descending of this fine group flows through beautiful forests to within 3500 feet of the sea-level, and sends forth a river laden with glacier mud and sand. On through British Columbia and southeastern Alaska the broad, sustained mountain-chain, extending along the coast, is generally glacier-bearing. The upper branches of nearly all the main cañons and fiords are occupied by glaciers, which gradually increase in size, and descend lower until the high region between Mount Fairweather and Mount St. Elias is reached, where a considerable number discharge into the waters of the ocean. This is preëminently the ice-land of Alaska and of the entire Pacific Coast.

Northward from here the glaciers gradually diminish in size and thickness, and melt at higher levels. In Prince William Sound and Cook's Inlet many fine glaciers are displayed, pouring from the surrounding mountains; but to the north of latitude 62° few, if any, glaciers remain, the ground being mostly low and the snowfall light. Between latitude 56° and 60° there are probably more than 5000 glaciers, not counting the smallest. Hundreds of the largest size descend through the forests to the level of the sea, or near it, though as far as my own observations have reached, after a pretty thorough examination of the region, not more than twenty-five discharge icebergs into the sea. All the long high-walled fiords into which these great glaciers of the first class flow are of course crowded with icebergs of every conceivable form, which are detached with thundering noise at intervals of a few minutes from an imposing ice-wall that is thrust forward into deep water. But these Pacific Coast icebergs are small as compared with those of Greenland and the Antarctic region, and only a few of them escape from the intricate system of channels, with which this portion of the coast is fringed, into the open sea. Nearly all of them are swashed and drifted by wind and tide back and forth in the fiords until finally melted by the ocean water, the sunshine, the warm winds, and the copious rains of summer. Only one glacier on the coast, observed by Prof. Russell, discharges its bergs directly into the open sea, at Icy Cape, opposite Mount St. Elias. The southernmost of the glaciers that reach the sea occupies a narrow, picturesque fiord about twenty miles to the northwest of the mouth of the Stikeen River, in latitude 56° 50′. The fiord is called by the natives "Hutli," or Thunder Bay, from the noise made by the discharge of the icebergs. About one degree farther north there are four of these complete glaciers, discharging at the heads of the long arms of Holkam Bay. At the head of the

Tahkoo Inlet, still farther north, there is one; and at the head and around the sides of Glacier Bay, trending in a general northerly direction from Cross Sound in latitude 58° to 59°, there are seven of these complete glaciers pouring bergs into the bay and its branches, and keeping up an eternal thundering. The largest of this group, the Muir, has upward of 200 tributaries, and a width below the confluence of the main tributaries of about twenty-five miles. Between the west side of this icy bay and the ocean all the ground, high and low, excepting the peaks of the Fairweather Range, is covered with a mantle of ice from 1000 to probably 3000 feet thick, which discharges by many distinct mouths.

This fragmentary ice-sheet, and the immense glaciers about Mount St. Elias, together with the multitude of separate river-like glaciers that load the slopes of the coast mountains, evidently once formed part of a continuous ice-sheet that flowed over all the region hereabouts, and only a comparatively short time ago extended as far southward as the mouth of the Strait of Juan de Fuca, probably farther. All the islands of the Alexander Archipelago, as well as the headlands and promontories of the mainland, display telling traces of this great mantle that are still fresh and unmistakable. They all have the forms of the greatest strength with reference to the action of a vast rigid press of oversweeping ice from the north and northwest, and their surfaces have a smooth, rounded, overrubbed appearance, generally free from angles. The intricate labyrinth of canals, channels, straits, passages, sounds, narrows, etc. between the islands, and extending into the mainland, of course manifest in their forms and trends and general characteristics the same subordination to the grinding action of universal glaciation as to their origin, and differ from the islands and banks of the fiords only in being portions of the pre-glacial margin of the continent more deeply eroded, and therefore covered by the ocean waters which flowed into them as the ice was melted out of them. The formation and extension of fiords in this manner is still going on, and may be witnessed in many places in Glacier Bay, Yakutat Bay, and adjacent regions. That the domain of the sea is being extended over the land by the wearing away of its shores, is well known, but in these icy regions of Alaska, and even as far south as Vancouver Island, the coast rocks have been so short a time exposed to wave-action they are but little wasted as yet. In these regions the extension of the sea effected by its own action in post-glacial time is scarcely appreciable as compared with that effected by ice-action.

Traces of the vanished glaciers made during the period of greater extension abound on the Sierra as far south as latitude 36°. Even the polished rock surfaces, the most evanescent of glacial records, are still found in a wonderfully perfect state of preservation on the upper half of the middle portion of the range, and form the most striking of all the glacial phenomena. They occur in large irregular patches in the summit and middle regions, and though they have been subjected to the action of the weather with its corroding storms for thousands of years, their mechanical excellence is such that they still reflect the sunbeams like glass, and attract the attention of every observer. The attention of the mountaineer is seldom arrested by moraines, however regular and high they may be, or by cañons, however deep, or by rocks, however noble in form and sculpture; but he stoops and rubs his hands admiringly on the shining surfaces and trios hard to account for their mysterious smoothness. He has seen the snow descending in avalanches, but concludes this cannot be the work of snow, for he finds it where no avalanches occur. Nor can water have done it, for he sees this smoothness glowing on the sides and tops of the highest domes. Only the winds of all the agents he knows seem capable of flowing in the directions indicated by the scoring. Indians, usually so little curious about geological phenomena, have come to me occasionally and asked me, "What makeum the ground so smooth at Lake Tenaya?" Even horses and dogs gaze wonderingly at the strange brightness of the ground, and smell the polished spaces and place their feet cautiously on them when they come to them for the first time, as if afraid of sinking. The most perfect of the polished pavements and walls lie at an elevation of from 7000 to 9000 feet above the sea, where the rock is compact silicious granite. Small dim patches may be found as low as 3000 feet on the driest and most enduring portions of sheer walls with a southern exposure, and on compact swelling bosses partially protected from rain by a covering of large boulders. On the north half of the range the striated and polished surfaces are less common, not only because this part of the chain is lower, but because the surface rocks are chiefly porous lavas subject to comparatively rapid waste. The ancient moraines also, though well preserved on most of the south half of the range, are nearly obliterated to the northward, but then material is found scattered and disintegrated.

A similar blurred condition of the superficial records of glacial action obtains throughout most of Oregon, Washington, British Columbia, and Alaska, due in great part to the action of excessive moisture. Even in southeastern Alaska, where the most extensive glaciers on the continent are, the more evanescent of the traces of their former greater extension, though comparatively recent, are more obscure than those of the ancient California glaciers whore the climate is drier and the rocks more resisting.

These general views of the glaciers of the Pacific Coast will enable my readers to see something of the changes that have taken place in California, and will throw light on the residual glaciers of the High Sierra.

Prior to the autumn of 1871 the glaciers of the Sierra were unknown. In October of that year I discovered the Black Mountain Glacier in a shadowy amphitheater between Black and Rod Mountains, two of the peaks of the Merced group. This group is the highest portion of a spur that straggles out from the main axis of the range in the direction of Yosemite Valley. At the time of this interesting discovery I was exploring the névé amphitheaters of the group, and tracing the courses of the ancient glaciers that once poured from its ample fountains through the Illilouette Basin and the Yosemite Valley, not expecting to find any active glaciers so far south in the land of sunshine.

Beginning on the northwestern extremity of the group, I explored the chief tributary basins in succession, their moraines, roches moutonnées, and splendid glacier pavements, taking them in regular succession without any reference to the time consumed in their study. The monuments of the tributary that poured its ice from between Red and Black Mountains I found to be the most interesting of them all; and when I saw its magnificent moraines extending in majestic curves from the spacious amphitheater between the mountains, I was exhilarated with the work that lay before me. It was one of the golden days of the Sierra Indian summer, when the rich sunshine glorifies every landscape however rocky and cold, and suggests anything rather than glaciers. The path of the vanished glacier was warm now, and shone in many places as if washed with silver. The tall pines growing on the moraines stood transfigured in the glowing light, the poplar groves on the levels of the basin were masses of orange-yellow, and the late-blooming goldenrods added gold to gold. Pushing on over my rosy glacial highway, I passed lake after lake set in solid basins of granite, and many a thicket and meadow watered by a stream that issues from the amphitheater and links the lakes together; now wading through plushy bogs knee-deep in yellow and purple sphagnum; now passing over bare rock. The main lateral moraines that bounded the view on either hand are from 100 to nearly 200 feet high, and about as regular as artificial embankments, and covered with a superb growth of Silver Fir and Pine. But this garden and forest luxuriance was speedily left behind. The trees were dwarfed as I ascended; patches of the alpine bryanthus and cassiope began to appear, and arctic willows pressed into flat carpets by the winter snow. The lakelets, which a few miles down the valley were so richly embroidered with flowery meadows, had here, at an elevation of 10,000 feet, only small brown mats of carex, leaving bare rocks around more than half their shores. Yet amid this alpine suppression the Mountain Pine bravely tossed his storm-beaten branches on the ledges and buttresses of Red Mountain, some specimens being over 100 feet high, and 24 feet in circumference, seemingly as fresh and vigorous as the giants of the lower zones.

Evening came on just as I got fairly within the portal of the main amphitheater. It is about a mile wide, and a little less than two miles long. The crumbling spurs and battlements of Red Mountain bound it on the north, the somber, rudely sculptured precipices of Black Mountain on the south, and a hacked, splintery col, curving around from mountain to mountain, shuts it in on the east.

I chose a camping-ground on the brink of one of the lakes where a thicket of Hemlock Spruce sheltered me from the night wind. Then, after making a tin-cupful of tea, I sat by my camp-fire reflecting on the grandeur and significance of the glacial records I had seen. As the night advanced the mighty rock walls of my mountain mansion seemed to come nearer, while the starry sky in glorious brightness stretched across like a ceiling from wall to wall, and fitted closely down into all the spiky irregularities of the summits. Then, after a long fireside rest and a glance at my note-book, I cut a few leafy branches for a bed, and fell into the clear, death-like sleep of the tired mountaineer.

Early next morning I set out to trace the grand old glacier that had done so much for the beauty of the Yosemite region back to its farthest fountains, enjoying the charm that every explorer feels in Nature's untrodden wildernesses. The voices of the mountains were still asleep. The wind scarce stirred the pine-needles. The sun was up, but it was yet too cold for the birds and the few burrowing animals that dwell here. Only the stream, cascading from pool to pool, seemed to be wholly awake. Yet the spirit of the opening day called to action. The sunbeams came streaming gloriously through the jagged openings of the col, glancing on the burnished pavements and lighting the silvery lakes, while every sun-touched rock burned white on its edges like melting iron in a furnace. Passing round the north shore of my camp lake I followed the central stream past many cascades from lakelet to lakelet. The scenery became more rigidly arctic, the Dwarf Pines and Hemlocks disappeared, and the stream was bordered with icicles. As the sun rose higher rocks were loosened on shattered portions of the cliffs, and came down in rattling avalanches, echoing wildly from crag to crag.

The main lateral moraines that extend from the jaws of the amphitheater into the Illilouette Basin are continued in straggling masses along the walls of the amphitheater, while separate boulders, hundreds of tons in weight, are left stranded here and there out in the middle of the channel. Here, also, I observed a series of small terminal moraines ranged along the south wall of the amphitheater, corresponding in size and form with the shadows cast by the highest portions. The meaning of this correspondence between moraines and shadows was afterward made plain. Tracing the stream back to the last of its chain of lakelets, I noticed a deposit of fine gray mud on the bottom except where the force of the entering current had prevented its settling. It looked like the mud worn from a grindstone, and I at once suspected its glacial origin, for the stream that was carrying it came gurgling out of the base of a raw moraine that seemed in process of formation. Not a plant or weather-stain was visible on its rough, unsettled surface. It is from 60 to over 100 feet high, and plunges forward at an angle of 38°. Cautiously picking my way, I gained the top of the moraine and was delighted to see a small but well characterized glacier swooping down from the gloomy precipices of Black Mountain in a finely graduated curve to the moraine on which I stood. The compact ice appeared on all the lower portions of the glacier, though gray with dirt and stones embedded in it. Farther up the ice disappeared beneath coarse granulated snow. The surface of the glacier was further characterized by dirt bands and the outcropping edges of the blue veins, showing the laminated structure of the ice. The uppermost crevasse, or "bergschrund," where the névé was attached to the mountain, was from 12 to 14 feet wide, and was bridged in a few places by the remains of snow avalanches. Creeping along the edge of the schrund, holding on with benumbed fingers, I discovered clear sections where the bedded structure was beautifully revealed. The surface snow, though sprinkled with stones shot down from the cliffs, was in some places almost pure, gradually becoming crystalline and changing to whitish porous ice of different shades of color, and this again changing at a depth of 20 or 30 feet to blue ice, some of the ribbon-like bands of which were nearly pure, and blended with the paler bands in the most gradual and delicate manner imaginable. A series of rugged zigzags enabled me to make my way down into the weird under-world of the crevasse. Its chambered hollows were hung with a multitude of clustered icicles, amid which pale, subdued light pulsed and shimmered with indescribable loveliness. Water dripped and tinkled overhead, and from far below came strange, solemn murmurings from currents that were feeling their way through veins and fissures in the dark. The chambers of a glacier are perfectly enchanting, notwithstanding one feels out of place in their frosty beauty. I was soon cold in my shirt-sleeves, and the leaning wall threatened to engulf me; yet it was hard to leave the delicious music of the water and the lovely light. Coming again to the surface, I noticed boulders of every size on their journeys to the terminal moraine—journeys of more than a hundred years, without a single stop, night or day, winter or summer.

The sun gave birth to a network of sweet-voiced rills that ran gracefully down the glacier, curling and swirling in their shining channels, and cutting clear sections through the porous surface-ice into the solid blue, where the structure of the glacier was beautifully illustrated.

The series of small terminal moraines which I had observed in the morning, along the south wall of the amphitheater, correspond in every way with the moraine of this glacier, and their distribution with reference to shadows was now understood. When the climatic changes came on that caused the melting and retreat of the main glacier that filled the amphitheater, a series of residual glaciers were left in the cliff shadows, under the protection of which they lingered, until they formed the moraines we are studying. Then, as the snow became still less abundant, all of them vanished in succession, except the one just described; and the cause of its longer life is sufficiently apparent in the greater area of snow-basin it drains, and its more perfect protection from wasting sunshine. How much longer this little glacier will last depends, of course, on the amount of snow it receives from year to year, as compared with melting waste.

After this discovery, I made excursions over all the High Sierra, pushing my explorations summer after summer, and discovered that what at first sight in the distance looked like extensive snow-fields, wore in great part glaciers, busily at work completing the sculpture of the summit-peaks so grandly blocked out by their giant predecessors.

On August 21, I set a series of stakes in the Maclure Glacier, near Mount Lyell, and found its rate of motion to be little more than an inch a day in the middle, showing a great contrast to the Muir Glacier in Alaska, which, near the front, flows at a rate of from five to ten feet in twenty-four hours. Mount Shasta has three glaciers, but Mount Whitney, although it is the highest mountain in the range, does not now cherish a single glacier. Small patches of lasting snow and ice occur on its northern slopes, but they are shallow, and present no well marked evidence of glacial motion. Its sides, however, are scored and polished in many places by the action of its ancient glaciers that flowed east and west as tributaries of the great glaciers that once filled the valleys of the Kern and Owen's rivers.

CHAPTER III

THE SNOW

The first snow that whitens the Sierra, usually falls about the end of October or early in November, to a depth of a few inches, after months of the most charming Indian summer weather imaginable. But in a few days, this light covering mostly melts from the slopes exposed to the sun and causes but little apprehension on the part of mountaineers who may be lingering among the high peaks at this time. The first general winter storm that yields snow that is to form a lasting portion of the season's supply, seldom breaks on the mountains before the end of November. Then, warned by the sky, cautions mountaineers, together with the wild sheep, deer, and most of the birds and bears, make haste to the lowlands or foot-hills; and burrowing marmots, mountain beavers, wood-rats, and such people go into winter quarters, some of them not again to see the light of day until the general awakening and resurrection of the spring in June or July. The first heavy fall is usually from about two to four feet in depth. Then, with intervals of splendid sunshine, storm succeeds storm, heaping snow on snow, until thirty to fifty feet has fallen. But on account of its settling and compacting, and the almost constant waste from melting and evaporation, the average depth actually found at any time seldom exceeds ten feet in the forest region, or fifteen feet along the slopes of the summit peaks.

Even during the coldest weather evaporation never wholly ceases, and the sunshine that abounds between the storms is sufficiently powerful to melt the surface more or less through all the winter months. Waste from melting also goes on to some extent on the bottom from heat stored up in the rocks, and given off slowly to the snow in contact with them, as is shown by the rising of the streams on all the higher regions after the first snowfall, and their steady sustained flow all winter.

The greater portion of the snow deposited around the lofty summits of the range falls in small crisp flakes and broken crystals, or, when accompanied by strong winds and low temperature, the crystals, instead of being locked together in their fall to form tufted flakes, are beaten and broken into meal and fine dust. But down in the forest region the greater portion comes gently to the ground, light and feathery, some of the flakes in mild weather being nearly an inch in diameter, and it is evenly distributed and kept from drifting to any great extent by the shelter afforded by the large trees. Every tree during the progress of gentle storms is loaded with, fairy bloom at the coldest and darkest time of year, bending the branches, and hushing every singing needle. But as soon as the storm is over, and the sun shines, the snow at once begins to shift and settle and fall from the branches in miniature avalanches, and the white forest soon becomes green again. The snow on the ground also settles and thaws every bright day, and freezes at night, until it becomes coarsely granulated, and loses every trace of its rayed crystalline structure, and then a man may walk firmly over its frozen surface as if on ice. The forest region up to an elevation of 7000 feet is usually in great part free from snow in June, but at this time the higher regions are still heavy-laden, and are not touched by spring weather to any considerable extent before the middle or end of July.

One of the most striking effects of the snow on the mountains is the burial of the rivers and small lakes.

As the snow fa's in the river

A moment white, then lost forever,

sang Burns, in illustrating the fleeting character of human pleasure. The first snowflakes that fall into the Sierra rivers vanish thus suddenly; but in great storms, when the temperature is low, the abundance of the snow at length chills the water nearly to the freezing point, and then, of course, it ceases to melt and consume the snow so suddenly. The falling flakes and crystals form, cloud-like masses of blue sludge, which are swept forward with the current and carried down to warmer climates many miles distant, while some are lodged against logs and rocks and projecting points of the banks, and last for days, piled high above the level of the water, and show white again, instead of being at once "lost forever," while the rivers themselves are at length lost for months during the snowy period. The snow is first built out from the banks in bossy, over-curling drifts, compacting and cementing until the streams are spanned. They then flow in the dark beneath a continuous covering across the snowy zone, which is about thirty miles wide. All the Sierra rivers and their tributaries in these high regions are thus lost every winter, as if another glacial period had come on. Not a drop of running water is to be seen excepting at a few points where large falls occur, though the rush and rumble of the heavier currents may still be heard. Toward spring, when the weather is warm during the day and frosty at night, repeated thawing and freezing and new layers of snow render the bridging-masses dense and firm, so that one may safely walk across the streams, or even lead a horse across them without danger of falling through. In June the thinnest parts of the winter ceiling, and those most exposed to sunshine, begin to give way, forming dark, rugged-edged, pit-like sinks, at the bottom of which the rushing water may be seen. At the end of June only here and there may the mountaineer find a secure snow-bridge. The most lasting of the winter bridges, thawing from below as well as from above, because of warm currents of air passing through the tunnels, are strikingly arched and sculptured; and by the occasional freezing of the oozing, dripping water of the ceiling they become brightly and picturesquely icy. In some of the reaches, where there is a free margin, we may walk through them. Small skylights appearing here and there, these tunnels are not very dark. The roaring river fills all the arching way with impressively loud reverberating music, which is sweetened at times by the ouzel, a bird that is not afraid to go wherever a stream may go, and to sing wherever a stream sings.

All the small alpine pools and lakelets are in like manner obliterated from the winter landscapes, either by being first frozen and then covered by snow, or by being filled in by avalanches. The first avalanche of the season shot into a lake basin may perhaps find the surface frozen. Then there is a grand crashing of breaking ice and dashing of waves mingled with the low, deep booming of the avalanche. Detached masses of the invading snow, mixed with fragments of ice, drift about in sludgy, island-like heaps, while the main body of it forms a talus with its base wholly or in part resting on the bottom of the basin, as controlled by its depth and the size of the avalanche. The next avalanche, of course, encroaches still farther, and so on with each in succession until the entire basin may be filled and its water sponged up or displaced. This huge mass of sludge, more or less mixed with sand, stones, and perhaps timber, is frozen to a considerable depth, and much sun-heat is required to thaw it. Some of these unfortunate lakelets are not clear of ice and snow until near the end of summer. Others are never quite free, opening only on the side opposite the entrance of the avalanches. Some show only a narrow crescent of water lying between the shore and sheer bluffs of icy compacted snow, masses of which breaking off float in front like icebergs in a miniature Arctic Ocean, while the avalanche heaps leaning back against the mountains look like small glaciers. The frontal cliffs are in some instances quite picturesque, and with the berg-dotted waters in front of them lighted with sunshine are exceedingly beautiful. It often happens that while one side of a lake basin is hopelessly snow-buried and frozen, the other, enjoying sunshine, is adorned with beautiful flower-gardens. Some of the smaller lakes are extinguished in an instant by a heavy avalanche either of rocks or snow. The rolling, sliding, ponderous mass entering on one side sweeps across the bottom and up the opposite side, displacing the water and even scraping the basin clean, and shoving the accumulated rocks and sediments up the farther bank and taking full possession. The dislodged water is in part absorbed, but most of it is sent around the front of the avalanche and down the channel of the outlet, roaring and hurrying as if frightened and glad to escape.

SNOW-BANNERS

The most magnificent storm phenomenon I ever saw, surpassing in showy grandeur the most imposing effects of clouds, floods, or avalanches, was the peaks of the High Sierra, back of Yosemite Valley, decorated with snow-banners. Many of the starry snow-flowers, out of which these banners are made, fall before they are ripe, while most of those that do attain perfect development as six-rayed crystals glint and chafe against one another in their fall through the frosty air, and are broken into fragments. This dry fragmentary snow is still further prepared for the formation of banners by the action of the wind. For, instead of finding rest at once, like the snow which falls into the tranquil depths of the forests, it is rolled over and over, beaten against rock-ridges, and swirled in pits and hollows, like boulders, pebbles, and sand in the pot-holes of a river, until finally the delicate angles of the crystals are worn off, and the whole mass is reduced to dust. And whenever storm-winds find this prepared snow-dust in a loose condition on exposed slopes, where there is a free upward sweep to leeward, it is tossed back into the sky, and borne onward from peak to peak in the form of banners or cloudy drifts, according to the velocity of the wind and the conformation of the slopes up or around which it is driven. While thus flying through the air, a small portion makes good its escape, and remains in the sky as vapor. But far the greater part, after being driven into the sky again and again, is at length locked fast in bossy drifts, or in the wombs of glaciers, some of it to remain silent and rigid for centuries before it is finally melted and sent singing down the mountainsides to the sea.

Yet, notwithstanding the abundance of winter snow-dust in the mountains, and the frequency of high winds, and the length of time the dust remains loose and exposed to their action, the occurrence of well-formed banners is, for causes we shall hereafter note, comparatively rare. I have seen only one display of this kind that seemed in every way perfect. This was in the winter of 1873, when the snow-laden summits were swept by a wild "norther." I happened at the time to be wintering in Yosemite Valley, that sublime Sierra temple where every day one may see the grandest sights. Yet even here the wild gala-day of the north wind seemed surpassingly glorious. I was awakened in the morning by the rocking of my cabin and the beating of pine-burs on the roof. Detached torrents and avalanches from the main wind-flood overhead were rushing wildly down the narrow side cañons, and over the precipitous walls, with loud resounding roar, rousing the pines to enthusiastic action, and making the whole valley vibrate as though it were an instrument being played.

But afar on the lofty exposed peaks of the range standing so high in the sky, the storm was expressing itself in still grander characters, which I was soon to see in all their glory. I had long been anxious to study some points in the structure of the ice-cone that is formed every winter at the foot of the upper Yosemite fall, but the blinding spray by which it is invested had hitherto prevented me from making a sufficiently near approach. This morning the entire body of the fall was torn into gauzy shreds, and blown horizontally along the face of the cliff, leaving the cone dry; and while making my way to the top of an overlooking ledge to seize so favorable an opportunity to examine the interior of the cone, the peaks of the Merced group came in sight over the shoulder of the South Dome, each waving a resplendent banner against the blue sky, as regular in form, and as firm in texture, as if woven of fine silk. So rare and splendid a phenomenon, of course, overbore all other considerations, and I at once let the ice-cone go, and began to force my way out of the valley to some dome or ridge sufficiently lofty to command a general view of the main summits, feeling assured that I should find them bannered still more gloriously; nor was I in the least disappointed. Indian Cañon, through which I climbed, was choked with snow that had been shot down in avalanches from the high cliffs on either side, rendering the ascent difficult; but inspired by the roaring storm, the tedious wallowing brought no fatigue, and in four hours I gained the top of a ridge above the valley, 8000 feet high. And there in bold relief, like a clear painting, appeared a most imposing scene. Innumerable peaks, black and sharp, rose grandly into the dark blue sky, their bases set in solid white, their sides streaked and splashed with snow, like ocean rocks with foam; and from every summit, all free and unconfused, was streaming a beautiful silky silvery banner, from half a mile to a mile in length, slender at the point of attachment, then widening gradually as it extended from the peak until it was about 1000 or 1500 feet in breadth, as near as I could estimate. The cluster of peaks called the "Crown of the Sierra," at the head of the Merced and Tuolumne rivers,—Mounts Dana, Gibbs, Conness, Lyell, Maclure, Ritter, with their nameless compeers,—each had its own refulgent banner, waving with a clearly visible motion in the sunglow, and there was not a single cloud in the sky to mar their simple grandeur. Fancy yourself standing on this Yosemite ridge looking eastward. You notice a strange garish glitter in the air. The gale drives wildly overhead with a fierce, tempestuous roar, but its violence is not felt, for you are looking through a sheltered opening in the woods as through a window. There, in the immediate foreground of your picture, rises a majestic forest of Silver Fir blooming in eternal freshness, the foliage yellow-green, and the snow beneath the trees strewn with their beautiful plumes, plucked off by the wind. Beyond, and extending over all the middle ground, are somber swaths of pine, interrupted by huge swelling ridges and domes; and just beyond the dark forest you see the monarchs of the High Sierra waving their magnificent banners. They are twenty miles away, but you would not wish them nearer, for every feature is distinct, and the whole glorious show is seen in its right proportions. After this general view, mark how sharply the dark snowless ribs and buttresses and summits of the peaks are defined, excepting the portions veiled by the banners, and how delicately their sides are streaked with snow, where it has come to rest in narrow flutings and gorges. Mark, too, how grandly the banners wave as the wind is deflected against their sides, and how trimly each is attached to the very summit of its peak, like a streamer at a masthead; how smooth and silky they are in texture, and how finely their fading fringes are penciled on the azure sky. See how dense and opaque they are at the point of attachment, and how filmy and translucent toward the end, so that the peaks back of them are seen dimly, as though you were looking through ground glass. Yet again observe how some of the longest, belonging to the loftiest summits, stream perfectly free all the way across intervening notches and passes from peak to peak, while others overlap and partly hide each other. And consider how keenly every particle of this wondrous cloth of snow is flashing out jets of light. These are the main features of the beautiful and terrible picture as seen from the forest window; and it would still be surpassingly glorious were the fore- and middle-grounds obliterated altogether, leaving only the black peaks, the white banners, and the blue sky.

Glancing now in a general way at the formation of snow-banners, we find that the main causes of the wondrous beauty and perfection of those we have been contemplating were the favorable direction and great force of the wind, the abundance of snow-dust, and the peculiar conformation of the slopes of the peaks. It is essential not only that the wind should move with great velocity and steadiness to supply a sufficiently copious and continuous stream of snow-dust, but that it should come from the north. No perfect banner is ever hung on the Sierra peaks by a south wind. Had the gale that day blown from the south, leaving other conditions unchanged, only a dull, confused, fog-like drift would have been produced; for the snow, instead of being spouted up over the tops of the peaks in concentrated currents to be drawn out as streamers, would have been shed off around the sides, and piled down into the glacier wombs. The cause of the concentrated action of the north wind is found in the peculiar form of the north sides of the peaks, where the amphitheaters of the residual glaciers are. In general the south sides are convex and irregular, while the north sides are concave both in their vertical and horizontal sections; the wind in ascending these curves converges toward the summits, carrying the snow in concentrating currents with it, shooting it almost straight up into the air above the peaks, from which it is then carried away in a horizontal direction.

This difference in form between the north and south sides of the peaks was almost wholly produced by the difference in the kind and quantity of the glaciation to which they have been subjected, the north sides having been hollowed by residual shadow-glaciers of a form that never existed on the sun-beaten sides.

It appears, therefore, that shadows in great part determine not only the forms of lofty icy mountains, but also those of the snow-banners that the wild winds hang on them.

CHAPTER IV

A NEAR VIEW OF THE HIGH SIERRA

Early one bright morning in the middle of Indian summer, while the glacier meadows were still crisp with frost crystals, I set out from the foot of Mount Lyell, on my way down to Yosemite Valley, to replenish my exhausted store of bread and tea. I had spent the past summer, as many preceding ones, exploring the glaciers that lie on the head waters of the San Joaquin, Tuolumne, Merced, and Owen's rivers; measuring and studying their movements, trends, crevasses, moraines, etc., and the part they had played during the period of their greater extension in the creation and development of the landscapes of this alpine wonderland. The time for this kind of work was nearly over for the year, and I began to look forward with delight to the approaching winter with its wondrous storms, when I would be warmly snow-bound in my Yosemite cabin with plenty of bread and books; but a tinge of regret came on when I considered that possibly I might not see this favorite region again until the next summer, excepting distant views from the heights about the Yosemite walls.

To artists, few portions of the High Sierra are, strictly speaking, picturesque. The whole massive uplift of the range is one great picture, not clearly divisible into smaller ones; differing much in this respect from the older, and what may be called, riper mountains of the Coast Range. All the landscapes of the Sierra, as we have seen, were born again, remodeled from base to summit by the developing ice-floods of the last glacial winter. But all those new landscapes were not brought forth simultaneously; some of the highest, where the ice lingered longest, are tens of centuries younger than those of the warmer regions below them. In general, the younger the mountain-landscapes,—younger, I mean, with reference to the time of their emergence from the ice of the glacial period,—the less separable are they into artistic bits capable of being made into warm, sympathetic, lovable pictures with appreciable humanity in them.

Here, however, on the head waters of the Tuolumne, is a group of wild peaks on which the geologist may say that the sun has but just begun to shine, which is yet in a high degree picturesque, and in its main features so regular and evenly balanced as almost to appear conventional—one somber cluster of snow-laden peaks with gray pine-fringed granite bosses braided around its base, the whole surging free into the sky from the head of a magnificent valley, whose lofty walls are beveled away on both sides so as to embrace it all without admitting anything not strictly belonging to it. The foreground was now aflame with autumn colors, brown and purple and gold, ripe in the mellow sunshine; contrasting brightly with the deep, cobalt blue of the sky, and the black and gray, and pure, spiritual white of the rocks and glaciers. Down through the midst, the young Tuolumne was seen pouring from its crystal fountains, now resting in glassy pools as if changing back again into ice, now leaping in white cascades as if turning to snow; gliding right and left between granite bosses, then sweeping on through the smooth, meadowy levels of the valley, swaying pensively from side to side with calm, stately gestures past dipping willows and sedges, and around groves of arrowy pine; and throughout its whole eventful course, whether flowing fast or slow, singing loud or low, ever filling the landscape with spiritual animation, and manifesting the grandeur of its sources in every movement and tone.

Pursuing my lonely way down the valley, I turned again and again to gaze on the glorious picture, throwing up my arms to inclose it as in a frame. After long ages of growth in the darkness beneath the glaciers, through sunshine and storms, it seemed now to be ready and waiting for the elected artist, like yellow wheat for the reaper; and I could not help wishing that I might carry colors and brushes with me on my travels, and learn to paint. In the mean time I had to be content with photographs on my mind and sketches in my note-books. At length, after I had rounded a precipitous headland that puts out from the west wall of the valley, every peak vanished from sight, and I pushed rapidly along the frozen meadows, over the divide between the waters of the Merced and Tuolumne, and down through the forests that clothe the slopes of Cloud's Rest, arriving in Yosemite in due time—which, with me, is any time. And, strange to say, among the first people I met here were two artists who, with letters of introduction, were awaiting my return. They inquired whether in the course of my explorations in the adjacent mountains I had ever come upon a landscape suitable for a large painting; whereupon I began a description of the one that had so lately excited my admiration. Then, as I went on further and further into details, their faces began to glow, and I offered to guide them to it, while they declared that they would gladly follow, far or near, whithersoever I could spare the time to lead them.

Since storms might come breaking down through the fine weather at any time, burying the colors in snow, and cutting off the artists' retreat, I advised getting ready at once.

I led them out of the valley by the Vernal and Nevada Falls, thence over the main dividing ridge to the Big Tuolumne Meadows, by the old Mono trail, and thence along the upper Tuolumne River to its head. This was my companions' first excursion into the High Sierra, and as I was almost always alone in my mountaineering, the way that the fresh beauty was reflected in their faces made for me a novel and interesting study. They naturally were affected most of all by the colors—the intense azure of the sky, the purplish grays of the granite, the red and browns of dry meadows, and the translucent purple and crimson of huckleberry bogs; the flaming yellow of aspen groves, the silvery flashing of the streams, and the bright green and blue of the glacier lakes. But the general expression of the scenery—rocky and savage—seemed sadly disappointing; and as they threaded the forest from ridge to ridge, eagerly scanning the landscapes as they were unfolded, they said: "All this is huge and sublime, but we see nothing as yet at all available for effective pictures. Art is long, and art is limited, you know; and here are foregrounds, middle-grounds, backgrounds, all alike; bare rock-waves, woods, groves, diminutive flecks of meadow, and strips of glittering water." "Never mind," I replied, "only bide a wee, and I will show you something you will like."

At length, toward the end of the second day, the Sierra Crown began to come into view, and when we had fairly rounded the projecting headland before mentioned, the whole picture stood revealed in the flush of the alpenglow. Their enthusiasm was excited beyond bounds, and the more impulsive of the two, a young Scotchman, dashed ahead, shouting and gesticulating and tossing his arms in the air like a madman. Here, at last, was a typical alpine landscape.

After feasting awhile on the view, I proceeded to make camp in a sheltered grove a little way back from the meadow, where pine-boughs could be obtained for beds, and where there was plenty of dry wood for fires, while the artists ran here and there, along the river-bends and up the sides of the cañon, choosing foregrounds for sketches. After dark, when our tea was made and a rousing fire had been built, we began to make our plans. They decided to remain several days, at the least, while I concluded to make an excursion in the mean time to the untouched summit of Ritter.

It was now about the middle of October, the springtime of snow-flowers. The first winter-clouds had already bloomed, and the peaks were strewn with fresh crystals, without, however, affecting the climbing to any dangerous extent. And as the weather was still profoundly calm, and the distance to the foot of the mountain only a little more than a day, I felt that I was running no great risk of being storm-bound.

Mount Ritter is king of the mountains of the middle portion of the High Sierra, as Shasta of the north and Whitney of the south sections. Moreover, as far as I know, it had never been climbed. I had explored the adjacent wilderness summer after summer, but my studies thus far had never drawn me to the top of it. Its height above sea-level is about 13,300 feet, and it is fenced round by steeply inclined glaciers, and cañons of tremendous depth and ruggedness, which render it almost inaccessible. But difficulties of this kind only exhilarate the mountaineer.

Next morning, the artists went heartily to their work and I to mine. Former experiences had given good reason to know that passionate storms, invisible as yet, might be brooding in the calm sun-gold; therefore, before bidding farewell, I warned the artists not to be alarmed should I fail to appear before a week or ten days, and advised them, in case a snow-storm should set in, to keep up big fires and shelter themselves as best they could, and on no account to become frightened and attempt to seek their way back to Yosemite alone through the drifts.

My general plan was simply this: to scale the cañon, wall, cross over to the eastern flank of the range, and then make my way southward to the northern spurs of Mount Ritter in compliance with the intervening topography; for to push on directly southward from camp through the innumerable peaks and pinnacles that adorn this portion of the axis of the range, however interesting, would take too much time, besides being extremely difficult and dangerous at this time of year.

All my first day was pure pleasure; simply mountaineering indulgence, crossing the dry pathways of the ancient glaciers, tracing happy streams, and learning the habits of the birds and marmots in the groves and rocks. Before I had gone a mile from camp, I came to the foot of a white cascade that beats its way down a rugged gorge in the cañon wall, from a height of about nine hundred feet, and pours its throbbing waters into the Tuolumne. I was acquainted with its fountains, which, fortunately, lay in my course. What a fine traveling companion it proved to be, what songs it sang, and how passionately it told the mountain's own joy! Gladly I climbed along its dashing border, absorbing its divine music, and bathing from time to time in waftings of irised spray. Climbing higher, higher, now beauty came streaming on the sight: painted meadows, late-blooming gardens, peaks of rare architecture, lakes here and there, shining like silver, and glimpses of the forested middle region and the yellow lowlands far in the west. Beyond the range I saw the so-called Mono Desert, lying dreamily silent in thick purple light—a desert of heavy sun-glare beheld from a desert of ice-burnished granite. Here the waters divide, shouting in glorious enthusiasm, and falling eastward to vanish in the volcanic sands and dry sky of the Great Basin, or westward to the Great Valley of California, and thence through the Bay of San Francisco and the Golden Gate to the sea.

Passing a little way down over the summit until I had reached an elevation of about 10,000 feet, I pushed on southward toward a group of savage peaks that stand guard about Ritter on the north and west, groping my way, and dealing instinctively with every obstacle as it presented itself. Here a huge gorge would be found cutting across my path, along the dizzy edge of which I scrambled until some less precipitous point was discovered where I might safely venture to the bottom and then, selecting some feasible portion of the opposite wall, reascend with the same slow caution. Massive, flat-topped spurs alternate with the gorges, plunging abruptly from the shoulders of the snowy peaks, and planting their feet in the warm desert. These were everywhere marked and adorned with characteristic sculptures of the ancient glaciers that swept over this entire region like one vast ice-wind, and the polished surfaces produced by the ponderous flood are still so perfectly preserved that in many places the sunlight reflected from them is about as trying to the eyes as sheets of snow.

God's glacial-mills grind slowly, but they have been kept in motion long enough in California to grind sufficient soil for a glorious abundance of life, though most of the grist has been carried to the lowlands, leaving these high regions comparatively lean and bare; while the post-glacial agents of erosion have not yet furnished sufficient available food over the general surface for more than a few tufts of the hardiest plants, chiefly carices and eriogonae. And it is interesting to learn in this connection that the sparseness and repressed character of the vegetation at this height is caused more by want of soil than by harshness of climate; for, here and there, in sheltered hollows (countersunk beneath the general surface) into which a few rods of well-ground moraine chips have been dumped, we find groves of spruce and pine thirty to forty feet high, trimmed around the edges with willow and huckleberry bushes, and oftentimes still further by an outer ring of tall grasses, bright with lupines, larkspurs, and showy columbines, suggesting a climate by no means repressingly severe. All the streams, too, and the pools at this elevation are furnished with little gardens wherever soil can be made to lie, which, though making scarce any show at a distance, constitute charming surprises to the appreciative observer. In these bits of leanness a few birds find grateful homes. Having no acquaintance with man, they fear no ill, and flock curiously about the stranger, almost allowing themselves to be taken in the hand. In so wild and so beautiful a region was spent my first day, every sight and sound inspiring, leading one far out of himself, yet feeding and building up his individuality.

Now came the solemn, silent evening. Long, blue, spiky shadows crept out across the snow-fields, while a rosy glow, at first scarce discernible, gradually deepened and suffused every mountain-top, flushing the glaciers and the harsh crags above them. This was the alpenglow, to me one of the most impressive of all the terrestrial manifestations of God. At the touch of this divine light, the mountains seemed to kindle to a rapt, religious consciousness, and stood hushed and waiting like devout worshipers. Just before the alpenglow began to fade, two crimson clouds came streaming across the summit like wings of flame, rendering the sublime scene yet more impressive; then came darkness and the stars.

Icy Ritter was still miles away, but I could proceed no farther that night. I found a good campground on the rim of a glacier basin about 11,000 feet above the sea. A small lake nestles in the bottom of it, from which I got water for my tea, and a storm-beaten thicket near by furnished abundance of resiny fire-wood. Somber peaks, hacked and shattered, circled half-way around the horizon, wearing a savage aspect in the gloaming, and a waterfall chanted solemnly across the lake on its way down from the foot of a glacier. The fall and the lake and the glacier were almost equally bare; while the scraggy pines anchored in the rock-fissures were so dwarfed and shorn by storm-winds that you might walk over their tops. In tone and aspect the scene was one of the most desolate I ever beheld. But the darkest scriptures of the mountains are illumined with bright passages of love that never fail to make themselves felt when one is alone.

I made my bed in a nook of the pine-thicket, where the branches were pressed and crinkled overhead like a roof, and bent down around the sides. These are the best bedchambers the high mountains afford—snug as squirrel-nests, well ventilated, full of spicy odors, and with plenty of wind-played needles to sing one asleep. I little expected company, but, creeping in through a low side-door, I found five or six birds nestling among the tassels. The night-wind began to blow soon after dark; at first only a gentle breathing, but increasing toward midnight to a rough gale that fell upon my leafy roof in ragged surges like a cascade, bearing wild sounds from the crags overhead. The waterfall sang in chorus, filling the old ice-fountain with its solemn roar, and seeming to increase in power as the night advanced—fit voice for such a landscape. I had to creep out many times to the fire during the night, for it was biting cold and I had no blankets. Gladly I welcomed the morning star.

The dawn in the dry, wavering air of the desert was glorious. Everything encouraged my undertaking and betokened success. There was no cloud in the sky, no storm-tone in the wind. Breakfast of bread and tea was soon made. I fastened a hard, durable crust to my belt by way of provision, in case I should be compelled to pass a night on the mountain-top; then, securing the remainder of my little stock against wolves and wood-rats, I set forth free and hopeful.

How glorious a greeting the sun gives the mountains! To behold this alone is worth the pains of any excursion a thousand times over. The highest peaks burned like islands in a sea of liquid shade. Then the lower peaks and spires caught the glow, and long lances of light, streaming through many a notch and pass, fell thick on the frozen meadows. The majestic form of Ritter was full in sight, and I pushed rapidly on over rounded rock-bosses and pavements, my iron-shod shoes making a clanking sound, suddenly hushed now and then in rugs of bryanthus, and sedgy lake-margins soft as moss. Here, too, in this so-called "land of desolation," I met cassiope, growing in fringes among the battered rocks. Her blossoms had faded long ago, but they were still clinging with happy memories to the evergreen sprays, and still so beautiful as to thrill every fiber of one's being. Winter and summer, you may hear her voice, the low, sweet melody of her purple bells. No evangel among all the mountain plants speaks Nature's love more plainly than cassiope. Where she dwells, the redemption of the coldest solitude is complete. The very rocks and glaciers seem to feel her presence, and become imbued with her own fountain sweetness. All things were warming and awakening. Frozen rills began to flow, the marmots came out of their nests in boulder-piles and climbed sunny rocks to bask, and the dun-headed sparrows were flitting about seeking their breakfasts. The lakes seen from every ridge-top were brilliantly rippled and spangled, shimmering like the thickets of the low Dwarf Pines. The rocks, too, seemed responsive to the vital heat—rock-crystals and snow-crystals thrilling alike. I strode on exhilarated, as if never more to feel fatigue, limbs moving of themselves, every sense unfolding like the thawing flowers, to take part in the new day harmony.

All along my course thus far, excepting when down in the cañons, the landscapes were mostly open to me, and expansive, at least on one side. On the left were the purple plains of Mono, reposing dreamily and warm; on the right, the near peaks springing keenly into the thin sky with more and more impressive sublimity. But these larger views were at length lost. Rugged spurs, and moraines, and huge, projecting buttresses began to shut me in. Every feature became more rigidly alpine, without, however, producing any chilling effect; for going to the mountains is like going home. We always find that the strangest objects in these fountain wilds are in some degree familiar, and we look upon them with a vague sense of having seen them before.

On the southern shore of a frozen lake, I encountered an extensive field of hard, granular snow, up which I scampered in fine tone, intending to follow it to its head, and cross the rocky spur against which it leans, hoping thus to come direct upon the base of the main Ritter peak. The surface was pitted with oval hollows, made by stones and drifted pine-needles that had melted themselves into the mass by the radiation of absorbed sun-heat. These afforded good footholds, but the surface curved more and more steeply at the head, and the pits became shallower and less abundant, until I found myself in danger of being shed off like avalanching snow. I persisted, however, creeping on all fours, and shuffling up the smoothest places on my back, as I had often done on burnished granite, until, after slipping several times, I was compelled to retrace my course to the bottom, and make my way around the west end of the lake, and thence up to the summit of the divide between the head waters of Rush Creek and the northernmost tributaries of the San Joaquin.

Arriving on the summit of this dividing crest, one of the most exciting pieces of pure wilderness was disclosed that I ever discovered in all my mountaineering. There, immediately in front, loomed the majestic mass of Mount Ritter, with a glacier swooping down its face nearly to my feet, then curving westward and pouring its frozen flood into a dark blue lake, whose shores were bound with precipices of crystalline snow; while a deep chasm drawn between the divide and the glacier separated the massive picture from everything else. I could see only the one sublime mountain, the one glacier, the one lake; the whole veiled with one blue shadow—rock, ice, and water close together without a single leaf or sign of life. After gazing spellbound, I began instinctively to scrutinize every notch and gorge and weathered buttress of the mountain, with reference to making the ascent. The entire front above the glacier appeared as one tremendous precipice, slightly receding at the top, and bristling with spires and pinnacles set above one another in formidable array. Massive lichen-stained battlements stood forward here and there, hacked at the top with angular notches, and separated by frosty gullies and recesses that have been veiled in shadow ever since their creation; while to right and left, as far as I could see, were huge, crumbling buttresses, offering no hope to the climber. The head of the glacier sends up a few finger-like branches through narrow couloirs; but these seemed too steep and short to be available, especially as I had no ax with which to cut steps, and the numerous narrow-throated gullies down which stones and snow are avalanched seemed hopelessly steep, besides being interrupted by vertical cliffs; while the whole front was rendered still more terribly forbidding by the chill shadow and the gloomy blackness of the rocks.

Descending the divide in a hesitating mood, I picked my way across the yawning chasm at the foot, and climbed out upon the glacier. There were no meadows now to cheer with their brave colors, nor could I hear the dun-headed sparrows, whose cheery notes so often relieve the silence of our highest mountains. The only sounds were the gurgling of small rills down in the veins and crevasses of the glacier, and now and then the rattling report of falling stones, with the echoes they shot out into the crisp air.

I could not distinctly hope to reach the summit from this side, yet I moved on across the glacier as if driven by fate. Contending with myself, the season is too far spent, I said, and even should I be successful, I might be storm-bound on the mountain; and in the cloud-darkness, with the cliffs and crevasses covered with snow, how could I escape? No, I must wait till next summer. I would only approach the mountain now, and inspect it, creep about its flanks, learn what I could of its history, holding myself ready to flee on the approach of the first storm-cloud. But we little know until tried how much of the uncontrollable there is in us, urging across glaciers and torrents, and up dangerous heights, let the judgment forbid as it may.

I succeeded in gaining the foot of the cliff on the eastern extremity of the glacier, and there discovered the mouth of a narrow avalanche gully, through which I began to climb, intending to follow it as far as possible, and at least obtain some fine wild views for my pains. Its general course is oblique to the plane of the mountain-face, and the metamorphic slates of which the mountain is built are cut by cleavage planes in such a way that they weather off in angular blocks, giving rise to irregular steps that greatly facilitate climbing on the sheer places. I thus made my way into a wilderness of crumbling spires and battlements, built together in bewildering combinations, and glazed in many places with a thin coating of ice, which I had to hammer off with stones. The situation was becoming gradually more perilous; but, having passed several dangerous spots,

I dared not think of descending; for, so steep was the entire ascent, one would inevitably fall to the glacier in case a single misstep were made. Knowing, therefore, the tried danger beneath, I became all the more anxious concerning the developments to be made above, and began to be conscious of a vague foreboding of what actually befell; not that I was given to fear, but rather because my instincts, usually so positive and true, seemed vitiated in some way, and were leading me astray. At length, after attaining an elevation of about 12,800 feet, I found myself at the foot of a sheer drop in the bed of the avalanche channel I was tracing, which seemed absolutely to bar further progress. It was only about forty-five or fifty feet high, and somewhat roughened by fissures and projections; but these seemed so slight and insecure, as footholds, that I tried hard to avoid the precipice altogether, by scaling the wall of the channel on either side. But, though less steep, the walls were smoother than the obstructing rock, and repeated efforts only showed that I must either go right ahead or turn back. The tried dangers beneath seemed even greater than that of the cliff in front; therefore, after scanning its face again and again, I began to scale it, picking my holds with intense caution. After gaining a point about halfway to the top, I was suddenly brought to a dead stop, with arms outspread, clinging close to the face of the rock, unable to move hand or foot either up or down. My doom appeared fixed. I must fall. There would be a moment of bewilderment, and then a lifeless rumble down the one general precipice to the glacier below.

When this final danger flashed upon me, I became nerve-shaken for the first time since setting foot on the mountains, and my mind seemed to fill with a stifling smoke. But this terrible eclipse lasted only a moment, when life blazed forth again with preternatural clearness. I seemed suddenly to become possessed of a new sense. The other self, bygone experiences, Instinct, or Guardian Angel,—call it what you will,—came forward and assumed control. Then my trembling muscles became firm again, every rift and flaw in the rock was seen as through a microscope, and my limbs moved with a positiveness and precision with which I seemed to have nothing at all to do. Had I been borne aloft upon wings, my deliverance could not have been more complete.

Above this memorable spot, the face of the mountain is still more savagely hacked and torn. It is a maze of yawning chasms and gullies, in the angles of which rise beetling crags and piles of detached boulders that seem to have been gotten ready to be launched below. But the strange influx of strength I had received seemed inexhaustible. I found a way without effort, and soon stood upon the topmost crag in the blessed light.

How truly glorious the landscape circled around this noble summit!—giant mountains, valleys innumerable, glaciers and meadows, rivers and lakes, with the wide blue sky bent tenderly over them all. But in my first hour of freedom from that terrible shadow, the sunlight in which I was laving seemed all in all.

Looking southward along the axis of the range, the eye is first caught by a row of exceedingly sharp and slender spires, which rise openly to a height of about a thousand feet, above a series of short, residual glaciers that lean back against their bases; their fantastic sculpture and the unrelieved sharpness with which they spring out of the ice rendering them peculiarly wild and striking. These are "The Minarets." Beyond them you behold a sublime wilderness of mountains, their snowy summits towering together in crowded abundance, peak beyond peak, swelling higher, higher as they sweep on southward, until the culminating point of the range is reached on Mount Whitney, near the head of the Kern River, at an elevation of nearly 14,700 feet above the level of the sea.

Westward, the general flank of the range is seen flowing sublimely away from the sharp summits, in smooth undulations; a sea of huge gray granite waves dotted with lakes and meadows, and fluted with stupendous cañons that grow steadily deeper as they recede in the distance. Below this gray region lies the dark forest zone, broken here and there by upswelling ridges and domes; and yet beyond lies a yellow, hazy belt, marking the broad plain of the San Joaquin, bounded on its farther side by the blue mountains of the coast.

Turning now to the northward, there in the immediate foreground is the glorious Sierra Crown, with Cathedral Peak, a temple of marvelous architecture, a few degrees to the left of it; the gray, massive form of Mammoth Mountain to the right; while Mounts Ord, Gibbs, Dana, Conness, Tower Peak, Castle Peak, Silver Mountain, and a host of noble companions, as yet nameless, make a sublime show along the axis of the range.

Eastward, the whole region seems a land of desolation covered with beautiful light. The torrid volcanic basin of Mono, with its one bare lake fourteen miles long; Owen's Valley and the broad lava table-land at its head, dotted with craters, and the massive Inyo Range, rivaling even the Sierra in height; these are spread, map-like, beneath you, with countless ranges beyond, passing and overlapping one another and fading on the glowing horizon.

At a distance of less than 3000 feet below the summit of Mount Ritter you may find tributaries of the San Joaquin and Owen's rivers, bursting forth from the ice and snow of the glaciers that load its flanks; while a little to the north of here are found the highest affluents of the Tuolumne and Merced. Thus, the fountains of four of the principal rivers of California are within a radius of four or five miles.

Lakes are seen gleaming in all sorts of places,—round, or oval, or square, like very mirrors; others narrow and sinuous, drawn close around the peaks like silver zones, the highest reflecting only rocks, snow, and the sky. But neither these nor the glaciers, nor the bits of brown meadow and moorland that occur here and there, are large enough to make any marked impression upon the mighty wilderness of mountains. The eye, rejoicing in its freedom, roves about the vast expanse, yet returns again and again to the fountain peaks. Perhaps some one of the multitude excites special attention, some gigantic castle with turret and battlement, or some Gothic cathedral more abundantly spired than Milan's. But, generally, when looking for the first time from an all-embracing standpoint like this, the inexperienced observer is oppressed by the incomprehensible grandeur, variety, and abundance of the mountains rising shoulder to shoulder beyond the reach of vision; and it is only after they have been studied one by one, long and lovingly, that their far-reaching harmonies become manifest. Then, penetrate the wilderness where you may, the main telling features, to which all the surrounding topography is subordinate, are quickly perceived, and the most complicated clusters of peaks stand revealed harmoniously correlated and fashioned like works of art—eloquent monuments of the ancient ice-rivers that brought them into relief from the general mass of the range. The cañons, too, some of them a mile deep, mazing wildly through the mighty host of mountains, however lawless and ungovernable at first sight they appear, are at length recognized as the necessary effects of causes which followed each other in harmonious sequence—Nature's poems carved on tables of stone—the simplest and most emphatic of her glacial compositions.

Could we have been here to observe during the glacial period, we should have overlooked a wrinkled ocean of ice as continuous as that now covering the landscapes of Greenland; filling every valley and cañon with only the tops of the fountain peaks rising darkly above the rock-encumbered ice-waves like islets in a stormy sea—those islets the only hints of the glorious landscapes now smiling in the sun. Standing here in the deep, brooding silence all the wilderness seems motionless, as if the work of creation were done. But in the midst of this outer steadfastness we know there is incessant motion and change. Ever and anon, avalanches are falling from yonder peaks. These cliff-bound glaciers, seemingly wedged and immovable, are flowing like water and grinding the rocks beneath them. The lakes are lapping their granite shores and wearing them away, and every one of these rills and young rivers is fretting the air into music, and carrying the mountains to the plains. Here are the roots of all the life of the valleys, and here more simply than elsewhere is the eternal flux of nature manifested. Ice changing to water, lakes to meadows, and mountains to plains. And while we thus contemplate Nature's methods of landscape creation, and, reading the records she has carved on the rocks, reconstruct, however imperfectly, the landscapes of the past, we also learn that as these we now behold have succeeded those of the pre-glacial age, so they in turn are withering and vanishing to be succeeded by others yet unborn.

But in the midst of these fine lessons and landscapes, I had to remember that the sun was wheeling far to the west, while a new way down the mountain had to be discovered to some point on the timber line where I could have a fire; for I had not even burdened myself with a coat. I first scanned the western spurs, hoping some way might appear through which I might reach the northern glacier, and cross its snout; or pass around the lake into which it flows, and thus strike my morning track. This route was soon sufficiently unfolded to show that, if practicable at all, it would require so much time that reaching camp that night would be out of the question. I therefore scrambled back eastward, descending the southern slopes obliquely at the same time. Here the crags seemed less formidable, and the head of a glacier that flows northeast came in sight, which I determined to follow as far as possible, hoping thus to make my way to the foot of the peak on the east side, and thence across the intervening cañons and ridges to camp.

The inclination of the glacier is quite moderate at the head, and, as the sun had softened the névé, I made safe and rapid progress, running and sliding, and keeping up a sharp outlook for crevasses. About half a mile from the head, there is an ice-cascade, where the glacier pours over a sharp declivity and is shattered into massive blocks separated by deep, blue fissures. To thread my way through the slippery mazes of this crevassed portion seemed impossible, and I endeavored to avoid it by climbing off to the shoulder of the mountain. But the slopes rapidly steepened and at length fell away in sheer precipices, compelling a return to the ice. Fortunately, the day had been warm enough to loosen the ice-crystals so as to admit of hollows being dug in the rotten portions of the blocks, thus enabling me to pick my way with far less difficulty than I had anticipated. Continuing down over the snout, and along the left lateral moraine, was only a confident saunter, showing that the ascent of the mountain by way of this glacier is easy, provided one is armed with an ax to cut steps here and there.

The lower end of the glacier was beautifully waved and barred by the outcropping edges of the bedded ice-layers which represent the annual snowfalls, and to some extent the irregularities of structure caused by the weathering of the walls of crevasses, and by separate snowfalls which have been followed by rain, hail, thawing and freezing, etc. Small rills were gliding and swirling over the melting surface with a smooth, oily appearance, in channels of pure ice—their quick, compliant movements contrasting most impressively with the rigid, invisible flow of the glacier itself, on whose back they all were riding.

Night drew near before I reached the eastern base of the mountain, and my camp lay many a rugged mile to the north; but ultimate success was assured. It was now only a matter of endurance and ordinary mountain-craft. The sunset was, if possible, yet more beautiful than that of the day before. The Mono landscape seemed to be fairly saturated with warm, purple light. The peaks marshaled along the summit were in shadow, but through every notch and pass streamed vivid sun-fire, soothing and irradiating their rough, black angles, while companies of small, luminous clouds hovered above them like very angels of light.

Darkness came on, but I found my way by the trends of the cañons and the peaks projected against the sky. All excitement died with the light, and then I was weary. But the joyful sound of the waterfall across the lake was heard at last, and soon the stars were seen reflected in the lake itself. Taking my bearings from these, I discovered the little pine thicket in which my nest was, and then I had a rest such as only a tired mountaineer may enjoy. After lying loose and lost for awhile, I made a sunrise fire, went down to the lake, dashed water on my head, and dipped a cupful for tea. The revival brought about by bread and tea was as complete as the exhaustion from excessive enjoyment and toil. Then I crept beneath the pine-tassels to bed. The wind was frosty and the fire burned low, but my sleep was none the less sound, and the evening constellations had swept far to the west before I awoke.

After thawing and resting in the morning sunshine, I sauntered home,—that is, back to the Tuolumne camp,—bearing away toward a cluster of peaks that hold the fountain snows of one of the north tributaries of Rush Creek. Here I discovered a group of beautiful glacier lakes, nestled together in a grand amphitheater. Toward evening, I crossed the divide separating the Mono waters from those of the Tuolumne, and entered the glacier basin that now holds the fountain snows of the stream that forms the upper Tuolumne cascades. This stream I traced down through its many dells and gorges, meadows and bogs, reaching the brink of the main Tuolumne at dusk.

A loud whoop for the artists was answered again and again. Their camp-fire came in sight, and half an hour afterward I was with them. They seemed unreasonably glad to see me. I had been absent only three days; nevertheless, though the weather was fine, they had already been weighing chances as to whether I would ever return, and trying to decide whether they should wait longer or begin to seek their way back to the lowlands. Now their curious troubles were over. They packed their precious sketches, and next morning we set out homeward bound, and in two days entered the Yosemite Valley from the north by way of Indian Cañon.

CHAPTER V

THE PASSES

The sustained grandeur of the High Sierra is strikingly illustrated by the great height of the passes. Between latitude 36° 20′ and 38° the lowest pass, gap, gorge, or notch of any kind cutting across the axis of the range, as far as I have discovered, exceeds 9000 feet in height above the level of the sea; while the average height of all that are in use, either by Indians or whites, is perhaps not less than 11,000 feet, and not one of these is a carriage-pass.

Farther north a carriage-road has been constructed through what is known as the Sonora Pass, on the head waters of the Stanislaus and Walker's rivers, the summit of which is about 10,000 feet above the sea. Substantial wagon-roads have also been built through the Carson and Johnson passes, near the head of Lake Tahoe, over which immense quantities of freight were hauled from California to the mining regions of Nevada, before the construction of the Central Pacific Railroad.

Still farther north, a considerable number of comparatively low passes occur, some of which are accessible to wheeled vehicles, and through these rugged defiles during the exciting years of the gold period long emigrant-trains with foot-sore cattle wearily toiled. After the toil-worn adventurers had escaped a thousand dangers and had crawled thousands of miles across the plains the snowy Sierra at last loomed in sight, the eastern wall of the land of gold. And as with shaded eyes they gazed through the tremulous haze of the desert, with what joy must they have descried the pass through which they were to enter the better land of their hopes and dreams!

Between the Sonora Pass and the southern extremity of the High Sierra, a distance of nearly 160 miles, there are only five passes through which trails conduct from one side of the range to the other. These are barely practicable for animals; a pass in these regions meaning simply any notch or cañon through which one may, by the exercise of unlimited patience, make out to lead a mule, or a sure-footed mustang; animals that can slide or jump as well as walk. Only three of the five passes may be said to be in use, viz.: the Kearsarge, Mono, and Virginia Creek; the tracks leading through the others being only obscure Indian trails, not graded in the least, and scarcely traceable by white men; for much of the way is over solid rock and earthquake avalanche taluses, where the unshod ponies of the Indians leave no appreciable sign. Only skilled mountaineers are able to detect the marks that serve to guide the Indians, such as slight abrasions of the looser rocks, the displacement of stones here and there, and bent bushes and weeds. A general knowledge of the topography is, then, the main guide, enabling one to determine where the trail ought to go—must go. One of these Indian trails crosses the range by a nameless pass between the head waters of the south and middle forks of the San Joaquin, the other between the north and middle forks of the same river, just to the south of "The Minarets"; this last being about 9000 feet high, is the lowest of the five. The Kearsarge is the highest, crossing the summit near the head of the south fork of King's River, about eight miles to the north of Mount Tyndall, through the midst of the most stupendous rock-scenery. The summit of this pass is over 12,000 feet above sea-level; nevertheless, it is one of the safest of the five, and is used every summer, from July to October or November, by hunters, prospectors, and stock-owners, and to some extent by enterprising pleasure-seekers also. For, besides the surpassing grandeur of the scenery about the summit, the trail, in ascending the western flank of the range, conducts through a grove of the giant Sequoias, and through the magnificent Yosemite Valley of the south fork of King's River. This is, perhaps, the highest traveled pass on the North American continent.

The Mono Pass lies to the east of Yosemite Valley, at the head of one of the tributaries of the south fork of the Tuolumne. This is the best known and most extensively traveled of all that exist in the High Sierra. A trail was made through it about the time of the Mono gold excitement, in the year 1858, by adventurous miners and prospectors—men who would build a trail down the throat of darkest Erebus on the way to gold. Though more than a thousand feet lower than the Kearsarge, it is scarcely less sublime in rock-scenery, while in snowy, falling water it far surpasses it. Being so favorably situated for the stream of Yosemite travel, the more adventurous tourists cross over through this glorious gateway to the volcanic region around Mono Lake. It has therefore gained a name and fame above every other pass in the range. According to the few barometrical observations made upon it, its highest point is 10,765 feet above the sea. The other pass of the five we have been considering is somewhat lower, and crosses the axis of the range a few miles to the north of the Mono Pass, at the head of the southernmost tributary of Walker's River. It is used chiefly by roaming bands of the Pah Ute Indians and "sheepmen."

But, leaving wheels and animals out of the question, the free mountaineer with a sack of bread on his shoulders and an ax to cut steps in ice and frozen snow can make his way across the range almost everywhere, and at any time of year when the weather is calm. To him nearly every notch between the peaks is a pass, though much patient step-cutting is at times required up and down steeply inclined glaciers, with cautious climbing over precipices that at first sight would seem hopelessly inaccessible.

In pursuing my studies, I have crossed from side to side of the range at intervals of a few miles all along the highest portion of the chain, with far less real danger than one would naturally count on. And what fine wildness was thus revealed—storms and avalanches, lakes and waterfalls, gardens and meadows, and interesting animals—only those will ever know who give the freest and most buoyant portion of their lives to climbing and seeing for themselves.

To the timid traveler, fresh from the sedimentary levels of the lowlands, these highways, however picturesque and grand, seem terribly forbidding—cold, dead, gloomy gashes in the bones of the mountains, and of all Nature's ways the ones to be most cautiously avoided. Yet they are full of the finest and most telling examples of Nature's love; and though hard to travel, none are safer. For they lead through regions that lie far above the ordinary haunts of the devil, and of the pestilence that walks in darkness. True, there are innumerable places where the careless step will be the last step; and a rock falling from the cliffs may crush without warning like lightning from the sky; but what then! Accidents in the mountains are less common than in the lowlands, and these mountain mansions are decent, delightful, even divine, places to die in, compared with the doleful chambers of civilization. Few places in this world are more dangerous than home. Fear not, therefore, to try the mountain-passes. They will kill care, save you from deadly apathy, set you free, and call forth every faculty into vigorous, enthusiastic action. Even the sick should try these so-called dangerous passes, because for every unfortunate they kill, they cure a thousand.

All the passes make their steepest ascents on the eastern flank. On this side the average rise is not far from a thousand feet to the mile, while on the west it is about two hundred feet. Another marked difference between the eastern and western portions of the passes is that the former begin at the very foot of the range, while the latter can hardly be said to begin lower than an elevation of from seven to ten thousand feet. Approaching the range from the gray levels of Mono and Owen's Valley on the east, the traveler sees before him the steep, short passes in full view, fenced in by rugged spurs that come plunging down from the shoulders of the peaks on either side, the courses of the more direct being disclosed from top to bottom without interruption. But from the west one sees nothing of the way he may be seeking until near the summit, after days have been spent in threading the forests growing on the main dividing ridges between the river cañons.

It is interesting to observe how surely the alp-crossing animals of every kind fall into the same trails. The more rugged and inaccessible the general character of the topography of any particular region, the more surely will the trails of white men, Indians, bears, wild sheep, etc., be found converging into the best passes. The Indians of the western slope venture cautiously over the passes in settled weather to attend dances, and obtain loads of pine-nuts and the larvae of a small fly that breeds in Mono and Owen's lakes, which, when dried, forms an important article of food; while the Pah Utes cross over from the east to hunt the deer and obtain supplies of acorns; and it is truly astonishing to see what immense loads the haggard old squaws make out to carry bare-footed through these rough passes, oftentimes for a distance of sixty or seventy miles. They are always accompanied by the men, who stride on, unburdened and erect, a little in advance, kindly stooping at difficult places to pile stepping-stones for their patient, pack-animal wives, just as they would prepare the way for their ponies.

Bears evince great sagacity as mountaineers, but although they are tireless and enterprising travelers they seldom cross the range. I have several times tracked them through the Mono Pass, but only in late years, after cattle and sheep had passed that way, when they doubtless were following to feed on the stragglers and on those that had been killed by falling over the rocks. Even the wild sheep, the best mountaineers of all, choose regular passes in making journeys across the summits. Deer seldom cross the range in either direction. I have never yet observed a single specimen of the mule-deer of the Great Basin west of the summit, and rarely one of the black-tailed species on the eastern slope, notwithstanding many of the latter ascend the range nearly to the summit every summer, to feed in the wild gardens and bring forth their young.

The glaciers are the pass-makers, and it is by them that the courses of all mountaineers are predestined. Without exception every pass in the Sierra was created by them without the slightest aid or predetermining guidance from any of the cataclysmic agents. I have seen elaborate statements of the amount of drilling and blasting accomplished in the construction of the railroad across the Sierra, above Donner Lake; but for every pound of rock moved in this way, the glaciers which descended east and west through this same pass, crushed and carried away more than a hundred tons.

The so-called practicable road-passes are simply those portions of the range more degraded by glacial action than the adjacent portions, and degraded in such a way as to leave the summits rounded, instead of sharp; while the peaks, from the superior strength and hardness of their rocks, or from more favorable position, having suffered less degradation, are left towering above the passes as if they had been heaved into the sky by some force acting from beneath.

The scenery of all the passes, especially at the head, is of the wildest and grandest description,—lofty peaks massed together and laden around their bases with ice and snow; chains of glacier lakes; cascading streams in endless variety, with glorious views, westward over a sea of rocks and woods, and eastward over strange ashy plains, volcanoes, and the dry, dead-looking ranges of the Great Basin. Every pass, however, possesses treasures of beauty all its own.

Having thus in a general way indicated the height, leading features, and distribution of the principal passes, I will now endeavor to describe the Mono

Pass in particular, which may, I think, be regarded as a fair example of the higher alpine passes in general.

The main portion of the Mono Pass is formed by Bloody Cañon, which begins at the summit of the range, and runs in a general east-northeasterly direction to the edge of the Mono Plain.

The first white men who forced a way through its somber depths were, as we have seen, eager gold-seekers. But the cañon was known and traveled as a pass by the Indians and mountain animals long before its discovery by white men, as is shown by the numerous tributary trails which come into it from every direction. Its name accords well with the character of the "early times" in California, and may perhaps have been suggested by the predominant color of the metamorphic slates in which it is in great part eroded; or more probably by blood-stains made by the unfortunate animals which were compelled to slip and shuffle awkwardly over its rough, cutting rocks. I have never known an animal, either mule or horse, to make its way through the cañon, either in going up or down, without losing more or less blood from wounds on the legs. Occasionally one is killed outright—falling headlong and rolling over precipices like a boulder. But such accidents are rarer than from the terrible appearance of the trail one would be led to expect; the more experienced when driven loose find their way over the dangerous places with a caution and sagacity that is truly wonderful. During the gold excitement it was at times a matter of considerable pecuniary importance to force a way through the cañon with pack-trains early in the spring while it was yet heavily blocked with snow; and then the mules with their loads had sometimes to be let down over the steepest drifts and avalanche beds by means of ropes.

A good bridle-path leads from Yosemite through many a grove and meadow up to the head of the cañon, a distance of about thirty miles. Here the scenery undergoes a sudden and startling condensation. Mountains, red, gray, and black, rise close at hand on the right, whitened around their bases with banks of enduring snow; on the left swells the huge red mass of Mount Gibbs, while in front the eye wanders down the shadowy cañon, and out on the warm plain of Mono, where the lake is seen gleaming like a burnished metallic disk, with clusters of lofty volcanic cones to the south of it.

When at length we enter the mountain gateway, the somber rocks seem aware of our presence, and seem to come thronging closer about us. Happily the ouzel and the old familiar robin are here to sing us welcome, and azure daisies beam with trustfulness and sympathy, enabling us to feel something of Nature's love even here, beneath the gaze of her coldest rocks.

The effect of this expressive outspokenness on the part of the cañon-rocks is greatly enhanced by the quiet aspect of the alpine meadows through which we pass just before entering the narrow gateway. The forests in which they lie, and the mountain-tops rising beyond them, seem quiet and tranquil. We catch their restful spirit, yield to the soothing influences of the sunshine, and saunter dreamily on through flowers and bees, scarce touched by a definite thought; then suddenly we find ourselves in the shadowy cañon, closeted with Nature in one of her wildest strongholds.

After the first bewildering impression begins to wear off, we perceive that it is not altogether terrible; for besides the reassuring birds and flowers we discover a chain of shining lakelets hanging down from the very summit of the pass, and linked together by a silvery stream. The highest are set in bleak, rough bowls, scantily fringed with brown and yellow sedges. Winter storms blow snow through the cañon in blinding drifts, and avalanches shoot from the heights. Then are these sparkling tarns filled and buried, leaving not a hint of their existence. In June and July they begin to blink and thaw out like sleepy eyes, the carices thrust up their short brown spikes, the daisies bloom in turn, and the most profoundly buried of them all is at length warmed and summered as if winter were only a dream.

Red Lake is the lowest of the chain, and also the largest. It seems rather dull and forbidding at first sight, lying motionless in its deep, dark bed. The cañon wall rises sheer from the water's edge on the south, but on the opposite side there is sufficient space and sunshine for a sedgy daisy garden, the center of which is brilliantly lighted with lilies, castilleias, larkspurs, and columbines, sheltered from the wind by leafy willows, and forming a most joyful outburst of plant-life keenly emphasized by the chill baldness of the onlooking cliffs.

After indulging here in a dozing, shimmering lake-rest, the happy stream sets forth again, warbling and trilling like an ouzel, ever delightfully confiding, no matter how dark the way; leaping, gliding, hither, thither, clear or foaming: manifesting the beauty of its wildness in every sound and gesture.

One of its most beautiful developments is the Diamond Cascade, situated a short distance below Red Lake. Here the tense, crystalline water is first dashed into coarse, granular spray mixed with dusty foam, and then divided into a diamond pattern by following the diagonal cleavage-joints that intersect the face of the precipice over which it pours. Viewed in front, it resembles a strip of embroidery of definite pattern, varying through the seasons with the temperature and the volume of water. Scarce a flower may be seen along its snowy border. A few bent pines look on from a distance, and small fringes of cassiope and rock-ferns are growing in fissures near the head, but these are so lowly and undemonstrative that only the attentive observer will be likely to notice them.

On the north wall of the cañon, a little below the Diamond Cascade, a glittering side stream makes its appearance, seeming to leap directly out of the sky. It first resembles a crinkled ribbon of silver hanging loosely down the wall, but grows wider as it descends, and dashes the dull rock with foam. A long rough talus curves up against this part of the cliff, overgrown with snow-pressed willows, in which the fall disappears with many an eager surge and swirl and plashing leap, finally beating its way down to its confluence with the main cañon stream.

Below this point the climate is no longer arctic. Butterflies become larger and more abundant, grasses with imposing spread of panicle wave above your shoulders, and the summery drone of the bumblebee thickens the air. The Dwarf Pine, the tree-mountaineer that climbs highest and braves the coldest blasts, is found scattered in storm-beaten clumps from the summit of the pass about half-way down the cañon. Here it is succeeded by the hardy Two-leaved Pine, which is speedily joined by the taller Yellow and Mountain Pines. These, with the burly juniper, and shimmering aspen, rapidly grow larger as the sunshine becomes richer, forming groves that block the view; or they stand more apart here and there in picturesque groups, that make beautiful and obvious harmony with the rocks and with one another. Blooming underbrush becomes abundant,—azalea, spiraea, and the brier-rose weaving fringes for the streams, and shaggy rugs to relieve the stern, unflinching rock-bosses.

Through this delightful wilderness, Cañon Creek roves without any constraining channel, throbbing and wavering; now in sunshine, now in thoughtful shade; falling, swirling, flashing from side to side in weariless exuberance of energy. A glorious milky way of cascades is thus developed, of which Bower Cascade, though one of the smallest, is perhaps the most beautiful of them all. It is situated in the lower region of the pass, just where the sunshine begins to mellow between the cold and warm climates. Here the glad creek, grown strong with tribute gathered from many a snowy fountain on the heights, sings richer strains, and becomes more human and lovable at every step. Now you may by its side find the rose and homely yarrow, and small meadows full of bees and clover. At the head of a low-browed rock, luxuriant dogwood bushes and willows arch over from bank to bank, embowering the stream with their leafy branches; and drooping plumes, kept in motion by the current, fringe the brow of the cascade in front. From this leafy covert the stream leaps out into the light in a fluted curve thick sown with sparkling crystals, and falls into a pool filled with brown boulders, out of which it creeps gray with foam-bells and disappears in a tangle of verdure like that from which it came.

Hence, to the foot of the cañon, the metamorphic slates give place to granite, whose nobler sculpture calls forth expressions of corresponding beauty from the stream in passing over it,—bright trills of rapids, booming notes of falls, solemn hushes of smooth-gliding sheets, all chanting and blending in glorious harmony. When, at length, its impetuous alpine life is done, it slips through a meadow with scarce an audible whisper, and falls asleep in Moraine Lake.

This water-bed is one of the finest I ever saw. Evergreens wave soothingly about it, and the breath of flowers floats over it like incense. Here our blessed stream rests from its rocky wanderings, all its mountaineering done,—no more foaming rock-leaping, no more wild, exulting song. It falls into a smooth, glassy sleep, stirred only by the night-wind, which, coming down the cañon, makes it croon and mutter in ripples along its broidered shores.

Leaving the lake, it glides quietly through the rushes, destined never more to touch the living rock. Henceforth its path lies through ancient moraines and reaches of ashy sage-plain, which nowhere afford rocks suitable for the development of cascades or sheer falls. Yet this beauty of maturity, though less striking, is of a still higher order, enticing us lovingly on through gentian meadows and groves of rustling aspen to Lake Mono, where, spirit-like, our happy stream vanishes in vapor, and floats free again in the sky.

Bloody Cañon, like every other in the Sierra, was recently occupied by a glacier, which derived its fountain snows from the adjacent summits, and descended into Mono Lake, at a time when its waters stood at a much higher level than now. The principal characters in which the history of the ancient glaciers is preserved are displayed here in marvelous freshness and simplicity, furnishing the student with extraordinary advantages for the acquisition of knowledge of this sort. The most striking passages are polished and striated surfaces, which in many places reflect the rays of the sun like smooth water. The dam of Red Lake is an elegantly modeled rib of metamorphic slate, brought into relief because of its superior strength, and because of the greater intensity of the glacial erosion of the rock immediately above it, caused by a steeply inclined tributary glacier, which entered the main trunk with a heavy down-thrust at the head of the lake.

Moraine Lake furnishes an equally interesting example of a basin formed wholly, or in part, by a terminal moraine dam curved across the path of a stream between two lateral moraines.

At Moraine Lake the cañon proper terminates, although apparently continued by the two lateral moraines of the vanished glacier. These moraines are about 300 feet high, and extend unbrokenly from the sides of the cañon into the plain, a distance of about five miles, curving and tapering in beautiful lines. Their sunward sides are gardens, their shady sides are groves; the former devoted chiefly to eriogonae, compositae, and graminae; a square rod containing five or six profusely flowered eriogonums of several species, about the same number of bahia and linosyris, and a few grass tufts; each species being planted trimly apart, with bare gravel between, as if cultivated artificially.

My first visit to Bloody Cañon was made in the summer of 1869, under circumstances well calculated to heighten the impressions that are the peculiar offspring of mountains. I came from the blooming tangles of Florida, and waded out into the plant-gold of the great valley of California, when its flora was as yet untrodden. Never before had I beheld congregations of social flowers half so extensive or half so glorious. Golden composite covered all the ground from the Coast Range to the Sierra like a stratum of curdled sunshine, in which I reveled for weeks, watching the rising and setting of their innumerable suns; then I gave myself up to be borne forward on the crest of the summer wave that sweeps annually up the Sierra and spends itself on the snowy summits.

At the Big Tuolumne Meadows I remained more than a month, sketching, botanizing, and climbing among the surrounding mountains. The mountaineer with whom I then happened to be camping was one of those remarkable men one so frequently meets in California, the hard angles and bosses of whose characters have been brought into relief by the grinding excitements of the gold period, until they resemble glacial landscapes. But at this late day, my friend's activities had subsided, and his craving for rest caused him to become a gentle shepherd and literally to lie down with the lamb.

Recognizing the unsatisfiable longings of my Scotch Highland instincts, he threw out some hints concerning Bloody Cañon, and advised me to explore it. "I have never seen it myself," he said, "for I never was so unfortunate as to pass that way. But I have heard many a strange story about it, and I warrant you will at least find it wild enough."

Then of course I made haste to see it. Early next morning I made up a bundle of bread, tied my note-book to my belt, and strode away in the bracing air, full of eager, indefinite hope. The plushy lawns that lay in my path served to soothe my morning haste. The sod in many places was starred with daisies and blue gentians, over which I lingered. I traced the paths of the ancient glaciers over many a shining pavement, and marked the gaps in the upper forests that told the power of the winter avalanches. Climbing higher, I saw for the first time the gradual dwarfing of the pines in compliance with climate, and on the summit discovered creeping mats of the arctic willow overgrown with silky catkins, and patches of the dwarf vaccinium with its round flowers sprinkled in the grass like purple hail; while in every direction the landscape stretched sublimely away in fresh wildness—a manuscript written by the hand of Nature alone.

At length, as I entered the pass, the huge rocks began to close around in all their wild, mysterious impressiveness, when suddenly, as I was gazing eagerly about me, a drove of gray hairy beings came in sight, lumbering toward me with a kind of boneless, wallowing motion like bears.

I never turn back, though often so inclined, and in this particular instance, amid such surroundings, everything seemed singularly unfavorable for the calm acceptance of so grim a company. Suppressing my fears, I soon discovered that although as hairy as bears and as crooked as summit pines, the strange creatures were sufficiently erect to belong to our own species. They proved to be nothing more formidable than Mono Indians dressed in the skins of sage-rabbits. Both the men and the women begged persistently for whisky and tobacco, and seemed so accustomed to denials that I found it impossible to convince them that I had none to give. Excepting the names of these two products of civilization, they seemed to understand not a word of English; but I afterward learned that they were on their way to Yosemite Valley to feast awhile on trout and procure a load of acorns to carry back through the pass to their huts on the shore of Mono Lake.

Occasionally a good countenance may be seen among the Mono Indians, but these, the first specimens I had seen, were mostly ugly, and some of them altogether hideous. The dirt on their faces was fairly stratified, and seemed so ancient and so undisturbed it might almost possess a geological significance. The older faces were, moreover, strangely blurred and divided into sections by furrows that looked like the cleavage-joints of rocks, suggesting exposure on the mountains in a castaway condition for ages. Somehow they seemed to have no right place in the landscape, and I was glad to see them fading out of sight down the pass.

Then came evening, and the somber cliffs were inspired with the ineffable beauty of the alpenglow. A solemn calm fell upon everything. All the lower portion of the cañon was in gloaming shadow, and I crept into a hollow near one of the upper lakelets to smooth the ground in a sheltered nook for a bed. When the short twilight faded, I kindled a sunny fire, made a cup of tea, and lay down to rest and look at the stars. Soon the night-wind began to flow and pour in torrents among the jagged peaks, mingling strange tones with those of the waterfalls sounding far below; and as I drifted toward sleep I began to experience an uncomfortable feeling of nearness to the furred Monos. Then the full moon looked down over the edge of the cañon wall, her countenance seemingly filled with intense concern, and apparently so near as to produce a startling effect as if she had entered my bedroom, forgetting all the world, to gaze on me alone.

The night was full of strange sounds, and I gladly welcomed the morning. Breakfast was soon done, and I set forth in the exhilarating freshness of the new day, rejoicing in the abundance of pure wildness so close about me. The stupendous rocks, hacked and scarred with centuries of storms, stood sharply out in the thin early light, while down in the bottom of the cañon grooved and polished bosses heaved and glistened like swelling sea-waves, telling a grand old story of the ancient glacier that poured its crushing floods above them.

Here for the first time I met the arctic daisies in all their perfection of purity and spirituality,—gentle mountaineers face to face with the stormy sky, kept safe and warm by a thousand miracles. I leaped lightly from rock to rock, glorying in the eternal freshness and sufficiency of Nature, and in the ineffable tenderness with which she nurtures her mountain darlings in the very fountains of storms. Fresh beauty appeared at every step, delicate rock-ferns, and groups of the fairest flowers. Now another lake came to view, now a waterfall. Never fell light in brighter spangles, never fell water in whiter foam. I seemed to float through the cañon enchanted, feeling nothing of its roughness, and was out in the Mono levels before I was aware.

Looking back from the shore of Moraine Lake, my morning ramble seemed all a dream. There curved Bloody Cañon, a mere glacial furrow 2000 feet deep, with smooth rocks projecting from the sides and braided together in the middle, like bulging, swelling muscles. Here the lilies were higher than my head, and the sunshine was warm enough for palms. Yet the snow around the arctic willows was plainly visible only four miles away, and between were narrow specimen zones of all the principal climates of the globe.

On the bank of a small brook that comes gurgling down the side of the left lateral moraine, I found a camp-fire still burning, which no doubt belonged to the gray Indians I had met on the summit, and I listened instinctively and moved cautiously forward, half expecting to see some of their grim faces peering out of the bushes.

Passing on toward the open plain, I noticed three well-defined terminal moraines curved gracefully across the cañon stream, and joined by long splices to the two noble laterals. These mark the halting-places of the vanished glacier when it was retreating into its summit shadows on the breaking-up of the glacial winter.

Five miles below the foot of Moraine Lake, just where the lateral moraines lose themselves in the plain, there was a field of wild rye, growing in magnificent waving bunches six to eight feet high, bearing heads from six to twelve inches long. Rubbing out some of the grains, I found them about five eighths of an inch long, dark-colored, and sweet. Indian women were gathering it in baskets, bending down large handfuls, beating it out, and fanning it in the wind. They were quite picturesque, coming through the rye, as one caught glimpses of them here and there, in winding lanes and openings, with splendid tufts arching above their heads, while their incessant chat and laughter showed their heedless joy.

Like the rye-field, I found the so-called desert of Mono blooming in a high state of natural cultivation with the wild rose, cherry, aster, and the delicate abronia; also innumerable gilias, phloxes, poppies, and bush-compositae. I observed their gestures and the various expressions of their corollas, inquiring how they could be so fresh and beautiful out in this volcanic desert. They told as happy a life as any plant-company I ever met, and seemed to enjoy even the hot sand and the wind.

But the vegetation of the pass has been in great part destroyed, and the same may be said of all the more accessible passes throughout the range. Immense numbers of starving sheep and cattle have been driven through them into Nevada, trampling the wild gardens and meadows almost out of existence. The lofty walls are untouched by any foot, and the falls sing on unchanged; but the sight of crushed flowers and stripped, bitten bushes goes far toward destroying the charm of wildness.

The cañon should be seen in winter. A good, strong traveler, who knows the way and the weather, might easily make a safe excursion through it from Yosemite Valley on snow-shoes during some tranquil time, when the storms are hushed. The lakes and falls would be buried then; but so, also, would be the traces of destructive feet, while the views of the mountains in their winter garb, and the ride at lightning speed down the pass between the snowy walls, would be truly glorious.

CHAPTER VI

THE GLACIER LAKES

Among the many unlooked-for treasures that are bound up and hidden away in the depths of Sierra solitudes, none more surely charm and surprise all kinds of travelers than the glacier lakes. The forests and the glaciers and the snowy fountains of the streams advertise their wealth in a more or less telling manner even in the distance, but nothing is seen of the lakes until we have climbed above them. All the upper branches of the rivers are fairly laden with lakes, like orchard trees with fruit. They lie embosomed in the deep woods, down in the grovy bottoms of cañons, high on bald tablelands, and around the feet of the icy peaks, mirroring back their wild beauty over and over again. Some conception of their lavish abundance may be made from the fact that, from one standpoint on the summit of Red Mountain, a day's journey to the east of Yosemite Valley, no fewer than forty-two are displayed within a radius of ten miles. The whole number in the Sierra can hardly be less than fifteen hundred, not counting the smaller pools and tarns, which are innumerable. Perhaps two thirds or more lie on the western flank of the range, and all are restricted to the alpine and subalpine regions. At the close of the last glacial period, the middle and foot-hill regions also abounded in lakes, all of which have long since vanished as completely as the magnificent ancient glaciers that brought them into existence.

Though the eastern flank of the range is excessively steep, we find lakes pretty regularly distributed throughout even the most precipitous portions. They are mostly found in the upper branches of the cañons, and in the glacial amphitheaters around the peaks.

Occasionally long, narrow specimens occur upon the steep sides of dividing ridges, their basins swung lengthwise like hammocks, and very rarely one is found lying so exactly on the summit of the range at the head of some pass that its waters are discharged down both flanks when the snow is melting fast. But, however situated, they soon cease to form surprises to the studious mountaineer; for, like all the love-work of Nature, they are harmoniously related to one another, and to all the other features of the mountains. It is easy, therefore, to find the bright lake-eyes in the roughest and most ungovernable-looking topography of any landscape countenance. Even in the lower regions, where they have been closed for many a century, their rocky orbits are still discernible, filled in with the detritus of flood and avalanche. A beautiful system of grouping in correspondence with the glacial fountains is soon perceived; also their extension in the direction of the trends of the ancient glaciers; and in general their dependence as to form, size, and position upon the character of the rocks in which their basins have been eroded, and the quantity and direction of application of the glacial force expended upon each basin.

In the upper cañons we usually find them in pretty regular succession, strung together like beads on the bright ribbons of their feeding-streams, which pour, white and gray with foam and spray, from one to the other, their perfect mirror stillness making impressive contrasts with the grand blare and glare of the connecting cataracts. In Lake Hollow, on the north side of the Hoffman spur, immediately above the great Tuolumne cañon, there are ten lovely lakelets lying near together in one general hollow, like eggs in a nest. Seen from above, in a general view, feathered with Hemlock Spruce, and fringed with sedge, they seem to me the most singularly beautiful and interestingly located lake-cluster I have ever yet discovered.

Lake Tahoe, 22 miles long by about 10 wide, and from 500 to over 1600 feet in depth, is the largest of all the Sierra lakes. It lies just beyond the northern limit of the higher portion of the range between the main axis and a spur that puts out on the east side from near the head of the Carson River. Its forested shores go curving in and out around many an emerald bay and pine-crowned promontory, and its waters are everywhere as keenly pure as any to be found among the highest mountains.

Donner Lake, rendered memorable by the terrible fate of the Donner party, is about three miles long, and lies about ten miles to the north of Tahoe, at the head of one of the tributaries of the Truckee. A few miles farther north lies Lake Independence, about the same size as Donner. But far the greater number of the lakes lie much higher and are quite small, few of them exceeding a mile in length, most of them less than half a mile.

Along the lower edge of the lake-belt, the smallest have disappeared by the filling-in of their basins, leaving only those of considerable size. But all along the upper freshly glaciated margin of the lake-bearing zone, every hollow, however small, lying within reach of any portion of the close network of streams, contains a bright, brimming pool; so that the landscape viewed from the mountain-tops seems to be sown broadcast with them. Many of the larger lakes are encircled with smaller ones like central gems girdled with sparkling brilliants. In general, however, there is no marked dividing line as to size. In order, therefore, to prevent confusion, I would state here that in giving numbers, I include none less than 500 yards in circumference.

In the basin of the Merced River, I counted 131, of which 111 are upon the tributaries that fall so grandly into Yosemite Valley. Pohono Creek, which forms the fall of that name, takes its rise in a beautiful lake, lying beneath the shadow of a lofty granite spur that puts out from Buena Vista peak. This is now the only lake left in the whole Pohono Basin. The Illilouette has sixteen, the Nevada no fewer than sixty-seven, the Tenaya eight, Hoffmann Creek five, and Yosemite Creek fourteen. There are but two other lake-bearing affluents of the Merced, viz., the South Fork with fifteen, and Cascade Creek with five, both of which unite with the main trunk below Yosemite.

The Merced River, as a whole, is remarkably like an elm-tree, and it requires but little effort on the part of the imagination to picture it standing upright, with all its lakes hanging upon its spreading branches, the topmost eighty miles in height. Now add all the other lake-bearing rivers of the Sierra, each in its place, and you will have a truly glorious spectacle,—an avenue the length and width of the range; the long, slender, gray shafts of the main trunks, the milky way of arching branches, and the silvery lakes, all clearly defined and shining on the sky. How excitedly such an addition to the scenery would be gazed at! Yet these lakeful rivers are still more excitingly beautiful and impressive in their natural positions to those who have the eyes to see them as they lie imbedded in their meadows and forests and glacier-sculptured rocks.

When a mountain lake is born,—when, like a young eye, it first opens to the light,—it is an irregular, expressionless crescent, inclosed in banks of rock and ice,—bare, glaciated rock on the lower side, the rugged snout of a glacier on the upper. In this condition it remains for many a year, until at length, toward the end of some auspicious cluster of seasons, the glacier recedes beyond the upper margin of the basin, leaving it open from shore to shore for the first time, thousands of years after its conception beneath the glacier that excavated its basin. The landscape, cold and bare, is reflected in its pure depths; the winds ruffle its glassy surface, and the sun fills it with throbbing spangles, while its waves begin to lap and murmur around its leafless shores,—sun-spangles during the day and reflected stars at night its only flowers, the winds and the snow its only visitors. Meanwhile, the glacier continues to recede, and numerous rills, still younger than the lake itself, bring down glacier-mud, sand-grains, and pebbles, giving rise to margin-rings and plats of soil. To these fresh soil-beds come many a waiting plant. First, a hardy carex with arching leaves and a spike of brown flowers; then, as the seasons grow warmer, and the soil-beds deeper and wider, other sedges take their appointed places, and these are joined by blue gentians, daisies, dodecatheons, violets, honeyworts, and many a lowly moss. Shrubs also hasten in time to the new gardens,—kalmia with its glossy leaves and purple flowers, the arctic willow, making soft woven carpets, together with the heathy bryanthus and cassiope, the fairest and dearest of them all. Insects now enrich the air, frogs pipe cheerily in the shallows, soon followed by the ouzel, which is the first bird to visit a glacier lake, as the sedge is the first of plants.

So the young lake grows in beauty, becoming more and more humanly lovable from century to century. Groves of aspen spring up, and hardy pines, and the Hemlock Spruce, until it is richly overshadowed and embowered. But while its shores are being enriched, the soil-beds creep out with incessant growth, contracting its area, while the lighter mud-particles deposited on the bottom cause it to grow constantly shallower, until at length the last remnant of the lake vanishes,—closed forever in ripe and natural old age. And now its feeding-stream goes winding on without halting through the new gardens and groves that have taken its place.

The length of the life of any lake depends ordinarily upon the capacity of its basin, as compared with the carrying power of the streams that flow into it, the character of the rocks over which these streams flow, and the relative position of the lake toward other lakes. In a series whose basins lie in the same cañon, and are fed by one and the same main stream, the uppermost will, of course, vanish first unless some other lake-filling agent comes in to modify the result; because at first it receives nearly all of the sediments that the stream brings down, only the finest of the mud-particles being carried through the highest of the series to the next below. Then the next higher, and the next would be successively filled, and the lowest would be the last to vanish. But this simplicity as to duration is broken in upon in various ways, chiefly through the action of side-streams that enter the lower lakes direct. For, notwithstanding many of these side tributaries are quite short, and, during late summer, feeble, they all become powerful torrents in springtime when the snow is melting, and carry not only sand and pine-needles, but large trunks and boulders tons in weight, sweeping them down their steeply inclined channels and into the lake basins with astounding energy. Many of these side affluents also have the advantage of access to the main lateral moraines of the vanished glacier that occupied the cañon, and upon these they draw for lake-filling material, while the main trunk stream flows mostly over clean glacier pavements, where but little moraine matter is ever left for them to carry. Thus a small rapid stream with abundance of loose transportable material within its reach may fill up an extensive basin in a few centuries, while a large perennial trunk stream, flowing over clean, enduring pavements, though ordinarily a hundred times larger, may not fill a smaller basin in thousands of years.

The comparative influence of great and small streams as lake-fillers is strikingly illustrated in Yosemite Valley, through which the Merced flows. The bottom of the valley is now composed of level meadow-lands and dry, sloping soil-beds planted with oak and pine, but it was once a lake stretching from wall to wall and nearly from one end of the valley to the other, forming one of the most beautiful cliff-bound sheets of water that ever existed in the Sierra. And though never perhaps seen by human eye, it was but yesterday, geologically speaking, since it disappeared, and the traces of its existence are still so fresh, it may easily be restored to the eye of imagination and viewed in all its grandeur, about as truly and vividly as if actually before us. Now we find that the detritus which fills this magnificent basin was not brought down from the distant mountains by the main streams that converge here to form the river, however powerful and available for the purpose at first sight they appear; but almost wholly by the small local tributaries, such as those of Indian Cañon, the Sentinel, and the Three Brothers, and by a few small residual glaciers which lingered in the shadows of the walls long after the main trunk glacier had receded beyond the head of the valley.

Had the glaciers that once covered the range been melted at once, leaving the entire surface bare from top to bottom simultaneously, then of course all the lakes would have come into existence at the same time, and the highest, other circumstances being equal, would, as we have seen, be the first to vanish. But because they melted gradually from the foot of the range upward, the lower lakes were the first to see the light and the first to be obliterated. Therefore, instead of finding the lakes of the present day at the foot of the range, we find them at the top. Most of the lower lakes vanished thousands of years before those now brightening the alpine landscapes were born. And in general, owing to the deliberation of the upward retreat of the glaciers, the lowest of the existing lakes are also the oldest, a gradual transition being apparent throughout the entire belt, from the older, forested, meadow-rimmed and contracted forms all the way up to those that are new born, lying bare and meadowless among the highest peaks.

A few small lakes unfortunately situated are extinguished suddenly by a single swoop of an avalanche, carrying down immense numbers of trees, together with the soil they were growing upon. Others are obliterated by land-slips, earthquake taluses, etc., but these lake-deaths compared with those resulting from the deliberate and incessant deposition of sediments, may be termed accidental. Their fate is like that of trees struck by lightning.

The lake-line is of course still rising, its present elevation being about 8000 feet above sea-level; somewhat higher than this toward the southern extremity of the range, lower toward the northern, on account of the difference in time of the withdrawal of the glaciers, due to difference in climate. Specimens occur here and there considerably below this limit, in basins specially protected from inwashing detritus, or exceptional in size. These, however, are not sufficiently numerous to make any marked irregularity in the line. The highest I have yet found lies at an elevation of about 12,000 feet, in a glacier womb, at the foot of one of the highest of the summit peaks, a few miles to the north of Mount Hitter. The basins of perhaps twenty-five or thirty are still in process of formation beneath the few lingering glaciers, but by the time they are born, an equal or greater number will probably have died. Since the beginning of the close of the ice-period the whole number in the range has perhaps never been greater than at present.

A rough approximation to the average duration of these mountain lakes may be made from data already suggested, but I cannot stop here to present the subject in detail. I must also forego, in the mean time, the pleasure of a full discussion of the interesting question of lake-basin formation, for which fine, clear, demonstrative material abounds in these mountains. In addition to what has been already given on the subject, I will only make this one statement. Every lake in the Sierra is a glacier lake. Their basins were not merely remodeled and scoured out by this mighty agent, but in the first place were eroded from the solid.

I must now make haste to give some nearer views of representative specimens lying at different elevations on the main lake-belt, confining myself to descriptions of the features most characteristic of each.

SHADOW LAKE

This is a fine specimen of the oldest and lowest of the existing lakes. It lies about eight miles above Yosemite Valley, on the main branch of the Merced, at an elevation of about 7350 feet above the sea; and is everywhere so securely cliff-bound that without artificial trails only wild animals can get down to its rocky shores from any direction. Its original length was about a mile and a half; now it is only half a mile in length by about a fourth of a mile in width, and over the lowest portion of the basin ninety-eight feet deep. Its crystal waters are clasped around on the north and south by majestic granite walls sculptured in true Yosemitic style into domes, gables, and battlemented headlands, which on the south come plunging down sheer into deep water, from a height of from 1500 to 2000 feet. The South Lyell glacier eroded this magnificent basin out of solid porphyritic granite while forcing its way westward from the summit fountains toward Yosemite, and the exposed rocks around the shores, and the projecting bosses of the walls, ground and burnished beneath the vast ice-flood, still glow with silvery radiance, notwithstanding the innumerable corroding storms that have fallen upon them. The general conformation of the basin, as well as the moraines laid along the top of the walls, and the grooves and scratches on the bottom and sides, indicate in the most unmistakable manner the direction pursued by this mighty ice-river, its great depth, and the tremendous energy it exerted in thrusting itself into and out of the basin; bearing down with superior pressure upon this portion of its channel, because of the greater declivity, consequently eroding it deeper than the other portions about it, and producing the lake-bowl as the necessary result.

With these magnificent ice-characters so vividly before us it is not easy to realize that the old glacier that made them vanished tens of centuries ago; for, excepting the vegetation that has sprung up, and the changes effected by an earthquake that hurled rock-avalanches from the weaker headlands, the basin as a whole presents the same appearance that it did when first brought to light. The lake itself, however, has undergone marked changes; one sees at a glance that it is growing old. More than two thirds of its original area is now dry land, covered with meadow-grasses and groves of pine and fir, and the level bed of alluvium stretching across from wall to wall at the head is evidently growing out all along its lakeward margin, and will at length close the lake forever.

Every lover of fine wildness would delight to saunter on a summer day through the flowery groves now occupying the filled-up portion of the basin. The curving shore is clearly traced by a ribbon of white sand upon which the ripples play; then comes a belt of broad-leafed sedges, interrupted here and there by impenetrable tangles of willows; beyond this there are groves of trembling aspen; then a dark, shadowy belt of Two-leaved Pine, with here and there a round carex meadow ensconced nest-like in its midst; and lastly, a narrow outer margin of majestic Silver Fir 200 feet high. The ground beneath the trees is covered with a luxuriant crop of grasses, chiefly triticum, bromus, and calamagrostis, with purple spikes and panicles arching to one's shoulders; while the open meadow patches glow throughout the summer with showy flowers,—heleniums, goldenrods, erigerons, lupines, castilleias, and lilies, and form favorite hiding and feeding-grounds for bears and deer.

The rugged south wall is feathered darkly along the top with an imposing array of spirey Silver Firs, while the rifted precipices all the way down to the water's edge are adorned with picturesque old junipers, their cinnamon-colored bark showing finely upon the neutral gray of the granite. These, with a few venturesome Dwarf Pines and Spruces, lean out over fissured ribs and tablets, or stand erect back in shadowy niches, in an indescribably wild and fearless manner. Moreover, the white-flowered Douglas spiraea and dwarf evergreen oak form graceful fringes along the narrower seams, wherever the slightest hold can be effected. Rock-ferns, too, are here, such as allosorus, pellaea, and cheilanthes, making handsome rosettes on the drier fissures; and the delicate maidenhair, cistoperis, and woodsia hide back in mossy grottoes, moistened by some trickling rill; and then the orange wall-flower holds up its showy panicles here and there in the sunshine, and bahia makes bosses of gold. But, notwithstanding all this plant beauty, the general impression in looking across the lake is of stern, unflinching rockiness; the ferns and flowers are scarcely seen, and not one fiftieth of the whole surface is screened with plant life.

The sunnier north wall is more varied in sculpture, but the general tone is the same. A few headlands, flat-topped and soil-covered, support clumps of cedar and pine; and up-curving tangles of chinquapin and live-oak, growing on rough earthquake taluses, girdle their bases. Small streams come cascading down between them, their foaming margins brightened with gay primulas, gilias, and mimuluses. And close along the shore on this side there is a strip of rocky meadow enameled with buttercups, daisies, and white violets, and the purple-topped grasses out on its beveled border dip their leaves into the water.

The lower edge of the basin is a dam-like swell of solid granite, heavily abraded by the old glacier, but scarce at all cut into as yet by the outflowing stream, though it has flowed on unceasingly since the lake came into existence.

As soon as the stream is fairly over the lake-lip it breaks into cascades, never for a moment halting, and scarce abating one jot of its glad energy, until it reaches the next filled-up basin, a mile below. Then swirling and curving drowsily through meadow and grove, it breaks forth anew into gray rapids and falls, leaping and gliding in glorious exuberance of wild bound and dance down into another and yet another filled-up lake basin. Then, after a long rest in the levels of Little Yosemite, it makes its grandest display in the famous Nevada Fall. Out of the clouds of spray at the foot of the fall the battered, roaring river gropes its way, makes another mile of cascades and rapids, rests a moment in Emerald Pool, then plunges over the grand cliff of the Vernal Fall, and goes thundering and chafing down a boulder-choked gorge of tremendous depth and wildness into the tranquil reaches of the old Yosemite lake basin.

The color-beauty about Shadow Lake during the Indian summer is much richer than one could hope to find in so young and so glacial a wilderness. Almost every leaf is tinted then, and the golden-rods are in bloom; but most of the color is given by the ripe grasses, willows, and aspens. At the foot of the lake you stand in a trembling aspen grove, every leaf painted like a butterfly, and away to right and left round the shores sweeps a curving ribbon of meadow, red and brown dotted with pale yellow, shading off here and there into hazy purple. The walls, too, are dashed with bits of bright color that gleam out on the neutral granite gray. But neither the walls, nor the margin meadow, nor yet the gay, fluttering grove in which you stand, nor the lake itself, flashing with spangles, can long hold your attention; for at the head of the lake there is a gorgeous mass of orange-yellow, belonging to the main aspen belt of the basin, which seems the very fountain whence all the color below it had flowed, and here your eye is filled and fixed. This glorious mass is about thirty feet high, and extends across the basin nearly from wall to wall. Rich bosses of willow flame in front of it, and from the base of these the brown meadow comes forward to the water's edge, the whole being relieved against the unyielding green of the coniferae, while thick sun-gold is poured over all.

During these blessed color-days no cloud darkens the sky, the winds are gentle, and the landscape rests, hushed everywhere, and indescribably impressive. A few ducks are usually seen sailing on the lake, apparently more for pleasure than anything else, and the ouzels at the head of the rapids sing always; while robins, grosbeaks, and the Douglas squirrels are busy in the groves, making delightful company, and intensifying the feeling of grateful sequestration without ruffling the deep, hushed calm and peace.

This autumnal mellowness usually lasts until the end of November. Then come days of quite another kind. The winter clouds grow, and bloom, and shed their starry crystals on every leaf and rock, and all the colors vanish like a sunset. The deer gather and hasten down their well-known trails, fearful of being snow-bound. Storm succeeds storm, heaping snow on the cliffs and meadows, and bending the slender pines to the ground in wide arches, one over the other, clustering and interlacing like lodged wheat. Avalanches rush and boom from the shelving heights, piling immense heaps upon the frozen lake, and all the summer glory is buried and lost. Yet in the midst of this hearty winter the sun shines warm at times, calling the Douglas squirrel to frisk in the snowy pines and seek out his hidden stores; and the weather is never so severe as to drive away the grouse and little nut-hatches and chickadees.

Toward May, the lake begins to open. The hot sun sends down innumerable streams over the cliffs, streaking them round and round with foam. The snow slowly vanishes, and the meadows show tintings of green. Then spring comes on apace; flowers and flies enrich the air and the sod, and the deer come back to the upper groves like birds to an old nest.

I first discovered this charming lake in the autumn of 1872, while on my way to the glaciers at the head of the river. It was rejoicing then in its gayest colors, untrodden, hidden in the glorious wildness like unmined gold. Year after year I walked its shores without discovering any other trace of humanity than the remains of an Indian camp-fire, and the thigh-bones of a deer that had been broken to get at the marrow. It lies out of the regular ways of Indians, who love to hunt in more accessible fields adjacent to trails. Their knowledge of deer-haunts had probably enticed them here some hunger-time when they wished to make sure of a feast; for hunting in this lake-hollow is like hunting in a fenced park. I had told the beauty of Shadow Lake only to a few friends, fearing it might come to be trampled and "improved" like Yosemite. On my last visit, as I was sauntering along the shore on the strip of sand between the water and sod, reading the tracks of the wild animals that live here, I was startled by a human track, which I at once saw belonged to some shepherd; for each step was turned out 35° or 40° from the general course pursued, and was also run over in an uncertain sprawling fashion at the heel, while a row of round dots on the right indicated the staff that shepherds carry. None but a shepherd could make such a track, and after tracing it a few minutes I began to fear that he might be seeking pasturage; for what else could he be seeking? Returning from the glaciers shortly afterward, nay worst fears were realized. A trail had been made down the mountain-side from the north, and all the gardens and meadows were destroyed by a horde of hoofed locusts, as if swept by a fire. The money-changers were in the temple.

ORANGE LAKE

Besides these larger cañon lakes, fed by the main cañon streams, there are many smaller ones lying aloft on the top of rock benches, entirely independent of the general drainage channels, and of course drawing their supplies from a very limited area. Notwithstanding they are mostly small and shallow, owing to their immunity from avalanche detritus and the inwashings of powerful streams, they often endure longer than others many times larger but less favorably situated. When very shallow they become dry toward the end of summer; but because their basins are ground out of seamless stone they suffer no loss save from evaporation alone; and the great depth of snow that falls, lasting into June, makes their dry season short in any case.

Orange Lake is a fair illustration of this bench form. It lies in the middle of a beautiful glacial pavement near the lower margin of the lake-line, about a mile and a half to the northwest of Shadow Lake. It is only about 100 yards in circumference. Next the water there is a girdle of carices with wide overarching leaves, then in regular order a shaggy ruff of huckleberry bushes, a zone of willows with here and there a bush of the Mountain Ash, then a zone of aspens with a few pines around the outside. These zones are of course concentric, and together form a wall beyond which the naked ice-burnished granite stretches away in every direction, leaving it conspicuously relieved, like a bunch of palms in a desert.

In autumn, when the colors are ripe, the whole circular grove, at a little distance, looks like a big handful of flowers set in a cup to be kept fresh—a tuft of goldenrods. Its feeding-streams are exceedingly beautiful, notwithstanding their inconstancy and extreme shallowness. They have no channel whatever, and consequently are left free to spread in thin sheets upon the shining granite and wander at will. In many places the current is less than a fourth of an inch deep, and flows with so little friction it is scarcely visible. Sometimes there is not a single foam-bell, or drifting pine-needle, or irregularity of any sort to manifest its motion. Yet when observed narrowly it is seen to form a web of gliding lacework exquisitely woven, giving beautiful reflections from its minute curving ripples and eddies, and differing from the water-laces of large cascades in being everywhere transparent. In spring, when the snow is melting, the lake-bowl is brimming full, and sends forth quite a large stream that slips glassily for 200 yards or so, until it comes to an almost vertical precipice 800 feet high, down which it plunges in a fine cataract; then it gathers its scattered waters and goes smoothly over folds of gently dipping granite to its confluence with the main cañon stream. During the greater portion of the year, however, not a single water sound will you hear either at head or foot of the lake, not oven the whispered lappings of ripple-waves along the shore; for the winds are fenced out. But the deep mountain silence is sweetened now and then by birds that stop here to rest and drink on their way across the cañon.

LAKE STARR KING

A beautiful variety of the bench-top lakes occurs just where the great lateral moraines of the main glaciers have been shoved forward in outswelling concentric rings by small residual tributary glaciers. Instead of being encompassed by a narrow ring of trees like Orange Lake, these lie embosomed in dense moraine woods, so dense that in seeking them you may pass them by again and again, although you may know nearly where they lie concealed.

Lake Starr King, lying to the north of the cone of that name, above the Little Yosemite Valley, is a fine specimen of this variety. The ouzels pass it by, and so do the ducks; they could hardly get into it if they would, without plumping straight down inside the circling trees.

Yet these isolated gems, lying like fallen fruit detached from the branches, are not altogether without inhabitants and joyous, animating visitors. Of course fishes cannot get into them, and this is generally true of nearly every glacier lake in the range, but they are all well stocked with happy frogs. How did the frogs get into them in the first place? Perhaps their sticky spawn was carried in on the feet of ducks or other birds, else their progenitors must have made some exciting excursions through the woods and up the sides of the cañons. Down in the still, pure depths of these hidden lakelets you may also find the larvae of innumerable insects and a great variety of beetles, while the air above them is thick with humming wings, through the midst of which fly-catchers are constantly darting. And in autumn, when the huckleberries are ripe, bands of robins and grosbeaks come to feast, forming altogether delightful little byworlds for the naturalist.

Pushing our way upward toward the axis of the range, we find lakes in greater and greater abundance, and more youthful in aspect. At an elevation of about 9000 feet above sea-level they seem to have arrived at middle age,—that is, their basins seem to be about half filled with alluvium. Broad sheets of meadow-land are seen extending into them, imperfect and boggy in many places and more nearly level than those of the older lakes below them, and the vegetation of their shores is of course more alpine. Kalmia, lodum, and cassiope fringe the meadow rocks, while the luxuriant, waving groves, so characteristic of the lower lakes, are represented only by clumps of the Dwarf Pine and Hemlock Spruce. These, however, are oftentimes very picturesquely grouped on rocky headlands around the outer rim of the meadows, or with still more striking effect crown some rocky islet.

Moreover, from causes that we cannot stop here to explain, the cliffs about these middle-aged lakes are seldom of the massive Yosemite type, but are more broken, and less sheer, and they usually stand back, leaving the shores comparatively free; while the few precipitous rocks that do come forward and plunge directly into deep water are seldom more than three or four hundred feet high.

I have never yet met ducks in any of the lakes of this kind, but the ouzel is never wanting where the feeding-streams are perennial. Wild sheep and deer may occasionally be seen on the meadows, and very rarely a bear. One might camp on the rugged shores of these bright fountains for weeks, without meeting any animal larger than the marmots that burrow beneath glacier boulders along the edges of the meadows.

The highest and youngest of all the lakes lie nestled in glacier wombs. At first sight, they seem pictures of pure bloodless desolation, miniature arctic seas, bound in perpetual ice and snow, and overshadowed by harsh, gloomy, crumbling precipices. Their waters are keen ultramarine blue in the deepest parts, lively grass-green toward the shore shallows and around the edges of the small bergs usually floating about in them. A few hardy sedges, frost-pinched every night, are occasionally found making soft sods along the sun-touched portions of their shores, and when their northern banks slope openly to the south, and are soil-covered, no matter how coarsely, they are sure to be brightened with flowers. One lake in particular now comes to mind which illustrates the floweriness of the sun-touched banks of these icy gems. Close up under the shadow of the Sierra Matterhorn, on the eastern slope of the range, lies one of the iciest of these glacier lakes at an elevation of about 12,000 feet. A short, ragged-edged glacier crawls into it from the south, and on the opposite side it is embanked and dammed by a series of concentric terminal moraines, made by the glacier when it entirely filled the basin. Half a mile below lies a second lake, at a height of 11,500 feet, about as cold and as pure as a snow-crystal. The waters of the first come gurgling down into it over and through the moraine dam, while a second stream pours into it direct from a glacier that lies to the southeast. Sheer precipices of crystalline snow rise out of deep water on the south, keeping perpetual winter on that side, but there is a fine summery spot on the other, notwithstanding the lake is only about 300 yards wide. Here, on August 25, 1873, I found a charming company of flowers, not pinched, crouching dwarfs, scarce able to look up, but warm and juicy, standing erect in rich cheery color and bloom. On a narrow strip of shingle, close to the water's edge, there were a few tufts of carex gone to seed; and a little way back up the rocky bank at the foot of a crumbling wall so inclined as to absorb and radiate as well as reflect a considerable quantity of sun-heat, was the garden, containing a thrifty thicket of Cowania covered with large yellow flowers; several bushes of the alpine ribes with berries nearly ripe and wildly acid; a few handsome grasses belonging to two distinct species, and one goldenrod; a few hairy lupines and radiant spragueas, whose blue and rose-colored flowers were set off to fine advantage amid green carices; and along a narrow seam in the very warmest angle of the wall a perfectly gorgeous fringe of Epilobium obcordatum with flowers an inch wide, crowded together in lavish profusion, and colored as royal a purple as ever was worn by any high-bred plant of the tropics; and best of all, and greatest of all, a noble thistle in full bloom, standing erect, head and shoulders above his companions, and thrusting out his lances in sturdy vigor as if growing on a Scottish brae. All this brave warm bloom among the raw stones, right in the face of the onlooking glaciers.

As far as I have been able to find out, these upper lakes are snow-buried in winter to a depth of about thirty-five or forty feet, and those most exposed to avalanches, to a depth of even a hundred feet or more. These last are, of course, nearly lost to the landscape. Some remain buried for years, when the snowfall is exceptionally great, and many open only on one side late in the season. The snow of the closed side is composed of coarse granules compacted and frozen into a firm, faintly stratified mass, like the névé of a glacier. The lapping waves of the open portion gradually undermine and cause it to break off in large masses like icebergs, which gives rise to a precipitous front like the discharging wall of a glacier entering the sea. The play of the lights among the crystal angles of these snow-cliffs, the pearly white of the outswelling bosses, the bergs drifting in front, aglow in the sun and edged with green water, and the deep blue disk of the lake itself extending to your feet,—this forms a picture that enriches all your afterlife, and is never forgotten. But however perfect the season and the day, the cold incompleteness of these young lakes is always keenly felt. We approach them with a kind of mean caution, and steal unconfidingly around their crystal shores, dashed and ill at ease, as if expecting to hear some forbidding voice. But the love-songs of the ouzels and the love-looks of the daisies gradually reassure us, and manifest the warm fountain humanity that pervades the coldest and most solitary of them all.

CHAPTER VII

THE GLACIER MEADOWS

After the lakes on the High Sierra come the glacier meadows. They are smooth, level, silky lawns, lying embedded in the upper forests, on the floors of the valleys, and along the broad backs of the main dividing ridges, at a height of about 8000 to 9500 feet above the sea.

They are nearly as level as the lakes whose places they have taken, and present a dry, even surface free from rock-heaps, mossy bogginess, and the frowsy roughness of rank, coarse-leaved, weedy, and shrubby vegetation. The sod is close and fine, and so complete that you cannot see the ground; and at the same time so brightly enameled with flowers and butterflies that it may well be called a garden-meadow, or meadow-garden; for the plushy sod is in many places so crowded with gentians, daisies, ivesias, and various species of orthocarpus that the grass is scarcely noticeable, while in others the flowers are only pricked in here and there singly, or in small ornamental rosettes.

The most influential of the grasses composing the sod is a delicate calamagrostis with fine filiform leaves, and loose, airy panicles that seem to float above the flowery lawn like a purple mist. But, write as I may, I cannot give anything like an adequate idea of the exquisite beauty of these mountain carpets as they lie smoothly outspread in the savage wilderness. What words are fine enough to picture them I to what shall we liken them? The flowery levels of the prairies of the old West, the luxuriant savannahs of the South, and the finest of cultivated meadows are coarse in comparison. One may at first sight compare them with the carefully tended lawns of pleasure-grounds; for they are as free from weeds as they, and as smooth, but here the likeness ends; for these wild lawns, with all their exquisite fineness, have no trace of that painful, licked, snipped, repressed appearance that pleasure-ground lawns are apt to have even when viewed at a distance. And, not to mention the flowers with which they are brightened, their grasses are very much finer both in color and texture, and instead of lying flat and motionless, matted together like a dead green cloth, they respond to the touches of every breeze, rejoicing in pure wildness, blooming and fruiting in the vital light.

Glacier meadows abound throughout all the alpine and subalpine regions of the Sierra in still greater numbers than the lakes. Probably from 2500 to 3000 exist between latitude 36° 30′ and 39°, distributed, of course, like the lakes, in concordance with all the other glacial features of the landscape.

On the head waters of the rivers there are what are called "Big Meadows," usually about from five to ten miles long. These occupy the basins of the ancient ice-seas, where many tributary glaciers came together to form the grand trunks. Most, however, are quite small, averaging perhaps but little more than three fourths of a mile in length.

One of the very finest of the thousands I have enjoyed lies hidden in an extensive forest of the Two-leaved Pine, on the edge of the basin of the ancient Tuolumne Mer de Glace, about eight miles to the west of Mount Dana.

Imagine yourself at the Tuolumne Soda Springs on the bank of the river, a day's journey above Yosemite Valley. You set off northward through a forest that stretches away indefinitely before you, seemingly unbroken by openings of any kind. As soon as you are fairly into the woods, the gray mountain-peaks, with their snowy gorges and hollows, are lost to view. The ground is littered with fallen trunks that lie crossed and recrossed like storm-lodged wheat; and besides this close forest of pines, the rich moraine soil supports a luxuriant growth of ribbon-leaved grasses—bromus, triticum, calamagrostis, agrostis, etc., which rear their handsome spikes and panicles above your waist. Making your way through the fertile wilderness,—finding lively bits of interest now and then in the squirrels and Clark crows, and perchance in a deer or bear,—after the lapse of an hour or two vertical bars of sunshine are seen ahead between the brown shafts of the pines, showing that you are approaching an open space, and then you suddenly emerge from the forest shadows upon a delightful purple lawn lying smooth and free in the light like a lake. This is a glacier meadow. It is about a mile and a half long by a quarter of a mile wide. The trees come pressing forward all around in close serried ranks, planting their feet exactly on its margin, and holding themselves erect, strict and orderly like soldiers on parade; thus bounding the meadow with exquisite precision, yet with free curving lines such as Nature alone can draw. With inexpressible delight you wade out into the grassy sun-lake, feeling yourself contained in one of Nature's most sacred chambers, withdrawn from the sterner influences of the mountains, secure from all intrusion, secure from yourself, free in the universal beauty. And notwithstanding the scene is so impressively spiritual, and you seem dissolved in it, yet everything about you is beating with warm, terrestrial, human love and life delightfully substantial and familiar. The resiny pines are types of health and steadfastness; the robins feeding on the sod belong to the same species you have known since childhood; and surely these daisies, larkspurs, and goldenrods are the very friend-flowers of the old home garden. Bees hum as in a harvest noon, butterflies waver above the flowers, and like them you lave in the vital sunshine, too richly and homogeneously joy-filled to be capable of partial thought. You are all eye, sifted through and through with light and beauty. Sauntering along the brook that meanders silently through the meadow from the east, special flowers call you back to discriminating consciousness. The sod comes curving down to the water's edge, forming bossy outswelling banks, and in some places overlapping countersunk boulders and forming bridges. Here you find mats of the curious dwarf willow scarce an inch high, yet sending up a multitude of gray silky catkins, illumined here and there with, the purple cups and bells of bryanthus and vaccinium.

Go where you may, you everywhere find the lawn divinely beautiful, as if Nature had fingered and adjusted every plant this very day. The floating grass panicles are scarcely felt in brushing through their midst, so flue are they, and none of the flowers have tall or rigid stalks. In the brightest places you find three species of gentians with different shades of blue, daisies pure as the sky, silky leaved ivesias with warm yellow flowers, several species of orthocarpus with blunt, bossy spikes, red and purple and yellow; the alpine goldenrod, pentstemon, and clover, fragrant and honeyful, with their colors massed and blended. Parting the grasses and looking more closely you may trace the branching of their shining stems, and note the marvelous beauty of their mist of flowers, the glumes and pales exquisitely penciled, the yellow dangling stamens, and feathery pistils. Beneath the lowest leaves you discover a fairy realm of mosses,—hypnum, dicranum, polytriclium, and many others,—their precious spore-cups poised daintily on polished shafts, curiously hooded, or open, showing the richly ornate peristomas worn like royal crowns. Creeping liverworts are here also in abundance, and several rare species of fungi, exceedingly small, and frail, and delicate, as if made only for beauty. Caterpillars, black beetles, and ants roam the wilds of this lower world, making their way through miniature groves and thickets like bears in a thick wood.

And how rich, too, is the life of the sunny air! Every leaf and flower seems to have its winged representative overhead. Dragon-flies shoot in vigorous zigzags through the dancing swarms, and a rich profusion of butterflies—the leguminosae of insects—make a fine addition to the general show. Many of these last are comparatively small at this elevation, and as yet almost unknown to science; but every now and then a familiar vanessa or papilio comes sailing past. Humming-birds, too, are quite common here, and the robin is always found along the margin of the stream, or out in the shallowest portions of the sod, and sometimes the grouse and mountain quail, with their broods of precious fluffy chickens. Swallows skim the grassy lake from end to end, fly-catchers come and go in fitful flights from the tops of dead spars, while woodpeckers swing across from side to side in graceful festoon curves,—birds, insects, and flowers all in their own way telling a deep summer joy.

The influences of pure nature seem to be so little known as yet, that it is generally supposed that complete pleasure of this kind, permeating one's very flesh and bones, unfits the student for scientific pursuits in which cool judgment and observation are required. But the effect is just the opposite. Instead of producing a dissipated condition, the mind is fertilized and stimulated and developed like sun-fed plants. All that we have seen here enables us to see with surer vision the fountains among the summit-peaks to the east whence flowed the glaciers that ground soil for the surrounding forest; and down at the foot of the meadow the moraine which formed the dam which gave rise to the lake that occupied this basin before the meadow was made; and around the margin the stones that were shoved back and piled up into a rude wall by the expansion of the lake ice during long bygone winters; and along the sides of the streams the slight hollows of the meadow which mark those portions of the old lake that were the last to vanish.

I would fain ask my readers to linger awhile in this fertile wilderness, to trace its history from its earliest glacial beginnings, and learn what we may of its wild inhabitants and visitors. How happy the birds are all summer and some of them all winter; how the pouched marmots drive tunnels under the snow, and how fine and brave a life the slandered coyote lives here, and the deer and bears! But, knowing well the difference between reading and seeing, I will only ask attention to some brief sketches of its varying aspects as they are presented throughout the more marked seasons of the year.

The summer life we have been depicting lasts with but little abatement until October, when the night frosts begin to sting, bronzing the grasses, and ripening the leaves of the creeping heathworts along the banks of the stream to reddish purple and crimson; while the flowers disappear, all save the goldenrods and a few daisies, that continue to bloom on unscathed until the beginning of snowy winter. In still nights the grass panicles and every leaf and stalk are laden with frost crystals, through which the morning sunbeams sift in ravishing splendor, transforming each to a precious diamond radiating the colors of the rainbow. The brook shallows are plaited across and across with slender lances of ice, but both these and the grass crystals are melted before midday, and, notwithstanding the great elevation of the meadow, the afternoons are still warm enough to revive the chilled butterflies and call them out to enjoy the late-flowering goldenrods. The divine alpenglow flushes the surrounding forest every evening, followed by a crystal night with hosts of lily stars, whose size and brilliancy cannot be conceived by those who have never risen above the lowlands.

Thus come and go the bright sun-days of autumn, not a cloud in the sky, week after week until near December. Then comes a sudden change. Clouds of a peculiar aspect with a slow, crawling gait gather and grow in the azure, throwing out satiny fringes, and becoming gradually darker until every lake-like rift and opening is closed and the whole bent firmament is obscured in equal structureless gloom. Then comes the snow, for the clouds are ripe, the meadows of the sky are in bloom, and shed their radiant blossoms like an orchard in the spring. Lightly, lightly they lodge in the brown grasses and in the tasseled needles of the pines, falling hour after hour, day after day, silently, lovingly,—all the winds hushed,—glancing and circling hither, thither, glinting against one another, rays interlocking in flakes as large as daisies; and then the dry grasses, and the trees, and the stones are all equally abloom again. Thunder-showers occur here during the summer months, and impressive it is to watch the coming of the big transparent drops, each a small world in itself,—one unbroken ocean without islands hurling free through the air like planets through space. But still more impressive to me is the coming of the snow-flowers,—falling stars, winter daisies,—giving bloom to all the ground alike. Raindrops blossom brilliantly in the rainbow, and change to flowers in the sod, but snow comes in full flower direct from the dark, frozen sky.

The later snow-storms are oftentimes accompanied by winds that break up the crystals, when the temperature is low, into single petals and irregular dusty fragments; but there is comparatively little drifting on the meadow, so securely is it embosomed in the woods. From December to May, storm succeeds storm, until the snow is about fifteen or twenty feet deep, but the surface is always as smooth as the breast of a bird.

Hushed now is the life that so late was beating warmly. Most of the birds have gone down below the snow-line, the plants sleep, and all the fly-wings are folded. Yet the sun beams gloriously many a cloudless day in midwinter, casting long lance shadows athwart the dazzling expanse. In June small flecks of the dead, decaying sod begin to appear, gradually widening and uniting with one another, covered with creeping rags of water during the day, and ice by night, looking as hopeless and unvital as crushed rocks just emerging from the darkness of the glacial period. Walk the meadow now! Scarce the memory of a flower will you find. The ground seems twice dead. Nevertheless, the annual resurrection is drawing near. The life-giving sun pours his floods, the last snow-wreath melts, myriads of growing points push eagerly through the steaming mold, the birds come back, new wings fill the air, and fervid summer life comes surging on, seemingly yet more glorious than before.

This is a perfect meadow, and under favorable circumstances exists without manifesting any marked changes for centuries. Nevertheless, soon or late it must inevitably grow old and vanish. During the calm Indian summer, scarce a sand-grain moves around its banks, but in flood-times and storm-times, soil is washed forward upon it and laid in successive sheets around its gently sloping rim, and is gradually extended to the center, making it dryer. Through a considerable period the meadow vegetation is not greatly affected thereby, for it gradually rises with the rising ground, keeping on the surface like water-plants rising on the swell of waves. But at length the elevation of the meadow-land goes on so far as to produce too dry a soil for the specific meadow-plants, when, of course, they have to give up their places to others fitted for the new conditions. The most characteristic of the newcomers at this elevation above the sea are principally sun-loving gilias, eriogonae, and compositae, and finally forest-trees. Henceforward the obscuring changes are so manifold that the original lake-meadow can be unveiled and seen only by the geologist.

Generally speaking, glacier lakes vanish more slowly than the meadows that succeed them, because, unless very shallow, a greater quantity of material is required to fill up their basins and obliterate them than is required to render the surface of the meadow too high and dry for meadow vegetation. Furthermore, owing to the weathering to which the adjacent rocks are subjected, material of the finer sort, susceptible of transportation by rains and ordinary floods, is more abundant during the meadow period than during the lake period. Yet doubtless many a fine meadow favorably situated exists in almost prime beauty for thousands of years, the process of extinction being exceedingly slow, as we reckon time. This is especially the case with meadows circumstanced like the one we have described—embosomed in deep woods, with the ground rising gently away from it all around, the network of tree-roots in which all the ground is clasped preventing any rapid torrential washing. But, in exceptional cases, beautiful lawns formed with great deliberation are overwhelmed and obliterated at once by the action of land-slips, earthquake avalanches, or extraordinary floods, just as lakes are.

In those glacier meadows that take the places of shallow lakes which have been fed by feeble streams, glacier mud and fine vegetable humus enter largely into the composition of the soil; and on account of the shallowness of this soil, and the seamless, water-tight, undrained condition of the rock-basins, they are usually wet, and therefore occupied by tall grasses and sedges, whose coarse appearance offers a striking contrast to that of the delicate lawn-making kind described above. These shallow-soiled meadows are oftentimes still further roughened and diversified by partially buried moraines and swelling bosses of the bed-rock, which, with the trees and shrubs growing upon them, produce a striking effect as they stand in relief like islands in the grassy level, or sweep across in rugged curves from one forest wall to the other.

Throughout the upper meadow region, wherever water is sufficiently abundant and low in temperature, in basins secure from flood-washing, handsome bogs are formed with a deep growth of brown and yellow sphagnum picturesquely ruined with patches of kalmia and ledum which ripen masses of beautiful color in the autumn. Between these cool, spongy bogs and the dry, flowery meadows there are many interesting varieties which are graduated into one another by the varied conditions already alluded to, forming a series of delightful studies.

HANGING MEADOWS

Another, very well-marked and interesting kind of meadow, differing greatly both in origin and appearance from the lake-meadows, is found lying aslant upon moraine-covered hillsides trending in the direction of greatest declivity, waving up and down over rock heaps and ledges, like rich green ribbons brilliantly illumined with tall flowers. They occur both in the alpine and subalpine regions in considerable numbers, and never fail to make telling features in the landscape. They are often a mile or more in length, but never very wide—usually from thirty to fifty yards. When the mountain or cañon side on which, they lie dips at the required angle, and other conditions are at the same time favorable, they extend from above the timber line to the bottom of a cañon or lake basin, descending in fine, fluent lines like cascades, breaking here and there into a kind of spray on large boulders, or dividing and flowing around on either side of some projecting islet. Sometimes a noisy stream goes brawling down through them, and again, scarcely a drop of water is in sight. They owe their existence, however, to streams, whether visible or invisible, the wildest specimens being found where some perennial fountain, as a glacier or snowbank or moraine spring sends down its waters across a rough sheet of soil in a dissipated web of feeble, oozing rivulets. These conditions give rise to a meadowy vegetation, whose extending roots still more obstruct the free flow of the waters, and tend to dissipate them out over a yet wider area. Thus the moraine soil and the necessary moisture requisite for the better class of meadow plants are at times combined about as perfectly as if smoothly outspread on a level surface. Where the soil happens to be composed of the finer qualities of glacial detritus and the water is not in excess, the nearest approach is made by the vegetation to that of the lake-meadow. But where, as is more commonly the case, the soil is coarse and bouldery, the vegetation is correspondingly rank. Tall, wide-leaved grasses take their places along the sides, and rushes and nodding carices in the wetter portions, mingled with the most beautiful and imposing flowers,—orange lilies and larkspurs seven or eight feet high, lupines, senecios, aliums, painted-cups, many species of mimulus and pentstemon, the ample boat-leaved veratrum alba, and the magnificent alpine columbine, with spurs an inch and a half long. At an elevation of from seven to nine thousand feet showy flowers frequently form the bulk of the vegetation; then the hanging meadows become hanging gardens.

In rare instances we find an alpine basin the bottom of which is a perfect meadow, and the sides nearly all the way round, rising in gentle curves, are covered with moraine soil, which, being saturated with melting snow from encircling fountains, gives rise to an almost continuous girdle of down-curving meadow vegetation that blends gracefully into the level meadow at the bottom, thus forming a grand, smooth, soft, meadow-lined mountain nest. It is in meadows of this sort that the mountain beaver (Haplodon) loves to make his home, excavating snug chambers beneath the sod, digging canals, turning the underground waters from channel to channel to suit his convenience, and feeding the vegetation.

Another kind of meadow or bog occurs on densely timbered hillsides where small perennial streams have been dammed at short intervals by fallen trees. Still another kind is found hanging down smooth, flat precipices, while corresponding leaning meadows rise to meet them.

There are also three kinds of small pot-hole meadows one of which is found along the banks of the main streams, another on the summits of rocky ridges, and the third on glacier pavements, all of them interesting in origin and brimful of plant beauty.

CHAPTER VIII

THE FORESTS

The coniferous forests of the Sierra are the grandest and most beautiful in the world, and grow in a delightful climate on the most interesting and accessible of mountain-ranges, yet strange to say they are not well known. More than sixty years ago David Douglas, an enthusiastic botanist and tree lover, wandered alone through fine sections of the Sugar Pine and Silver Fir woods wild with delight. A few years later, other botanists made short journeys from the coast into the lower woods. Then came the wonderful multitude of miners into the foot-hill zone, mostly blind with gold-dust, soon followed by "sheepmen," who, with wool over their eyes, chased their flocks through all the forest belts from one end of the range to the other. Then the Yosemite Valley was discovered, and thousands of admiring tourists passed through sections of the lower and middle zones on their way to that wonderful park, and gained fine glimpses of the Sugar Pines and Silver Firs along the edges of dusty trails and roads. But few indeed, strong and free with eyes undimmed with care, have gone far enough and lived long enough with the trees to gain anything like a loving conception of their grandeur and significance as manifested in the harmonies of their distribution and varying aspects throughout the seasons, as they stand arrayed in their winter garb rejoicing in storms, putting forth their fresh leaves in the spring while steaming with resiny fragrance, receiving the thunder-showers of summer, or reposing heavy-laden with ripe cones in the rich sungold of autumn. For knowledge of this kind one must dwell with the trees and grow with them, without any reference to time in the almanac sense.

The distribution of the general forest in belts is readily perceived. These, as we have seen, extend in regular order from one extremity of the range to the other; and however dense and somber they may appear in general views, neither on the rocky heights nor down in the leafiest hollows will you find anything to remind you of the dank, malarial selvas of the Amazon and Orinoco, with, their "boundless contiguity of shade," the monotonous uniformity of the Deodar forests of the Himalaya, the Black Forest of Europe, or the dense dark woods of Douglas Spruce where rolls the Oregon. The giant pines, and firs, and Sequoias hold their arms open to the sunlight, rising above one another on the mountain benches, marshaled in glorious array, giving forth the utmost expression of grandeur and beauty with inexhaustible variety and harmony.

The inviting openness of the Sierra woods is one of their most distinguishing characteristics. The trees of all the species stand more or less apart in groves, or in small, irregular groups, enabling one to find a way nearly everywhere, along sunny colonnades and through openings that have a smooth, park-like surface, strewn with brown needles and burs. Now you cross a wild garden, now a meadow, now a ferny, willowy stream; and ever and anon you emerge from all the groves and flowers upon some granite pavement or high, bare ridge commanding superb views above the waving sea of evergreens far and near.

One would experience but little difficulty in riding on horseback through the successive belts all the way up to the storm-beaten fringes of the icy peaks. The deep cañons, however, that extend from the axis of the range, cut the belts more or less completely into sections, and prevent the mounted traveler from tracing them lengthwise.

This simple arrangement in zones and sections brings the forest, as a whole, within the comprehension of every observer. The different species are ever found occupying the same relative positions to one another, as controlled by soil, climate, and the comparative vigor of each species in taking and holding the ground; and so appreciable are these relations, one need never be at a loss in determining, within a few hundred feet, the elevation above sea-level by the trees alone; for, notwithstanding some of the species range upward for several thousand feet, and all pass one another more or less, yet even those possessing the greatest vertical range are available in this connection, in as much as they take on new forms corresponding with the variations in altitude.

Crossing the treeless plains of the Sacramento and San Joaquin from the west and reaching the Sierra foot-hills, you enter the lower fringe of the forest, composed of small oaks and pines, growing so far apart that not one twentieth of the surface of the ground is in shade at clear noonday. After advancing fifteen or twenty miles, and making an ascent of from two to three thousand feet, you reach the lower margin of the main pine belt, composed of the gigantic Sugar Pine, Yellow Pine, Incense Cedar, and Sequoia. Next you come to the magnificent Silver Fir belt, and lastly to the upper pine belt, which sweeps up the rocky acclivities of the summit peaks in a dwarfed, wavering fringe to a height of from ten to twelve thousand feet.

This general order of distribution, with reference to climate dependent on elevation, is perceived at once, but there are other harmonies, as far-reaching in this connection, that become manifest only after patient observation and study. Perhaps the most interesting of these is the arrangement of the forests in long, curving bands, braided together into lace-like patterns, and outspread in charming variety. The key to this beautiful harmony is the ancient glaciers; where they flowed the trees followed, tracing their wavering courses along cañons, over ridges, and over high, rolling plateaus. The Cedars of Lebanon, says Hooker, are growing upon one of the moraines of an ancient glacier. All the forests of the Sierra are growing upon moraines. But moraines vanish like the glaciers that make them. Every storm that falls upon them wastes them, cutting gaps, disintegrating boulders, and carrying away their decaying material into new formations, until at length they are no longer recognizable by any save students, who trace their transitional forms down from the fresh moraines still in process of formation, through those that are more and more ancient, and more and more obscured by vegetation and all kinds of post-glacial weathering.

Had the ice-sheet that once covered all the range been melted simultaneously from the foot-hills to the summits, the flanks would, of course, have been left almost bare of soil, and these noble forests would be wanting. Many groves and thickets would undoubtedly have grown up on lake and avalanche beds, and many a fair flower and shrub would have found food and a dwelling-place in weathered nooks and crevices, but the Sierra as a whole would have been a bare, rocky desert.

It appears, therefore, that the Sierra forests in general indicate the extent and positions of the ancient moraines as well as they do lines of climate. For forests, properly speaking, cannot exist without soil; and, since the moraines have been deposited upon the solid rock, and only upon elected places, leaving a considerable portion of the old glacial surface bare, we find luxuriant forests of pine and fir abruptly terminated by scored and polished pavements on which not even a moss is growing, though soil alone is required to fit them for the growth of trees 200 feet in height.

THE NUT PINE

(Pinus Sabiniana)

The Nut Pine, the first conifer met in ascending the range from the west, grows only on the torrid foothills, seeming to delight in the most ardent sun-heat, like a palm; springing up here and there singly, or in scattered groups of five or six, among scrubby White Oaks and thickets of ceanothus and manzanita; its extreme upper limit being about 4000 feet above the sea, its lower about from 500 to 800 feet.

This tree is remarkable for its airy, widespread, tropical appearance, which suggests a region of palms, rather than cool, resiny pine woods. No one would take it at first sight to be a conifer of any kind, it is so loose in habit and so widely branched, and its foliage is so thin and gray. Full-grown specimens are from forty to fifty feet in height, and from two to three feet in diameter. The trunk usually divides into three or four main branches, about fifteen and twenty feet from the ground, which, after bearing away from one another, shoot straight up and form separate summits; while the crooked subordinate branches aspire, and radiate, and droop in ornamental sprays. The slender, grayish-green needles are from eight to twelve inches long, loosely tasseled, and inclined to droop in handsome curves, contrasting with the stiff, dark-colored trunk and branches in a very striking manner. No other tree of my acquaintance, so substantial in body, is in its foliage so thin and so pervious to the light. The sunbeams sift through even the leafiest trees with scarcely any interruption, and the weary, heated traveler finds but little protection in their shade.

The generous crop of nutritious nuts which the Nut Pine yields makes it a favorite with Indians, bears, and squirrels. The cones are most beautiful, measuring from five to eight inches in length, and not much less in thickness, rich chocolate-brown in color, and protected by strong, down-curving hooks which terminate the scales. Nevertheless, the little Douglas squirrel can open them. Indians gathering the ripe nuts make a striking picture. The men climb the trees like bears and beat off the cones with sticks, or recklessly cut off the more fruitful branches with hatchets, while the squaws gather the big, generous cones, and roast them until the scales open sufficiently to allow the hard-shelled seeds to be beaten out. Then, in the cool evenings, men, women, and children, with their capacity for dirt greatly increased by the soft resin with which they are all bedraggled, form circles around camp-fires, on the bank of the nearest stream, and lie in easy independence cracking nuts and laughing and chattering, as heedless of the future as the squirrels.

Pinus tuberculata

This curious little pine is found at an elevation of from 1500 to 3000 feet, growing in close, willowy groves. It is exceedingly slender and graceful in habit, although trees that chance to stand alone outside the groves sweep forth long, curved branches, producing a striking contrast to the ordinary grove form. The foliage is of the same peculiar gray-green color as that of the Nut Pine, and is worn about as loosely, so that the body of the tree is scarcely obscured by it.

At the age of seven or eight years it begins to bear cones, not on branches, but on the main axis, and, as they never fall off, the trunk is soon picturesquely dotted with them. The branches also become fruitful after they attain sufficient size. The average size of the older trees is about thirty or forty feet in height, and twelve to fourteen inches in diameter. The cones are about four inches long, exceedingly hard, and covered with a sort of silicious varnish and gum, rendering them impervious to moisture, evidently with a view to the careful preservation of the seeds.

No other conifer in the range is so closely restricted to special localities. It is usually found apart, standing deep in chaparral on sunny hill-and cañon-sides where there is but little depth of soil, and, where found at all, it is quite plentiful; but the ordinary traveler, following carriage-roads and trails, may ascend the range many times without meeting it.

While exploring the lower portion of the Merced Cañon I found a lonely miner seeking his fortune in a quartz vein on a wild mountain-side planted with this singular tree. He told me that he called it the Hickory Pine, because of the whiteness and toughness of the wood. It is so little known, however, that it can hardly be said to have a common name. Most mountaineers refer to it as "that queer little pine-tree covered all over with burs." In my studies of this species I found a very interesting and significant group of facts, whose relations will be seen almost as soon as stated:

1st. All the trees in the groves I examined, however unequal in size, are of the same age.

2d. Those groves are all planted on dry hillsides covered with chaparral, and therefore are liable to be swept by fire.

3d. There are no seedlings or saplings in or about the living groves, but there is always a fine, hopeful crop springing up on the ground once occupied by any grove that has been destroyed by the burning of the chaparral.

4th. The cones never fall off and never discharge their seeds until the tree or branch to which they belong dies.

A full discussion of the bearing of these facts upon one another would perhaps be out of place here, but I may at least call attention to the admirable adaptation of the tree to the fire-swept regions where alone it is found. After a grove has been destroyed, the ground is at once sown lavishly with all the seeds ripened during its whole life, which seem to have been carefully held in store with reference to such a calamity. Then a young grove immediately springs up, giving beauty for ashes.

SUGAR PINE

(Pinus Lambertiana)

This is the noblest pine yet discovered, surpassing all others not merely in size but also in kingly beauty and majesty.

It towers sublimely from every ridge and cañon of the range, at an elevation of from three to seven thousand feet above the sea, attaining most perfect development at a height of about 5000 feet.

Full-grown specimens are commonly about 220 feet high, and from six to eight feet in diameter near the ground, though some grand old patriarch is occasionally met that has enjoyed five or six centuries of storms, and attained a thickness of ten or even twelve feet, living on undecayed, sweet and fresh in every fiber.

In southern Oregon, where it was first discovered by David Douglas, on the head waters of the Umpqua, it attains still grander dimensions, one specimen having been measured that was 245 feet high, and over eighteen feet in diameter three feet from the ground. The discoverer was the Douglas for whom the noble Douglas Spruce is named, and many other plants which will keep his memory sweet and fresh as long as trees and flowers are loved. His first visit to the Pacific Coast was made in the year 1825. The Oregon Indians watched him with curiosity as he wandered in the woods collecting specimens, and, unlike the fur-gathering strangers they had hitherto known, caring nothing about trade. And when at length they came to know him better, and saw that from year to year the growing things of the woods and prairies were his only objects of pursuit, they called him "The Man of Grass," a title of which he was proud. During his first summer on the waters of the Columbia he made Fort Vancouver his headquarters, making excursions from this Hudson Bay post in every direction. On one of his long trips he saw in an Indian's pouch some of the seeds of a new species of pine which he learned were obtained from a very large tree far to the southward of the Columbia. At the end of the next summer, returning to Fort Vancouver after the setting in of the winter rains, bearing in mind the big pine he had heard of, he set out on an excursion up the Willamette Valley in search of it; and how he fared, and what dangers and hardships he endured, are best told in his own journal, from which I quote as follows:

> October 26, 1826. Weather dull. Cold and cloudy. When my friends in England are made acquainted with my travels I fear they will think I have told them nothing but my miseries.... I quitted my camp early in the morning to survey the neighboring country, leaving my guide to take charge of the horses until my return in the evening. About an hour's walk from the camp I met an Indian, who on perceiving me instantly strung his bow, placed on his left arm a sleeve of raccoon skin and stood on the defensive. Being quite sure that conduct was prompted by fear and not by hostile intentions, the poor fellow having probably never seen such a being as myself before, I laid my gun at my feet on the ground and waved my hand for him to come to me, which he did slowly and with great caution. I then made him place his bow and quiver of arrows beside my gun, and striking a light gave him a smoke out of my own pipe and a present of a few beads. With my pencil I made a rough sketch of the cone and pine tree which I wanted to obtain, and drew his attention to it, when he instantly pointed with his hand to the hills fifteen or twenty miles distant towards the south; and when I expressed my intention of going thither, cheerfully set out to accompany me. At midday I reached my long-wished-for pines, and lost no time in examining them and endeavoring to collect specimens and seeds. New and strange things seldom fail to make strong impressions, and are therefore frequently over-rated; so that, lest I should never see my friends in England to inform them verbally of this most beautiful and immensely grand tree, I

shall here state the dimensions of the largest I could find among several that had been blown down by the wind. At 3 feet from the ground its circumference is 57 feet 9 inches; at 134 feet, 17 feet 5 inches; the extreme length 245 feet.... As it was impossible either to climb the tree or hew it down, I endeavored to knock off the cones by firing at them with ball, when the report of my gun brought eight Indians, all of them painted with red earth, armed with bows, arrows, bone-tipped spears, and flint-knives. They appeared anything but friendly. I explained to them what I wanted, and they seemed satisfied and sat down to smoke; but presently I saw one of them string his bow, and another sharpen his flint knife with a pair of wooden pincers and suspend it off the wrist of his right hand. Further testimony of their intentions was unnecessary. To save myself by flight was impossible, so without hesitation I stepped back about five paces, cocked my gun, drew one of the pistols out of my belt, and holding it in my left hand and the gun in my right, showed myself determined to fight for my life. As much as possible I endeavored to preserve my coolness, and thus we stood looking at one another without making any movement or uttering a word for perhaps ten minutes, when one at last, who seemed to be the leader, gave a sign that they wished for some tobacco; this I signified that they should have if they fetched a quantity of cones. They went off immediately in search of them, and no sooner were they all out of sight than I picked up my three cones and some twigs of the trees and made the quickest possible retreat, hurrying back to the camp, which I reached before dusk.... I now write lying on the grass with my gun cocked beside me, and penning these lines by the light of my Columbian candle, namely, an ignited piece of rosin-wood.

This grand pine discovered under such, exciting circumstances Douglas named in honor of his friend Dr. Lambert of London.

The trunk is a smooth, round, delicately tapered shaft, mostly without limbs, and colored rich purplish-brown, usually enlivened with tufts of yellow lichen. At the top of this magnificent bole, long, curving branches sweep gracefully outward and downward, sometimes forming a palm-like crown, but far more nobly impressive than any palm crown I ever beheld. The needles are about three inches long, finely tempered and arranged in rather close tassels at the ends of slender branchlets that clothe the long, outsweeping limbs. How well they sing in the wind, and how strikingly harmonious an effect is made by the immense cylindrical cones that depend loosely from the ends of the main branches! No one knows what Nature can do in the way of pine-burs until he has seen those of the Sugar Pine. They are commonly from fifteen to eighteen inches long, and three in diameter; green, shaded with dark purple on their sunward sides. They are ripe in September and October. Then the flat scales open and the seeds take wing, but the empty cones become still more beautiful and effective, for their diameter is nearly doubled by the spreading of the scales, and their color changes to a warm yellowish-brown; while they remain swinging on the tree all the following winter and summer, and continue effectively beautiful even on the ground many years after they fall. The wood is deliciously fragrant, and fine in grain and texture; it is of a rich cream-yellow, as if formed of condensed sunbeams. Retinospora obtusa, Siebold, the glory of Eastern forests, is called "Fu-si-no-ki" (tree of the sun) by the Japanese; the Sugar Pine is the sun-tree of the Sierra. Unfortunately it is greatly prized by the lumbermen, and in accessible places is always the first tree in the woods to feel their steel. But the regular lumbermen, with their saw-mills, have been, less generally destructive thus far than the shingle-makers. The wood splits freely, and there is a constant demand for the shingles. And because an ax, and saw, and frow are all the capital required for the business, many of that drifting, unsteady class of men so large in California engage in it for a few months in the year. When prospectors, hunters, ranch hands, etc., touch their "bottom dollar" and find themselves out of employment, they say, "Well, I can at least go to the Sugar Pines and make shingles." A few posts are set in the ground, and a single length cut from the first tree felled produces boards enough for the walls and roof of a cabin; all the rest the lumberman makes is for sale, and he is speedily independent. No gardener or haymaker is more sweetly perfumed than these rough mountaineers while engaged in this business, but the havoc they make is most deplorable.

The sugar, from which the common name is derived, is to my taste the best of sweets—better than maple sugar. It exudes from the heart-wood, where wounds have been made, either by forest fires, or the ax, in the shape of irregular, crisp, candy-like kernels, which are crowded together in masses of considerable size, like clusters of resin-beads. When fresh, it is perfectly white and delicious, but, because most of the wounds on which it is found have been made by fire, the exuding sap is stained on the charred surface, and the hardened sugar becomes brown. Indians are fond of it, but on account of its laxative properties only small quantities may be eaten. Bears, so fond of sweet things in general, seem never to taste it; at least I have failed to find any trace of their teeth in this connection.

No lover of trees will ever forget his first meeting with the Sugar Pine, nor will he afterward need a poet to call him to "listen what the pine-tree saith." In most pine-trees there is a sameness of expression, which, to most people, is apt to become monotonous; for the typical spiry form, however beautiful, affords but little scope for appreciable individual character. The Sugar Pine is as free from conventionalities of form and motion as any oak. No two are alike, even to the most inattentive observer; and, notwithstanding they are ever tossing out their immense arms in what might seem most extravagant gestures, there is a majesty and repose about them that precludes all possibility of the grotesque, or even picturesque, in their general expression. They are the priests of pines, and seem ever to be addressing the surrounding forest. The Yellow Pine is found growing with them on warm hillsides, and the White Silver Fir on cool northern slopes; but, noble as these are, the Sugar Pine is easily king, and spreads his arms above them in blessing while they rock and wave in sign of recognition. The main branches are sometimes found to be forty feet in length, yet persistently simple, seldom dividing at all, excepting near the end; but anything like a bare cable appearance is prevented by the small, tasseled branchlets that extend all around them; and when these superb limbs sweep out symmetrically on all sides, a crown sixty or seventy feet wide is formed, which, gracefully poised on the summit of the noble shaft, and filled with sunshine, is one of the most glorious forest objects conceivable. Commonly, however, there is a great preponderance of limbs toward the east, away from the direction of the prevailing winds.

No other pine seems to me so unfamiliar and self-contained. In approaching it, we feel as if in the presence of a superior being, and begin to walk with a light step, holding our breath. Then, perchance, while we gaze awe-stricken, along comes a merry squirrel, chattering and laughing, to break the spell, running up the trunk with no ceremony, and gnawing off the cones as if they were made only for him; while the carpenter-woodpecker hammers away at the bark, drilling holes in which to store his winter supply of acorns.

Although so wild and unconventional when full-grown, the Sugar Pine is a remarkably proper tree in youth. The old is the most original and independent in appearance of all the Sierra evergreens; the young is the most regular,—a strict follower of coniferous fashions,—slim, erect, with leafy, supple branches kept exactly in place, each tapering in outline and terminating in a spiry point. The successive transitional forms presented between the cautious neatness of youth and bold freedom of maturity offer a delightful study. At the age of fifty or sixty years, the shy, fashionable form begins to be broken up. Specialized branches push out in the most unthought-of places, and bend with the great cones, at once marking individual character, and this being constantly augmented from year to year by the varying action of the sunlight, winds, snow-storms, etc., the individuality of the tree is never again lost in the general forest.

The most constant companion of this species is the Yellow Pine, and a worthy companion it is.

The Douglas Spruce, Libocedrus, Sequoia, and the White Silver Fir are also more or less associated with it; but on many deep-soiled mountain-sides, at an elevation of about 5000 feet above the sea, it forms the bulk of the forest, filling every swell and hollow and down-plunging ravine. The majestic crowns, approaching each other in bold curves, make a glorious canopy through which the tempered sunbeams pour, silvering the needles, and gilding the massive boles, and flowery, park-like ground, into a scene of enchantment.

On the most sunny slopes the white-flowered fragrant chamoebatia is spread like a carpet, brightened during early summer with the crimson Sarcodes, the wild rose, and innumerable violets and gilias. Not even in the shadiest nooks will you find any rank, untidy weeds or unwholesome darkness. On the north sides of ridges the boles are more slender, and the ground is mostly occupied by an underbrush of hazel, ceanothus, and flowering dogwood, but never so densely as to prevent the traveler from sauntering where he will; while the crowning branches are never impenetrable to the rays of the sun, and never so interblended as to lose their individuality.

View the forest from beneath or from some commanding ridge-top; each tree presents a study in itself, and proclaims the surpassing grandeur of the species.

YELLOW, OR SILVER PINE

(Pinus ponderosa)

The Silver, or Yellow, Pine, as it is commonly called, ranks second among the pines of the Sierra as a lumber tree, and almost rivals the Sugar Pine in stature and nobleness of port. Because of its superior powers of enduring variations of climate and soil, it has a more extensive range than any other conifer growing on the Sierra. On the western slope it is first met at an elevation of about 2000 feet, and extends nearly to the upper limit of the timber line. Thence, crossing the range by the lowest passes, it descends to the eastern base, and pushes out for a considerable distance into the hot volcanic plains, growing bravely upon well-watered moraines, gravelly lake basins, arctic ridges, and torrid lava-beds; planting itself upon the lips of craters, flourishing vigorously even there, and tossing ripe cones among the ashes and cinders of Nature's hearths.

The average size of full-grown trees on the western slope, where it is associated with the Sugar Pine, is a little less than 200 feet in height and from five to six feet in diameter, though specimens may easily be found that are considerably larger. I measured one, growing at an elevation of 4000 feet in the valley of the Merced, that is a few inches over eight feet in diameter, and 220 feet high.

Where there is plenty of free sunshine and other conditions are favorable, it presents a striking contrast in form to the Sugar Pine, being a symmetrical spire, formed of a straight round trunk, clad with innumerable branches that are divided over and over again. About one half of the trunk is commonly branchless, but where it grows at all close, three fourths or more become naked; the tree presenting then a more slender and elegant shaft than any other tree in the woods. The bark is mostly arranged in massive plates, some of them measuring four or five feet in length by eighteen inches in width, with a thickness of three or four inches, forming a quite marked and distinguishing feature. The needles are of a fine, warm, yellow-green color, six to eight inches long, firm and elastic, and crowded in handsome, radiant tassels on the upturning ends of the branches. The cones are about three or four inches long, and two and a half wide, growing in close, sessile clusters among the leaves.

The species attains its noblest form in filled-up lake basins, especially in those of the older yosemites, and so prominent a part does it form of their groves that it may well be called the Yosemite Pine. Ripe specimens favorably situated are almost always 200 feet or more in height, and the branches clothe the trunk nearly to the ground, as seen in the illustration.

The Jeffrey variety attains its finest development in the northern portion of the range, in the wide basins of the McCloud and Pitt rivers, where it forms magnificent forests scarcely invaded by any other tree. It differs from the ordinary form in size, being only about half as tall, and in its redder and more closely furrowed bark, grayish-green foliage, less divided branches, and larger cones; but intermediate forms come in which make a clear separation impossible, although some botanists regard it as a distinct species. It is this variety that climbs storm-swept ridges, and wanders out among the volcanoes of the Great Basin. Whether exposed to extremes of heat or cold, it is dwarfed like every other tree, and becomes all knots and angles, wholly unlike the majestic forms we have been sketching. Old specimens, bearing cones about as big as pineapples, may sometimes be found clinging to rifted rocks at an elevation of seven or eight thousand feet, whose highest branches scarce reach above one's shoulders.

I have oftentimes feasted on the beauty of these noble trees when they were towering in all their winter grandeur, laden with snow—one mass of bloom; in summer, too, when the brown, staminate clusters hang thick among the shimmering needles, and the big purple burs are ripening in the mellow light; but it is during cloudless wind-storms that these colossal pines are most impressively beautiful. Then they bow like willows, their leaves streaming forward all in one direction, and, when the sun shines upon them at the required angle, entire groves glow as if every leaf were burnished silver. The fall of tropic light on the royal crown of a palm is a truly glorious spectacle, the fervid sun-flood breaking upon the glossy leaves in long lance-rays, like mountain water among boulders. But to me there is something more impressive in the fall of light upon these Silver Pines. It seems beaten to the finest dust, and is shed off in myriads of minute sparkles that seem to come from the very heart of the trees, as if, like rain falling upon fertile soil, it had been absorbed, to reappear in flowers of light.

This species also gives forth the finest music to the wind. After listening to it in all kinds of winds, night and day, season after season, I think I could approximate to my position on the mountains by this pine-music alone. If you would catch the tones of separate needles, climb a tree. They are well tempered, and give forth no uncertain sound, each standing out, with no interference excepting during heavy gales; then you may detect the click of one needle upon another, readily distinguishable from their free, wing-like hum. Some idea of their temper may be drawn from the fact that, notwithstanding they are so long, the vibrations that give rise to the peculiar shimmering of the light are made at the rate of about two hundred and fifty per minute.

When a Sugar Pine and one of this species equal in size are observed together, the latter is seen to be far more simple in manners, more lithely graceful, and its beauty is of a kind more easily appreciated; but then, it is, on the other hand, much less dignified and original in demeanor. The Silver Pine seems eager to shoot aloft. Even while it is drowsing in autumn sun-gold, you may still detect a skyward aspiration. But the Sugar Pine seems too unconsciously noble, and too complete in every way, to leave room for even a heavenward care.

DOUGLAS SPRUCE

(Pseudotsuga Douglasii)

This tree is the king of the spruces, as the Sugar Pine is king of pines. It is by far the most majestic spruce I ever beheld in any forest, and one of the largest and longest lived of the giants that flourish throughout the main pine belt, often attaining a height of nearly 200 feet, and a diameter of six or seven. Where the growth is not too close, the strong, spreading branches come more than halfway down the trunk, and these are hung with innumerable slender, swaying sprays, that are handsomely feathered with the short leaves which radiate at right angles all around them. This vigorous spruce is ever beautiful, welcoming the mountain winds and the snow as well as the mellow summer light, and maintaining its youthful freshness undiminished from century to century through a thousand storms.

It makes its finest appearance in the months of June and July. The rich brown buds with which its sprays are tipped swell and break about this time, revealing the young leaves, which at first are bright yellow, making the tree appear as if covered with gay blossoms; while the pendulous bracted cones with their shell-like scales are a constant adornment.

The young trees are mostly gathered into beautiful family groups, each sapling exquisitely symmetrical. The primary branches are whorled regularly around the axis, generally in fives, while each is draped with long, feathery sprays, that descend in curves as free and as finely drawn as those of falling water.

In Oregon and Washington it grows in dense forests, growing tall and mast-like to a height of 300 feet, and is greatly prized as a lumber tree. But in the Sierra it is scattered among other trees, or forms small groves, seldom ascending higher than 5500 feet, and never making what would be called a forest. It is not particular in its choice of soil—wet or dry, smooth or rocky, it makes out to live well on them all. Two of the largest specimens I have measured are in Yosemite Valley, one of which is more than eight feet in diameter, and is growing upon the terminal moraine of the residual glacier that occupied the South Fork Canon; the other is nearly as large, growing upon angular blocks of granite that have been shaken from the precipitous front of the Liberty Cap near the Nevada Fall. No other tree seems so capable of adapting itself to earthquake taluses, and many of these rough boulder-slopes are occupied by it almost exclusively, especially in yosemite gorges moistened by the spray of waterfalls.

INCENSE CEDAR

(Libocedrus decurrens)

The Incense Cedar is another of the giants quite generally distributed throughout this portion of the forest, without exclusively occupying any considerable area, or even making extensive groves. It ascends to about 5000 feet on the warmer hillsides, and reaches the climate most congenial to it at about from 3000 to 4000 feet, growing vigorously at this elevation on all kinds of soil, and in particular it is capable of enduring more moisture about its roots than any of its companions, excepting only the Sequoia.

The largest specimens are about 150 feet high, and seven feet in diameter. The bark is brown, of a singularly rich tone very attractive to artists, and the foliage is tinted with a warmer yellow than that of any other evergreen in the woods. Casting your eye over the general forest from some ridge-top, the color alone of its spiry summits is sufficient to identify it in any company.

In youth, say up to the age of seventy or eighty years, no other tree forms so strictly tapered a cone from top to bottom. The branches swoop outward and downward in bold curves, excepting the younger ones near the top, which aspire, while the lowest droop to the ground, and all spread out in flat, ferny plumes, beautifully fronded, and imbricated upon one another. As it becomes older, it grows strikingly irregular and picturesque. Large special branches put out at right angles from the trunk, form big, stubborn elbows, and then shoot up parallel with the axis. Very old trees are usually dead at the top, the main axis protruding above ample masses of green plumes, gray and lichen-covered, and drilled full of acorn holes by the woodpeckers. The plumes are exceedingly beautiful; no waving fern-frond in shady dell is more unreservedly beautiful in form and texture, or half so inspiring in color and spicy fragrance. In its prime, the whole tree is thatched with them, so that they shed off rain and snow like a roof, making fine mansions for storm-bound birds and mountaineers. But if you would see the Libocedrus in all its glory, you must go to the woods in winter. Then it is laden with myriads of four-sided staminate cones about the size of wheat grains,—

winter wheat,—producing a golden tinge, and forming a noble illustration of Nature's immortal vigor and virility. The fertile cones are about three fourths of an inch long, borne on the outside of the plumy branchlets, where they serve to enrich still more the surpassing beauty of this grand winter-blooming goldenrod.

WHITE SILVER FIR

(Abies concolor)

We come now to the most regularly planted of all the main forest belts, composed almost exclusively of two noble firs—A. concolor and A. magnifica. It extends with no marked interruption for 450 miles, at an elevation of from 5000 to nearly 9000 feet above the sea. In its youth A. concolor is a charmingly symmetrical tree with branches regularly whorled in level collars around its whitish-gray axis, which terminates in a strong, hopeful shoot. The leaves are in two horizontal rows, along branchlets that commonly are less than eight years old, forming handsome plumes, pinnated like the fronds of ferns. The cones are grayish-green when ripe, cylindrical, about from three to four inches long by one and a half to two inches wide, and stand upright on the upper branches.

Full-grown trees, favorably situated as to soil and exposure, are about 200 feet high, and five or six feet in diameter near the ground, though larger specimens are by no means rare.

As old age creeps on, the bark becomes rougher and grayer, the branches lose their exact regularity, many are snow-bent or broken off, and the main axis often becomes double or otherwise irregular from accidents to the terminal bud or shoot; but throughout all the vicissitudes of its life on the mountains, come what may, the noble grandeur of the species is patent to every eye.

MAGNIFICENT SILVER FIR, OR RED FIR

(Abies magnifica)

This is the most charmingly symmetrical of all the giants of the Sierra woods, far surpassing its companion species in this respect, and easily distinguished from it by the purplish-red bark, which is also more closely furrowed than that of the white, and by its larger cones, more regularly whorled and fronded branches, and by its leaves, which are shorter, and grow all around the branchlets and point upward.

In size, these two Silver Firs are about equal, the magnifica perhaps a little the taller. Specimens from 200 to 250 feet high are not rare on well-ground moraine soil, at an elevation of from 7500 to 8500 feet above sea-level. The largest that I measured stands back three miles from the brink of the north wall of Yosemite Valley. Fifteen years ago it was 240 feet high, with a diameter of a little more than five feet.

Happy the man with the freedom and the love to climb one of these superb trees in full flower and fruit. How admirable the forest-work of Nature is then seen to be, as one makes his way up through the midst of the broad, fronded branches, all arranged in exquisite order around the trunk, like the whorled leaves of lilies, and each branch and branchlet about as strictly pinnate as the most symmetrical fern-frond. The staminate cones are seen growing straight downward from the under side of the young branches in lavish profusion, making fine purple clusters amid the grayish-green foliage. On the topmost branches the fertile cones are set firmly on end like small casks. They are about six inches long, three wide, covered with a fine gray down, and streaked with crystal balsam that seems to have been poured upon each cone from above.

Both the Silver Firs live 250 years or more when the conditions about them are at all favorable. Some venerable patriarch may often be seen, heavily storm-marked, towering in severe majesty above the rising generation, with a protecting grove of saplings pressing close around his feet, each dressed with such loving care that not a leaf seems wanting. Other companies are made up of trees near the prime of life, exquisitely harmonized to one another in form and gesture, as if Nature had culled them one by one with nice discrimination from all the rest of the woods.

It is from this tree, called Red Fir by the lumberman, that mountaineers always cut boughs to sleep on when they are so fortunate as to be within its limits. Two rows of the plushy branches overlapping along the middle, and a crescent of smaller plumes mixed with ferns and flowers for a pillow, form the very best bed imaginable. The essences of the pressed leaves seem to fill every pore of one's body, the sounds of falling water make a soothing hush, while the spaces between the grand spires afford noble openings through which to gaze dreamily into the starry sky. Even in the matter of sensuous ease, any combination of cloth, steel springs, and feathers seems vulgar in comparison.

The fir woods are delightful sauntering-grounds at any time of year, but most so in autumn. Then the noble trees are hushed in the hazy light, and drip with balsam; the cones are ripe, and the seeds, with their ample purple wings, mottle the air like flocks of butterflies; while deer feeding in the flowery openings between the groves, and birds and squirrels in the branches, make a pleasant stir which enriches the deep, brooding calm of the wilderness, and gives a peculiar impressiveness to every tree. No wonder the enthusiastic Douglas went wild with joy when he first discovered this species. Even in the Sierra, where so many noble evergreens challenge admiration, we linger among these colossal firs with fresh love, and extol their beauty again and again, as if no other in the world could henceforth claim our regard.

It is in these woods the great granite domes rise that are so striking and characteristic a feature of the Sierra. And here too we find the best of the garden meadows. They lie level on the tops of the dividing ridges, or sloping on the sides of them, embedded in the magnificent forest. Some of these meadows are in great part occupied by Veratrumalba, which here grows rank and tall, with boat-shaped leaves thirteen inches long and twelve inches wide, ribbed like those of cypripedium. Columbine grows on the drier margins with tall larkspurs and lupines waist-deep in grasses and sedges; several species of castilleia also make a bright show in beds of blue and white violets and daisies. But the glory of these forest meadows is a lily—L. parvum. The flowers are orange-colored and quite small, the smallest I ever saw of the true lilies; but it is showy nevertheless, for it is seven to eight feet high and waves magnificent racemes of ten to twenty flowers or more over one's head, while it stands out in the open ground with just enough of grass and other plants about it to make a fringe for its feet and show it off to best advantage.

A dry spot a little way back from the margin of a Silver Fir lily garden makes a glorious campground, especially where the slope is toward the east and opens a view of the distant peaks along the summit of the range. The tall lilies are brought forward in all their glory by the light of your blazing camp-fire, relieved against the outer darkness, and the nearest of the trees with their whorled branches tower above you like larger lilies, and the sky seen through the garden opening seems one vast meadow of white lily stars.

In the morning everything is joyous and bright, the delicious purple of the dawn changes softly to daffodil yellow and white; while the sunbeams pouring through the passes between the peaks give a margin of gold to each of them. Then the spires of the firs in the hollows of the middle region catch the glow, and your camp grove is filled with light. The birds begin to stir, seeking sunny branches on the edge of the meadow for sun-baths after the cold night, and looking for their breakfasts, every one of them as fresh as a lily and as charmingly arrayed. Innumerable insects begin to dance, the deer withdraw from the open glades and ridge-tops to their leafy hiding-places in the chaparral, the flowers open and straighten their petals as the dew vanishes, every pulse beats high, every life-cell rejoices, the very rocks seem to tingle with life, and God is felt brooding over everything great and small.

BIG TREE

(Sequoia gigantea)

Between the heavy pine and Silver Fir belts we find the Big Tree, the king of all the conifers in the world, "the noblest of a noble race." It extends in a widely interrupted belt from a small grove on the middle fork of the American River to the head of Deer Creek, a distance of about 260 miles, the northern limit being near the thirty-ninth parallel, the southern a little below the thirty-sixth, and the elevation of the belt above the sea varies from about 5000 to 8000 feet. From the American River grove to the forest on King's River the species occurs only in small isolated groups so sparsely distributed along the belt that three of the gaps in it are from forty to sixty miles wide. But from King's River southward the Sequoia is not restricted to mere groves, but extends across the broad rugged basins of the Kaweah and Tule rivers in noble forests, a distance of nearly seventy miles, the continuity of this part of the belt being broken only by deep cañons. The Fresno, the largest of the northern groves, occupies an area of three or four square miles, a short distance to the southward of the famous Mariposa Grove. Along the beveled rim of the cañon of the south fork of King's River there is a majestic forest of Sequoia about six miles long by two wide. This is the northernmost assemblage of Big Trees that may fairly be called a forest. Descending the precipitous divide between the King's River and Kaweah you enter the grand forests that form the main continuous portion of the belt. Advancing southward the giants become more and more irrepressibly exuberant, heaving their massive crowns into the sky from every ridge and slope, and waving onward in graceful compliance with the complicated topography of the region. The finest of the Kaweah section of the belt is on the broad ridge between Marble Creek and the middle fork, and extends from the granite headlands overlooking the hot plains to within a few miles of the cool glacial fountains of the summit peaks. The extreme upper limit of the belt is reached between the middle and south forks of the Kaweah at an elevation of 8400 feet. But the finest block of Big Tree forest in the entire belt is on the north fork of Tule River. In the northern groves there are comparatively few young trees or saplings. But here for every old, storm-stricken giant there are many in all the glory of prime vigor, and for each of these a crowd of eager, hopeful young trees and saplings growing heartily on moraines, rocky ledges, along watercourses, and in the moist alluvium of meadows, seemingly in hot pursuit of eternal life.

But though the area occupied by the species increases so much from north to south there is no marked increase in the size of the trees. A height of 275 feet and a diameter near the ground of about 20 feet is perhaps about the average size of full-grown trees favorably situated; specimens 25 feet in diameter are not very rare, and a few are nearly 300 feet high. In the Calaveras Grove there are four trees over 300 feet in height, the tallest of which by careful measurement is 325 feet. The largest I have yet met in the course of my explorations is a majestic old scarred monument in the King's River forest. It is 35 feet 8 inches in diameter inside the bark four feet from the ground. Under the most favorable conditions these giants probably live 5000 years or more, though few of even the larger trees are more than half as old. I never saw a Big Tree that had died a natural death; barring accidents they seem to be immortal, being exempt from all the diseases that afflict and kill other trees. Unless destroyed by man, they live on indefinitely until burned, smashed by lightning, or cast down by storms, or by the giving way of the ground on which they stand. The age of one that was felled in the Calaveras Grove, for the sake of having its stump for a dancing-floor, was about 1300 years, and its diameter, measured across the stump, 24 feet inside the bark. Another that was cut down in the King's River forest was about the same size, but nearly a thousand years older (2200 years), though not a very old-looking tree. It was felled to procure a section for exhibition, and thus an opportunity was given to count its annual rings of growth. The colossal scarred monument in the King's River forest mentioned above is burned half through, and I spent a day in making an estimate of its age, clearing away the charred surface with an ax and carefully counting the annual rings with the aid of a pocket-lens. The wood-rings in the section I laid bare were so involved and contorted in some places that I was not able to determine its age exactly, but I counted over 4000 rings, which showed that this tree was in its prime, swaying in the Sierra winds, when Christ walked the earth. No other tree in the world, as far as I know, has looked down on so many centuries as the Sequoia, or opens such impressive and suggestive views into history.

So exquisitely harmonious and finely balanced are even the very mightiest of these monarchs of the woods in all their proportions and circumstances there never is anything overgrown or monstrous-looking about them. On coming in sight of them for the first time, you are likely to say, "Oh, see what beautiful, noble-looking trees are towering there among the firs and pines!"—their grandeur being in the mean time in great part invisible, but to the living eye it will be manifested sooner or later, stealing slowly on the senses, like the grandeur of Niagara, or the lofty Yosemite domes. Their great size is hidden from the inexperienced observer as long as they are seen at a distance in one harmonious view. When, however, you approach them and walk round them, you begin to wonder at their colossal size and seek a measuring-rod. These giants bulge considerably at the base, but not more than is required for beauty and safety; and the only reason that this bulging seems in some cases excessive is that only a comparatively small section of the shaft is seen at once in near views. One that I measured in the King's River forest was 25 feet in diameter at the ground, and 10 feet in diameter 200 feet above the ground, showing that the taper of the trunk as a whole is charmingly fine. And when you stand back far enough to see the massive columns from the swelling instep to the lofty summit dissolving in a dome of verdure, you rejoice in the unrivaled display of combined grandeur and beauty. About a hundred feet or more of the trunk is usually branchless, but its massive simplicity is relieved by the bark furrows, which instead of making an irregular network run evenly parallel, like the fluting of an architectural column, and to some extent by tufts of slender sprays that wave lightly in the winds and cast flecks of shade, seeming to have been pinned on here and there for the sake of beauty only. The young trees have slender simple branches down to the ground, put on with strict regularity, sharply aspiring at the top, horizontal about half-way down, and drooping in handsome curves at the base. By the time the sapling is five or six hundred years old this spiry, feathery, juvenile habit merges into the firm, rounded dome form of middle age, which in turn takes on the eccentric picturesqueness of old age. No other tree in the Sierra forest has foliage so densely massed or presents outlines so firmly drawn and so steadily subordinate to a special type. A knotty ungovernable-looking branch five to eight feet thick may be seen pushing out abruptly from the smooth trunk, as if sure to throw the regular curve into confusion, but as soon as the general outline is reached it stops short and dissolves in spreading bosses of law-abiding sprays, just as if every tree were growing beneath some huge, invisible bell-glass, against whose sides every branch was being pressed and molded, yet somehow indulging in so many small departures from the regular form that there is still an appearance of freedom.

The foliage of the saplings is dark bluish-green in color, while the older trees ripen to a warm brownish-yellow tint like Libocedrus. The bark is rich cinnamon-brown, purplish in young trees and in shady portions of the old, while the ground is covered with brown leaves and burs forming color-masses of extraordinary richness, not to mention the flowers and underbrush that rejoice about them in their seasons. Walk the Sequoia woods at any time of year and you will say they are the most beautiful and majestic on earth. Beautiful and impressive contrasts meet you everywhere: the colors of tree and flower, rock and sky, light and shade, strength and frailty, endurance and evanescence, tangles of supple hazel-bushes, tree-pillars about as rigid as granite domes, roses and violets, the smallest of their kind, blooming around the feet of the giants, and rugs of the lowly chamaebatia where the sunbeams fall. Then in winter the trees themselves break forth in bloom, myriads of small four-sided staminate cones crowd the ends of the slender sprays, coloring the whole tree, and when ripe dusting the air and the ground with golden pollen. The fertile cones are bright grass-green, measuring about two inches in length by one and a half in thickness, and are made up of about forty firm rhomboidal scales densely packed, with from five to eight seeds at the base of each. A single cone, therefore, contains from two to three hundred seeds, which are about a fourth of an inch long by three sixteenths wide, including a thin, flat margin that makes them go glancing and wavering in their fall like a boy's kite. The fruitfulness of Sequoia may be illustrated by two specimen branches one and a half and two inches in diameter on which I counted 480 cones. No other Sierra conifer produces nearly so many seeds. Millions are ripened annually by a single tree, and in a fruitful year the product of one of the northern groves would be enough to plant all the mountain-ranges of the world. Nature takes care, however, that not one seed in a million shall germinate at all, and of those that do perhaps not one in ten thousand is suffered to live through the many vicissitudes of storm, drought, fire, and snow-crushing that beset their youth.

The Douglas squirrel is the happy harvester of most of the Sequoia cones. Out of every hundred perhaps ninety fall to his share, and unless cut off by his ivory sickle they shake out their seeds and remain on the tree for many years. Watching the squirrels at their harvest work in the Indian summer is one of the most delightful diversions imaginable. The woods are calm and the ripe colors are blazing in all their glory; the cone-laden trees stand motionless in the warm, hazy air, and you may see the crimson-crested woodcock, the prince of Sierra woodpeckers, drilling some dead limb or fallen trunk with his bill, and ever and anon filling the glens with his happy cackle. The humming-bird, too, dwells in these noble woods, and may oftentimes be seen glancing among the flowers or resting wing-weary on some leafless twig; here also are the familiar robin of the orchards, and the brown and grizzly bears so obviously fitted for these majestic solitudes; and the Douglas squirrel, making more hilarious, exuberant, vital stir than all the bears, birds, and humming wings together.

As soon as any accident happens to the crown of these Sequoias, such as being stricken off by lightning or broken by storms, then the branches beneath the wound, no matter how situated, seem to be excited like a colony of bees that have lost their queen, and become anxious to repair the damage. Limbs that have grown outward for centuries at right angles to the trunk begin to turn upward to assist in making a new crown, each speedily assuming the special form of true summits. Even in the case of mere stumps, burned half through, some mere ornamental tuft will try to go aloft and do its best as a leader in forming a new head.

Groups of two or three of these grand trees are often found standing close together, the seeds from which they sprang having probably grown on ground cleared for their reception by the fall of a large tree of a former generation. These patches of fresh, mellow soil beside the upturned roots of the fallen giant may be from forty to sixty feet wide, and they are speedily occupied by seedlings. Out of these seedling-thickets perhaps two or three may become trees, forming those close groups called "three graces," "loving couples," etc. For even supposing that the trees should stand twenty or thirty feet apart while young, by the time they are full-grown their trunks will touch and crowd against each other and even appear as one in some cases.

It is generally believed that this grand Sequoia was once far more widely distributed over the Sierra; but after long and careful study I have come to the conclusion that it never was, at least since the close of the glacial period, because a diligent search along the margins of the groves, and in the gaps between, fails to reveal a single trace of its previous existence beyond its present bounds. Notwithstanding, I feel confident that if every Sequoia in the range were to die to-day, numerous monuments of their existence would remain, of so imperishable a nature as to be available for the student more than ten thousand years hence.

In the first place we might notice that no species of coniferous tree in the range keeps its individuals so well together as Sequoia; a mile is perhaps the greatest distance of any straggler from the main body, and all of those stragglers that have come under my observation are young, instead of old monumental trees, relics of a more extended growth.

Again, Sequoia trunks frequently endure for centuries after they fall. I have a specimen block, cut from a fallen trunk, which is hardly distinguishable from specimens cut from living trees, although the old trunk-fragment from which it was derived has lain in the damp forest more than 380 years, probably thrice as long. The time measure in the case is simply this: when the ponderous trunk to which the old vestige belonged fell, it sunk itself into the ground, thus making a long, straight ditch, and in the middle of this ditch a Silver Fir is growing that is now four feet in diameter and 380 years old, as determined by cutting it half through and counting the rings, thus demonstrating that the remnant of the trunk that made the ditch has lain on the ground more than 380 years. For it is evident that to find the whole time, we must add to the 380 years the time that the vanished portion of the trunk lay in the ditch before being burned out of the way, plus the time that passed before the seed from which the monumental fir sprang fell into the prepared soil and took root. Now, because Sequoia trunks are never wholly consumed in one forest fire, and those fires recur only at considerable intervals, and because Sequoia ditches after being cleared are often left unplanted for centuries, it becomes evident that the trunk remnant in question may probably have lain a thousand years or more. And this instance is by no means a rare one.

But admitting that upon those areas supposed to have been once covered with Sequoia every tree may have fallen, and every trunk may have been burned or buried, leaving not a remnant, many of the ditches made by the fall of the ponderous trunks, and the bowls made by their upturning roots, would remain patent for thousands of years after the last vestige of the trunks that made them had vanished. Much of this ditch-writing would no doubt be quickly effaced by the flood-action of overflowing streams and rain-washing; but no inconsiderable portion would remain enduringly engraved on ridge-tops beyond such destructive action; for, where all the conditions are favorable, it is almost imperishable. Now these historic ditches and root bowls occur in all the present Sequoia groves and forests, but as far as I have observed, not the faintest vestige of one presents itself outside of them.

We therefore conclude that the area covered by Sequoia has not been diminished during the last eight or ten thousand years, and probably not at all in post-glacial times.

Is the species verging to extinction? What are its relations to climate, soil, and associated trees?

All the phenomena bearing on these questions also throw light, as we shall endeavor to show, upon the peculiar distribution of the species, and sustain the conclusion already arrived at on the question of extension.

In the northern groups, as we have seen, there are few young trees or saplings growing up around the failing old ones to perpetuate the race, and in as much as those aged Sequoias, so nearly childless, are the only ones commonly known, the species, to most observers, seems doomed to speedy extinction, as being nothing more than an expiring remnant, vanquished in the so-called struggle for life by pines and firs that have driven it into its last strongholds in moist glens where climate is exceptionally favorable. But the language of the majestic continuous forests of the south creates a very different impression. No tree of all the forest is more enduringly established in concordance with climate and soil. It grows heartily everywhere—on moraines, rocky ledges, along watercourses, and in the deep, moist alluvium of meadows, with a multitude of seedlings and saplings growing up around the aged, seemingly abundantly able to maintain the forest in prime vigor. For every old storm-stricken tree, there is one or more in all the glory of prime; and for each of these many young trees and crowds of exuberant saplings. So that if all the trees of any section of the main Sequoia forest were ranged together according to age, a very promising curve would be presented, all the way up from last year's seedlings to giants, and with the young and middle-aged portion of the curve many times longer than the old portion. Even as far north as the Fresno, I counted 536 saplings and seedlings growing promisingly upon a piece of rough avalanche soil not exceeding two acres in area. This soil bed is about seven years old, and has been seeded almost simultaneously by pines, firs, Libocedrus, and Sequoia, presenting a simple and instructive illustration of the struggle for life among the rival species; and it was interesting to note that the conditions thus far affecting them have enabled the young Sequoias to gain a marked advantage.

In every instance like the above I have observed that the seedling Sequoia is capable of growing on both drier and wetter soil than its rivals, but requires more sunshine than they; the latter fact being clearly shown wherever a Sugar Pine or fir is growing in close contact with a Sequoia of about equal age and size, and equally exposed to the sun; the branches of the latter in such cases are always less leafy. Toward the south, however, where the Sequoia becomes more exuberant and numerous, the rival trees become less so; and where they mix with Sequoias, they mostly grow up beneath them, like slender grasses among stalks of Indian corn. Upon a bed of sandy flood-soil I counted ninety-four Sequoias, from one to twelve feet high, on a patch, of ground once occupied by four large

Sugar Pines which lay crumbling beneath them,—an instance of conditions which have enabled Sequoias to crowd out the pines.

I also noted eighty-six vigorous saplings upon a piece of fresh ground prepared for their reception by fire. Thus fire, the great destroyer of Sequoia, also furnishes bare virgin ground, one of the conditions essential for its growth from the seed. Fresh ground is, however, furnished in sufficient quantities for the constant renewal of the forests without fire, viz., by the fall of old trees. The soil is thus upturned and mellowed, and many trees are planted for every one that falls. Land-slips and floods also give rise to bare virgin ground; and a tree now and then owes its existence to a burrowing wolf or squirrel, but the most regular supply of fresh soil is furnished by the fall of aged trees.

The climatic changes in progress in the Sierra, bearing on the tenure of tree life, are entirely misapprehended, especially as to the time and the means employed by Nature in effecting them. It is constantly asserted in a vague way that the Sierra was vastly wetter than now, and that the increasing drought will of itself extinguish Sequoia, leaving its ground to other trees supposed capable of nourishing in a drier climate. But that Sequoia can and does grow on as dry ground as any of its present rivals, is manifest in a thousand places. "Why, then," it will be asked, "are Sequoias always found in greatest abundance in well-watered places where streams are exceptionally abundant?" Simply because a growth of Sequoias creates those streams. The thirsty mountaineer knows well that in every Sequoia grove he will find running water, but it is a mistake to suppose that the water is the cause of the grove being there; on the contrary, the grove is the cause of the water being there. Drain off the water and the trees will remain, but cut off the trees, and the streams will vanish. Never was cause more completely mistaken for effect than in the case of these related phenomena of Sequoia woods and perennial streams, and I confess that at first I shared in the blunder.

When attention is called to the method of Sequoia stream-making, it will be apprehended at once. The roots of this immense tree fill the ground, forming a thick sponge that absorbs and holds back the rains and melting snows, only allowing them to ooze and flow gently. Indeed, every fallen leaf and rootlet, as well as long clasping root, and prostrate trunk, may be regarded as a dam hoarding the bounty of storm-clouds, and dispensing it as blessings all through the summer, instead of allowing it to go headlong in short-lived floods. Evaporation is also checked by the dense foliage to a greater extent than by any other Sierra tree, and the air is entangled in masses and broad sheets that are quickly saturated; while thirsty winds are not allowed to go sponging and licking along the ground.

So great is the retention of water in many places in the main belt, that bogs and meadows are created by the killing of the trees. A single trunk falling across a stream in the woods forms a dam 200 feet long, and from ten to thirty feet high, giving rise to a pond which kills the trees within its reach. These dead trees fall in turn, thus making a clearing, while sediments gradually accumulate changing the pond into a bog, or meadow, for a growth of carices and sphagnum. In some instances a series of small bogs or meadows rise above one another on a hillside, which are gradually merged into one another, forming sloping bogs, or meadows, which make striking features of Sequoia woods, and since all the trees that have fallen into them have been preserved, they contain records of the generations that have passed since they began to form.

Since, then, it is a fact that thousands of Sequoias are growing thriftily on what is termed dry ground, and even clinging like mountain pines to rifts in granite precipices; and since it has also been shown that the extra moisture found in connection with the denser growths is an effect of their presence, instead of a cause of their presence, then the notions as to the former extension of the species and its near approach to extinction, based upon its supposed dependence on greater moisture, are seen to be erroneous.

The decrease in the rain- and snow-fall since the close of the glacial period in the Sierra is much less than is commonly guessed. The highest post-glacial watermarks are well preserved in all the upper river channels, and they are not greatly higher than the spring floodmarks of the present; showing conclusively that no extraordinary decrease has taken place in the volume of the upper tributaries of post-glacial Sierra streams since they came into existence. But in the mean time, eliminating all this complicated question of climatic change, the plain fact remains that the present rain- and snow-fall is abundantly sufficient for the luxuriant growth of Sequoia forests. Indeed, all my observations tend to show that in a prolonged drought the Sugar Pines and firs would perish before the Sequoia, not alone because of the greater longevity of individual trees, but because the species can endure more drought, and make the most of whatever moisture falls.

Again, if the restriction and irregular distribution of the species be interpreted as a result of the desiccation of the range, then instead of increasing as it does in individuals toward the south where the rainfall is less, it should diminish.

If, then, the peculiar distribution of Sequoia has not been governed by superior conditions of soil as to fertility or moisture, by what has it been governed?

In the course of my studies I observed that the northern groves, the only ones I was at first acquainted with, were located on just those portions of the general forest soil-belt that were first laid bare toward the close of the glacial period when the ice-sheet began to break up into individual glaciers. And while searching the wide basin of the San Joaquin, and trying to account for the absence of Sequoia where every condition seemed favorable for its growth, it occured to me that this remarkable gap in the Sequoia belt is located exactly in the basin of the vast ancient mer de glace of the San Joaquin and King's River basins, which poured its frozen floods to the plain, fed by the snows that fell on more than fifty miles of the summit. I then perceived that the next great gap in the belt to the northward, forty miles wide, extending between the Calaveras and Tuolumne groves, occurs in the basin of the great ancient mer de glace of the Tuolumne and Stanislaus basins, and that the smaller gap between the Merced and Mariposa groves occurs in the basin of the smaller glacier of the Merced. The wider the ancient glacier, the wider the corresponding gap in the Sequoia belt.

Finally, pursuing my investigations across the basins of the Kaweah and Tule, I discovered that the Sequoia belt attained its greatest development just where, owing to the topographical peculiarities of the region, the ground had been most perfectly protected from the main ice-rivers that continued to pour past from the summit fountains long after the smaller local glaciers had been melted.

Taking now a general view of the belt, beginning at the south, we see that the majestic ancient glaciers were shed off right and left down the valleys of Kern and King's rivers by the lofty protective spurs outspread embracingly above the warm Sequoia-filled basins of the Kaweah and Tule. Then, next northward, occurs the wide Sequoia-less channel, or basin, of the ancient San Joaquin and King's River mer de glace; then the warm, protected spots of Fresno and Mariposa groves; then the Sequoia-less channel of the ancient Merced glacier; next the warm, sheltered ground of the Merced and Tuolumne groves; then the Sequoia-less channel of the grand ancient mer de glace of the Tuolumne and Stanislaus; then the warm old ground of the Calaveras and Stanislaus groves. It appears, therefore, that just where, at a certain period in the history of the Sierra, the glaciers were not, there the Sequoia is, and just where the glaciers were, there the Sequoia is not.

What the other conditions may have been that enabled Sequoia to establish itself upon these oldest and warmest portions of the main glacial soil-belt, I cannot say. I might venture to state, however, in this connection, that since the Sequoia forests present a more and more ancient aspect as they extend southward, I am inclined to think that the species was distributed from the south, while the Sugar Pine, its great rival in the northern groves, seems to have come around the head of the Sacramento valley and down the Sierra from the north; consequently, when the Sierra soil-beds were first thrown open to preemption on the melting of the ice-sheet, the Sequoia may have established itself along the available portions of the south half of the range prior to the arrival of the Sugar Pine, while the Sugar Pine took possession of the north half prior to the arrival of Sequoia.

But however much uncertainty may attach to this branch of the question, there are no obscuring shadows upon the grand general relationship we have pointed out between the present distribution of Sequoia and the ancient glaciers of the Sierra. And when we bear in mind that all the present forests of the Sierra are young, growing on moraine soil recently deposited, and that the flank of the range itself, with all its landscapes, is new-born, recently sculptured, and brought to the light of day from beneath the ice mantle of the glacial winter, then a thousand lawless mysteries disappear, and broad harmonies take their places.

But although all the observed phenomena bearing on the post-glacial history of this colossal tree point to the conclusion that it never was more widely distributed on the Sierra since the close of the glacial epoch; that its present forests are scarcely past prime, if, indeed, they have reached prime; that the post-glacial day of the species is probably not half done; yet, when from a wider outlook the vast antiquity of the genus is considered, and its ancient richness in species and individuals; comparing our Sierra Giant and Sequoia sempervirens of the Coast Range, the only other living species of Sequoia, with the twelve fossil species already discovered and described by Heer and Lesquereux, some of which seem to have flourished over vast areas in the Arctic regions and in Europe and our own territories, during tertiary and cretaceous times,—then indeed it becomes plain that our two surviving species, restricted to narrow belts within the limits of California, are mere remnants of the genus, both as to species and individuals, and that they probably are verging to extinction. But the verge of a period beginning in cretaceous times may have a breadth of tens of thousands of years, not to mention the possible existence of conditions calculated to multiply and reëxtend both species and individuals. This, however, is a branch of the question into which I do not now purpose to enter.

In studying the fate of our forest king, we have thus far considered the action of purely natural causes only; but, unfortunately, man is in the woods, and waste and pure destruction are making rapid headway. If the importance of forests were at all understood, even from an economic standpoint, their preservation would call forth the most watchful attention of government. Only of late years by means of forest reservations has the simplest groundwork for available legislation been laid, while in many of the finest groves every species of destruction is still moving on with accelerated speed.

In the course of my explorations I found no fewer than five mills located on or near the lower edge of the Sequoia belt, all of which were cutting considerable quantities of Big Tree lumber. Most of the Fresno group are doomed to feed the mills recently erected near them, and a company of lumbermen are now cutting the magnificent forest on King's River. In these milling operations waste far exceeds use, for after the choice young manageable trees on any given spot have been felled, the woods are fired to clear the ground of limbs and refuse with reference to further operations, and, of course, most of the seedlings and saplings are destroyed.

These mill ravages, however, are small as compared with the comprehensive destruction caused by "sheepmen." Incredible numbers of sheep are driven to the mountain pastures every summer, and their course is ever marked by desolation. Every wild garden is trodden down, the shrubs are stripped of leaves as if devoured by locusts, and the woods are burned. Running fires are set everywhere, with a view to clearing the ground of prostrate trunks, to facilitate the movements of the flocks and improve the pastures. The entire forest belt is thus swept and devastated from one extremity of the range to the other, and, with the exception of the resinous Pinus contorta, Sequoia suffers most of all. Indians burn off the underbrush in certain localities to facilitate deer-hunting, mountaineers and lumbermen carelessly allow their camp-fires to run; but the fires of the sheepmen, or muttoneers, form more than ninety per cent. of all destructive fires that range the Sierra forests.

It appears, therefore, that notwithstanding our forest king might live on gloriously in Nature's keeping, it is rapidly vanishing before the fire and steel of man; and unless protective measures be speedily invented and applied, in a few decades, at the farthest, all that will be left of Sequoia gigantea will be a few hacked and scarred monuments.

TWO-LEAVED, OR TAMARACK, PINE

(Pinus contorta, var.Marrayana)

This species forms the bulk of the alpine forests, extending along the range, above the fir zone, up to a height of from 8000 to 9500 feet above the sea, growing in beautiful order upon moraines that are scarcely changed as yet by post-glacial weathering. Compared with the giants of the lower zones, this is a small tree, seldom attaining a height of a hundred feet. The largest specimen I ever measured was ninety feet in height, and a little over six in diameter four feet from the ground. The average height of mature trees throughout the entire belt is probably not far from fifty or sixty feet, with a diameter of two feet. It is a well-proportioned, rather handsome little pine, with grayish-brown bark, and crooked, much-divided branches, which cover the greater portion of the trunk, not so densely, however, as to prevent its being seen. The lower limbs curve downward, gradually take a horizontal position about half-way up the trunk, then aspire more and more toward the summit, thus forming a sharp, conical top. The foliage is short and rigid, two leaves in a fascicle, arranged in comparatively long, cylindrical tassels at the ends of the tough, up-curving branchlets. The cones are about two inches long, growing in stiff clusters among the needles, without making any striking effect, except while very young, when they are of a vivid crimson color, and the whole tree appears to be dotted with brilliant flowers. The sterile cones are still more showy, on account of their great abundance, often giving a reddish-yellow tinge to the whole mass of the foliage, and filling the air with pollen.

No other pine on the range is so regularly planted as this one. Moraine forests sweep along the sides of the high, rocky valleys for miles without interruption; still, strictly speaking, they are not dense, for flecks of sunshine and flowers find their way into the darkest places, where the trees grow tallest and thickest. Tall, nutritious grasses are specially abundant beneath them, growing over all the ground, in sunshine and shade, over extensive areas like a farmer's crop, and serving as pasture for the multitude of sheep that are driven from the arid plains every summer as soon as the snow is melted.

The Two-leaved Pine, more than any other, is subject to destruction by fire. The thin bark is streaked and sprinkled with resin, as though it had been showered down upon it like rain, so that even the green trees catch fire readily, and during strong winds whole forests are destroyed, the flames leaping from tree to tree, forming one continuous belt of roaring fire that goes surging and racing onward above the bending woods, like the grass-fires of a prairie. During the calm, dry season of Indian summer, the fire creeps quietly along the ground, feeding on the dry needles and burs; then, arriving at the foot of a tree, the resiny bark is ignited, and the heated air ascends in a powerful current, increasing in velocity, and dragging the flames swiftly upward; then the leaves catch fire, and an immense column of flame, beautifully spired on the edges, and tinted a rose-purple hue, rushes aloft thirty or forty feet above the top of the tree, forming a grand spectacle, especially on a dark night. It lasts, however, only a few seconds, vanishing with magical rapidity, to be succeeded by others along the fire-line at irregular intervals for weeks at a time—tree after tree flashing and darkening, leaving the trunks and branches hardly scarred. The heat, however, is sufficient to kill the trees, and in a few years the bark shrivels and falls off. Belts miles in extent are thus killed and left standing with the branches on, peeled and rigid, appearing gray in the distance, like misty clouds. Later the branches drop off, leaving a forest of bleached spars. At length the roots decay, and the forlorn trunks are blown down during some storm, and piled one upon another encumbering the ground until they are consumed by the next fire, and leave it ready for a fresh crop.

The endurance of the species is shown by its wandering occasionally out over the lava plains with the Yellow Pine, and climbing moraineless mountain-sides with the Dwarf Pine, clinging to any chance support in rifts and crevices of storm-beaten rocks—always, however, showing the effects of such hardships in every feature.

Down in sheltered lake hollows, on beds of rich alluvium, it varies so far from the common form as frequently to be taken for a distinct species. Here it grows in dense sods, like grasses, from forty to eighty feet high, bending all together to the breeze and whirling in eddying gusts more lithely than any other tree in the woods. I have frequently found specimens fifty feet high less than five inches in diameter. Being thus slender, and at the same time well clad with leafy boughs, it is oftentimes bent to the ground when laden with soft snow, forming beautiful arches in endless variety, some of which last until the melting of the snow in spring.

MOUNTAIN PINE

(Pinus monticola)

The Mountain Pine is king of the alpine woods, brave, hardy, and long-lived, towering grandly above its companions, and becoming stronger and more imposing just where other species begin to crouch and disappear. At its best it is usually about ninety feet high and five or six in diameter, though a specimen is often met considerably larger than this. The trunk is as massive and as suggestive of enduring strength as that of an oak. About two thirds of the trunk is commonly free of limbs, but close, fringy tufts of sprays occur all the way down, like those which adorn the colossal shafts of Sequoia. The bark is deep reddish-brown upon trees that occupy exposed situations near its upper limit, and furrowed rather deeply, the main furrows running nearly parallel with each other, and connected by conspicuous cross furrows, which, with one exception, are, as far as I have noticed, peculiar to this species.

The cones are from four to eight inches long, slender, cylindrical, and somewhat curved, resembling those of the common White Pine of the Atlantic coast. They grow in clusters of about from three to six or seven, becoming pendulous as they increase in weight, chiefly by the bending of the branches.

This species is nearly related to the Sugar Pine, and, though not half so tall, it constantly suggests its noble relative in the way that it extends its long arms and in general habit. The Mountain Pine is first met on the upper margin of the fir zone, growing singly in a subdued, inconspicuous form, in what appear as chance situations, without making much impression on the general forest. Continuing up through the Two-leaved Pines in the same scattered growth, it begins to show its character, and at an elevation of about 10,000 feet attains its noblest development near the middle of the range, tossing its tough arms in the frosty air, welcoming storms and feeding on them, and reaching the grand old age of 1000 years.

JUNIPER, OR RED CEDAR

(Juniperus occidentalis)

The Juniper is preëminently a rock tree, occupying the baldest domes and pavements, where there is scarcely a handful of soil, at a height of from 7000 to 9500 feet. In such situations the trunk is frequently over eight feet in diameter, and not much more in height. The top is almost always dead in old trees, and great stubborn limbs push out horizontally that are mostly broken and bare at the ends, but densely covered and embedded here and there with bossy mounds of gray foliage. Some are mere weathered stumps, as broad as long, decorated with a few leafy sprays, reminding one of the crumbling towers of some ancient castle scantily draped with ivy. Only upon the head waters of the Carson have I found this species established on good moraine soil. Here it flourishes with the Silver and Two-leaved Pines, in great beauty and luxuriance, attaining a height of from forty to sixty feet, and manifesting but little of that rocky angularity so characteristic a feature throughout the greater portion, of its range. Two of the largest, growing at the head of Hope Valley, measured twenty-nine feet three inches and twenty-five feet six inches in circumference, respectively, four feet from the ground. The bark is of a bright cinnamon color, and, in thrifty trees, beautifully braided and reticulated, flaking off in thin, lustrous ribbons that are sometimes used by Indians for tent-matting. Its fine color and odd picturesqueness always catch an artist's eye, but to me the Juniper seems a singularly dull and taciturn tree, never speaking to one's heart. I have spent many a day and night in its company, in all kinds of weather, and have ever found it silent, cold, and rigid, like a column of ice. Its broad stumpiness, of course, precludes all possibility of waving, or even shaking; but it is not this rocky steadfastness that constitutes its silence. In calm, sun-days the Sugar Pine preaches the grandeur of the mountains like an apostle without moving a leaf.

On level rocks it dies standing, and wastes insensibly out of existence like granite, the wind exerting about as little control over it alive or dead as it does over a glacier boulder. Some are undoubtedly over 2000 years old. All the trees of the alpine woods suffer, more or less, from avalanches, the Two-leaved Pine most of all. Gaps two or three hundred yards wide, extending from the upper limit of the tree-line to the bottoms of valleys and lake basins, are of common occurrence in all the upper forests, resembling the clearings of settlers in the old backwoods. Scarcely a tree is spared, even the soil is scraped away, while the thousands of uprooted pines and spruces are piled upon one another heads downward, and tucked snugly in along the sides of the clearing in two windrows, like lateral moraines. The pines lie with branches wilted and drooping like weeds. Not so the burly junipers. After braving in silence the storms of perhaps a dozen or twenty centuries, they seem in this, their last calamity, to become somewhat communicative, making sign of a very unwilling acceptance of their fate, holding themselves well up from the ground on knees and elbows, seemingly ill at ease, and anxious, like stubborn wrestlers, to rise again.

HEMLOCK SPRUCE

(Tsuga Pattoniana)

The Hemlock Spruce is the most singularly beautiful of all the California coniferae. So slender is its axis at the top, that it bends over and droops like the stalk of a nodding lily. The branches droop also, and divide into innumerable slender, waving sprays, which are arranged in a varied, eloquent harmony that is wholly indescribable. Its cones are purple, and hang free, in the form of little tassels two inches long from all the sprays from top to bottom. Though exquisitely delicate and feminine in expression, it grows best where the snow lies deepest, far up in the region of storms, at an elevation of from 9000 to 9500 feet, on frosty northern slopes; but it is capable of growing considerably higher, say 10,500 feet. The tallest specimens, growing in sheltered hollows somewhat beneath the heaviest wind-currents, are from eighty to a hundred feet high, and from two to four feet in diameter. The very largest specimen I ever found was nineteen feet seven inches in circumference four feet from the ground, growing on the edge of Lake Hollow, at an elevation of 9250 feet above the level of the sea. At the age of twenty or thirty years it becomes fruitful, and hangs out its beautiful purple cones at the ends of the slender sprays, where they swing free in the breeze, and contrast delightfully with the cool green foliage. They are translucent when young, and their beauty is delicious. After they are fully ripe, they spread their shell-like scales and allow the brown-winged seeds to fly in the mellow air, while the empty cones remain to beautify the tree until the coming of a fresh crop.

The staminate cones of all the coniferae are beautiful, growing in bright clusters, yellow, and rose, and crimson. Those of the Hemlock Spruce are the most beautiful of all, forming little conelets of blue flowers, each on a slender stem.

Under all conditions, sheltered or storm-beaten, well-fed or ill-fed, this tree is singularly graceful in habit. Even at its highest limit upon exposed ridge-tops, though compelled to crouch in dense thickets, huddled close together, as if for mutual protection, it still manages to throw out its sprays in irrepressible loveliness; while on well-ground moraine soil it develops a perfectly tropical luxuriance of foliage and fruit, and is the very loveliest tree in the forest; poised in thin white sunshine, clad with branches from head to foot, yet not in the faintest degree heavy or bunchy, it towers in unassuming majesty, drooping as if unaffected with the aspiring tendencies of its race, loving the ground while transparently conscious of heaven and joyously receptive of its blessings, reaching out its branches like sensitive tentacles, feeling the light and reveling in it. No other of our alpine conifers so finely veils its strength. Its delicate branches yield to the mountains' gentlest breath; yet is it strong to meet the wildest onsets of the gale,—strong not in resistance, but compliance, bowing, snow-laden, to the ground, gracefully accepting burial month after month in the darkness beneath the heavy mantle of winter.

When the first soft snow begins to fall, the flakes lodge in the leaves, weighing down the branches against the trunk. Then the axis bends yet lower and lower, until the slender top touches the ground, thus forming a fine ornamental arch. The snow still falls lavishly, and the whole tree is at length buried, to sleep and rest in its beautiful grave as though dead. Entire groves of young trees, from ten to forty feet high, are thus buried every winter like slender grasses. But, like the violets and daisies which the heaviest snows crush not, they are safe. It is as though this were only Nature's method of putting her darlings to sleep instead of leaving them exposed to the biting storms of winter.

Thus warmly wrapped they await the summer resurrection. The snow becomes soft in the sunshine, and freezes at night, making the mass hard and compact, like ice, so that during the months of April and May you can ride a horse over the prostrate groves without catching sight of a single leaf. At length the down-pouring sunshine sets them free. First the elastic tops of the arches begin to appear, then one branch after another, each springing loose with a gentle rustling sound, and at length the whole tree, with the assistance of the winds, gradually unbends and rises and settles back into its place in the warm air, as dry and feathery and fresh as young ferns just out of the coil.

Some of the finest groves I have yet found are on the southern slopes of Lassen's Butte. There are also many charming companies on the head waters of the Tuolumne, Merced, and San Joaquin, and, in general, the species is so far from being rare that you can scarcely fail to find groves of considerable extent in crossing the range, choose what pass you may. The Mountain Pine grows beside it, and more frequently the two-leaved species; but there are many beautiful groups, numbering 1000 individuals, or more, without a single intruder.

I wish I had space to write more of the surpassing beauty of this favorite spruce. Every tree-lover is sure to regard it with special admiration; apathetic mountaineers, even, seeking only game or gold, stop to gaze on first meeting it, and mutter to themselves: "That's a mighty pretty tree," some of them adding, "d——d pretty!" In autumn, when its cones are ripe, the little striped tamias, and the Douglas squirrel, and the Clark crow make a happy stir in its groves. The deer love to lie down beneath its spreading branches; bright streams from the snow that is always near ripple through its groves, and bryanthus spreads precious carpets in its shade. But the best words only hint its charms. Come to the mountains and see.

DWARF PINE

(Pinus albicaulis)

This species forms the extreme edge of the timber line throughout nearly the whole extent of the range on both flanks. It is first met growing in company with Pinus contorta, var. Murrayana, on the upper margin of the belt, as an erect tree from fifteen to thirty feet high and from one to two feet in thickness; thence it goes straggling up the flanks of the summit peaks, upon moraines or crumbling ledges, wherever it can obtain a foothold, to an elevation of from 10,000 to 12,000 feet, where it dwarfs to a mass of crumpled, prostrate branches, covered with slender, upright shoots, each tipped with a short, close-packed tassel of leaves. The bark is smooth and purplish, in some places almost white. The fertile cones grow in rigid clusters upon the upper branches, dark chocolate in color while young, and bear beautiful pearly seeds about the size of peas, most of which are eaten by two species of tamias and the notable Clark crow. The staminate cones occur in clusters, about an inch wide, down among the leaves, and, as they are colored bright rose-purple, they give rise to a lively, flowery appearance little looked for in such a tree.

Pines are commonly regarded as sky-loving trees that must necessarily aspire or die. This species forms a marked exception, creeping lowly, in compliance with the most rigorous demands of climate, yet enduring bravely to a more advanced age than many of its lofty relatives in the sun-lands below. Seen from a distance, it would never be taken for a tree of any kind. Yonder, for example, is Cathedral Peak, some three miles away, with a scattered growth of this pine creeping like mosses over the roof and around the beveled edges of the north gable, nowhere giving any hint of an ascending axis. When approached quite near it still appears matted and heathy, and is so low that one experiences no great difficulty in walking over the top of it. Yet it is seldom absolutely prostrate, at its lowest usually attaining a height of three or four feet, with a main trunk, and branches outspread and intertangled above it, as if in ascending they had been checked by a ceiling, against which they had grown and been compelled to spread horizontally. The winter snow is indeed such a ceiling, lasting half the year; while the pressed, shorn surface is made yet smoother by violent winds, armed with cutting sand-grains, that beat down any shoot that offers to rise much above the general level, and carve the dead trunks and branches in beautiful patterns.

During stormy nights I have often camped snugly beneath the interlacing arches of this little pine. The needles, which have accumulated for centuries, make fine beds, a fact well known to other mountaineers, such as deer and wild sheep, who paw out oval hollows and lie beneath the larger trees in safe and comfortable concealment.

The longevity of this lowly dwarf is far greater than would be guessed. Here, for example, is a specimen, growing at an elevation of 10,700 feet, which seems as though it might be plucked up by the roots, for it is only three and a half inches in diameter, and its topmost tassel is hardly three feet above the ground. Cutting it half through and counting the annual rings with the aid of a lens, we find its age to be no less than 255 years. Here is another telling specimen about the same height, 426 years old, whose trunk is only six inches in diameter; and one of its supple branchlets, hardly an eighth of an inch in diameter inside the bark, is seventy-five years old, and so filled with oily balsam, and so well seasoned by storms, that we may tie it in knots like a whip-cord.

WHITE PINE

(Pinus flexilis)

This species is widely distributed throughout the Rocky Mountains, and over all the higher of the many ranges of the Great Basin, between the Wahsatch Mountains and the Sierra, where it is known as White Pine. In the Sierra it is sparsely scattered along the eastern flank, from Bloody Cañon southward nearly to the extremity of the range, opposite the village of Lone Pine, nowhere forming any appreciable portion of the general forest. From its peculiar position, in loose, straggling parties, it seems to have been derived from the Basin ranges to the eastward, where it is abundant.

It is a larger tree than the Dwarf Pine. At an elevation of about 9000 feet above the sea, it often attains a height of forty or fifty feet, and a diameter of from three to five feet. The cones open freely when ripe, and are twice as large as those of the albicaulis, and the foliage and branches are more open, having a tendency to sweep out in free, wild curves, like those of the Mountain Pine, to which it is closely allied. It is seldom found lower than 9000 feet above sea-level, but from this elevation it pushes upward over the roughest ledges to the extreme limit of tree-growth, where, in its dwarfed, storm-crushed condition, it is more like the white-barked species.

Throughout Utah and Nevada it is one of the principal timber-trees, great quantities being cut every year for the mines. The famous White Pine Mining District, White Pine City, and the White Pine Mountains have derived their names from it.

NEEDLE PINE

(Pinus aristata)

This species is restricted in the Sierra to the southern portion of the range, about the head waters of Kings and Kern rivers, where it forms extensive forests, and in some places accompanies the Dwarf Pine to the extreme limit of tree-growth.

It is first met at an elevation of between 9000 and 10,000 feet, and runs up to 11,000 without seeming to suffer greatly from the climate or the leanness of the soil. It is a much finer tree than the Dwarf Pine. Instead of growing in clumps and low, heathy mats, it manages in some way to maintain an erect position, and usually stands single. Wherever the young trees are at all sheltered, they grow up straight and arrowy, with delicately tapered bole, and ascending branches terminated with glossy, bottle-brush tassels. At middle age, certain limbs are specialized and pushed far out for the bearing of cones, after the manner of the Sugar Pine; and in old age these branches droop and cast about in every direction, giving rise to very picturesque effects. The trunk becomes deep brown and rough, like that of the Mountain Pine, while the young cones are of a strange, dull, blackish-blue color, clustered on the upper branches. When ripe they are from three to four inches long, yellowish brown, resembling in every way those of the Mountain Pine. Excepting the Sugar Pine, no tree on the mountains is so capable of individual expression, while in grace of form and movement it constantly reminds one of the Hemlock Spruce.

The largest specimen I measured was a little over five feet in diameter and ninety feet in height, but this is more than twice the ordinary size.

This species is common throughout the Rocky Mountains and most of the short ranges of the Great Basin, where it is called the Fox-tail Pine, from its long dense leaf-tassels. On the Hot Creek, White Pine, and Golden Gate ranges it is quite abundant. About a foot or eighteen inches of the ends of the branches is densely packed with stiff outstanding needles which radiate like an electric fox or squirrel's tail. The needles have a glossy polish, and the sunshine sifting through them makes them burn with silvery luster, while their number and elastic temper tell delightfully in the winds. This tree is here still more original and picturesque than in the Sierra, far surpassing not only its companion conifers in this respect, but also the most noted of the lowland oaks. Some stand firmly erect, feathered with radiant tassels down to the ground, forming slender tapering towers of shining verdure; others, with two or three specialized branches pushed out at right angles to the trunk and densely clad with tasseled sprays, take the form of beautiful ornamental crosses. Again in the same woods you find trees that are made up of several boles united near the ground, spreading at the sides in a plane parallel to the axis of the mountain, with the elegant tassels hung in charming order between them, making a harp held against the main wind lines where they are most effective in playing the grand storm harmonies. And besides these there are many variable arching forms, alone or in groups, with innumerable tassels drooping beneath the arches or radiant above them, and many lowly giants of no particular form that have braved the storms of a thousand years. But whether old or young, sheltered or exposed to the wildest gales, this tree is ever found irrepressibly and extravagantly picturesque, and offers a richer and more varied series of forms to the artist than any other conifer I know of.

NUT PINE

(Pinus monophylla)

The Nut Pine covers or rather dots the eastern flank of the Sierra, to which it is mostly restricted, in grayish, bush-like patches, from the margin of the sage-plains to an elevation of from 7000 to 8000 feet.

A more contentedly fruitful and unaspiring conifer could not be conceived. All the species we have been sketching make departures more or less distant from the typical spire form, but none goes so far as this. Without any apparent exigency of climate or soil, it remains near the ground, throwing out crooked, divergent branches like an orchard apple-tree, and seldom pushes a single shoot higher than fifteen or twenty feet above the ground.

The average thickness of the trunk is, perhaps, about ten or twelve inches. The leaves are mostly undivided, like round awls, instead of being separated, like those of other pines, into twos and threes and fives. The cones are green while growing, and are usually found over all the tree, forming quite a marked feature as seen against the bluish-gray foliage. They are quite small, only about two inches in length, and give no promise of edible nuts; but when we come to open them, we find that about half the entire bulk of the cone is made up of sweet, nutritious seeds, the kernels of which are nearly as large as those of hazel-nuts.

This is undoubtedly the most important food-tree on the Sierra, and furnishes the Mono, Carson, and Walker River Indians with more and better nuts than all the other species taken together. It is the Indians' own tree, and many a white man have they killed for cutting it down.

In its development Nature seems to have aimed at the formation of as great a fruit-bearing surface as possible. Being so low and accessible, the cones are readily beaten off with poles, and the nuts procured by roasting them until the scales open. In bountiful seasons a single Indian will gather thirty or forty bushels of them—a fine squirrelish employment.

Of all the conifers along the eastern base of the Sierra, and on all the many mountain groups and short ranges of the Great Basin, this foodful little pine is the commonest tree, and the most important. Nearly every mountain is planted with it to a height of from 8000 to 9000 feet above the sea. Some are covered from base to summit by this one species, with only a sparse growth of juniper on the lower slopes to break the continuity of its curious woods, which, though dark-looking at a distance, are almost shadeless, and have none of the damp, leafy glens and hollows so characteristic of other pine woods. Tens of thousands of acres occur in continuous belts. Indeed, viewed comprehensively the entire Basin seems to be pretty evenly divided into level plains dotted with sage-bushes and mountain-chains covered with Nut Pines. No slope is too rough, none too dry, for these bountiful orchards of the red man.

The value of this species to Nevada is not easily overestimated. It furnishes charcoal and timber for the mines, and, with the juniper, supplies the ranches with fuel and rough fencing. In fruitful seasons the nut crop is perhaps greater than the California wheat crop, which exerts so much influence throughout the food markets of the world. When, the crop is ripe, the Indians make ready the long beating-poles; bags, baskets, mats, and sacks are collected; the women out at service among the settlers, washing or drudging, assemble at the family huts; the men leave their ranch work; old and young, all are mounted on ponies and start in great glee to the nut-lands, forming curiously picturesque cavalcades; flaming scarfs and calico skirts stream loosely over the knotty ponies, two squaws usually astride of each, with baby midgets bandaged in baskets slung on their backs or balanced on the saddle-bow; while nut-baskets and water-jars project from each side, and the long beating-poles make angles in every direction. Arriving at some well-known central point where grass and water are found, the squaws with baskets, the men with poles ascend the ridges to the laden trees, followed by the children. Then the beating begins right merrily, the burs fly in every direction, rolling down the slopes, lodging here and there against rocks and sage-bushes, chased and gathered by the women and children with fine natural gladness. Smoke-columns speedily mark the joyful scene of their labors as the roasting-fires are kindled, and, at night, assembled in gay circles garrulous as jays, they begin the first nut feast of the season.

The nuts are about half an inch long and a quarter of an inch in diameter, pointed at the top, round at the base, light brown in general color, and, like many other pine seeds, handsomely dotted with purple, like birds' eggs. The shells are thin and may be crushed between the thumb and finger. The kernels are white, becoming brown by roasting, and are sweet to every palate, being eaten by birds, squirrels, dogs, horses, and men. Perhaps less than one bushel in a thousand of the whole crop is ever gathered. Still, besides supplying their own wants, in times of plenty the Indians bring large quantities to market; then they are eaten around nearly every fireside in the State, and are even fed to horses occasionally instead of barley.

Of other trees growing on the Sierra, but forming a very small part of the general forest, we may briefly notice the following:

Chamoecyparis Lawsoniana is a magnificent tree in the coast ranges, but small in the Sierra. It is found only well to the northward along the banks of cool streams on the upper Sacramento toward Mount Shasta. Only a few trees of this species, as far as I have seen, have as yet gained a place in the Sierra woods. It has evidently been derived from the coast range by way of the tangle of connecting mountains at the head of the Sacramento Valley.

In shady dells and on cool stream banks of the northern Sierra we also find the Yew (Taxus brevifolia).

The interesting Nutmeg Tree (Torreya Californica) is sparsely distributed along the western flank of the range at an elevation of about 4000 feet, mostly in gulches and cañons. It is a small, prickly leaved, glossy evergreen, like a conifer, from twenty to fifty feet high, and one to two feet in diameter. The fruit resembles a green-gage plum, and contains one seed, about the size of an acorn, and like a nutmeg, hence the common name. The wood is fine-grained and of a beautiful, creamy yellow color like box, sweet-scented when dry, though the green leaves emit a disagreeable odor.

Betula occidentalis, the only birch, is a small, slender tree restricted to the eastern flank of the range along stream-sides below the pine-belt, especially in Owen's Valley.

Alder, Maple, and Nuttall's Flowering Dogwood make beautiful bowers over swift, cool streams at an elevation of from 3000 to 5000 feet, mixed more or less with willows and cottonwood; and above these in lake basins the aspen forms fine ornamental groves, and lets its light shine gloriously in the autumn months.

The Chestnut Oak (Quercus densiflora) seems to have come from the coast range around the head of the Sacramento Valley, like the Chamaecyparis, but as it extends southward along the lower edge of the main pine-belt it grows smaller until it finally dwarfs to a mere chaparral bush. In the coast mountains it is a fine, tall, rather slender tree, about from sixty to seventy-five feet high, growing with the grand Sequoia sempervirens, or Redwood. But unfortunately it is too good to live, and is now being rapidly destroyed for tan-bark.

Besides the common Douglas Oak and the grand Quercus Wislizeni of the foot-hills, and several small ones that make dense growths of chaparral, there are two mountain-oaks that grow with the pines up to an elevation of about 5000 feet above the sea, and greatly enhance the beauty of the yosemite parks. These are the Mountain Live Oak and the Kellogg Oak, named in honor of the admirable botanical pioneer of California. Kellogg's Oak (Quercus Kelloggii) is a firm, bright, beautiful tree, reaching a height of sixty feet, four to seven feet in diameter, with wide-spreading branches, and growing at an elevation of from 3000 to 5000 feet in sunny valleys and flats among the evergreens, and higher in a dwarfed state. In the cliff-bound parks about 4000 feet above the sea it is so abundant and effective it might fairly be called the Yosemite Oak. The leaves make beautiful masses of purple in the spring, and yellow in ripe autumn; while its acorns are eagerly gathered by Indians, squirrels, and woodpeckers. The

Mountain Live Oak (Q. Chrysolepis) is a tough, rugged mountaineer of a tree, growing bravely and attaining noble dimensions on the roughest earthquake taluses in deep cañons and yosemite valleys. The trunk is usually short, dividing near the ground into great, wide-spreading limbs, and these again into a multitude of slender sprays, many of them cord-like and drooping to the ground, like those of the Great White Oak of the lowlands (Q. lobata). The top of the tree where there is plenty of space is broad and bossy, with a dense covering of shining leaves, making delightful canopies, the complicated system of gray, interlacing, arching branches as seen from beneath being exceedingly rich and picturesque. No other tree that I know dwarfs so regularly and completely as this under changes of climate due to changes in elevation. At the foot of a cañon 4000 feet above the sea you may find magnificent specimens of this oak fifty feet high, with craggy, bulging trunks, five to seven feet in diameter, and at the head of the cañon, 2500 feet higher, a dense, soft, low, shrubby growth of the same species, while all the way up the cañon between these extremes of size and habit a perfect gradation may be traced. The largest I have seen was fifty feet high, eight feet in diameter, and about seventy-five feet in spread. The trunk was all knots and buttresses, gray like granite, and about as angular and irregular as the boulders on which it was growing—a type of steadfast, unwedgeable strength.

CHAPTER IX

THE DOUGLAS SQUIRREL

(Sciurus Douglasii)

The Douglas Squirrel is by far the most interesting and influential of the California sciuridae, surpassing every other species in force of character, numbers, and extent of range, and in the amount of influence he brings to bear upon the health and distribution of the vast forests he inhabits.

Go where you will throughout the noble woods of the Sierra Nevada, among the giant pines and spruces of the lower zones, up through the towering Silver Firs to the storm-bent thickets of the summit peaks, you everywhere find this little squirrel the master-existence. Though only a few inches long, so intense is his fiery vigor and restlessness, he stirs every grove with wild life, and makes himself more important than even the huge bears that shuffle through the tangled underbrush beneath him. Every wind is fretted by his voice, almost every bole and branch feels the sting of his sharp feet. How much the growth of the trees is stimulated by this means it is not easy to learn, but his action in manipulating their seeds is more appreciable. Nature has made him master forester and committed most of her coniferous crops to his paws. Probably over fifty per cent. of all the cones ripened on the Sierra are cut off and handled by the Douglas alone, and of those of the Big Trees perhaps ninety per cent. pass through his hands: the greater portion is of course stored away for food to last during the winter and spring, but some of them are tucked separately into loosely covered holes, where some of the seeds germinate and become trees. But the Sierra is only one of the many provinces over which he holds sway, for his dominion extends over all the Redwood Belt of the Coast Mountains, and far northward throughout the majestic forests of Oregon, Washington, and British Columbia. I make haste to mention these facts, to show upon how substantial a foundation the importance I ascribe to him rests.

The Douglas is closely allied to the Red Squirrel or Chickaree of the eastern woods. Ours may be a lineal descendant of this species, distributed westward to the Pacific by way of the Great Lakes and the Rocky Mountains, and thence southward along our forested ranges. This view is suggested by the fact that our species becomes redder and more Chickaree-like in general, the farther it is traced back along the course indicated above. But whatever their relationship, and the evolutionary forces that have acted upon them, the Douglas is now the larger and more beautiful animal.

From the nose to the root of the tail he measures about eight inches; and his tail, which he so effectively uses in interpreting his feelings, is about six inches in length. He wears dark bluish-gray over the back and half-way down the sides, bright buff on the belly, with a stripe of dark gray, nearly black, separating the upper and under colors; this dividing stripe, however, is not very sharply defined. He has long black whiskers, which gives him a rather fierce look when observed closely, strong claws, sharp as fish-hooks, and the brightest of bright eyes, full of telling speculation.

A King's River Indian told me that they call him "Pillillooeet," which, rapidly pronounced with the first syllable heavily accented, is not unlike the lusty exclamation he utters on his way up a tree when excited. Most mountaineers in California call him the Pine Squirrel; and when I asked an old trapper whether he knew our little forester, he replied with brightening countenance: "Oh, yes, of course I know him; everybody knows him. When I'm huntin' in the woods, I often find out where the deer are by his barkin' at 'em. I call 'em Lightnin' Squirrels, because they're so mighty quick and peert."

All the true squirrels are more or less birdlike in speech and movements; but the Douglas is preëminently so, possessing, as he does, every attribute peculiarly squirrelish enthusiastically concentrated. He is the squirrel of squirrels, flashing from branch to branch of his favorite evergreens crisp and glossy and undiseased as a sunbeam. Give him wings and he would outfly any bird in the woods. His big gray cousin is a looser animal, seemingly light enough to float on the wind; yet when leaping from limb to limb, or out of one tree-top to another, he sometimes halts to gather strength, as if making efforts concerning the upshot of which he does not always feel exactly confident. But the Douglas, with his denser body, leaps and glides in hidden strength, seemingly as independent of common muscles as a mountain stream. He threads the tasseled branches of the pines, stirring their needles like a rustling breeze; now shooting across openings in arrowy lines; now launching in curves, glinting deftly from side to side in sudden zigzags, and swirling in giddy loops and spirals around the knotty trunks; getting into what seem to be the most impossible situations without sense of danger; now on his haunches, now on his head; yet ever graceful, and punctuating his most irrepressible outbursts of energy with little dots and dashes of perfect repose. He is, without exception, the wildest animal I ever saw,—a fiery, sputtering little bolt of life, luxuriating in quick oxygen and the woods' best juices. One can hardly think of such a creature being dependent, like the rest of us, on climate and food. But, after all, it requires no long acquaintance to learn he is human, for he works for a living. His busiest time is in the Indian summer. Then he gathers burs and hazel-nuts like a plodding farmer, working continuously every day for hours; saying not a word; cutting off the ripe cones at the top of his speed, as if employed by the job, and examining every branch in regular order, as if careful that not one should escape him; then, descending, he stores them away beneath logs and stumps, in anticipation of the pinching hunger days of winter. He seems himself a kind of coniferous fruit,—both fruit and flower. The resiny essences of the pines pervade every pore of his body, and eating his flesh is like chewing gum.

One never tires of this bright chip of nature,—this brave little voice crying in the wilderness,—of observing his many works and ways, and listening to his curious language. His musical, piny gossip is as savory to the ear as balsam to the palate; and, though he has not exactly the gift of song, some of his notes are as sweet as those of a linnet—almost flute-like in softness, while others prick and tingle like thistles. He is the mocking-bird of squirrels, pouring forth mixed chatter and song like a perennial fountain; barking like a dog, screaming like a hawk, chirping like a blackbird or a sparrow; while in bluff, audacious noisiness he is a very jay.

In descending the trunk of a tree with the intention of alighting on the ground, he preserves a cautious silence, mindful, perhaps, of foxes and wildcats; but while rocking safely at home in the pine-tops there is no end to his capers and noise; and woe to the gray squirrel or chipmunk that ventures to set foot on his favorite tree! No matter how slyly they trace the furrows of the bark, they are speedily discovered, and kicked down-stairs with comic vehemence, while a torrent of angry notes comes rushing from his whiskered lips that sounds remarkably like swearing. He will even attempt at times to drive away dogs and men, especially if he has had no previous knowledge of them. Seeing a man for the first time, he approaches nearer and nearer, until within a few feet; then, with an angry outburst, he makes a sudden rush, all teeth and eyes, as if about to eat you up. But, finding that the big, forked animal doesn't scare, he prudently beats a retreat, and sets himself up to reconnoiter on some overhanging branch, scrutinizing every movement you make with ludicrous solemnity. Gathering courage, he ventures down the trunk again, churring and chirping, and jerking nervously up and down in curious loops, eyeing you all the time, as if snowing off and demanding your admiration. Finally, growing calmer, he settles down in a comfortable posture on some horizontal branch commanding a good view, and beats time with his tail to a steady "Chee-up! chee-up!" or, when somewhat less excited, "Pee-ah!" with the first syllable keenly accented, and the second drawn out like the scream of a hawk,—repeating this slowly and more emphatically at first, then gradually faster, until a rate of about 150 words a minute is reached; usually sitting all the time on his haunches, with paws resting on his breast, which pulses visibly with each word. It is remarkable, too, that, though articulating distinctly, he keeps his mouth shut most of the time, and speaks through his nose. I have occasionally observed him even eating Sequoia seeds and nibbling a troublesome flea, without ceasing or in any way confusing his "Pee-ah! pee-ah!" for a single moment.

While ascending trees all his claws come into play, but in descending the weight of his body is sustained chiefly by those of the hind feet; still in neither case do his movements suggest effort, though if you are near enough you may see the bulging strength of his short, bear-like arms, and note his sinewy fists clinched in the bark.

Whether going up or down, he carries his tail extended at full length in line with his body, unless it be required for gestures. But while running along horizontal limbs or fallen trunks, it is frequently folded forward over the back, with the airy tip daintily upcurled. In cool weather it keeps him warm. Then, after he has finished his meal, you may see him crouched close on some level limb with his tail-robe neatly spread and reaching forward to his ears, the electric, outstanding hairs quivering in the breeze like pine-needles. But in wet or very cold weather he stays in his nest, and while curled up there his comforter is long enough to come forward around his nose. It is seldom so cold, however, as to prevent his going out to his stores when hungry.

Once as I lay storm-bound on the upper edge of the timber line on Mount Shasta, the thermometer nearly at zero and the sky thick with driving snow, a Douglas came bravely out several times from one of the lower hollows of a Dwarf Pine near my camp, faced the wind without seeming to feel it much, frisked lightly about over the mealy snow, and dug his way down to some hidden seeds with wonderful precision, as if to his eyes the thick snow-covering were glass.

No other of the Sierra animals of my acquaintance is better fed, not even the deer, amid abundance of sweet herbs and shrubs, or the mountain sheep, or omnivorous bears. His food consists of grass-seeds, berries, hazel-nuts, chinquapins, and the nuts and seeds of all the coniferous trees without exception,—Pine, Fir, Spruce, Libocedrus, Juniper, and Sequoia,—he is fond of them all, and they all agree with him, green or ripe. No cone is too large for him to manage, none so small as to be beneath his notice. The smaller ones, such as those of the Hemlock, and the Douglas Spruce, and the Two-leaved Pine, he cuts off and eats on a branch of the tree, without allowing them to fall; beginning at the bottom of the cone and cutting away the scales to expose the seeds; not gnawing by guess, like a bear, but turning them round and round in regular order, in compliance with their spiral arrangement.

When thus employed, his location in the tree is betrayed by a dribble of scales, shells, and seed-wings, and, every few minutes, by the fall of the stripped axis of the cone. Then of course he is ready for another, and if you are watching you may catch a glimpse of him as he glides silently out to the end of a branch and see him examining the cone-clusters until he finds one to his mind; then, leaning over, pull back the springy needles out of his way, grasp the cone with his paws to prevent its falling, snip it off in an incredibly short time, seize it with jaws grotesquely stretched, and return to his chosen seat near the trunk. But the immense size of the cones of the Sugar Pine—from fifteen to twenty inches in length—and those of the Jeffrey variety of the Yellow Pine compel him to adopt a quite different method. He cuts them off without attempting to hold them, then goes down and drags them from where they have chanced to fall up to the bare, swelling ground around the instep of the tree, where he demolishes them in the same methodical way, beginning at the bottom and following the scale-spirals to the top.

From a single Sugar Pine cone he gets from two to four hundred seeds about half the size of a hazel-nut, so that in a few minutes he can procure enough to last a week. He seems, however, to prefer those of the two Silver First above all others; perhaps because they are most easily obtained, as the scales drop off when ripe without needing to be cut. Both species are filled with an exceedingly pungent, aromatic oil, which spices all his flesh, and is of itself sufficient to account for his lightning energy.

You may easily know this little workman by his chips. On sunny hillsides around the principal trees they lie in big piles,—bushels and basketfuls of them, all fresh and clean, making the most beautiful kitchen-middens imaginable. The brown and yellow scales and nut-shells are as abundant and as delicately penciled and tinted as the shells along the sea-shore; while the beautiful red and purple seed-wings mingled with them would lead one to fancy that innumerable butterflies had there met their fate.

He feasts on all the species long before they are ripe, but is wise enough to wait until they are matured before he gathers them into his barns. This is in October and November, which with him are the two busiest months of the year. All kinds of burs, big and little, are now cut off and showered down alike, and the ground is speedily covered with them. A constant thudding and bumping is kept up; some of the larger cones chancing to fall on old logs make the forest reëcho with the sound. Other nut-eaters less industrious know well what is going on, and hasten to carry away the cones as they fall. But however busy the harvester may be, he is not slow to descry the pilferers below, and instantly leaves his work to drive them away. The little striped tamias is a thorn in his flesh, stealing persistently, punish him as he may. The large Gray Squirrel gives trouble also, although the Douglas has been accused of stealing from him. Generally, however, just the opposite is the case.

The excellence of the Sierra evergreens is well known to nurserymen throughout the world, consequently there is considerable demand for the seeds. The greater portion of the supply has hitherto been procured by chopping down the trees in the more accessible sections of the forest alongside of bridle-paths that cross the range. Sequoia seeds at first brought from twenty to thirty dollars per pound, and therefore were eagerly sought after. Some of the smaller fruitful trees were cut down in the groves not protected by government, especially those of Fresno and King's River. Most of the Sequoias, however, are of so gigantic a size that the seedsmen have to look for the greater portion of their supplies to the Douglas, who soon learns he is no match for these freebooters. He is wise enough, however, to cease working the instant he perceives them, and never fails to embrace every opportunity to recover his burs whenever they happen to be stored in any place accessible to him, and the busy seedsman often finds on returning to camp that the little Douglas has exhaustively spoiled the spoiler. I know one seed-gatherer who, whenever he robs the squirrels, scatters wheat or barley beneath the trees as conscience-money.

The want of appreciable life remarked by so many travelers in the Sierra forests is never felt at this time of year. Banish all the humming insects and the birds and quadrupeds, leaving only Sir Douglas, and the most solitary of our so-called solitudes would still throb with ardent life. But if you should go impatiently even into the most populous of the groves on purpose to meet him, and walk about looking up among the branches, you would see very little of him. But lie down at the foot of one of the trees and straightway he will come. For, in the midst of the ordinary forest sounds, the falling of burs, piping of quails, the screaming of the Clark Crow, and the rustling of deer and bears among the chaparral, he is quick to detect your strange footsteps, and will hasten to make a good, close inspection of you as soon as you are still. First, you may hear him sounding a few notes of curious inquiry, but more likely the first intimation of his approach will be the prickly sounds of his feet as he descends the tree overhead, just before he makes his savage onrush to frighten you and proclaim your presence to every squirrel and bird in the neighborhood. If you remain perfectly motionless, he will come nearer and nearer, and probably set your flesh a-tingle by frisking across your body. Once, while I was seated at the foot of a Hemlock Spruce in one of the most inaccessible of the San Joaquin yosemites engaged in sketching, a reckless fellow came up behind me, passed under my bended arm, and jumped on my paper. And one warm afternoon, while an old friend of mine was reading out in the shade of his cabin, one of his Douglas neighbors jumped from the gable upon his head, and then with admirable assurance ran down over his shoulder and on to the book he held in his hand.

Our Douglas enjoys a large social circle; for, besides his numerous relatives, Sciurus fossor, Tamias quadrivitatus, T. Townsendii, Spermophilus Beccheyi, S. Douglasii, he maintains intimate relations with the nut-eating birds, particularly the Clark Crow (Picicorvus columbianus) and the numerous woodpeckers and jays. The two spermophiles are astonishingly abundant in the lowlands and lower foot-hills, but more and more sparingly distributed up through the Douglas domains,—seldom venturing higher than six or seven thousand feet above the level of the sea. The gray sciurus ranges but little higher than this. The little striped tamias alone is associated with him everywhere. In the lower and middle zones, where they all meet, they are tolerably harmonious—a happy family, though very amusing skirmishes may occasionally be witnessed. Wherever the ancient glaciers have spread forest soil there you find our wee hero, most abundant where depth of soil and genial climate have given rise to a corresponding luxuriance in the trees, but following every kind of growth up the curving moraines to the highest glacial fountains.

Though I cannot of course expect all my readers to sympathize fully in my admiration of this little animal, few, I hope, will think this sketch of his life too long. I cannot begin to tell here how much he has cheered my lonely wanderings during all the years I have been pursuing my studies in these glorious wilds; or how much unmistakable humanity I have found in him. Take this for example: One calm, creamy Indian summer morning, when the nuts were ripe, I was camped in the upper pine-woods of the south fork of the San Joaquin, where the squirrels seemed to be about as plentiful as the ripe burs. They were taking an early breakfast before going to their regular harvest-work. While I was busy with my own breakfast I heard the thudding fall of two or three heavy cones from a Yellow Pine near me. I stole noiselessly forward within about twenty feet of the base of it to observe. In a few moments down came the Douglas. The breakfast-burs he had cut off had rolled on the gently sloping ground into a clump of ceanothus bushes, but he seemed to know exactly where they were, for he found them at once, apparently without searching for them. They were more than twice as heavy as himself, but after turning them into the right position for getting a good hold with his long sickle-teeth he managed to drag them up to the foot of the tree from which he had cut them, moving backward. Then seating himself comfortably, he held them on end, bottom up, and demolished them at his ease. A good deal of nibbling had to be done before he got anything to eat, because the lower scales are barren, but when he had patiently worked his way up to the fertile ones he found two sweet nuts at the base of each, shaped like trimmed hams, and spotted purple like birds' eggs. And notwithstanding these cones were dripping with soft balsam, and covered with prickles, and so strongly put together that a boy would be puzzled to cut them open with a jack-knife, he accomplished his meal with easy dignity and cleanliness, making less effort apparently than a man would in eating soft cookery from a plate.

Breakfast done, I whistled a tune for him before he went to work, curious to see how he would be affected by it. He had not seen me all this while; but the instant I began to whistle he darted up the tree nearest to him, and came out on a small dead limb opposite me, and composed himself to listen. I sang and whistled more than a dozen airs, and as the music changed his eyes sparkled, and he turned his head quickly from side to side, but made no other response. Other squirrels, hearing the strange sounds, came around on all sides, also chipmunks and birds. One of the birds, a handsome, speckle-breasted thrush, seemed even more interested than the squirrels. After listening for awhile on one of the lower dead sprays of a pine, he came swooping forward within a few feet of my face, and remained fluttering in the air for half a minute or so, sustaining himself with whirring wing-beats, like a humming-bird in front of a flower, while I could look into his eyes and see his innocent wonder.

By this time my performance must have lasted nearly half an hour. I sang or whistled "Bonnie Boon," "Lass o' Gowrie," "O'er the Water to Charlie," "Bonnie Woods o' Cragie Lee," etc., all of which seemed to be listened to with bright interest, my first Douglas sitting patiently through it all, with his telling eyes fixed upon me until I ventured to give the "Old Hundredth," when he screamed his Indian name, Pillillooeet, turned tail, and darted with ludicrous haste up the tree out of sight, his voice and actions in the case leaving a somewhat profane impression, as if he had said, "I'll be hanged if you get me to hear anything so solemn and unpiny." This acted as a signal for the general dispersal of the whole hairy tribe, though the birds seemed willing to wait further developments, music being naturally more in their line.

What there can be in that grand old church-tune that is so offensive to birds and squirrels I can't imagine. A year or two after this High Sierra concert, I was sitting one fine day on a hill in the Coast Range where the common Ground Squirrels were abundant. They were very shy on account of being hunted so much; but after I had been silent and motionless for half an hour or so they began to venture out of their holes and to feed on the seeds of the grasses and thistles around me as if I were no more to be feared than a tree-stump. Then it occurred to me that this was a good opportunity to find out whether they also disliked "Old Hundredth." Therefore I began to whistle as nearly as I could remember the same familiar airs that had pleased the mountaineers of the Sierra. They at once stopped eating, stood erect, and listened patiently until I came to "Old Hundredth," when with ludicrous haste every one of them rushed to their holes and bolted in, their feet twinkling in the air for a moment as they vanished.

No one who makes the acquaintance of our forester will fail to admire him; but he is far too self-reliant and warlike ever to be taken for a darling.

How long the life of a Douglas Squirrel may be, I don't know. The young seem to sprout from knot-holes, perfect from the first, and as enduring as their own trees. It is difficult, indeed, to realize that so condensed a piece of sun-fire should ever become dim or die at all. He is seldom killed by hunters, for he is too small to encourage much of their attention, and when pursued in settled regions becomes excessively shy, and keeps close in the furrows of the highest trunks, many of which are of the same color as himself. Indian boys, however, lie in wait with unbounded patience to shoot them with arrows. In the lower and middle zones a few fall a prey to rattlesnakes. Occasionally he is pursued by hawks and wildcats, etc. But, upon the whole, he dwells safely in the deep bosom of the woods, the most highly favored of all his happy tribe. May his tribe increase!

CHAPTER X

A WIND-STORM IN THE FORESTS

The mountain winds, like the dew and rain, sunshine and snow, are measured and bestowed with love on the forests to develop their strength and beauty. However restricted the scope of other forest influences, that of the winds is universal. The snow bends and trims the upper forests every winter, the lightning strikes a single tree here and there, while avalanches mow down thousands at a swoop as a gardener trims out a bed of flowers. But the winds go to every tree, fingering every leaf and branch and furrowed bole; not one is forgotten; the Mountain Pine towering with outstretched arms on the rugged buttresses of the icy peaks, the lowliest and most retiring tenant of the dells; they seek and find them all, caressing them tenderly, bending them in lusty exercise, stimulating their growth, plucking off a leaf or limb as required, or removing an entire tree or grove, now whispering and cooing through the branches like a sleepy child, now roaring like the ocean; the winds blessing the forests, the forests the winds, with ineffable beauty and harmony as the sure result.

After one has seen pines six feet in diameter bending like grasses before a mountain gale, and ever and anon some giant falling with a crash that shakes the hills, it seems astonishing that any, save the lowest thickset trees, could ever have found a period sufficiently stormless to establish themselves; or, once established, that they should not, sooner or later, have been blown down. But when the storm is over, and we behold the same forests tranquil again, towering fresh and unscathed in erect majesty, and consider what centuries of storms have fallen upon them since they were first planted,—hail, to break the tender seedlings; lightning, to scorch and shatter; snow, winds, and avalanches, to crush and overwhelm,—while the manifest result of all this wild storm-culture is the glorious perfection we behold; then faith in Nature's forestry is established, and we cease to deplore the violence of her most destructive gales, or of any other storm-implement whatsoever.

There are two trees in the Sierra forests that are never blown down, so long as they continue in sound health. These are the Juniper and the Dwarf Pine of the summit peaks. Their stiff, crooked roots grip the storm-beaten ledges like eagles' claws, while their lithe, cord-like branches bend round compliantly, offering but slight holds for winds, however violent. The other alpine conifers—the Needle Pine, Mountain Pine, Two-leaved Pine, and Hemlock Spruce—are never thinned out by this agent to any destructive extent, on account of their admirable toughness and the closeness of their growth. In general the same is true of the giants of the lower zones. The kingly Sugar Pine, towering aloft to a height of more than 200 feet, offers a fine mark to storm-winds; but it is not densely foliaged, and its long, horizontal arms swing round compliantly in the blast, like tresses of green, fluent algae in a brook; while the Silver Firs in most places keep their ranks well together in united strength. The Yellow or Silver Pine is more frequently overturned than any other tree on the Sierra, because its leaves and branches form a larger mass in proportion to its height, while in many places it is planted sparsely, leaving open lanes through which storms may enter with full force. Furthermore, because it is distributed along the lower portion of the range, which was the first to be left bare on the breaking up of the ice-sheet at the close of the glacial winter, the soil it is growing upon has been longer exposed to post-glacial weathering, and consequently is in a more crumbling, decayed condition than the fresher soils farther up the range, and therefore offers a less secure anchorage for the roots.

While exploring the forest zones of Mount Shasta, I discovered the path of a hurricane strewn with thousands of pines of this species. Great and small had been uprooted or wrenched off by sheer force, making a clean gap, like that made by a snow avalanche. But hurricanes capable of doing this class of work are rare in the Sierra, and when we have explored the forests from one extremity of the range to the other, we are compelled to believe that they are the most beautiful on the face of the earth, however we may regard the agents that have made them so.

There is always something deeply exciting, not only in the sounds of winds in the woods, which exert more or less influence over every mind, but in their varied waterlike flow as manifested by the movements of the trees, especially those of the conifers. By no other trees are they rendered so extensively and impressively visible, not even by the lordly tropic palms or tree-ferns responsive to the gentlest breeze. The waving of a forest of the giant Sequoias is indescribably impressive and sublime, but the pines seem to me the best interpreters of winds. They are mighty waving goldenrods, ever in tune, singing and writing wind-music all their long century lives. Little, however, of this noble tree-waving and tree-music will you see or hear in the strictly alpine portion of the forests. The burly Juniper, whose girth sometimes more than equals its height, is about as rigid as the rocks on which it grows. The slender lash-like sprays of the Dwarf Pine stream out in wavering ripples, but the tallest and slenderest are far too unyielding to wave even in the heaviest gales. They only shake in quick, short vibrations. The Hemlock Spruce, however, and the Mountain Pine, and some of the tallest thickets of the Two-leaved species bow in storms with considerable scope and gracefulness. But it is only in the lower and middle zones that the meeting of winds and woods is to be seen in all its grandeur.

One of the most beautiful and exhilarating storms I ever enjoyed in the Sierra occurred in December, 1874, when I happened to be exploring one of the tributary valleys of the Yuba River. The sky and the ground and the trees had been thoroughly rain-washed and were dry again. The day was intensely pure, one of those incomparable bits of California winter, warm and balmy and full of white sparkling sunshine, redolent of all the purest influences of the spring, and at the same time enlivened with one of the most bracing wind-storms conceivable. Instead of camping out, as I usually do, I then chanced to be stopping at the house of a friend. But when the storm began to sound, I lost no time in pushing out into the woods to enjoy it. For on such occasions Nature has always something rare to show us, and the danger to life and limb is hardly greater than one would experience crouching deprecatingly beneath a roof.

It was still early morning when I found myself fairly adrift. Delicious sunshine came pouring over the hills, lighting the tops of the pines, and setting free a steam of summery fragrance that contrasted strangely with the wild tones of the storm. The air was mottled with pine-tassels and bright green plumes, that went flashing past in the sunlight like birds pursued. But there was not the slightest dustiness, nothing less pure than leaves, and ripe pollen, and flecks of withered bracken and moss. I heard trees falling for hours at the rate of one every two or three minutes; some uprooted, partly on account of the loose, water-soaked condition of the ground; others broken straight across, where some weakness caused by fire had determined the spot. The gestures of the various trees made a delightful study. Young Sugar Pines, light and feathery as squirrel-tails, were bowing almost to the ground; while the grand old patriarchs, whose massive boles had been tried in a hundred storms, waved solemnly above them, their long, arching branches streaming fluently on the gale, and every needle thrilling and ringing and shedding off keen lances of light like a diamond. The Douglas Spruces, with long sprays drawn out in level tresses, and needles massed in a gray, shimmering glow, presented a most striking appearance as they stood in bold relief along the hilltops. The madroños in the dells, with their red bark and large glossy leaves tilted every way, reflected the sunshine in throbbing spangles like those one so often sees on the rippled surface of a glacier lake. But the Silver Pines were now the most impressively beautiful of all. Colossal spires 200 feet in height waved like supple golden-rods chanting and bowing low as if in worship, while the whole mass of their long, tremulous foliage was kindled into one continuous blaze of white sun-fire. The force of the gale was such that the most steadfast monarch of them all rocked down to its roots with a motion plainly perceptible when one leaned against it. Nature was holding high festival, and every fiber of the most rigid giants thrilled with glad excitement.

I drifted on through the midst of this passionate music and motion, across many a glen, from ridge to ridge; often halting in the lee of a rock for shelter, or to gaze and listen. Even when the grand anthem had swelled to its highest pitch, I could distinctly hear the varying tones of individual trees,—Spruce, and Fir, and Pine, and leafless Oak,—and even the infinitely gentle rustle of the withered grasses at my feet. Each was expressing itself in its own way,—singing its own song, and making its own peculiar gestures,—manifesting a richness of variety to be found in no other forest I have yet seen. The coniferous woods of Canada, and the Carolinas, and Florida, are made up of trees that resemble one another about as nearly as blades of grass, and grow close together in much the same way. Coniferous trees, in general, seldom possess individual character, such as is manifest among Oaks and Elms. But the California forests are made up of a greater number of distinct species than any other in the world. And in them we find, not only a marked differentiation into special groups, but also a marked individuality in almost every tree, giving rise to storm effects indescribably glorious.

Toward midday, after a long, tingling scramble through copses of hazel and ceanothus, I gained the summit of the highest ridge in the neighborhood; and then it occurred to me that it would be a fine thing to climb one of the trees to obtain a wider outlook and get my ear close to the Aeolian music of its topmost needles. But under the circumstances the choice of a tree was a serious matter. One whose instep was not very strong seemed in danger of being blown down, or of being struck by others in case they should fall; another was branchless to a considerable height above the ground, and at the same time too large to be grasped with arms and legs in climbing; while others were not favorably situated for clear views. After cautiously casting about, I made choice of the tallest of a group of Douglas Spruces that were growing close together like a tuft of grass, no one of which seemed likely to fall unless all the rest fell with it. Though comparatively young, they were about 100 feet high, and their lithe, brushy tops were rocking and swirling in wild ecstasy. Being accustomed to climb trees in making botanical studies, I experienced no difficulty in reaching the top of this one, and never before did I enjoy so noble an exhilaration of motion. The slender tops fairly flapped and swished in the passionate torrent, bending and swirling backward and forward, round and round, tracing indescribable combinations of vertical and horizontal curves, while I clung with muscles firm braced, like a bobolink on a reed.

In its widest sweeps my tree-top described an arc of from twenty to thirty degrees, but I felt sure of its elastic temper, having seen others of the same species still more severely tried—bent almost to the ground indeed, in heavy snows—without breaking a fiber. I was therefore safe, and free to take the wind into my pulses and enjoy the excited forest from my superb outlook. The view from here must be extremely beautiful in any weather. Now my eye roved over the piny hills and dales as over fields of waving grain, and felt the light running in ripples and broad swelling undulations across the valleys from ridge to ridge, as the shining foliage was stirred by corresponding waves of air. Oftentimes these waves of reflected light would break up suddenly into a kind of beaten foam, and again, after chasing one another in regular order, they would seem to bend forward in concentric curves, and disappear on some hillside, like sea-waves on a shelving shore. The quantity of light reflected from the bent needles was so great as to make whole groves appear as if covered with snow, while the black shadows beneath the trees greatly enhanced the effect of the silvery splendor.

Excepting only the shadows there was nothing somber in all this wild sea of pines. On the contrary, notwithstanding this was the winter season, the colors were remarkably beautiful. The shafts of the pine and libocedrus were brown and purple, and most of the foliage was well tinged with yellow; the laurel groves, with the pale undersides of their leaves turned upward, made masses of gray; and then there was many a dash of chocolate color from clumps of manzanita, and jet of vivid crimson from the bark of the madroños, while the ground on the hillsides, appearing here and there through openings between the groves, displayed masses of pale purple and brown.

The sounds of the storm corresponded gloriously with this wild exuberance of light and motion. The profound bass of the naked branches and boles booming like waterfalls; the quick, tense vibrations of the pine-needles, now rising to a shrill, whistling hiss, now falling to a silky murmur; the rustling of laurel groves in the dells, and the keen metallic click of leaf on leaf—all this was heard in easy analysis when the attention was calmly bent.

The varied gestures of the multitude were seen to fine advantage, so that one could recognize the different species at a distance of several miles by this means alone, as well as by their forms and colors, and the way they reflected the light. All seemed strong and comfortable, as if really enjoying the storm, while responding to its most enthusiastic greetings. We hear much nowadays concerning the universal struggle for existence, but no struggle in the common meaning of the word was manifest here; no recognition of danger by any tree; no deprecation; but rather an invincible gladness as remote from exultation as from fear.

I kept my lofty perch for hours, frequently closing my eyes to enjoy the music by itself, or to feast quietly on the delicious fragrance that was streaming past. The fragrance of the woods was less marked than that produced during warm rain, when so many balsamic buds and leaves are steeped like tea; but, from the chafing of resiny branches against each other, and the incessant attrition of myriads of needles, the gale was spiced to a very tonic degree. And besides the fragrance from these local sources there were traces of scents brought from afar. For this wind came first from the sea, rubbing against its fresh, briny waves, then distilled through the redwoods, threading rich ferny gulches, and spreading itself in broad undulating currents over many a flower-enameled ridge of the coast mountains, then across the golden plains, up the purple foot-hills, and into these piny woods with the varied incense gathered by the way.

Winds are advertisements of all they touch, however much or little we may be able to read them; telling their wanderings even by their scents alone. Mariners detect the flowery perfume of land-winds far at sea, and sea-winds carry the fragrance of dulse and tangle far inland, where it is quickly recognized, though mingled with the scents of a thousand land-flowers. As an illustration of this, I may tell here that I breathed sea-air on the Firth of Forth, in Scotland, while a boy; then was taken to Wisconsin, where I remained nineteen years; then, without in all this time having breathed one breath of the sea, I walked quietly, alone, from the middle of the Mississippi Valley to the Gulf of Mexico, on a botanical excursion, and while in Florida, far from the coast, my attention wholly bent on the splendid tropical vegetation about me, I suddenly recognized a sea-breeze, as it came sifting through the palmettos and blooming vine-tangles, which at once awakened and set free a thousand dormant associations, and made me a boy again in Scotland, as if all the intervening years had been annihilated.

Most people like to look at mountain rivers, and bear them in mind; but few care to look at the winds, though far more beautiful and sublime, and though they become at times about as visible as flowing water. When the north winds in winter are making upward sweeps over the curving summits of the High Sierra, the fact is sometimes published with flying snow-banners a mile long. Those portions of the winds thus embodied can scarce be wholly invisible, even to the darkest imagination. And when we look around over an agitated forest, we may see something of the wind that stirs it, by its effects upon the trees. Yonder it descends in a rush of water-like ripples, and sweeps over the bending pines from hill to hill. Nearer, we see detached plumes and leaves, now speeding by on level currents, now whirling in eddies, or, escaping over the edges of the whirls, soaring aloft on grand, upswelling domes of air, or tossing on flame-like crests. Smooth, deep currents, cascades, falls, and swirling eddies, sing around every tree and leaf, and over all the varied topography of the region with telling changes of form, like mountain rivers conforming to the features of their channels.

After tracing the Sierra streams from their fountains to the plains, marking where they bloom white in falls, glide in crystal plumes, surge gray and foam-filled in boulder-choked gorges, and slip through the woods in long, tranquil reaches—after thus learning their language and forms in detail, we may at length hear them chanting all together in one grand anthem, and comprehend them all in clear inner vision, covering the range like lace. But even this spectacle is far less sublime and not a whit more substantial than what we may behold of these storm-streams of air in the mountain woods.

We all travel the milky way together, trees and men; but it never occurred to me until this storm-day, while swinging in the wind, that trees are travelers, in the ordinary sense. They make many journeys, not extensive ones, it is true; but our own little journeys, away and back again, are only little more than tree-wavings—many of them not so much.

When the storm began to abate, I dismounted and sauntered down through the calming woods. The storm-tones died away, and, turning toward the east, I beheld the countless hosts of the forests hushed and tranquil, towering above one another on the slopes of the hills like a devout audience. The setting sun filled them with amber light, and seemed to say, while they listened, "My peace I give unto you."

As I gazed on the impressive scene, all the so-called ruin of the storm was forgotten, and never before did these noble woods appear so fresh, so joyous, so immortal.

CHAPTER XI

THE RIVER FLOODS

The Sierra rivers are flooded every spring by the melting of the snow as regularly as the famous old Nile. They begin to rise in May, and in June high-water mark is reached. But because the melting does not go on rapidly over all the fountains, high and low, simultaneously, and the melted snow is not reinforced at this time of year by rain, the spring floods are seldom very violent or destructive. The thousand falls, however, and the cascades in the cañons are then in full bloom, and sing songs from one end of the range to the other. Of course the snow on the lower tributaries of the rivers is first melted, then that on the higher fountains most exposed to sunshine, and about a month later the cooler, shadowy fountains send down their treasures, thus allowing the main trunk streams nearly six weeks to get their waters hurried through the foot-hills and across the lowlands to the sea. Therefore very violent spring floods are avoided, and will be as long as the shading, restraining forests last. The rivers of the north half of the range are still less subject to sudden floods, because their upper fountains in great part lie protected from the changes of the weather beneath thick folds of lava, just as many of the rivers of Alaska lie beneath folds of ice, coming to the light farther down the range in large springs, while those of the high Sierra lie on the surface of solid granite, exposed to every change of temperature. More than ninety per cent. of the water derived from the snow and ice of Mount Shasta is at once absorbed and drained away beneath the porous lava folds of the mountain, where mumbling and groping in the dark they at length find larger fissures and tunnel-like caves from which they emerge, filtered and cool, in the form of large springs, some of them so large they give birth to rivers that set out on their journeys beneath the sun without any visible intermediate period of childhood. Thus the Shasta River issues from a large lake-like spring in Shasta Valley, and about two thirds of the volume of the McCloud River gushes forth suddenly from the face of a lava bluff in a roaring spring seventy-five yards wide.

These spring rivers of the north are of course shorter than those of the south whose tributaries extend up to the tops of the mountains. Fall River, an important tributary of the Pitt or Upper Sacramento, is only about ten miles long, and is all falls, cascades, and springs from its head to its confluence with the Pitt. Bountiful springs, charmingly embowered, issue from the rocks at one end of it, a snowy fall a hundred and eighty feet high thunders at the other, and a rush of crystal rapids sing and dance between. Of course such streams are but little affected by the weather. Sheltered from evaporation their flow is nearly as full in the autumn as in the time of general spring floods. While those of the high Sierra diminish to less than the hundredth part of their springtime prime, shallowing in autumn to a series of silent pools among the rocks and hollows of their channels, connected by feeble, creeping threads of water, like the sluggish sentences of a tired writer, connected by a drizzle of "ands" and "buts." Strange to say, the greatest floods occur in winter, when one would suppose all the wild waters would be muffled and chained in frost and snow. The same long, all-day storms of the so-called Rainy Season in California, that give rain to the lowlands, give dry frosty snow to the mountains. But at rare intervals warm rains and warm winds invade the mountains and push back the snow line from 2000 feet to 8000, or even higher, and then come the big floods.

I was usually driven down out of the High Sierra about the end of November, but the winter of 1874 and 1875 was so warm and calm that I was tempted to seek general views of the geology and topography of the basin of Feather River in January. And I had just completed a hasty survey of the region, and made my way down to winter quarters, when one of the grandest flood-storms that I ever saw broke on the mountains. I was then in the edge of the main forest belt at a small foot-hill town called Knoxville, on the divide between the waters of the Feather and Yuba rivers. The cause of this notable flood was simply a sudden and copious fall of warm wind and rain on the basins of these rivers at a time when they contained a considerable quantity of snow. The rain was so heavy and long-sustained that it was, of itself, sufficient to make a good wild flood, while the snow which the warm wind and rain melted on the upper and middle regions of the basins was sufficient to make another flood equal to that of the rain. Now these two distinct harvests of flood waters were gathered simultaneously and poured out on the plain in one magnificent avalanche. The basins of the Yuba and Feather, like many others of the Sierra, are admirably adapted to the growth of floods of this kind. Their many tributaries radiate far and wide, comprehending extensive areas, and the tributaries are steeply inclined, while the trunks are comparatively level. While the flood-storm was in progress the thermometer at Knoxville ranged between 44° and 50°; and when warm wind and warm rain fall simultaneously on snow contained in basins like these, both the rain and that portion of the snow which the rain and wind melt are at first sponged up and held back until the combined mass becomes sludge, which at length, suddenly dissolving, slips and descends all together to the trunk channel; and since the deeper the stream the faster it flows, the flooded portion of the current above overtakes the slower foot-hill portion below it, and all sweeping forward together with a high, overcurling front, debouches on the open plain with a violence and suddenness that at first seem wholly unaccountable. The destructiveness of the lower portion of this particular flood was somewhat augmented by mining gravel in the river channels, and by levees which gave way after having at first restrained and held back the accumulating waters. These exaggerating conditions did not, however, greatly influence the general result, the main effect having been caused by the rare combination of flood factors indicated above. It is a pity that but few people meet and enjoy storms so noble as this in their homes in the mountains, for, spending themselves in the open levels of the plains, they are likely to be remembered more by the bridges and houses they carry away than by their beauty or the thousand blessings they bring to the fields and gardens of Nature.

On the morning of the flood, January 19th, all the Feather and Yuba landscapes were covered with running water, muddy torrents filled every gulch and ravine, and the sky was thick with rain. The pines had long been sleeping in sunshine; they were now awake, roaring and waving with the beating storm, and the winds sweeping along the curves of hill and dale, streaming through the woods, surging and gurgling on the tops of rocky ridges, made the wildest of wild storm melody.

It was easy to see that only a small part of the rain reached the ground in the form of drops. Most of it was thrashed into dusty spray like that into which small waterfalls are divided when they dash on shelving rocks. Never have I seen water coming from the sky in denser or more passionate streams. The wind chased the spray forward in choking drifts, and compelled me again and again to seek shelter in the dell copses and back of large trees to rest and catch my breath. Wherever I went, on ridges or in hollows, enthusiastic water still flashed and gurgled about my ankles, recalling a wild winter flood in Yosemite when a hundred waterfalls came booming and chanting together and filled the grand valley with a sea-like roar.

After drifting an hour or two in the lower woods, I set out for the summit of a hill 900 feet high, with a view to getting as near the heart of the storm as possible. In order to reach it I had to cross Dry Creek, a tributary of the Yuba that goes crawling along the base of the hill on the northwest. It was now a booming river as large as the Tuolumne at ordinary stages, its current brown with mining-mud washed down from many a "claim," and mottled with sluice-boxes, fence-rails, and logs that had long lain above its reach. A slim foot-bridge stretched across it, now scarcely above the swollen current. Here I was glad to linger, gazing and listening, while the storm was in its richest mood—the gray rain-flood above, the brown river-flood beneath. The language of the river was scarcely less enchanting than that of the wind and rain; the sublime overboom of the main bouncing, exulting current, the swash and gurgle of the eddies, the keen dash and clash of heavy waves breaking against rocks, and the smooth, downy hush of shallow currents feeling their way through the willow thickets of the margin. And amid all this varied throng of sounds I heard the smothered bumping and rumbling of boulders on the bottom as they were shoving and rolling forward against one another in a wild rush, after having lain still for probably 100 years or more.

The glad creek rose high above its banks and wandered from its channel out over many a briery sand-flat and meadow. Alders and willows waist-deep were bearing up against the current with nervous trembling gestures, as if afraid of being carried away, while supple branches bending confidingly, dipped lightly and rose again, as if stroking the wild waters in play. Leaving the bridge and passing on through the storm-thrashed woods, all the ground seemed to be moving. Pine-tassels, flakes of bark, soil, leaves, and broken branches were being swept forward, and many a rock-fragment, weathered from exposed ledges, was now receiving its first rounding and polishing in the wild streams of the storm. On they rushed through every gulch and hollow, leaping, gliding, working with a will, and rejoicing like living creatures.

Nor was the flood confined to the ground. Every tree had a water system of its own spreading far and wide like miniature Amazons and Mississippis.

Toward midday, cloud, wind, and rain reached their highest development. The storm was in full bloom, and formed, from my commanding outlook on the hilltop, one of the most glorious views I ever beheld. As far as the eye could reach, above, beneath, around, wind-driven rain filled the air like one vast waterfall. Detached clouds swept imposingly up the valley, as if they were endowed with independent motion and had special work to do in replenishing the mountain wells, now rising above the pine-tops, now descending into their midst, fondling their arrowy spires and soothing every branch and leaf with gentleness in the midst of all the savage sound and motion. Others keeping near the ground glided behind separate groves, and brought them forward into relief with admirable distinctness; or, passing in front, eclipsed whole groves in succession, pine after pine melting in their gray fringes and bursting forth again seemingly clearer than before.

The forms of storms are in great part measured, and controlled by the topography of the regions where they rise and over which they pass. When, therefore, we attempt to study them from the valleys, or from gaps and openings of the forest, we are confounded by a multitude of separate and apparently antagonistic impressions. The bottom of the storm is broken up into innumerable waves and currents that surge against the hillsides like sea-waves against a shore, and these, reacting on the nether surface of the storm, erode immense cavernous hollows and cañons, and sweep forward the resulting detritus in long trains, like the moraines of glaciers. But, as we ascend, these partial, confusing effects disappear and the phenomena are beheld united and harmonious.

The longer I gazed into the storm, the more plainly visible it became. The drifting cloud detritus gave it a kind of visible body, which explained many perplexing phenomena, and published its movements in plain terms, while the texture of the falling mass of rain rounded it out and rendered it more complete. Because raindrops differ in size they fall at different velocities and overtake and clash against one another, producing mist and spray. They also, of course, yield unequal compliance to the force of the wind, which gives rise to a still greater degree of interference, and passionate gusts sweep off clouds of spray from the groves like that torn from wave-tops in a gale. All these factors of irregularity in density, color, and texture of the general rain mass tend to make it the more appreciable and telling. It is then seen as one grand flood rushing over bank and brae, bending the pines like weeds, curving this way and that, whirling in huge eddies in hollows and dells, while the main current pours grandly over all, like ocean currents over the landscapes that lie hidden at the bottom of the sea.

I watched the gestures of the pines while the storm was at its height, and it was easy to see that they were not distressed. Several large Sugar Pines stood near the thicket in which I was sheltered, bowing solemnly and tossing their long arms as if interpreting the very words of the storm while accepting its wildest onsets with passionate exhilaration. The lions were feeding. Those who have observed sunflowers feasting on sunshine during the golden days of Indian summer know that none of their gestures express thankfulness. Their celestial food is too heartily given, too heartily taken to leave room for thanks. The pines were evidently accepting the benefactions of the storm in the same whole-souled manner; and when I looked down among the budding hazels, and still lower to the young violets and fern-tufts on the rocks, I noticed the same divine methods of giving and taking, and the same exquisite adaptations of what seems an outbreak of violent and uncontrollable force to the purposes of beautiful and delicate life. Calms like sleep come upon landscapes, just as they do on people and trees, and storms awaken them in the same way. In the dry midsummer of the lower portion of the range the withered hills and valleys seem to lie as empty and expressionless as dead shells on a shore. Even the highest mountains may be found occasionally dull and uncommunicative as if in some way they had lost countenance and shrunk to less than half their real stature. But when the lightnings crash and echo in the cañons, and the clouds come down wreathing and crowning their bald snowy heads, every feature beams with expression and they rise again in all their imposing majesty.

Storms are fine speakers, and tell all they know, but their voices of lightning, torrent, and rushing wind are much less numerous than the nameless still, small voices too low for human ears; and because we are poor listeners we fail to catch much that is fairly within reach. Our best rains are heard mostly on roofs, and winds in chimneys; and when by choice or compulsion we are pushed into the heart of a storm, the confusion made by cumbersome equipments and nervous haste and mean fear, prevent our hearing any other than the loudest expressions. Yet we may draw enjoyment from storm sounds that are beyond hearing, and storm movements we cannot see. The sublime whirl of planets around their suns is as silent as raindrops oozing in the dark among the roots of plants. In this great storm, as in every other, there were tones and gestures inexpressibly gentle manifested in the midst of what is called violence and fury, but easily recognized by all who look and listen for them. The rain brought out the colors of the woods with delightful freshness, the rich brown of the bark of the trees and the fallen burs and leaves and dead ferns; the grays of rocks and lichens; the light purple of swelling buds, and the warm yellow greens of the libocedrus and mosses. The air was steaming with delightful fragrance, not rising and wafting past in separate masses, but diffused through all the atmosphere. Pine woods are always fragrant, but most so in spring when the young tassels are opening and in warm weather when the various gums and balsams are softened by the sun. The wind was now chafing their innumerable needles and the warm rain was steeping them. Monardella grows here in large beds in the openings, and there is plenty of laurel in dells and manzanita on the hillsides, and the rosy, fragrant chamoebatia carpets the ground almost everywhere. These, with the gums and balsams of the woods, form the main local fragrance-fountains of the storm. The ascending clouds of aroma wind-rolled and rain-washed became pure like light and traveled with the wind as part of it. Toward the middle of the afternoon the main flood cloud lifted along its western border revealing a beautiful section of the Sacramento Valley some twenty or thirty miles away, brilliantly sun-lighted and glistering with rain-sheets as if paved with silver. Soon afterward a jagged bluff-like cloud with a sheer face appeared over the valley of the Yuba, dark-colored and roughened with numerous furrows like some huge lava-table. The blue Coast Range was seen stretching along the sky like a beveled wall, and the somber, craggy Marysville Buttes rose impressively out of the flooded plain like islands out of the sea. Then the rain began to abate and I sauntered down through the dripping bushes reveling in the universal vigor and freshness that inspired all the life about me. How clean and unworn and immortal the woods seemed to be!—the lofty cedars in full bloom laden with golden pollen and their washed plumes shining; the pines rocking gently and settling back into rest, and the evening sunbeams spangling on the broad leaves of the madroños, their tracery of yellow boughs relieved against dusky thickets of Chestnut Oak; liverworts, lycopodiums, ferns were exulting in glorious revival, and every moss that had ever lived seemed to be coming crowding back from the dead to clothe each trunk and stone in living green. The steaming ground seemed fairly to throb and tingle with life; smilax, fritillaria, saxifrage, and young violets were pushing up as if already conscious of the summer glory, and innumerable green and yellow buds were peeping and smiling everywhere.

As for the birds and squirrels, not a wing or tail of them was to be seen while the storm was blowing. Squirrels dislike wet weather more than cats do; therefore they were at home rocking in their dry nests. The birds were hiding in the dells out of the wind, some of the strongest of them pecking at acorns and manzanita berries, but most were perched on low twigs, their breast feathers puffed out and keeping one another company through the hard time as best they could.

When I arrived at the village about sundown, the good people bestirred themselves, pitying my bedraggled condition as if I were some benumbed castaway snatched from the sea, while I, in turn, warm with excitement and reeking like the ground, pitied them for being dry and defrauded of all the glory that Nature had spread round about them that day.

CHAPTER XII

SIERRA THUNDER-STORMS

The weather of spring and summer in the middle region of the Sierra is usually well flecked with rains and light dustings of snow, most of which are far too obviously joyful and life-giving to be regarded as storms; and in the picturesque beauty and clearness of outlines of their clouds they offer striking contrasts to those boundless, all-embracing cloud-mantles of the storms of winter. The smallest and most perfectly individualized specimens present a richly modeled cumulous cloud rising above the dark woods, about 11 A.M., swelling with a visible motion straight up into the calm, sunny sky to a height of 12,000 to 14,000 feet above the sea, its white, pearly bosses relieved by gray and pale purple shadows in the hollows, and showing outlines as keenly defined as those of the glacier-polished domes. In less than an hour it attains full development and stands poised in the blazing sunshine like some colossal mountain, as beautiful in form and finish as if it were to become a permanent addition to the landscape. Presently a thunderbolt crashes through the crisp air, ringing like steel on steel, sharp and clear, its startling detonation breaking into a spray of echoes against the cliffs and cañon walls. Then down comes a cataract of rain. The big drops sift through the pine-needles, plash and patter on the granite pavements, and pour down the sides of ridges and domes in a network of gray, bubbling rills. In a few minutes the cloud withers to a mesh of dim filaments and disappears, leaving the sky perfectly clear and bright, every dust-particle wiped and washed out of it. Everything is refreshed and invigorated, a steam of fragrance rises, and the storm is finished—one cloud, one lightning-stroke, and one dash of rain. This is the Sierra mid-summer thunder-storm reduced to its lowest terms. But some of them attain much larger proportions, and assume a grandeur and energy of expression hardly surpassed by those bred in the depths of winter, producing those sudden floods called "cloud-bursts," which are local, and to a considerable extent periodical, for they appear nearly every day about the same time for weeks, usually about eleven o'clock, and lasting from five minutes to an hour or two. One soon becomes so accustomed to see them that the noon sky seems empty and abandoned without them, as if Nature were forgetting something. When the glorious pearl and alabaster clouds of these noonday storms are being built I never give attention to anything else. No mountain or mountain-range, however divinely clothed with light, has a more enduring charm than those fleeting mountains of the sky—floating fountains bearing water for every well, the angels of the streams and lakes; brooding in the deep azure, or sweeping softly along the ground over ridge and dome, over meadow, over forest, over garden and grove; lingering with cooling shadows, refreshing every flower, and soothing rugged rock-brows with a gentleness of touch and gesture wholly divine.

The most beautiful and imposing of the summer storms rise just above the upper edge of the Silver Fir zone, and all are so beautiful that it is not easy to choose any one for particular description. The one that I remember best fell on the mountains near Yosemite Valley, July 19, 1869, while I was encamped in the Silver Fir woods. A range of bossy cumuli took possession of the sky, huge domes and peaks rising one beyond another with deep cañons between them, bending this way and that in long curves and reaches, interrupted here and there with white upboiling masses that looked like the spray of waterfalls. Zigzag lances of lightning followed each other in quick succession, and the thunder was so gloriously loud and massive it seemed as if surely an entire mountain was being shattered at every stroke. Only the trees were touched, however, so far as I could see,—a few firs 200 feet high, perhaps, and five to six feet in diameter, were split into long rails and slivers from top to bottom and scattered to all points of the compass. Then came the rain in a hearty flood, covering the ground and making it shine with a continuous sheet of water that, like a transparent film or skin, fitted closely down over all the rugged anatomy of the landscape.

It is not long, geologically speaking, since the first raindrop fell on the present landscapes of the Sierra; and in the few tens of thousands of years of stormy cultivation they have been blest with, how beautiful they have become! The first rains fell on raw, crumbling moraines and rocks without a plant. Now scarcely a drop can fail to find a beautiful mark: on the tops of the peaks, on the smooth glacier pavements, on the curves of the domes, on moraines full of crystals, on the thousand forms of yosemitic sculpture with their tender beauty of balmy, flowery vegetation, laving, plashing, glinting, pattering; some falling softly on meadows, creeping out of sight, seeking and finding every thirsty rootlet, some through the spires of the woods, sifting in dust through the needles, and whispering good cheer to each of them; some falling with blunt tapping sounds, drumming on the broad leaves of veratrum, cypripedium, saxifrage; some falling straight into fragrant corollas, kissing the lips of lilies, glinting on the sides of crystals, on shining grains of gold; some falling into the fountains of snow to swell their well-saved stores; some into the lakes and rivers, patting the smooth glassy levels, making dimples and bells and spray, washing the mountain windows, washing the wandering winds; some plashing into the heart of snowy falls and cascades as if eager to join in the dance and the song and beat the foam yet finer. Good work and happy work for the merry mountain raindrops, each one of them a brave fall in itself, rushing from the cliffs and hollows of the clouds into the cliffs and hollows of the mountains; away from the thunder of the sky into the thunder of the roaring rivers. And how far they have to go, and how many cups to fill—cassiope-cups, holding half a drop, and lake basins between the hills, each replenished with equal care—every drop God's messenger sent on its way with glorious pomp and display of power—silvery new-born stars with lake and river, mountain and valley—all that the landscape holds—reflected in their crystal depths.

CHAPTER XIII

THE WATER-OUZEL

The waterfalls of the Sierra are frequented by only one bird,—the Ouzel or Water Thrush (Cinclus Mexicanus, SW.). He is a singularly joyous and lovable little fellow, about the size of a robin, clad in a plain waterproof suit of bluish gray, with a tinge of chocolate on the head and shoulders. In form he is about as smoothly plump and compact as a pebble that has been whirled in a pot-hole, the flowing contour of his body being interrupted only by his strong feet and bill, the crisp wing-tips, and the up-slanted wren-like tail. Among all the countless waterfalls I have met in the course of ten years' exploration in the Sierra, whether among the icy peaks, or warm foot-hills, or in the profound yosemitic cañons of the middle region, not one was found without its Ouzel. No cañon is too cold for this little bird, none too lonely, provided it be rich in falling water. Find a fall, or cascade, or rushing rapid, anywhere upon a clear stream, and there you will surely find its complementary Ouzel, flitting about in the spray, diving in foaming eddies, whirling like a leaf among beaten foam-bells; ever vigorous and enthusiastic, yet self-contained, and neither seeking nor shunning your company.

If disturbed while dipping about in the margin shallows, he either sets off with a rapid whir to some other feeding-ground up or down the stream, or alights on some half-submerged rock or snag out in the current, and immediately begins to nod and courtesy like a wren, turning his head from side to side with many other odd dainty movements that never fail to fix the attention of the observer.

He is the mountain streams' own darling, the humming-bird of blooming waters, loving rocky ripple-slopes and sheets of foam as a bee loves flowers, as a lark loves sunshine and meadows. Among all the mountain birds, none has cheered me so much in my lonely wanderings,—none so unfailingly. For both in winter and summer he sings, sweetly, cheerily, independent alike of sunshine and of love, requiring no other inspiration than the stream on which he dwells. While water sings, so must he, in heat or cold, calm or storm, ever attuning his voice in sure accord; low in the drought of summer and the drought of winter, but never silent.

During the golden days of Indian summer, after most of the snow has been melted, and the mountain streams have become feeble,—a succession of silent pools, linked together by shallow, transparent currents and strips of silvery lacework,—then the song of the Ouzel is at its lowest ebb. But as soon as the winter clouds have bloomed, and the mountain treasuries are once more replenished with snow, the voices of the streams and ouzels increase in strength and richness until the flood season of early summer. Then the torrents chant their noblest anthems, and then is the flood-time of our songster's melody. As for weather, dark days and sun days are the same to him. The voices of most song-birds, however joyous, suffer a long winter eclipse; but the Ouzel sings on through all the seasons and every kind of storm. Indeed no storm can be more violent than those of the waterfalls in the midst of which he delights to dwell. However dark and boisterous the weather, snowing, blowing, or cloudy, all the same he sings, and with never a note of sadness. No need of spring sunshine to thaw his song, for it never freezes. Never shall you hear anything wintry from his warm breast; no pinched cheeping, no wavering notes between sorrow and joy; his mellow, fluty voice is ever tuned to downright gladness, as free from dejection as cock-crowing.

It is pitiful to see wee frost-pinched sparrows on cold mornings in the mountain groves shaking the snow from their feathers, and hopping about as if anxious to be cheery, then hastening back to their hidings out of the wind, puffing out their breast-feathers over their toes, and subsiding among the leaves, cold and breakfastless, while the snow continues to fall, and there is no sign of clearing. But the Ouzel never calls forth a single touch of pity; not because he is strong to endure, but rather because he seems to live a charmed life beyond the reach of every influence that makes endurance necessary.

One wild winter morning, when Yosemite Valley was swept its length from west to east by a cordial snow-storm, I sallied forth to see what I might learn and enjoy. A sort of gray, gloaming-like darkness filled the valley, the huge walls were out of sight, all ordinary sounds were smothered, and even the loudest booming of the falls was at times buried beneath the roar of the heavy-laden blast. The loose snow was already over five feet deep on the meadows, making extended walks impossible without the aid of snow-shoes. I found no great difficulty, however, in making my way to a certain ripple on the river where one of my ouzels lived. He was at home, busily gleaning his breakfast among the pebbles of a shallow portion of the margin, apparently unaware of anything extraordinary in the weather. Presently he flew out to a stone against which the icy current was beating, and turning his back to the wind, sang as delightfully as a lark in springtime.

After spending an hour or two with my favorite, I made my way across the valley, boring and wallowing through the drifts, to learn as definitely as possible how the other birds were spending their time. The Yosemite birds are easily found during the winter because all of them excepting the Ouzel are restricted to the sunny north side of the valley, the south side being constantly eclipsed by the great frosty shadow of the wall. And because the Indian Cañon groves, from their peculiar exposure, are the warmest, the birds congregate there, more especially in severe weather.

I found most of the robins cowering on the lee side of the larger branches where the snow could not fall upon them, while two or three of the more enterprising were making desperate efforts to reach the mistletoe berries by clinging nervously to the under side of the snow-crowned masses, back downward, like woodpeckers. Every now and then they would dislodge some of the loose fringes of the snow-crown, which would come sifting down on them and send them screaming back to camp, where they would subside among their companions with a shiver, muttering in low, querulous chatter like hungry children.

Some of the sparrows were busy at the feet of the larger trees gleaning seeds and benumbed insects, joined now and then by a robin weary of his unsuccessful attempts upon the snow-covered berries. The brave woodpeckers were clinging to the snowless sides of the larger boles and overarching branches of the camp trees, making short nights from side to side of the grove, pecking now and then at the acorns they had stored in the bark, and chattering aimlessly as if unable to keep still, yet evidently putting in the time in a very dull way, like storm-bound travelers at a country tavern. The hardy nut-hatches were threading the open furrows of the trunks in their usual industrious manner, and uttering their quaint notes, evidently less distressed than their neighbors. The Steller jays were of course making more noisy stir than all the other birds combined; ever coming and going with loud bluster, screaming as if each had a lump of melting sludge in his throat, and taking good care to improve the favorable opportunity afforded by the storm to steal from the acorn stores of the woodpeckers. I also noticed one solitary gray eagle braving the storm on the top of a tall pine-stump just outside the main grove. He was standing bolt upright with his back to the wind, a tuft of snow piled on his square shoulders, a monument of passive endurance. Thus every snow-bound bird seemed more or less uncomfortable if not in positive distress.

The storm was reflected in every gesture, and not one cheerful note, not to say song, came from a single bill; their cowering, joyless endurance offering a striking contrast to the spontaneous, irrepressible gladness of the Ouzel, who could no more help exhaling sweet song than a rose sweet fragrance. He must sing though the heavens fall. I remember noticing the distress of a pair of robins during the violent earthquake of the year 1872, when the pines of the Valley, with strange movements, flapped and waved their branches, and beetling rock-brows came thundering down to the meadows in tremendous avalanches. It did not occur to me in the midst of the excitement of other observations to look for the ouzels, but I doubt not they were singing straight on through it all, regarding the terrible rock-thunder as fearlessly as they do the booming of the waterfalls.

What may be regarded as the separate songs of the Ouzel are exceedingly difficult of description, because they are so variable and at the same time so confluent. Though I have been acquainted with my favorite ten years, and during most of this time have heard him sing nearly every day, I still detect notes and strains that seem new to me. Nearly all of his music is sweet and tender, lapsing from his round breast like water over the smooth lip of a pool, then breaking farther on into a sparkling foam of melodious notes, which, glow with subdued enthusiasm, yet without expressing much of the strong, gushing ecstasy of the bobolink or skylark.

The more striking strains are perfect arabesques of melody, composed of a few full, round, mellow notes, embroidered with delicate trills which fade and melt in long slender cadences. In a general way his music is that of the streams refined and spiritualized. The deep booming notes of the falls are in it, the trills of rapids, the gurgling of margin eddies, the low whispering of level reaches, and the sweet tinkle of separate drops oozing from the ends of mosses and falling into tranquil pools.

The Ouzel never sings in chorus with other birds, nor with his kind, but only with the streams. And like flowers that bloom beneath the surface of the ground, some of our favorite's best song-blossoms never rise above the surface of the heavier music of the water. I have often observed him singing in the midst of beaten spray, his music completely buried beneath the water's roar; yet I knew he was surely singing by his gestures and the movements of his bill.

His food, as far as I have noticed, consists of all kinds of water insects, which in summer are chiefly procured along shallow margins. Here he wades about ducking his head under water and deftly turning over pebbles and fallen leaves with his bill, seldom choosing to go into deep water where he has to use his wings in diving.

He seems to be especially fond of the larvae; of mosquitos, found in abundance attached to the bottom of smooth rock channels where the current is shallow. When feeding in such places he wades up-stream, and often while his head is under water the swift current is deflected upward along the glossy curves of his neck and shoulders, in the form of a clear, crystalline shell, which fairly incloses him like a bell-glass, the shell being broken and re-formed as he lifts and dips his head; while ever and anon he sidles out to where the too powerful current carries him off his feet; then he dexterously rises on the wing and goes gleaning again in shallower places.

But during the winter, when the stream-banks are embossed in snow, and the streams themselves are chilled nearly to the freezing-point, so that the snow falling into them in stormy weather is not wholly dissolved, but forms a thin, blue sludge, thus rendering the current opaque—then he seeks the deeper portions of the main rivers, where he may dive to clear water beneath the sludge. Or he repairs to some open lake or mill-pond, at the bottom of which he feeds in safety.

When thus compelled to betake himself to a lake, he does not plunge into it at once like a duck, but always alights in the first place upon some rock or fallen pine along the shore. Then flying out thirty or forty yards, more or less, according to the character of the bottom, he alights with a dainty glint on the surface, swims about, looks down, finally makes up his mind, and disappears with a sharp stroke of his wings. After feeding for two or three minutes he suddenly reappears, showers the water from his wings with one vigorous shake, and rises abruptly into the air as if pushed up from beneath, comes back to his perch, sings a few minutes, and goes out to dive again; thus coming and going, singing and diving at the same place for hours.

The Ouzel is usually found singly; rarely in pairs, excepting during the breeding season, and very rarely in threes or fours. I once observed three thus spending a winter morning in company, upon a small glacier lake, on the Upper Merced, about 7500 feet above the level of the sea. A storm had occurred during the night, but the morning sun shone unclouded, and the shadowy lake, gleaming darkly in its setting of fresh snow, lay smooth and motionless as a mirror. My camp chanced to be within a few feet of the water's edge, opposite a fallen pine, some of the branches of which leaned out over the lake. Here my three dearly welcome visitors took up their station, and at once began to embroider the frosty air with their delicious melody, doubly delightful to me that particular morning, as I had been somewhat apprehensive of danger in breaking my way down through the snow-choked cañons to the lowlands.

The portion of the lake bottom selected for a feeding-ground lies at a depth of fifteen or twenty feet below the surface, and is covered with a short growth of algae and other aquatic plants,—facts I had previously determined while sailing over it on a raft. After alighting on the glassy surface, they occasionally indulged in a little play, chasing one another round about in small circles; then all three would suddenly dive together, and then come ashore and sing.

The Ouzel seldom swims more than a few yards on the surface, for, not being web-footed, he makes rather slow progress, but by means of his strong, crisp wings he swims, or rather flies, with celerity under the surface, often to considerable distances. But it is in withstanding the force of heavy rapids that his strength of wing in this respect is most strikingly manifested. The following may be regarded as a fair illustration of his power of sub-aquatic flight. One stormy morning in winter when the Merced River was blue and green with unmelted snow, I observed one of my ouzels perched on a snag out in the midst of a swift-rushing rapid, singing cheerily, as if everything was just to his mind; and while I stood on the bank admiring him, he suddenly plunged into the sludgy current, leaving his song abruptly broken off. After feeding a minute or two at the bottom, and when one would suppose that he must inevitably be swept far down-stream, he emerged just where he went down, alighted on the same snag, showered the water-beads from his feathers, and continued his unfinished song, seemingly in tranquil ease as if it had suffered no interruption.

The Ouzel alone of all birds dares to enter a white torrent. And though strictly terrestrial in structure, no other is so inseparably related to water, not even the duck, or the bold ocean albatross, or the stormy-petrel. For ducks go ashore as soon as they finish feeding in undisturbed places, and very often make long flights over land from lake to lake or field to field. The same is true of most other aquatic birds. But the Ouzel, born on the brink of a stream, or on a snag or boulder in the midst of it, seldom leaves it for a single moment. For, notwithstanding he is often on the wing, he never flies overland, but whirs with, rapid, quail-like beat above the stream, tracing all its windings. Even when the stream is quite small, say from five to ten feet wide, he seldom shortens his flight by crossing a bend, however abrupt it may be; and even when disturbed by meeting some one on the bank, he prefers to fly over one's head, to dodging out over the ground. When, therefore, his flight along a crooked stream is viewed endwise, it appears most strikingly wavered—a description on the air of every curve with lightning-like rapidity.

The vertical curves and angles of the most precipitous torrents he traces with the same rigid fidelity, swooping down the inclines of cascades, dropping sheer over dizzy falls amid the spray, and ascending with the same fearlessness and ease, seldom seeking to lessen the steepness of the acclivity by beginning to ascend before reaching the base of the fall. No matter though it may be several hundred feet in height he holds straight on, as if about to dash headlong into the throng of booming rockets, then darts abruptly upward, and, after alighting at the top of the precipice to rest a moment, proceeds to feed and sing. His flight is solid and impetuous, without any intermission of wing-beats,—one homogeneous buzz like that of a laden bee on its way home. And while thus buzzing freely from fall to fall, he is frequently heard giving utterance to a long outdrawn train of unmodulated notes, in no way connected with his song, but corresponding closely with his flight in sustained vigor.

Were the flights of all the ouzels in the Sierra traced on a chart, they would indicate the direction of the flow of the entire system of ancient glaciers, from about the period of the breaking up of the ice-sheet until near the close of the glacial winter; because the streams which the ouzels so rigidly follow are, with the unimportant exceptions of a few side tributaries, all flowing in channels eroded for them out of the solid flank of the range by the vanished glaciers,—the streams tracing the ancient glaciers, the ouzels tracing the streams. Nor do we find so complete compliance to glacial conditions in the life of any other mountain bird, or animal of any kind. Bears frequently accept the pathways laid down by glaciers as the easiest to travel; but they often leave them and cross over from cañon to cañon. So also, most of the birds trace the moraines to some extent, because the forests are growing on them. But they wander far, crossing the cañons from grove to grove, and draw exceedingly angular and complicated courses.

The Ouzel's nest is one of the most extraordinary pieces of bird architecture I ever saw, odd and novel in design, perfectly fresh and beautiful, and in every way worthy of the genius of the little builder. It is about a foot in diameter, round and bossy in outline, with a neatly arched opening near the bottom, somewhat like an old-fashioned brick oven, or Hottentot's hut. It is built almost exclusively of green and yellow mosses, chiefly the beautiful fronded hypnum that covers the rocks and old drift-logs in the vicinity of waterfalls. These are deftly interwoven, and felted together into a charming little hut; and so situated that many of the outer mosses continue to flourish as if they had not been plucked. A few fine, silky-stemmed grasses are occasionally found interwoven with the mosses, but, with the exception of a thin layer lining the floor, their presence seems accidental, as they are of a species found growing with the mosses and are probably plucked with them. The site chosen for this curious mansion is usually some little rock-shelf within reach of the lighter particles of the spray of a waterfall, so that its walls are kept green and growing, at least during the time of high water.

No harsh lines are presented by any portion of the nest as seen in place, but when removed from its shelf, the back and bottom, and sometimes a portion of the top, is found quite sharply angular, because it is made to conform to the surface of the rock upon which and against which it is built, the little architect always taking advantage of slight crevices and protuberances that may chance to offer, to render his structure stable by means of a kind of gripping and dovetailing.

In choosing a building-spot, concealment does not seem to be taken into consideration; yet notwithstanding the nest is large and guilelessly exposed to view, it is far from being easily detected, chiefly because it swells forward like any other bulging moss-cushion growing naturally in such situations. This is more especially the case where the nest is kept fresh by being well sprinkled. Sometimes these romantic little huts have their beauty enhanced by rock-ferns and grasses that spring up around the mossy walls, or in front of the door-sill, dripping with crystal beads.

Furthermore, at certain hours of the day, when the sunshine is poured down at the required angle, the whole mass of the spray enveloping the fairy establishment is brilliantly irised; and it is through so glorious a rainbow atmosphere as this that some of our blessed ouzels obtain their first peep at the world.

Ouzels seem so completely part and parcel of the streams they inhabit, they scarce suggest any other origin than the streams themselves; and one might almost be pardoned in fancying they come direct from the living waters, like flowers from the ground. At least, from whatever cause, it never occurred to me to look for their nests until more than a year after I had made the acquaintance of the birds themselves, although I found one the very day on which I began the search. In making my way from Yosemite to the glaciers at the heads of the Merced and Tuolumne rivers, I camped in a particularly wild and romantic portion of the Nevada cañon where in previous excursions I had never failed to enjoy the company of my favorites, who were attracted here, no doubt, by the safe nesting-places in the shelving rocks, and by the abundance of food and falling water. The river, for miles above and below, consists of a succession of small falls from ten to sixty feet in height, connected by flat, plume-like cascades that go flashing from fall to fall, free and almost channelless, over waving folds of glacier-polished granite.

On the south side of one of the falls, that portion of the precipice which is bathed by the spray presents a series of little shelves and tablets caused by the development of planes of cleavage in the granite, and by the consequent fall of masses through the action of the water. "Now here," said I, "of all places, is the most charming spot for an Ouzel's nest." Then carefully scanning the fretted face of the precipice through the spray, I at length noticed a yellowish moss-cushion, growing on the edge of a level tablet within five or six feet of the outer folds of the fall. But apart from the fact of its being situated where one acquainted with the lives of ouzels would fancy an Ouzel's nest ought to be, there was nothing in its appearance visible at first sight, to distinguish it from other bosses of rock-moss similarly situated with reference to perennial spray; and it was not until I had scrutinized it again and again, and had removed my shoes and stockings and crept along the face of the rock within eight or ten feet of it, that I could decide certainly whether it was a nest or a natural growth.

In these moss huts three or four eggs are laid, white like foam-bubbles; and well may the little birds hatched from them sing water songs, for they hear them all their lives, and even before they are born.

I have often observed the young just out of the nest making their odd gestures, and seeming in every way as much at home as their experienced parents, like young bees on their first excursions to the flower fields. No amount of familiarity with people and their ways seems to change them in the least. To all appearance their behavior is just the same on seeing a man for the first time, as when they have seen him frequently.

On the lower reaches of the rivers where mills are built, they sing on through the din of the machinery, and all the noisy confusion of dogs, cattle, and workmen. On one occasion, while a wood-chopper was at work on the river-bank, I observed one cheerily singing within reach of the flying chips. Nor does any kind of unwonted disturbance put him in bad humor, or frighten him out of calm self-possession. In passing through a narrow gorge, I once drove one ahead of me from rapid to rapid, disturbing him four times in quick succession where he could not very well fly past me on account of the narrowness of the channel. Most birds under similar circumstances fancy themselves pursued, and become suspiciously uneasy; but, instead of growing nervous about it, he made his usual dippings, and sang one of his most tranquil strains. When observed within a few yards their eyes are seen to express remarkable gentleness and intelligence; but they seldom allow so near a view unless one wears clothing of about the same color as the rocks and trees, and knows how to sit still. On one occasion, while rambling along the shore of a mountain lake, where the birds, at least those born that season, had never seen a man, I sat down to rest on a large stone close to the water's edge, upon which it seemed the ouzels and sandpipers were in the habit of alighting when they came to feed on that part of the shore, and some of the other birds also, when they came down to wash or drink. In a few minutes, along came a whirring Ouzel and alighted on the stone beside me, within reach of my hand. Then suddenly observing me, he stooped nervously as if about to fly on the instant, but as I remained as motionless as the stone, he gained confidence, and looked me steadily in the face for about a minute, then flew quietly to the outlet and began to sing. Next came a sandpiper and gazed at me with much the same guileless expression of eye as the Ouzel. Lastly, down with a swoop came a Steller's jay out of a fir-tree, probably with the intention of moistening his noisy throat. But instead of sitting confidingly as my other visitors had done, he rushed off at once, nearly tumbling heels over head into the lake in his suspicious confusion, and with loud screams roused the neighborhood.

Love for song-birds, with their sweet human voices, appears to be more common and unfailing than love for flowers. Every one loves flowers to some extent, at least in life's fresh morning, attracted by them as instinctively as humming-birds and bees. Even the young Digger Indians have sufficient love for the brightest of those found growing on the mountains to gather them and braid them, as decorations for the hair. And I was glad to discover, through the few Indians that could be induced to talk on the subject, that they have names for the wild rose and the lily, and other conspicuous flowers, whether available as food or otherwise. Most men, however, whether savage or civilized, become apathetic toward all plants that have no other apparent use than the use of beauty. But fortunately one's first instinctive love of song-birds is never wholly obliterated, no matter what the influences upon our lives may be. I have often been delighted to see a pure, spiritual glow come into the countenances of hard business-men and old miners, when a song-bird chanced to alight near them. Nevertheless, the little mouthful of meat that swells out the breasts of some song-birds is too often the cause of their death. Larks and robins in particular are brought to market in hundreds. But fortunately the Ouzel has no enemy so eager to eat his little body as to follow him into the mountain solitudes. I never knew him to be chased even by hawks.

An acquaintance of mine, a sort of foot-hill mountaineer, had a pet cat, a great, dozy, overgrown creature, about as broad-shouldered as a lynx. During the winter, while the snow lay deep, the mountaineer sat in his lonely cabin among the pines smoking his pipe and wearing the dull time away. Tom was his sole companion, sharing his bed, and sitting beside him on a stool with much the same drowsy expression of eye as his master. The good-natured bachelor was content with his hard fare of soda-bread and bacon, but Tom, the only creature in the world acknowledging dependence on him, must needs be provided with fresh meat. Accordingly he bestirred himself to contrive squirrel-traps, and waded the snowy woods with his gun, making sad havoc among the few winter birds, sparing neither robin, sparrow, nor tiny nuthatch, and the pleasure of seeing Tom eat and grow fat was his great reward.

One cold afternoon, while hunting along the river-bank, he noticed a plain-feathered little bird skipping about in the shallows, and immediately raised his gun. But just then the confiding songster began to sing, and after listening to his summery melody the charmed hunter turned away, saying, "Bless your little heart, I can't shoot you, not even for Tom."

Even so far north as icy Alaska, I have found my glad singer. When I was exploring the glaciers between Mount Fairweather and the Stikeen River, one cold day in November, after trying in vain to force a way through the innumerable icebergs of Sum Dum Bay to the great glaciers at the head of it, I was weary and baffled and sat resting in my canoe convinced at last that I would have to leave this part of my work for another year. Then I began to plan my escape to open water before the young ice which was beginning to form should shut me in. While I thus lingered drifting with the bergs, in the midst of these gloomy forebodings and all the terrible glacial desolation and grandeur, I suddenly heard the well-known whir of an Ouzel's wings, and, looking up, saw my little comforter coming straight across the ice from the shore. In a second or two he was with me, flying three times round my head with a happy salute, as if saying, "Cheer up, old friend; you see I'm here, and all's well." Then he flew back to the shore, alighted on the topmost jag of a stranded iceberg, and began to nod and bow as though he were on one of his favorite boulders in the midst of a sunny Sierra cascade.

The species is distributed all along the mountain-ranges of the Pacific Coast from Alaska to Mexico, and east to the Rocky Mountains. Nevertheless, it is as yet comparatively little known. Audubon and Wilson did not meet it. Swainson was, I believe, the first naturalist to describe a specimen from Mexico. Specimens were shortly afterward procured by Drummond near the sources of the Athabasca

River, between the fifty-fourth and fifty-sixth parallels; and it has been collected by nearly all of the numerous exploring expeditions undertaken of late through our Western States and Territories; for it never fails to engage the attention of naturalists in a very particular manner.

Such, then, is our little cinclus, beloved of every one who is so fortunate as to know him. Tracing on strong wing every curve of the most precipitous torrents from one extremity of the Sierra to the other; not fearing to follow them through their darkest gorges and coldest snow-tunnels; acquainted with every waterfall, echoing their divine music; and throughout the whole of their beautiful lives interpreting all that we in our unbelief call terrible in the utterances of torrents and storms, as only varied expressions of God's eternal love.

CHAPTER XIV

THE WILD SHEEP

(Ovis montana)

The wild sheep ranks highest among the animal mountaineers of the Sierra. Possessed of keen sight and scent, and strong limbs, he dwells secure amid the loftiest summits, leaping unscathed from crag to crag, up and down the fronts of giddy precipices, crossing foaming torrents and slopes of frozen snow, exposed to the wildest storms, yet maintaining a brave, warm life, and developing from generation to generation in perfect strength and beauty.

Nearly all the lofty mountain-chains of the globe are inhabited by wild sheep, most of which, on account of the remote and all but inaccessible regions where they dwell, are imperfectly known as yet. They are classified by different naturalists under from five to ten distinct species or varieties, the best known being the burrhel of the Himalaya (Ovis burrhel, Blyth); the argali, the large wild sheep of central and northeastern Asia (O. ammon, Linn., or Caprovis argali); the Corsican mouflon (O. musimon, Pal.); the aoudad of the mountains of northern Africa (Ammotragus tragelaphus); and the Rocky Mountain bighorn (O. montana, Cuv.). To this last-named species belongs the wild sheep of the Sierra. Its range, according to the late Professor Baird of the Smithsonian Institution, extends "from the region of the upper Missouri and Yellowstone to the Rocky Mountains and the high grounds adjacent to them on the eastern slope, and as far south as the Rio Grande. Westward it extends to the coast ranges of Washington, Oregon, and California, and follows the highlands some distance into Mexico." Throughout the vast region bounded on the east by the Wahsatch Mountains and on the west by the Sierra there are more than a hundred subordinate ranges and mountain groups, trending north and south, range beyond range, with summits rising from eight to twelve thousand feet above the level of the sea, probably all of which, according to my own observations, is, or has been, inhabited by this species.

Compared with the argali, which, considering its size and the vast extent of its range, is probably the most important of all the wild sheep, our species is about the same size, but the horns are less twisted and less divergent. The more important characteristics are, however, essentially the same, some of the best naturalists maintaining that the two are only varied forms of one species. In accordance with this view, Cuvier conjectures that since central Asia seems to be the region where the sheep first appeared, and from which it has been distributed, the argali may have been distributed over this continent from Asia by crossing

Bering Strait on ice. This conjecture is not so ill founded as at first sight would appear; for the Strait is only about fifty miles wide, is interrupted by three islands, and is jammed with ice nearly every winter. Furthermore the argali is abundant on the mountains adjacent to the Strait at East Cape, where it is well known to the Tschuckchi hunters and where I have seen many of their horns.

On account of the extreme variability of the sheep under culture, it is generally supposed that the innumerable domestic breeds have all been derived from the few wild species; but the whole question is involved in obscurity. According to Darwin, sheep have been domesticated from a very ancient period, the remains of a small breed, differing from any now known, having been found in the famous Swiss lake-dwellings.

Compared with the best-known domestic breeds, we find that our wild species is much larger, and, instead of an all-wool garment, wears a thick over-coat of hair like that of the deer, and an under-covering of fine wool. The hair, though rather coarse, is comfortably soft and spongy, and lies smooth, as if carefully tended with comb and brush. The predominant color during most of the year is brownish-gray, varying to bluish-gray in the autumn; the belly and a large, conspicuous patch on the buttocks are white; and the tail, which is very short, like that of a deer, is black, with a yellowish border. The wool is white, and grows in beautiful spirals down out of sight among the shining hair, like delicate climbing vines among stalks of corn.

The horns of the male are of immense size, measuring in their greater diameter from five to six and a half inches, and from two and a half to three feet in length around the curve. They are yellowish-white in color, and ridged transversely, like those of the domestic ram. Their cross-section near the base is somewhat triangular in outline, and flattened toward the tip. Rising boldly from the top of the head, they curve gently backward and outward, then forward and outward, until about three fourths of a circle is described, and until the flattened, blunt tips are about two feet or two and a half feet apart. Those of the female are flattened throughout their entire length, are less curved than those of the male, and much smaller, measuring less than a foot along the curve.

A ram and ewe that I obtained near the Modoc lava-beds, to the northeast of Mount Shasta, measured as follows:

	Ram.		Ewe.	
	ft.	in.	ft.	in.
Height at shoulders	3	6	3	0
Girth around shoulders	3	11	3	3¾
Length from nose to root of tail	5	10¼	4	3½

Length of ears 0 4¾ 0 5

Length of tail 0 4½ 0 4½

Length of horns around curve 2 9 0 11½

Distance across from tip to tip of horns 2 5½

Circumference of horns at base 1 4 0 6

The measurements of a male obtained in the Rocky Mountains by Audubon vary but little as compared with the above. The weight of his specimen was 344 pounds, which is, perhaps, about an average for full-grown males. The females are about a third lighter.

Besides these differences in size, color, hair, etc., as noted above, we may observe that the domestic sheep, in a general way, is expressionless, like a dull bundle of something only half alive, while the wild is as elegant and graceful as a deer, every movement manifesting admirable strength and character. The tame is timid; the wild is bold. The tame is always more or less ruffled and dirty; while the wild is as smooth and clean as the flowers of his mountain pastures.

The earliest mention that I have been able to find of the wild sheep in America is by Father Picolo, a Catholic missionary at Monterey, in the year 1797, who, after describing it, oddly enough, as "a kind of deer with a sheep-like head, and about as large as a calf one or two years old," naturally hurries on to remark: "I have eaten of these beasts; their flesh is very tender and delicious." Mackenzie, in his northern travels, heard the species spoken of by the Indians as "white buffaloes." And Lewis and Clark tell us that, in a time of great scarcity on the head waters of the Missouri, they saw plenty of wild sheep, but they were "too shy to be shot."

A few of the more energetic of the Pah Ute Indians hunt the wild sheep every season among the more accessible sections of the High Sierra, in the neighborhood of passes, where, from having been pursued, they have become extremely wary; but in the rugged wilderness of peaks and cañons, where the foaming tributaries of the San Joaquin and King's rivers take their rise, they fear no hunter save the wolf, and are more guileless and approachable than their tame kindred.

While engaged in the work of exploring high regions where they delight to roam I have been greatly interested in studying their habits. In the months of November and December, and probably during a considerable portion of midwinter, they all flock together, male and female, old and young. I once found a complete band of this kind numbering upward of fifty, which, on being alarmed, went bounding away across a jagged lava-bed at admirable speed, led by a majestic old ram, with the lambs safe in the middle of the flock.

In spring and summer, the full-grown rams form separate bands of from three to twenty, and are usually found feeding along the edges of glacier meadows, or resting among the castle-like crags of the high summits; and whether quietly feeding, or scaling the wild cliffs, their noble forms and the power and beauty of their movements never fail to strike the beholder with lively admiration.

Their resting-places seem to be chosen with reference to sunshine and a wide outlook, and most of all to safety. Their feeding-grounds are among the most beautiful of the wild gardens, bright with daisies and gentians and mats of purple bryanthus, lying hidden away on rocky headlands and cañon sides, where sunshine is abundant, or down in the shady glacier valleys, along the banks of the streams and lakes, where the plushy sod is greenest. Here they feast all summer, the happy wanderers, perhaps relishing the beauty as well as the taste of the lovely flora on which they feed.

When the winter storms set in, loading their highland pastures with snow, then, like the birds, they gather and go to lower climates, usually descending the eastern flank of the range to the rough, volcanic table-lands and treeless ranges of the Great Basin adjacent to the Sierra. They never make haste, however, and seem to have no dread of storms, many of the strongest only going down leisurely to bare, wind-swept ridges, to feed on bushes and dry bunch-grass, and then returning up into the snow. Once I was snow-bound on Mount Shasta for three days, a little below the timber line. It was a dark and stormy time, well calculated to test the skill and endurance of mountaineers. The snow-laden gale drove on night and day in hissing, blinding floods, and when at length it began to abate, I found that a small band of wild sheep had weathered the storm in the lee of a clump of Dwarf Pines a few yards above my storm-nest, where the snow was eight or ten feet deep. I was warm back of a rock, with blankets, bread, and fire. My brave companions lay in the snow, without food, and with only the partial shelter of the short trees, yet they made no sign of suffering or faint-heartedness.

In the months of May and June, the wild sheep bring forth their young in solitary and almost inaccessible crags, far above the nesting-rocks of the eagle. I have frequently come upon the beds of the ewes and lambs at an elevation of from 12,000 to 13,000 feet above sea-level. These beds are simply oval-shaped hollows, pawed out among loose, disintegrating rock-chips and sand, upon some sunny spot commanding a good outlook, and partially sheltered from the winds that sweep those lofty peaks almost without intermission. Such is the cradle of the little mountaineer, aloft in the very sky; rocked in storms, curtained in clouds, sleeping in thin, icy air; but, wrapped in his hairy coat, and nourished by a strong, warm mother, defended from the talons of the eagle and the teeth of the sly coyote, the bonny lamb grows apace. He soon learns to nibble the tufted rock-grasses and leaves of the white spirsea; his horns begin to shoot, and before summer is done he is strong and agile, and goes forth with the flock, watched by the same divine love that tends the more helpless human lamb in its cradle by the fireside.

Nothing is more commonly remarked by noisy, dusty trail-travelers in the Sierra than the want of animal life—no song-birds, no deer, no squirrels, no game of any kind, they say. But if such could only go away quietly into the wilderness, sauntering afoot and alone with natural deliberation, they would soon learn that these mountain mansions are not without inhabitants, many of whom, confiding and gentle, would not try to shun their acquaintance.

In the fall of 1873 I was tracing the South Fork of the San Joaquin up its wild cañon to its farthest glacier fountains. It was the season of alpine Indian summer. The sun beamed lovingly; the squirrels were nutting in the pine-trees, butterflies hovered about the last of the goldenrods, the willow and maple thickets were yellow, the meadows brown, and the whole sunny, mellow landscape glowed like a countenance in the deepest and sweetest repose. On my way over the glacier-polished rocks along the river, I came to an expanded portion of the cañon, about two miles long and half a mile wide, which formed a level park inclosed with picturesque granite walls like those of Yosemite Valley. Down through the middle of it poured the beautiful river shining and spangling in the golden light, yellow groves on its banks, and strips of brown meadow; while the whole park was astir with wild life, some of which even the noisiest and least observing of travelers must have seen had they been with me. Deer, with their supple, well-grown fawns, bounded from thicket to thicket as I advanced; grouse kept rising from the brown grass with a great whirring of wings, and, alighting on the lower branches of the pines and poplars, allowed a near approach, as if curious to see me. Farther on, a broad-shouldered wildcat showed himself, coming out of a grove, and crossing the river on a flood-jamb of logs, halting for a moment to look back. The bird-like tamias frisked about my feet everywhere among the pine-needles and seedy grass-tufts; cranes waded the shallows of the river-bends, the kingfisher rattled from perch to perch, and the blessed ouzel sang amid the spray of every cascade. Where may lonely wanderer find a more interesting family of mountain-dwellers, earth-born companions and fellow-mortals? It was afternoon when I joined them, and the glorious landscape began to fade in the gloaming before I awoke from their enchantment. Then I sought a camp-ground on the river-bank, made a cupful of tea, and lay down to sleep on a smooth place among the yellow leaves of an aspen grove. Next day I discovered yet grander landscapes and grander life. Following the river over huge, swelling rock-bosses through a majestic cañon, and past innumerable cascades, the scenery in general became gradually wilder and more alpine. The Sugar Pine and Silver Firs gave place to the hardier Cedar and Hemlock Spruce. The cañon walls became more rugged and bare, and gentians and arctic daisies became more abundant in the gardens and strips of meadow along the streams. Toward the middle of the afternoon I came to another valley, strikingly wild and original in all its features, and perhaps never before touched by human foot. As regards area of level bottom-land, it is one of the very smallest of the Yosemite type, but its walls are sublime, rising to a height of from 2000 to 4000 feet above the river. At the head of the valley the main cañon forks, as is found to be the case in all yosemites. The formation of this one is due chiefly to the action of two great glaciers, whose fountains lay to the eastward, on the flanks of Mounts Humphrey and Emerson and a cluster of nameless peaks farther south.

The gray, boulder-chafed river was singing loudly through the valley, but above its massy roar I heard the booming of a waterfall, which drew me eagerly on; and just as I emerged from the tangled groves and brier-thickets at the head of the valley, the main fork of the river came in sight, falling fresh from its glacier fountains in a snowy cascade, between granite walls 2000 feet high. The steep incline down which the glad waters thundered seemed to bar all farther progress. It was not long, however, before I discovered a crooked seam in the rock, by which I was enabled to climb to the edge of a terrace that crosses the cañon, and divides the cataract nearly in the middle. Here I sat down to take breath and make some entries in my note book, taking advantage, at the same time, of my elevated position above the trees to gaze back over the valley into the heart of the noble landscape, little knowing the while what neighbors were near.

After spending a few minutes in this way, I chanced to look across the fall, and there stood three sheep quietly observing me. Never did the sudden appearance of a mountain, or fall, or human friend more forcibly seize and rivet my attention. Anxiety to observe accurately held me perfectly still. Eagerly I marked the flowing undulations of their firm, braided muscles, their strong legs, ears, eyes, heads, their graceful rounded necks, the color of their hair, and the bold, upsweeping curves of their noble horns. When they moved I watched every gesture, while they, in no wise disconcerted either by my attention or by the tumultuous roar of the water, advanced deliberately alongside the rapids, between the two divisions of the cataract, turning now and then to look at me. Presently they came to a steep, ice-burnished acclivity, which they ascended by a succession of quick, short, stiff-legged leaps, reaching the top without a struggle. This was the most startling feat of mountaineering I had ever witnessed, and, considering only the mechanics of the thing, my astonishment could hardly have been greater had they displayed wings and taken to flight. "Surefooted" mules on such ground would have fallen and rolled like loosened boulders. Many a time, where the slopes are far lower, I have been compelled to take off my shoes and stockings, tie them to my belt, and creep barefooted, with the utmost caution. No wonder then, that I watched the progress of these animal mountaineers with keen sympathy, and exulted in the boundless sufficiency of wild nature displayed in their invention, construction, and keeping. A few minutes later I caught sight of a dozen more in one band, near the foot of the upper fall. They were standing on the same side of the river with me, only twenty-five or thirty yards away, looking as unworn and perfect as if created on the spot. It appeared by their tracks, which I had seen in the Little Yosemite, and by their present position, that when I came up the cañon they were all feeding together down in the valley, and in their haste to reach high ground, where they could look about them to ascertain the nature of the strange disturbance, they were divided, three ascending on one side the river, the rest on the other.

The main band, headed by an experienced chief, now began to cross the wild rapids between the two divisions of the cascade. This was another exciting feat; for, among all the varied experiences of mountaineers, the crossing of boisterous, rock-dashed torrents is found to be one of the most trying to the nerves. Yet these fine fellows walked fearlessly to the brink, and jumped from boulder to boulder, holding themselves in easy poise above the whirling, confusing current, as if they were doing nothing extraordinary.

In the immediate foreground of this rare picture there was a fold of ice-burnished granite, traversed by a few bold lines in which rock-ferns and tufts of bryanthus were growing, the gray cañon walls on the sides, nobly sculptured and adorned with brown cedars and pines; lofty peaks in the distance, and in the middle ground the snowy fall, the voice and soul of the landscape; fringing bushes beating time to its thunder-tones, the brave sheep in front of it, their gray forms slightly obscured in the spray, yet standing out in good, heavy relief against the close white water, with their huge horns rising like the upturned roots of dead pine-trees, while the evening sunbeams streaming up the cañon colored all the picture a rosy purple and made it glorious. After crossing the river, the dauntless climbers, led by their chief, at once began to scale the cañon wall, turning now right, now left, in long, single file, keeping well apart out of one another's way, and leaping in regular succession from crag to crag, now ascending slippery dome-curves, now walking leisurely along the edges of precipices, stopping at times to gaze down at me from some flat-topped rock, with heads held aslant, as if curious to learn what I thought about it, or whether I was likely to follow them. After reaching the top of the wall, which, at this place, is somewhere between 1500 and 2000 feet high, they were still visible against the sky as they lingered, looking down in groups of twos or threes.

Throughout the entire ascent they did not make a single awkward step, or an unsuccessful effort of any kind. I have frequently seen tame sheep in mountains jump upon a sloping rock-surface, hold on tremulously a few seconds, and fall back baffled and irresolute. But in the most trying situations, where the slightest want or inaccuracy would have been fatal, these always seemed to move in comfortable reliance on their strength and skill, the limits of which they never appeared to know. Moreover, each one of the flock, while following the guidance of the most experienced, yet climbed with intelligent independence as a perfect individual, capable of separate existence whenever it should wish or be compelled to withdraw from the little clan. The domestic sheep, on the contrary, is only a fraction of an animal, a whole flock being required to form an individual, just as numerous flowerets are required to make one complete sunflower.

Those shepherds who, in summer, drive their flocks to the mountain pastures, and, while watching them night and day, have seen them frightened by bears and storms, and scattered like wind-driven chaff, will, in some measure, be able to appreciate the self-reliance and strength and noble individuality of Nature's sheep.

Like the Alp-climbing ibex of Europe, our mountaineer is said to plunge headlong down the faces of sheer precipices, and alight on his big horns. I know only two hunters who claim to have actually witnessed this feat; I never was so fortunate. They describe the act as a diving head-foremost. The horns are so large at the base that they cover the upper portion of the head down nearly to a level with the eyes, and the skull is exceedingly strong. I struck an old, bleached specimen on Mount Ritter a dozen blows with my ice-ax without breaking it. Such skulls would not fracture very readily by the wildest rock-diving, but other bones could hardly be expected to hold together in such a performance; and the mechanical difficulties in the way of controlling their movements, after striking upon an irregular surface, are, in themselves, sufficient to show this boulder-like method of progression to be impossible, even in the absence of all other evidence on the subject; moreover, the ewes follow wherever the rams may lead, although their horns are mere spikes. I have found many pairs of the horns of the old rams considerably battered, doubtless a result of fighting. I was particularly interested in the question, after witnessing the performances of this San Joaquin band upon the glaciated rocks at the foot of the falls; and as soon as I procured specimens and examined their feet, all the mystery disappeared. The secret, considered in connection with exceptionally strong muscles, is simply this: the wide posterior portion of the bottom of the foot, instead of wearing down and becoming flat and hard, like the feet of tame sheep and horses, bulges out in a soft, rubber-like pad or cushion, which not only grips and holds well on smooth rocks, but fits into small cavities, and down upon or against slight protuberances. Even the hardest portions of the edge of the hoof are comparatively soft and elastic; furthermore, the toes admit of an extraordinary amount of both lateral and vertical movement, allowing the foot to accommodate itself still more perfectly to the irregularities of rock surfaces, while at the same time increasing the gripping power.

At the base of Sheep Rock, one of the winter strongholds of the Shasta flocks, there lives a stock-raiser who has had the advantage of observing the movements of wild sheep every winter; and, in the course of a conversation with him on the subject of their diving habits, he pointed to the front of a lava headland about 150 feet high, which is only eight or ten degrees out of the perpendicular. "There," said he, "I followed a band of them fellows to the back of that rock yonder, and expected to capture them all, for I thought I had a dead thing on them. I got behind them on a narrow bench that runs along the face of the wall near the top and comes to an end where they couldn't get away without falling and being killed; but they jumped off, and landed all right, as if that were the regular thing with them."

"What!" said I, "jumped 150 feet perpendicular! Did you see them do it?"

"No," he replied, "I didn't see them going down, for I was behind them; but I saw them go off over the brink, and then I went below and found their tracks where they struck on the loose rubbish at the bottom. They just sailed right off, and landed on their feet right side up. That is the kind of animal they is—beats anything else that goes on four legs."

On another occasion, a flock that was pursued by hunters retreated to another portion of this same cliff where it is still higher, and, on being followed, they were seen jumping down in perfect order, one behind another, by two men who happened to be chopping where they had a fair view of them and could watch their progress from top to bottom of the precipice. Both ewes and rams made the frightful descent without evincing any extraordinary concern, hugging the rock closely, and controlling the velocity of their half falling, half leaping movements by striking at short intervals and holding back with their cushioned, rubber feet upon small ledges and roughened inclines until near the bottom, when they "sailed off" into the free air and alighted on their feet, but with their bodies so nearly in a vertical position that they appeared to be diving.

It appears, therefore, that the methods of this wild mountaineering become clearly comprehensible as soon as we make ourselves acquainted with the rocks, and the kind of feet and muscles brought to bear upon them.

The Modoc and Pah Ute Indians are, or rather have been, the most successful hunters of the wild sheep in the regions that have come under my own observation. I have seen large numbers of heads and horns in the caves of Mount Shasta and the Modoc lava-beds, where the Indians had been feasting in stormy weather; also in the cañons of the Sierra opposite Owen's Valley; while the heavy obsidian arrow-heads found on some of the highest peaks show that this warfare has long been going on.

In the more accessible ranges that stretch across the desert regions of western Utah and Nevada, considerable numbers of Indians used to hunt in company like packs of wolves, and being perfectly acquainted with the topography of their hunting-grounds, and with the habits and instincts of the game, they were pretty successful. On the tops of nearly every one of the Nevada mountains that I have visited, I found small, nest-like inclosures built of stones, in which, as I afterward learned, one or more Indians would lie in wait while their companions scoured the ridges below, knowing that the alarmed sheep would surely run to the summit, and when they could be made to approach with the wind they were shot at short range.

Still larger bands of Indians used to make extensive hunts upon some dominant mountain much frequented by the sheep, such as Mount Grant on the Wassuck Range to the west of Walker Lake. On some particular spot, favorably situated with reference to the well-known trails of the sheep, they built a high-walled corral, with long guiding wings diverging from the gateway; and into this inclosure they sometimes succeeded in driving the noble game. Great numbers of Indians were of course required, more, indeed, than they could usually muster, counting in squaws, children, and all; they were compelled, therefore, to build rows of dummy hunters out of stones, along the ridge-tops which they wished to prevent the sheep from crossing. And, without discrediting the sagacity of the game, these dummies were found effective; for, with a few live Indians moving about excitedly among them, they could hardly be distinguished at a little distance from men, by any one not in the secret. The whole ridge-top then seemed to be alive with hunters.

The only animal that may fairly be regarded as a companion or rival of the sheep is the so-called Rocky Mountain goat (Aplocerus montana, Rich.), which, as its name indicates, is more antelope than goat. He, too, is a brave and hardy climber, fearlessly crossing the wildest summits, and braving the severest storms, but he is shaggy, short-legged, and much less dignified in demeanor than the sheep. His jet-black horns are only about five or six inches in length, and the long, white hair with which he is covered obscures the expression of his limbs. I have never yet seen a single specimen in the Sierra, though possibly a few flocks may have lived on Mount Shasta a comparatively short time ago.

The ranges of these two mountaineers are pretty distinct, and they see but little of each other; the sheep being restricted mostly to the dry, inland mountains; the goat or chamois to the wet, snowy glacier-laden mountains of the northwest coast of the continent in Oregon, Washington, British Columbia, and Alaska. Probably more than 200 dwell on the icy, volcanic cone of Mount Rainier; and while I was exploring the glaciers of Alaska I saw flocks of these admirable mountaineers nearly every day, and often followed their trails through the mazes of bewildering crevasses, in which they are excellent guides.

Three species of deer are found in California,—the black-tailed, white-tailed, and mule deer. The first mentioned (Cervus Columbianus) is by far the most abundant, and occasionally meets the sheep during the summer on high glacier meadows, and along the edge of the timber line; but being a forest animal, seeking shelter and rearing its young in dense thickets, it seldom visits the wild sheep in its higher homes. The antelope, though not a mountaineer, is occasionally met in winter by the sheep while feeding along the edges of the sage-plains and bare volcanic hills to the east of the Sierra. So also is the mule deer, which is almost restricted in its range to this eastern region. The white-tailed species belongs to the coast ranges.

Perhaps no wild animal in the world is without enemies, but highlanders, as a class, have fewer than lowlanders. The wily panther, slipping and crouching among long grass and bushes, pounces upon the antelope and deer, but seldom crosses the bald, craggy thresholds of the sheep. Neither can the bears be regarded as enemies; for, though they seek to vary their every-day diet of nuts and berries by an occasional meal of mutton, they prefer to hunt tame and helpless flocks. Eagles and coyotes, no doubt, capture an unprotected lamb at times, or some unfortunate beset in deep, soft snow, but these cases are little more than accidents. So, also, a few perish in long-continued snow-storms, though, in all my mountaineering, I have not found more than five or six that seemed to have met their fate in this way. A little band of three were discovered snow-bound in Bloody Canon a few years ago, and were killed with an ax by mountaineers, who chanced to be crossing the range in winter.

Man is the most dangerous enemy of all, but even from him our brave mountain-dweller has little to fear in the remote solitudes of the High Sierra. The golden plains of the Sacramento and San Joaquin were lately thronged with bands of elk and antelope, but, being fertile and accessible, they were required for human pastures. So, also, are many of the feeding-grounds of the deer—hill, valley, forest, and meadow—but it will be long before man will care to take the highland castles of the sheep. And when we consider here how rapidly entire species of noble animals, such as the elk, moose, and buffalo, are being pushed to the very verge of extinction, all lovers of wildness will rejoice with me in the rocky security of Ovis montana, the bravest of all the Sierra mountaineers.

CHAPTER XV

IN THE SIERRA FOOT-HILLS

Murphy's camp is a curious old mining-town in Calaveras County, at an elevation of 2400 feet above the sea, situated like a nest in the center of a rough, gravelly region, rich in gold. Granites, slates, lavas, limestone, iron ores, quartz veins, auriferous gravels, remnants of dead fire-rivers and dead water-rivers are developed here side by side within a radius of a few miles, and placed invitingly open before the student like a book, while the people and the region beyond the camp furnish mines of study of never-failing interest and variety.

When I discovered this curious place, I was tracing the channels of the ancient pre-glacial rivers, instructive sections of which have been laid bare here and in the adjacent regions by the miners. Rivers, according to the poets, "go on forever"; but those of the Sierra are young as yet and have scarcely learned the way down to the sea, while at least one generation of them have died and vanished together with most of the basins they drained. All that remains of them to tell their history is a series of interrupted fragments of channels, mostly choked with gravel, and buried beneath broad, thick sheets of lava. These are known as the "Dead Rivers of California," and the gravel deposited in them is comprehensively called the "Blue Lead." In some places the channels of the present rivers trend in the same direction, or nearly so, as those of the ancient rivers; but, in general, there is little correspondence between them, the entire drainage having been changed, or, rather, made new. Many of the hills of the ancient landscapes have become hollows, and the old hollows have become hills. Therefore the fragmentary channels, with their loads of auriferous gravel, occur in all kinds of unthought-of places, trending obliquely, or even at right angles to the present drainage, across the tops of lofty ridges or far beneath them, presenting impressive illustrations of the magnitude of the changes accomplished since those ancient streams were annihilated. The last volcanic period preceding the regeneration of the Sierra landscapes seems to have come on over all the range almost simultaneously, like the glacial period, notwithstanding lavas of different age occur together in many places, indicating numerous periods of activity in the Sierra fire-fountains. The most important of the ancient river-channels in this region is a section that extends from the south side of the town beneath Coyote Creek and the ridge beyond it to the Cañon of the Stanislaus; but on account of its depth below the general surface of the present valleys the rich gold gravels it is known to contain cannot be easily worked on a large scale. Their extraordinary richness may be inferred from the fact that many claims were profitably worked in them by sinking shafts to a depth of 200 feet or more, and hoisting the dirt by a windlass. Should the dip of this ancient channel be such as to make the Stanislaus Cañon available as a dump, then the grand deposit might be worked by the hydraulic method, and although a long, expensive tunnel would be required, the scheme might still prove profitable, for there is "millions in it."

The importance of these ancient gravels as gold fountains is well known to miners. Even the superficial placers of the present streams have derived much of their gold from them. According to all accounts, the Murphy placers have been very rich—"terrific rich," as they say here. The hills have been cut and scalped, and every gorge and gulch and valley torn to pieces and disemboweled, expressing a fierce and desperate energy hard to understand. Still, any kind of effort-making is better than inaction, and there is something sublime in seeing men working in dead earnest at anything, pursuing an object with glacier-like energy and persistence. Many a brave fellow has recorded a most eventful chapter of life on these Calaveras rocks. But most of the pioneer miners are sleeping now, their wild day done, while the few survivors linger languidly in the washed-out gulches or sleepy village like harried bees around the ruins of their hive. "We have no industry left now," they told me, "and no men; everybody and everything hereabouts has gone to decay. We are only bummers—out of the game, a thin scatterin' of poor, dilapidated cusses, compared with what we used to be in the grand old gold-days. We were giants then, and you can look around here and see our tracks." But although these lingering pioneers are perhaps more exhausted than the mines, and about as dead as the dead rivers, they are yet a rare and interesting set of men, with much gold mixed with the rough, rocky gravel of their characters; and they manifest a breeding and intelligence little looked for in such surroundings as theirs. As the heavy, long-continued grinding of the glaciers brought out the features of the Sierra, so the intense experiences of the gold period have brought out the features of these old miners, forming a richness and variety of character little known as yet. The sketches of Bret Harte, Hayes, and Miller have not exhausted this field by any means. It is interesting to note the extremes possible in one and the same character: harshness and gentleness, manliness and childishness, apathy and fierce endeavor. Men who, twenty years ago, would not cease their shoveling to save their lives, now play in the streets with children. Their long, Micawber-like waiting after the exhaustion of the placers has brought on an exaggerated form of dotage. I heard a group of brawny pioneers in the street eagerly discussing the quantity of tail required for a boy's kite; and one graybeard undertook the sport of flying it, volunteering the information that he was a boy, "always was a boy, and d—n a man who was not a boy inside, however ancient outside!" Mines, morals, politics, the immortality of the soul, etc., were discussed beneath shade-trees and in saloons, the time for each being governed apparently by the temperature. Contact with Nature, and the habits of observation acquired in gold-seeking, had made them all, to some extent, collectors, and, like wood-rats, they had gathered all kinds of odd specimens into their cabins, and now required me to examine them. They were themselves the oddest and most interesting specimens. One of them offered to show me around the old diggings, giving me fair warning before setting out that I might not like him, "because," said he, "people say I'm eccentric. I notice everything, and gather beetles and snakes and anything that's queer; and so some don't like me, and call me eccentric. I'm always trying to find out things. Now, there's a weed; the Indians eat it for greens. What do you call those long-bodied flies with big heads?" "Dragon-flies," I suggested. "Well, their jaws work sidewise, instead of up and down, and grasshoppers' jaws work the same way, and therefore I think they are the same species. I always notice everything like that, and just because I do, they say I'm eccentric," etc.

Anxious that I should miss none of the wonders of their old gold-field, the good people had much to say about the marvelous beauty of Cave City Cave, and advised me to explore it. This I was very glad to do, and finding a guide who knew the way to the mouth of it, I set out from Murphy the next morning.

The most beautiful and extensive of the mountain caves of California occur in a belt of metamorphic limestone that is pretty generally developed along the western flank of the Sierra from the McCloud River on the north to the Kaweah on the south, a distance of over 400 miles, at an elevation of from 2000 to 7000 feet above the sea. Besides this regular belt of caves, the California landscapes are diversified by long imposing ranks of sea caves, rugged and variable in architecture, carved in the coast headlands and precipices by centuries of wave-dashing; and innumerable lava-caves, great and small, originating in the unequal flowing and hardening of the lava sheets in which they occur, fine illustrations of which are presented in the famous Modoc Lava Beds, and around the base of icy Shasta. In this comprehensive glance we may also notice the shallow wind-worn caves in stratified sandstones along the margins of the plains; and the cave-like recesses in the Sierra slates and granites, where bears and other mountaineers find shelter during the fall of sudden storms. In general, however, the grand massive uplift of the Sierra, as far as it has been laid-bare to observation, is about as solid and caveless as a boulder.

Fresh beauty opens one's eyes wherever it is really seen, but the very abundance and completeness of the common beauty that besets our steps prevents its being absorbed and appreciated. It is a good thing, therefore, to make short excursions now and then to the bottom of the sea among dulse and coral, or up among the clouds on mountain-tops, or in balloons, or even to creep like worms into dark holes and caverns underground, not only to learn something of what is going on in those out-of-the-way places, but to see better what the sun sees on our return to common every-day beauty.

Our way from Murphy's to the cave lay across a series of picturesque, moory ridges in the chaparral region between the brown foot-hills and the forests, a flowery stretch of rolling hill-waves breaking here and there into a kind of rocky foam on the higher summits, and sinking into delightful bosky hollows embowered with vines. The day was a fine specimen of California summer, pure sunshine, unshaded most of the time by a single cloud. As the sun rose higher, the heated air began to flow in tremulous waves from every southern slope. The sea-breeze that usually comes up the foot-hills at this season, with cooling on its wings, was scarcely perceptible. The birds were assembled beneath leafy shade, or made short, languid flights in search of food, all save the majestic buzzard; with broad wings outspread he sailed the warm air unwearily from ridge to ridge, seeming to enjoy the fervid sunshine like a butterfly. Squirrels, too, whose spicy ardor no heat or cold may abate, were nutting among the pines, and the innumerable hosts of the insect kingdom were throbbing and wavering unwearied as sunbeams.

This brushy, berry-bearing region used to be a deer and bear pasture, but since the disturbances of the gold period these fine animals have almost wholly disappeared. Here, also, once roamed the mastodon and elephant, whose bones are found entombed in the river gravels and beneath thick folds of lava. Toward noon, as we were riding slowly over bank and brae, basking in the unfeverish sun-heat, we witnessed the upheaval of a new mountain-range, a Sierra of clouds abounding in landscapes as truly sublime and beautiful—if only we have a mind to think so and eyes to see—as the more ancient rocky Sierra beneath it, with its forests and waterfalls; reminding us that, as there is a lower world of caves, so, also, there is an upper world of clouds. Huge, bossy cumuli developed with astonishing rapidity from mere buds, swelling with visible motion into colossal mountains, and piling higher, higher, in long massive ranges, peak beyond peak, dome over dome, with many a picturesque valley and shadowy cave between; while the dark firs and pines of the upper benches of the Sierra were projected against their pearl bosses with exquisite clearness of outline. These cloud mountains vanished in the azure as quickly as they were developed, leaving no detritus; but they were not a whit less real or interesting on this account. The more enduring hills over which we rode were vanishing as surely as they, only not so fast, a difference which is great or small according to the standpoint from which it is contemplated.

At the bottom of every dell we found little homesteads embosomed in wild brush and vines wherever the recession of the hills left patches of arable ground. These secluded flats are settled mostly by Italians and Germans, who plant a few vegetables and grape-vines at odd times, while their main business is mining and prospecting. In spite of all the natural beauty of these dell cabins, they can hardly be called homes. They are only a better kind of camp, gladly abandoned whenever the hoped-for gold harvest has been gathered. There is an air of profound unrest and melancholy about the best of them. Their beauty is thrust upon them by exuberant Nature, apart from which they are only a few logs and boards rudely jointed and without either ceiling or floor, a rough fireplace with corresponding cooking utensils, a shelf-bed, and stool. The ground about them is strewn with battered prospecting-pans, picks, sluice-boxes, and quartz specimens from many a ledge, indicating the trend of their owners' hard lives.

The ride from Murphy's to the cave is scarcely two hours long, but we lingered among quartz-ledges and banks of dead river gravel until long after noon. At length emerging from a narrow-throated gorge, a small house came in sight set in a thicket of fig-trees at the base of a limestone hill. "That," said my guide, pointing to the house, "is Cave City, and the cave is in that gray hill." Arriving at the one house of this one-house city, we were boisterously welcomed by three drunken men who had come to town to hold a spree. The mistress of the house tried to keep order, and in reply to our inquiries told us that the cave guide was then in the cave with a party of ladies. "And must we wait until he returns?" we asked. No, that was unnecessary; we might take candles and go into the cave alone, provided we shouted from time to time so as to be found by the guide, and were careful not to fall over the rocks or into the dark pools. Accordingly taking a trail from the house, we were led around the base of the hill to the mouth of the cave, a small inconspicuous archway, mossy around the edges and shaped like the door of a water-ouzel's nest, with no appreciable hint or advertisement of the grandeur of the many crystal chambers within. Lighting our candles, which seemed to have no illuminating power in the thick darkness, we groped our way onward as best we could along narrow lanes and alleys, from chamber to chamber, around rustic columns and heaps of fallen rocks, stopping to rest now and then in particularly beautiful places—fairy alcoves furnished with admirable variety of shelves and tables, and round bossy stools covered with sparkling crystals. Some of the corridors were muddy, and in plodding along these we seemed to be in the streets of some prairie village in spring-time. Then we would come to handsome marble stairways conducting right and left into upper chambers ranged above one another three or four stories high, floors, ceilings, and walls lavishly decorated with innumerable crystalline forms. After thus wandering exploringly, and alone for a mile or so, fairly enchanted, a murmur of voices and a gleam of light betrayed the approach of the guide and his party, from whom, when they came up, we received a most hearty and natural stare, as we stood half concealed in a side recess among stalagmites. I ventured to ask the dripping, crouching company how they had enjoyed their saunter, anxious to learn how the strange sunless scenery of the underworld had impressed them. "Ah, it's nice! It's splendid!" they all replied and echoed. "The Bridal Chamber back here is just glorious! This morning we came down from the Calaveras Big Tree Grove, and the trees are nothing to it." After making this curious comparison they hastened sunward, the guide promising to join us shortly on the bank of a deep pool, where we were to wait for him. This is a charming little lakelet of unknown depth, never yet stirred by a breeze, and its eternal calm excites the imagination even more profoundly than the silvery lakes of the glaciers rimmed with meadows and snow and reflecting sublime mountains.

Our guide, a jolly, rollicking Italian, led us into the heart of the hill, up and down, right and left, from chamber to chamber more and more magnificent, all a-glitter like a glacier cave with icicle-like stalactites and stalagmites combined in forms of indescribable beauty. We were shown one large room that was occasionally used as a dancing-hall; another that was used as a chapel, with natural pulpit and crosses and pews, sermons in every stone, where a priest had said mass. Mass-saying is not so generally developed in connection with natural wonders as dancing. One of the first conceits excited by the giant Sequoias was to cut one of them down and dance on its stump. We have also seen dancing in the spray of Niagara; dancing in the famous Bower Cave above Coulterville; and nowhere have I seen so much dancing as in Yosemite. A dance on the inaccessible South Dome would likely follow the making of an easy way to the top of it.

It was delightful to witness here the infinite deliberation of Nature, and the simplicity of her methods in the production of such mighty results, such perfect repose combined with restless enthusiastic energy. Though cold and bloodless as a landscape of polar ice, building was going on in the dark with incessant activity. The archways and ceilings were everywhere hung with down-growing crystals, like inverted groves of leafless saplings, some of them large, others delicately attenuated, each tipped with a single drop of water, like the terminal bud of a pine-tree. The only appreciable sounds were the dripping and tinkling of water failing into pools or faintly plashing on the crystal floors.

In some places the crystal decorations are arranged in graceful flowing folds deeply plicated like stiff silken drapery. In others straight lines of the ordinary stalactite forms are combined with reference to size and tone in a regularly graduated system like the strings of a harp with musical tones corresponding thereto; and on these stone harps we played by striking the crystal strings with a stick. The delicious liquid tones they gave forth seemed perfectly divine as they sweetly whispered and wavered through the majestic halls and died away in faintest cadence,—the music of fairy-land. Here we lingered and reveled, rejoicing to find so much music in stony silence, so much splendor in darkness, so many mansions in the depths of the mountains, buildings ever in process of construction, yet ever finished, developing from perfection to perfection, profusion without overabundance; every particle visible or invisible in glorious motion, marching to the music of the spheres in a region regarded as the abode of eternal stillness and death.

The outer chambers of mountain caves are frequently selected as homes by wild beasts. In the Sierra, however, they seem to prefer homes and hiding-places in chaparral and beneath shelving precipices, as I have never seen their tracks in any of the caves. This is the more remarkable because notwithstanding the darkness and oozing water there is nothing uncomfortably cellar-like or sepulchral about them.

When we emerged into the bright landscapes of the sun everything looked brighter, and we felt our faith in Nature's beauty strengthened, and saw more clearly that beauty is universal and immortal, above, beneath, on land and sea, mountain and plain, in heat and cold, light and darkness.

CHAPTER XVI

THE BEE-PASTURES

When California was wild, it was one sweet bee-garden throughout its entire length, north and south, and all the way across from the snowy Sierra to the ocean.

Wherever a bee might fly within the bounds of this virgin wilderness—through the redwood forests, along the banks of the rivers, along the bluffs and headlands fronting the sea, over valley and plain, park and grove, and deep, leafy glen, or far up the piny slopes of the mountains—throughout every belt and section of climate up to the timber line, bee-flowers bloomed in lavish, abundance. Here they grew more or less apart in special sheets and patches of no great size, there in broad, flowing folds hundreds of miles in length—zones of polleny forests, zones of flowery chaparral, stream-tangles of rubus and wild rose, sheets of golden composite, beds of violets, beds of mint, beds of bryanthus and clover, and so on, certain species blooming somewhere all the year round.

But of late years plows and sheep have made sad havoc in these glorious pastures, destroying tens of thousands of the flowery acres like a fire, and banishing many species of the best honey-plants to rocky cliffs and fence-corners, while, on the other hand, cultivation thus far has given no adequate compensation, at least in kind; only acres of alfalfa for miles of the richest wild pasture, ornamental roses and honeysuckles around cottage doors for cascades of wild roses in the dells, and small, square orchards and orange-groves for broad mountain-belts of chaparral.

The Great Central Plain of California, during the months of March, April, and May, was one smooth, continuous bed of honey-bloom, so marvelously rich that, in walking from one end of it to the other, a distance of more than 400 miles, your foot would press about a hundred flowers at every step. Mints, gilias, nemophilas, castilleias, and innumerable compositae were so crowded together that, had ninety-nine per cent. of them been taken away, the plain would still have seemed to any but Californians extravagantly flowery. The radiant, honeyful corollas, touching and overlapping, and rising above one another, glowed in the living light like a sunset sky—one sheet of purple and gold, with the bright Sacramento pouring through the midst of it from the north, the San Joaquin from the south, and their many tributaries sweeping in at right angles from the mountains, dividing the plain into sections fringed with trees.

Along the rivers there is a strip of bottom-land, countersunk beneath the general level, and wider toward the foot-hills, where magnificent oaks, from three to eight feet in diameter, cast grateful masses of shade over the open, prairie-like levels. And close along the water's edge there was a fine jungle of tropical luxuriance, composed of wild-rose and bramble bushes and a great variety of climbing vines, wreathing and interlacing the branches and trunks of willows and alders, and swinging across from summit to summit in heavy festoons. Here the wild bees reveled in fresh bloom long after the flowers of the drier plain had withered and gone to seed. And in midsummer, when the "blackberries" were ripe, the Indians came from the mountains to feast—men, women, and babies in long, noisy trains, often joined by the farmers of the neighborhood, who gathered this wild fruit with commendable appreciation of its superior flavor, while their home orchards were full of ripe peaches, apricots, nectarines, and figs, and their vineyards were laden with grapes. But, though these luxuriant, shaggy river-beds were thus distinct from the smooth, treeless plain, they made no heavy dividing lines in general views. The whole appeared as one continuous sheet of bloom bounded only by the mountains.

When I first saw this central garden, the most extensive and regular of all the bee-pastures of the State, it seemed all one sheet of plant gold, hazy and vanishing in the distance, distinct as a new map along the foot-hills at my feet.

Descending the eastern slopes of the Coast Range through beds of gilias and lupines, and around many a breezy hillock and bush-crowned headland, I at length waded out into the midst of it. All the ground was covered, not with grass and green leaves, but with radiant corollas, about ankle-deep next the foot-hills, knee-deep or more five or six miles out. Here were bahia, madia, madaria, burrielia, chrysopsis, corethrogyne, grindelia, etc., growing in close social congregations of various shades of yellow, blending finely with the purples of clarkia, orthocarpus, and oenothera, whose delicate petals were drinking the vital sunbeams without giving back any sparkling glow.

Because so long a period of extreme drought succeeds the rainy season, most of the vegetation is composed of annuals, which spring up simultaneously, and bloom together at about the same height above the ground, the general surface being but slightly ruffled by the taller phacelias, pentstemons, and groups of Salvia carduacea, the king of the mints.

Sauntering in any direction, hundreds of these happy sun-plants brushed against my feet at every step, and closed over them as if I were wading in liquid gold. The air was sweet with fragrance, the larks sang their blessed songs, rising on the wing as I advanced, then sinking out of sight in the polleny sod, while myriads of wild bees stirred the lower air with their monotonous hum—monotonous, yet forever fresh and sweet as every-day sunshine. Hares and spermophiles showed themselves in considerable numbers in shallow places, and small bands of antelopes were almost constantly in sight, gazing curiously from some slight elevation, and then bounding swiftly away with unrivaled grace of motion. Yet I could discover no crushed flowers to mark their track, nor, indeed, any destructive action of any wild foot or tooth whatever.

The great yellow days circled by uncounted, while I drifted toward the north, observing the countless forms of life thronging about me, lying down almost anywhere on the approach of night. And what glorious botanical beds I had! Oftentimes on awaking I would find several new species leaning over me and looking me full in the face, so that my studies would begin before rising.

About the first of May I turned eastward, crossing the San Joaquin River between the mouths of the Tuolumne and Merced, and by the time I had reached the Sierra foot-hills most of the vegetation had gone to seed and become as dry as hay.

All the seasons of the great plain are warm or temperate, and bee-flowers are never wholly wanting; but the grand springtime—the annual resurrection—is governed by the rains, which usually set in about the middle of November or the beginning of December. Then the seeds, that for six months have lain on the ground dry and fresh as if they had been gathered into barns, at once unfold their treasured life. The general brown and purple of the ground, and the dead vegetation of the preceding year, give place to the green of mosses and liverworts and myriads of young leaves. Then one species after another comes into flower, gradually overspreading the green with yellow and purple, which lasts until May.

The "rainy season" is by no means a gloomy, soggy period of constant cloudiness and rain. Perhaps nowhere else in North America, perhaps in the world, are the months of December, January, February, and March so full of bland, plant-building sunshine. Referring to my notes of the winter and spring of 1868-69, every day of which I spent out of doors, on that section of the plain lying between the Tuolumne and Merced rivers, I find that the first rain of the season fell on December 18th. January had only six rainy days—that is, days on which rain fell; February three, March five, April three, and May three, completing the so-called rainy season, which was about an average one. The ordinary rain-storm of this region is seldom very cold or violent. The winds, which in settled weather come from the northwest, veer round into the opposite direction, the sky fills gradually and evenly with one general cloud, from which, the rain falls steadily, often for days in succession, at a temperature of about 45° or 50°.

More than seventy-five per cent. of all the rain of this season came from the northwest, down the coast over southeastern Alaska, British Columbia, Washington, and Oregon, though the local winds of these circular storms blow from the southeast. One magnificent local storm from the northwest fell on March 21. A massive, round-browed cloud came swelling and thundering over the flowery plain in most imposing majesty, its bossy front burning white and purple in the full blaze of the sun, while warm rain poured from its ample fountains like a cataract, beating down flowers and bees, and flooding the dry watercourses as suddenly as those of Nevada are flooded by the so-called "cloudbursts." But in less than half an hour not a trace of the heavy, mountain-like cloud-structure was left in the sky, and the bees were on the wing, as if nothing more gratefully refreshing could have been sent them.

By the end of January four species of plants were in flower, and five or six mosses had already adjusted their hoods and were in the prime of life; but the flowers were not sufficiently numerous as yet to affect greatly the general green of the young leaves. Violets made their appearance in the first week of February, and toward the end of this month the warmer portions of the plain were already golden with myriads of the flowers of rayed composite.

This was the full springtime. The sunshine grew warmer and richer, new plants bloomed every day; the air became more tuneful with humming wings, and sweeter with the fragrance of the opening flowers. Ants and ground squirrels were getting ready for their summer work, rubbing their benumbed limbs, and sunning themselves on the husk-piles before their doors, and spiders were busy mending their old webs, or weaving new ones.

In March, the vegetation was more than doubled in depth and color; claytonia, calandrinia, a large white gilia, and two nemophilas were in bloom, together with a host of yellow composite, tall enough now to bend in the wind and show wavering ripples of shade.

In April, plant-life, as a whole, reached its greatest height, and the plain, over all its varied surface, was mantled with a close, furred plush of purple and golden corollas. By the end of this month, most of the species had ripened their seeds, but undecayed, still seemed to be in bloom from the numerous corolla-like involucres and whorls of chaffy scales of the composite. In May, the bees found in flower only a few deep-set liliaceous plants and eriogonums.

June, July, August, and September is the season of rest and sleep,—a winter of dry heat,—followed in October by a second outburst of bloom at the very driest time of the year. Then, after the shrunken mass of leaves and stalks of the dead vegetation crinkle and turn to dust beneath the foot, as if it had been baked in an oven, Hemizonia virgata, a slender, unobtrusive little plant, from six inches to three feet high, suddenly makes its appearance in patches miles in extent, like a resurrection of the bloom of April. I have counted upward of 3000 flowers, five eighths of an inch in diameter, on a single plant. Both its leaves and stems are so slender as to be nearly invisible, at a distance of a few yards, amid so showy a multitude of flowers. The ray and disk flowers are both yellow, the stamens purple, and the texture of the rays is rich and velvety, like the petals of garden pansies. The prevailing wind turns all the heads round to the southeast, so that in facing northwestward we have the flowers looking us in the face. In my estimation, this little plant, the last born of the brilliant host of compositae that glorify the plain, is the most interesting of all. It remains in flower until November, uniting with two or three species of wiry eriogonums, which continue the floral chain around December to the spring flowers of January. Thus, although the main bloom and honey season is only about three months long, the floral circle, however thin around some of the hot, rainless months, is never completely broken.

How long the various species of wild bees have lived in this honey-garden, nobody knows; probably ever since the main body of the present flora gained possession of the land, toward the close of the glacial period. The first brown honey-bees brought to California are said to have arrived in San Francisco in March, 1853. A bee-keeper by the name of Shelton purchased a lot, consisting of twelve swarms, from some one at Aspinwall, who had brought them from New York. When landed at San Francisco, all the hives contained live bees, but they finally dwindled to one hive, which was taken to San José. The little immigrants flourished and multiplied in the bountiful pastures of the Santa Clara Valley, sending off three swarms the first season. The owner was killed shortly afterward, and in settling up his estate, two of the swarms were sold at auction for $105 and $110 respectively. Other importations were made, from time to time, by way of the Isthmus, and, though great pains were taken to insure success, about one half usually died on the way. Four swarms were brought safely across the plains in 1859, the hives being placed in the rear end of a wagon, which was stopped in the afternoon to allow the bees to fly and feed in the floweriest places that were within reach until dark, when the hives were closed.

In 1855, two years after the time of the first arrivals from New York, a single swarm was brought over from San José, and let fly in the Great Central Plain. Bee-culture, however, has never gained much attention here, notwithstanding the extraordinary abundance of honey-bloom, and the high price of honey during the early years. A few hives are found here and there among settlers who chanced to have learned something about the business before coming to the State. But sheep, cattle, grain, and fruit raising are the chief industries, as they require less skill and care, while the profits thus far have been greater. In 1856 honey sold here at from one and a half to two dollars per pound. Twelve years later the price had fallen to twelve and a half cents. In 1868 I sat down to dinner with a band of ravenous sheep-shearers at a ranch on the San Joaquin, where fifteen or twenty hives were kept, and our host advised us not to spare the large pan of honey he had placed on the table, as it was the cheapest article he had to offer. In all my walks, however, I have never come upon a regular bee-ranch in the Central Valley like those so common and so skilfully managed in the southern counties of the State. The few pounds of honey and wax produced are consumed at home, and are scarcely taken into account among the coarser products of the farm. The swarms that escape from their careless owners have a weary, perplexing time of it in seeking suitable homes. Most of them make their way to the foot-hills of the mountains, or to the trees that line the banks of the rivers, where some hollow log or trunk may be found. A friend of mine, while out hunting on the San Joaquin, came upon an old coon trap, hidden among some tall grass, near the edge of the river, upon which he sat down to rest. Shortly afterward his attention was attracted to a crowd of angry bees that were flying excitedly about his head, when he discovered that he was sitting upon their hive, which was found to contain more than 200 pounds of honey. Out in the broad, swampy delta of the Sacramento and San Joaquin rivers, the little wanderers have been known to build their combs in a bunch of rushes, or stiff, wiry grass, only slightly protected from the weather, and in danger every spring of being carried away by floods. They have the advantage, however, of a vast extent of fresh pasture, accessible only to themselves.

The present condition of the Grand Central Garden is very different from that we have sketched. About twenty years ago, when the gold placers had been pretty thoroughly exhausted, the attention of fortune-seekers—not home-seekers—was, in great part, turned away from the mines to the fertile plains, and many began experiments in a kind of restless, wild agriculture. A load of lumber would be hauled to some spot on the free wilderness, where water could be easily found, and a rude box-cabin built. Then a gang-plow was procured, and a dozen mustang ponies, worth ten or fifteen dollars apiece, and with these hundreds of acres were stirred as easily as if the land had been under cultivation for years, tough, perennial roots being almost wholly absent. Thus a ranch was established, and from these bare wooden huts, as centers of desolation, the wild flora vanished in ever-widening circles. But the arch destroyers are the shepherds, with their flocks of hoofed locusts, sweeping over the ground like a fire, and trampling down every rod that escapes the plow as completely as if the whole plain were a cottage garden-plot without a fence. But notwithstanding these destroyers, a thousand swarms of bees may be pastured here for every one now gathering honey. The greater portion is still covered every season with a repressed growth of bee-flowers, for most of the species are annuals, and many of them are not relished by sheep or cattle, while the rapidity of their growth enables them to develop and mature their seeds before any foot has time to crush them. The ground is, therefore, kept sweet, and the race is perpetuated, though only as a suggestive shadow of the magnificence of its wildness.

The time will undoubtedly come when the entire area of this noble valley will be tilled like a garden, when the fertilizing waters of the mountains, now flowing to the sea, will be distributed to every acre, giving rise to prosperous towns, wealth, arts, etc. Then, I suppose, there will be few left, even among botanists, to deplore the vanished primeval flora. In the mean time, the pure waste going on—the wanton destruction of the innocents—is a sad sight to see, and the sun may well be pitied in being compelled to look on.

The bee-pastures of the Coast Ranges last longer and are more varied than those of the great plain, on account of differences of soil and climate, moisture, and shade, etc. Some of the mountains are upward of 4000 feet in height, and small streams, springs, oozy bogs, etc., occur in great abundance and variety in the wooded regions, while open parks, flooded with sunshine, and hill-girt valleys lying at different elevations, each with its own peculiar climate and exposure, possess the required conditions for the development of species and families of plants widely varied.

Next the plain there is, first, a series of smooth hills, planted with a rich and showy vegetation that differs but little from that of the plain itself—as if the edge of the plain had been lifted and bent into flowing folds, with all its flowers in place, only toned down a little as to their luxuriance, and a few new species introduced, such as the hill lupines, mints, and gilias. The colors show finely when thus held to view on the slopes; patches of red, purple, blue, yellow, and white, blending around the edges, the whole appearing at a little distance like a map colored in sections.

Above this lies the park and chaparral region, with oaks, mostly evergreen, planted wide apart, and blooming shrubs from three to ten feet high; manzanita and ceanothus of several species, mixed with rhamnus, cercis, pickeringia, cherry, amelanchier, and adenostoma, in shaggy, interlocking thickets, and many species of hosackia, clover, monardella, castilleia, etc., in the openings.

The main ranges send out spurs somewhat parallel to their axes, inclosing level valleys, many of them quite extensive, and containing a great profusion of sun-loving bee-flowers in their wild state; but these are, in great part, already lost to the bees by cultivation.

Nearer the coast are the giant forests of the redwoods, extending from near the Oregon line to Santa Cruz. Beneath the cool, deep shade of these majestic trees the ground is occupied by ferns, chiefly woodwardia and aspidiums, with only a few flowering plants—oxalis, trientalis, erythronium, fritillaria, smilax, and other shade-lovers. But all along the redwood belt there are sunny openings on hill-slopes looking to the south, where the giant trees stand back, and give the ground to the small sunflowers and the bees. Around the lofty redwood walls of these little bee-acres there is usually a fringe of Chestnut Oak, Laurel, and Madroño, the last of which is a surpassingly beautiful tree, and a great favorite with the bees. The trunks of the largest specimens are seven or eight feet thick, and about fifty feet high; the bark red and chocolate colored, the leaves plain, large, and glossy, like those of Magnolia grandiflora, while the flowers are yellowish-white, and urn-shaped, in well-proportioned panicles, from five to ten inches long. When in full bloom, a single tree seems to be visited at times by a whole hive of bees at once, and the deep hum of such a multitude makes the listener guess that more than the ordinary work of honey-winning must be going on.

How perfectly enchanting and care-obliterating are these withdrawn gardens of the woods—long vistas opening to the sea—sunshine sifting and pouring upon the flowery ground in a tremulous, shifting mosaic, as the light-ways in the leafy wall open and close with the swaying breeze—shining leaves and flowers, birds and bees, mingling together in springtime harmony, and soothing fragrance exhaling from a thousand thousand fountains! In these balmy, dissolving days, when the deep heart-beats of Nature are felt thrilling rocks and trees and everything alike, common business and friends are happily forgotten, and even the natural honey-work of bees, and the care of birds for their young, and mothers for their children, seem slightly out of place.

To the northward, in Humboldt and the adjacent counties, whole hillsides are covered with rhododendron, making a glorious melody of bee-bloom in the spring. And the Western azalea, hardly less flowery, grows in massy thickets three to eight feet high around the edges of groves and woods as far south as San Luis Obispo, usually accompanied by manzanita; while the valleys, with their varying moisture and shade, yield a rich variety of the smaller honey-flowers, such as mentha, lycopus, micromeria, audibertia, trichostema, and other mints; with vaccinium, wild strawberry, geranium, calais, and goldenrod; and in the cool glens along the stream-banks, where the shade of trees is not too deep, spiraea, dog-wood, heteromeles, and calycanthus, and many species of rubus form interlacing tangles, some portion of which continues in bloom for months.

Though the coast region was the first to be invaded and settled by white men, it has suffered less from a bee point of view than either of the other main divisions, chiefly, no doubt, because of the unevenness of the surface, and because it is owned and protected instead of lying exposed to the flocks of the wandering "sheepmen." These remarks apply more particularly to the north half of the coast. Farther south there is less moisture, less forest shade, and the honey flora is less varied.

The Sierra region is the largest of the three main divisions of the bee-lands of the State, and the most regularly varied in its subdivisions, owing to their gradual rise from the level of the Central Plain to the alpine summits. The foot-hill region is about as dry and sunful, from the end of May until the setting in of the winter rains, as the plain. There are no shady forests, no damp glens, at all like those lying at the same elevations in the Coast Mountains. The social compositae of the plain, with a few added species, form the bulk of the herbaceous portion of the vegetation up to a height of 1500 feet or more, shaded lightly here and there with oaks and Sabine Pines, and interrupted by patches of ceanothus and buckeye. Above this, and just below the forest region, there is a dark, heath-like belt of chaparral, composed almost exclusively of Adenostoma fasciculata, a bush belonging to the rose family, from five to eight feet high, with small, round leaves in fascicles, and bearing a multitude of small white flowers in panicles on the ends of the upper branches. Where it occurs at all, it usually covers all the ground with a close, impenetrable growth, scarcely broken for miles.

Up through the forest region, to a height of about 9000 feet above sea-level, there are ragged patches of manzanita, and five or six species of ceanothus, called deer-brush or California lilac. These are the most important of all the honey-bearing bushes of the Sierra. Chamaebatia foliolosa, a little shrub about a foot high, with flowers like the strawberry, makes handsome carpets beneath the pines, and seems to be a favorite with the bees; while pines themselves furnish unlimited quantities of pollen and honey-dew. The product of a single tree, ripening its pollen at the right time of year, would be sufficient for the wants of a whole hive. Along the streams there is a rich growth of lilies, larkspurs, pedicularis, castilleias, and clover. The alpine region contains the flowery glacier meadows, and countless small gardens in all sorts of places full of potentilla of several species, spraguea, ivesia, epilobium, and goldenrod, with beds of bryanthus and the charming cassiope covered with sweet bells. Even the tops of the mountains are blessed with flowers,—dwarf phlox, polemonium, ribes, hulsea, etc. I have seen wild bees and butterflies feeding at a height of 13,000 feet above the sea. Many, however, that go up these dangerous heights never come down again. Some, undoubtedly, perish in storms, and I have found thousands lying dead or benumbed on the surface of the glaciers, to which they had perhaps been attracted by the white glare, taking them for beds of bloom.

From swarms that escaped their owners in the lowlands, the honey-bee is now generally distributed throughout the whole length of the Sierra, up to an elevation of 8000 feet above sea-level. At this height they flourish without care, though the snow every winter is deep. Even higher than this several bee-trees have been cut which contained over 200 pounds of honey.

The destructive action of sheep has not been so general on the mountain pastures as on those of the great plain, but in many places it has been more complete, owing to the more friable character of the soil, and its sloping position. The slant digging and down-raking action of hoofs on the steeper slopes of moraines has uprooted and buried many of the tender plants from year to year, without allowing them time to mature their seeds. The shrubs, too, are badly bitten, especially the various species of ceanothus. Fortunately, neither sheep nor cattle care to feed on the manzanita, spiraea, or adenostoma; and these fine honey-bushes are too stiff and tall, or grow in places too rough and inaccessible, to be trodden under foot. Also the cañon walls and gorges, which form so considerable a part of the area of the range, while inaccessible to domestic sheep, are well fringed with honey-shrubs, and contain thousands of lovely bee-gardens, lying hid in narrow side-cañons and recesses fenced with avalanche taluses, and on the top of flat, projecting headlands, where only bees would think to look for them.

But, on the other hand, a great portion of the woody plants that escape the feet and teeth of the sheep are destroyed by the shepherds by means of running fires, which are set everywhere during the dry autumn for the purpose of burning off the old fallen trunks and underbrush, with a view to improving the pastures, and making more open ways for the flocks. These destructive sheep-fires sweep through nearly the entire forest belt of the range, from one extremity to the other, consuming not only the underbrush, but the young trees and seedlings on which the permanence of the forests depends; thus setting in motion a long train of evils which will certainly reach far beyond bees and beekeepers.

The plow has not yet invaded the forest region to any appreciable extent, neither has it accomplished much in the foot-hills. Thousands of bee-ranches might be established along the margin of the plain, and up to a height of 4000 feet, wherever water could be obtained. The climate at this elevation admits of the making of permanent homes, and by moving the hives to higher pastures as the lower pass out of bloom, the annual yield of honey would be nearly doubled. The foot-hill pastures, as we have seen, fail about the end of May, those of the chaparral belt and lower forests are in full bloom in June, those of the upper and alpine region in July, August, and September. In Scotland, after the best of the Lowland bloom is past, the bees are carried in carts to the Highlands, and set free on the heather hills. In France, too, and in Poland, they are carried from pasture to pasture among orchards and fields in the same way, and along the rivers in barges to collect the honey of the delightful vegetation of the banks. In Egypt they are taken far up the Nile, and floated slowly home again, gathering the honey-harvest of the various fields on the way, timing their movements in accord with the seasons. Were similar methods pursued in California the productive season would last nearly all the year.

The average elevation of the north half of the Sierra is, as we have seen, considerably less than that of the south half, and small streams, with the bank and meadow gardens dependent upon them, are less abundant. Around the head waters of the Yuba, Feather, and Pitt rivers, the extensive tablelands of lava are sparsely planted with pines, through which the sunshine reaches the ground with little interruption. Here flourishes a scattered, tufted growth of golden applopappus, linosyris, bahia, wyetheia, arnica, artemisia, and similar plants; with manzanita, cherry, plum, and thorn in ragged patches on the cooler hill-slopes. At the extremities of the Great Central Plain, the Sierra and Coast Ranges curve around and lock together in a labyrinth of mountains and valleys, throughout which their floras are mingled, making at the north, with its temperate climate and copious rainfall, a perfect paradise for bees, though, strange to say, scarcely a single regular bee-ranch has yet been established in it.

Of all the upper flower fields of the Sierra, Shasta is the most honeyful, and may yet surpass in fame the celebrated honey hills of Hybla and hearthy Hymettus. Regarding this noble mountain from a bee point of view, encircled by its many climates, and sweeping aloft from the torrid plain into the frosty azure, we find the first 5000 feet from the summit generally snow-clad, and therefore about as honeyless as the sea. The base of this arctic region is girdled by a belt of crumbling lava measuring about 1000 feet in vertical breadth, and is mostly free from snow in summer. Beautiful lichens enliven the faces of the cliffs with their bright colors, and in some of the warmer nooks there are a few tufts of alpine daisies, wall-flowers and pentstemons; but, notwithstanding these bloom freely in the late summer, the zone as a whole is almost as honeyless as the icy summit, and its lower edge may be taken as the honey-line. Immediately below this comes the forest zone, covered with a rich growth of conifers, chiefly Silver Firs, rich in pollen and honey-dew, and diversified with countless garden openings, many of them less than a hundred yards across. Next, in orderly succession, comes the great bee zone. Its area far surpasses that of the icy summit and both the other zones combined, for it goes sweeping majestically around the entire mountain, with a breadth of six or seven miles and a circumference of nearly a hundred miles.

Shasta, as we have already seen, is a fire-mountain created by a succession of eruptions of ashes and molten lava, which, flowing over the lips of its several craters, grew outward and upward like the trunk of a knotty exogenous tree. Then followed a strange contrast. The glacial winter came on, loading the cooling mountain with ice, which flowed slowly outward in every direction, radiating from the summit in the form of one vast conical glacier—a down-crawling mantle of ice upon a fountain of smoldering fire, crushing and grinding for centuries its brown, flinty lavas with incessant activity, and thus degrading and remodeling the entire mountain. When, at length, the glacial period began to draw near its close, the ice-mantle was gradually melted off around the bottom, and, in receding and breaking into its present fragmentary condition, irregular rings and heaps of moraine matter were stored upon its flanks. The glacial erosion of most of the Shasta lavas produces detritus, composed of rough, sub-angular boulders of moderate size and of porous gravel and sand, which yields freely to the transporting power of running water. Magnificent floods from the ample fountains of ice and snow working with sublime energy upon this prepared glacial detritus, sorted it out and carried down immense quantities from the higher slopes, and reformed it in smooth, delta-like beds around the base; and it is these flood-beds joined together that now form the main honey-zone of the old volcano.

Thus, by forces seemingly antagonistic and destructive, has Mother Nature accomplished her beneficent designs—now a flood of fire, now a flood of ice, now a flood of water; and at length an outburst of organic life, a milky way of snowy petals and wings, girdling the rugged mountain like a cloud, as if the vivifying sunbeams beating against its sides had broken into a foam of plant-bloom and bees, as sea-waves break and bloom on a rock shore.

In this flowery wilderness the bees rove and revel, rejoicing in the bounty of the sun, clambering eagerly through bramble and hucklebloom, ringing the myriad bells of the manzanita, now humming aloft among polleny willows and firs, now down on the ashy ground among gilias and buttercups, and anon plunging deep into snowy banks of cherry and buckthorn. They consider the lilies and roll into them, and, like lilies, they toil not, for they are impelled by sun-power, as water-wheels by water-power; and when the one has plenty of high-pressure water, the other plenty of sunshine, they hum and quiver alike. Sauntering in the Shasta bee-lands in the sun-days of summer, one may readily infer the time of day from the comparative energy of bee-movements alone—drowsy and moderate in the cool of the morning, increasing in energy with the ascending sun, and, at high noon, thrilling and quivering in wild ecstasy, then gradually declining again to the stillness of night. In my excursions among the glaciers I occasionally meet bees that are hungry, like mountaineers who venture too far and remain too long above the bread-line; then they droop and wither like autumn leaves. The Shasta bees are perhaps better fed than any others in the Sierra. Their field-work is one perpetual feast; but, however exhilarating the sunshine or bountiful the supply of flowers, they are always dainty feeders. Humming-moths and hummingbirds seldom set foot upon a flower, but poise on the wing in front of it, and reach forward as if they were sucking through straws. But bees, though, as dainty as they, hug their favorite flowers with profound cordiality, and push their blunt, polleny faces against them, like babies on their mother's bosom. And fondly, too, with eternal love, does Mother Nature clasp her small bee-babies, and suckle them, multitudes at once, on her warm Shasta breast.

Besides the common honey-bee there are many other species here—fine mossy, burly fellows, who were nourished on the mountains thousands of sunny seasons before the advent of the domestic species. Among these are the bumblebees, mason-bees, carpenter-bees, and leaf-cutters. Butterflies, too, and moths of every size and pattern; some broad-winged like bats, flapping slowly, and sailing in easy curves; others like small, flying violets, shaking about loosely in short, crooked flights close to the flowers, feasting luxuriously night and day. Great numbers of deer also delight to dwell in the brushy portions of the bee-pastures.

Bears, too, roam the sweet wilderness, their blunt, shaggy forms harmonizing well with the trees and tangled bushes, and with the bees, also, notwithstanding the disparity in size. They are fond of all good things, and enjoy them to the utmost, with but little troublesome discrimination—flowers and leaves as well as berries, and the bees themselves as well as their honey. Though the California bears have as yet had but little experience with honeybees, they often succeed in reaching their bountiful stores, and it seems doubtful whether bees themselves enjoy honey with so great a relish. By means of their powerful teeth and claws they can gnaw and tear open almost any hive conveniently accessible. Most honey-bees, however, in search of a home are wise enough to make choice of a hollow in a living tree, a considerable distance above the ground, when such places are to be had; then they are pretty secure, for though the smaller black and brown bears climb well, they are unable to break into strong hives while compelled to exert themselves to keep from falling, and at the same time to endure the stings of the fighting bees without having their paws free to rub them off. But woe to the black bumblebees discovered in their mossy nests in the ground! With a few strokes of their huge paws the bears uncover the entire establishment, and, before time is given for a general buzz, bees old and young, larvae, honey, stings, nest, and all are taken in one ravishing mouthful.

Not the least influential of the agents concerned in the superior sweetness of the Shasta flora are its storms—storms I mean that are strictly local, bred and born on the mountain. The magical rapidity with which they are grown on the mountain-top, and bestow their charity in rain and snow, never fails to astonish the inexperienced lowlander. Often in calm, glowing days, while the bees are still on the wing, a storm-cloud may be seen far above in the pure ether, swelling its pearl bosses, and growing silently, like a plant. Presently a clear, ringing discharge of thunder is heard, followed by a rush of wind that comes sounding over the bending woods like the roar of the ocean, mingling raindrops, snow-flowers, honey-flowers, and bees in wild storm harmony.

Still more impressive are the warm, reviving days of spring in the mountain pastures. The blood of the plants throbbing beneath the life-giving sunshine seems to be heard and felt. Plant growth goes on before our eyes, and every tree in the woods, and every bush and flower is seen as a hive of restless industry. The deeps of the sky are mottled with singing wings of every tone and color; clouds of brilliant chrysididae dancing and swirling in exquisite rhythm, golden-barred vespidae, dragon-flies, butterflies, grating cicadas, and jolly, rattling grasshoppers, fairly enameling the light.

On bright, crisp mornings a striking optical effect may frequently be observed from the shadows of the higher mountains while the sunbeams are pouring past overhead. Then every insect, no matter what may be its own proper color, burns white in the light. Gauzy-winged hymenoptera, moths, jet-black beetles, all are transfigured alike in pure, spiritual white, like snowflakes.

In Southern California, where bee-culture has had so much skilful attention of late years, the pasturage is not more abundant, or more advantageously varied as to the number of its honey-plants and their distribution over mountain and plain, than that of many other portions of the State where the industrial currents flow in other channels. The famous White Sage (Audibertia), belonging to the mint family, flourishes here in all its glory, blooming in May, and yielding great quantities of clear, pale honey, which is greatly prized in every market it has yet reached. This species grows chiefly in the valleys and low hills. The Black Sage on the mountains is part of a dense, thorny chaparral, which is composed chiefly of adenostoma, ceanothus, manzanita, and cherry—not differing greatly from that of the southern portion of the Sierra, but more dense and continuous, and taller, and remaining longer in bloom. Stream-side gardens, so charming a feature of both the Sierra and Coast Mountains, are less numerous in Southern California, but they are exceedingly rich in honey-flowers, wherever found,—melilotus, columbine, collinsia, verbena, zauschneria, wild rose, honeysuckle, philadelphus, and lilies rising from the warm, moist dells in a very storm of exuberance. Wild buckwheat of many species is developed in abundance over the dry, sandy valleys and lower slopes of the mountains, toward the end of summer, and is, at this time, the main dependence of the bees, reinforced here and there by orange groves, alfalfa fields, and small home gardens.

The main honey months, in ordinary seasons, are April, May, June, July, and August; while the other months are usually flowery enough to yield sufficient for the bees.

According to Mr. J.T. Gordon, President of the Los Angeles County Bee-keepers' Association, the first bees introduced into the county were a single hive, which cost $150 in San Francisco, and arrived in September, 1854. In April, of the following year, this hive sent out two swarms, which were sold for $100 each. From this small beginning the bees gradually multiplied to about 3000 swarms in the year 1873. In 1876 it was estimated that there were between 15,000 and 20,000 hives in the county, producing an annual yield of about 100 pounds to the hive—in some exceptional cases, a much greater yield.

In San Diego County, at the beginning of the season of 1878, there were about 24,000 hives, and the shipments from the one port of San Diego for the same year, from July 17 to November 10, were 1071 barrels, 15,544 cases, and nearly 90 tons. The largest bee-ranches have about a thousand hives, and are carefully and skilfully managed, every scientific appliance of merit being brought into use. There are few bee-keepers, however, who own half as many as this, or who give their undivided attention to the business. Orange culture, at present, is heavily overshadowing every other business.

A good many of the so-called bee-ranches of Los Angeles and San Diego counties are still of the rudest pioneer kind imaginable. A man unsuccessful in everything else hears the interesting story of the profits and comforts of bee-keeping, and concludes to try it; he buys a few colonies, or gets them, from some overstocked ranch on shares, takes them back to the foot of some cañon, where the pasturage is fresh, squats on the land, with, or without, the permission of the owner, sets up his hives, makes a box-cabin for himself, scarcely bigger than a bee-hive, and awaits his fortune.

Bees suffer sadly from famine during the dry years which occasionally occur in the southern and middle portions of the State. If the rainfall amounts only to three or four inches, instead of from twelve to twenty, as in ordinary seasons, then sheep and cattle die in thousands, and so do these small, winged cattle, unless they are carefully fed, or removed to other pastures. The year 1877 will long be remembered as exceptionally rainless and distressing. Scarcely a flower bloomed on the dry valleys away from the stream-sides, and not a single grain-field depending upon rain was reaped. The seed only sprouted, came up a little way, and withered. Horses, cattle, and sheep grew thinner day by day, nibbling at bushes and weeds, along the shallowing edges of streams, many of which were dried up altogether, for the first time since the settlement of the country.

In the course of a trip I made during the summer of that year through Monterey, San Luis Obispo, Santa Barbara, Ventura, and Los Angeles counties, the deplorable effects of the drought were everywhere visible—leafless fields, dead and dying cattle, dead bees, and half-dead people with dusty, doleful faces. Even the birds and squirrels were in distress, though their suffering was less painfully apparent than that of the poor cattle. These were falling one by one in slow, sure starvation along the banks of the hot, sluggish streams, while thousands of buzzards correspondingly fat were sailing above them, or standing gorged on the ground beneath the trees, waiting with easy faith for fresh carcasses. The quails, prudently considering the hard times, abandoned all thought of pairing. They were too poor to marry, and so continued in flocks all through the year without attempting to rear young. The ground-squirrels, though an exceptionally industrious and enterprising race, as every farmer knows, were hard pushed for a living; not a fresh leaf or seed was to be found save in the trees, whose bossy masses of dark green foliage presented a striking contrast to the ashen baldness of the ground beneath them. The squirrels, leaving their accustomed feeding-grounds, betook themselves to the leafy oaks to gnaw out the acorn stores of the provident woodpeckers, but the latter kept up a vigilant watch upon their movements. I noticed four woodpeckers in league against one squirrel, driving the poor fellow out of an oak that they claimed. He dodged round the knotty trunk from side to side, as nimbly as he could in his famished condition, only to find a sharp bill everywhere. But the fate of the bees that year seemed the saddest of all. In different portions of Los Angeles and San Diego counties, from one half to three fourths of them died of sheer starvation. Not less than 18,000 colonies perished in these two counties alone, while in the adjacent counties the death-rate was hardly less.

Even the colonies nearest to the mountains suffered this year, for the smaller vegetation on the foot-hills was affected by the drought almost as severely as that of the valleys and plains, and even the hardy, deep-rooted chaparral, the surest dependence of the bees, bloomed sparingly, while much of it was beyond reach. Every swarm could have been saved, however, by promptly supplying them with food when their own stores began to fail, and before they became enfeebled and discouraged; or by cutting roads back into the mountains, and taking them into the heart of the flowery chaparral. The Santa Lucia, San Rafael, San Gabriel, San Jacinto, and San Bernardino ranges are almost untouched as yet save by the wild bees. Some idea of their resources, and of the advantages and disadvantages they offer to bee-keepers, may be formed from an excursion that I made into the San Gabriel Range about the beginning of August of "the dry year." This range, containing most of the characteristic features of the other ranges just mentioned, overlooks the Los Angeles vineyards and orange groves from the north, and is more rigidly inaccessible in the ordinary meaning of the word than any other that I ever attempted to penetrate. The slopes are exceptionally steep and insecure to the foot, and they are covered with thorny bushes from five to ten feet high. With the exception of little spots not visible in general views, the entire surface is covered with them, massed in close hedge growth, sweeping gracefully down into every gorge and hollow, and swelling over every ridge and summit in shaggy, ungovernable exuberance, offering more honey to the acre for half the year than the most crowded clover-field. But when beheld from the open San Gabriel Valley, beaten with dry sunshine, all that was seen of the range seemed to wear a forbidding aspect. From base to summit all seemed gray, barren, silent, its glorious chaparral appearing like dry moss creeping over its dull, wrinkled ridges and hollows.

Setting out from Pasadena, I reached the foot of the range about sundown; and being weary and heated with my walk across the shadeless valley, concluded to camp for the night. After resting a few moments, I began to look about among the flood-boulders of Eaton Creek for a camp-ground, when I came upon a strange, dark-looking man who had been chopping cord-wood. He seemed surprised at seeing me, so I sat down with him on the live-oak log he had been cutting, and made haste to give a reason for my appearance in his solitude, explaining that I was anxious to find out something about the mountains, and meant to make my way up Eaton Creek next morning. Then he kindly invited me to camp with him, and led me to his little cabin, situated at the foot of the mountains, where a small spring oozes out of a bank overgrown with wild-rose bushes. After supper, when the daylight was gone, he explained that he was out of candles; so we sat in the dark, while he gave me a sketch of his life in a mixture of Spanish and English. He was born in Mexico, his father Irish, his mother Spanish. He had been a miner, rancher, prospector, hunter, etc., rambling always, and wearing his life away in mere waste; but now he was going to settle down. His past life, he said, was of "no account," but the future was promising. He was going to "make money and marry a Spanish woman." People mine here for water as for gold. He had been running a tunnel into a spur of the mountain back of his cabin. "My prospect is good," he said, "and if I chance to strike a good, strong flow, I'll soon be worth $5000 or $10,000. For that flat out there," referring to a small, irregular patch of bouldery detritus, two or three acres in size, that had been deposited by Eaton Creek during some flood season,—"that flat is large enough for a nice orange-grove, and the bank behind the cabin will do for a vineyard, and after watering my own trees and vines I will have some water left to sell to my neighbors below me, down the valley. And then," he continued, "I can keep bees, and make money that way, too, for the mountains above here are just full of honey in the summer-time, and one of my neighbors down here says that he will let me have a whole lot of hives, on shares, to start with. You see I've a good thing; I'm all right now." All this prospective affluence in the sunken, boulder-choked flood-bed of a mountain-stream! Leaving the bees out of the count, most fortune-seekers would as soon think of settling on the summit of Mount Shasta. Next morning, wishing my hopeful entertainer good luck, I set out on my shaggy excursion.

About half an hour's walk above the cabin, I came to "The Fall," famous throughout the valley settlements as the finest yet discovered in the San Gabriel Mountains. It is a charming little thing, with a low, sweet voice, singing like a bird, as it pours from a notch in a short ledge, some thirty-five or forty feet into a round mirror-pool. The face of the cliff back of it, and on both sides, is smoothly covered and embossed with mosses, against which the white water shines out in showy relief, like a silver instrument in a velvet case. Hither come the San Gabriel lads and lassies, to gather ferns and dabble away their hot holidays in the cool water, glad to escape from their commonplace palm-gardens and orange-groves. The delicate maidenhair grows on fissured rocks within reach of the spray, while broad-leaved maples and sycamores cast soft, mellow shade over a rich profusion of bee-flowers, growing among boulders in front of the pool—the fall, the flowers, the bees, the ferny rocks, and leafy shade forming a charming little poem of wildness, the last of a series extending down the flowery slopes of Mount San Antonio through the rugged, foam-beaten bosses of the main Eaton Canon.

From the base of the fall I followed the ridge that forms the western rim of the Eaton basin to the summit of one of the principal peaks, which is about 5000 feet above sea-level. Then, turning eastward, I crossed the middle of the basin, forcing a way over its many subordinate ridges and across its eastern rim, having to contend almost everywhere with the floweriest and most impenetrable growth of honey-bushes I had ever encountered since first my mountaineering began. Most of the Shasta chaparral is leafy nearly to the ground; here the main stems are naked for three or four feet, and interspiked with dead twigs, forming a stiff chevaux de frise through which even the bears make their way with difficulty. I was compelled to creep for miles on all fours, and in following the bear-trails often found tufts of hair on the bushes where they had forced themselves through.

For 100 feet or so above the fall the ascent was made possible only by tough cushions of club-moss that clung to the rock. Above this the ridge weathers away to a thin knife-blade for a few hundred yards, and thence to the summit of the range it carries a bristly mane of chaparral. Here and there small openings occur on rocky places, commanding fine views across the cultivated valley to the ocean. These I found by the tracks were favorite outlooks and resting-places for the wild animals—bears, wolves, foxes, wildcats, etc.—which abound here, and would have to be taken into account in the establishment of bee-ranches. In the deepest thickets I found wood-rat villages—groups of huts four to six feet high, built of sticks and leaves in rough, tapering piles, like musk-rat cabins. I noticed a good many bees, too, most of them wild. The tame honey-bees seemed languid and wing-weary, as if they had come all the way up from the flowerless valley.

After reaching the summit I had time to make only a hasty survey of the basin, now glowing in the sunset gold, before hastening down into one of the tributary cañons in search, of water. Emerging from a particularly tedious breadth of chaparral, I found myself free and erect in a beautiful park-like grove of Mountain Live Oak, where the ground was planted with aspidiums and brier-roses, while the glossy foliage made a close canopy overhead, leaving the gray dividing trunks bare to show the beauty of their interlacing arches. The bottom of the cañon was dry where I first reached it, but a bunch of scarlet mimulus indicated water at no great distance, and I soon discovered about a bucketful in a hollow of the rock. This, however, was full of dead bees, wasps, beetles, and leaves, well steeped and simmered, and would, therefore, require boiling and filtering through fresh charcoal before it could be made available. Tracing the dry channel about a mile farther down to its junction with a larger tributary cañon, I at length discovered a lot of boulder pools, clear as crystal, brimming full, and linked together by glistening streamlets just strong enough to sing audibly. Flowers in full bloom adorned their margins, lilies ten feet high, larkspur, columbines, and luxuriant ferns, leaning and overarching in lavish abundance, while a noble old Live Oak spread its rugged arms over all. Here I camped, making my bed on smooth cobblestones.

Next day, in the channel of a tributary that heads on Mount San Antonio, I passed about fifteen or twenty gardens like the one in which I slept—lilies in every one of them, in the full pomp of bloom. My third camp was made near the middle of the general basin, at the head of a long system of cascades from ten to 200 feet high, one following the other in close succession down a rocky, inaccessible cañon, making a total descent of nearly 1700 feet. Above the cascades the main stream passes through a series of open, sunny levels, the largest of which are about an acre in size, where the wild bees and their companions were feasting on a showy growth of zauschneria, painted cups, and monardella; and gray squirrels were busy harvesting the burs of the Douglas Spruce, the only conifer I met in the basin.

The eastern slopes of the basin are in every way similar to those we have described, and the same may be said of other portions of the range. From the highest summit, far as the eye could reach, the landscape was one vast bee-pasture, a rolling wilderness of honey-bloom, scarcely broken by bits of forest or the rocky outcrops of hilltops and ridges.

Behind the San Bernardino Range lies the wild "sage-brush country," bounded on the east by the Colorado River, and extending in a general northerly direction to Nevada and along the eastern base of the Sierra beyond Mono Lake.

The greater portion of this immense region, including Owen's Valley, Death Valley, and the Sink of the Mohave, the area of which is nearly one fifth that of the entire State, is usually regarded as a desert, not because of any lack in the soil, but for want of rain, and rivers available for irrigation. Very little of it, however, is desert in the eyes of a bee.

Looking now over all the available pastures of California, it appears that the business of beekeeping is still in its infancy. Even in the more enterprising of the southern counties, where so vigorous a beginning has been made, less than a tenth of their honey resources have as yet been developed; while in the Great Plain, the Coast Ranges, the Sierra Nevada, and the northern region about Mount Shasta, the business can hardly be said to exist at all. What the limits of its developments in the future may be, with the advantages of cheaper transportation and the invention of better methods in general, it is not easy to guess. Nor, on the other hand, are we able to measure the influence on bee interests likely to follow the destruction of the forests, now rapidly falling before fire and the ax. As to the sheep evil, that can hardly become greater than it is at the present day. In short, notwithstanding the wide-spread deterioration and destruction of every kind already effected, California, with her incomparable climate and flora, is still, as far as I know, the best of all the bee-lands of the world.

STICKEEN

My dear dumb friend, low lying there,
A willing vassal at my feet;
Glad partner of my home and fare,
My shadow in the street;

I look into your great brown eyes,
Where love and loyal homage shine,
And wonder where the difference lies
Between your soul and mine!

I scan the whole broad earth around
For that one heart which, leal and true,
Bears friendship without end or bound,
And find the prize in you.

Ah, Blanco! did I worship God
As truly as you worship me,
Or follow where my Master trod
With your humility:

Did I sit fondly at His feet
As you, dear Blanco, sit at mine,
And watch Him with a love as sweet,
My life would grow divine!

STICKEEN

In the summer of 1880 I set out from Fort Wrangel in a canoe to continue the exploration of the icy region of southeastern Alaska, begun in the fall of 1879. After the necessary provisions, blankets, etc., had been collected and stowed away, and my Indian crew were in their places ready to start, while a crowd of their relatives and friends on the wharf were bidding them good-by and good-luck, my companion, the Rev. S.H. Young, for whom we were waiting, at last came aboard, followed by a little black dog, that immediately made himself at home by curling up in a hollow among the baggage. I like dogs, but this one seemed so small and worthless that I objected to his going, and asked the missionary why he was taking him.

"Such a little helpless creature will only be in the way," I said; "you had better pass him up to the Indian boys on the wharf, to be taken home to play with the children. This trip is not likely to be good for toy-dogs. The poor silly thing will be in rain and snow for weeks or months, and will require care like a baby."

But his master assured me that he would be no trouble at all; that he was a perfect wonder of a dog, could endure cold and hunger like a bear, swim like a seal, and was wondrous wise and cunning, etc., making out a list of virtues to show he might be the most interesting member of the party.

Nobody could hope to unravel the lines of his ancestry. In all the wonderfully mixed and varied dog-tribe I never saw any creature very much like him, though in some of his sly, soft, gliding motions and gestures he brought the fox to mind. He was short-legged and bunchy-bodied, and his hair, though smooth, was long and silky and slightly waved, so that when the wind was at his back it ruffled, making him look shaggy. At first sight his only noticeable feature was his fine tail, which was about as airy and shady as a squirrel's, and was carried curling forward almost to his nose. On closer inspection you might notice his thin sensitive ears, and sharp eyes with cunning tan-spots above them. Mr. Young told me that when the little fellow was a pup about the size of a woodrat he was presented to his wife by an Irish prospector at Sitka, and that on his arrival at Fort Wrangel he was adopted with enthusiasm by the Stickeen Indians as a sort of new good-luck totem, was named "Stickeen" for the tribe, and became a universal favorite; petted, protected, and admired wherever he went, and regarded as a mysterious fountain of wisdom.

On our trip he soon proved himself a queer character—odd, concealed, independent, keeping invincibly quiet, and doing many little puzzling things that piqued my curiosity. As we sailed week after week through the long intricate channels and inlets among the innumerable islands and mountains of the coast, he spent most of the dull days in sluggish ease, motionless, and apparently as unobserving as if in deep sleep. But I discovered that somehow he always knew what was going on. When the Indians were about to shoot at ducks or seals, or when anything along the shore was exciting our attention, he would rest his chin on the edge of the canoe and calmly look out like a dreamy-eyed tourist. And when he heard us talking about making a landing, he immediately roused himself to see what sort of a place we were coming to, and made ready to jump overboard and swim ashore as soon as the canoe neared the beach. Then, with a vigorous shake to get rid of the brine in his hair, he ran into the woods to hunt small game. But though always the first out of the canoe, he was always the last to get into it. When we were ready to start he could never be found, and refused to come to our call. We soon found out, however, that though we could not see him at such times, he saw us, and from the cover of the briers and huckleberry bushes in the fringe of the woods was watching the canoe with wary eye. For as soon as we were fairly off he came trotting down the beach, plunged into the surf, and swam after us, knowing well that we would cease rowing and take him in. When the contrary little vagabond came alongside, he was lifted by the neck, held at arm's length a moment to drip, and dropped aboard. We tried to cure him of this trick by compelling him to swim a long way, as if we had a mind to abandon him; but this did no good: the longer the swim the better he seemed to like it.

Though capable of great idleness, he never failed to be ready for all sorts of adventures and excursions. One pitch-dark rainy night we landed about ten o'clock at the mouth of a salmon stream when the water was phosphorescent. The salmon were running, and the myriad fins of the onrushing multitude were churning all the stream into a silvery glow, wonderfully beautiful and impressive in the ebon darkness. To get a good view of the show I set out with one of the Indians and sailed up through the midst of it to the foot of a rapid about half a mile from camp, where the swift current dashing over rocks made the luminous glow most glorious. Happening to look back down the stream, while the Indian was catching a few of the struggling fish, I saw a long spreading fan of light like the tail of a comet, which we thought must be made by some big strange animal that was pursuing us. On it came with its magnificent train, until we imagined we could see the monster's head and eyes; but it was only Stickeen, who, finding I had left the camp, came swimming after me to see what was up.

When we camped early, the best hunter of the crew usually went to the woods for a deer, and Stickeen was sure to be at his heels, provided I had not gone out. For, strange to say, though I never carried a gun, he always followed me, forsaking the hunter and even his master to share my wanderings. The days that were too stormy for sailing I spent in the woods, or on the adjacent mountains, wherever my studies called me; and Stickeen always insisted on going with me, however wild the weather, gliding like a fox through dripping huckleberry bushes and thorny tangles of panax and rubus, scarce stirring their rain-laden leaves;

wading and wallowing through snow, swimming icy streams, skipping over logs and rocks and the crevasses of glaciers with the patience and endurance of a determined mountaineer, never tiring or getting discouraged. Once he followed me over a glacier the surface of which was so crusty and rough that it cut his feet until every step was marked with blood; but he trotted on with Indian fortitude until I noticed his red track, and, taking pity on him, made him a set of moccasins out of a handkerchief. However great his troubles he never asked help or made any complaint, as if, like a philosopher, he had learned that without hard work and suffering there could be no pleasure worth having.

Yet none of us was able to make out what Stickeen was really good for. He seemed to meet danger and hardships without anything like reason, insisted on having his own way, never obeyed an order, and the hunter could never set him on anything, or make him fetch the birds he shot. His equanimity was so steady it seemed due to want of feeling; ordinary storms were pleasures to him, and as for mere rain, he flourished in it like a vegetable. No matter what advances you might make, scarce a glance or a tail-wag would you get for your pains. But though he was apparently as cold as a glacier and about as impervious to fun, I tried hard to make his acquaintance, guessing there must be something worth while hidden beneath so much courage, endurance, and love of wild-weathery adventure. No superannuated mastiff or bulldog grown old in office surpassed this fluffy midget in stoic dignity. He sometimes reminded me of a small, squat, unshakable desert cactus. For he never displayed a single trace of the merry, tricksy, elfish fun of the terriers and collies that we all know, nor of their touching affection and devotion. Like children, most small dogs beg to be loved and allowed to love; but Stickeen seemed a very Diogenes, asking only to be let alone: a true child of the wilderness, holding the even tenor of his hidden life with the silence and serenity of nature. His strength of character lay in his eyes. They looked as old as the hills, and as young, and as wild. I never tired of looking into them: it was like looking into a landscape; but they were small and rather deep-set, and had no explaining lines around them to give out particulars. I was accustomed to look into the faces of plants and animals, and I watched the little sphinx more and more keenly as an interesting study. But there is no estimating the wit and wisdom concealed and latent in our lower fellow mortals until made manifest by profound experiences; for it is through suffering that dogs as well as saints are developed and made perfect.

After exploring the Sumdum and Tahkoo fiords and their glaciers, we sailed through Stephen's Passage into Lynn Canal and thence through Icy Strait into Cross Sound, searching for unexplored inlets leading toward the great fountain ice-fields of the Fairweather Range. Here, while the tide was in our favor, we were accompanied by a fleet of icebergs drifting out to the ocean from Glacier Bay. Slowly we paddled around Vancouver's Point, Wimbledon, our frail canoe tossed like a feather on the massive heaving swells coming in past Cape Spenser. For miles the sound is bounded by precipitous mural cliffs, which, lashed with wave-spray and their heads hidden in clouds, looked terribly threatening and stern. Had our canoe been crushed or upset we could have made no landing here, for the cliffs, as high as those of Yosemite, sink sheer into deep water. Eagerly we scanned the wall on the north side for the first sign of an opening fiord or harbor, all of us anxious except Stickeen, who dozed in peace or gazed dreamily at the tremendous precipices when he heard us talking about them. At length we made the joyful discovery of the mouth of the inlet now called "Taylor Bay," and about five o'clock reached the head of it and encamped in a spruce grove near the front of a large glacier.

While camp was being made, Joe the hunter climbed the mountain wall on the east side of the fiord in pursuit of wild goats, while Mr. Young and I went to the glacier. We found that it is separated from the waters of the inlet by a tide-washed moraine, and extends, an abrupt barrier, all the way across from wall to wall of the inlet, a distance of about three miles. But our most interesting discovery was that it had recently advanced, though again slightly receding. A portion of the terminal moraine had been plowed up and shoved forward, uprooting and overwhelming the woods on the east side. Many of the trees were down and buried, or nearly so, others were leaning away from the ice-cliffs, ready to fall, and some stood erect, with the bottom of the ice plow still beneath their roots and its lofty crystal spires towering high above their tops. The spectacle presented by these century-old trees standing close beside a spiry wall of ice, with their branches almost touching it, was most novel and striking. And when I climbed around the front, and a little way up the west side of the glacier, I found that it had swelled and increased in height and width in accordance with its advance, and carried away the outer ranks of trees on its bank.

On our way back to camp after these first observations I planned a far-and-wide excursion for the morrow. I awoke early, called not only by the glacier, which had been on my mind all night, but by a grand flood-storm. The wind was blowing a gale from the north and the rain was flying with the clouds in a wide passionate horizontal flood, as if it were all passing over the country instead of falling on it. The main perennial streams were booming high above their banks, and hundreds of new ones, roaring like the sea, almost covered the lofty gray walls of the inlet with white cascades and falls. I had intended making a cup of coffee and getting something like a breakfast before starting, but when I heard the storm and looked out I made haste to join it; for many of Nature's finest lessons are to be found in her storms, and if careful to keep in right relations with them, we may go safely abroad with them, rejoicing in the grandeur and beauty of their works and ways, and chanting with the old Norsemen, "The blast of the tempest aids our oars, the hurricane is our servant and drives us whither we wish to go." So, omitting breakfast, I put a piece of bread in my pocket and hurried away.

Mr. Young and the Indians were asleep, and so, I hoped, was Stickeen; but I had not gone a dozen rods before he left his bed in the tent and came boring through the blast after me. That a man should welcome storms for their exhilarating music and motion, and go forth to see God making landscapes, is reasonable enough; but what fascination could there be in such tremendous weather for a dog? Surely nothing akin to human enthusiasm for scenery or geology. Anyhow, on he came, breakfastless, through the choking blast. I stopped and did my best to turn him back. "Now don't," I said, shouting to make myself heard in the storm, "now don't, Stickeen. What has got into your queer noddle now? You must be daft. This wild day has nothing for you. There is no game abroad, nothing but weather. Go back to camp and keep warm, get a good breakfast with your master, and be sensible for once. I can't carry you all day or feed you, and this storm will kill you."

But Nature, it seems, was at the bottom of the affair, and she gains her ends with dogs as well as with men, making us do as she likes, shoving and pulling us along her ways, however rough, all but killing us at times in getting her lessons driven hard home. After I had stopped again and again, shouting good warning advice, I saw that he was not to be shaken off; as well might the earth try to shake off the moon. I had once led his master into trouble, when he fell on one of the topmost jags of a mountain and dislocated his arm; now the turn of his humble companion was coming. The pitiful little wanderer just stood there in the wind, drenched and blinking, saying doggedly, "Where thou goest I will go." So at last I told him to come on if he must, and gave him a piece of the bread I had in my pocket; then we struggled on together, and thus began the most memorable of all my wild days.

The level flood, driving hard in our faces, thrashed and washed us wildly until we got into the shelter of a grove on the east side of the glacier near the front, where we stopped awhile for breath and to listen and look out. The exploration of the glacier was my main object, but the wind was too high to allow excursions over its open surface, where one might be dangerously shoved while balancing for a jump on the brink of a crevasse. In the mean time the storm was a fine study. Here the end of the glacier, descending an abrupt swell of resisting rock about five hundred feet high, leans forward and falls in ice cascades. And as the storm came down the glacier from the north, Stickeen and I were beneath the main current of the blast, while favorably located to see and hear it. What a psalm the storm was singing, and how fresh the smell of the washed earth and leaves, and how sweet the still small voices of the storm! Detached wafts and swirls were coming through the woods, with music from the leaves and branches and furrowed boles, and even from the splintered rocks and ice-crags overhead, many of the tones soft and low and flute-like, as if each leaf and tree, crag and spire were a tuned reed. A broad torrent, draining the side of the glacier, now swollen by scores of new streams from the mountains, was rolling boulders along its rocky channel, with thudding, bumping, muffled sounds, rushing towards the bay with tremendous energy, as if in haste to get out of the mountains; the waters above and beneath calling to each other, and all to the ocean, their home.

Looking southward from our shelter, we had this great torrent and the forested mountain wall above it on our left, the spiry ice-crags on our right, and smooth gray gloom ahead. I tried to draw the marvelous scene in my note-book, but the rain blurred the page in spite of all my pains to shelter it, and the sketch was almost worthless. When the wind began to abate, I traced the east side of the glacier. All the trees standing on the edge of the woods were barked and bruised, showing high-ice mark in a very telling way, while tens of thousands of those that had stood for centuries on the bank of the glacier farther out lay crushed and being crushed. In many places I could see down fifty feet or so beneath the margin of the glacier-mill, where trunks from one to two feet in diameter were being ground to pulp against outstanding rock-ribs and bosses of the bank.

About three miles above the front of the glacier I climbed to the surface of it by means of axe-steps made easy for Stickeen. As far as the eye could reach, the level, or nearly level, glacier stretched away indefinitely beneath the gray sky, a seemingly boundless prairie of ice. The rain continued, and grew colder, which I did not mind, but a dim snowy look in the drooping clouds made me hesitate about venturing far from land. No trace of the west shore was visible, and in case the clouds should settle and give snow, or the wind again become violent, I feared getting caught in a tangle of crevasses. Snow-crystals, the flowers of the mountain clouds, are frail, beautiful things, but terrible when flying on storm-winds in darkening, benumbing swarms or when welded together into glaciers full of deadly crevasses. Watching the weather, I sauntered about on the crystal sea. For a mile or two out I found the ice remarkably safe. The marginal crevasses were mostly narrow, while the few wider ones were easily avoided by passing around them, and the clouds began to open here and there.

Thus encouraged, I at last pushed out for the other side; for Nature can make us do anything she likes. At first we made rapid progress, and the sky was not very threatening, while I took bearings occasionally with a pocket compass to enable me to find my way back more surely in case the storm should become blinding; but the structure lines of the glacier were my main guide. Toward the west side we came to a closely crevassed section in which we had to make long, narrow tacks and doublings, tracing the edges of tremendous transverse and longitudinal crevasses, many of which were from twenty to thirty feet wide, and perhaps a thousand feet deep—beautiful and awful. In working a way through them I was severely cautious, but Stickeen came on as unhesitating as the flying clouds. The widest crevasse that I could jump he would leap without so much as halting to take a look at it. The weather was now making quick changes, scattering bits of dazzling brightness through the wintry gloom; at rare intervals, when the sun broke forth wholly free, the glacier was seen from shore to shore with a bright array of encompassing mountains partly revealed, wearing the clouds as garments, while the prairie bloomed and sparkled with irised light from myriads of washed crystals. Then suddenly all the glorious show would be darkened and blotted out.

Stickeen seemed to care for none of these things, bright or dark, nor for the crevasses, wells, moulins, or swift flashing streams into which he might fall. The little adventurer was only about two years old, yet nothing seemed novel to him, nothing daunted him. He showed neither caution nor curiosity, wonder nor fear, but bravely trotted on as if glaciers were playgrounds. His stout, muffled body seemed all one skipping muscle, and it was truly wonderful to see how swiftly and to all appearance heedlessly he flashed across nerve-trying chasms six or eight feet wide. His courage was so unwavering that it seemed to be due to dullness of perception, as if he were only blindly bold; and I kept warning him to be careful. For we had been close companions on so many wilderness trips that I had formed the habit of talking to him as if he were a boy and understood every word.

We gained the west shore in about three hours; the width of the glacier here being about seven miles. Then I pushed northward in order to see as far back as possible into the fountains of the Fairweather Mountains, in case the clouds should rise. The walking was easy along the margin of the forest, which, of course, like that on the other side, had been invaded and crushed by the swollen, overflowing glacier. In an hour or so, after passing a massive headland, we came suddenly on a branch of the glacier, which, in the form of a magnificent ice-cascade two miles wide, was pouring over the rim of the main basin in a westerly direction, its surface broken into wave-shaped blades and shattered blocks, suggesting the wildest updashing, heaving, plunging motion of a great river cataract. Tracing it down three or four miles, I found that it discharged into a lake, filling it with icebergs.

I would gladly have followed the lake outlet to tide-water, but the day was already far spent, and the threatening sky called for haste on the return trip to get off the ice before dark. I decided therefore to go no farther, and, after taking a general view of the wonderful region, turned back, hoping to see it again under more favorable auspices. We made good speed up the cañon of the great ice-torrent, and out on the main glacier until we had left the west shore about two miles behind us. Here we got into a difficult network of crevasses, the gathering clouds began to drop misty fringes, and soon the dreaded snow came flying thick and fast. I now began to feel anxious about finding a way in the blurring storm.

Stickeen showed no trace of fear. He was still the same silent, able little hero. I noticed, however, that after the storm-darkness came on he kept close up behind me. The snow urged us to make still greater haste, but at the same time hid our way. I pushed on as best I could, jumping innumerable crevasses, and for every hundred rods or so of direct advance traveling a mile in doubling up and down in the turmoil of chasms and dislocated ice-blocks. After an hour or two of this work we came to a series of longitudinal crevasses of appalling width, and almost straight and regular in trend, like immense furrows. These I traced with firm nerve, excited and strengthened by the danger, making wide jumps, poising cautiously on their dizzy edges after cutting hollows for my feet before making the spring, to avoid possible slipping or any uncertainty on the farther sides, where only one trial is granted—exercise at once frightful and inspiring. Stickeen followed seemingly without effort.

Many a mile we thus traveled, mostly up and down, making but little real headway in crossing, running instead of walking most of the time as the danger of being compelled to spend the night on the glacier became threatening. Stickeen seemed able for anything. Doubtless we could have weathered the storm for one night, dancing on a flat spot to keep from freezing, and I faced the threat without feeling anything like despair; but we were hungry and wet, and the wind from the mountains was still thick with snow and bitterly cold, so of course that night would have seemed a very long one. I could not see far enough through the blurring snow to judge in which general direction the least dangerous route lay, while the few dim, momentary glimpses I caught of mountains through rifts in the flying clouds were far from encouraging either as weather signs or as guides. I had simply to grope my way from crevasse to crevasse, holding a general direction by the ice-structure, which was not to be seen everywhere, and partly by the wind. Again and again I was put to my mettle, but Stickeen followed easily, his nerve apparently growing more unflinching as the danger increased. So it always is with mountaineers when hard beset. Running hard and jumping, holding every minute of the remaining daylight, poor as it was, precious, we doggedly persevered and tried to hope that every difficult crevasse we overcame would prove to be the last of its kind. But on the contrary, as we advanced they became more deadly trying.

At length our way was barred by a very wide and straight crevasse, which I traced rapidly northward a mile or so without finding a crossing or hope of one; then down the glacier about as far, to where it united with another uncrossable crevasse. In all this distance of perhaps two miles there was only one place where I could possibly jump it, but the width of this jump was the utmost I dared attempt, while the danger of slipping on the farther side was so great that I was loath to try it. Furthermore, the side I was on was about a foot higher than the other, and even with this advantage the crevasse seemed dangerously wide. One is liable to underestimate the width of crevasses where the magnitudes in general are great, I therefore stared at this one mighty keenly, estimating its width and the shape of the edge on the farther side, until I thought that I could jump it if necessary, but that in case I should be compelled to jump back from the lower side I might fail. Now, a cautious mountaineer seldom takes a step on unknown ground which seems at all dangerous that he cannot retrace in case he should be stopped by unseen obstacles ahead. This is the rule of mountaineers who live long, and, though in haste, I compelled myself to sit down and calmly deliberate before I broke it.

Retracing my devious path in imagination as if it were drawn on a chart, I saw that I was recrossing the glacier a mile or two farther up stream than the course pursued in the morning, and that I was now entangled in a section I had not before seen. Should I risk this dangerous jump, or try to regain the woods on the west shore, make a fire, and have only hunger to endure while waiting for a new day? I had already crossed so broad a stretch of dangerous ice that I saw it would be difficult to get back to the woods through the storm, before dark, and the attempt would most likely result in a dismal night-dance on the glacier; while just beyond the present barrier the surface seemed more promising, and the east shore was now perhaps about as near as the west. I was therefore eager to go on. But this wide jump was a dreadful obstacle.

At length, because of the dangers already behind me, I determined to venture against those that might be ahead, jumped and landed well, but with so little to spare that I more than ever dreaded being compelled to take that jump back from the lower side. Stickeen followed, making nothing of it, and we ran eagerly forward, hoping we were leaving all our troubles behind. But within the distance of a few hundred yards we were stopped by the widest crevasse yet encountered. Of course I made haste to explore it, hoping all might yet be remedied by finding a bridge or a way around either end. About three-fourths of a mile upstream I found that it united with the one we had just crossed, as I feared it would. Then, tracing it down, I found it joined the same crevasse at the lower end also, maintaining throughout its whole course a width of forty to fifty feet. Thus to my dismay I discovered that we were on a narrow island about two miles long, with two barely possible ways of escape: one back by the way we came, the other ahead by an almost inaccessible sliver-bridge that crossed the great crevasse from near the middle of it!

After this nerve-trying discovery I ran back to the sliver-bridge and cautiously examined it. Crevasses, caused by strains from variations in the rate of motion of different parts of the glacier and convexities in the channel, are mere cracks when they first open, so narrow as hardly to admit the blade of a pocket-knife, and gradually widen according to the extent of the strain and the depth of the glacier. Now some of these cracks are interrupted, like the cracks in wood, and in opening, the strip of ice between overlapping ends is dragged out, and may maintain a continuous connection between the sides, just as the two sides of a slivered crack in wood that is being split are connected. Some crevasses remain open for months or even years, and by the melting of their sides continue to increase in width long after the opening strain has ceased; while the sliver-bridges, level on top at first and perfectly safe, are at length melted to thin, vertical, knife-edged blades, the upper portion being most exposed to the weather; and since the exposure is greatest in the middle, they at length curve downward like the cables of suspension bridges. This one was evidently very old, for it had been weathered and wasted until it was the most dangerous and inaccessible that ever lay in my way. The width of the crevasse was here about fifty feet, and the sliver crossing diagonally was about seventy feet long; its thin knife-edge near the middle was depressed twenty-five or thirty feet below the level of the glacier, and the upcurving ends were attached to the sides eight or ten feet below the brink. Getting down the nearly vertical wall to the end of the sliver and up the other side were the main difficulties, and they seemed all but insurmountable. Of the many perils encountered in my years of wandering on mountains and glaciers none seemed so plain and stern and merciless as this. And it was presented when we were wet to the skin and hungry, the sky dark with quick driving snow, and the night near. But we were forced to face it. It was a tremendous necessity.

Beginning, not immediately above the sunken end of the bridge, but a little to one side, I cut a deep hollow on the brink for my knees to rest in. Then, leaning over, with my short-handled axe I cut a step sixteen or eighteen inches below, which on account of the sheerness of the wall was necessarily shallow. That step, however, was well made; its floor sloped slightly inward and formed a good hold for my heels. Then, slipping cautiously upon it, and crouching as low as possible, with my left side toward the wall, I steadied myself against the wind with my left hand in a slight notch, while with the right I cut other similar steps and notches in succession, guarding against losing balance by glinting of the axe, or by wind-gusts, for life and death were in every stroke and in the niceness of finish of every foothold.

After the end of the bridge was reached I chipped it down until I had made a level platform six or eight inches wide, and it was a trying thing to poise on this little slippery platform while bending over to get safely astride of the sliver. Crossing was then comparatively easy by chipping off the sharp edge with short, careful strokes, and hitching forward an inch or two at a time, keeping my balance with my knees pressed against the sides. The tremendous abyss on either hand I studiously ignored. To me the edge of that blue sliver was then all the world. But the most trying part of the adventure, after working my way across inch by inch and chipping another small platform, was to rise from the safe position astride and to cut a step-ladder in the nearly vertical face of the wall,—chipping, climbing, holding on with feet and fingers in mere notches. At such times one's whole body is eye, and common skill and fortitude are replaced by power beyond our call or knowledge. Never before had I been so long under deadly strain. How I got up that cliff I never could tell. The thing seemed to have been done by somebody else. I never have held death in contempt, though in the course of my explorations I have oftentimes felt that to meet one's fate on a noble mountain, or in the heart of a glacier, would be blessed as compared with death from disease, or from some shabby lowland accident. But the best death, quick and crystal-pure, set so glaringly open before us, is hard enough to face, even though we feel gratefully sure that we have already had happiness enough for a dozen lives.

But poor Stickeen, the wee, hairy, sleekit beastie, think of him! When I had decided to dare the bridge, and while I was on my knees chipping a hollow on the rounded brow above it, he came behind me, pushed his head past my shoulder, looked down and across, scanned the sliver and its approaches with his mysterious eyes, then looked me in the face with a startled air of surprise and concern, and began to mutter and whine; saying as plainly as if speaking with words, "Surely, you are not going into that awful place." This was the first time I had seen him gaze deliberately into a crevasse, or into my face with an eager, speaking, troubled look. That he should have recognized and appreciated the danger at the first glance showed wonderful sagacity. Never before had the daring midget seemed to know that ice was slippery or that there was any such thing as danger anywhere. His looks and tones of voice when he began to complain and speak his fears were so human that I unconsciously talked to him in sympathy as I would to a frightened boy, and in trying to calm his fears perhaps in some measure moderated my own. "Hush your fears, my boy," I said, "we will get across safe, though it is not going to be easy. No right way is easy in this rough world. We must risk our lives to save them. At the worst we can only slip, and then how grand a grave we will have, and by and by our nice bones will do good in the terminal moraine."

But my sermon was far from reassuring him: he began to cry, and after taking another piercing look at the tremendous gulf, ran away in desperate excitement, seeking some other crossing. By the time he got back, baffled of course, I had made a step or two. I dared not look back, but he made himself heard; and when he saw that I was certainly bent on crossing he cried aloud in despair. The danger was enough to daunt anybody, but it seems wonderful that he should have been able to weigh and appreciate it so justly. No mountaineer could have seen it more quickly or judged it more wisely, discriminating between real and apparent peril.

When I gained the other side, he screamed louder than ever, and after running back and forth in vain search for a way of escape, he would return to the brink of the crevasse above the bridge, moaning and wailing as if in the bitterness of death. Could this be the silent, philosophic Stickeen? I shouted encouragement, telling him the bridge was not so bad as it looked, that I had left it flat and safe for his feet, and he could walk it easily. But he was afraid to try. Strange so small an animal should be capable of such big, wise fears. I called again and again in a reassuring tone to come on and fear nothing; that he could come if he would only try. He would hush for a moment, look down again at the bridge, and shout his unshakable conviction that he could never, never come that way; then lie back in despair, as if howling, "O-o-oh! what a place! No-o-o, I can never go-o-o down there!" His natural composure and courage had vanished utterly in a tumultuous storm of fear. Had the danger been less, his distress would have seemed ridiculous. But in this dismal, merciless abyss lay the shadow of death, and his heartrending cries might well have called Heaven to his help. Perhaps they did. So hidden before, he was now transparent, and one could see the workings of his heart and mind like the movements of a clock out of its case. His voice and gestures, hopes and fears, were so perfectly human that none could mistake them; while he seemed to understand every word of mine. I was troubled at the thought of having to leave him out all night, and of the danger of not finding him in the morning. It seemed impossible to get him to venture. To compel him to try through fear of being abandoned, I started off as if leaving him to his fate, and disappeared back of a hummock; but this did no good; he only lay down and moaned in utter hopeless misery. So, after hiding a few minutes, I went back to the brink of the crevasse and in a severe tone of voice shouted across to him that now I must certainly leave him, I could wait no longer, and that, if he would not come, all I could promise was that I would return to seek him next day. I warned him that if he went back to the woods the wolves would kill him, and finished by urging him once more by words and gestures to come on, come on.

He knew very well what I meant, and at last, with the courage of despair, hushed and breathless, he crouched down on the brink in the hollow I had made for my knees, pressed his body against the ice as if trying to get the advantage of the friction of every hair, gazed into the first step, put his little feet together and slid them slowly, slowly over the edge and down into it, bunching all four in it and almost standing on his head. Then, without lifting his feet, as well as I could see through the snow, he slowly worked them over the edge of the step and down into the next and the next in succession in the same way, and gained the end of the bridge. Then, lifting his feet with the regularity and slowness of the vibrations of a seconds pendulum, as if counting and measuring one-two-three, holding himself steady against the gusty wind, and giving separate attention to each little step, he gained the foot of the cliff, while I was on my knees leaning over to give him a lift should he succeed in getting within reach of my arm. Here he halted in dead silence, and it was here I feared he might fail, for dogs are poor climbers. I had no cord. If I had had one, I would have dropped a noose over his head and hauled him up. But while I was thinking whether an available cord might be made out of clothing, he was looking keenly into the series of notched steps and finger-holds I had made, as if counting them, and fixing the position of each one of them in his mind. Then suddenly up he came in a springy rush, hooking his paws into the steps and notches so quickly that I could not see how it was done, and whizzed past my head, safe at last!

And now came a scene! "Well done, well done, little boy! Brave boy!" I cried, trying to catch and caress him; but he would not be caught. Never before or since have I seen anything like so passionate a revulsion from the depths of despair to exultant, triumphant, uncontrollable joy. He flashed and darted hither and thither as if fairly demented, screaming and shouting, swirling round and round in giddy loops and circles like a leaf in a whirlwind, lying down, and rolling over and over, sidewise and heels over head, and pouring forth a tumultuous flood of hysterical cries and sobs and gasping mutterings. When I ran up to him to shake him, fearing he might die of joy, he flashed off two or three hundred yards, his feet in a mist of motion; then, turning suddenly, came back in a wild rush and launched himself at my face, almost knocking me down, all the time screeching and screaming and shouting as if saying, "Saved! saved! saved!" Then away again, dropping suddenly at times with his feet in the air, trembling and fairly sobbing. Such passionate emotion was enough to kill him. Moses' stately song of triumph after escaping the Egyptians and the Red Sea was nothing to it. Who could have guessed the capacity of the dull, enduring little fellow for all that most stirs this mortal frame? Nobody could have helped crying with him!

But there is nothing like work for toning down excessive fear or joy. So I ran ahead, calling him in as gruff a voice as I could command to come on and stop his nonsense, for we had far to go and it would soon be dark. Neither of us feared another trial like this. Heaven would surely count one enough for a lifetime. The ice ahead was gashed by thousands of crevasses, but they were common ones. The joy of deliverance burned in us like fire, and we ran without fatigue, every muscle with immense rebound glorying in its strength. Stickeen flew across everything in his way, and not till dark did he settle into his normal fox-like trot. At last the cloudy mountains came in sight, and we soon felt the solid rock beneath our feet, and were safe. Then came weakness. Danger had vanished, and so had our strength. We tottered down the lateral moraine in the dark, over boulders and tree trunks, through the bushes and devil-club thickets of the grove where we had sheltered ourselves in the morning, and across the level mud-slope of the terminal moraine. We reached camp about ten o'clock, and found a big fire and a big supper. A party of Hoona Indians had visited Mr. Young, bringing a gift of porpoise meat and wild strawberries, and Hunter Joe had brought in a wild goat. But we lay down, too tired to eat much, and soon fell into a troubled sleep. The man who said, "The harder the toil, the sweeter the rest," never was profoundly tired. Stickeen kept springing up and muttering in his sleep, no doubt dreaming that he was still on the brink of the crevasse; and so did I, that night and many others long afterward, when I was overtired.

Thereafter Stickeen was a changed dog. During the rest of the trip, instead of holding aloof, he always lay by my side, tried to keep me constantly in sight, and would hardly accept a morsel of food, however tempting, from any hand but mine. At night, when all was quiet about the camp-fire, he would come to me and rest his head on my knee with a look of devotion as if I were his god. And often as he caught my eye he seemed to be trying to say, "Wasn't that an awful time we had together on the glacier?"

Nothing in after years has dimmed that Alaska storm-day. As I write it all comes rushing and roaring to mind as if I were again in the heart of it. Again I see the gray flying clouds with their rain-floods and snow, the ice-cliffs towering above the shrinking forest, the majestic ice-cascade, the vast glacier outspread before its white mountain fountains, and in the heart of it the tremendous crevasse,—emblem of the valley of the shadow of death,—low clouds trailing over it, the snow falling into it; and on its brink I see little Stickeen, and I hear his cries for help and his shouts of joy. I have known many dogs, and many a story I could tell of their wisdom and devotion; but to none do I owe so much as to Stickeen. At first the least promising and least known of my dog-friends, he suddenly became the best known of them all. Our storm battle for life brought him to light, and through him as through a window I have ever since been looking with deeper sympathy into all my fellow mortals.

None of Stickeen's friends knows what finally became of him. After my work for the season was done I departed for California, and I never saw the dear little fellow again. In reply to anxious inquiries his master wrote me that in the summer of 1883 he was stolen by a tourist at Fort Wrangel and taken away on a steamer. His fate is wrapped in mystery. Doubtless he has left this world—crossed the last crevasse—and gone to another. But he will not be forgotten. To me Stickeen is immortal.

OUR NATIONAL PARKS

CHAPTER I

The Wild Parks and Forest Reservations of the West

"Keep not standing fix'd and rooted,
Briskly venture, briskly roam;
Head and hand, where'er thou foot it,
And stout heart are still at home.
In each land the sun does visit
We are gay, whate'er betide:
To give room for wandering is it
That the world was made so wide."

The tendency nowadays to wander in wildernesses is delightful to see. Thousands of tired, nerve-shaken, over-civilized people are beginning to find out that going to the mountains is going home; that wildness is a necessity; and that mountain parks and reservations are useful not only as fountains of timber and irrigating rivers, but as fountains of life. Awakening from the stupefying effects of the vice of over-industry and the deadly apathy of luxury, they are trying as best they can to mix and enrich their own little ongoings with those of Nature, and to get rid of rust and disease. Briskly venturing and roaming, some are washing off sins and cobweb cares of the devil's spinning in all-day storms on mountains; sauntering in rosiny pinewoods or in gentian meadows, brushing through chaparral, bending down and parting sweet, flowery sprays; tracing rivers to their sources, getting in touch with the nerves of Mother Earth; jumping from rock to rock, feeling the life of them, learning the songs of them, panting in whole-souled exercise, and rejoicing in deep, long-drawn breaths of pure wildness. This is fine and natural and full of promise. So also is the growing interest in the care and preservation of forests and wild places in general, and in the half wild parks and gardens of towns. Even the scenery habit in its most artificial forms, mixed with spectacles, silliness, and kodaks; its devotees arrayed more gorgeously than scarlet tanagers, frightening the wild game with red umbrellas,—even this is encouraging, and may well be regarded as a hopeful sign of the times.

All the Western mountains are still rich in wildness, and by means of good roads are being brought nearer civilization every year. To the sane and free it will hardly seem necessary to cross the continent in search of wild beauty, however easy the way, for they find it in abundance wherever they chance to be. Like Thoreau they see forests in orchards and patches of huckleberry brush, and oceans in ponds and drops of dew. Few in these hot, dim, strenuous times are quite sane or free; choked with care like clocks full of dust, laboriously doing so much good and making so much money,—or so little,—they are no longer good for themselves.

When, like a merchant taking a list of his goods, we take stock of our wildness, we are glad to see how much of even the most destructible kind is still unspoiled. Looking at our continent as scenery when it was all wild, lying between beautiful seas, the starry sky above it, the starry rocks beneath it, to compare its sides, the East and the West, would be like comparing the sides of a rainbow. But it is no longer equally beautiful. The rainbows of to-day are, I suppose, as bright as those that first spanned the sky; and some of our landscapes are growing more beautiful from year to year, notwithstanding the clearing, trampling work of civilization. New plants and animals are enriching woods and gardens, and many landscapes wholly new, with divine sculpture and architecture, are just now coming to the light of day as the mantling folds of creative glaciers are being withdrawn, and life in a thousand cheerful, beautiful forms is pushing into them, and new-born rivers are beginning to sing and shine in them. The old rivers, too, are growing longer, like healthy trees, gaining new branches and lakes as the residual glaciers at their highest sources on the mountains recede, while the rootlike branches in the flat deltas are at same time spreading farther and wider into the seas and making new lands.

Under the control of the vast mysterious forces of the interior of the earth all the continents and islands are slowly rising or sinking. Most of the mountains are diminishing in size under the wearing action of the weather, though a few are increasing in height and girth, especially the volcanic ones, as fresh floods of molten rocks are piled on their summits and spread in successive layers, like the wood-rings of trees, on their sides. New mountains, also, are being created from time to time as islands in lakes and seas, or as subordinate cones on the slopes of old ones, thus in some measure balancing the waste of old beauty with new. Man, too, is making many far-reaching changes. This most influential half animal, half angel is rapidly multiplying and spreading, covering the seas and lakes with ships, the land with huts, hotels, cathedrals, and clustered city shops and homes, so that soon, it would seem, we may have to go farther than Nansen to find a good sound solitude. None of Nature's landscapes are ugly so long as they are wild; and much, we can say comfortingly, must always be in great part wild, particularly the sea and the sky, the floods of light from the stars, and the warm, unspoilable heart of the earth, infinitely beautiful, though only dimly visible to the eye of imagination. The geysers, too, spouting from the hot underworld; the steady, long-lasting glaciers on the mountains, obedient only to the sun;

Yosemite domes and the tremendous grandeur of rocky cañons and mountains in general,—these must always be wild, for man can change them and mar them hardly more than can the butterflies that hover above them. But the continent's outer beauty is fast passing away, especially the plant part of it, the most destructible and most universally charming of all.

Only thirty years ago, the great Central Valley of California, five hundred miles long and fifty miles wide, was one bed of golden and purple flowers. Now it is ploughed and pastured out of existence, gone forever,—scarce a memory of it left in fence corners and along the bluffs of the streams. The gardens of the Sierra, also, and the noble forests in both the reserved and unreserved portions are sadly hacked and trampled, notwithstanding, the ruggedness of the topography,—all excepting those of the parks guarded by a few soldiers. In the noblest forests of the world, the ground, once divinely beautiful, is desolate and repulsive, like a face ravaged by disease. This is true also of many other Pacific Coast and Rocky Mountain valleys and forests. The same fate, sooner or later, is awaiting them all, unless awakening public opinion comes forward to stop it. Even the great deserts in Arizona, Nevada, Utah, and New Mexico, which offer so little to attract settlers, and which a few years ago pioneers were afraid of, as places of desolation and death, are now taken as pastures at the rate of one or two square miles per cow, and of course their plant treasures are passing away,—the delicate abronias, phloxes, gilias, etc. Only a few of the bitter, thorny, unbitable shrubs are left, and the sturdy cactuses that defend themselves with bayonets and spears.

Most of the wild plant wealth of the East also has vanished,—gone into dusty history. Only vestiges of its glorious prairie and woodland wealth remain to bless humanity in boggy, rocky, unploughable places. Fortunately, some of these are purely wild, and go far to keep Nature's love visible. White water-lilies, with rootstocks deep and safe in mud, still send up every summer a Milky Way of starry, fragrant flowers around a thousand lakes, and many a tuft of wild grass waves its panicles on mossy rocks, beyond reach of trampling feet, in company with saxifrages, bluebells, and ferns. Even in the midst of farmers fields, precious sphagnum bogs, too soft for the feet of cattle, are preserved with their charming plants unchanged,—chiogenes, Andromeda, Kalmia, Linnæa, Arethusa, etc. Calypso borealis still hides in the arbor vitæ swamps of Canada, and away to the southward there are a few unspoiled swamps, big ones, where miasma, snakes, and alligators, like guardian angels, defend their treasures and keep them as pure as paradise. And beside a' that and a' that, the East is blessed with good winters and blossoming clouds that shed white flowers over all the land, covering every scar and making the saddest landscape divine at least once a year.

The most extensive, least spoiled, and most unspoilable of the gardens of the continent are the vast tundras of Alaska. In summer they extend smooth, even, undulating, continuous beds of flowers and leaves from about lat. 62° to the shores of the Arctic Ocean; and in winter sheets of snowflowers make all the country shine, one mass of white radiance like a star. Nor are these Arctic plant people the pitiful frost-pinched unfortunates they are guessed to be by those who have never seen them. Though lowly in stature, keeping near the frozen ground as if loving it, they are bright and cheery, and speak Nature's love as plainly as their big relatives of the South. Tenderly happed and tucked in beneath downy snow to sleep through the long, white winter, they make haste to bloom in the spring without trying to grow tall, though some rise high enough to ripple and wave in the wind, and display masses of color,—yellow, purple, and blue,—so rich that they look like beds of rainbows, and are visible miles and miles away.

As early as June one may find the showy Geum glaciale in flower, and the dwarf willows putting forth myriads of fuzzy catkins, to be followed quickly, especially on the dryer ground, by mertensia, eritrichium, polemonium, oxytropis, astragalus, lathyrus, lupinus, myosotis, dodecatheon, arnica, chrysanthemum, nardosmia, saussurea, senecio, erigeron, matrecaria, caltha, valeriana, stellaria, Tofieldia, polygonum, papaver, phlox, lychnis, cheiranthus, Linnæa, and a host of drabas, saxifrages, and heathworts, with bright stars and bells in glorious profusion, particularly Cassiope, Andromeda, ledum, pyrola, and vaccinium,—Cassiope the most abundant and beautiful of them all. Many grasses also grow here, and wave fine purple spikes and panicles over the other flowers,—poa, aira, calamagrostis, alopecurus, trisetum, elymus, festuca, glyceria, etc. Even ferns are found thus far north, carefully and comfortably unrolling their precious fronds,—aspidium, cystopteris, and woodsia, all growing on a sumptuous bed of mosses and lichens; not the scaly lichens seen on rails and trees and fallen logs to the southward, but massive, roundheaded, finely colored plants like corals, wonderfully beautiful, worth going round the world to see. I should like to mention all the plant friends I found in a summer's wanderings in this cool reserve, but I fear few would care to read their names, although everybody, I am sure, would love them could they see them blooming and rejoicing at home.

On my last visit to the region about Kotzebue Sound, near the middle of September, 1881, the weather was so fine and mellow that it suggested the Indian summer of the Eastern States. The winds were hushed, the tundra glowed in creamy golden sunshine, and the colors of the ripe foliage of the heathworts, willows, and birch—red, purple, and yellow, in pure bright tones—were enriched with those of berries which were scattered everywhere, as if they had been showered from the clouds like hail. When I was back a mile or two from the shore, reveling in this color-glory, and thinking how fine it would be could I cut a square of the tundra sod of conventional picture size, frame it, and hang it among the paintings on my study walls at home, saying to myself, "Such a Nature painting taken at random from any part of the thousand-mile bog would make the other pictures look dim and coarse," I heard merry shouting, and, looking round, saw a band of Eskimos—men, women, and children, loose and hairy like wild animals—running towards me. I could not guess at first what they were seeking, for they seldom leave the shore; but soon they told me, as they threw themselves down, sprawling and laughing, on the mellow bog, and began to feast on the berries. A lively picture they made, and a pleasant one, as they frightened the whirring ptarmigans, and surprised their oily stomachs with the beautiful acid berries of many kinds, and filled sealskin bags with them to carry away for festive days in winter.

Nowhere else on my travels have I seen so much warm-blooded, rejoicing life as in this grand Arctic reservation, by so many regarded as desolate. Not only are there whales in abundance along the shores, and innumerable seals, walruses, and white bears, but on the tundras great herds of fat reindeer and wild sheep, foxes, hares, mice, piping marmots, and birds. Perhaps more birds are born here than in any other region of equal extent on the continent. Not only do strong-winged hawks, eagles, and water-fowl, to whom the length of the continent is merely a pleasant excursion, come up here every summer in great numbers, but also many short-winged warblers, thrushes, and finches, repairing hither to rear their young in safety, reinforce the plant bloom with their plumage, and sweeten the wilderness with song; flying all the way, some of them, from Florida, Mexico, and Central America. In coming north they are coming home, for they were born here, and they go south only to spend the winter months, as New Englanders go to Florida. Sweet-voiced troubadours, they sing in orange groves and vine-clad magnolia woods in winter, in thickets of dwarf birch and alder in summer, and sing and chatter more or less all the way back and forth, keeping the whole country glad. Oftentimes, in New England, just as the last snow-patches are melting and the sap in the maples begins to flow, the blessed wanderers may be heard about orchards and the edges of fields where they have stopped to glean a scanty meal, not tarrying long, knowing they have far to go. Tracing the footsteps of spring, they arrive in their tundra homes in June or July, and set out on their return journey in September, or as soon as their families are able to fly well.

This is Nature's own reservation, and every lover of wildness will rejoice with me that by kindly frost it is so well defended. The discovery lately made that it is sprinkled with gold may cause some alarm; for the strangely exciting stuff makes the timid bold enough for anything, and the lazy destructively industrious. Thousands at least half insane are now pushing their way into it, some by the southern passes over the mountains, perchance the first mountains they have ever seen,—sprawling, struggling, gasping for breath, as, laden with awkward, merciless burdens of provisions and tools, they climb over rough-angled boulders and cross thin miry bogs. Some are going by the mountains and rivers to the eastward through Canada, tracing the old romantic ways of the Hudson Bay traders; others by Bering Sea and the Yukon, sailing all the way, getting glimpses perhaps of the famous fur-seals, the ice-floes, and the innumerable islands and bars of the great Alaska river. In spite of frowning hardships and the frozen ground, the Klondike gold will increase the crusading crowds for years to come, but comparatively little harm will be done. Holes will be burned and dug into the hard ground here and there, and into the quartz-ribbed mountains and hills; ragged towns like beaver and muskrat villages will be built, and mills and locomotives will make rumbling, screeching, disenchanting noises; but the miner's pick will not be followed far by the plough, at least not until Nature is ready to unlock the frozen soil-beds with her slow-turning climate key. On the other hand, the roads of the pioneer miners will lead many a lover of wildness into the heart of the reserve, who without them would never see it.

In the meantime, the wildest health and pleasure grounds accessible and available to tourists seeking escape from care and dust and early death are the parks and reservations of the West. There are four national parks,[1] —the Yellowstone, Yosemite, General Grant, and Sequoia,—all within easy reach, and thirty forest reservations, a magnificent realm of woods, most of which, by railroads and trails and open ridges, is also fairly accessible, not only to the determined traveler rejoicing in difficulties, but to those (may their tribe increase) who, not tired, not sick, just naturally take wing every summer in search of wildness. The forty million acres of these reserves are in the main unspoiled as yet, though sadly wasted and threatened on their more open margins by the axe and fire of the lumberman and prospector, and by hoofed locusts, which, like the winged ones, devour every leaf within reach, while the shepherds and owners set fires with the intention of making a blade of grass grow in the place of every tree, but with the result of killing both the grass and the trees.

[1] There are now (1909) twelve parks and one hundred and fifty forest reservations, besides twenty "national monuments.".

In the million acre Black Hills Reserve of South Dakota, the easternmost of the great forest reserves, made for the sake of the farmers and miners, there are delightful, reviving sauntering-grounds in open parks of yellow pine, planted well apart, allowing plenty of sunshine to warm the ground. This tree is one of the most variable and most widely distributed of American pines. It grows sturdily on all kinds of soil and rocks, and, protected by a mail of thick bark, defies frost and fire and disease alike, daring every danger in firm, calm beauty and strength. It occurs here mostly on the outer hills and slopes where no other tree can grow. The ground beneath it is yellow most of the summer with showy Wythia, arnica, applopappus, solidago, and other sun-loving plants, which, though they form no heavy entangling growth, yet give abundance of color and make all the woods a garden. Beyond the yellow pine woods there lies a world of rocks of wildest architecture, broken, splintery, and spiky, not very high, but the strangest in form and style of grouping imaginable. Countless towers and spires, pinnacles and slender domed columns, are crowded together, and feathered with sharp-pointed Engelmann spruces, making curiously mixed forests,—half trees, half rocks. Level gardens here and there in the midst of them offer charming surprises, and so do the many small lakes with lilies on their meadowy borders, and bluebells, anemones, daises, castilleias, comandras, etc., together forming landscapes delightfully novel, and made still wilder by many interesting animals,—elk, deer, beavers, wolves, squirrels, and birds. Not very long ago this was the richest of all the red man's hunting-grounds hereabout. After the season's buffalo hunts were over,—as described by Parkman, who, with a picturesque cavalcade of Sioux savages, passed through these famous hills in 1846,—every winter deficiency was here made good, and hunger was unknown until, in spite of most determined, fighting, killing opposition, the white gold-hunters entered the fat game reserve and spoiled it. The Indians are dead now, and so are most of the hardly less striking free trappers of the early romantic Rocky Mountain times. Arrows, bullets, scalping-knives, need no longer be feared; and all the wilderness is peacefully open.

The Rocky Mountain reserves are the Teton, Yellowstone, Lewis and Clark, Bitter Root, Priest River and Flathead, comprehending more than twelve million acres of mostly unclaimed, rough, forest-covered mountains in which the great rivers of the country take their rise. The commonest tree in most of them is the brave, indomitable, and altogether admirable Pinus contorta, widely distributed in all kinds of climate and soil, growing cheerily in frosty Alaska, breathing the damp salt air of the sea as well as the dry biting blasts of the Arctic interior, and making itself at home on the most dangerous flame-swept slopes and bridges of the Rocky Mountains in immeasurable abundance and variety of forms. Thousands of acres of this species are destroyed by running fires nearly every summer, but a new growth springs quickly from the ashes. It is generally small, and yields few sawlogs of commercial value, but is of incalculable importance to the farmer and miner; supplying fencing, mine timbers, and firewood, holding the porous soil on steep slopes, preventing landslips and avalanches, and giving kindly, nourishing shelter to animals and the widely outspread sources of the life-giving rivers. The other trees are mostly spruce, mountain pine, cedar, juniper, larch, and balsam fir; some of them, especially on the western slopes of the mountains, attaining grand size and furnishing abundance of fine timber.

Perhaps the least known of all this grand group of reserves is the Bitter Root, of more than four million acres. It is the wildest, shaggiest block of forest wildness in the Rocky Mountains, full of happy, healthy, storm-loving trees, full of streams that dance and sing in glorious array, and full of Nature's animals,—elk, deer, wild sheep, bears, cats, and innumerable smaller people.

In calm Indian summer, when the heavy winds are hushed, the vast forests covering hill and dale, rising and falling over the rough topography and vanishing in the distance, seem lifeless. No moving thing is seen as we climb the peaks, and only the low, mellow murmur of falling water is heard, which seems to thicken the silence. Nevertheless, how many hearts with warm red blood in them are beating under cover of the woods, and how many teeth and eyes are shining! A multitude of animal people, intimately related to us, but of whose lives we know almost nothing, are as busy about their own affairs as we are about ours: beavers are building and mending dams and huts for winter, and storing them with food; bears are studying winter quarters as they stand thoughtful in open spaces, while the gentle breeze ruffles the long hair on their backs; elk and deer, assembling on the heights, are considering cold pastures where they will be farthest away from the wolves; squirrels and marmots are busily laying up provisions and lining their nests against coming frost and snow foreseen; and countless thousands of birds are forming parties and gathering their young about them for flight to the southlands; while butterflies and bees, apparently with no thought of hard times to come, are hovering above the late-blooming goldenrods, and, with countless other insect folk, are dancing and humming right merrily in the sunbeams and shaking all the air into music.

Wander here a whole summer, if you can. Thousands of God's wild blessings will search you and soak you as if you were sponge, and the big days will go by uncounted. If you are business-tangled, and so burdened with duty that only weeks can be got out of the heavy-laden year, then go to the Flathead Reserve; for it is easily and quickly reached by the Great Northern Railroad. Get off the track at Belton Station, and in a few minutes you will find yourself in the midst of what you are sure to say is the best care-killing scenery on the continent,—beautiful lakes derived straight from glaciers, lofty mountains steeped in lovely nemophila-blue skies and clad with forests and glaciers, mossy, ferny waterfalls in their hollows, nameless and numberless, and meadowy gardens abounding in the best of everything. When you are calm enough for discriminating observation, you will find the king of the larches, one of the best of the Western giants, beautiful, picturesque, and regal in port, easily the grandest of all the larches in the world. It grows to a height of one hundred and fifty to two hundred feet, with a diameter at the ground of five to eight feet, throwing out its branches into the light as no other tree does. To those who before have seen only the European larch or the Lyall species of the eastern Rocky Mountains, or the little tamarack or hackmatack of the Eastern States and Canada, this Western king must be a revelation.

Associated with this grand tree in the making of the Flathead forests is the large and beautiful mountain pine, or Western white pine (Pinus monticola), the invincible contorta or lodge-pole pine, and spruce and cedar. The forest floor is covered with the richest beds of Linnæa borealis I ever saw, thick fragrant carpets, enriched with shining mosses here and there, and with Clintonia, pyrola, moneses, and vaccinium, weaving hundred-mile beds of bloom that would have made blessed old Linnæus weep for joy.

Lake McDonald, full of brisk trout, is in the heart of this forest, and Avalanche Lake is ten miles above McDonald, at the feet of a group of glacier-laden mountains. Give a month at least to this precious reserve. The time will not be taken from the sum of your life. Instead of shortening, it will indefinitely lengthen it and make you truly immortal. Nevermore will time seem short or long, and cares will never again fall heavily on you, but gently and kindly as gifts from heaven.

The vast Pacific Coast reserves in Washington and Oregon—the Cascade, Washington, Mount Rainier, Olympic, Bull Run, and Ashland, named in order of size—include more than 12,500,000 acres of magnificent forests of beautiful and gigantic trees. They extend over the wild, unexplored Olympic Mountains and both flanks of the Cascade Range, the wet and the dry. On the east side of the Cascades the woods are sunny and open, and contain principally yellow pine, of moderate size, but of great value as a cover for the irrigating streams that flow into the dry interior, where agriculture on a grand scale is being carried on. Along the moist, balmy, foggy, west flank of the mountains, facing the sea, the woods reach their highest development, and, excepting the California redwoods, are the heaviest on the continent. They are made up mostly of the Douglas spruce (Pseudotsuga taxifolia), with the giant arbor vitæ, or cedar, and several species of fir and hemlock in varying abundance, forming a forest kingdom unlike any other, in which limb meets limb, touching and overlapping in bright, lively, triumphant exuberance, two hundred and fifty, three hundred, and even four hundred feet above the shady, mossy ground. Over all the other species the Douglas spruce reigns supreme. It is not only a large tree, the tallest in America next to the redwood, but a very beautiful one, with bright green drooping foliage, handsome pendent cones, and a shaft exquisitely straight and round and regular. Forming extensive forests by itself in many places, it lifts its spiry tops into the sky close together with as even a growth as a well-tilled field of grain. No ground has been better tilled for wheat than these Cascade Mountains for trees: they were ploughed by mighty glaciers, and harrowed and mellowed and outspread by the broad streams that flowed from the ice-ploughs as they were withdrawn at the close of the glacial period.

In proportion to its weight when dry, Douglas spruce timber is perhaps stronger than that of any other large conifer in the country, and being tough, durable, and elastic, it is admirably suited for ship-building, piles, and heavy timbers in general; but its hardness and liability to warp when it is cut into boards render it unfit for fine work. In the lumber markets of California it is called "Oregon pine." When lumbering is going on in the best Douglas woods, especially about Puget Sound, many of the long, slender boles are saved for spars; and so superior is their quality that they are called for in almost every shipyard in the world, and it is interesting to follow their fortunes. Felled and peeled and dragged to tide-water, they are raised again as yards and masts for ships, given iron roots and canvas foliage, decorated with flags, and sent to sea, where in glad motion they go cheerily over the ocean prairie in every latitude and longitude, singing and bowing responsive to the same winds that waved them when they were in the woods. After standing in one place for centuries they thus go round the world like tourists, meeting many a friend from the old home forest; some traveling like themselves, some standing head downward in muddy harbors, holding up the platforms of wharves, and others doing all kinds of hard timber work, showy or hidden.

This wonderful tree also grows far northward in British Columbia, and southward along the coast and middle regions of Oregon and California; flourishing with the redwood wherever it can find an opening, and with the sugar pine, yellow pine, and libocedrus in the Sierra. It extends into the San Gabriel, San Bernardino, and San Jacinto Mountains of southern California. It also grows well on the Wasatch Mountains, where it is called "red pine," and on many parts of the Rocky Mountains and short interior ranges of the Great Basin. But though thus widely distributed, only in Oregon, Washington, and some parts of British Columbia does it reach perfect development.

To one who looks from some high standpoint over its vast breadth, the forest on the west side of the Cascades seems all one dim, dark, monotonous field, broken only by the white volcanic cones along the summit of the range. Back in the untrodden wilderness a deep furred carpet of brown and yellow mosses covers the ground like a garment, pressing about the feet of the trees, and rising in rich bosses softly and kindly over every rock and mouldering trunk, leaving no spot uncared for; and dotting small prairies, and fringing the meadows and the banks of streams not seen in general views, we find, besides the great conifers, a considerable number of hard-wood trees,—oak, ash, maple, alder, wild apple, cherry, arbutus, Nuttall's flowering dogwood, and in some places chestnuts. In a few favored spots the broad-leaved maple grows to a height of a hundred feet in forests by itself, sending out large limbs in magnificent interlacing arches covered with mosses and ferns, thus forming lofty sky-gardens, and rendering the underwoods delightfully cool. No finer forest ceiling is to be found than these maple arches, while the floor, ornamented with tall ferns and rubus vines, and cast into hillocks by the bulging, moss-covered roots of the trees, matches it well.

Passing from beneath the heavy shadows of the woods, almost anywhere one steps into lovely gardens of lilies, orchids, heathworts, and wild roses. Along the lower slopes, especially in Oregon, where the woods are less dense, there are miles of rhododendron, making glorious masses of purple in the spring, while all about the streams and the lakes and the beaver meadows there is a rich tangle of hazel, plum, cherry, crab-apple, cornel, gaultheria, and rubus, with myriads of flowers and abundance of other more delicate bloomers, such as erythronium, brodiæa, fritillaria, calochortus, Clintonia, and the lovely hider of the north, Calypso. Beside all these bloomers there are wonderful ferneries about the many misty waterfalls, some of the fronds ten feet high, others the most delicate of their tribe, the maidenhair fringing the rocks within reach of the lightest dust of the spray, while the shading trees on the cliffs above them, leaning over, look like eager listeners anxious to catch every tone of the restless waters. In the autumn berries of every color and flavor abound, enough for birds, bears, and everybody, particularly about the stream-sides and meadows where sunshine reaches the ground: huckleberries, red, blue, and black, some growing close to the ground others on bushes ten feet high; gaultheria berries, called "sal-al" by the Indians; salmon berries, an inch in diameter, growing in dense prickly tangles, the flowers, like wild roses, still more beautiful than the fruit; raspberries, gooseberries, currants, blackberries, and strawberries. The underbrush and meadow fringes are in great part made up of these berry bushes and vines; but in the depths of the woods there is not much underbrush of any kind,—only a thin growth of rubus, huckleberry, and vine-maple.

Notwithstanding the outcry against the reservations last winter in Washington, that uncounted farms, towns, and villages were included in them, and that all business was threatened or blocked, nearly all the mountains in which the reserves lie are still covered with virgin forests. Though lumbering has long been carried on with tremendous energy along their boundaries, and home-seekers have explored the woods for openings available for farms, however small, one may wander in the heart of the reserves for weeks without meeting a human being, Indian or white man, or any conspicuous trace of one. Indians used to ascend the main streams on their way to the mountains for wild goats, whose wool furnished them clothing. But with food in abundance on the coast there was little to draw them into the woods, and the monuments they have left there are scarcely more conspicuous than those of birds and squirrels; far less so than those of the beavers, which have dammed streams and made clearings that will endure for centuries. Nor is there much in these woods to attract cattle-keepers. Some of the first settlers made farms on the small bits of prairie and in the comparatively open Cowlitz and Chehalis valleys of Washington; but before the gold period most of the immigrants from the Eastern States settled in the fertile and open Willamette Valley of Oregon. Even now, when the search for tillable land is so keen, excepting the bottom-lands of the rivers around Puget Sound, there are few cleared spots in all western Washington. On every meadow or opening of any sort some one will be found keeping cattle, raising hops, or cultivating patches of grain, but these spots are few and far between. All the larger spaces were taken long ago; therefore most of the newcomers build their cabins where the beavers built theirs. They keep a few cows, laboriously widen their little meadow openings by hacking, girdling, and burning the rim of the close-pressing forest, and scratch and plant among the huge blackened logs and stamps, girdling and killing themselves in killing the trees.

Most of the farm lands of Washington and Oregon, excepting the valleys of the Willamette and Rogue rivers, lie on the east side of the mountains. The forests on the eastern slopes of the Cascades fail altogether ere the foot of the range is reached, stayed by drought as suddenly as on the west side they are stopped by the sea; showing strikingly how dependent are these forest giants on the generous rains and fogs so often complained of in the coast climate. The lower portions of the reserves are solemnly soaked and poulticed in rain and fog during the winter months, and there is a sad dearth of sunshine, but with a little knowledge of woodcraft any one may enjoy an excursion into these woods even in the rainy season. The big, gray days are exhilarating, and the colors of leaf and branch and mossy bole are then at their best. The mighty trees getting their food are seen to be wide-awake, every needle thrilling in the welcome nourishing storms, chanting and bowing low in glorious harmony, while every raindrop and snowflake is seen as a beneficent messenger from the sky. The snow that falls on the lower woods is mostly soft, coming through the trees in downy tufts, loading their branches, and bending them down against the trunks until they look like arrows, while a strange muffled silence prevails, making everything impressively solemn. But these lowland snowstorms and their effects quickly vanish. The snow melts in a day or two, sometimes in a few hours, the bent branches spring up again, and all the forest work is left to the fog and the rain. At the same time, dry snow is falling on the upper forests and mountain tops. Day after day, often for weeks, the big clouds give their flowers without ceasing, as if knowing how important is the work they have to do. The glinting, swirling swarms thicken the blast, and the trees and rocks are covered to a depth of ten to twenty feet. Then the mountaineer, snug in a grove with bread and fire, has nothing to do but gaze and listen and enjoy. Ever and anon the deep, low roar of the storm is broken by the booming of avalanches, as the snow slips from the overladen heights and crushes down the long white slopes to fill the fountain hollows. All the smaller streams are crushed and buried, and the young groves of spruce and fir near the edge of the timber-line are gently bowed to the ground and put to sleep, not again to see the light of day or stir branch or leaf until the spring.

These grand reservations should draw thousands of admiring visitors at least in summer, yet they are neglected as if of no account, and spoilers are allowed to ruin them as fast as they like.[2] A few peeled spars cut here were set up in London, Philadelphia, and Chicago, where they excited wondering attention; but the countless hosts of living trees rejoicing at home on the mountains are scarce considered at all. Most travelers here are content with what they can see from car windows or the verandas of hotels, and in going from place to place cling to their precious trains and stages like wrecked sailors to rafts. When an excursion into the woods is proposed, all sorts of dangers are imagined,—snakes, bears, Indians. Yet it is far safer to wander in God's woods than to travel on black highways or to stay at home. The snake danger is so slight it is hardly worth mentioning. Bears are a peaceable people, and mind their own business, instead of going about like the devil seeking whom they may devour. Poor fellows, they have been poisoned, trapped, and shot at until they have lost confidence in brother man, and it is not now easy to make their acquaintance. As to Indians, most of them are dead or civilized into useless innocence. No American wilderness that I know of is so dangerous as a city home "with all the modern improvements." One should go to the woods for safety, if for nothing else. Lewis and Clark, in their famous trip across the continent in 1804-1805, did not lose a single man by Indians or animals, though all the West was then wild. Captain Clark was bitten on the hand as he lay asleep. That was one bite among more than a hundred men while traveling nine thousand sand miles. Loggers are far more likely to be met than Indians or bears in the reserves or about their boundaries, brown weather-tanned men with faces furrowed like bark, tired-looking, moving slowly, swaying like the trees they chop. A little of everything in the woods is fastened to their clothing, rosiny and smeared with balsam, and rubbed into it, so that their scanty outer garments grow thicker with use and never wear out. Many a forest giant have these old woodmen felled, but, round-shouldered and stooping, they too are leaning over and tottering to their fall. Others, however, stand ready to take their places, stout young fellows, erect as saplings; and always the foes of trees outnumber their friends. Far up the white peaks one can hardly fail to meet the wild goat, or American chamois,—an admirable mountaineer, familiar with woods and glaciers as well as rocks,—and in leafy thickets deer will be found; while gliding about unseen there are many sleek furred animals enjoying their beautiful lives, and birds also, notwithstanding few are noticed in hasty walks. The ousel sweetens the glens and gorges where the streams flow fastest, and every grove has its singers, however silent it seems,—thrushes, linnets, warblers; humming-birds glint about the fringing bloom of the meadows and peaks, and the lakes are stirred into lively pictures by water-fowl.

> [2] The outlook over forest affairs is now encouraging. Popular interest, more practical than sentimental in whatever touches the welfare of the country's forests, is growing rapidly, and a hopeful beginning has been made by the Government in real protection for the reservations as well as for the parks. From July 1, 1900, there have been 9 superintendents, 39 supervisors, and from 330 to 445 rangers of reservations.

The Mount Rainier Forest Reserve should be made a national park and guarded while yet its bloom is on;[3] for if in the making of the West Nature had what we call parks in mind,—places for rest, inspiration, and prayers,—this Rainier region must surely be one of them. In the centre of it there is a lonely mountain capped with ice; from the ice-cap glaciers radiate in every direction, and young rivers from the glaciers; while its flanks, sweeping down in beautiful curves, are clad with forests and gardens, and filled with birds and animals. Specimens of the best of Nature's treasures have been lovingly gathered here and arranged in simple symmetrical beauty within regular bounds.

> [3] This was done shortly after the above was written. "One of the most important measures taken during the past year in connection with forest reservations was the action of Congress in withdrawing from the Mount Rainier Forest Reserve a portion of the region immediately surrounding Mount Rainier and setting it apart as a national park." (Report of Commissioner of General Land Office, for the year ended June, 1899.) But the park as it now stands is far too small.

Of all the fire-mountains which, like beacons, once blazed along the Pacific Coast, Mount Rainier is the noblest in form, has the most interesting forest cover, and, with perhaps the exception of Shasta, is the highest and most flowery. Its massive white dome rises out of its forests, like a world by itself, to a height of fourteen thousand to fifteen thousand feet. The forests reach to a height of a little over six thousand feet, and above the forests there is a zone of the loveliest flowers, fifty miles in circuit and nearly two miles wide, so closely planted and luxuriant that it seems as if Nature, glad to make an open space between woods so dense and ice so deep, were economizing the precious ground, and trying to see how many of her darlings she can get together in one mountain wreath,—daisies, anemones, geraniums, columbines, erythroniums, larkspurs, etc., among which we wade knee-deep and waist-deep, the bright corollas in myriads touching petal to petal. Picturesque detached groups of the spiry Abies lasiocarpa stand like islands along the lower margin of the garden zone, while on the upper margin there are extensive beds of bryanthus, Cassiope, Kalmia, and other heathworts, and higher still saxifrages and drabas, more and more lowly, reach up to the edge of the ice. Altogether this is the richest subalpine garden I ever found, a perfect floral elysium. The icy dome needs none of man's care, but unless the reserve is guarded the flower bloom will soon be killed, and nothing of the forests will be left but black stump monuments.

The Sierra of California is the most openly beautiful and useful of all the forest reserves, and the largest excepting the Cascade Reserve of Oregon and the Bitter Root of Montana and Idaho. It embraces over four million acres of the grandest scenery and grandest trees on the continent, and its forests are planted just where they do the most good, not only for beauty, but for farming in the great San Joaquin Valley beneath them. It extends southward from the Yosemite National Park to the end of the range, a distance of nearly two hundred miles. No other coniferous forest in the world contains so many species or so many large and beautiful trees,—Sequoia gigantea, king of conifers, "the noblest of a noble race," as Sir Joseph Hooker well says; the sugar pine, king of all the world's pines, living or extinct; the yellow pine, next in rank, which here reaches most perfect development, forming noble towers of verdure two hundred feet high; the mountain pine, which braves the coldest blasts far up the mountains on grim, rocky slopes; and five others, flourishing each in its place, making eight species of pine in one forest, which is still further enriched by the great Douglas spruce, libocedrus, two species of silver fir, large trees and exquisitely beautiful, the Paton hemlock, the most graceful of evergreens, the curious tumion, oaks of many species, maples, alders, poplars, and flowering dogwood, all fringed with flowery underbrush, manzanita, ceanothus, wild rose, cherry, chestnut, and rhododendron. Wandering at random through these friendly, approachable woods, one comes here and there to the loveliest lily gardens, some of the lilies ten feet high, and the smoothest gentian meadows, and Yosemite valleys known only to mountaineers. Once I spent a night by a camp-fire on Mount Shasta with Asa Gray and Sir Joseph Hooker, and, knowing that they were acquainted with all the great forests of the world, I asked whether they knew any coniferous forest that rivaled that of the Sierra. They unhesitatingly said: "No. In the beauty and grandeur of individual trees, and in number and variety of species, the Sierra forests surpass all others."

This Sierra Reserve, proclaimed by the President of the United States in September, 1893, is worth the most thoughtful care of the government for its own sake, without considering its value as the fountain of the rivers on which the fertility of the great San Joaquin Valley depends. Yet it gets no care at all. In the fog of tariff, silver, and annexation politics it is left wholly unguarded, though the management of the adjacent national parks by a few soldiers shows how well and how easily it can be preserved. In the meantime, lumbermen are allowed to spoil it at their will, and sheep in uncountable ravenous hordes to trample it and devour every green leaf within reach; while the shepherds, like destroying angels, set innumerable fires, which burn not only the undergrowth of seedlings on which the permanence of the forest depends, but countless thousands of the venerable giants. If every citizen could take one walk through this reserve, there would be no more trouble about its care; for only in darkness does vandalism flourish.[4] The reserves of southern California,—the San Gabriel, San Bernardino, San Jacinto, and Trabuco,—though not large, only about two million acres together, are perhaps the best appreciated. Their slopes are covered with a close, almost impenetrable growth of flowery bushes, beginning on the sides of the fertile coast valleys and the dry interior plains. Their higher ridges, however, and mountains are open, and fairly well forested with sugar pine, yellow pine, Douglas spruce, libocedrus, and white fir. As timber fountains they amount to little, but as bird and bee pastures, cover for the precious streams that irrigate the lowlands, and quickly available retreats from dust and heat and care, their value is incalculable.

Good roads have been graded into them, by which in a few hours lowlanders can get well up into the sky and find refuge in hospitable camps and club-houses, where, while breathing reviving ozone, they may absorb the beauty about them, and look comfortably down on the busy towns and the most beautiful orange groves ever planted since gardening began.

[4] See footnote 2.

The Grand Cañon Reserve of Arizona, of nearly two million acres, or the most interesting part of it, as well as the Rainier region, should be made into a national park, on account of their supreme grandeur and beauty. Setting out from Flagstaff, a station on the Atchison, Topeka, and Santa Fé Railroad, on the way to the cañon you pass through beautiful forests of yellow pine,—like those of the Black Hills, but more extensive,—and curious dwarf forests of nut pine and juniper, the spaces between the miniature trees planted with many interesting species of eriogonum, yucca, and cactus. After riding or walking seventy-five miles through these pleasure-grounds, the San Francisco and other mountains, abounding in flowery parklike openings and smooth shallow valleys with long vistas which in fineness of finish and arrangement suggest the work of a consummate landscape artist, watching you all the way, you come to the most tremendous cañon in the world. It is abruptly countersunk in the forest plateau, so that you see nothing of it until you are suddenly stopped on its brink, with its immeasurable wealth of divinely colored and sculptured buildings before you and beneath you. No matter how far you have wandered hitherto, or how many famous gorges and valleys you have seen, this one, the Grand Cañon of the Colorado, will seem as novel to you, as unearthly in the color and grandeur and quantity of its architecture, as if you had found it after death, on some other star; so incomparably lovely and grand and supreme is it above all the other cañons in our fire-moulded, earthquake-shaken, rain-washed, wave-washed, river and glacier sculptured world. It is about six thousand feet deep where you first see it, and from rim to rim ten to fifteen miles wide. Instead of being dependent for interest upon waterfalls, depth, wall sculpture, and beauty of parklike floor, like most other great cañons, it has not waterfalls in sight, and no appreciable floor spaces. The big river has just room enough to flow and roar obscurely, here and there groping its way as best it can, like a weary, murmuring, overladen traveler trying to escape from the tremendous, bewildering labyrinthic abyss, while its roar serves only to deepen the silence. Instead of being filled with air, the vast space between the walls is crowded with Nature's grandest buildings,—a sublime city of them, painted in every color, and adorned with richly fretted cornice and battlement spire and tower in endless variety of style and architecture. Every architectural invention of man has been anticipated, and far more, in this grandest of God's terrestrial cities.

CHAPTER II

The Yellowstone National Park

Of the four national parks of the West, the Yellowstone is far the largest. It is a big, wholesome wilderness on the broad summit of the Rocky Mountains, favored with abundance of rain and snow,—a place of fountains where the greatest of the American rivers take their rise. The central portion is a densely forested and comparatively level volcanic plateau with an average elevation of about eight thousand feet above the sea, surrounded by an imposing host of mountains belonging to the subordinate Gallatin, Wind River, Teton, Absaroka, and snowy ranges. Unnumbered lakes shine in it, united by a famous band of streams that rush up out of hot lava beds, or fall from the frosty peaks in channels rocky and bare, mossy and bosky, to the main rivers, singing cheerily on through every difficulty, cunningly dividing and finding their way east and went to the two far-off seas.

Glacier meadows and beaver meadows are out-spread with charming effect along the banks of the streams, parklike expanses in the woods, and innumerable small gardens in rocky recesses of the mountains, some of them containing more petals than leaves, while the whole wilderness is enlivened with happy animals.

Beside the treasures common to most mountain regions that are wild and blessed with a kind climate, the park is full of exciting wonders. The wildest geysers in the world, in bright, triumphant bands, are dancing and singing in it amid thousands of boiling springs, beautiful and awful, their basins arrayed in gorgeous colors like gigantic flowers; and hot paint-pots, mud springs, mud volcanoes, mush and broth caldrons whose contents are of every color and consistency, plash and heave and roar in bewildering abundance. In the adjacent mountains, beneath the living trees the edges of petrified forests are exposed to view, like specimens on the shelves of a museum, standing on ledges tier above tier where they grew, solemnly silent in rigid crystalline beauty after swaying in the winds thousands of centuries ago, opening marvelous views back into the years and climates and life of the past. Here, too, are hills of sparkling crystals, hills of sulphur, hills of glass, hills of cinders and ashes, mountains of every style of architecture, icy or forested, mountains covered with honey-bloom sweet as Hymettus, mountains boiled soft like potatoes and colored like a sunset sky. A' that and a' that, and twice as muckle's a' that, Nature has on show in the Yellowstone Park. Therefore it is called Wonderland, and thousands of tourists and travelers stream into it every summer, and wander about in it enchanted.

Fortunately, almost as soon as it was discovered it was dedicated and set apart for the benefit of the people, a piece of legislation that shines benignly amid the common dust-and-ashes history of the public domain, for which the world must thank Professor Hayden above all others; for he led the first scientific exploring party into it, described it, and with admirable enthusiasm urged Congress to preserve it. As delineated in the year 1872, the park, contained about 3344 square miles. On March 30, 1891 it was to all intents and purposes enlarged by the Yellowstone National Park Timber Reserve, and in December, 1897, by the Teton Forest Reserve; thus nearly doubling its original area, and extending the southern boundary far enough to take in the sublime Teton range and the famous pasture-lands of the big Rocky Mountain game animals. The withdrawal of this large tract from the public domain did not harm to any one; for its height, 6000 to over 13,000 feet above the sea, and its thick mantle of volcanic rocks, prevent its ever being available for agriculture or mining, while on the other hand its geographical position, reviving climate, and wonderful scenery combine to make it a grand health, pleasure, and study resort,—a gathering-place for travelers from all the world.

The national parks are not only withdrawn from sale and entry like the forest reservations, but are efficiently managed and guarded by small troops of United States cavalry, directed by the Secretary of the Interior. Under this care the forests are flourishing, protected from both axe and fire; and so, of course, are the shaggy beds of underbrush and the herbaceous vegetation. The so-called curiosities, also, are preserved, and the furred and feathered tribes, many of which, in danger of extinction a short time ago, are now increasing in numbers,—a refreshing thing to see amid the blind, ruthless destruction that is going on in the adjacent regions. In pleasing contrast to the noisy, ever changing management, or mismanagement, of blundering, plundering, money-making vote-sellers who receive their places from boss politicians as purchased goods, the soldiers do their duty so quietly that the traveler is scarce aware of their presence.

This is the coolest and highest of the parks. Frosts occur every month of the year. Nevertheless, the tenderest tourist finds it warm enough in summer. The air is electric and full of ozone, healing, reviving, exhilarating, kept pure by frost and fire, while the scenery is wild enough to awaken the dead. It is a glorious place to grow in and rest in; camping on the shores of the lakes, in the warm openings of the woods golden with sunflowers, on the banks of the streams, by the snowy waterfalls, beside the exciting wonders or away from them in the scallops of the mountain walls sheltered from every wind, on smooth silky lawns enameled with gentians, up in the fountain hollows of the ancient glaciers between the peaks, where cool pools and brooks and gardens of precious plants charmingly embowered are never wanting, and good rough rocks with every variety of cliff and scaur are invitingly near for outlooks and exercise.

From these lovely dens you may make excursions whenever you like into the middle of the park, where the geysers and hot springs are reeking and spouting in their beautiful basins, displaying an exuberance of color and strange motion and energy admirably calculated to surprise and frighten, charm and shake up the least sensitive out of apathy into newness of life.

However orderly your excursions or aimless, again and again amid the calmest, stillest scenery you will be brought to a standstill hushed and awe-stricken before phenomena wholly new to you. Boiling springs and huge deep pools of purest green and azure water, thousands of them, are plashing and heaving in these high, cool mountains as if a fierce furnace fire were burning beneath each one of them; and a hundred geysers, white torrents of boiling water and steam, like inverted waterfalls, are ever and anon rushing up out of the hot, black underworld. Some of these ponderous geyser columns are as large as sequoias,—five to sixty feet in diameter, one hundred and fifty to three hundred feet high,—and are sustained at this great height with tremendous energy for a few minutes, or perhaps nearly an hour, standing rigid and erect, hissing, throbbing, booming, as if thunderstorms were raging beneath their roots, their sides roughened or fluted like the furrowed bark of trees, their tops dissolving in feathery branches, while the irised spray, like misty bloom is at times blown aside, revealing the massive shafts shining against a background of pine-covered hills. Some of them lean more or less, as if storm-bent, and instead of being round are flat or fan-shaped, issuing from irregular slits in silex pavements with radiate structure, the sunbeams sifting through them in ravishing splendor. Some are broad and round-headed like oaks; others are low and bunchy, branching near the ground like bushes; and a few are hollow in the centre like big daisies or water-lilies. No frost cools them, snow never covers them nor lodges in their branches; winter and summer they welcome alike; all of them, of whatever form or size, faithfully rising and sinking in fairy rhythmic dance night and day, in all sorts of weather, at varying periods of minutes, hours, or weeks, growing up rapidly, uncontrollable as fate, tossing their pearly branches in the wind, bursting into bloom and vanishing like the frailest flowers,—plants of which Nature raises hundreds or thousands of crops a year with no apparent exhaustion of the fiery soil.

The so-called geyser basins, in which this rare sort of vegetation is growing, are mostly open valleys on the central plateau that were eroded by glaciers after the greater volcanic fires had ceased to burn. Looking down over the forests as you approach them from the surrounding heights, you see a multitude of white columns, broad, reeking masses, and irregular jets and puffs of misty vapor ascending from the bottom of the valley, or entangled like smoke among the neighboring trees, suggesting the factories of some busy town or the camp-fires of an army. These mark the position of each mush-pot, paint-pot, hot spring, and geyser, or gusher, as the Icelandic words mean. And when you saunter into the midst of them over the bright sinter pavements, and see how pure and white and pearly gray they are in the shade of the mountains, and how radiant in the sunshine, you are fairly enchanted. So numerous they are and varied, Nature seems to have gathered them from all the world as specimens of her rarest fountains, to show in one place what she can do. Over four thousand hot springs have been counted in the park, and a hundred geysers; how many more there are nobody knows.

These valleys at the heads of the great rivers may be regarded as laboratories and kitchens, in which, amid a thousand retorts and pots, we may see Nature at work as chemist or cook, cunningly compounding an infinite variety of mineral messes; cooking whole mountains; boiling and steaming flinty rocks to smooth paste and mush,—yellow, brown, red, pink, lavender, gray, and creamy white,—making the most beautiful mud in the world; and distilling the most ethereal essences. Many of these pots and caldrons have been boiling thousands of years. Pots of sulphurous mush, stringy and lumpy, and pots of broth as black as ink, are tossed and stirred with constant care, and thin transparent essences, too pure and fine to be called water, are kept simmering gently in beautiful sinter cups and bowls that grow ever more beautiful the longer they are used. In some of the spring basins, the waters, though still warm, are perfectly calm, and shine blandly in a sod of overleaning grass and flowers, as if they were thoroughly cooked at last, and set aside to settle and cool. Others are wildly boiling over as if running to waste, thousands of tons of the precious liquids being thrown into the air to fall in scalding floods on the clean coral floor of the establishment, keeping onlookers at a distance. Instead of holding limpid pale green or azure water, other pots and craters are filled with scalding mud, which is tossed up from three or four feet to thirty feet, in sticky, rank-smelling masses, with gasping, belching, thudding sounds, plastering the branches of neighboring trees; every flask, retort, hot spring, and geyser has something special in it, no two being the same in temperature, color, or composition.

In these natural laboratories one needs stout faith to feel at ease. The ground sounds hollow underfoot, and the awful subterranean thunder shakes one's mind as the ground is shaken, especially at night in the pale moonlight, or when the sky is overcast with storm-clouds. In the solemn gloom, the geysers, dimly visible, look like monstrous dancing ghosts, and their wild songs and the earthquake thunder replying to the storms overhead seem doubly terrible, as if divine government were at an end. But the trembling hills keep their places. The sky clears, the rosy dawn is reassuring, and up comes the sun like a god, pouring his faithful beams across the mountains and forest, lighting each peak and tree and ghastly geyser alike, and shining into the eyes of the reeking springs, clothing them with rainbow light, and dissolving the seeming chaos of darkness into varied forms of harmony. The ordinary work of the world goes on. Gladly we see the flies dancing in the sun-beams, birds feeding their young, squirrels gathering nuts, and hear the blessed ouzel singing confidingly in the shallows of the river,—most faithful evangel, calming every fear, reducing everything to love.

The variously tinted sinter and travertine formations, outspread like pavements over large areas of the geyser valleys, lining the spring basins and throats of the craters, and forming beautiful coral-like rims and curbs about them, always excite admiring attention; so also does the play of the waters from which they are deposited. The various minerals in them are rich in colors, and these are greatly heightened by a smooth, silky growth of brilliantly colored confervæ which lines many of the pools and channels and terraces. No bed of flower-bloom is more exquisite than these myriads of minute plants, visible only in mass, growing in the hot waters. Most of the spring borders are low and daintily scalloped, crenelated, and beaded with sinter pearls. Some of the geyser craters are massive and picturesque, like ruined castles or old burned-out sequoia stumps, and are adorned on a grand scale with outbulging, cauliflower-like formations. From these as centres the silex pavements slope gently away in thin, crusty, overlapping layers, slightly interrupted in some places by low terraces. Or, as in the case of the Mammoth Hot Springs, at the north end of the park, where the building waters issue from the side of a steep hill, the deposits form a succession of higher and broader terraces of white travertine tinged with purple, like the famous Pink Terrace at Rotomahana, New Zealand, draped in front with clustering stalactites, each terrace having a pool of indescribably beautiful water upon it in a basin with a raised rim that glistens with confervæ,—the whole, when viewed at a distance of a mile or two, looking like a broad, massive cascade pouring over shelving rocks in snowy purpled foam.

The stones of this divine masonry, invisible particles of lime or silex, mined in quarries no eye has seen, go to their appointed places in gentle, tinkling, transparent currents or through the dashing turmoil of floods, as surely guided as the sap of plants streaming into bole and branch, leaf and flower. And thus from century to century this beauty-work has gone on and is going on.

Passing through many a mile of pine and spruce woods, toward the centre of the park you come to the famous Yellowstone Lake. It is about twenty miles long and fifteen wide, and lies at a height of nearly 8000 feet above the level of the sea, amid dense black forests and snowy mountains. Around its winding, wavering shores, closely forested and picturesquely varied with promontories and bays, the distance is more than 100 miles. It is not very deep, only from 200 to 300 feet, and contains less water than the celebrated Lake Tahoe of the California Sierra, which is nearly the same size, lies at a height of 6400 feet, and is over 1600 feet deep. But no other lake in North America of equal area lies so high as the Yellowstone, or gives birth to so noble a river. The terraces around its shores show that at the close of the glacial period its surface was about 160 feet higher than it is now, and its area nearly twice as great.

It is full of trout, and a vast multitude of birds—swans, pelicans, geese, ducks, cranes, herons, curlews, plovers, snipe—feed in it and upon its shores; and many forest animals come out of the woods, and wade a little way in shallow, sandy places to drink and look about them, and cool themselves in the free flowing breezes.

In calm weather it is a magnificent mirror for the woods and mountains and sky, now pattered with hail and rain, now roughened with sudden storms that send waves to fringe the shores and wash its border of gravel and sand. The Absaroka Mountains and the Wind River Plateau on the east and south pour their gathered waters into it, and the river issues from the north side in a broad, smooth, stately current, silently gliding with such serene majesty that one fancies it knows the vast journey of four thousand miles that lies before it, and the work it has to do. For the first twenty miles its course is in a level, sunny valley lightly fringed with trees, through which it flows in silvery reaches stirred into spangles here and there by ducks and leaping trout, making no sound save a low whispering among the pebbles and the dipping willows and sedges of its banks. Then suddenly, as if preparing for hard work; it rushes eagerly, impetuously forward rejoicing in its strength, breaks into foam-bloom, and goes thundering down into the Grand Cañon in two magnificent falls, one hundred and three hundred feet high.

The cañon is so tremendously wild and impressive that even these great falls cannot hold your attention. It is about twenty miles long and a thousand feet deep,—a weird, unearthly-looking gorge of jagged, fantastic architecture, and most brilliantly colored. Here the Washburn range, forming the northern rim of the Yellowstone basin, made up mostly of beds of rhyolite decomposed by the action of thermal waters, has been cut through and laid open to view by the river; and a famous section it has made. It is not the depth or the shape of the cañon nor the waterfall, nor the green and gray river chanting its brave song as it goes foaming on its way, that most impresses the observer, but the colors of the decomposed volcanic rocks. With few exceptions, the traveler in strange lands finds that, however much the scenery and vegetation in different countries may change, Mother Earth is ever familiar and the same. But here the very ground is changed, as if belonging to some other world. The walls of the cañon from top to bottom burn in a perfect glory of color, confounding and dazzling when the sun is shining,—white, yellow, green, blue, vermilion, and various other shades of red indefinitely blending. All the earth hereabouts seems to be paint. Millions of tons of it lie in sight, exposed to wind and weather as if of no account, yet marvelously fresh and bright, fast colors not to be washed out or bleached out by either sunshine or storms. The effect is so novel and awful, we imagine that even a river might be afraid to enter such a place. But the rich and gentle beauty of the vegetation is reassuring. The lovely Linnæa borealis hangs her twin bells over the brink of the cliffs, forests and gardens extend their treasures in smiling confidence on either side, nuts and berries ripen well whatever may be going on below; blind fears varnish, and the grand gorge seems a kindly, beautiful part of the general harmony, full of peace and joy and good will.

The park is easy of access. Locomotives drag you to its northern boundary at Cinnabar, and horses and guides do the rest. From Cinnabar you will be whirled in coaches along the foaming Gardiner River to Mammoth Hot Springs; thence through woods and meadows, gulches and ravines along branches of the Upper Gallatin, Madison, and Firehole rivers to the main geyser basins; thence over the Continental Divide and back again, up and down through dense pine, spruce, and fir woods to the magnificent Yellowstone Lake, along its northern shore to the outlet, down the river to the falls and Grand Cañon, and thence back through the woods to Mammoth Hot Springs and Cinnabar; stopping here and there at the so-called points of interest among the geysers, springs, paint-pots, mud volcanoes, etc., where you will be allowed a few minutes or hours to saunter over the sinter pavements, watch the play of a few of the geysers, and peer into some of the most beautiful and terrible of the craters and pools. These wonders you will enjoy, and also the views of the mountains, especially the Gallatin and Absaroka ranges, the long, willowy glacier and beaver meadows, the beds of violets, gentians, phloxes, asters, phacelias, goldenrods, eriogonums, and many other flowers, some species giving color to whole meadows and hillsides. And you will enjoy your short views of the great lake and river and cañon. No scalping Indians will you see. The Blackfeet and Bannocks that once roamed here are gone; so are the old beaver-catchers, the Coulters and Bridgers, with all their attractive buckskin and romance. There are several bands of buffaloes in the park, but you will not thus cheaply in tourist fashion see them nor many of the other large animals hidden in the wilderness. The song-birds, too, keep mostly out of sight of the rushing tourist, though off the roads thrushes, warblers, orioles, grosbeaks, etc., keep the air sweet and merry. Perhaps in passing rapids and falls you may catch glimpses of the water-ouzel, but in the whirling noise you will not hear his song. Fortunately, no road noise frightens the Douglas squirrel, and his merry play and gossip will amuse you all through the woods. Here and there a deer may be seen crossing the road, or a bear. Most likely, however, the only bears you will see are the half tame ones that go to the hotels every night for dinner-table scraps,—yeast-powder biscuit, Chicago canned stuff, mixed pickles, and beefsteaks that have proved too tough for the tourists.

Among the gains of a coach trip are the acquaintances made and the fresh views into human nature; for the wilderness is a shrewd touchstone, even thus lightly approached, and brings many a curious trait to view. Setting out, the driver cracks his whip, and the four horses go off at half gallop, half trot, in trained, showy style, until out of sight of the hotel. The coach is crowded, old and young side by side, blooming and fading, full of hope and fun and care. Some look at the scenery or the horses, and all ask questions, an odd mixed lot of them: "Where is the umbrella? What is the name of that blue flower over there? Are you sure the little bag is aboard? Is that hollow yonder a crater? How is your throat this morning? How high did you say the geysers spout? How does the elevation affect your head? Is that a geyser reeking over there in the rocks, or only a hot spring?" A long ascent is made, the solemn mountains come to view, small cares are quenched, and all become natural and silent, save perhaps some unfortunate expounder who has been reading guidebook geology, and rumbles forth foggy subsidences and upheavals until he is danger of being heaved overboard. The driver will give you the names of the peaks and meadows and streams as you come to them, call attention to the glass road, tell how hard it was to build,—how the obsidian cliffs naturally pushed the surveyor's lines to the right, and the industrious beavers, by flooding the valley in front of the cliff, pushed them to the left.

Geysers, however, are the main objects, and as soon as they come in sight other wonders are forgotten. All gather around the crater of the one that is expected to play first. During the eruptions of the smaller geysers, such as the Beehive and Old Faithful, though a little frightened at first, all welcome the glorious show with enthusiasm, and shout, "Oh, how wonderful, beautiful, splendid, majestic!" Some venture near enough to stroke the column with a stick, as if it were a stone pillar or a tree, so firm and substantial and permanent it seems. While tourists wait around a large geyser, such as the Castle or the Giant, there is a chatter of small talk in anything but solemn mood; and during the intervals between the preliminary splashes and upheavals some adventurer occasionally looks down the throat of the crater, admiring the silex formations and wondering whether Hades is as beautiful. But when, with awful uproar as if avalanches were falling and storms thundering in the depths, the tremendous outburst begins, all run away to a safe distance, and look on, awe-stricken and silent, in devout, worshiping wonder.

The largest and one of the most wonderfully beautiful of the springs is the Prismatic, which the guide will be sure to show you. With a circumference of 300 yards, it is more like a lake than a spring. The water is pure deep blue in the centre, fading to green on the edges, and its basin and the slightly terraced pavement about it are astonishingly bright and varied in color. This one of the multitude of Yellowstone fountains is of itself object enough for a trip across the continent. No wonder that so many fine myths have originated in springs; that so many fountains were held sacred in the youth of the world, and had miraculous virtues ascribed to them. Even in these cold, doubting, questioning, scientific times many of the Yellowstone fountains seem able to work miracles. Near the Prismatic Spring is the great Excelsior Geyser, which is said to throw a column of boiling water 60 to 70 feet in diameter to a height of from 50 to 300 feet, at irregular periods. This is the greatest of all the geysers yet discovered anywhere. The Firehole River, which sweeps past it, is, at ordinary states, a stream about 100 yards wide and 3 feet deep; but when the geyser is in eruption, so great is the quantity of water discharged that the volume of the river is doubled, and it is rendered too hot and rapid to be forded.

Geysers are found in many other volcanic regions,—in Iceland, New Zealand, Japan, the Himalayas, the Eastern Archipelago, South America, the Azores, and elsewhere; but only in Iceland, New Zealand, and this Rocky Mountain park do they display their grandest forms, and of these three famous regions the Yellowstone is easily first, both in the number and in the size of its geysers. The greatest height of the column of the Great Geyser of Iceland actually measured was 212 feet, and of the Strokhr 162 feet.

In New Zealand, the Te Pueia at Lake Taupo, the Waikite at Rotorna, and two others are said to lift their waters occasionally to a height of 100 feet, while the celebrated Te Tarata at Rotomahana sometimes lifts a boiling column 20 feet in diameter to a height of 60 feet. But all these are far surpassed by the Excelsior. Few tourists, however, will see the Excelsior in action, or a thousand other interesting features of the park that lie beyond the wagon roads and the hotels. The regular trips—from three to five days—are too short. Nothing can be done well at a speed of forty miles a day. The multitude of mixed, novel impressions rapidly piled on one another make only a dreamy, bewildering, swirling blur, most of which is unrememberable. Far more time should be taken. Walk away quietly in any direction and taste the freedom of the mountaineer. Camp out among the grass and gentians of glacier meadows, in craggy garden nooks full of Nature's darlings. Climb the mountains and get their good tidings. Nature's peace will flow into you as sunshine flows into trees. The winds will blow their own freshness into you, and the storms their energy, while cares will drop off like autumn leaves. As age comes on, one source of enjoyment after another is closed, but Nature's sources never fail. Like a generous host, she offers here brimming cups in endless variety, served in a grand hall, the sky its ceiling, the mountains its walls, decorated with glorious paintings and enlivened with bands of music ever playing. The petty discomforts that beset the awkward guest, the unskilled camper, are quickly forgotten, while all that is precious remains. Fears vanish as soon as one is fairly free in the wilderness.

Most of the dangers that haunt the unseasoned citizen are imaginary; the real ones are perhaps too few rather than too many for his good. The bears that always seem to spring up thick as trees, in fighting, devouring attitudes before the frightened tourist whenever a camping trip is proposed, are gentle now, finding they are no longer likely to be shot; and rattlesnakes, the other big irrational dread of over-civilized people, are scarce here, for most of the park lies above the snake-line. Poor creatures, loved only by their Maker, they are timid and bashful, as mountaineers know; and though perhaps not possessed of much of that charity that suffers long and is kind, seldom, either by mistake or by mishap, do harm to any one. Certainly they cause not the hundredth part of the pain and death that follow the footsteps of the admired Rocky Mountain trapper. Nevertheless, again and again, in season and out of season, the question comes up, "What are rattlesnakes good for?" As if nothing that does not obviously make for the benefit of man had any right to exist; as if our ways were God's ways. Long ago, an Indian to whom a French traveler put this old question replied that their tails were good for toothache, and their heads for fever. Anyhow, they are all, head and tail, good for themselves, and we need not begrudge them their share of life.

Fear nothing. No town park you have been accustomed to saunter in is so free from danger as the Yellowstone. It is a hard place to leave. Even its names in your guidebook are attractive, and should draw you far from wagon-roads,—all save the early ones, derived from the infernal regions: Hell Roaring River, Hell Broth Springs, The Devil's Caldron, etc. Indeed, the whole region was at first called Coulter's Hell, from the fiery brimstone stories told by trapper Coulter, who left the Lewis and Clark expedition and wandered through the park, in the year 1807, with a band of Bannock Indians. The later names, many of which we owe to Mr. Arnold Hague of the U. S. Geological Survey, are so telling and exhilarating that they set our pulses dancing and make us begin to enjoy the pleasures of excursions ere they are commenced. Three River Peak, Two Ocean Pass, Continental Divide, are capital geographical descriptions, suggesting thousands of miles of rejoicing streams and all that belongs to them. Big Horn Pass, Bison Peak, Big Game Ridge, bring brave mountain animals to mind. Birch Hills, Garnet Hills, Amethyst Mountain, Storm Peak, Electric Peak, Roaring Mountain, are bright, bracing names. Wapiti, Beaver, Tern, and Swan lakes, conjure up fine pictures, and so also do Osprey and Ouzel falls. Antelope Creek, Otter, Mink, and Grayling creeks, Geode, Jasper, Opal, Carnelian, and Chalcedony creeks, are lively and sparkling names that help the streams to shine; and Azalea, Stellaria, Arnica, Aster, and Phlox creeks, what pictures these bring up! Violet, Morning Mist, Hygeia, Beryl, Vermilion, and Indigo springs, and many beside, give us visions of fountains more beautifully arrayed than Solomon in all his purple and golden glory. All these and a host of others call you to camp. You may be a little cold some nights, on mountain tops above the timber-line, but you will see the stars, and by and by you can sleep enough in your town bed, or at least in your grave. Keep awake while you may in mountain mansions so rare.

If you are not very strong, try to climb Electric Peak when a big bossy, well-charged thunder-cloud is on it, to breathe the ozone set free, and get yourself kindly shaken and shocked. You are sure to be lost in wonder and praise, and every hair of your head will stand up and hum and sing like an enthusiastic congregation.

After this reviving experience, you should take a look into a few of the tertiary volumes of the grand geological library of the park, and see how God writes history. No technical knowledge is required; only a calm day and a calm mind. Perhaps nowhere else in the Rocky Mountains have the volcanic forces been so busy. More than ten thousand square miles hereabouts have been covered to a depth of at least five thousand feet with material spouted from chasms and craters during the tertiary period, forming broad sheets of basalt, andesite, rhyolite, etc., and marvelous masses of ashes, sand, cinders, and stones now consolidated into conglomerates, charged with the remains of plants and animals that lived in the calm, genial periods that separated the volcanic outbursts.

Perhaps the most interesting and telling of these rocks to the hasty tourist, are those that make up the mass of Amethyst Mountain. On its north side it presents a section two thousand feet high of roughly stratified beds of sand, ashes, and conglomerates coarse and fine, forming the untrimmed edges of a wonderful set of volumes lying on their sides,—books a million years old, well bound, miles in size, with full-page illustrations. On the ledges of this one section we see trunks and stumps of fifteen or twenty ancient forests ranged one above another, standing where they grew, or prostrate and broken like the pillars of ruined temples in desert sands,—a forest fifteen or twenty stories high, the roots of each spread above the tops of the next beneath it, telling wonderful tales of the bygone centuries, with their winters and summers, growth and death, fire, ice, and flood.

There were giants in those days. The largest of the standing opal and agate stumps and prostrate sections of the trunks are from two or three to fifty feet in height or length, and from five to ten feet in diameter; and so perfect is the petrifaction that the annual rings and ducts are clearer and more easily counted than those of living trees, centuries of burial having brightened the records instead of blurring them. They show that the winters of the tertiary period gave as decided a check to vegetable growth as do those of the present time. Some trees favorably located grew rapidly, increasing twenty inches in diameter in as many years, while others of the some species, on poorer soil or overshadowed, increased only two or three inches in the same time.

Among the roots and stumps on the old forest floors we find the remains of ferns and bushes, and the seeds and leaves of trees like those now growing on the southern Alleghanies,—such as magnolia, sassafras, laurel, linden, persimmon, ash, alder, dogwood. Studying the lowest of these forests, the soil it grew on and the deposits it is buried in, we see that it was rich in species, and flourished in a genial, sunny climate. When its stately trees were in their glory, volcanic fires broke forth from chasms and craters, like larger geysers, spouting ashes, cinders, stones and mud, which fell on the doomed forest like hail and snow; sifting, hurtling through the leaves and branches, choking the streams, covering the ground, crushing bushes and ferns, rapidly deepening, packing around the trees and breaking them, rising higher until the topmost boughs of the giants were buried, leaving not a leaf or twig in sight, so complete was the desolation. At last the volcanic storm began to abate, the fiery soil settled; mud floods and boulder floods passed over it, enriching it, cooling it; rains fell and mellow sunshine, and it became fertile and ready for another crop. Birds, and the winds, and roaming animals brought seeds from more fortunate woods, and a new forest grew up on the top of the buried one. Centuries of genial growing seasons passed. The seedling trees became giants, and with strong outreaching branches spread a leafy canopy over the gray land.

The sleeping subterranean fires again awake and shake the mountains, and every leaf trembles. The old craters, with perhaps new ones, are opened, and immense quantities of ashes, pumice, and cinders are again thrown into the sky. The sun, and shorn of his beams, glows like a dull red ball, until hidden in sulphurous clouds. Volcanic snow, hail, and floods fall on the new forest, burying it alive, like the one beneath its roots. Then come another noisy band of mud floods and boulder floods, mixing, settling, enriching the new ground, more seeds, quickening sunshine and showers; and a third noble magnolia forest is carefully raised on the top of the second. And so on. Forest was planted above forest and destroyed, as if Nature were ever repenting, undoing the work she had so industriously done, and burying it.

Of course this destruction was creation, progress in the march of beauty through death. How quickly these old monuments excite and hold the imagination! We see the old stone stumps budding and blossoming and waving in the wind as magnificent trees, standing shoulder to shoulder, branches interlacing in grand varied round-headed forests; see the sunshine of morning and evening gilding their mossy trunks, and at high noon spangling on the thick glossy leaves of the magnolia, filtering through translucent canopies of linden and ash, and falling in mellow patches on the ferny floor; see the shining after rain, breathe the exhaling fragrance, and hear the winds and birds and the murmur of brooks and insects. We watch them from season to season; see the swelling buds when the sap begins to flow in the spring, the opening leaves and blossoms, the ripening of summer fruits, the colors of autumn, and the maze of leafless branches and sprays in winter; and we see the sudden oncome of the storms that overwhelmed them.

One calm morning at sunrise I saw the oaks and pines in Yosemite Valley shaken by an earthquake, their tops swishing back and forth, and every branch and needle shuddering as if in distress like the frightened screaming birds. One may imagine the trembling, rocking, tumultuous waving of those ancient Yellowstone woods, and the terror of their inhabitants when the first foreboding shocks were felt, the sky grew dark, and rock-laden floods began to roar. But though they were close pressed and buried, cut off from sun and wind, all their happy leaf-fluttering and waving done, other currents coursed through them, fondling and thrilling every fibre, and beautiful wood was replaced by beautiful stone. Now their rocky sepulchres are partly open, and show forth the natural beauty of death.

After the forest times and fire times had passed away, and the volcanic furnaces were banked and held in abeyance, another great change occurred. The glacial winter came on. The sky was again darkened, not with dust and ashes, but with snow which fell in glorious abundance, piling deeper, deeper, slipping from the overladen heights in booming avalanches, compacting into glaciers, that flowed over all the landscape, wiping off forests, grinding, sculpturing, fashioning the comparatively featureless lava beds into the beautiful rhythm of hill and dale and ranges of mountains we behold to-day; forming basins for lakes, channels for streams, few soils for forests, gardens, and meadows. While this ice-work was going on, the slumbering volcanic fires were boiling the subterranean waters, and with curious chemistry decomposing the rocks, making beauty in the darkness; these forces, seemingly antagonistic, working harmoniously together. How wild their meetings on the surface were we may imagine. When the glacier period began, geysers and hot springs were playing in grander volume, it may be, than those of to-day. The glaciers flowed over them while they spouted and thundered, carrying away their fine sinter and travertine structures, and shortening their mysterious channels.

The soils made in the down-grinding required to bring the present features of the landscape into relief are possibly no better than were some of the old volcanic soils that were carried away, and which, as we have seen, nourished magnificent forests, but the glacial landscapes are incomparably more beautiful than the old volcanic ones were. The glacial winter has passed away, like the ancient summers and fire periods, though in the chronology of the geologist all these times are recent. Only small residual glaciers on the cool northern slopes of the highest mountains are left of the vast all-embracing ice-mantle, as solfataras and geysers are all that are left of the ancient volcanoes.

Now the post-glacial agents are at work on the grand old palimpsest of the park region, inscribing new characters; but still in its main telling features it remains distinctly glacial. The moraine soils are being leveled, sorted, refined, re-formed, and covered with vegetation; the polished pavements and scoring and other superficial glacial inscriptions on the crumbling lavas are being rapidly obliterated; gorges are being cut in the decomposed rhyolites and loose conglomerates, and turrets and pinnacles seem to be springing up like growing trees; while the geysers are depositing miles of sinter and travertine. Nevertheless, the ice-work is scarce blurred as yet. These later effects are only spots and wrinkles on the grand glacial countenance of the park.

Perhaps you have already said that you have seen enough for a lifetime. But before you go away you should spend at least one day and a night on a mountain top, for a last general, calming, settling view. Mount Washburn is a good one for the purpose, because it stands in the middle of the park, is unencumbered with other peaks, and is so easy of access that the climb to its summit is only a saunter. First your eye goes roving around the mountain rim amid the hundreds of peaks; some with plain flowing skirts, others abruptly precipitous and defended by sheer battlemented escarpments; flat-topped or round; heaving like sea-waves or spired and turreted like Gothic cathedrals; streaked with snow in the ravines, and darkened with files of adventurous trees climbing the ridges. The nearer peaks are perchance clad in sapphire blue, others far off in creamy white. In the broad glare of noon they seem to shrink and crouch to less than half their real stature, and grow dull and uncommunicative,—mere dead, draggled heaps of waste ashes and stone, giving no hint of the multitude of animals enjoying life in their fastnesses, or of the bright bloom-bordered streams and lakes. But when storms blow they awake and arise, wearing robes of cloud and mist in majestic speaking attitudes like gods. In the color glory of morning and evening they become still more impressive; steeped in the divine light of the alpenglow their earthiness disappears, and, blending with the heavens, they seem neither high nor low.

Over all the central plateau, which from here seems level, and over the foothills and lower slopes of the mountains, the forests extends like a black uniform bed of weeds, interrupted only by lakes and meadows and small burned spots called parks,—all of them, except the Yellowstone Lake, being mere dots and spangles in general views, made conspicuous by their color and brightness. About eighty-five per cent of the entire area of the park is covered with trees, mostly the indomitable lodge-pole pine (Pinus contorta, var. Murrayana), with a few patches and sprinklings of Douglas spruce, Engelmann spruce, silver fir (Abies lasiocarpa), Pinus flexilis, and a few alders, aspens, and birches. The Douglas spruce is found only on the lowest portions, the silver fir on the highest, and the Engelmann spruce on the dampest places, best defended from fire. Some fine specimens of the flexilis pine are growing on the margins of openings,—wide-branching, sturdy trees, as broad as high, with trunks five feet in diameter, leafy and shady, laden with purple cones and rose-colored flowers. The Engelmann spruce and sub-alpine silver fir are beautiful and notable trees, but as the plateau became drier and fires began to run, they were driven up the mountains, and into the wet spots and islands where we now find them, leaving nearly all the park to the lodge-pole pine, which, though as thin-skinned as they and as easily killed by fire, takes pains to store up its seeds in firmly closed cones, and holds them from three to nine years, so that, let the fire come when it may, it is ready to die and ready to live again in a new generation. For when the killing fires have devoured the leaves and thin resinous bark, many of the cones, only scorched, open as soon as the smoke clears away; the hoarded store of seeds is sown broadcast on the cleared ground, and a new growth immediately springs up triumphant out of the ashes. Therefore, this tree not only holds its ground, but extends its conquests farther after every fire. Thus the evenness and closeness of its growth are accounted for. In one part of the forest that I examined, the growth was about as close as a cane-brake. The trees were from four to eight inches in diameter, one hundred feet high, and one hundred and seventy-five years old. The lower limbs die young and drop off for want of light. Life with these close-planted trees is a race for light, more light, and so they push straight for the sky. Mowing off ten feet from the top of the forest would make it look like a crowded mass of telegraph-poles; for only the sunny tops are leafy. A sapling ten years old, growing in the sunshine, has as many leaves as a crowded tree one or two hundred years old. As fires are multiplied and the mountains become drier, this wonderful lodge-pole pine bids fair to obtain possession of nearly all the forest ground in the West.

How still the woods seem from here, yet how lively a stir the hidden animals are making; digging, gnawing, biting, eyes shining, at work and play, getting food, rearing young, roving through the underbrush, climbing the rocks, wading solitary marshes, tracing the banks of the lakes and streams! Insect swarms are dancing in the sunbeams, burrowing in the ground, diving, swimming,—a cloud of witnesses telling Nature's joy. The plants are as busy as the animals, every cell in a swirl of enjoyment, humming like a hive, singing the old new song of creation. A few columns and puffs of steam are seen rising above the treetops, some near, but most of them far off, indicating geysers and hot springs, gentle-looking and noiseless as noiseless as downy clouds, softly hinting the reaction going on between the surface and the hot interior. From here you see them better than when you are standing beside them, frightened and confused, regarding them as lawless cataclysms. The shocks and out-bursts of earthquakes, volcanoes, geysers, storms, the pounding of waves, the uprush of sap in plants, each and all tell the orderly love-beats of Nature's heart.

Turning to the eastward, you have the Grand Cañon and reaches of the river in full view; and yonder to the southward lies the great lake, the largest and most important of all the high fountains of the Missouri-Mississippi, and the last to be discovered.

In the year 1541, when De Soto, with a romantic band of adventurers, was seeking gold and glory and the fountain of youth, he found the Mississippi a few hundred miles above its mouth, and made his grave beneath its floods. La Salle, in 1682, after discovering the Ohio, one of the largest and most beautiful branches of the Mississippi, traced the latter to the sea from the mouth of the Illinois, through adventures and privations not easily realized now. About the same time Joliet and Father Marquette reached the "Father of Waters" by way of the Wisconsin, but more than a century passed ere its highest sources in these mountains were seen. The advancing stream of civilization has ever followed its guidance toward the west, but none of the thousand tribes of Indians living on its banks could tell the explorer whence it came. From those romantic De Soto and La Salle days to these times of locomotives and tourists, how much has the great river seen and done! Great as it now is, and still growing longer through the ground of its delta and the basins of receding glaciers at its head, it was immensely broader toward the close of the glacial period, when the ice-mantle of the mountains was melting: then with its three hundred thousand miles of branches out-spread over the plains and valleys of the continent, laden with fertile mud, it made the biggest and most generous bed of soil in the world.

Think of this mighty stream springing in the first place in vapor from the sea, flying on the wind, alighting on the mountains in hail and snow and rain, lingering in many a fountain feeding the trees and grass; then gathering its scattered waters, gliding from its noble lake, and going back home to the sea, singing all the way! On it sweeps, through the gates of the mountains, across the vast prairies and plains, through many a wild, gloomy forest, cane-brake, and sunny savanna; from glaciers and snowbanks and pine woods to warm groves of magnolia and palm; geysers dancing at its head keeping time with the sea-waves at its mouth; roaring and gray in rapids, booming in broad, bossy falls, murmuring, gleaming in long, silvery reaches, swaying now hither, now thither, whirling, bending in huge doubling, eddying folds, serene, majestic, ungovernable, overflowing all its metes and bounds, frightening the dwellers upon its banks; building, wasting, uprooting, planting; engulfing old islands and making new ones, taking away fields and towns as if in sport, carrying canoes and ships of commerce in the midst of its spoils and drift, fertilizing the continent as one vast farm. Then, its work done, it gladly vanishes in its ocean home, welcomed by the waiting waves.

Thus naturally, standing here in the midst of its fountains, we trace the fortunes of the great river. And how much more comes to mind as we overlook this wonderful wilderness! Fountains of the Columbia and Colorado lie before us, interlaced with those of the Yellowstone and Missouri, and fine it would be to go with them to the Pacific; but the sun is already in the west, and soon our day will be done.

Yonder is Amethyst Mountain, and other mountains hardly less rich in old forests, which now seem to spring up again in their glory; and you see the storms that buried them,—the ashes and torrents laden with boulders and mud, the centuries of sunshine, and the dark, lurid nights. You see again the vast floods of lava, red-hot and white-hot, pouring out from gigantic geysers, usurping the basins of lakes and streams, absorbing or driving away their hissing, screaming waters, flowing around hills and ridges, submerging every subordinate feature. Then you see the snow and glaciers taking possession of the land, making new landscapes. How admirable it is that, after passing through so many vicissitudes of frost and fire and flood, the physiognomy and even the complexion of the landscape should still be so divinely fine!

Thus reviewing the eventful past, we see Nature working with enthusiasm like a man, blowing her volcanic forges like a blacksmith blowing his smithy fires, shoving glaciers over the landscapes like a carpenter shoving his planes, clearing, ploughing, harrowing, irrigating, planting, and sowing broadcast like a farmer and gardener, doing rough work and fine work, planting sequoias and pines, rosebushes and daisies; working in gems, filling every crack and hollow with them; distilling fine essences; painting plants and shells, clouds, mountains, all the earth and heavens, like an artist,—ever working toward beauty higher and higher. Where may the mind find more stimulating, quickening pasturage? A thousand Yellowstone wonders are calling, "Look up and down and round about you!" And a multitude of still, small voices may be heard directing you to look through all this transient, shifting show of things called "substantial" into the truly substantial, spiritual world whose forms flesh and wood, rock and water, air and sunshine, only veil and conceal, and to learn that here is heaven and the dwelling-place of the angles.

The sun is setting; long, violet shadows are growing out over the woods from the mountains along the western rim of the park; the Absaroka range is baptized in the divine light of the alpenglow, and its rocks and trees are transfigured. Next to the light of the dawn on high mountain tops, the alpenglow is the most impressive of all the terrestrial manifestations of God.

Now comes the gloaming. The alpenglow is fading into earthy, murky gloom, but do not let your town habits draw you away to the hotel. Stay on this good fire-mountain and spend the night among the stars. Watch their glorious bloom until the dawn, and get one more baptism of light. Then, with fresh heart, go down to your work, and whatever your fate, under whatever ignorance or knowledge you may afterward chance to suffer, you will remember these fine, wild views, and look back with joy to your wanderings in the blessed old Yellowstone Wonderland.

CHAPTER III

The Yosemite National Park

Of all the mountain ranges I have climbed, I like the Sierra Nevada the best. Though extremely rugged, with its main features on the grandest scale in height and depth, it is nevertheless easy of access and hospitable; and its marvelous beauty, displayed in striking and alluring forms, wooes the admiring wanderer on and on, higher and higher, charmed and enchanted. Benevolent, solemn, fateful, pervaded with divine light, every landscape glows like a countenance hallowed in eternal repose; and every one of its living creatures, clad in flesh and leaves, and every crystal of its rocks, whether on the surface shining in the sun or buries miles deep in what we call darkness, is throbbing and pulsing with the heartbeats of God. All the world lies warm in one heart, yet the Sierra seems to get more light than other mountains. The weather is mostly sunshine embellished with magnificent storms, and nearly everything shines from base to summit,—the rocks, streams, lakes, glaciers, irised falls, and the forests of silver fir and silver pine. And how bright is the shining after summer showers and dewy nights, and after frosty nights in spring and autumn, when the morning sunbeams are pouring through the crystals on the bushes and grass, and in winter through the snow-laden trees!

The average cloudiness for the whole year is perhaps less than ten hundredths. Scarcely a day of all the summer is dark, though there is no lack of magnificent thundering cumuli. They rise in the warm midday hours, mostly over the middle region, in June and July, like new mountain ranges, higher Sierras, mightily augmenting the grandeur of the scenery while giving rain to the forests and gardens and bringing forth their fragrance. The wonderful weather and beauty inspire everybody to be up and doing. Every summer day is a workday to be confidently counted on, the short dashes of rain forming, not interruptions, but rests. The big blessed storm days of winter, when the whole range stands white, are not a whit less inspiring and kind. Well may the Sierra be called the Range of Light, not the Snowy Range; for only in winter is it white; while all the year it is bright.

Of this glorious range the Yosemite National Park is a central section, thirty-six miles in length and forty-eight miles in breadth. The famous Yosemite Valley lies in the heart of it, and it includes the head waters of the Tuolumne and Merced rivers, two of the most songful streams in the world; innumerable lakes and waterfalls and smooth silky lawns; the noblest forests, the loftiest granite domes, the deepest ice-sculptured cañons, the brightest crystalline pavements, and snowy mountains soaring into the sky twelve and thirteen thousand feet, arrayed in open ranks and spiry pinnacled groups partially separated by tremendous cañons and amphitheatres; gardens on their sunny brows avalanches thundering down their long white slopes, cataracts roaring gray and foaming in the crooked rugged gorges, and glaciers in their shadowy recesses working in silence, slowly completing their sculpture; new-born lakes at their feet, blue and green, free or encumbered with drifting icebergs like miniature Arctic Oceans, shining, sparkling, calm as stars.

Nowhere will you see the majestic operations of nature more clearly revealed beside the frailest, most gentle and peaceful things. Nearly all the park is a profound solitude. Yet it is full of charming company, full of God's thoughts, a place of peace and safety amid the most exalted grandeur and eager enthusiastic action, a new song, a place of beginnings abounding in first lessons on life, mountain-building, eternal, invincible, unbreakable order; with sermons in stones, storms, trees, flowers, and animals brimful of humanity. During the last glacial period, just past, the former features of the range were rubbed off as a chalk sketch from a blackboard, and a new beginning was made. Hence the wonderful clearness and freshness of the rocky pages.

But to get all this into words is a hopeless task. The leanest sketch of each feature would need a whole chapter. Nor would any amount of space, however industriously scribbled, be of much avail. To defrauded town toilers, parks in magazine articles are like pictures of bread to the hungry. I can write only hints to incite good wanderers to come to the feast.

While this glorious park embraces big, generous samples of the very best of the Sierra treasure, it is, fortunately, at the same time, the most accessible portion. It lies opposite San Francisco, at a distance of about one hundred and forty miles. Railroads connected with all the continent reach into the foothills, and three good carriage roads, from Big Oak Flat, Coulterville, and Raymond, run into Yosemite Valley. Another, called the Tioga road, runs from Crocker's Station on the Yosemite Big Oak Flat road near the Tuolumne Big Tree Grove, right across the park to the summit of the range by way of Lake Tenaya, the Big Tuolumne Meadows, and Mount Dana. These roads, with many trials that radiate from Yosemite Valley, bring most of the park within reach of everybody, well or half well.

The three main natural divisions of the park, the lower, middle, and alpine regions, are fairly well defined in altitude, topographical features, and vegetation. The lower, with an average elevation of about five thousand feet, is the region of the great forests, made up of sugar pine, the largest and most beautiful of all the pines in the world; the silvery yellow pine, the next in rank; Douglas spruce, libocedrus, the white and red silver firs, and the Sequoia gigantea, or "big tree," the king of conifers, the noblest of a noble race. On warm slopes next the foothills there are a few Sabine nut pines; oaks make beautiful groves in the cañon valleys; and poplar, alder, maple, laurel, and Nuttall's flowering dogwood shade the banks of the streams. Many of the pines are more than two hundred feet high, but they are not crowded together. The sunbeams streaming through their feathery arches brighten the ground, and you walk beneath the radiant ceiling in devout subdued mood, as if you were in a grand cathedral with mellow light sifting through colored windows, while the flowery pillared aisles open enchanting vistas in every direction. Scarcely a peak or ridge in the whole region rises bare above the forests, though they are thinly planted in some places where the soil is shallow. From the cool breezy heights you look abroad over a boundless waving sea of evergreens, covering hill and ridge and smooth-flowing slope as far as the eye can reach, and filling every hollow and down-plunging ravine in glorious triumphant exuberance.

Perhaps the best general view of the pine forests of the park, and one of the best in the range, is obtained from the top of the Merced and Tuolumne divide near Hazel Green. On the long, smooth, finely folded slopes of the main ridge, at a height of five to six thousand feet above the sea, they reach most perfect development and are marshaled to view in magnificent towering ranks, their colossal spires and domes and broad palmlike crowns, deep in the kind sky, rising above one another,—a multitude of giants in perfect health and beauty,—sun-fed mountaineers rejoicing in their strength, chanting with the winds, in accord with the falling waters. The ground is mostly open and inviting to walkers. The fragrant chamæbatia is outspread in rich carpets miles in extent; the manzanita, in orchard-like groves, covered with pink bell-shaped flowers in the spring, grows in openings facing the sun, hazel and buckthorn in the dells; warm brows are purple with mint, yellow with sunflowers and violets; and tall lilies ring their bells around the borders of meadows and along the ferny, mossy banks of the streams. Never was mountain forest more lavishly furnished.

Hazel Green is a good place quietly to camp and study, to get acquainted with the trees and birds, to drink the reviving water and weather, and to watch the changing lights of the big charmed days. The rose light of the dawn, creeping higher among the stars, changes to daffodil yellow; then come the level enthusiastic sunbeams pouring across the feathery ridges, touching pine after pine, spruce and fir, libocedrus and lordly sequoia, searching every recess, until all are awakened and warmed. In the white noon they shine in silvery splendor, every needle and cell in bole and branch thrilling and tingling with ardent life; and the whole landscape glows with consciousness, like the face of a god. The hours go by uncounted. The evening flames with purple and gold. The breeze that has been blowing from the lowlands dies away, and far and near the mighty host of trees baptized in the purple flood stand hushed and thoughtful, awaiting the sun's blessing and farewell,—as impressive a ceremony as if it were never to rise again. When the daylight fades, the night breeze from the snowy summits begins to blow, and the trees, waving and rustling beneath the stars, breathe free again.

It is hard to leave such camps and woods; nevertheless, to the large majority of travelers the middle region of the park is still more interesting, for it has the most striking features of all the Sierra scenery,—the deepest sections of the famous cañons, of which the Yosemite Valley, Hetch-Hetchy Valley, and many smaller ones are wider portions, with level parklike floors and walls of immense height and grandeur of sculpture. This middle region holds also the greater number of the beautiful glacier lakes and glacier meadows, the great granite domes, and the most brilliant and most extensive of the glacier pavements. And though in large part it is severely rocky and bare, it is still rich in trees. The magnificent silver fir (Abies magnifica), which ranks with the giants, forms a continuous belt across the park above the pines at an elevation of from seven to nine thousand feet, and north and south of the park boundaries to the extremities of the range, only slightly interrupted by the main cañons. The two-leaved or tamarack pine makes another less regular belt along the upper margin of the region, while between these two belts, and mingling with them, in groves or scattered, are the mountain hemlock, the most graceful of evergreens; the noble mountain pine; the Jeffrey form of the yellow pine, with big cones and long needles; and the brown, burly, sturdy Western juniper. All these, except the juniper, which grows on bald rocks, have plenty of flowery brush about them, and gardens in open spaces.

Here, too, lies the broad, shining heavily sculptured region of primeval granite, which best tells the story of the glacial period on the Pacific side of the continent. No other mountain chain on the globe, as far as I know, is so rich as the Sierra in bold, striking, well-preserved glacial monuments, easily understood by anybody capable of patient observation. Every feature is more or less glacial, and this park portion of the range is the brightest and clearest of all. Not a peak, ridge, dome, cañon, lake basin, garden, forest, or stream but in some way explains the past existence and modes of action of flowing, grinding, sculpturing, soil-making, scenery-making ice. For, notwithstanding the post-glacial agents—air, rain, frost, rivers, earthquakes, avalanches—have been at work upon the greater part of the range for tens of thousands of stormy years, engraving their own characters over those of the ice, the latter are so heavily emphasized and enduring they still rise in sublime relief, clear and legible through every after inscription. The streams have traced only shallow wrinkles as yet, and avalanche, wind, rain, and melting snow have made blurs and scars, but the change effected on the face of the landscape is not greater than is made on the face of a mountaineer by a single year of weathering.

Of all the glacial phenomena presented here, the most striking and attractive to travelers are the polished pavements, because they are so beautiful, and their beauty is of so rare a kind,—unlike any part of the loose earthy lowlands where people dwell and earn their bread. They are simply flat or gently undulating areas of solid resisting granite, the unchanged surface over which the ancient glaciers flowed. They are found in the most perfect condition at an elevation of from eight to nine thousand feet above sea level. Some are miles in extent, only slightly blurred or scarred by spots that have at last yielded to the weather; while the best preserved portions are brilliantly polished, and reflect the sunbeams as calm water or glass, shining as if rubbed and burnished every day, notwithstanding they have been exposed to plashing, corroding rains, dew, frost, and melting sloppy snows for thousands of years.

The attention of hunters and prospectors, who see so much in their wild journeys, is seldom attracted by moraines, however regular and artificial-looking; or rocks, however boldly sculptured; or cañons, however deep and sheer-walled. But when they come to these pavements, they go down on their knees and rub their hands admiringly on the glistening surface, and try hard to account for its mysterious smoothness and brightness. They may have seen the winter avalanches come down the mountains, through the woods, sweeping away the trees and scouring the ground; but they conclude that this cannot be the work of avalanches, because the striæ show that the agent, whatever it was, flowed along and around and over the top of high ridges and domes, and also filled the deep cañons. Neither can they see how water could be the agent, for the strange polish is found thousands of feet above the reach of any conceivable flood. Only the winds seem capable of moving over the face of the country in the directions indicated by the lines and grooves.

The pavements are particularly fine around Lake Tenaya, and have suggested the Indian name Py-we-ack, the Lake of the Shining Rocks. Indians seldom trouble themselves with geological questions, but a Mono Indian once came to me and asked if I could tell him what made the rocks so smooth at Tenaya. Even dogs and horses, on their first journeys into this region, study geology to the extent of gazing wonderingly at the strange brightness of the ground, and pawing it and smelling it, as if afraid of falling or sinking.

In the production of this admirable hard finish, the glaciers in many places exerted a pressure of more than a hundred tons to the square foot, planing down granite, slate, and quartz alike, showing their structure, and making beautiful mosaics where large feldspar crystals form the greater part of the rock. On such pavements the sunshine is at times dazzling, as if the surface were of burnished silver.

Here, also, are the brightest of the Sierra landscapes in general. The regions lying at the same elevation to the north and south were perhaps subjected to as long and intense a glaciation; but because the rocks are less resisting, their polished surfaces have mostly given way to the weather, leaving here and there only small imperfect patches on the most enduring portions of cañon walls protected from the action of rain and snow, and on hard bosses kept comparatively dry by boulders. The short, steeply inclined cañons of the east flank of the range are in some places brightly polished, but they are far less magnificent than those of the broad west flank.

One of the best general views of the middle region of the park is to be had from the top of a majestic dome which long ago I named the Glacier Monument. It is situated a few miles to the north of Cathedral Peak, and rises to a height of about fifteen hundred feet above its base and ten thousand above the sea. At first sight it seems sternly inaccessible, but a good climber will find that it may be scaled on the south side. Approaching it from this side you pass through a dense bryanthus-fringed grove of mountain hemlock, catching glimpses now and then of the colossal dome towering to an immense height above the dark evergreens; and when at last you have made your way across woods, wading through azalea and ledum thickets, you step abruptly out of the tree shadows and mossy leafy softness upon a bare porphyry pavement, and behold the dome unveiled in all its grandeur. Fancy a nicely proportioned monument, eight or ten feet high, hewn from one stone, standing in a pleasure ground; magnify it to a height of fifteen hundred feet, retaining its simplicity of form and fineness, and cover its surface with crystals; then you may gain an idea of the sublimity and beauty of this ice-burnished dome, one of many adorning this wonderful park.

In making the ascent, one finds that the curve of the base rapidly steepens, until one is in danger of slipping; but feldspar crystals, two or three inches long, that have been weathered into relief, afford slight footholds. The summit is in part burnished, like the sides and base, the striæ and scratches indicating that the mighty Tuolumne Glacier, two or three thousand feet deep, overwhelmed it while it stood firm like a boulder at the bottom of a river. The pressure it withstood must have been enormous. Had it been less solidly built, it would have been ground and crushed into moraine fragments, like the general mass of the mountain flank in which at first it lay imbedded; for it is only a hard residual knob or knot with a concentric structure of superior strength, brought into relief by the removal of the less resisting rock about it,—an illustration in stone of the survival of the strongest and most favorably situated.

Hardly less wonderful, when we contemplate the storms it has encountered since first it saw the light, is its present unwasted condition. The whole quantity of postglacial wear and tear it has suffered has not diminished its stature a single inch, as may be readily shown by measuring from the level of the unchanged polished portions of the surface. Indeed, the average postglacial denudation of the entire region, measured in the same way, is found to be less than two inches,—a mighty contrast to that of the ice; for the glacial denudation here has been not less than a mile; that is, in developing the present landscapes, an amount of rock a mile in average thickness has been silently carried away by flowing ice during the last glacial period.

A few erratic boulders nicely poised on the founded summit of the monument tell an interesting story. They came from a mountain on the crest of the range, about twelve miles to the eastward, floating like chips on the frozen sea, and were stranded here when the top of the monument emerged to the light of day, while the companions of these boulders, whose positions chanced to be over the slopes where they could not find rest, were carried farther on by the shallowing current.

The general view from the summit consists of a sublime assemblage of iceborn mountains and rocks and long wavering ridges, lakes and streams and meadows, moraines in wide-sweeping belts, and beds covered and dotted with forests and groves,—hundreds of square miles of them composed in wild harmony. The snowy mountains on the axis of the range, mostly sharp-peaked and crested, rise in a noble array along the sky to the eastward and northward; the gray-pillared Hoffman spur and the Yosemite domes and a countless number of others to the westward; Cathedral Peak with its many spires and companion peaks and domes to the southward; and a smooth billowy multitude of rocks, from fifty feet or less to a thousand feet high, which from their peculiar form seem to be rolling on westward, fill most of the middle ground. Immediately beneath you are the Big Tuolumne Meadows, with an ample swath of dark pine woods on either side, enlivened by the young river, that is seen sparkling and shimmering as it sways from side to side, tracing as best it can its broad glacial channel.

The ancient Tuolumne Glacier, lavishly flooded by many a noble affluent from the snow-laden flanks of Mounts Dana, Gibbs, Lyell, Maclure, and others nameless as yet, poured its majestic overflowing current, four or five miles wide, directly against the high outstanding mass of Mount Hoffman, which divided and deflected it right and left, just as a river is divided against an island that stands in the middle of its channel. Two distinct glaciers were thus formed, one of which flowed through the Big Tuolumne Cañon and Hetch-Hetchy Valley, while the other swept upward five hundred feet in a broad current across the divide between the basins of the Tuolumne and Merced into the Tenaya basin, and thence down through the Tenaya Cañon and Yosemite Valley.

The maplike distinctness and freshness of this glacial landscape cannot fail to excite the attention of every observer, no matter how little of its scientific significance he may at first recognize. These bald, glossy, westward-leaning rocks in the open middle ground, with their rounded backs and shoulders toward the glacier fountains of the summit mountains and their split angular fronts looking in the opposite direction, every one of them displaying the form of greatest strength with reference to physical structure and glacial action, show the tremendous force with which through unnumbered centuries the ice flood swept over them, and also the direction of the flow; while the mountains, with their sharp summits and abraded sides, indicate the height to which the glacier rose; and the moraines, curving and swaying in beautiful lines, mark the boundaries of the main trunk and its tributaries as they existed toward the close of the glacial winter. None of the commercial highways of the sea or land, marked with buoys and lamps, fences and guideboards, is so unmistakably indicated as are these channels of the vanished Tuolumne glaciers.

The action of flowing ice, whether in the form of river-like glaciers or broad mantling folds, is but little understood as compared with that of other sculpturing agents. Rivers work openly where people dwell, and so do the rain, and the sea thundering on all the shores of the world; and the universal ocean of air, through unseen, speaks aloud in a thousand voices and explains its modes of working and its power. But glaciers, back in their cold solitudes, work apart from men, exerting their tremendous energies in silence and darkness. Coming in vapor from the sea, flying invisible on the wind, descending in snow, changing to ice, white, spiritlike, they brood outspread over the predestined landscapes, working on unwearied through unmeasured ages, until in the fullness of time the mountains and valleys are brought forth, channels furrowed for the rivers, basins made for meadows and lakes, and soil beds spread for the forests and fields that man and beast may be fed. Then vanishing like clouds, they melt into streams and go singing back home to the sea.

To an observer upon this adamantine old monument in the midst of such scenery, getting glimpses of the thoughts of God, the day seems endless, the sun stands still. Much faithless fuss is made over the passage in the Bible telling of the standing still of the sun for Joshua. Here you may learn that the miracle occurs for every devout mountaineer, for everybody doing anything worth doing, seeing anything worth seeing. One day is as a thousand years, a thousand years as one day, and while yet in the flesh you enjoy immortality.

From the monument you will find an easy way down through the woods and along the Big Tuolumne Meadows to Mount Dana, the summit of which commands a grand telling view of the alpine region. The scenery all the way is inspiring, and you saunter on without knowing that you are climbing. The spacious sunny meadows, through the midst of which the bright river glides, extend with but little interruption ten miles to the eastward, dark woods rising on either side to the limit of tree growth, and above the woods a picturesque line of gray peaks and spires dotted with snow banks; while, on the axis of the Sierra, Mount Dana and his noble compeers repose in massive sublimity, their vast size and simple flowing contours contrasting in the most striking manner with the clustering spires and thin-pinnacled crests crisply outlined on the horizon to the north and south of them.

Tracing the silky lawns, gradually ascending, gazing at the sublime scenery more and more openly unfolded, noting the avalanche gaps in the upper forests, lingering over beds of blue gentians and purple-flowered bryanthus and cassiope, and dwarf willows an inch high in close-felted gray carpets, brightened here and there with kalmia and soft creeping mats of vaccinium sprinkled with pink bells that seem to have been showered down from the sky like hail,—thus beguiled and enchanted, you reach the base of the mountain wholly unconscious of the miles you have walked. And so on to the summit. For all the way up the long red slate slopes, that in the distance seemed barren, you find little garden beds and tufts of dwarf phlox, ivesia, and blue arctic daisies that go straight to your heart, blessed fellow mountaineers kept safe and warm by a thousand miracles. You are now more than thirteen thousand feet above the sea, and to the north and south you behold a sublime wilderness of mountains in glorious array, their snowy summits towering together in crowded, bewildering abundance, shoulder to shoulder, peak beyond peak. To the east lies the Great Basin, barren-looking and silent, apparently a land of pure desolation, rich only in beautiful light. Mono Lake, fourteen miles long, is outspread below you at a depth of nearly seven thousand feet, its shores of volcanic ashes and sand, treeless and sunburned; a group of volcanic cones, with well-formed, unwasted craters rises to the south of the lake; while up from its eastern shore innumerable mountains with soft flowing outlines extend range beyond range, gray, and pale purple, and blue,—the farthest gradually fading on the flowing horizon. Westward you look down and over the countless moraines, glacier meadows, and grand sea of domes and rock waves of the upper Tuolumne basin, the Cathedral and Hoffman mountains with their wavering lines and zones of forest, the wonderful region to the north of the Tuolumne Cañon, and across the dark belt of silver firs to the pale mountains of the coast.

In the icy fountains of the Mount Lyell and Ritter groups of peaks, to the south of Dana, three of the most important of the Sierra rivers—the Tuolumne, Merced, and San Joaquin—take their rise, their highest tributaries being within a few miles of one another as they rush forth on their adventurous courses from beneath snow banks and glaciers.

Of the small shrinking glaciers of the Sierra, remnants of the majestic system that sculptured the range, I have seen sixty-five. About twenty-five of them are in the park, and eight are in sight from Mount Dana.

The glacier lakes are sprinkled over all the alpine and subalpine regions, gleaming like eyes beneath heavy rock brows, tree-fringed or bare, embosomed in the woods, or lying in open basins with green and purple meadows around them; but the greater number are in the cool shadowy hollows of the summit mountains not far from the glaciers, the highest lying at an elevation of from eleven to nearly twelve thousand feet above the sea. The whole number in the

Sierra, not counting the smallest, can hardly be less than fifteen hundred, of which about two hundred and fifty are in the park. From one standpoint, on Red Mountain, I counted forty-two, most of them within a radius of ten miles. The glacier meadows, which are spread over the filled-up basins of vanished lakes and form one of the most charming features of the scenery, are still more numerous than the lakes.

An observer stationed here, in the glacial period, would have overlooked a wrinkled mantle of ice as continuous as that which now covers the continent of Greenland; and of all the vast landscape now shining in the sun, he would have seen only the tops of the summit peaks, rising darkly like storm-beaten islands, lifeless and hopeless, above rock-encumbered ice waves. If among the agents that nature has employed in making these mountains there be one that above all other deserves the name of Destroyer, it is the glacier. But we quickly learn that destruction is creation. During the dreary centuries through which the Sierra lay in darkness, crushed beneath the ice folds of the glacial winter, there was a steady invincible advance toward the warm life and beauty of to-day; and it is just where the glaciers crushed most destructively that the greatest amount of beauty is made manifest. But as these landscapes have succeeded the preglacial landscapes, so they in turn are giving place to others already planned and foreseen. The granite domes and pavements, apparently imperishable, we take as symbols of permanence, while these crumbling peaks, down whose frosty gullies avalanches are ever falling, are symbols of change and decay. Yet all alike, fast or slow, are surely vanishing away.

Nature is ever at work building and pulling down, creating and destroying, keeping everything whirling and flowing, allowing no rest but in rhythmical motion, chasing everything in endless song out of one beautiful form into another.

CHAPTER IV

The Forests of the Yosemite Park

The coniferous forests of the Yosemite Park, and of the Sierra in general, surpass all others of their kind in America or indeed in the world, not only in the size and beauty of the trees, but in the number of species assembled together, and the grandeur of the mountains they are growing on. Leaving the workaday lowlands, and wandering into the heart of the mountains, we find a new world, and stand beside the majestic pines and firs and sequoias silent and awe-stricken, as if in the presence of superior beings new arrived from some other star, so calm and bright and godlike they are.

Going to the woods is going home; for I suppose we came from the woods originally. But in some of nature's forests the adventurous traveler seems a feeble, unwelcome creature; wild beasts and the weather trying to kill him, the rank, tangled vegetation, armed with spears and stinging needles, barring his way and making life a hard struggle. Here everything is hospitable and kind, as if planned for your pleasure, ministering to every want of body and soul. Even the storms are friendly and seem to regard you as a brother, their beauty and tremendous fateful earnestness charming alike. But the weather is mostly sunshine, both winter and summer and the clear sunny brightness of the park is one of its most striking characteristics. Even the heaviest portions of the main forest belt, where the trees are tallest and stand closest, are not in the least gloomy. The sunshine falls in glory through the colossal spires and crowns, each a symbol of health and strength, the noble shafts faithfully upright like the pillars of temples, upholding a roof of infinite leafy interlacing arches and fretted skylights. The more open portions are like spacious parks, carpeted with small shrubs, or only with the fallen needles sprinkled here and there with flowers. In some places, where the ground is level or slopes gently, the trees are assembled in groves, and the flowers and underbrush in trim beds and thickets as in landscape gardens or the lovingly planted grounds of homes; or they are drawn up in orderly rows around meadows and lakes and along the brows of cañons. But in general the forests are distributed in wide belts in accordance with climate and the comparative strength of each kind in gaining and holding possession of the ground, while anything like monotonous uniformity is prevented by the grandly varied topography, and by the arrangement of the best soilbeds in intricate patterns like embroidery; for these soilbeds are the moraines of ancient glaciers more or less modified by weathering and stream action, and the trees trace them over the hills and ridges, and far up the sides of the mountains, rising with even growth on levels, and towering above one another on the long rich slopes prepared for them by the vanished glaciers.

Had the Sierra forests been cheaply accessible, the most valuable of them commercially would ere this have fallen a prey to the lumberman. Thus far the redwood of the Coast Mountains and the Douglas spruce of Oregon and Washington have been more available for lumber than the pine of the Sierra. It cost less to go a thousand miles up the coast for timber, where the trees came down to the shores of navigable rivers and bays, than fifty miles up the mountains. Nevertheless, the superior value of the sugar pine for many purposes has tempted capitalists to expend large sums on flumes and railroads to reach the best forests, though perhaps none of these enterprises has paid. Fortunately, the lately established system of parks and reservations has put a stop to any great extension of the business hereabouts in its most destructive forms. And as the Yosemite Park region has escaped the millmen, and the all-devouring hordes of hoofed locusts have been banished, it is still in the main a pure wilderness, unbroken by axe clearings except on the lower margin, where a few settlers have opened spots beside hay meadows for their cabins and gardens. But these are mere dots of cultivation, in no appreciable degree disturbing the grand solitude. Twenty or thirty years ago a good many trees were felled for their seeds; traces of this destructive method of seed-collecting are still visible along the trails; but these as well as the shingle-makers ruins are being rapidly overgrown, the gardens and beds of underbrush once devastated by sheep are blooming again in all their wild glory, and the park is a paradise that makes even the loss of Eden seem insignificant.

On the way to Yosemite Valley, you get some grand views over the forests of the Merced and Tuolumne basins and glimpses of some of the finest trees by the roadside without leaving your seat in the stage. But to learn how they live and behave in pure wildness, to see them in their varying aspects through the seasons and weather, rejoicing in the great storms, in the spiritual mountain light, putting forth their new leaves and flowers when all the streams are in flood and the birds are singing, and sending away their seeds in the thoughtful Indian summer when all the landscape is glowing in deep calm enthusiasm,—for this you must love them and live with them, as free from schemes and cares and time as the trees themselves.

And surely nobody will find anything hard in this. Even the blind must enjoy these woods, drinking their fragrance, listening to the music of the winds in their groves, and fingering their flowers and plumes and cones and richly furrowed boles. The kind of study required is as easy and natural as breathing. Without any great knowledge of botany or wood-craft, in a single season you may learn the name and something more of nearly every kind of tree in the park.

With few exceptions all the Sierra trees are growing in the park,—nine species of pine, two of silver fir, one each of Douglas spruce, libocedrus, hemlock, juniper, and sequoia,—sixteen conifers in all, and about the same number of round-headed trees, oaks, maples, poplars, laurel, alder, dogwood, tumion, etc.

The first of the conifers you meet in going up the range from the west is the digger nut-pine (Pinus Sabiniana), a remarkably open, airy, wide-branched tree, forty to sixty feet high, with long, sparse, grayish green foliage and large cones. At a height of fifteen to thirty feet from the ground the trunk usually divides into several main branches, which, after bearing away from one another, shoot straight up and form separate heads as if the axis of the tree had been broken, while the secondary branches divide again and again into rather slender sprays loosely tasseled, with leaves eight to twelve inches long. The yellow and purple flowers are about an inch long, the staminate in showy clusters. The big, rough, burly cones, five to eight or ten inches in length and five or six in diameter, are rich brown in color when ripe, and full of hard-shelled nuts that are greatly prized by Indians and squirrels. This strange-looking pine, enjoying hot sunshine like a palm, is sparsely distributed along the driest part of the Sierra among small oaks and chaparral, and with its gray mist of foliage, strong trunk and branches, and big cones seen in relief on the glowing sky, forms the most striking feature of the foothill vegetation.

Pinus attenuata is a small, slender, arrowy tree, with pale green leaves in threes, clustered flowers half an inch long, brownish yellow and crimson, and cones whorled in conspicuous clusters around the branches and also around the trunk. The cones never fall off or open until the tree dies. They are about four inches long, exceedingly strong and solid, and varnished with hard resin forming a waterproof and almost worm and squirrel proof package, in which the seeds are kept fresh and safe during the lifetime of the tree. Sometimes one of the trunk cones is overgrown and imbedded in the heart wood like a knot, but nearly all are pushed out and kept on the surface by the pressure of the successive layers of wood against the base.

This admirable little tree grows on brushy, sun-beaten slopes, which from their position and the inflammable character of the vegetation are most frequently fire-swept. These grounds it is able to hold against all comers, however big and strong, by saving its seeds until death, when all it has produced are scattered over the bare cleared ground, and a new generation quickly springs out of the ashes. Thus the curious fact that all the trees of extensive groves and belts are of the same age is accounted for, and their slender habit; for the lavish abundance of seed sown at the same time makes a crowded growth, and the seedlings with an even start rush up in a hurried race for light and life.

Only a few of the attenuata and Sabiniana pines are within the boundaries of the park, the former on the side of the Merced Cañon, the latter on the walls of Hetch-Hetchy Valley and in the cañon below it.

The nut-pine (Pinus monophylla) is a small, hardy, contended-looking tree, about fifteen or twenty feet high and a foot in diameter. In its youth the close radiating and aspiring branches form a handsome broad-based pyramid, but when fully grown it becomes round-topped, knotty, and irregular, throwing out crooked divergent limbs like an apple tree. The leaves are pale grayish green, about an inch and a half long, and instead of being divided into clusters they are single, round, sharp-pointed, and rigid like spikes, amid which in the spring the red flowers glow brightly. The cones are only about two inches in length and breadth, but nearly half of their bulk is made up of sweet nuts.

This fruitful little pine grows on the dry east side of the park, along the margin of the Mono sage plain, and is the commonest tree of the short mountain ranges of the Great Basins. Tens of thousands of acres are covered with it, forming bountiful orchards for the Red-man. Being so low and accessible, the cones are easily beaten off with poles, and the nuts procured by roasting until the scales open. To the tribes of the desert and sage plains these seeds are the staff of life. They are eaten either raw or parched, or in the form of mush or cakes after being pounded into meal. The time of nut harvest in the autumn is the Indian's merriest time of all the year. An industrious squirrelish family can gather fifty or sixty bushels in a single month before the snow comes, and then their bread for the winter is sure.

The white pine (Pinus flexilis) is widely distributed through the Rocky Mountains and the ranges of the Great Basin, where in many places it grows to a good size, and is an important timber tree where none better is to be found. In the park it is sparsely scattered along the eastern flank of the range from Mono Pass southward, above the nut-pine, at an elevation of from eight to ten thousand feet, dwarfing to a tangled bush near the timber-line, but under favorable conditions attaining a height of forty or fifty feet, with a diameter of three to five. The long branches show a tendency to sweep out in bold curves, like those of the mountain and sugar pines to which it is closely related. The needles are in clusters of five, closely packed on the ends of the branchlets. The cones are about five inches long,—the smaller ones nearly oval, the larger cylindrical. But the most interesting feature of the tree is its bloom, the vivid red pistillate flowers glowing among the leaves like coals of fire.

The dwarfed pine or white-barked pine (Pinus albicaulis) is sure to interest every observer on account of its curious low matted habit, and the great height on the snowy mountains at which it bravely grows. It forms the extreme edge of the timber-line on both flanks of the summit mountains—if so lowly a tree can be called timber—at an elevation of ten to twelve thousand feet above the level of the sea. Where it is first met on the lower limit of its range it may be thirty or forty feet high, but farther up the rocky wind-swept slopes, where the snow lies deep and heavy for six months of the year, it makes shaggy clumps and beds, crinkled and pressed flat, over which you can easily walk. Nevertheless in this crushed, down-pressed, felted condition it clings hardily to life, puts forth fresh leaves every spring on the ends of its tasseled branchlets, blooms bravely in the lashing blasts with abundance of gay red and purple flowers, matures its seeds in the short summers, and often outlives the favored giants of the sun lands far below. One of the trees that I examined was only about three feet high, with a stem six inches in diameter at the ground, and branches that spread out horizontally as if they had grown up against a ceiling; yet it was four hundred and twenty-six years old, and one of its supple branchlets, about an eighth of an inch in diameter inside the bark, was seventy-five years old, and so tough that I tied it into knots. At the age of this dwarf many of the sugar and yellow pines and sequoias are seven feet in diameter and over two hundred feet high.

In detached clumps never touched by fire the fallen needles of centuries of growth make fine elastic mattresses for the weary mountaineer, while the tasseled branchlets spread a roof over him, and the dead roots, half resin, usually found in abundance, make capital camp-fires, unquenchable in thickest storms of rain or snow. Seen from a distance the belts and patches darkening the mountain sides look like mosses on a roof, and bring to mind Dr. Johnson's remarks on the trees of Scotland. His guide, anxious for the honor of Mull, was still talking of its woods and pointing them out. "Sir," said Johnson, "I saw at Tobermory what they called a wood, which I unluckily took for heath. If you show me what I shall take for furze, it will be something."

The mountain pine (Pinus monticola) is far the largest of the Sierra tree mountaineers. Climbing nearly as high as the dwarf albicaulis, it is still a giant in size, bold and strong, standing erect on the storm-beaten peaks and ridges, tossing its cone-laden branches in the rough winds, living a thousand years, and reaching its greatest size—ninety to a hundred feet in height, six to eight in diameter—just where other trees, its companions, are dwarfed. But it is not able to endure burial in snow so long as the albicaulis and flexilis. Therefore, on the upper limit of its range it is found on slopes which, from their steepness or exposure, are least snowy. Its soft graceful beauty in youth, and its leaves, cones, and outsweeping feathery branches constantly remind you of the sugar pine, to which it is closely allied. An admirable tree, growing nobler in form and size the colder and balder the mountains about it.

The giants of the main forest in the favored middle region are the sequoia, sugar pine, yellow pine, libocedrus, Douglas spruce, and the two silver firs. The park sequoias are restricted to two small groves, a few miles apart, on the Tuolumne and Merced divide, about seventeen miles from Yosemite Valley. The Big Oak Flat road to the valley runs through the Tuolumne Grove, the Coulterville through the Merced. The more famous and better known Mariposa Grove, belonging to the state, lies near the southwest corner of the park, a few miles above Wawona.

The sugar pine (Pinus Lambertiana) is first met in the park in open, sunny, flowery woods, at an elevation of about thirty-five hundred feet above the sea, attains full development at a height between five and six thousand feet, and vanishes at the level of eight thousand feet. In many places, especially on the northern slopes of the main ridges between the rivers, it forms the bulk of the forest, but mostly it is intimately associated with its noble companions, above which it covers in glorious majesty on every hill, ridge, and plateau from one extremity of the range to the other, a distance of five hundred miles,—the largest, noblest, and most beautiful of all the seventy or eighty species of pine trees in the world, and of all the conifers second only to King Sequoia.

A good many are from two hundred to two hundred and twenty feet in height, with a diameter at four feet from the ground of six to eight feet, and occasionally a grand patriarch, seven or eight hundred years old, is found that is ten or even twelve feet in diameter and two hundred and forty feet high, with a magnificent crown seventy feet wide. David Douglas, who discovered "this most beautiful and immensely grand tree" in the fall of 1826 in southern Oregon, says that the largest of several that had been blown down, "at three feet from the ground was fifty-seven feet nine inches in circumference" (or fully eighteen feet in diameter); "at one hundred and thirty-four feet, seventeen feet five inches; extreme length, two hundred and forty-five feet." Probably for fifty-seven we should read thirty-seven for the base measurement, which would make it correspond with the other dimensions; for none of this species with anything like so great a girth has since been seen. A girth of even thirty feet is uncommon. A fallen specimen that I measured was nine feet three inches in diameter inside the bark at four feet from the ground, and six feet in diameter at a hundred feet from the ground. A comparatively young tree, three hundred and thirty years old, that had been cut down, measured seven feet across the stump, was three feet three inches in diameter at a height of one hundred and fifty feet, and two hundred and ten feet in length.

The trunk is a round, delicately tapered shaft with finely furrowed purplish-brown bark, usually free of limbs for a hundred feet or more. The top is furnished with long and comparatively slender branches, which sweep gracefully downward and outward, feathered with short tasseled branchlets, and divided only at the ends, forming a palmlike crown fifty to seventy-five feet wide, but without the monotonous uniformity of palm crowns or of the spires of most conifers. The old trees are as tellingly varied and picturesque as oaks. No two are alike, and we are tempted to stop and admire every one we come to, whether as it stands silent in the calm balsam-scented sunshine or waving in accord with enthusiastic storms. The leaves are about three or four inches long, in clusters of five, finely tempered, bright lively green, and radiant. The flowers are but little larger than those of the dwarf pine, and far less showy. The immense cylindrical cones, fifteen to twenty or even twenty-four inches long and three in diameter, hang singly or in clusters, like ornamental tassels, at the ends of the long branches, green, flushed with purple on the sunward side. Like those of almost all the pines they ripen in the autumn of the second season from the flower, and the seeds of all that have escaped the Indians, bears, and squirrels take wing and fly to their places. Then the cones become still more effective as ornaments, for by the spreading of the scales the diameter is nearly doubled, and the color changes to a rich brown. They remain on the tree the following winter and summer; therefore few fertile trees are ever found without them. Nor even after they fall is the beauty work of these grand cones done, for they make a fine show on the flowery, needle-strewn ground. The wood is pale yellow, fine in texture, and deliciously fragrant. The sugar, which gives name to the tree, exudes from the heart wood on wounds made by fire or the axe, and forms irregular crisp white candy-like masses. To the taste of most people it is as good as maple sugar, though it cannot be eaten in large quantities.

No traveler, whether a tree lover or not, will ever forget his first walk in a sugar-pine forest. The majestic crowns approaching one another make a glorious canopy, through the feathery arches of which the sunbeams pour, silvering the needles and gilding the stately columns and the ground into a scene of enchantment.

The yellow pine (Pinus ponderosa) is surpassed in size and nobleness of port only by its kingly companion. Full-grown trees in the main forest where it is associated with the sugar pine, are about one hundred and seventy-five feet high, with a diameter of five to six feet, though much larger specimens may easily be found. The largest I ever measured was little over eight feet in diameter four feet above the ground, and two hundred and twenty feet high. Where there is plenty of sunshine and other conditions are favorable, it is a massive symmetrical spire, formed of a strong straight shaft clad with innumerable branches, which are divided again and again into stout branchlets laden with bright shining needles and green or purple cones. Where the growth is at all close half or more of the trunk is branchless. The species attains its greatest size and most majestic form in open groves on the deep, well-drained soil of lake basins at an elevation of about four thousand feet. There nearly all the old trees are over two hundred feet high, and the heavy, leafy, much-divided branches sumptuously clothe the trunk almost to the ground. Such trees are easily climbed, and in going up the winding stairs of knotty limbs to the top you will gain a most telling and memorable idea of the height, the richness and intricacy of the branches, and the marvelous abundance and beauty of the long shining elastic foliage. In tranquil weather, you will see the firm outstanding needles in calm content, shimmering and throwing off keen minute rays of light like lances of ice; but when heavy winds are blowing, the strong towers bend and wave in the blast with eager wide-awake enthusiasm, and every tree in the grove glows and flashes in one mass of white sunfire.

Both the yellow and sugar pines grow rapidly on good soil where they are not crowded. At the age of a hundred years they are about two feet in diameter and a hundred or more high. They are then very handsome, though very unlike: the sugar pine, lithe, feathery, closely clad with ascending branches; the yellow, open, showing its axis from the ground to the top, its whorled branches but little divided as yet, spreading and turning up at the ends with magnificent tassels of long stout bright needles, the terminal shoot with its leaves being often three or four feet long and a foot and a half wide, the most hopeful looking and the handsomest tree-top in the woods. But instead of increasing, like its companion, in wildness and individuality of form with age, it becomes more evenly and compactly spiry. The bark is usually very thick, four to six inches at the ground and arranged in large plates, some of them on the lower part of the trunk four or five feet long and twelve to eighteen inches wide, forming a strong defense against fire. The leaves are in threes, and from three inches to a foot long. The flowers appear in May: the staminate pink or brown, in conspicuous clusters two or three inches wide; the pistillate crimson, a fourth of an inch wide, and mostly hidden among the leaves on the tips of the branchlets. The cones vary from about three to ten inches in length, two to five in width, and grow in sessile outstanding clusters near the ends of the upturned branchlets.

Being able to endure fire and hunger and many climates this grand tree is widely distributed: eastward from the coast across the broad Rocky Mountain ranges to the Black Hills of Dakota, a distance of more than a thousand miles, and southward from British Columbia, near latitude 51°, to Mexico, about fifteen hundred miles. South of the Columbia River it meets the sugar pine, and accompanies it all the way down along the Coast and Cascade mountains and the Sierra and southern ranges to the mountains of the peninsula of Lower California, where they find their southmost homes together. Pinus ponderosa is extremely variable, and much bother it gives botanists who try to catch and confine the unmanageable proteus in two or a dozen species,—Jeffreyi, deflexa, Apacheca latifolia, etc. But in all its wanderings, in every form, it manifests noble strength. Clad in thick bark like a warrior in mail, it extends its bright ranks over all the high ranges of the wild side of the continent: flourishes in the drenching fog and rain of the northern coast at the level of the sea, in the snow-laden blasts of the mountains, and the white glaring sunshine of the interior plateaus and plains, on the borders of mirage-haunted deserts, volcanoes, and lava beds, waving its bright plumes in hot winds undaunted, blooming every year for centuries, and tossing big ripe cones among the cinders and ashes of nature's hearths.

The Douglas spruce grows with the great pines, especially on the cool north sides of ridges and cañons, and is here nearly as large as the yellow pine, but less abundant. The wood is strong and tough, the bark thick and deeply furrowed, and on vigorous, quick-growing trees the stout, spreading branches are covered with innumerable slender, swaying sprays, handsomely clothed with short leaves. The flowers are about three fourths of an inch in length, red or greenish, not so showy as the pendulous bracted cones. But in June and July, when the young bright yellow leaves appear, the entire tree seems to be covered with bloom.

It is this grand tree that forms the famous forests of western Oregon, Washington, and the adjacent coast regions of British Columbia, where it attains its greatest size and is most abundant, making almost pure forests over thousands of square miles, dark and close and almost inaccessible, many of the trees towering with straight, imperceptibly tapered shafts to a height of three hundred feet, their heads together shutting out the light,—one of the largest, most widely distributed, and most important of all the Western giant.

The incense cedar (Libocedrus decurrens), when full grown, is a magnificent tree, one hundred and twenty to nearly two hundred feet high, five to eight and occasionally twelve feet in diameter, with cinnamon-colored bark and warm yellow-green foliage, and in general appearance like an arbor vitæ. It is distributed through the main forest from an elevation of three to six thousand feet, and in sheltered portions of cañons on the warm sides to seven thousand five hundred. In midwinter, when most trees are asleep, it puts forth its flowers. The pistillate are pale green and inconspicuous; but the staminate are yellow, about one fourth of an inch long, and are produced in myriads, tingeing all the branches with gold, and making the tree as it stands in the snow look like a gigantic goldenrod. Though scattered rather sparsely amongst its companions in the open woods, it is seldom out of sight, and its bright brown shafts and warm masses of plumy foliage make a striking feature of the landscape. While young and growing fast in an open situation no other tree of its size in the park forms so exactly tapered a pyramid. The branches, outspread in flat plumes and beautifully fronded, sweep gracefully downward and outward, except those near the top, which aspire; the lowest droop to the ground, overlapping one another, shedding off rain and snow, and making fine tents for storm-bound mountaineers and birds. In old age it becomes irregular and picturesque, mostly from accidents: running fires, heavy wet snow breaking the branches, lightning shattering the top, compelling it to try to make new summits out of side branches, etc. Still it frequently lives more than a thousand years, invincibly beautiful, and worthy its place beside the Douglas spruce and the great pines.

This unrivaled forest is still further enriched by two majestic silver firs, Abies magnifica and Abies concolor, bands of which come down from the main fir belt by cool shady ridges and glens. Abies magnifica is the noblest of its race, growing on moraines, at an elevation of seven thousand to eight thousand five hundred feet above the sea, to a height of two hundred or two hundred and fifty feet, and five to seven in diameter; and with these noble dimensions there is a richness and symmetry and perfection of finish not to be found in any other tree in the Sierra. The branches are whorled, in fives mostly, and stand out from the straight red purple bole in level or, on old trees, in drooping collars, every branch regularly pinnated like fern fronds, and clad with silvery needles, making broad plumes singularly rich and sumptuous.

The flowers are in their prime about the middle of June: the staminate red, growing on the underside of the branchlets in crowded profusion, giving a rich color to nearly all the tree; the pistillate greenish yellow tinged with pink, standing erect on the upper side of the topmost branches; while the tufts of young leaves, about as brightly colored as those of the Douglas spruce, push out their fragrant brown buds a few weeks later, making another grand show.

The cones mature in a single season from the flowers. When full grown they are about six to eight inches long, three or four in diameter, blunt, massive, cylindrical, greenish gray in color, covered with a fine silvery down, and beaded with transparent balsam, very rich and precious-looking, standing erect like casks on the topmost branches. If possible, the inside of the cone is still more beautiful. The scales and bracts are tinged with red, and the seed wings are purple with bright iridescence.

Abies concolor, the white silver fir, grows best about two thousand feet lower than the magnifica. It is nearly as large, but the branches are less regularly pinnated and whorled, the leaves are longer, and instead of standing out around the branchlets or turning up and clasping them they are mostly arranged in two horizontal or ascending rows, and the cones are less than half as large. The bark of the magnifica is reddish purple and closely furrowed, that of the concolor is gray and widely furrowed,—a noble pair, rivaled only by the Abies grandis, amabilis, and nobilis of the forests of Oregon, Washington, and the Northern California Coast Range. But none of these northern species form pure forests that in extent and beauty approach those of the Sierra.

The seeds of the conifers are curiously formed and colored, white, brown, purple, plain or spotted like birds eggs, and expecting the juniper they are all handsomely and ingeniously winged with reference to their distribution. They are a sort of cunningly devised flying machines,—one-winged birds, birds with but one feather,—and they take but one flight, all save those which, after flying from the cone-nest in calm weather, chance to alight on branches where they have to wait for a wind. And though these seed wings are intended for only a moment's use, they are as thoughtfully colored and fashioned as the wings of birds, and require from one to two seasons to grow. Those of the pine, fir, hemlock, and spruce are curved in such manner that, in being dragged through the air by the seeds, they are made to revolve, whirling the seeds in a close spiral, and sustaining them long enough to allow the winds to carry them to considerable distances,—a style of flying full of quick merry motion, strikingly contrasted to the sober dignified sailing of seeds on tufts of feathery pappus. Surely no merrier adventurers ever set out to seek their fortunes. Only in the fir woods are large flocks seen; for, unlike the cones of the pine, spruce, hemlock, etc., which let the seeds escape slowly, one or two at a time, by spreading the scales, the fir cones when ripe fall to pieces, and let nearly all go at once in favorable weather. All along the Sierra for hundreds of miles, on dry breezy autumn days, the sunny spaces in the woods among the colossal spires are in a whirl with these shining purplewinged wanderers, notwithstanding the harvesting squirrels have been working at the top of their speed for weeks trying to cut off every cone before the seeds were ready to swarm and fly. Sequoia seeds have flat wings, and glint and glance in their flight like a boy's kite. The dispersal of juniper seeds is effected by the plum and cherry plan of hiring birds at the cost of their board, and thus obtaining the use of a pair of extra good wings.

Above the great fir belt, and below the ragged beds and fringes of the dwarf pine, stretch the broad dark forests of Pinus contorta, var. Murrayana, usually called tamarack pine. On broad fields of moraine material it forms nearly pure forests at an elevation of about eight or nine thousand feet above the sea, where it is a small, well proportioned tree, fifty or sixty feet high and one or two in diameter, with thin gray bark, crooked much-divided straggling branches, short needles in clusters of two, bright yellow and crimson flowers, and small prickly cones. The very largest I ever measured was ninety feet in height, and a little over six feet in diameter four feet above the ground. On moist well-drained soil in sheltered hollows along streamsides it grows tall and slender with ascending branches, making graceful arrowy spires fifty to seventy-five feet high, with stems only five or six inches thick.

The most extensive forest of this pine in the park lies to the north of the Big Tuolumne Meadows,—a famous deer pasture and hunting ground of the Mono Indians. For miles over wide moraine beds there is an even, nearly pure growth, broken only by glacier meadows, around which the trees stand in trim array, their sharp spires showing to fine advantage both in green flowery summer and white winter. On account of the closeness of its growth in many places, and the thinness and gumminess of its bark, it is easily killed by running fires, which work wide-spread destruction in its ranks; but a new generation rises quickly from the ashes, for all or a part of its seeds are held in reserve for a year or two or many years, and when the tree is killed the cones open and the seeds are scattered over the burned ground like those of the attenuata.

Next to the mountain hemlock and the dwarf pine this species best endures burial in heavy snow, while in braving hunger and cold on rocky ridgetops it is not surpassed by any. It is distributed from Alaska to Southern California, and inland across the Rocky Mountains, taking many forms in accordance with demands of climate, soil, rivals, and enemies; growing patiently in bogs and on sand dunes beside the sea where it is pelted with salt scud, on high snowy mountains and down in the throats of extinct volcanoes; springing up with invincible vigor after every devastating fire and extending its conquests farther.

The sturdy storm-enduring red cedar (Juniperus occidentalis) delights to dwell on the tops of granite domes and ridges and glacier pavements of the upper pine belt, at an elevation of seven to ten thousand feet, where it can get plenty of sunshine and snow and elbow-room without encountering quick-growing overshadowing rivals. They never make anything like a forest, seldom come together even in groves, but stand out separate and independent in the wind, clinging by slight joints to the rock, living chiefly on snow and thin air, and maintaining tough health on this diet for two thousand years or more, every feature and gesture expressing steadfast dogged endurance. The largest are usually about six or eight feet in diameter, and fifteen or twenty in height. A very few are ten feet in diameter, and on isolated moraine heaps forty to sixty feet in height. Many are mere stumps, as broad as high, broken by avalanches and lightning, picturesquely tufted with dense gray scalelike foliage, and giving no hint of dying. The staminate flowers are like those of the libocedrus, but smaller; the pistillate are inconspicuous. The wood is red, fine-grained, and fragrant; the bark bright cinnamon and red, and in thrifty trees is strikingly braided and reticulated, flaking off in thin lustrous ribbons, which the Indians used to weave into matting and coarse cloth. These brown unshakable pillars, standing solitary on polished pavements with bossy masses of foliage in their arms, are exceedingly picturesque, and never fail to catch the eye of the artist. They seem sole survivors of some ancient race, wholly unacquainted with their neighbors.

I have spent a good deal of time, trying to determine their age, but on account of dry rot which honeycombs most of the old ones, I never got a complete count of the largest. Some are undoubtedly more than two thousand years old; for though on good moraine soil they grow about as fast as oaks, on bare pavements and smoothly glaciated overswept granite ridges in the dome region they grow extremely slowly. One on the Starr King ridge, only two feet eleven inches in diameter, was eleven hundred and forty years old. Another on the same ridge, only one foot seven and a half inches in diameter, had reached the age of eight hundred and thirty-four years. The first fifteen inches from the bark of a medium-sized tree—six feet in diameter—on the north Tenaya pavement had eight hundred and fifty-nine layers of wood, or fifty-seven to the inch. Beyond this the count was stopped by dry rot and scars of old wounds. The largest I examined was thirty-three feet in girth, or nearly ten in diameter; and though I failed to get anything like a complete count, I learned enough from this and many other specimens to convince me that most of the trees eight to ten feet thick standing on pavements are more than twenty centuries of age rather than less. Barring accidents, for all I can see, they would live forever. When killed, they waste out of existence about as slowly as granite. Even when overthrown by avalanches, after standing so long, they refuse to lie at rest, leaning stubbornly on their big elbows as if anxious to rise, and while a single root holds to the rock putting forth fresh leaves with a grim never-say-die and never-lie-down expression.

As the juniper is the most stubborn and unshakable of trees, the mountain hemlock (Tsuga Mertensiana) is the most graceful and pliant and sensitive, responding to the slightest touches of the wind. Until it reaches a height of fifty or sixty feet it is sumptuously clothed down to the ground with drooping branches, which are divided into countless delicate waving sprays, grouped and arranged in most indescribably beautiful ways, and profusely sprinkled with handsome brown cones. The flowers also are peculiarly beautiful and effective; the pistillate very dark rich purple; the staminate blue of so fine and pure a tone that the best azure of the high sky seems to be condensed in them.

Though apparently the most delicate and feminine of all the mountain trees, it grows best where the snow lies deepest, at an elevation of from nine thousand to nine thousand five hundred feet, in hollows on the northern slopes of mountains and ridges. But under all circumstances and conditions of weather and soil, sheltered from the main currents of the winds or in blank exposure to them, well fed or starved, it is always singularly graceful in habit. Even at its highest limit in the park, ten thousand five hundred feet above the sea on exposed ridgetops, where it crouches and huddles close together in low thickets like those of the dwarf pine, it still contrives to put forth its sprays and branches in forms of irrepressible beauty, while on moist well-drained moraines it displays a perfectly tropical luxuriance of foliage, flower, and fruit.

In the first winter storms the snow is oftentimes soft, and lodges in the dense leafy branches, pressing them down against the trunk, and the slender drooping axis bends lower and lower as the load increases, until the top touches the ground and an ornamental arch is made. Then, as storm succeeds storm and snow is heaped on snow, the whole tree is at last buried, not again to see the light or move leaf or limb until set free by the spring thaws in June or July. Not the young saplings only are thus carefully covered and put to sleep in the whitest of white beds for five or six months of the year, but trees thirty and forty feet high. From April to May, then the snow is compacted, you may ride over the prostrate groves without seeing a single branch or leaf of them. In the autumn they are full of merry life, when Clark crows, squirrels, and chipmunks are gathering the abundant crop of seeds while the deer rest beneath the thick concealing branches. The finest grove in the park is near Mount Conness, and the trail from the Tuolumne soda springs to the mountain runs through it. Many of the trees in this grove are three to four or five feet in diameter and about a hundred feet high.

The mountain hemlock is widely distributed from near the south extremity of the high Sierra northward along the Cascade Mountains of Oregon and Washington and the coast ranges of British Columbia to Alaska, where it was first discovered in 1827. Its northmost limit, so far as I have observed, is in the icy fiords of Prince William's Sound in latitude 61°, where it forms pure forests at the level of the sea, growing tall and majestic on the banks of the great glaciers, waving in accord with the mountain winds and the thunder of the falling icebergs. Here as in the Sierra it is ineffably beautiful, the very loveliest evergreen in America.

Of the round-headed dicotyledonous trees in the park the most influential are the black and goldcup oaks. They occur in some parts of the main forest belt, scattered among the big pines like a heavier chaparral, but form extensive groves and reach perfect development only in the Yosemite valleys and flats of the main cañons. The California black oak (Quercus Californica) is one of the largest and most beautiful of the Western oaks, attaining under favorable conditions a height of sixty to a hundred feet, with a trunk three to seven feet in diameter, wide-spreading picturesque branches, and smooth lively green foliage handsomely scalloped, purple in the spring, yellow and red in autumn. It grows best in sunny open groves on ground covered with ferns, chokecherry, brier rose, rubus, mints, goldenrods, etc. Few, if any, of the famous oak groves of Europe, however extensive, surpass these in the size and strength and bright, airy beauty of the trees, the color and fragrance of the vegetation beneath them, the quality of the light that fills their leafy arches, and in the grandeur of the surrounding scenery. The finest grove in the park is in one of the little Yosemite valleys of the Tuolumne Cañon, a few miles above Hetch-Hetchy.

The mountain live-oak, or goldcup oak (Quercus chrysolepis), forms extensive groves on earthquake and avalanche taluses and terraces in cañons and Yosemite valleys, from about three to five thousand feet above the sea. In tough, sturdy, unwedgeable strength this is the oak of oaks. In general appearance it resembles the great live-oak of the Southern states. It has pale gray dark, a short, uneven, heavily buttressed trunk which usually divides a few feet above the ground into strong wide-reaching limbs, forming noble arches, and ending in an intricate maze of small branches and sprays, the outer ones frequently drooping in long tresses to the ground like those of the weeping willow, covered with small simple polished leaves, making a canopy broad and bossy, on which the sunshine falls in glorious brightness. The acorn cups are shallow, thick-walled, and covered with yellow fuzzy dust. The flowers appear in May and June with a profusion of pollened tresses, followed by the bronze-colored young leaves.

No tree in the park is a better measure of altitude. In cañons, at an elevation of four thousand, feet you may easily find a tree six or eight feet in diameter; and at the head of a side cañon, three thousand feet higher, up which you can climb in less than two hours, you find the knotty giant dwarfed to a slender shrub, with leaves like those of huckleberry bushes, still bearing acorns, and seemingly contented, forming dense patches of chaparral, on the top of which you may make your bed and sleep softly like a Highlander in heather. About a thousand feet higher it is still smaller, making fringes about a foot high around boulders and along seams in pavements and the brows of cañons, giving hand-holds here and there on cliffs hard to climb. The largest I have measured were from twenty-five to twenty-seven feet in girth, fifty to sixty feet high, and the spread of the limbs was about double the height.

The principal riverside trees are poplar, alder, willow, broad-leaved maple, and Nuttall's flowering dogwood. The poplar (Populus trichocarpa), often called balm of Gilead from the gum on its buds, is a tall, stately tree, towering above its companions and gracefully embowering the banks of the main streams at an elevation of about four thousand feet. Its abundant foliage turns bright yellow in the fall, and the Indian-summer sunshine sifts through it in delightful tones over the slow-gliding waters when they are at their lowest ebb.

The flowering dogwood is brighter still in these brooding days, for every branch of its broad head is then a brilliant crimson flame. In the spring, when the streams are in flood, it is the whitest of trees, white as a snow bank with its magnificent flowers four to eight inches in width, making a wonderful show, and drawing swarms of moths and butterflies.

The broad-leaved maple is usually found in the coolest boulder-choked cañons, where the streams are gray and white with foam, over which it spreads its branches in beautiful arches from bank to bank, forming leafy tunnels full of soft green light and spray,—favorite homes of the water ousel. Around the glacier lakes, two or three thousand feet higher, the common aspen grows in fringing lines and groves which are brilliantly colored in autumn, reminding you of the color glory of the Eastern woods.

Scattered here and there or in groves the botanist will find a few other trees, mostly small,—the mountain mahogany, cherry, chestnut-oak, laurel, and nutmeg. The California nutmeg (Tumion Californicum) is a handsome evergreen, belonging to the yew family, with pale bark, prickly leaves, fruit like a green-gage plum, and seed like a nutmeg. One of the best groves of it in the park is at the Cascades below Yosemite.

But the noble oaks and all these rock-shading, stream-embowering trees are as nothing amid the vast abounding billowy forests of conifers. During my first years in the Sierra I was ever calling on everybody within reach to admire them, but I found no one half warm enough until Emerson came. I had read his essays, and felt sure that of all men he would best interpret the sayings of these noble mountains and trees. Nor was my faith weakened when I met him in Yosemite. He seemed as serene as a sequoia, his head in the empyrean; and forgetting his age, plans, duties, ties of every sort, I proposed an immeasurable camping trip back in the heart of the mountains. He seemed anxious to go, but considerately mentioned his party. I said: "Never mind. The mountains are calling; run away, and let plans and parties and dragging lowland duties all 'gang tapsal-teerie'. We'll go up a cañon singing your own song, 'Good-by, proud world! I'm going home,' in divine earnest. Up there lies a new heaven and a new earth; let us go to the show." But alas, it was too late,—too near the sundown of his life. The shadows were growing long, and he leaned on his friends. His party, full of indoor philosophy, failed to see the natural beauty and fullness of promise of my wild plan, and laughed at it in good-natured ignorance, as if it were necessarily amusing to imagine that Boston people might be led to accept Sierra manifestations of God at the price of rough camping. Anyhow, they would have none of it, and held Mr. Emerson to the hotels and trails.

After spending only five tourist days in Yosemite he was led away, but I saw him two days more; for I was kindly invited to go with the party as far as the Mariposa big trees. I told Mr. Emerson that I would gladly go to the sequoias with him, if he would camp in the grove. He consented heartily, and I felt sure that we would have at least one good wild memorable night around a sequoia camp-fire. Next day we rode through the magnificent forests of the Merced basin, and I kept calling his attention to the sugar pines, quoting his wood-notes, "Come listen what the pine tree saith," etc., pointing out the noblest as kings and high priests, the most eloquent and commanding preachers of all the mountain forests, stretching forth their century-old arms in benediction over the worshiping congregations crowded about them. He gazed in devout admiration, saying but little, while his fine smile faded away.

Early in the afternoon, when we reached Clark's Station, I was surprised to see the party dismount. And when I asked if we were not going up into the grove to camp they said: "No; it would never do to lie out in the night air. Mr. Emerson might take cold; and you know, Mr. Muir, that would be a dreadful thing." In vain I urged, that only in homes and hotels were colds caught, that nobody ever was known to take cold camping in these woods, that there was not a single cough or sneeze in all the Sierra. Then I pictured the big climate-changing, inspiring fire I would make, praised the beauty and fragrance of sequoia flame, told how the great trees would stand about us transfigured in the purple light, while the stars looked down between the great domes; ending by urging them to come on and make an immortal Emerson night of it. But the house habit was not to be overcome, nor the strange dread of pure night air, though it is only cooled day air with a little dew in it. So the carpet dust and unknowable reeks were preferred. And to think of this being a Boston choice! Sad commentary on culture and the glorious transcendentalism.

Accustomed to reach whatever place I started for, I was going up the mountain alone to camp, and wait the coming of the party next day. But since Emerson was so soon to vanish, I concluded to stop with him. He hardly spoke a word all the evening, yet it was a great pleasure simply to be near him, warming in the light of his face as at a fire. In the morning we rode up the trail through a noble forest of pine and fir into the famous Mariposa Grove, and stayed an hour or two, mostly in ordinary tourist fashion,—looking at the biggest giants, measuring them with a tape line, riding through prostrate fire-bored trunks, etc., though Mr. Emerson was alone occasionally, sauntering about as if under a spell. As we walked through a fine group, he quoted, "There were giants in those days," recognizing the antiquity of the race. To commemorate his visit, Mr. Galen Clark, the guardian of the grove, selected the finest of the unnamed trees and requested him to give it a name. He named it Samoset, after the New England sachem, as the best that occurred to him.

The poor bit of measured time was soon spent, and while the saddles were being adjusted I again urged Emerson to stay. "You are yourself a sequoia," I said. "Stop and get acquainted with your big brethren." But he was past his prime, and was now as a child in the hands of his affectionate but sadly civilized friends, who seemed as full of old-fashioned conformity as of bold intellectual independence. It was the afternoon of the day and the afternoon of his life, and his course was now westward down all the mountains into the sunset. The party mounted and rode away in wondrous contentment, apparently, tracing the trail through ceanothus and dogwood bushes, around the bases of the big trees, up the slope of the sequoia basin, and over the divide. I followed to the edge of the grove. Emerson lingered in the rear of the train, and when he reached the top of the ridge, after all the rest of the party were over and out of sight, he turned his horse, took off his hat and waved me a last good-by. I felt lonely, so sure had I been that Emerson of all men would be the quickest to see the mountains and sing them. Gazing awhile on the spot where he vanished, I sauntered back into the heart of the grove, made a bed of sequoia plumes and ferns by the side of a stream, gathered a store of firewood, and then walked about until sundown. The birds, robins, thrushes, warblers, etc., that had kept out of sight, came about me, now that all was quiet, and made cheer. After sundown I built a great fire, and as usual had it all to myself. And though lonesome for the first time in these forests, I quickly took heart again,—the trees had not gone to Boston, nor the birds; and as I sat by the fire, Emerson was still with me in spirit, though I never again saw him in the flesh. He sent books and wrote, cheering me on; advised me not to stay too long in solitude. Soon he hoped that my guardian angel would intimate that my probation was at a close. Then I was to roll up my herbariums, sketches, and poems (though I never knew I had any poems), and come to his house; and when I tired of him and his humble surroundings, he would show me to better people.

But there remained many a forest to wander through, many a mountain and glacier to cross, before I was to see his Wachusett and Monadnock, Boston and Concord. It was seventeen years after our parting on the Wawona ridge that I stood beside his grave under a pine tree on the hill above Sleepy Hollow. He had gone to higher Sierras, and, as I fancied, was again waving his hand in friendly recognition.

CHAPTER V

The Wild Gardens of the Yosemite Park

When California was wild, it was the floweriest part of the continent. And perhaps it is so still, notwithstanding the lowland flora has in great part vanished before the farmers' flocks and ploughs. So exuberant was the bloom of the main valley of the state, it would still have been extravagantly rich had ninety-nine out of every hundred of its crowded flowers been taken away,—far flowerier than the beautiful prairies of Illinois and Wisconsin, or the savannas of the Southern states. In the early spring it was a smooth, evenly planted sheet of purple and gold, one mass of bloom more than four hundred miles long, with scarce a green leaf in sight.

Still more interesting is the rich and wonderfully varied flora of the mountains. Going up the Sierra across the Yosemite Park to the Summit peaks, thirteen thousand feet high, you find as much variety in the vegetation as in the scenery. Change succeeds change with bewildering rapidity, for in a few days you pass through as many climates and floras, ranged one above another, as you would in walking along the lowlands to the Arctic Ocean.

And to the variety due to climate there is added that caused by the topographical features of the different regions. Again, the vegetation is profoundly varied by the peculiar distribution of the soil and moisture. Broad and deep moraines, ancient and well weathered, are spread over the lower regions, rough and comparatively recent and unweathered moraines over the middle and upper regions, alternating with bare ridges and domes and glacier-polished pavements, the highest in the icy recesses of the peaks, raw and shifting, some of them being still in process of formation, and of course scarcely planted as yet.

Besides these main soilbeds there are many others comparatively small, reformation of both glacial and weather soils, sifted, sorted out, and deposited by running water and the wind on gentle slopes and in all sorts of hollows, potholes, valleys, lake basins, etc.,—some in dry and breezy situations, others sheltered and kept moist by lakes, streams, and waftings of waterfall spray, making comfortable homes for plants widely varied. In general, glaciers give soil to high and low places almost alike, while water currents are dispensers of special blessings, constantly tending to make the ridges poorer and the valleys richer. Glaciers mingle all kinds of material together, mud particles and boulders fifty feet in diameter: water, whether in oozing currents or passionate torrents, discriminates both in the size and shape of the material it carries. Glacier mud is the finest meal ground for any use in the Park, and its transportation into lakes and as foundations for flowery garden meadows was the first work that the young rivers were called on to do. Bogs occur only in shallow alpine basins where the climate is cool enough for sphagnum, and where the surrounding topographical conditions are such that they are safe, even in the most copious rains and thaws, from the action of flood currents capable of carrying rough gravel and sand, but where the water supply is nevertheless constant. The mosses dying from year to year gradually give rise to those rich spongy peat-beds in which so many of our best alpine plants delight to dwell. The strong winds that occasionally sweep the high Sierra play a more important part in the distribution of special soil-beds than is at first sight recognized, carrying forward considerable quantities of sand gravel, flakes of mica, etc., and depositing them in fields and beds beautifully ruffled and embroidered and adapted to the wants of some of the hardiest and handsomest of the alpine shrubs and flowers. The more resisting of the smooth, solid, glacier-polished domes and ridges can hardly be said to have any soil at all, while others beginning to give way to the weather are thinly sprinkled with coarse angular gravel. Some of them are full of crystals, which as the surface of the rock is decomposed are set free, covering the summits and rolling down the sides in minute avalanches, giving rise to zones and beds of crystalline soil. In some instances the various crystals occur only here and there, sprinkled in the gray gravel like daisies in a sod; but in others half or more is made up of crystals, and the glow of the imbedded or loosely strewn gems and their colored gleams and glintings at different times of the day when the sun is shining might well exhilarate the flowers that grow among them, and console them for being so completely outshone.

These radiant sheets and belts and dome-encircling rings of crystals are the most beautiful of all the Sierra soil-beds, while the huge taluses ranged along the walls of the great cañons are the deepest and roughest. Instead of being slowly weathered and accumulated from the cliffs overhead like common taluses, they were all formed suddenly and simultaneously by an earthquake that occurred at least three centuries ago. Though thus hurled into existence at a single effort, they are the least changeable and destructible of all the soil formations in the range. Excepting those which were launched directly into the channels of rivers, scarcely one of their wedged and interlocked boulders has been moved since the day of their creation, and though mostly made up of huge angular blocks of granite, many of them from ten to fifty feet cube, trees and shrubs make out to live and thrive on them, and even delicate herbaceous plants,—draperia, collomia, zauschneria, etc.,—soothing their rugged features with gardens and groves. In general views of the Park scarce a hint is given of its floral wealth. Only by patiently, lovingly sauntering about in it will you discover that it is all more or less flowery, the forests as well as the open spaces, and the mountain tops and rugged slopes around the glaciers as well as the sunny meadows.

Even the majestic cañon cliffs, seemingly absolutely flawless for thousands of feet and necessarily doomed to eternal sterility, are cheered with happy flowers on invisible niches and ledges wherever the slightest grip for a root can be found; as if Nature, like an enthusiastic gardener, could not resist the temptation to plant flowers everywhere. On high, dry rocky summits and plateaus, most of the plants are so small they make but little show even when in bloom. But in the opener parts of the main forests, the meadows, stream banks, and the level floors of Yosemite valleys the vegetation is exceedingly rich in flowers, some of the lilies and larkspurs being from eight to ten feet high. And on the upper meadows there are miles of blue gentians and daisies, white and blue violets; and great breadths of rosy purple heathworts covering rocky moraines with a marvelous abundance of bloom, enlivened by humming-birds, butterflies and a host of other insects as beautiful as flowers. In the lower and middle regions, also, many of the most extensive beds of bloom are in great part made by shrubs,—adenostoma, manzanita, ceanothus, chamæbatia, cherry, rose, rubus, spiræa, shad, laurel, azalea, honeysuckle, calycanthus, ribes, philadelphus, and many others, the sunny spaces about them bright and fragrant with mints, lupines, geraniums, lilies, daisies, goldenrods, castilleias, gilias, pentstemons, etc.

Adenostoma fasciculatum is a handsome, hardy, heathlike shrub belonging to the rose family, flourishing on dry ground below the pine belt, and often covering areas of twenty or thirty square miles of rolling sun-beaten hills and dales with a dense, dark green, almost impenetrable chaparral, which in the distance looks like Scotch heather. It is about six to eight feet high, has slender elastic branches, red shreddy bark, needle-shaped leaves, and small white flowers in panicles about a foot long, making glorious sheets of fragrant bloom in the spring. To running fires it offers no resistance, vanishing with the few other flowery shrubs and vines and liliaceous plants that grow with it about as fast as dry grass, leaving nothing but ashes. But with wonderful vigor it rises again and again in fresh beauty from the root, and calls back to its hospitable mansions the multitude of wild animals that had to flee for their lives.

As soon as you enter the pine woods you meet the charming little Chamæbatia foliolosa, one of the handsomest of the Park shrubs, next in fineness and beauty to the heathworts of the alpine regions. Like adenostoma it belongs to the rose family, is from twelve to eighteen inches high, has brown bark, slender branches, white flowers like those of the strawberry, and thricepinnate glandular, yellow-green leaves, finely cut and fernlike, as if unusual pains had been taken in fashioning them. Where there is plenty of sunshine at an elevation of three thousand to six thousand feet, it makes a close, continuous growth, leaf touching leaf over hundreds of acres, spreading a handsome mantle beneath the yellow and sugar pines. Here and there a lily rises above it, an arching bunch of tall bromus, and at wide intervals a rosebush or clump of ceanothus or manzanita, but there are no rough weeds mixed with it,—no roughness of any sort.

Perhaps the most widely distributed of all the Park shrubs and of the Sierra in general, certainly the most strikingly characteristic, are the many species of manzanita (Arctostaphylos). Though one species, the Uva-ursa, or bearberry,—the kinikinic of the Western Indians,—extends around the world, the greater part of them are California. They are mostly from four to ten feet high, round-headed, with innumerable branches, brown or red bark, pale green leaves set on edge, and a rich profusion of small, pink, narrow-throated, urn-shaped flowers like those of arbutus. The branches are knotty, zigzaggy, and about as rigid as bones, and the bark is so thin and smooth, both trunk and branches seem to be naked, looking as if they had been peeled, polished, and painted red. The wood also is red, hard, and heavy.

These grand bushes seldom fail to engage the attention of the traveler and hold it, especially if he has to pass through closely planted fields of them such as grow on moraine slopes at an elevation of about seven thousand feet, and in cañons choked with earthquake boulders; for they make the most uncompromisingly stubborn of all chaparral. Even bears take pains to go around the stoutest patches of possible, and when compelled to force a passage leave tufts of hair and broken branches to mark their way, while less skillful mountaineers under like circumstances sometimes lose most of their clothing and all their temper.

The manzanitas like sunny ground. On warm ridges and sandy flats at the foot of sun-beaten cañon cliffs, some of the tallest specimens have well-defined trunks six inches of a foot or more thick, and stand apart in orchard-like growths which in bloomtime are among the finest garden sights in the Park. The largest I ever saw had a round, slightly fluted trunk nearly four feet in diameter, which at a height of only eighteen inches from the ground dissolved into a wilderness of branches, rising and spreading to a height and width of about twelve feet. In spring every bush over all the mountains is covered with rosy flowers, in autumn with fruit. The red pleasantly acid berries, about the size of peas, are like little apples, and the hungry mountaineer is glad to eat them, though half their bulk is made up of hard seeds. Indians, bears, coyotes, foxes, birds, and other mountain people live on them for months.

Associated with manzanita there are six or seven species of ceanothus, flowery, fragrant, and altogether delightful shrubs, growing in glorious abundance in the forests on sunny or half-shaded ground, up to an elevation of about nine thousand feet above the sea. In the sugar-pine woods the most beautiful species is C. integerrimus, often called California lilac, or deer brush. It is five or six feet high, smooth, slender, willowy, with bright foliage and abundance of blue flowers in close, showy panicles. Two species, prostatus and procumbens, spread handsome blue-flowered mats and rugs on warm ridges beneath the pines, and offer delightful beds to the tired mountaineers. The commonest species, C. cordulatus, is mostly restricted to the silver fir belt. It is white-flowered and thorny, and makes extensive thickets of tangled chaparral, far too dense to wade through, and too deep and loose to walk on, though it is pressed flat every winter by ten or fifteen feet of snow.

Above these thorny beds, sometimes mixed with them, a very wild, red-fruited cherry grows in magnificent tangles, fragrant and white as snow when in bloom. The fruit is small and rather bitter, not so good as the black, puckery chokecherry that grows in the cañons, but thrushes, robins, chipmunks like it. Below the cherry tangles, chinquapin and goldcup oak spread generous mantles of chaparral, and with hazel and ribes thickets in adjacent glens help to clothe and adorn the rocky wilderness, and produce food for the many mouths Nature has to fill. Azalea occidentalis is the glory of cool streams and meadows. It is from two to five feet high, has bright green leaves and a rich profusion of large, fragrant white and yellow flowers, which are in prime beauty in June, July, and August, according to the elevation (from three thousand to six thousand feet.) Only the purple-flowered rhododendron of the redwood forests rivals or surpasses it in superb abounding bloom.

Back a little way from the azalea-bordered streams, a small wild rose makes thickets, often several acres in extent, deliciously fragrant on dewy mornings and after showers, the fragrance mingled with the music of birds nesting in them. And not far from these rose gardens Rubus Nutkanus covers the ground with broad velvety leaves and pure white flowers as large as those of its neighbor the rose, and finer in texture; followed at the end of summer by soft red berries good for bird and beast and man also. This is the commonest and the most beautiful of the whole blessed flowery fruity genus.

The glory of the alpine region in bloomtime are the heathworts, cassiope, bryanthus, kalmia, and vaccinium, enriched here and there by the alpine honeysuckle, Lonicera conjugialis, and by the purple-flowered Primula suffruticosa, the only primrose discovered in California, and the only shrubby species in the genus. The lowly, hardy, adventurous cassiope has exceedingly slender creeping branches, scalelike leaves, and pale pink or white waxen bell flowers. Few plants, large or small, so well endure hard weather and rough ground over so great a range. In July it spreads a wavering, interrupted belt of the loveliest bloom around glacier lakes and meadows and across wild moory expanses, between roaring streams, all along the Sierra, and northward beneath cold skies by way of the mountain chains of Oregon, Washington, British Columbia, and Alaska, to the Arctic regions; gradually descending, until at the north end of the continent it reaches the level of the sea; blooming as profusely and at about the same time on mossy frozen tundras as on the high Sierra moraines.

Bryanthus, the companion of cassiope, accompanies it as far north as southeastern Alaska, where together they weave thick plushy beds on rounded mountain tops above the glaciers. It grows mostly at slightly lower elevations; the upper margin of what may be called the bryanthus belt in the Sierra uniting with and overlapping the lower margin of the cassiope. The wide bell-shaped flowers are bright purple, about three fourths of an inch in diameter, hundreds to the square yard, the young branches, mostly erect, being covered with them. No Highlander in heather enjoys more luxurious rest than the Sierra mountaineer in a bed of blooming bryanthus. And imagine the show on calm dewy mornings, when there is a radiant globe in the throat of every flower, and smaller gems on the needle-shaped leaves, the sunbeams pouring through them.

In the same wild, cold region the tiny Vaccinium myrtillus, mixed with kalmia and dwarf willows, spreads thinner carpets, the downpressed matted leaves profusely sprinkled with pink bells; and on higher sandy slopes you will find several alpine species of eriogonum with gorgeous bossy masses of yellow bloom, and the lovely Arctic daisy with many blessed companions; charming plants, gentle mountaineers, Nature's darlings, which seem always the finer the higher and stormier their homes.

Many interesting ferns are distributed over the Park from the foothills to a little above the timber line. The greater number are rock ferns, pellæa, cheilanthes, polypodium, adiantum, woodsia, cryptogramme, etc., with small tufted fronds, lining glens and gorges and fringing the cliffs and moraines. The most important of the larger species are woodwardia, aspidium, asplenium, and the common pteris. Woodwardia radicans is a superb fern five to eight feet high, growing in vaselike clumps where the ground is level, and on slopes in a regular thatch, frond over frond, like shingles on a roof. Its range in the Park is from the western boundary up to about five thousand feet, mostly on benches of the north walls of cañons watered by small outspread streams. It is far more abundant in the Coast Mountains beneath the noble redwoods, where it attains a height of ten to twelve feet. The aspidiums are mostly restricted to the moist parts of the lower forests, Asplenium filix-fœmina to marshy streams. The hardy, broad-shouldered Pteris aquilina, the commonest of ferns, grows tall and graceful on sunny flats and hillsides, at elevations between three thousand and six thousand feet. Those who know it only in the Eastern states can form no fair conception of its stately beauty in the sunshine of the Sierra. On the level sandy floors of Yosemite valleys it often attains a height of six to eight feet in fields thirty or forty acres in extent, the magnificent fronds outspread in a nearly horizontal position, forming a ceiling beneath which one may walk erect in delightful mellow shade. No other fern does so much for the color glory of autumn, with its browns and reds and yellows changing and interblending. Even after lying dead all winter beneath the snow it spreads a lively brown mantle over the desolate ground, until the young fronds with a noble display of faith and hope come rolling up into the light through the midst of the beautiful ruins. A few weeks suffice for their development, then, gracefully poised each in its place, they manage themselves in every exigency of weather as if they had passed through a long course of training. I have seen solemn old sugar pines thrown into momentary confusion by the sudden onset of a storm, tossing their arms excitedly as if scarce awake, and wondering what had happened, but I never noticed surprise or embarrassment in the behavior of this noble pteris.

Of five species of pellæa in the Park, the handsome andromedæfolia, growing in brushy foothills with Adiantum emarginatum, is the largest. P. Breweri, the hardiest and at the same time the most fragile of the genus, grows in dense tufts among rocks on storm-beaten mountain sides along the upper margin of the fern line. It is a charming little fern, four or five inches high, has shining bronze-colored stalks which are about as brittle as glass, and pale green pinnate fronds. Its companions on the lower part of its range are Cryptogramme acrostichoides and Phegopteris alpestris, the latter soft and tender, not at all like a rock fern, though it grows on rocks where the snow lies longest. P. Bridgesii, with blue-green, narrow, simply pinnate fronds, is about the same size as Breweri and ranks next to it as a mountaineer, growing in fissures and round boulders on glacier pavements. About a thousand feet lower we find the smaller and more abundant P. densa, on ledges and boulder-strewn fissured pavements, watered until late in summer by oozing currents from snow-banks or thin outspread streams from moraines, growing in close sods,—its little bright green triangular tripinnate fronds, about an inch in length, as innumerable as leaves of grass. P. ornithopus has twice or thrice pinnate fronds, is dull in color, and dwells on hot rocky hillsides among chaparral.

Three species of Cheilanthes,—Californica, gracillima, and myriophylla, with beautiful two to four pinnate fronds, an inch to five inches long, adorn the stupendous walls of the cañons, however dry and sheer. The exceedingly delicate and interesting Californica is rare, the others abundant at from three thousand to seven thousand feet elevation, and are often accompanied by the little gold fern, Gymnogramme triangularis, and rarely by the curious little Botrychium simplex, the smallest of which are less than an inch high.

The finest of all the rock ferns is Adiantum pedatum, lover of waterfalls and the lightest waftings of irised spray. No other Sierra fern is so constant a companion of white spray-covered streams, or tells so well their wild thundering music. The homes it loves best are cave-like hollows beside the main falls, where it can float its plumes on their dewy breath, safely sheltered from the heavy spray-laden blasts. Many of these moss-lined chambers, so cool, so moist, and brightly colored with rainbow light, contain thousands of these happy ferns, clinging to the emerald walls by the slightest holds, reaching out the most wonderfully delicate fingered fronds on dark glossy stalks, sensitive, tremulous, all alive, in an attitude of eager attention; throbbing in unison with every motion and tone of the resounding waters, compliant to their faintest impulses, moving each division of the frond separately at times as if fingering the music, playing on invisible keys.

Considering the lilies as you go up the mountains, the first you come to is L. Pardalinum, with large orange-yellow, purple-spotted flowers big enough for babies bonnets. It is seldom found higher than thirty-five hundred feet above the sea, grows in magnificent groups of fifty to a hundred or more, in romantic waterfall dells in the pine woods shaded by overarching maple and willow, alder and dogwood, with bushes in front of the embowering trees for a border, and ferns and sedges in front of the bushes; while the bed of black humus in which the bulbs are set is carpeted with mosses and liverworts. These richly furnished lily gardens are the pride of the falls on the lower tributaries of the Tuolumne and Merced rivers, falls not like those of Yosemite valleys,—coming from the sky with rock-shaking thunder tones,—but small, with low, kind voices cheerily singing in calm leafy bowers, self-contained, keeping their snowy skirts well about them, yet furnishing plenty of spray for the lilies.

The Washington lily (L. Washingtonianum) is white, deliciously fragrant, moderate in size, with three to ten flowered racemes. The largest I ever measured was eight feet high, the raceme two feet long, with fifty-two flowers, fifteen of them open; the others had faded or were still in the bud. This famous lily is distributed over the sunny portions of the sugar-pine woods, never in large garden companies like pardalinum, but widely scattered, standing up to the waist in dense ceanothus and manzanita chaparral, waving its lovely flowers above the blooming wilderness of brush, and giving their fragrance to the breeze. These stony, thorny jungles are about the last places in the mountains in which one would look for lilies. But though they toil not nor spin, like other people under adverse circumstances, they have to do the best they can. Because their large bulbs are good to eat they are dug up by Indians and bears; therefore, like hunted animals, they seek refuge in the chaparral, where among the boulders and tough tangled roots they are comparatively safe. This is the favorite Sierra lily, and it is now growing in all the best parks and gardens of the world.

The showiest gardens in the Park lie imbedded in the silver fir forests on the top of the main dividing ridges or hang likely gayly colored scarfs down their sides. Their wet places are in great part taken up by veratrum, a robust broad-leaved plant determined to be seen, and habenaria and spiranthes; the drier parts by tall columbines, larkspurs, castilleias, lupines, hosackias, erigerons, valerian, etc., standing deep in grass, with violets here and there around the borders. But the finest feature of these forest gardens is Lilium parvum. It varies greatly in size, the tallest being from six to nine feet high, with splendid racemes of ten to fifty small orange-colored flowers, which rock and wave with great dignity above the other flowers in the infrequent winds that fall over the protecting wall of trees. Though rather frail-looking it is strong, reaching prime vigor and beauty eight thousand feet above the sea, and in some places venturing as high as eleven thousand.

Calochortus, or Mariposa tulip, is a unique genus of many species confined to the California side of the continent; charming plants, somewhat resembling the tulips of Europe, but far finer. The richest calochortus region lies below the western boundary of the Park; still five or six species are included. C. Nuttallii is common on moraines in the forests of the two-leaved pine; and C. cæruleus and nudus, very slender, lowly species, may be found in moist garden spots near Yosemite. C. albus, with pure white flowers, growing in shady places among the foothill shrubs, is, I think, the very loveliest of all the lily family,—a spotless soul, plant saint, that every one must love and so be made better. It puts the wildest mountaineer on his good behavior. With this plant the whole world would seem rich though none other existed. Next after Calochortus, Brodiæa is the most interesting genus. Nearly all the many species have beautiful showy heads of blue, lilac, and yellow flowers, enriching the gardens of the lower pine region. Other liliaceous plants likely to attract attention are the blue-flowered camassia, the bulbs of which are prized as food by Indians; fritillaria, smilacina, chloragalum, and the twining climbing stropholirion.

The common orchidaceous plants are corallorhiza, goodyera, spiranthes, and habenaria. Cypripedium montanum, the only moccasin flower I have seen in the Park, is a handsome, thoughtful-looking plant living beside cool brooks. The large oval lip is white, delicately veined with purple; the other petals and sepals purple, strap-shaped, and elegantly curved and twisted.

To tourists the most attractive of all the flowers of the forest is the snow plant (Sarcodes sanguinea). It is a bright red, fleshy, succulent pillar that pushes up through the dead needles in the pine and fir woods like a gigantic asparagus shoot. The first intimation of its coming is a loosening and upbulging of the brown stratum of decomposed needles on the forest floor, in the cracks of which you notice fiery gleams; presently a blunt dome-shaped head an inch or two in diameter appears, covered with closely imbricated scales and bracts. In a week or so it grows to a height of six to twelve inches. Then the long fringed bracts spread and curl aside, allowing the twenty or thirty five-lobed bell-shaped flowers to open and look straight out from the fleshy axis. It is said to grow up through the snow; on the contrary it always waits until the ground is warm, though with other early flowers it is occasionally buried or half buried for a day or two by spring storms. The entire plant—flowers, bracts, stem, scales, and roots—is red. But notwithstanding its glowing color and beautiful flowers, it is singularly unsympathetic and cold. Everybody admires it as a wonderful curiosity, but nobody loves it. Without fragrance, rooted in decaying vegetable matter, it stands beneath the pines and firs lonely, silent, and about as rigid as a graveyard monument.

Down in the main cañons adjoining the azalea and rose gardens there are fine beds of herbaceous plants,—tall mints and sunflowers, iris, œnothera, brodiæa, and bright beds of erythræa on the ferny meadows. Bolandera, sedum, and airy, feathery, purple-flowered heuchera adorn mossy nooks near falls, the shading trees wreathed and festooned with wild grapevines and clematis; while lightly shaded flats are covered with gilia and eunanus of many species, hosackia, arnica, chænactis, gayophytum, gnaphalium, monardella, etc.

Thousands of the most interesting gardens in the Park are never seen, for they are small and lie far up on ledges and terraces of the sheer cañon walls, wherever a strip of soil, however narrow and shallow, can rest. The birds, winds, and down-washing rains have planted them with all sorts of hardy mountain flowers, and where there is sufficient moisture they flourish in profusion. Many of them are watered by little streams that seem lost on the tremendous precipices, clinging to the face of the rock in lacelike strips, and dripping from ledge to ledge, too silent to be called falls, pathless wanderers from the upper meadows, which for centuries have been seeking a way down to the rivers they belong to, without having worn as yet any appreciable channel, mostly evaporated or given to the plants they meet before reaching the foot of the cliffs. To these unnoticed streams the finest of the cliff gardens owe their luxuriance and freshness of beauty. In the larger ones ferns and showy flowers flourish in wonderful profusion,—woodwardia, columbine, collomia, castilleia, draperia, geranium, erythræa, pink and scarlet mimulus, hosackia, saxifrage, sunflowers and daisies, with azalea, spiræa, and calycanthus, a few specimens of each that seem to have been culled from the large gardens above and beneath them. Even lilies are occasionally found in these irrigated cliff gardens, swinging their bells over the giddy precipices, seemingly as happy as their relatives down in the waterfall dells. Most of the cliff gardens, however, are dependent on summer showers, and though from the shallowness of the soil beds they are often dry, they still display a surprising number of bright flowers,—scarlet zauschneria, purple bush penstemon, mints, gilias, and bosses of glowing golden bahia. Nor is there any lack of commoner plants; the homely yarrow is often found in them, and sweet clover and honeysuckle for the bees.

In the upper cañons, where the walls are inclined at so low an angle that they are loaded with moraine material, through which perennial streams percolate in broad diffused currents, there are long wavering garden beds, that seem to be descending through the forest like cascades, their fluent lines suggesting motion, swaying from side to side of the forested banks, surging up here and there over island-like boulder piles, or dividing and flowing around them. In some of these floral cascades the vegetation is chiefly sedges and grasses ruffled with willows; in others, showy flowers like those of the lily gardens on the main divides. Another curious and picturesque series of wall gardens are made by thin streams that ooze slowly from moraines and slip gently over smooth glaciated slopes. From particles of sand and mud they carry, a pair of lobe-shaped sheets of soil an inch or two thick are gradually formed, one of them hanging down from the brow of the slope, the other leaning up from the foot of it like stalactite and stalagmite, the soil being held together by the flowery, moisture-loving plants growing in it.

Along the rocky parts of the cañon bottoms between lake basins, where the streams flow fast over glacier-polished granite, there are rows of pothole gardens full of ferns, daisies, golden-rods, and other common plants of the neighborhood nicely arranged like bouquets, and standing out in telling relief on the bare shining rock banks. And all the way up the cañons to the Summit mountains, wherever there is soil of any sort, there is no lack of flowers, however short the summer may be. Within eight or ten feet of a snow bank lingering beneath a shadow, you may see belated ferns unrolling their fronds in September, and sedges hurrying up their brown spikes on ground that has been free from snow only eight or ten days, and likely to be covered again within a few weeks; the winter in the coolest of these shadow gardens being about eleven months long, while spring, summer, and autumn are hurried and crowded into one month. Again, under favorable conditions, alpine gardens three or four thousand feet higher than the last are in their prime in June. Between the Summit peaks at the head of the cañons surprising effects are produced where the sunshine falls direct on rocky slopes and reverberates among boulders. Toward the end of August, in one of these natural hothouses on the north shore of a glacier lake 11,500 feet above the sea, I found a luxuriant growth of hairy lupines, thistles, goldenrods, shrubby potentilla, spraguea, and the mountain epilobium with thousands of purple flowers an inch wide, while the opposite shore, at a distance of only three hundred yards, was bound in heavy avalanche snow,—flowery summer on one side, winter on the other. And I know a bench garden on the north wall of Yosemite in which a few flowers are in bloom all winter; the massive rocks about it storing up sunshine enough in summer to melt the snow about as fast as it falls. When tired of the confinement of my cabin I used to camp out in it in January, and never failed to find flowers, and butterflies also, except during snowstorms and a few days after.

From Yosemite one can easily walk in a day to the top of Mount Hoffman, a massive gray mountain that rises in the centre of the Park, with easy slopes adorned with castellated piles and crests on the south side, rugged precipices banked with perpetual snow on the north. Most of the broad summit is comparatively level and smooth, and covered with crystals of quartz, mica, hornblende, feldspar, garnet, zircon, tourmaline, etc., weathered out and strewn loosely as if sown broadcast; their radiance so dazzling in some places as to fairly hide the multitude of small flowers that grow among them; myriads of keen lance rays infinitely fine, white or colored, making an almost continuous glow over all the ground, with here and there throbbing, spangling lilies of light, on the larger gems. At first sight only these crystal sunflowers are noticed, but looking closely you discover minute gilias, ivesias, eunanus, phloxes, etc., in thousands, showing more petals than leaves; and larger plants in hollows and on the borders of rills,—lupines, potentillas, daisies, harebells, mountain columbine, astragalus, fringed with heathworts. You wander about from garden to garden enchanted, as if walking among stars, gathering the brightest gems, each and all apparently doing their best with eager enthusiasm, as if everything depended on faithful shining; and considering the flowers basking in the glorious light, many of them looking like swarms of small moths and butterflies that were resting after long dances in the sunbeams. Now your attention is called to colonies of woodchucks and pikas, the mounds in front of their burrows glittering like heaps of jewelry,—romantic ground to live in or die in. Now you look abroad over the vast round landscape bounded by the down-curving sky, nearly all the Park in it displayed like a map,—forests, meadows, lakes, rock waves, and snowy mountains. Northward lies the basin of Yosemite Creek, paved with bright domes and lakes like larger crystals; eastward, the meadowy, billowy Tuolumne region and the Summit peaks in glorious array; southward, Yosemite; and westward, the boundless forests. On no other mountain that I know of are you more likely to linger. It is a magnificent camp ground. Clumps of dwarf pine furnish rosiny roots and branches for fuel, and the rills pure water. Around your camp fire the flowers seem to be looking eagerly at the light, and the crystals shine unweariedly, making fine company as you lie at rest in the very heart of the vast, serene, majestic night.

The finest of the glacier meadow gardens lie at an elevation of about nine thousand feet, imbedded in the upper pine forests like lakes of light. They are smooth and level, a mile or two long, and the rich, well-drained ground is completely covered with a soft, silky, plushy sod enameled with flowers, not one of which is in the least weedy or coarse. In some places the sod is so crowded with showy flowers that the grasses are scarce noticed, in others they are rather sparingly scattered; while every leaf and flower seems to have its winged representative in the swarms of happy flower-like insects that enliven the air above them.

With the winter snowstorms wings and petals are folded, and for more than half the year the meadows are snow-buried ten or fifteen feet deep. In June they begin to thaw out, small patches of the dead sloppy sod appear, gradually increasing in size until they are free and warm again, face to face with the sky; myriads of growing points push through the steaming mould, frogs sing cheeringly, soon joined by the birds, and the merry insects come back as if suddenly raised from the dead. Soon the ground is green with mosses and liverworts and dotted with small fungi, making the first crop of the season. Then the grass leaves weave a new sod, and the exceedingly slender panicles rise above it like a purple mist, speedily followed by potentilla, ivesia, bossy orthocarpus, yellow and purple, and a few pentstemons. Later come the daisies and goldenrods, asters and gentians. Of the last there are three species, small and fine, with varying tones of blue, and in glorious abundance, coloring extensive patches where the sod is shallowest. Through the midst flows a stream only two or three feet wide, silently gliding as if careful not to disturb the hushed calm of the solitude, its banks embossed by the common sod bent down to the water's edge, and trimmed with mosses and violets; slender grass panicles lean over like miniature pine trees, and here and there on the driest places small mats of heathworts are neatly spread, enriching without roughening the bossy down-curling sod. In spring and summer the weather is mostly crisp, exhilarating sunshine, though magnificent mountain ranges of cumuli are often upheaved about noon, their shady hollows tinged with purple ineffably fine, their snowy sun-beaten bosses glowing against the sky, casting cooling shadows for an hour or two, then dissolving in a quick washing rain. But for days in succession there are no clouds at all, or only faint wisps and pencilings scarcely discernible.

Toward the end of August the sunshine grows hazy, announcing the coming of Indian summer, the outlines of the landscapes are softened and mellowed, and more and more plainly are the mountains clothed with light, white tinged with pale purple, richest in the morning and evening. The warm, brooding days are full of life and thoughts of life to come, ripening seeds with next summer in them or a hundred summers. The nights are unspeakably impresssive and calm; frost crystals of wondrous beauty grow on the grass,—each carefully planned and finished as if intended to endure forever. The sod becomes yellow and brown, but the late asters and gentians, carefully closing their flower at night, do not seem to feel the frost; no nipped, wilted plants of any kind are to be seen; even the early snowstorms fail to blight them. At last the precious seeds are ripe, all the work of the season is done, and the sighing pines tell the coming of winter and rest.

Ascending the range you find that many of the higher meadows slope considerably, from the amount of loose material washed into their basins; and sedges and rushes are mixed with the grasses or take their places, though all are still more or less flowery and bordered with heathworts, sibbaldea, and dwarf willows. Here and there you come to small bogs, the wettest smooth and adorned with parnassia and butter-cups, others tussocky and ruffled like bits of Arctic tundra, their mosses and lichens interwoven with dwarf shrubs. On boulder piles the red iridescent oxyria abounds, and on sandy, gravelly slopes several species of shrubby, yellow-flowered eriogonum, some of the plants, less than a foot high, being very old, a century or more as is shown by the rings made by the annual whorls of leaves on the big roots. Above these flower-dotted slopes the gray, savage wilderness of crags and peaks seems lifeless and bare. Yet all the way up to the tops of the highest mountains, commonly supposed to be covered with eternal snow, there are bright garden spots crowded with flowers, their warm colors calling to mind the sparks and jets of fire on polar volcanoes rising above a world of ice. The principal mountain-top plants are phloxes, drabas, saxifrages, silene, cymopterus, hulsea, and polemonium, growing in detached stripes and mats,—the highest streaks and splashes of the summer wave as it breaks against these wintry heights. The most beautiful are the phloxes (douglasii and cæspitosum), and the red-flowered silene, with innumerable flowers hiding the leaves. Though herbaceous plants, like the trees and shrubs, are dwarfed as they ascend, two of these mountain dwellers, Hulsea algida and Polemonium confertum, are notable exceptions. The yellow-flowered hulsea is eight to twelve inches high, stout, erect,—the leaves, three to six inches long, secreting a rosiny, fragrant gum, standing up boldly on the grim lichen-stained crags, and never looking in the least tired or discouraged. Both the ray and disk flowers are yellow; the heads are nearly two inches wide, and are eagerly sought for by roving bee mountaineers. The polemonium is quite as luxuriant and tropical-looking as its companion, about the same height, glandular, fragrant, its blue flowers closely packed in eight or ten heads, twenty to forty in head. It is never far from hulsea, growing at elevations of between eleven and thirteen thousand feet wherever a little hollow or crevice favorably situated with a handful of wind-driven soil can be found.

From these frosty Arctic sky gardens you may descend in one straight swoop to the abronia, mentzelia, and œnothera gardens of Mono, where the sunshine is warm enough for palms.

But the greatest of all the gardens is the belt of forest trees, profusely covered in the spring with blue and purple, red and yellow blossoms, each tree with a gigantic panicle of flowers fifty to a hundred feet long. Yet strange to say they are seldom noticed. Few travel through the woods when they are in bloom, the flowers of some of the showiest species opening before the snow is off the ground. Nevertheless, one would think the news of such gigantic flowers would quickly spread, and travelers from all the world would make haste to the show. Eager inquiries are made for the bloomtime of rhododendron-covered mountains and for the bloom-time of Yosemite streams, that they may be enjoyed in their prime; but the far grander outburst of tree bloom covering a thousand mountains—who inquires about that? That the pistillate flowers of the pines and fires should escape the eyes of careless lookers is less to be wondered at, since they mostly grow aloft on the topmost branches, and can hardly be seen from the foot of the trees. Yet even these make a magnificent show from the top of an overlooking ridge when the sunbeams are pouring through them. But the far more numerous staminate flowers of the pines in large rosy clusters, and those of the silver firs in countless thousands on the under side of the branches, cannot be hid, stand where you may. The mountain hemlock also is gloriously colored with a profusion of lovely blue and purple flowers, a spectacle to gods and men. A single pine or hemlock or silver fir in the prime of its beauty about the middle of June is well worth the pains of the longest journey; how much more broad forests of them thousands of miles long!

One of the best ways to see tree flowers is to climb one of the tallest trees and to get into close tingling touch with them, and then look broad. Speaking of the benefits of tree climbing, Thoreau says: "I found my account in climbing a tree once. It was a tall white pine, on the top of a hill; and though I got well pitched, I was well paid for it, for I discovered new mountains in the horizon which I had never seen before. I might have walked about the foot of the tree for threescore years and ten, and yet I certainly should never have seen them. But, above all, I discovered around me,—it was near the middle of June,—on the ends of the topmost branches, a few minute and delicate red conelike blossoms, the fertile flower of the white pine looking heavenward. I carried straightway to the village the topmost spire, and showed it to stranger jurymen who walked the streets,—for it was court week,—and to farmers and lumbermen and woodchoppers and hunters, and not one had ever seen the like before, but they wondered as at a star dropped down."

The same marvelous blindness prevails here, although the blossoms are a thousandfold more abundant and telling. Once when I was collecting flowers of the red silver fir near a summer tourist resort on the mountains above Lake Tahoe, I carried a handful of flowery branches to the boarding house, where they quickly attracted a wondering, admiring crowd of men, women, and children. "Oh, where did you get these?" they cried. "How pretty they are—mighty handsome—just too lovely for anything—where do they grow?" "On the commonest trees about you," I replied. "You are now standing beside one of them, and it is in full bloom; look up." And I pointed to a blossom-laden Abies magnifica, about a hundred and twenty feet high, in front of the house, used as a hitching post. And seeing its beauty for the first time, their wonder could hardly have been greater or more sincere had their silver fir hitching post blossomed for them at that moment as suddenly as Aaron's rod.

The mountain hemlock extends an almost continuous belt along the Sierra and northern ranges to Prince William's Sound, accompanied part of the way by the pines; our two silver firs, to Mount Shasta, thence the fir belt is continued through Oregon, Washington, and British Columbia by four other species, Abies nobilis, grandis, amabilis, and lasiocarpa; while the magnificent Sitka spruce, with large, bright, purple flowers, adorns the coast region from California to Cook's Inlet and Kodiak. All these, interblending, form one flowery belt—one garden blooming in June, rocking its myriad spires in the hearty weather, bowing and swirling, enjoying clouds and the winds and filling them with balsam; covering thousands of miles of the wildest mountains, clothing the long slopes by the sea, crowning bluffs and headlands and innumerable islands, and, fringing the banks of the glaciers, one wild wavering belt of the noblest flowers in the world, worth a lifetime of love work to know it.

CHAPTER VI

Among the Animals of the Yosemite

The Sierra bear, brown or gray, the sequoia of the animals, tramps over all the park, though few travelers have the pleasure of seeing him. On he fares through the majestic forests and cañons, facing all sorts of weather, rejoicing in his strength, everywhere at home, harmonizing with the trees and rocks and shaggy chaparral. Happy fellow! his lines have fallen in pleasant places,—lily gardens in silver-fir forests, miles of bushes in endless variety and exuberance of bloom over hill-waves and valleys and along the banks of streams, cañons full of music and waterfalls, parks fair as Eden,—places in which one might expect to meet angels rather than bears.

In this happy land no famine comes nigh him. All the year round his bread is sure, for some of the thousand kinds that he likes are always in season and accessible, ranged on the shelves of the mountains like stores in a pantry. From one to another, from climate to climate, up and down he climbs, feasting on each in turn,—enjoying as great variety as if he traveled to far-off countries north and south. To him almost every thing is food except granite. Every tree helps to feed him, every bush and herb, with fruits and flowers, leaves and bark; and all the animals he can catch,—badgers, gophers, ground squirrels, lizards, snakes, etc., and ants, bees, wasps, old and young, together with their eggs and larvæ and nests. Craunched and hashed, down all go to his marvelous stomach, and vanish as if cast into a fire. What digestion! A sheep or a wounded deer or a pig he eats warm, about as quickly as a boy eats a buttered muffin; or should the meat be a month old, it still is welcomed with tremendous relish. After so gross a meal as this, perhaps the next will be strawberries and clover, or raspberries with mushrooms and nuts, or puckery acorns and chokecherries. And as if fearing that anything eatable in all his dominions should escape being eaten, he breaks into cabins to look after sugar, dried apples, bacon, etc. Occasionally he eats the mountaineer's bed; but when he has had a full meal of more tempting dainties he usually leaves it undisturbed, though he has been known to drag it up through a hole in the roof, carry it to the foot of a tree, and lie down on it to enjoy a siesta. Eating everything, never is he himself eaten except by man, and only man is an enemy to be feared. "B'ar meat," said a hunter from whom I was seeking information, "b'ar meat is the best meat in the mountains; their skins make the best beds, and their grease the best butter. Biscuit shortened with b'ar grease goes as far as beans; a man will walk all day on a couple of them biscuit."

In my first interview with a Sierra bear we were frightened and embarrassed, both of us, but the bear's behavior was better than mine. When I discovered him, he was standing in a narrow strip of meadow, and I was concealed behind a tree on the side of it. After studying this appearance as he stood at rest, I rushed toward him to frighten him, that I might study his gait in running. But, contrary to all I had heard about the shyness of bears, he did not run at all; and when I stopped short within a few steps of him, as he held his ground in a fighting attitude, my mistake was monstrously plain. I was then put on my good behavior, and never afterward forgot the right manners of the wilderness.

This happened on my first Sierra excursion in the forest to the north of Yosemite Valley. I was eager to meet the animals, and many of them came to me as if willing to show themselves and make my acquaintance; but the bears kept out of my way.

An old mountaineer, in reply to my questions, told me that bears were very shy, all save grim old grizzlies, and that I might travel the mountains for years without seeing one, unless I gave my mind to them and practiced the stealthy ways of hunters. Nevertheless, it was only a few weeks after I had received this information that I met the one mentioned above, and obtained instruction at first-hand.

I was encamped in the woods about a mile back of the rim of Yosemite, beside a stream that falls into the valley by the way of Indian Cañon. Nearly every day for weeks I went to the top of the North Dome to sketch; for it commands a general view of the valley, and I was anxious to draw every tree and rock and waterfall. Carlo, a St. Bernard dog, was my companion,—a fine, intelligent fellow that belonged to a hunter who was compelled to remain all summer on the hot plains, and who loaned him to me for the season for the sake of having him in the mountains, where he would be so much better off. Carlo knew bears through long experience, and he it was who led me to my first interview, though he seemed as much surprised as the bear at my unhunter-like behavior. One morning in June, just as the sunbeams began to stream through the trees, I set out for a day's sketching on the dome; and before we had gone half a mile from camp Carlo snuffed the air and looked cautiously ahead, lowered his bushy tail, drooped his ears, and began to step softly like a cat, turning every few yards and looking me in the face with a telling expression, saying plainly enough, "There is a bear a little way ahead." I walked carefully in the indicated direction, until I approached a small flowery meadow that I was familiar with, then crawled to the foot of a tree on its margin, bearing in mind what I had been told about the shyness of bears. Looking out cautiously over the instep of the tree, I saw a big, burly cinnamon bear about thirty yards off, half erect, his paws resting on the trunk of a fir that had fallen into the meadow, his hips almost buried in grass and flowers. He was listening attentively and trying to catch the scent, showing that in some way he was aware of our approach. I watched his gestures, and tried to make the most of my opportunity to learn what I could about him, fearing he would not stay long. He made a fine picture, standing alert in the sunny garden walled in by the most beautiful firs in the world.

After examining him at leisure, noting the sharp muzzle thrust inquiringly forward, the long shaggy hair on his broad chest, the stiff ears nearly buried in hair, and the slow, heavy way in which he moved his head, I foolishly made a rush on him, throwing up my arms and shouting to frighten him, to see him run. He did not mind the demonstration much; only pushed his head farther forward, and looked at me sharply as if asking, "What now? If you want to fight, I'm ready." Then I began to fear that on me would fall the work of running. But I was afraid to run, lest he should be encouraged to pursue me; therefore I held my ground, staring him in the face within a dozen yards or so, putting on as bold a look as I could, and hoping the influence of the human eye would be as great as it is said to be. Under these strained relations the interview seemed to last a long time. Finally, the bear, seeing how still I was, calmly withdrew his huge paws from the log, gave me a piercing look, as if warning me not to follow him, turned, and walked slowly up the middle of the meadow into the forest; stopping every few steps and looking back to make sure that I was not trying to take him at a disadvantage in a rear attack. I was glad to part with him, and greatly enjoyed the vanishing view as he waded through the lilies and columbines.

Thenceforth I always tried to give bears respectful notice of my approach, and they usually kept well out of my way. Though they often came around my camp in the night, only once afterward, as far as I know, was I very near one of them in daylight. This time it was a grizzly I met; and as luck would have it, I was even nearer to him than I had been to the big cinnamon. Though not a large specimen, he seemed formidable enough at a distance of less than a dozen yards. His shaggy coat was well grizzled, his head almost white. When I first caught sight of him he was eating acorns under a Kellogg oak, at a distance of perhaps seventy-five yards, and I tried to slip past without disturbing him. But he had either heard my steps on the gravel or caught my scent, for he came straight toward me, stopping every rod or so to look and listen: and as I was afraid to be seen running, I crawled on my hands and knees a little way to one side and hid behind a libocedrus, hoping he would pass me unnoticed. He soon came up opposite me, and stood looking ahead, while I looked at him, peering past the bulging trunk of the tree. At last, turning his head, he caught sight of mine, stared sharply a minute or two, and then, with fine dignity, disappeared in a manzanita-covered earthquake talus.

Considering how heavy and broad-footed bears are, it is wonderful how little harm they do in the wilderness. Even in the well-watered gardens of the middle region, where the flowers grow tallest, and where during warm weather the bears wallow and roll, no evidence of destruction is visible. On the contrary, under nature's direction, the massive beasts act as gardeners. On the forest floor, carpeted with needles and brush, and on the tough sod of glacier meadows, bears make no mark; but around the sandy margin of lakes their magnificent tracks form grand lines of embroidery. Their well-worn trails extend along the main cañons on either side, and though dusty in some places make no scar on the landscape. They bite and break off the branches of some of the pines and oaks to get the nuts, but this pruning is so light that few mountaineers ever notice it; and though they interfere with the orderly lichen-veiled decay of fallen trees, tearing them to pieces to reach the colonies of ants that inhabit them, the scattered ruins are quickly pressed back into harmony by snow and rain and over-leaning vegetation.

The number of bears that make the Park their home may be guessed by the number that have been killed by the two best hunters, Duncan and old David Brown. Duncan began to be known as a bear-killer about the year 1865. He was then roaming the woods, hunting and prospecting on the south fork of the Merced. A friend told me that he killed his first bear near his cabin at Wawona; that after mustering courage to fire he fled, without waiting to learn the effect of his shot. Going back in a few hours he found poor Bruin dead, and gained courage to try again. Duncan confessed to me, when we made an excursion together in 1875, that he was at first mortally afraid of bears, but after killing a half dozen he began to keep count of his victims, and became ambitious to be known as a great bear-hunter. In nine years he had killed forty-nine, keeping count by notches cut on one of the timbers of his cabin on the shore of Crescent Lake, near the south boundary of the Park. He said the more he knew about bears, the more he respected them and the less he feared them. But at the same time he grew more and more cautious, and never fired until he had every advantage, no matter how long he had to wait and how far he had to go before he got the bear just right as to the direction of the wind, the distance, and the way of escape in case of accident; making allowance also for the character of the animal, old or young, cinnamon or grizzly. For old grizzlies, he said, he had no use whatever, and he was mighty careful to avoid their acquaintance. He wanted to kill an even hundred; then he was going to confine himself to safer game. There was not much money in bears, anyhow, and a round hundred was enough for glory.

I have not seen or heard of him lately, and do not know how his bloody count stands. On my excursions, I occasionally passed his cabin. It was full of meat and skins hung in bundles from the rafters, and the ground about it was strewn with bones and hair,—infinitely less tidy than a bear's den. He went as hunter and guide with a geological survey party for a year or two, and was very proud of the scientific knowledge, he picked up. His admiring fellow mountaineers, he said, gave him credit for knowing not only the botanical names of all the trees and bushes, but also the "botanical names of the bears."

The most famous hunter of the region was David Brown, an old pioneer, who early in the gold period established his main camp in a little forest glade on the north fork of the Merced, which is still called "Brown's Flat." No finer solitude for a hunter and prospector could be found; the climate is delightful all the year, and the scenery of both earth and sky is a perpetual feast. Though he was not much of a "scenery fellow," his friends say that he knew a pretty place when he saw it as well as any one, and liked mightily to get on the top of a commanding ridge to "look off."

When out of provisions, he would take down his old-fashioned long-barreled rifle from its deer-horn rest over the fireplace and set out in search of game. Seldom did he have to go far for venison, because the deer liked the wooded slopes of Pilot Peak ridge, with its open spots where they could rest and look about them, and enjoy the breeze from the sea in warm weather, free from troublesome flies, while they found hiding-places and fine aromatic food in the deer-brush chaparral. A small, wise dog was his only companion, and well the little mountaineer understood the object of every hunt, whether deer or bears, or only grouse hidden in the fir-tops. In deer-hunting Sandy had little to do, trotting behind his master as he walked noiselessly through the fragrant woods, careful not to step heavily on dry twigs, scanning open spots in the chaparral where the deer feed in the early morning and toward sunset, peering over ridges and swells as new outlooks were reached, and along alder and willow fringed flats and streams, until he found a young buck, killed it, tied its legs together, threw it on his shoulder, and so back to camp. But when bears were hunted, Sandy played an important part as leader, and several times saved his master's life; and it was as a bear-hunter that David Brown became famous. His method, as I had it from a friend who had passed many an evening in his cabin listening to his long stories of adventure, was simply to take a few pounds of flour and his rifle, and go slowly and silently over hill and valley in the loneliest part of the wilderness, until little Sandy came upon the fresh track of a bear, then follow it to the death, paying no heed to time. Wherever the bear went he went, however rough the ground, led by Sandy, who looked back from time to time to see how his master was coming on, and regulated his pace accordingly, never growing weary or allowing any other track to divert him. When high ground was reached a halt was made, to scan the openings in every direction, and perchance Bruin would be discovered sitting upright on his haunches, eating manzanita berries; pulling down the fruit-laden branches with his paws and pressing them together, so as to get substantial mouthfuls, however mixed with leaves and twigs. The time of year enabled the hunter to determine approximately where the game would be found: in spring and early summer, in lush grass and clover meadows and in berry tangles along the banks of streams, or on pea-vine and lupine clad slopes; in late summer and autumn, beneath the pines, eating the cones cut off by the squirrels, and in oak groves at the bottom of cañons, munching acorns, manzanita berries, and cherries; and after snow had fallen, in alluvial bottoms, feeding on ants and yellow-jacket wasps. These food places were always cautiously approached, so as to avoid the chance of sudden encounters.

"Whenever," said the hunter, "I saw a bear before he saw me, I had no trouble in killing him. I just took lots of time to learn what he was up to and how long he would be likely to stay, and to study the direction of the wind and the lay of the land. Then I worked round to leeward of him, no matter how far I had to go; crawled and dodged to within a hundred yards, near the foot of a tree that I could climb, but which was too small for a bear to climb. There I looked well to the priming of my rifle, took off my boots so as to climb quickly if necessary, and, with my rifle in rest and Sandy behind me, waited until my bear stood right, when I made a sure, or at least a good shot back of the fore leg. In case he showed fight, I got up the tree I had in mind, before he could reach me. But bears are slow and awkward with their eyes, and being to windward they could not scent me, and often I got in a second shot before they saw the smoke. Usually, however, they tried to get away when they were hurt, and I let them go a good safe while before I ventured into the brush after them. Then Sandy was pretty sure to find them dead; if not, he barked bold as a lion to draw attention, or rushed in and nipped them behind, enabling me to get to a safe distance and watch a chance for a finishing shot.

"Oh yes, bear-hunting is a mighty interesting business, and safe enough if followed just right, though, like every other business, especially the wild kind, it has its accidents, and Sandy and I have had close calls at times. Bears are nobody's fools, and they know enough to let men alone as a general thing, unless they are wounded, or cornered, or have cubs. In my opinion, a hungry old mother would catch and eat a man, if she could; which is only fair play, anyhow, for we eat them. But nobody, as far as I know, has been eaten up in these rich mountains. Why they never tackle a fellow when he is lying asleep I never could understand. They could gobble us mighty handy, but I suppose it's nature to respect a sleeping man."

Sheep-owners and their shepherds have killed a great many bears, mostly by poison and traps of various sorts. Bears are fond of mutton, and levy heavy toll on every flock driven into the mountains. They usually come to the corral at night, climb in, kill a sheep with a stroke of the paw, carry it off a little distance, eat about half of it, and return the next night for the other half; and so on all summer, or until they are themselves killed. It is not, however, by direct killing, but by suffocation through crowding against the corral wall in fright, that the greatest losses are incurred. From ten to fifteen sheep are found dead, smothered in the corral, after every attack; or the walls are broken, and the flock is scattered far and wide. A flock may escape the attention of these marauders for a week or two in the spring; but after their first taste of the fine mountain-fed meat the visits are persistently kept up, in spite of all precautions. Once I spent a night with two

Portuguese shepherds, who were greatly troubled with bears, from two to four or five visiting them almost every night. Their camp was near the middle of the Park, and the wicked bears, they said, were getting worse and worse. Not waiting now until dark, they came out of the brush in broad daylight, and boldly carried off as many sheep as they liked. One evening, before sundown, a bear, followed by two cubs, came for an early supper, as the flock was being slowly driven toward the camp. Joe, the elder of the shepherds, warned by many exciting experiences, promptly climbed a tall tamarack pine, and left the freebooters to help themselves; while Antone, calling him a coward, and declaring that he was not going to let bears eat up his sheep before his face, set the dogs on them, and rushed toward them with a great noise and a stick. The frightened cubs ran up a tree, and the mother ran to meet the shepherd and dogs. Antone stood astonished for a moment, eying the oncoming bear; then fled faster than Joe had, closely pursued. He scrambled to the roof of their little cabin, the only refuge quickly available; and fortunately, the bear, anxious about her young, did not climb after him,—only held him in mortal terror a few minutes, glaring and threatening, then hastened back to her cubs, called them down, went to the frightened, huddled flock, killed a sheep, and feasted in peace. Antone piteously entreated cautious Joe to show him a good safe tree, up which he climbed like a sailor climbing a mast, and held on as long as he could with legs crossed, the slim pine recommended by Joe being nearly branchless. "So you, too, are a bear coward as well as Joe," I said, after hearing the story. "Oh, I tell you," he replied, with grand solemnity, "bear face close by look awful; she just as soon eat me as not. She do so as eef all my sheeps b'long every one to her own self. I run to bear no more. I take tree every time."

After this the shepherds corraled the flock about an hour before sundown, chopped large quantities of dry wood and made a circle of fires around the corral every night, and one with a gun kept watch on a stage built in a pine by the side of the cabin, while the other slept. But after the first night or two this fire fence did no good, for the robbers seemed to regard the light as an advantage, after becoming used to it.

On the night I spent at their camp the show made by the wall of fire when it was blazing in its prime was magnificent,—the illumined trees around about relieved against solid darkness, and the two thousand sheep lying down in one gray mass, sprinkled with gloriously brilliant gems, the effect of the firelight in their eyes. It was nearly midnight when a pair of the freebooters arrived. They walked boldly through a gap in the fire circle, killed two sheep, carried them out, and vanished in the dark woods, leaving ten dead in a pile, trampled down and smothered against the corral fence; while the scared watcher in the tree did not fire a single shot, saying he was afraid he would hit some of the sheep, as the bears got among them before he could get a good sight.

In the morning I asked the shepherds why they did not move the flock to a new pasture. "Oh, no use!" cried Antone. "Look my dead sheeps. We move three four time before, all the same bear come by the track. No use. To-morrow we go home below. Look my dead sheeps. Soon all dead."

Thus were they driven out of the mountains more than a month before the usual time. After Uncle Sam's soldiers, bears are the most effective forest police, but some of the shepherds are very successful in killing them. Altogether, by hunters, mountaineers, Indians, and sheepmen, probably five or six hundred have been killed within the bounds of the Park, during the last thirty years. But they are not in danger of extinction. Now that the Park is guarded by soldiers, not only has the vegetation in great part come back to the desolate ground, but all the wild animals are increasing in numbers. No guns are allowed in the Park except under certain restrictions, and after a permit has been obtained from the officer in charge. This has stopped the barbarous slaughter of bears, and especially of deer, by shepherds, hunters, and hunting tourists, who, it would seem, can find no pleasure without blood.

The Sierra deer—the blacktail—spend the winters in the brushy and exceedingly rough region just below the main timber-belt, and are less accessible to hunters there than when they are passing through the comparatively open forests to and from their summer pastures near the summits of the range. They go up the mountains early in the spring as the snow melts, not waiting for it all to disappear; reaching the high Sierra about the first of June, and the coolest recesses at the base of the peaks a month or so later. I have tracked them for miles over compacted snow from three to ten feet deep.

Deer are capital mountaineers, making their way into the heart of the roughest mountains; seeking not only pasturage, but a cool climate, and safe hidden places in which to bring forth their young. They are not supreme as rock-climbing animals; they take second rank, yielding the first to the mountain sheep, which dwell above them on the highest crags and peaks. Still, the two meet frequently; for the deer climbs all the peaks save the lofty summits above the glaciers, crossing piles of angular boulders, roaring swollen streams, and sheer-walled cañons by fords and passes that would try the nerves of the hardiest mountaineers,—climbing with graceful ease and reserve of strength that cannot fail to arouse admiration. Everywhere some species of deer seems to be at home,—on rough or smooth ground, lowlands or highlands, in swamps and barrens and the densest woods, in varying climates, hot or cold, over all the continent; maintaining glorious health, never making an awkward step. Standing, lying down, walking, feeding, running even for life, it is always invincibly graceful, and adds beauty and animation to every landscape,—a charming animal, and a great credit to nature.

I never see one of the common blacktail deer, the only species in the Park, without fresh admiration; and since I never carry a gun I see them well: lying beneath a juniper or dwarf pine, among the brown needles on the brink of some cliff or the end of a ridge commanding a wide outlook; feeding in sunny openings among chaparral, daintily selecting aromatic leaves and twigs; leading their fawns out of my way, or making them lie down and hide; bounding past through the forest, or curiously advancing and retreating again and again.

One morning when I was eating breakfast in a little garden spot on the Kaweah, hedged around with chaparral, I noticed a deer's head thrust through the bushes, the big beautiful eyes gazing at me. I kept still, and the deer ventured forward a step, then snorted and withdrew. In a few minutes she returned, and came into the open garden, stepping with infinite grace, followed by two others. After showing themselves for a moment, they bounded over the hedge with sharp, timid snorts and vanished. But curiosity brought them back with still another, and all four came into my garden, and, satisfied that I meant them no ill, began to feed, actually eating breakfast with me, like tame, gentle sheep around a shepherd,—rare company, and the most graceful in movements and attitudes. I eagerly watched them while they fed on ceanothus and wild cherry, daintily culling single leaves here and there from the side of the hedge, turning now and then to ship a few leaves of mint from the midst of the garden flowers. Grass they did not eat at all. No wonder the contents of the deer's stomach are eaten by the Indians.

While exploring the upper cañon of the north fork of the San Joaquin, one evening, the sky threatening rain, I searched for a dry bed, and made choice of a big juniper that had been pushed down by a snow avalanche, but was resting stubbornly on its knees high enough to let me lie under its broad trunk. Just below my shelter there was another juniper on the very brink of a precipice, and, examining it, I found a deer-bed beneath it, completely protected and concealed by drooping branches,—a fine refuge and lookout as well as resting-place. About an hour before dark I heard the clear, sharp snorting of a deer, and looking down on the brushy, rocky cañon bottom, discovered an anxious doe that no doubt had her fawns concealed near by. She bounded over the chaparral and up the farther slope of the wall, often stopping to look back and listen,—a fine picture of vivid, eager alertness. I sat perfectly still, and as my shirt was colored like the juniper bark I was not easily seen. After a little she came cautiously toward me, sniffing the air and grazing, and her movements, as she descended the cañon side over boulder piles and brush and fallen timber, were admirably strong and beautiful; she never strained or made apparent efforts, although jumping high here and there. As she drew nigh she sniffed anxiously, trying the air in different directions until she caught my scent; then bounded off, and vanished behind a small grove of firs. Soon she came back with the same caution and insatiable curiosity,—

coming and going five or six times. While I sat admiring her, a Douglas squirrel, evidently excited by her noisy alarms, climbed a boulder beneath me, and witnessed her performances as attentively as I did, while a risky chipmunk, too restless or hungry for such shows, busied himself about his supper in a thicket of shadbushes, the fruit of which was then ripe, glancing about on the slender twigs lightly as a sparrow.

Toward the end of the Indian summer, when the young are strong, the deer begin to gather in little bands of from six to fifteen or twenty, and on the approach of the first snowstorm they set out on their march down the mountains to their winter quarters; lingering usually on warm hillsides and spurs eight or ten miles below the summits, as if loath to leave. About the end of November, a heavy, far-reaching storm drives them down in haste along the dividing ridges between the rivers, led by old experienced bucks whose knowledge of the topography is wonderful.

It is when the deer are coming down that the Indians set out on their grand fall hunt. Too lazy to go into the recesses of the mountains away from trails, they wait for the deer to come out, and then waylay them. This plan also has the advantage of finding them in bands. Great preparations are made. Old guns are mended, bullets moulded, and the hunters wash themselves and fast to some extent, to insure good luck, as they say. Men and women, old and young, set forth together. Central camps are made on the well-known highways of the deer, which are soon red with blood. Each hunter comes in laden, old crones as well as maidens smiling on the luckiest. All grow fat and merry. Boys, each armed with an antlered head, play at buck-fighting, and plague the industrious women, who are busily preparing the meat for transportation, by stealing up behind them and throwing fresh hides over them. But the Indians are passing away here as everywhere, and their red camps on the mountains are fewer every year.

There are panthers, foxes, badgers, porcupines, and coyotes in the Park, but not in large numbers. I have seen coyotes well back in the range at the head of the Tuolumne Meadows as early as June 1st, before the snow was gone, feeding on marmots; but they are far more numerous on the inhabited lowlands around ranches, where they enjoy life on chickens, turkeys, quail eggs, ground squirrels, hares, etc., and all kinds of fruit. Few wild sheep, I fear, are left hereabouts; for, though safe on the high peaks, they are driven down the eastern slope of the mountains when the deer are driven down the western, to ridges and outlying spurs where the snow does not fall to a great depth, and there they are within reach of the cattlemen's rifles.

The two squirrels of the Park, the Douglas and the California gray, keep all the woods lively. The former is far more abundant and more widely distributed, being found all the way up from the foothills to the dwarf pines on the Summit peaks. He is the most influential of the Sierra animals, though small, and the brightest of all the squirrels I know,—a squirrel of squirrels, quick mountain vigor and valor condensed, purely wild, and as free from disease as a sunbeam. One cannot think of such an animal ever being weary or sick. He claims all the woods, and is inclined to drive away even men as intruders. How he scolds, and what faces he makes! If not so comically small he would be a dreadful fellow. The gray, Sciurus fossor, is the handsomest, I think, of all the large American squirrels. He is something like the Eastern gray, but is brighter and clearer in color, and more lithe and slender. He dwells in the oak and pine woods up to a height of about five thousand feet above the sea, is rather common in Yosemite Valley, Hetch-Hetchy, Kings River Cañon, and indeed in all the main cañons and Yosemites, but does not like the high fir-covered ridges. Compared with the Douglas, the gray is more than twice as large; nevertheless, he manages to make his way through the trees with less stir than his small, peppery neighbor, and is much less influential in every way. In the spring, before the pine-nuts and hazel-nuts are ripe, he examines last year's cones for the few seeds that may be left in them between the half-open scales, and gleans fallen nuts and seeds on the ground among the leaves, after making sure that no enemy is nigh. His fine tail floats, now behind, now above him, level or gracefully curled, light and radiant as dry thistledown. His body seems hardly more substantial than his tail. The Douglas is a firm, emphatic bolt of life, fiery, pungent, full of brag and show and fight, and his movements have none of the elegant deliberation of the gray. They are so quick and keen they almost sting the onlooker, and the acrobatic harlequin gyrating show he makes of himself turns one giddy to see. The gray is shy and oftentimes stealthy, as if half expecting to find an enemy in every tree and bush and behind every log; he seems to wish to be let alone, and manifests no desire to be seen, or admired, or feared. He is hunted by the Indians, and this of itself is cause enough for caution. The Douglas is less attractive for game, and probably increasing in numbers in spite of every enemy. He goes his ways bold as a lion, up and down and across, round and round, the happiest, merriest of all the hairy tribe, and at the same time tremendously earnest and solemn, sunshine incarnate, making every tree tingle with his electric toes. If you prick him, you cannot think he will bleed. He seems above the chance and change that beset common mortals, though in busily gathering burs and nuts he shows that he has to work for a living, like the rest of us. I never found a dead Douglas. He gets into the world and out of it without being noticed; only in prime is he seen, like some little plants that are visible only when in bloom.

The little striped Tamias quadrivittatus is one of the most amiable and delightful of all the mountain tree-climbers. A brighter, cheerier chipmunk does not exist. He is smarter, more arboreal and squirrel-like, than the familiar Eastern species, and is distributed as widely on the Sierra as the Douglas. Every forest, however dense or open, every hilltop and cañon, however brushy or bare, is cheered and enlivened by this happy little animal. You are likely to notice him first on the lower edge of the coniferous belt, where the Sabine and yellow pines meet; and thence upward, go where you may, you will find him every day, even in winter, unless the weather is stormy. He is an exceedingly interesting little fellow, full of odd, quaint ways, confiding, thinking no evil; and without being a squirrel—a true shadow-tail—he lives the life of a squirrel, and has almost all squirrelish accomplishments without aggressive quarrelsomeness.

I never weary of watching him as he frisks about the bushes, gathering seeds and berries; poising on slender twigs of wild cherry, shad, chinquapin, buckthorn, bramble; skimming along prostrate trunks or over the grassy, needle-strewn forest floor; darting from boulder to boulder on glacial pavements and the tops of the great domes. When the seeds of the conifers are ripe, he climbs the trees and cuts off the cones for a winter store, working diligently, though not with the tremendous lighting energy of the Douglas, who frequently drives him out of the best trees. Then he lies in wait, and picks up a share of the burs cut off by his domineering cousin, and stores them beneath logs and in hollows. Few of the Sierra animals are so well liked as this little airy, fluffy half squirrel, half spermophile. So gentle, confiding, and busily cheery and happy, he takes one's heart and keeps his place among the best-loved of the mountain darlings. A diligent collector of seeds, nuts, and berries, of course he is well fed, though never in the least dumpy with fat. On the contrary, he looks like a mere fluff of fur, weighing but little more than a field mouse, and of his frisky, birdlike liveliness without haste there is no end. Douglas can bark with his mouth closed, but little quad always opens his when he talks or sings. He has a considerable variety of notes which correspond with his movements, some of them sweet and liquid, like water dripping into a pool with tinkling sound. His eyes are black and animated, shining like dew. He seems dearly to like teasing a dog, venturing within a few feet of it, then frisking away with a lively chipping and low squirrelish churring; beating time to his music, such as it is, with his tail, which at each chip and churr describes a half circle. Not even Douglas is surer footed or takes greater risks. I have seen him running about on sheer Yosemite cliffs, holding on with as little effort as a fly and as little thought of danger, in places where, if he had made the least slip, he would have fallen thousands of feet. How fine it would be could mountaineers move about on precipices with the same sure grip!

Before the pine-nuts are ripe, grass seeds and those of the many species of ceanothus, with strawberries, raspberries, and the soft red thimbleberries of Rubus nutkanus, form the bulk of his food, and a neater eater is not to be found in the mountains. Bees powdered with pollen, poking their blunt noses into the bells of flowers, are comparatively clumsy and boorish. Frisking along some fallen pine or fir, when the grass seeds are ripe, he looks about him, considering which of the tufts he sees is likely to have the best, runs out to it, selects what he thinks is sure to be a good head, cuts it off, carries it to the top of the log, sits upright and nibbles out the grain without getting awns in his mouth, turning the head round, holding it and fingering it as if playing on a flute; then skips for another and another, bringing them to the same dining-log.

The woodchuck (Arctomys monax) dwells on high bleak ridges and boulder piles; and a very different sort of mountaineer is he,—bulky, fat, aldermanic, and fairly bloated at times by hearty indulgence in the lush pastures of his airy home. And yet he is by no means a dull animal. In the midst of what we regard as storm-beaten desolation, high in the frosty air, beside the glaciers he pipes and whistles right cheerily and lives to a good old age. If you are as early a riser as he is, you may oftentimes see him come blinking out of his burrow to meet the first beams of the morning and take a sunbath on some favorite flat-topped boulder. Afterward, well warmed, he goes to breakfast in one of his garden hollows, eats heartily like a cow in clover until comfortably swollen, then goes a-visiting, and plays and loves and fights.

In the spring of 1875, when I was exploring the peaks and glaciers about the head of the middle fork of the San Joaquin, I had crossed the range from the head of Owen River, and one morning, passing around a frozen lake where the snow was perhaps ten feet deep, I was surprised to find the fresh track of a woodchuck plainly marked, the sun having softened the surface. What could the animal be thinking of, coming out so early while all the ground was snow-buried? The steady trend of his track showed he had a definite aim, and fortunately it was toward a mountain thirteen thousand feet high that I meant to climb. So I followed to see if I could find out what he was up to. From the base of the mountain the track pointed straight up, and I knew by the melting snow that I was not far behind him. I lost the track on a crumbling ridge, partly projecting through the snow, but soon discovered it again. Well toward the summit of the mountain, in an open spot on the south side, nearly inclosed by disintegrating pinnacles among which the sun heat reverberated, making an isolated patch of warm climate, I found a nice garden, full of rock cress, phlox, silene, draba, etc., and a few grasses; and in this garden I overtook the wanderer, enjoying a fine fresh meal, perhaps the first of the season. How did he know the way to this one garden spot, so high and far off, and what told him that it was in bloom while yet the snow was ten feet deep over his den? For this it would seem he would need more botanical, topographical, and climatological knowledge than most mountaineers are possessed of.

The shy, curious mountain beaver, Haplodon, lives on the heights, not far from the woodchuck. He digs canals and controls the flow of small streams under the sod. And it is startling when one is camped on the edge of a sloping meadow near the homes of these industrious mountaineers, to be awakened in the still night by the sound of water rushing and gurgling under one's head in a newly formed canal. Pouched gophers also have a way of awakening nervous campers that is quite as exciting as the Haplodon's paln; that is, by a series of firm upward pushes when they are driving tunnels and shoving up the dirt. One naturally cries out, "Who's there?" and then discovering the cause, "All right. Go on. Good-night." and goes to sleep again.

The haymaking pika, bob-tailed spermophile, and wood-rat are also among the most interesting of the Sierra animals. The last Neotoma is scarcely at all like the common rat, is nearly twice as large, has a delicate, soft, brownish fur, white on the belly, large ears thin and translucent, eyes full and liquid and mild in expression, nose blunt and squirrelish, slender claws sharp as needles, and as his limbs are strong he can climb about as well as a squirrel; while no rat or squirrel has so innocent a look, is so easily approached, or in general expresses so much confidence in one's good intentions. He seems too fine for the thorny thickets he inhabits, and his big, rough hut is as unlike himself as possible. No other animal in these mountains makes nests so large and striking in appearance as his. They are built of all kinds of sticks (broken branches, and old rotten moss-grown chunks and green twigs, smooth or thorny, cut from the nearest bushes), mixed with miscellaneous rubbish and curious odds and ends,—bits of cloddy earth, stones, bones, bits of deer-horn, etc.: the whole simply piled in conical masses on the ground in chaparral thickets. Some of these cabins are five or six feet high, and occasionally a dozen or more are grouped together; less, perhaps, for society's sake than for advantages of food and shelter.

Coming through deep, stiff chaparral in the heart of the wilderness, heated and weary in forcing a way, the solitary explorer, happening into one of these curious neotoma villages, is startled at the strange sight, and may imagine he is in an Indian village, and feel anxious as to the reception he will get in a place so wild. At first, perhaps, not a single inhabitant will be seen, or at most only two or three seated on the tops of their huts as at the doors, observing the stranger with the mildest of mild eyes. The nest in the centre of the cabin is made of grass and films of bark chewed to tow, and lined with feathers and the down of various seeds. The thick, rough walls seem to be built for defense against enemies—fox, coyote, etc.—as well as for shelter, and the delicate creatures in their big, rude homes, suggest tender flowers, like those of Salvia carduacea, defended by thorny involucres.

Sometimes the home is built in the forks of an oak, twenty or thirty feet from the ground, and even in garrets. Among housekeepers who have these bushmen as neighbors or guests they are regarded as thieves, because they carry away and pile together everything transportable (knives, forks, tin cups, spoons, spectacles, combs, nails, kindling-wood, etc., as well as eatables of all sorts), to strengthen their fortifications or to shine among rivals. Once, far back in the high Sierra, they stole my snow-goggles, the lid of my teapot, and my aneroid barometer; and one stormy night, when encamped under a prostrate cedar, I was awakened by a gritting sound on the granite, and by the light of my fire I discovered a handsome neotoma beside me, dragging away my ice-hatchet, pulling with might and main by a buckskin string on the handle. I threw bits of bark at him and made a noise to frighten him, but he stood scolding and chattering back at me, his fine eyes shining with an air of injured innocence.

A great variety of lizards enliven the warm portions of the Park. Some of them are more than a foot in length, others but little larger than grasshoppers. A few are snaky and repulsive at first sight, but most of the species are handsome and attractive, and bear acquaintance well; we like them better the farther we see into their charming lives. Small fellow mortals, gentle and guileless, they are easily tamed, and have beautiful eyes, expressing the clearest innocence, so that, in spite of prejudices brought from cool, lizardless countries, one must soon learn to like them. Even the horned toad of the plains and foothills, called horrid, is mild and gentle, with charming eyes, and so are the snakelike species found in the underbrush of the lower forests. These glide in curves with all the ease and grace of snakes, while their small, undeveloped limbs drag for the most part as useless appendages. One specimen that I measured was fourteen inches long, and as far as I saw it made no use whatever of its diminutive limbs.

Most of them glint and dart on the sunny rocks and across open spaces from bush to bush, swift as dragonflies and humming-birds, and about as brilliantly colored. They never make a long-sustained run, whatever their object, but dart direct as arrows for a distance of ten or twenty feet, then suddenly stop, and as suddenly start again. These stops are necessary as rests, for they are short-winded, and when pursued steadily are soon run out of breath, pant pitifully, and may easily be caught where no retreat in bush or rock is quickly available.

If you stay with them a week or two and behave well, these gentle saurians, descendants of an ancient race of giants, will soon know and trust you, come to your feet, play, and watch your every motion with cunning curiosity. You will surely learn to like them, not only the bright one, gorgeous as the rainbow, but the little ones, gray as lichened granite, and scarcely bigger than grasshoppers; and they will teach you that scales may cover as fine a nature as hair or feathers or anything tailored.

There are many snakes in the cañons and lower forests, but they are mostly handsome and harmless. Of all the tourists and travelers who have visited Yosemite and the adjacent mountains, not one has been bitten by a snake of any sort, while thousands have been charmed by them. Some of them vie with the lizards in beauty of color and dress patterns. Only the rattlesnake is venomous, and he carefully keeps his venom to himself as far as man is concerned, unless his life is threatened.

Before I learned to respect rattlesnakes I killed two, the first on the San Joaquin plain. He was coiled comfortably around a tuft of bunch-grass, and I discovered him when he was between my feet as I was stepping over him. He held his head down and did not attempt to strike, although in danger of being trampled. At that time, thirty years ago, I imagined that rattlesnakes should be killed wherever found. I had no weapon of any sort, and on the smooth plain there was not a stick or a stone within miles; so I crushed him by jumping on him, as the deer are said to do. Looking me in the face he saw I meant mischief, and quickly cast himself into a coil, ready to strike in defense. I knew he could not strike when traveling, therefore I threw handfuls of dirt and grass sods at him, to tease him out of coil. He held his ground a few minutes, threatening and striking, and then started off to get rid of me. I ran forward and jumped on him; but he drew back his head so quickly my heel missed, and he also missed his stroke at me. Persecuted, tormented, again and again he tried to get away, bravely striking out to protect himself; but at last my heel came squarely down, sorely wounding him, and a few more brutal stampings crushed him. I felt degraded by the killing business, farther from heaven, and I made up my mind to try to be at least as fair and charitable as the snakes themselves, and to kill no more save in self-defense.

The second killing might also, I think, have been avoided, and I have always felt somewhat sore and guilty about it. I had built a little cabin in Yosemite, and for convenience in getting water, and for the sake of music and society, I led a small stream from Yosemite Creek into it. Running along the side of the wall it was not in the way, and it had just fall enough to ripple and sing in low, sweet tones, making delightful company, especially at night when I was lying awake. Then a few frogs came in and made merry with the stream,—and one snake, I suppose to catch the frogs.

Returning from my long walks, I usually brought home a large handful of plants, partly for study, partly for ornament, and set them in a corner of the cabin, with their stems in the stream to keep them fresh. One day, when I picked up a handful that had begun to fade, I uncovered a large coiled rattler that had been hiding behind the flowers. Thus suddenly brought to light face to face with the rightful owner of the place, the poor reptile was desperately embarrassed, evidently realizing that he had no right in the cabin. It was not only fear that he showed, but a good deal of downright bashfulness and embarrassment, like that of a more than half honest person caught under suspicious circumstances behind a door. Instead of striking or threatening to strike, though coiled and ready, he slowly drew his head down as far as he could, with awkward, confused kinks in his neck and a shamefaced expression, as if wishing the ground would open and hide him. I have looked into the eyes of so many wild animals that I feel sure I did not mistake the feelings of this unfortunate snake. I did not want to kill him, but I had many visitors, some of them children, and I oftentimes came in late at night; so I judged he must die.

Since then I have seen perhaps a hundred or more in these mountains, but I have never intentionally disturbed them, nor have they disturbed me to any great extent, even by accident, though in danger of being stepped on. Once, while I was on my knees kindling a fire, one glided under the arch made by my arm. He was only going away from the ground I had selected for a camp, and there was not the slightest danger, because I kept still and allowed him to go in peace. The only time I felt myself in serious danger was when I was coming out of the Tuolumne Cañon by a steep side cañon toward the head of Yosemite Creek. On an earthquake talus, a boulder in my way presented a front so high that I could just reach the upper edge of it while standing on the next below it. Drawing myself up, as soon as my head was above the flat top of it I caught sight of a coiled rattler. My hands had alarmed him, and he was ready for me; but even with this provocation, and when my head came in sight within a foot of him, he did not strike. The last time I sauntered through the big cañon I saw about two a day. One was not coiled, but neatly folded in a narrow space between two cobble-stones on the side of the river, his head below the level of them, ready to shoot up like a Jack-in-the-box for frogs or birds. My foot spanned the space above within an inch or two of his head, but he only held it lower. In making my way through a particularly tedious tangle of buckthorn, I parted the branches on the side of an open spot and threw my bundle of bread into it; and when, with my arms free, I was pushing through after it, I saw a small rattlesnake dragging his tail from beneath my bundle. When he caught sight of me he eyed me angrily, and with an air of righteous indignation seemed to be asking why I had thrown that stuff on him. He was so small that I was inclined to slight him, but he struck out so angrily that I drew back, and approached the opening from the other side. But he had been listening, and when I looked through the brush I found him confronting me, still with a come-in-if-you-dare expression. In vain I tried to explain that I only wanted my bread; he stoutly held the ground in front of it; so I went back a dozen rods and kept still for half an hour, and when I returned he had gone.

One evening, near sundown, in a very rough, boulder-choked portion of the cañon, I searched long for a level spot for a bed, and at last was glad to find a patch of flood-sand on the river-bank, and a lot of driftwood close by for a campfire. But when I threw down my bundle, I found two snakes in possession of the ground. I might have passed the night even in this snake den without danger, for I never knew a single instance of their coming into camp in the night; but fearing that, in so small a space, some late comers, not aware of my presence, might get stepped on when I was replenishing the fire, to avoid possible crowding I encamped on one of the earthquake boulders.

There are two species of Crotalus in the Park, and when I was exploring the basin of Yosemite Creek I thought I had discovered a new one. I saw a snake with curious divided appendages on its head. Going nearer, I found that the strange headgear was only the feet of a frog. Cutting a switch, I struck the snake lightly until he disgorged the poor frog, or rather allowed it to back out. On its return to the light from one of the very darkest of death valleys, it blinked a moment with a sort of dazed look, then plunged into a stream, apparently happy and well.

Frogs abound in all the bogs, marshes, pools, and lakes, however cold and high and isolated. How did they manage to get up these high mountains? Surely not by jumping. Long and dry excursions through weary miles of boulders and brush would be trying to frogs. Most likely their stringy spawn is carried on the feet of ducks, cranes, and other waterbirds. Anyhow, they are most thoroughly distributed, and flourish famously. What a cheery, hearty set they are, and how bravely their krink and tronk concerts enliven the rocky wilderness!

None of the high-lying mountain lakes or branches of the rivers above sheer falls had fish of any sort until stocked by the agency of man. In the high Sierra, the only river in which trout exist naturally is the middle fork of Kings River. There are no sheer falls on this stream; some of the rapids, however, are so swift and rough, even at the lowest stage of water, that it is surprising any fish can climb them. I found trout in abundance in this fork up to seventy-five hundred feet. They also run quite high on the Kern. On the Merced they get no higher than Yosemite Valley, four thousand feet, all the forks of the river being barred there by sheer falls, and on the main Tuolumne they are stopped by a fall below Hetch-Hetchy, still lower than Yosemite. Though these upper waters are inaccessible to the fish, one would suppose their eggs might have been planted there by some means. Nature has so many ways of doing such things. In this case she waited for the agency of man, and now many of these hitherto fishless lakes and streams are full of fine trout, stocked by individual enterprise, Walton clubs etc., in great part under the auspices of the United States Fish Commission. A few trout carried into Hetch-Hetchy in a common water-bucket have multiplied wonderfully fast. Lake Tenaya, at an elevation of over eight thousand feet, was stocked eight years ago by Mr. Murphy, who carried a few trout from Yosemite. Many of the small streams of the eastern slope have also been stocked with trout transported over the passes in tin cans on the backs of mules. Soon, it would seem, all the streams of the range will be enriched by these lively fish, and will become the means of drawing thousands of visitors into the mountains. Catching trout with a bit of bent wire is a rather trivial business, but fortunately people fish better than they know. In most cases it is the man who is caught. Trout-fishing regarded as bait for catching men, for the saving of both body and soul, is important, and deserves all the expense and care bestowed on it.

CHAPTER VII

Among the Birds of the Yosemite

Travelers in the Sierra forests usually complain of the want of life. "The trees," they say, "are fine, but the empty stillness is deadly; there are no animals to be seen, no birds. We have not heard a song in all the woods." And no wonder! They go in large parties with mules and horses; they make a great noise; they are dressed in outlandish unnatural colors; every animal shuns them. Even the frightened pines would run away if they could. But Nature-lovers, devout, silent, open-eyed, looking and listening with love, find no lack of inhabitants in these mountain mansions, and they come to them gladly. Not to mention the large animals or the small insect people, every waterfall has its ouzel and every tree its squirrel or tamias or bird: tiny nuthatch threading the furrows of the bark, sheerily whispering to itself as it deftly pries off loose scales and examines the curled edges of lichens, or Clarke crow or jay examining the cones, or some singer—oriole, tanager, warbler—resting, feeding, attending to domestic affairs. Hawks and eagles sail overhead, grouse walk in happy flocks below, and song sparrows sing in every bed of chaparral. There is no crowding, to be sure. Unlike the low Eastern trees, those of the Sierra in the main forest belt average nearly two hundred feet in height, and of course many birds are required to make much show in them, and many voices to fill them. Nevertheless, the whole range, from foothills to snowy summits, is shaken into song every summer; and though low and thin in winter, the music never ceases.

The sage cock (Centrocercus urophasianus) is the largest of the Sierra game-birds and the king of American grouse. It is an admirably strong, hardy, handsome, independent bird, able with comfort to bid defiance to heat, cold, drought, hunger, and all sorts of storms, living on whatever seeds or insects chance to come in its way, or simply on the leaves of sage-brush, everywhere abundant on its desert range. In winter, when the temperature is oftentimes below zero, and heavy snowstorms are blowing, he sits beneath a sage bush and allows himself to be covered, poking his head now and then through the snow to feed on the leaves of his shelter. Not even the Arctic ptarmigan is hardier in braving frost and snow and wintry darkness. When in full plumage he is a beautiful bird, with a long, firm, sharp-pointed tail, which in walking is slightly raised and swings sidewise back and forth with each step. The male is handsomely marked with black and white on the neck, back, and wings, weighs five or six pounds, and measures about thirty inches in length. The female is clad mostly in plain brown, and is not so large. They occasionally wander from the sage plains into the open nut-pine and juniper woods, but never enter the main coniferous forest. It is only in the broad, dry, half-desert sage plains that they are quite at home, where the weather is blazing hot in summer, cold in winter. If any one passes through a flock, all squat on the gray ground and hold their heads low, hoping to escape observation; but when approached within a rod or so, they rise with a magnificent burst of wing-beats, looking about as big as turkeys and making a noise like a whirlwind.

On the 28th of June, at the head of Owen's Valley, I caught one of the young that was then just able to fly. It was seven inches long, of a uniform gray color, blunt-billed, and when captured cried lustily in a shrill piping voice, clear in tone as a boy's small willow whistle. I have seen flocks of from ten to thirty or forty on the east margin of the Park, where the Mono Desert meets the gray foothills of the Sierra; but since cattle have been pastured there they are becoming rarer every year.

Another magnificent bird, the blue or dusky grouse, next in size to the sage cock, is found all through the main forest belt, though not in great numbers. They like best the heaviest silver-fir woods near garden and meadow openings, where there is but little underbrush to cover the approach of enemies. When a flock of these brave birds, sauntering and feeding on the sunny, flowery levels of some hidden meadow or Yosemite valley far back in the heart of the mountains, see a man for the first time in their lives, they rise with hurried notes of surprise and excitement and alight on the lowest branches of the trees, wondering what the wanderer may be, and showing great eagerness to get a good view of the strange vertical animal. Knowing nothing of guns, they allow you to approach within a half dozen paces, then quietly hop a few branches higher or fly to the next tree without a thought of concealment, so that you may observe them as long as you like, near enough to see the fine shading of their plumage, the feathers on their toes, and the innocent wonderment in their beautiful wild eyes. But in the neighborhood of roads and trails they soon become shy, and when disturbed fly into the highest, leafiest trees, and suddenly become invisible, so well do they know how to hide and keep still and make use of their protective coloring. Nor can they be easily dislodged ere they are ready to go. In vain the hunter goes round and round some tall pine or fir into which he has perhaps seen a dozen enter, gazing up through the branches, straining his eyes while his gun is held ready; not a feather can he see unless his eyes have been sharpened by long experience and knowledge of the blue grouse's habits. Then, perhaps, when he is thinking that the tree must be hollow and that the birds have all gone inside, they burst forth with a startling whir of wing-beats, and after gaining full speed go skating swiftly away through the forest arches in a long, silent, wavering slide, with wings held steady.

During the summer they are most of the time on the ground, feeding on insects, seeds, berries, etc., around the margins of open spots and rocky moraines, playing and sauntering, taking sun baths and sand baths, and drinking at little pools and rills during the heat of the day. In winter they live mostly in the trees, depending on buds for food, sheltering beneath dense overlapping branches at night and during storms on the leeside of the trunk, sunning themselves on the southside limbs in fine weather, and sometimes diving into the mealy snow to flutter and wallow, apparently for exercise and fun.

I have seen young broods running beneath the firs in June at a height of eight thousand feet above the sea. On the approach of danger, the mother with a peculiar cry warns the helpless midgets to scatter and hide beneath leaves and twigs, and even in plain open places it is almost impossible to discover them. In the meantime the mother feigns lameness, throws herself at your feet, kicks and gasps and flutters, to draw your attention from the chicks. The young are generally able to fly about the middle of July; but even after they can fly well they are usually advised to run and hide and lie still, no matter how closely approached, while the mother goes on with her loving, lying acting, apparently as desperately concerned for their safety as when they were featherless infants. Sometimes, however, after carefully studying the circumstances, she tells them to take wing; and up and away in a blurry birr and whir they scatter to all points of the compass, as if blown up with gunpowder, dropping cunningly out of sight three or four hundred yards off, and keeping quiet until called, after the danger is supposed to be past. If you walk on a little way without manifesting any inclination to hunt them, you may sit down at the foot of a tree near enough to see and hear the happy reunion. One touch of nature makes the whole world kin; and it is truly wonderful how love-telling the small voices of these birds are, and how far they reach through the woods into one another's hearts and into ours. The tones are so perfectly human and so full of anxious affection, few mountaineers can fail to be touched by them.

They are cared for until full grown. On the 20th of August, as I was passing along the margin of a garden spot on the head-waters of the San Joaquin, a grouse rose from the ruins of an old juniper that had been uprooted and brought down by an avalanche from a cliff overhead. She threw herself at my feet, limped and fluttered and gasped, showing, as I thought, that she had a nest and was raising a second brood. Looking for the eggs, I was surprised to see a strong-winged flock nearly as large as the mother fly up around me.

Instead of seeking a warmer climate when the winter storms set in, these hardy birds stay all the year in the high Sierra forests, and I have never known them to suffer in any sort of weather. Able to live on the buds of pine, spruce, and fir, they are forever independent in the matter of food supply, which gives so many of us trouble, dragging us here and there away from our best work. How gladly I would live on pine buds, however pitchy, for the sake of this grand independence! With all his superior resources, man makes more distracting difficulty concerning food than any other of the family.

The mountain quail, or plumed partridge (Oreortyx pictus plumiferus) is common in all the upper portions of the Park, though nowhere in numbers. He ranges considerably higher than the grouse in summer, but is unable to endure the heavy storms of winter. When his food is buried, he descends the range to the brushy foothills, at a height of from two to three thousand feet above sea; but like every true mountaineer, he is quick to follow the spring back into the highest mountains. I think he is the very handsomest and most interesting of all the American partridges, larger and handsomer than the famous Bob White, or even the fine California valley quail, or the Massena partridge of Arizona and Mexico. That he is not so regarded, is because as a lonely mountaineer he is not half known.

His plumage is delicately shaded, brown above, white and rich chestnut below and on the sides, with many dainty markings of black and white and gray here and there, while his beautiful head plume, three or four inches long, nearly straight, composed of two feathers closely folded so as to appear as one, is worn jauntily slanted backward like a single feather in a boy's cap, giving him a very marked appearance. They wander over the lonely mountains in family flocks of from six to fifteen, beneath ceanothus, manzanita, and wild cherry thickets, and over dry sandy flats, glacier meadows, rocky ridges, and beds of Bryanthus around glacier lakes, especially in autumn, when the berries of the upper gardens are ripe, uttering low clucking notes to enable them to keep together. When they are so suddenly disturbed that they are afraid they cannot escape the danger by running into thickets, they rise with a fine hearty whir and scatter in the brush over an area of half a square mile or so, a few of them diving into leafy trees. But as soon as the danger is past, the parents with a clear piping note call them together again. By the end of July the young are two thirds grown and fly well, though only dire necessity can compel them to try their wings. In gait, gestures, habits, and general behavior they are like domestic chickens, but infinitely finer, searching for insects and seeds, looking to this side and that, scratching among fallen leaves, jumping up to pull down grass heads, and clucking and muttering in low tones.

Once when I was seated at the foot of a tree on the head-waters of the Merced, sketching, I heard a flock up the valley behind me, and by their voices gradually sounding nearer I knew that they were feeding toward me. I kept still, hoping to see them. Soon one came within three or four feet of me, without noticing me any more than if I were a stump or a bulging part of the trunk against which I was leaning, my clothing being brown, nearly like the bark. Presently along came another and another, and it was delightful to get so near a view of these handsome chickens perfectly undisturbed, observe their manners, and hear their low peaceful notes. At last one of them caught my eye, gazed in silent wonder for a moment, then uttered a peculiar cry, which was followed by a lot of hurried muttered notes that sounded like speech. The others, of course, saw me as soon as the alarm was sounded, and joined the wonder talk, gazing and chattering, astonished but not frightened. Then all with one accord ran back with the news to the rest of the flock. "What is it? what is it? Oh, you never saw the like," they seemed to be saying. "Not a deer, or a wolf, or a bear; come see, come see." "Where? where?" "Down there by that tree." Then they approached cautiously, past the tree, stretching their necks, and looking up in turn as if knowing from the story told them just where I was. For fifteen or twenty minutes they kept coming and going, venturing within a few feet of me, and discussing the wonder in charming chatter. Their curiosity at last satisfied, they began to scatter and feed again, going back in the direction they had come from; while I, loath to part with them, followed noiselessly, crawling beneath the bushes, keeping them in sight for an hour or two, learning their habits, and finding out what seeds and berries they like best.

The valley quail is not a mountaineer, and seldom enters the Park except at a few of the lowest places on the western boundary. It belongs to the brushy foothills and plains, orchards and wheatfields, and is a hundred times more numerous than the mountain quail. It is a beautiful bird, about the size of the Bob White, and has a handsome crest of four or five feathers an inch long, recurved, standing nearly erect at times or drooping forward. The loud calls of these quails in the spring—Pe-check-ah, Pe-check-a, Hoy, Hoy—are heard far and near over all the lowlands. They have vastly increased in numbers since the settlement of the country, notwithstanding the immense numbers killed every season by boys and pot-hunters as well as the regular leggined sportsmen from the towns; for man's destructive action is more than counterbalanced by increased supply of food from cultivation, and by the destruction of their enemies—coyotes, skunks, foxes, hawks, owls, etc.—which not only kill the old birds, but plunder their nests. Where coyotes and skunks abound, scarce one pair in a hundred is successful in raising a brood. So well aware are these birds of the protection afforded by man, even now that the number of their wild enemies has been greatly diminished, that they prefer to nest near houses, notwithstanding they are so shy. Four or five pairs rear their young around our cottage every spring. One year a pair nested in a straw pile within four or five feet of the stable door, and did not leave the eggs when the men led the horses back and forth within a foot or two. For many seasons a pair nested in a tuft of pampas grass in the garden; another pair in an ivy vine on the cottage roof, and when the young were hatched, it was interesting to see the parents getting the fluffy dots down. They were greatly excited, and their anxious calls and directions to their many babes attracted our attention. They had no great difficulty in persuading the young birds to pitch themselves from the main roof to the porch roof among the ivy, but to get them safely down from the latter to the ground, a distance of ten feet, was most distressing. It seemed impossible the frail soft things could avoid being killed. The anxious parents led them to a point above a spiræa bush, that reached nearly to the eaves, which they seemed to know would break the fall. Anyhow they led their chicks to this point, and with infinite coaxing and encouragement got them to tumble themselves off. Down they rolled and sifted through the soft leaves and panicles to the pavement, and, strange to say, all got away unhurt except one that lay as if dead for a few minutes. When it revived, the joyful parents, with their brood fairly launched on the journey of life, proudly led them down the cottage hill, through the garden, and along an osage orange hedge into the cherry orchard. These charming birds even enter towns and villages, where the gardens are of good size and guns are forbidden, sometimes going several miles to feed, and returning every evening to their roosts in ivy or brushy trees and shrubs.

Geese occasionally visit the Park, but never stay long. Sometimes on their way across the range, a flock wanders into Hetch-Hetchy or Yosemite to rest or get something to eat, and if shot at, are often sorely bewildered in seeking a way out. I have seen them rise from the meadow or river, wheel round in a spiral until a height of four or five hundred feet was reached, then form ranks and try to fly over the wall. But Yosemite magnitudes seem to be as deceptive to geese as to men, for they would suddenly find themselves against the cliffs not a fourth of the way to the top. Then turning in confusion, and screaming at the strange heights, they would try the opposite side, and so until exhausted they were compelled to rest, and only after discovering the river cañon could they make their escape. Large, harrow-shaped flocks may often be seen crossing the range in the spring, at a height of at least fourteen thousand feet. Think of the strength of wing required to sustain so heavy a bird in air so thin. At this elevation it is but little over half as dense as at the sea level. Yet they hold bravely on in beautifully dressed ranks, and have breath enough to spare for loud honking. After the crest of the Sierra is passed it is only a smooth slide down the sky to the waters of Mono, where they may rest as long as they like.

Ducks of five or six species, among which are the mallard and wood duck, go far up into the heart of the mountains in the spring, and of course come down in the fall with the families they have reared. A few, as if loath to leave the mountains, pass the winter in the lower valleys of the Park at a height of three thousand to four thousand feet, where the main streams are never wholly frozen over, and snow never falls to a great depth or lies long. In summer they are found up to a height of eleven thousand feet on all the lakes and branches of the rivers except the smallest, and those beside the glaciers incumbered with drifting ice and snow. I found mallards and wood ducks at Lake Tenaya, June 1, before the ice-covering was half melted, and a flock of young ones in Bloody Cañon Lake, June 20. They are usually met in pairs, never in large flocks. No place is too wild or rocky or solitary for these brave swimmers, no stream too rapid. In the roaring, resounding cañon torrents, they seem as much at home as in the tranquil reaches and lakes of the broad glacial valleys. Abandoning themselves to the wild play of the waters, they go drifting confidingly through blinding, thrashing spray, dancing on boulder-dashed waves, tossing in beautiful security on rougher water than is usually encountered by sea birds when storms are blowing.

A mother duck with her family of ten little ones, waltzing round and round in a pot-hole ornamented with foam bells, huge rocks leaning over them, cascades above and below and beside them, made one of the most interesting bird pictures I ever saw.

I have never found the great northern diver in the Park lakes. Most of them are inaccessible to him. He might plump down into them, but would hardly be able to get out of them, since, with his small wings and heavy body, a wide expanse of elbow room is required in rising. Now and then one may be seen in the lower Sierra lakes to the northward about Lassens Butte and Shasta, at a height of four thousand to five thousand feet, making the loneliest places lonelier with the wildest of wild cries.

Plovers are found along the sandy shores of nearly all the mountain lakes, tripping daintily on the water's edge, picking up insects; and it is interesting to learn how few of these familiar birds are required to make a solitude cheerful.

Sandhill cranes are sometimes found in comparatively small marshes, mere dots in the mighty forest. In such spots, at an elevation of from six thousand to eight thousand feet above the sea, they are occasionally met in pairs as early as the end of May, while the snow is still deep in the surrounding fir and sugar-pine woods. And on sunny days in autumn, large flocks may be seen sailing at a great height above the forests, shaking the crisp air into rolling waves with their hearty koor-r-r, koor-r-r, uck-uck, soaring in circles for hours together on their majestic wings, seeming to float without effort like clouds, eying the wrinkled landscape outspread like a map mottled with lakes and glaciers and meadows and streaked with shadowy cañons and streams, and surveying every frog marsh and sandy flat within a hundred miles.

Eagles and hawks are oftentimes seen above the ridges and domes. The greatest height at which I have observed them was about twelve thousand feet, over the summits of Mount Hoffman, in the middle region of the Park. A few pairs had their nests on the cliffs of this mountain, and could be seen every day in summer, hunting marmots, mountain beavers, pikas, etc. A pair of golden eagles have made their home in Yosemite ever since I went there thirty years ago. Their nest is on the Nevada Fall Cliff, opposite the Liberty Cap. Their screams are rather pleasant to hear in the vast gulfs between the granite cliffs, and they help the owls in keeping the echoes busy.

But of all the birds of the high Sierra, the strangest, noisiest, and most notable is the Clarke crow (Nucifraga columbiana). He is a foot long and nearly two feet in extent of wing, ashy gray in general color, with black wings, white tail, and a strong, sharp bill, with which he digs into the pine cones for the seeds on which he mainly subsists. He is quick, boisterous, jerky, and irregular in his movements and speech, and makes a tremendously loud and showy advertisement of himself,—swooping and diving in deep curves across gorges and valleys from ridge to ridge, alighting on dead spars, looking warily about him, and leaving his dry springy perches, trembling from the vigor of his kick as he launches himself for a new flight, screaming from time to time loud enough to be heard more than a mile in still weather. He dwells far back on the high stormbeaten margin of the forest, where the mountain pine, juniper, and hemlock grow wide apart on glacier pavements and domes and rough crumbling ridges, and the dwarf pine makes a low crinkled growth along the flanks of the Summit peaks. In so open a region, of course, he is well seen. Everybody notices him, and nobody at first knows what to make of him. One guesses he must be a woodpecker; another a crow or some sort of jay, another a magpie. He seems to be a pretty thoroughly mixed and fermented compound of all these birds, has all their strength, cunning, shyness, thievishness, and wary, suspicious curiosity combined and condensed. He flies like a woodpecker, hammers dead limbs for insects, digs big holes in pine cones to get at the seeds, cracks nuts held between his toes, cries like a crow or Stellar jay,—but in a far louder, harsher, and more forbidding tone of voice,—and besides his crow caws and screams, has a great variety of small chatter talk, mostly uttered in a fault-finding tone. Like the magpie, he steals articles that can be of no use to him. Once when I made my camp in a grove at Cathedral Lake, I chanced to leave a cake of soap on the shore where I had been washing, and a few minutes afterward I saw my soap flying past me through the grove, pushed by a Clarke crow.

In winter, when the snow is deep, the cones of the mountain pines are empty, and the juniper, hemlock, and dwarf pine orchard buried, he comes down to glean seeds in the yellow pine forests, startling the grouse with his loud screams. But even in winter, in calm weather, he stays in his high mountain home, defying the bitter frost. Once I lay snowbound through a three days' storm at the timber-line on Mount Shasta; and while the roaring snow-laden blast swept by, one of these brave birds came to my camp, and began hammering at the cones on the topmost branches of half-buried pines, without showing the slightest distress. I have seen Clarke crows feeding their young as early as June 19, at a height of more than ten thousand feet, when nearly the whole landscape was snow-covered.

They are excessively shy, and keep away from the traveler as long as they think they are observed; but when one goes on without seeming to notice them, or sits down and keeps still, their curiosity speedily gets the better of their caution, and they come flying from tree to tree, nearer and nearer, and watch every motion. Few, I am afraid, will ever learn to like this bird, he is so suspicious and self-reliant, and his voice is so harsh that to most ears the scream of the eagle will seem melodious compared with it. Yet the mountaineer who has battled and suffered and struggled must admire his strength and endurance,—the way he faces the mountain weather, cleaves the icy blasts, cares for his young, and digs a living from the stern wilderness.

Higher yet than Nucifraga dwells the little dun-headed sparrow (Leucosticte tephrocotis). From early spring to late autumn he is to be found only on the snowy, icy peaks at the head of the glacier cirques and cañons. His feeding grounds in spring are the snow sheets between the peaks, and in midsummer and autumn the glaciers. Many bold insects go mountaineering almost as soon as they are born, ascending the highest summits on the mild breezes that blow in from the sea every day during steady weather; but comparatively few of these adventurers find their way down or see a flower bed again. Getting tired and chilly, they alight on the snow fields and glaciers, attracted perhaps by the glare, take cold, and die. There they lie as if on a white cloth purposely outspread for them, and the dun sparrows find them a rich and varied repast requiring no pursuit,—bees and butterflies on ice, and many spicy beetles, a perpetual feast, on tables big for guests so small, and in vast banqueting halls ventilated by cool breezes that ruffle the feathers of the fairy brownies. Happy fellows, no rivals come to dispute possession with them. No other birds, not even hawks, as far as I have noticed, live so high. They see people so seldom, they flutter around the explorer with the liveliest curiosity, and come down a little way, sometimes nearly a mile, to meet him and conduct him into their icy homes.

When I was exploring the Merced group, climbing up the grand cañon between the Merced and Red mountains into the fountain amphitheatre of an ancient glacier, just as I was approaching the small active glacier that leans back in the shadow of Merced Mountain, a flock of twenty or thirty of these little birds, the first I had seen, came down the cañon to meet me, flying low, straight toward me as if they meant to fly in my face. Instead of attacking me or passing by, they circled round my head, chirping and fluttering for a minute or two, then turned and escorted me up the cañon, alighting on the nearest rocks on either hand, and flying ahead a few yards at a time to keep even with me.

I have not discovered their winter quarters. Probably they are in the desert ranges to the eastward, for I never saw any of them in Yosemite, the winter refuge of so many of the mountain birds.

Humming-birds are among the best and most conspicuous of the mountaineers, flashing their ruby throats in countless wild gardens far up the higher slopes, where they would be least expected. All one has to do to enjoy the company of these mountain-loving midgets is to display a showy blanket or handkerchief.

The arctic bluebird is another delightful mountaineer, singing a wild, cheery song and "carrying the sky on his back" over all the gray ridges and domes of the subalpine region.

A fine, hearty, good-natured lot of woodpeckers dwell in the Park, and keep it lively all the year round. Among the most notable of these are the magnificent log cock (Ceophlœus pileatus), the prince of Sierra woodpeckers, and only second in rank, as far as I know, of all the woodpeckers of the world; the Lewis woodpecker, large, black, glossy, that flaps and flies like a crow, does but little hammering, and feeds in great part on wild cherries and berries; and the carpenter, who stores up great quantities of acorns in the bark of trees for winter use. The last-named species is a beautiful bird, and far more common than the others. In the woods of the West he represents the Eastern red-head. Bright, cheerful, industrious, not in the least shy, the carpenters give delightful animation to the open Sierra forests at a height of from three thousand to fifty-five hundred feet, especially in autumn, when the acorns are ripe. Then no squirrel works harder at his pine-nut harvest than these woodpeckers at their acorn harvest, drilling holes in the thick, corky bark of the yellow pine and incense cedar, in which to store the crop for winter use,—a hole for each acorn, so nicely adjusted as to size that when the acorn, point foremost, is driven in, it fits so well that it cannot be drawn out without digging around it. Each acorn is thus carefully stored in a dry bin, perfectly protected from the weather,—a most laborious method of stowing away a crop, a granary for each kernel. Yet the birds seem never to weary at the work, but go on so diligently that they seem determined to save every acorn in the grove. They are never seen eating acorns at the time they are storing them, and it is commonly believed that they never eat them or intend to eat them, but that the wise birds store them and protect them from the depredations of squirrels and jays, solely for the sake of the worms they are supposed to contain. And because these worms are too small for use at the time the acorns drop, they are shut up like lean calves and steers, each in a separate stall with abundance of food, to grow big and fat by the time they will be most wanted, that is, in winter, when insects are scarce and stall-fed worms most valuable. So these woodpeckers are supposed to be a sort of cattle-raisers, each with a drove of thousands, rivaling the ants that raise grain and keep herds of plant lice for milk cows. Needless to say the story is not true, though some naturalists, even, believe it. When Emerson was in the Park, having heard the worm story and seen the great pines plugged full of acorns, he asked (just to pump me, I suppose), "Why do the woodpeckers take the trouble to put acorns into the bark of the trees?" "For the same reason," I replied, "that bees store honey and squirrels nuts." "But they tell me, Mr. Muir, that woodpeckers don't eat acorns." "Yes, they do," I said, "I have seen them eating them. During snowstorms they seem to eat little besides acorns. I have repeatedly interrupted them at their meals, and seen the perfectly sound, half-eaten acorns. They eat them in the shell as some people eat eggs." "But what about the worms?" "I suppose," I said, "that when they come to a wormy one they eat both worm and acorn. Anyhow, they eat the sound ones when they can't find anything they like better, and from the time they store them until they are used they guard them, and woe to the squirrel or jay caught stealing." Indians, in times of scarcity, frequently resort to these stores and chop them out with hatchets; a bushel or more may be gathered from a single cedar or pine.

The common robin, with all his familiar notes and gestures, is found nearly everywhere throughout the Park,—in shady dells beneath dogwoods and maples, along the flowery banks of the streams, tripping daintily about the margins of meadows in the fir and pine woods, and far beyond on the shores of glacier lakes and the slopes of the peaks. How admirable the constitution and temper of this cheery, graceful bird, keeping glad health over so vast and varied a range. In all America he is at home, flying from plains to mountains, up and down, north and south, away and back, with the seasons and supply of food. Oftentimes in the High Sierra, as you wander through the solemn woods, awestricken and silent, you will hear the reassuring voice of this fellow wanderer ringing out sweet and clear as if saying, "Fear not, fear not. Only love is here." In the severest solitudes he seems as happy as in gardens and apple orchards.

The robins enter the Park as soon as the snow melts, and go on up the mountains, gradually higher, with the opening flowers, until the topmost glacier meadows are reached in June and July. After the short summer is done, they descend like most other summer visitors in concord with the weather, keeping out of the first heavy snows as much as possible, while lingering among the frost-nipped wild cherries on the slopes just below the glacier meadows. Thence they go to the lower slopes of the forest region, compelled to make haste at times by heavy all-day storms, picking up seeds or benumbed insects by the way; and at last all, save a few that winter in Yosemite valleys, arrive in the vineyards and orchards and stubble-fields of the lowlands in November, picking up fallen fruit and grain, and awakening old-time memories among the white-headed pioneers, who cannot fail to recognize the influence of so homelike a bird. They are then in flocks of hundreds, and make their way into the gardens of towns as well as into the parks and fields and orchards about the bay of San Francisco, where many of the wanderers are shot for sport and the morsel of meat on their breasts. Man then seems a beast of prey. Not even genuine piety can make the robin-killer quite respectable. Saturday is the great slaughter day in the bay region. Then the city pot-hunters, with a rag-tag of boys, go forth to kill, kept in countenance by a sprinkling of regular sportsmen arrayed in self-conscious majesty and leggins, leading dogs and carrying hammerless, breech-loading guns of famous makers. Over the fine landscapes the killing goes forward with shameful enthusiasm. After escaping countless dangers, thousands fall, big bagfuls are gathered, many are left wounded to die slowly, no Red Cross Society to help them. Next day, Sunday, the blood and leggins vanish from the most devout of the bird-butchers, who go to church, carrying gold-headed canes instead of guns. After hymns, prayers, and sermon they go home to feast, to put God's song birds to use, put them in their dinners instead of in their hearts, eat them, and suck the pitiful little drumsticks. It is only race living on race, to be sure, but Christians singing Divine Love need not be driven to such straits while wheat and apples grow and the shops are full of dead cattle. Song birds for food! Compared with this, making kindlings of pianos and violins would be pious economy.

The larks come in large flocks from the hills and mountains in the fall, and are slaughtered as ruthlessly as the robins. Fortunately, most of our song birds keep back in leafy hidings, and are comparatively inaccessible.

The water ouzel, in his rocky home amid foaming waters, seldom sees a gun, and of all the singers I like him the best. He is a plainly dressed little bird, about the size of a robin, with short, crisp, but rather broad wings, and a tail of moderate length, slanted up, giving him, with his nodding, bobbing manners, a wrennish look. He is usually seen fluttering about in the spray of falls and the rapid cascading portions of the main branches of the rivers. These are his favorite haunts; but he is often seen also on comparatively level reaches and occasionally on the shores of mountain lakes, especially at the beginning of winter, when heavy snowfalls have blurred the streams with sludge. Though not a water-bird in structure, he gets his living in the water, and is never seen away from the immediate margin of streams. He dives fearlessly into rough, boiling eddies and rapids to feed at the bottom, flying under water seemingly as easily as in the air. Sometimes he wades in shallow places, thrusting his head under from time to time in a nodding, frisky way that is sure to attract attention. His flight is a solid whir of wing-beats like that of a partridge, and in going from place to place along his favorite string of rapids he follows the windings of the stream, and usually alights on some rock or snag on the bank or out in the current, or rarely on the dry limb of an overhanging tree, perching like a tree bird when it suits his convenience. He has the oddest, neatest manners imaginable, and all his gestures as he flits about in the wild, dashing waters bespeak the utmost cheerfulness and confidence. He sings both winter and summer, in all sorts of weather,—a sweet, fluty melody, rather low, and much less keen and accentuated than from the brisk vigor of his movements one would be led to expect.

How romantic and beautiful is the life of this brave little singer on the wild mountain streams, building his round bossy nest of moss by the side of a rapid or fall, where it is sprinkled and kept fresh and green by the spray! No wonder he sings well, since all the air about him is music; every breath he draws is part of a song, and he gets his first music lessons before he is born; for the eggs vibrate in time with the tones of the waterfalls. Bird and stream are inseparable, songful and wild, gentle and strong,—the bird ever in danger in the midst of the stream's mad whirlpools, yet seemingly immortal. And so I might go on, writing words, words, words; but to what purpose? Go see him and love him, and through him as through a window look into Nature's warm heart.

CHAPTER VIII

The Fountains and Streams of the Yosemite National Park

"Come let's to the fields, the meads, and the mountains,

The forests invite us, the streams and the fountains."

Carlyle, Translations, vol. iii.

The joyful, songful streams of the Sierra are among the most famous and interesting in the world, and draw the admiring traveler on and on through their wonderful cañons, year after year, unwearied. After long wanderings with them, tracing them to their fountains, learning their history and the forms they take in their wild works and ways throughout the different seasons of the year, we may then view them together in one magnificent show, outspread over all the range like embroidery, their silvery branches interlacing on a thousand mountains, singing their way home to the sea: the small rills, with hard roads to travel, dropping from ledge to ledge, pool to pool, like chains of sweet-toned bells, slipping gently over beds of pebbles and sand, resting in lakes, shining, spangling, shimmering, lapping the shores with whispering ripples, and shaking over-leaning bushes and grass; the larger streams and rivers in the cañons displaying noble purity and beauty with ungovernable energy, rushing down smooth inclines in wide foamy sheets fold over fold, springing up here and there in magnificent whirls, scattering crisp clashing spray for the sunbeams to iris, bursting with hoarse reverberating roar through rugged gorges and boulder dams, booming in falls, gliding, glancing with cool soothing murmuring, through long forested reaches richly embowered,—filling the grand cañons with glorious song, and giving life to all the landscape.

The present rivers of the Sierra are still young, and have made but little mark as yet on the grand cañons prepared for them by the ancient glaciers. Only a very short geological time ago they all lay buried beneath the glaciers they drained, singing in low smothered or silvery ringing tones in crystal channels, while the summer weather melted the ice and snow of the surface or gave showers. At first only in warm weather was any part of these buried rivers displayed in the light of day; for as soon as frost prevailed the surface rills vanished, though the streams beneath the ice and in the body of it flowed on all the year.

When, toward the close of the glacial period, the ice mantle began to shrink and recede from the lowlands, the lower portions of the rivers were developed, issuing from cavelike openings on the melting margin and growing longer as the ice withdrew; while for many a century the tributaries and upper portions of the trunks remained covered. In the fullness of time these also were set free in the sunshine, to take their places in the newborn landscapes; each tributary with its smaller branches being gradually developed like the main trunks, as the climatic changes went on. At first all of them were muddy with glacial detritus, and they became clear only after the glaciers they drained had receded beyond lake basins in which the sediments were dropped.

This early history is clearly explained by the present rivers of southeastern Alaska. Of those draining glaciers that discharge into arms of the sea, only the rills on the surface of the ice, and upboiling, eddying, turbid currents in the tide water in front of the terminal ice wall, are visible. Where glaciers, in the first stage of decadence, have receded from the shore, short sections of the trunks of the rivers that are to take their places may be seen rushing out from caverns and tunnels in the melting front,—rough, roaring, detritus-laden torrents, foaming and tumbling over outspread terminal moraines to the sea, perhaps without a single bush or flower to brighten their raw, shifting banks. Again, in some of the warmer cañons and valleys from which the trunk glaciers have been melted, the main trunks of the rivers are well developed, and their banks planted with fine forests, while their upper branches, lying high on the snowy mountains, are still buried beneath shrinking residual glaciers; illustrating every state of development, from icy darkness to light, and from muddiness to crystal clearness.

Now that the hard grinding sculpture work of the glacial period is done, the whole bright band of Sierra rivers run clear all the year, except when the snow is melting fast in the warm spring weather, and during extraordinary winter floods and the heavy thunderstorms of summer called cloud-bursts. Even then they are not muddy above the foothill mining region, unless the moraines have been loosened and the vegetation destroyed by sheep; for the rocks of the upper basins are clean, and the most able streams find but little to carry save the spoils of the forests,—trees, branches, flakes of bark, cones, leaves, pollen dust, etc.,—with scales of mica, sand grains, and boulders, which are rolled along the bottom of the steep parts of the main channels. Short sections of a few of the highest tributaries heading in glaciers are of course turbid with finely ground rock mud, but this is dropped in the first lakes they enter.

On the northern part of the range, mantled with porous fissured volcanic rocks, the fountain waters sink and flow below the surface for considerable distances, groping their way in the dark like the draining streams of glaciers, and at last bursting forth in big generous springs, filtered and cool and exquisitely clear. Some of the largest look like lakes, their waters welling straight up from the bottom of deep rock basins in quiet massive volume giving rise to young rivers. Others issue from horizontal clefts in sheer bluffs, with loud tumultuous roaring that may be heard half a mile or more. Magnificent examples of these great northern spring fountains, twenty or thirty feet deep and ten to nearly a hundred yards wide, abound on the main branches of the Feather, Pitt, McCloud, and Fall rivers.

The springs of the Yosemite Park, and the high Sierra in general, though many times more numerous, are comparatively small, oozing from moraines and snowbanks in thin, flat irregular currents which remain on the surface or near it, the rocks of the south half of the range being mostly flawless impervious granite; and since granite is but slightly soluble, the streams are particularly pure. Nevertheless, though they are all clear, and in the upper and main central forest regions delightfully lively and cool, they vary somewhat in color and taste as well as temperature, on account of differences, however slight, in exposure, and in the rocks and vegetation with which they come in contact. Some are more exposed than others to winds and sunshine in their falls and thin plumelike cascades; the amount of dashing, mixing, and airing the waters of each receive varies considerably; and there is always more or less variety in the kind and quantity of the vegetation they flow through, and in the time they lie in shady or sunny lakes and bogs.

The water of one of the branches of the north fork of Owens River, near the southeastern boundary of the Park, at an elevation of ninety-five hundred feet above the sea, is the best I ever found. It is not only delightfully cool and bright, but brisk, sparkling, exhilarating, and so positively delicious to the taste that a party of friends I led to it twenty-five years ago still praise it, and refer to it as "that wonderful champagne water;" though, comparatively, the finest wine is a coarse and vulgar drink. The party camped about a week in a pine grove on the edge of a little round sedgy meadow through which the stream ran bank full, and drank its icy water on frosty mornings, before breakfast, and at night about as eagerly as in the heat of the day; lying down and taking massy draughts direct from the brimming flood, lest the touch of a cup might disturb its celestial flavor. On one of my excursions I took pains to trace this stream to its head springs. It is mostly derived from snow that lies in heavy drifts and avalanche heaps on or near the axis of the range. It flows first in flat sheets over coarse sand or shingle derived from a granite ridge and the metamorphic slates of Red Mountain. Then, gathering its many small branches, it runs through beds of moraine material, and a series of lakelets and meadows and frosty juicy bogs bordered with heathworts and linked together by short bouldery reaches. Below these, growing strong with tribute drawn from many a snowy fountain on either side, the glad stream goes dashing and swirling through clumps of the white-barked pine, and tangled willow and alder thickets enriched by the fragrant herbaceous vegetation usually found about them. And just above the level camp meadow it is chafed and churned and beaten white over and over again in crossing a talus of big earthquake boulders, giving it a very thorough airing. But to what the peculiar indefinable excellence of this water is due I don't know; for other streams in adjacent cañons are aired in about the same way, and draw traces of minerals and plant essences from similar sources. The best mineral water yet discovered in the Park flows from the Tuolumne soda springs, on the north side of the Big Meadow. Mountaineers like it and ascribe every healing virtue to it, but in no way can any of these waters be compared with the Owens River champagne.

It is a curious fact that the waters of some of the Sierra lakes and streams are invisible, or nearly so, under certain weather conditions. This is noticed by mountaineers, hunters, and prospectors, wide-awake, sharp-eyed observers, little likely to be fooled by fine whims. One of these mountain men, whom I had nursed while a broken leg was mending, always gratefully reported the wonders he found. One, returning from a trip on the head waters of the Tuolumne, he came running eagerly, crying: "Muir, I've found the queerest lake in the mountains! It's high up where nothing grows; and when it isn't shiny you can't see it, and you walk right into it as if there was nothing there. The first you know of that lake you are in it, and get tripped up by the water, and hear the splash." The waters of Illilouette Creek are nearly invisible in the autumn; so that, in following the channel, jumping from boulder to boulder after a shower, you will frequently drag your feet in the apparently surfaceless pools.

Excepting a few low, warm slopes, fountain snow usually covers all the Yosemite Park from November or December to May, most of it until June or July, while on the coolest parts of the north slopes of the mountains, at a height of eleven to thirteen thousand feet, it is perpetual. It seldom lies at a greater depth than two or three feet on the lower margin, ten feet over the middle forested region, or fifteen to twenty feet in the shadowy cañons and cirques among the peaks of the Summit, except where it is drifted, or piled in avalanche heaps at the foot of long converging slopes to form perennial fountains.

The first crop of snow crystals that whitens the mountains and refreshes the streams usually falls in September or October, in the midst of charming Indian summer weather, often while the goldenrods and gentians are in their prime; but these Indian summer snows, like some of the late ones that bury the June gardens, vanish in a day or two, and garden work goes on with accelerated speed. The grand winter storms that load the mountains with enduring fountain snow seldom set in before the end of November. The fertile clouds, descending, glide about and hover in brooding silence, as if thoughtfully examining the forests and streams with reference to the work before them; then small flakes or single crystals appear, glinting and swirling in zigzags and spirals; and soon the thronging feathery masses fill the sky and make darkness like night, hurrying wandering mountaineers to their winter quarters. The first fall is usually about two to four feet deep. Then, with intervals of bright weather, not very cold, storm succeeds storm, heaping snow on snow, until from thirty to fifty or sixty feet has fallen; but on account of heavy settling and compacting, and the waste from evaporation and melting, the depth in the middle region, as stated above, rarely exceeds ten feet. Evaporation never wholly ceases, even in the coldest weather, and the sunshine between storms melts the surface more or less. Waste from melting also goes on at the bottom from summer heat stored in the rocks, as is shown by the rise of the streams after the first general storm, and their steady sustained flow all winter.

In the deep sugar-pine and silver-fir woods, up to a height of eight thousand feet, most of the snow lies where it falls, in one smooth universal fountain, until set free in the streams. But in the lighter forests of the two-leaved pine, and on the bleak slopes above the timber line, there is much wild drifting during storms accompanied by high winds, and for a day or two after they have fallen, when the temperature is low, and the snow dry and dusty. Then the trees, bending in the darkening blast, roar like feeding lions; the frozen lakes are buried; so also are the streams, which now flow in dark tunnels, as if another glacial period had come. On high ridges, where the winds have a free sweep, magnificent overcurling cornices are formed, which, with the avalanche piles, last as fountains almost all summer; and when an exceptionally high wind is blowing from the north, the snow, rolled, drifted, and ground to dust, is driven up the converging northern slopes of the peaks and sent flying for miles in the form of bright wavering banners, displayed in wonderful clearness and beauty against the sky.

The greatest storms, however, are usually followed by a deep, peculiar silence, especially profound and solemn in the forests; and the noble trees stand hushed and motionless, as if under a spell, until the morning sunbeams begin to sift through their laden spires. Then the snow, shifting and falling from the top branches, strikes the lower ones in succession, and dislodges bossy masses all the way down. Thus each tree is enveloped in a hollow conical avalanche of fairy fineness, silvery white, irised on the outside; while the relieved branches spring up and wave with startling effect in the general stillness, as if moving of their own volition. These beautiful tree avalanches, hundreds of which may be seen falling at once on fine mornings after storms, pile their snow in raised rings around corresponding hollows beneath the trees, making the forest mantle somewhat irregular, but without greatly influencing its duration and the flow of the streams.

The large storm avalanches are most abundant on the Summit peaks of the range. They descend the broad, steep slopes, as well as narrow gorges and couloirs, with grand roaring and booming, and glide in graceful curves out on the glaciers they so bountifully feed.

Down in the main cañons of the middle region broad masses are launched over the brows of cliffs three or four thousand feet high, which, worn to dust by friction in falling so far through the air, oftentimes hang for a minute or two in front of the tremendous precipices like gauzy half-transparent veils, gloriously beautiful when the sun is shining through them. Most of the cañon avalanches, however, flow in regular channels, like the cascades of tributary streams. When the snow first gives way on the upper slopes of their basins a dull muffled rush and rumble is heard, which, increasing with heavy deliberation, seems to draw rapidly nearer with appalling intensity of tone. Presently the wild floods comes in sight, bounding out over bosses and sheer places, leaping from bench to bench, spreading and narrowing and throwing off clouds of whirling diamond dust like a majestic foamy cataract. Compared with cascades and falls, avalanches are short-lived, and the sharp clashing sounds so common in dashing water are usually wanting; but in their deep thunder tones and pearly purple-tinged whiteness, and in dress, gait, gestures, and general behavior, they are much alike.

Besides these common storm avalanches there are two other kinds, the annual and the century, which still further enrich the scenery, though their influence on fountains is comparatively small. Annual avalanches are composed of heavy compacted snow which has been subjected to frequent alternations of frost and thaw. They are developed on cañon and mountain sides, the greater number of them, at elevations of from nine to ten thousand feet, where the slopes are so inclined that the dry snows of winter accumulate and hold fast until the spring thaws sap their foundations and make them slippery. Then away in grand style go the ponderous icy masses, adorned with crystalline spray without any cloudy snow dust; some of the largest descending more than a mile with even, sustained energy and directness like thunderbolts. The grand century avalanches, that mow wide swaths through the upper forests, occur on shady mountain sides about ten to twelve thousand feet high, where, under ordinary conditions, the snow accumulated from winter to winter lies at rest for many years, allowing trees fifty to a hundred feet high to grow undisturbed on the slopes below them. On their way through the forests they usually make a clean sweep, stripping off the soil as well as the trees, clearing paths two or three hundred yards wide from the timber line to the glacier meadows, and piling the uprooted trees, head downward, in windrows along the sides like lateral moraines. Sears and broken branches on the standing trees bordering the gaps record the side depth of the overwhelming flood; and when we come to count the annual wood rings of the uprooted trees, we learn that some of these colossal avalanches occur only once in about a century, or even at still wider intervals.

Few mountaineers go far enough, during the snowy months, to see many avalanches, and fewer still know the thrilling exhilaration of riding on them. In all my wild mountaineering I have enjoyed only one avalanche ride; and the start was so sudden, and the end came so soon, I thought but little of the danger that goes with this sort of travel, though one thinks fast at such times. One calm, bright morning in Yosemite, after a hearty storm had given three or four feet of fresh snow to the mountains, being eager to see as many avalanches as possible, and gain wide views of the peaks and forests arrayed in their new robes, before the sunshine had time to change or rearrange them, I set out early to climb by a side cañon to the top of a commanding ridge a little over three thousand feet above the valley. On account of the looseness of the snow that blocked the cañon I knew the climb would be trying, and estimated it might require three or four hours. But it proved far more difficult than I had foreseen. Most of the way I sank waist-deep, in some places almost out of sight; and after spending the day to within half an hour of sundown in this loose, baffling snow work, I was still several hundred feet below the summit. Then my hopes were reduced to getting up in time for the sunset, and a quick, sparkling home-going beneath the stars. But I was not to get top views of any sort that day; for deep trampling near the cañon head; where the snow was strained, started an avalanche, and I was swished back down to the foot of the cañon as if by enchantment. The plodding, wallowing ascent of about a mile had taken all day, the undoing descent perhaps a minute.

When the snow suddenly gave way, I instinctively threw myself on my back and spread my arms, to try to keep from sinking. Fortunately, though the grade of the cañon was steep, it was not interrupted by step levels or precipices big enough to cause outbounding or free plunging. On no part of the rush was I buried. I was only moderately imbedded on the surface or a little below it, and covered with a hissing back-streaming veil of dusty snow particles; and as the whole mass beneath or about me joined in the flight I felt no friction, though tossed here and there, and lurched from side to side. And when the torrent swedged and came to rest, I found myself on the top of the crumpled pile, without a single bruise or scar. Hawthorne says that steam has spiritualized travel, notwithstanding the smoke, friction, smells, and clatter of boat and rail riding. This flight in a milky way of snow flowers was the most spiritual of all my travels; and, after many years, the mere thought of it is still an exhilaration.

In the spring, after all the avalanches are down and the snow is melting fast, it is glorious to hear the streams sing out on the mountains. Every fountain swelling, countless rills hurry together to the rivers at the call of the sun,—beginning to run and sing soon after sunrise, increasing until toward sundown, then gradually failing through the cold frosty hours of the night. Thus the volume of the upper rivers, even in flood time, is nearly doubled during the day, rising and falling as regularly as the tides of the sea. At the height of flood, in the warmest June weather, they seem fairly to shout for joy, and clash their upleaping waters together like clapping of hands; racing down the cañons with white manes flying in glorious exuberance of strength, compelling huge sleeping boulders to wake up and join in the dance and song to swell their chorus.

Then the plants also are in flood; the hidden sap singing into leaf and flower, responding as faithfully to the call of the sun as the streams from the snow, gathering along the outspread roots like rills in their channels on the mountains, rushing up the stems of herb and tree, swirling in their myriad cells like streams in potholes, spreading along the branches and breaking into foamy bloom, while fragrance, like a finer music, rises and flows with the winds.

About the same may be said of the spring gladness of blood when the red streams surge and sing in accord with the swelling plants and rivers, inclining animals and everybody to travel in hurrahing crowds like floods, while exhilarating melody in color and fragrance, form and motion, flows to the heart through all the quickening senses.

In early summer the streams are in bright prime, running crystal clear, deep and full, but not overflowing their banks,—about as deep through the night as the day, the variation so marked in spring being now too slight to be noticed. Nearly all the weather is cloudless sunshine, and everything is at its brightest,—lake, river, garden, and forest, with all their warm, throbbing life. Most of the plants are in full leaf and flower; the blessed ousels have built their mossy huts, and are now singing their sweetest song on spray-sprinkled ledges beside the waterfalls.

In tranquil, mellow autumn, when the year's work is about done, when the fruits are ripe, birds and seeds out of their nests, and all the landscape is glowing like a benevolent countenance at rest, then the streams are at their lowest ebb,—their wild rejoicing soothed to thoughtful calm. All the smaller tributaries whose branches do not reach back to the perennial fountains of the Summit peaks shrink to whispering, tinkling currents. The snow of their basins gone, they are now fed only by small moraine springs, whose waters are mostly evaporated in passing over warm pavements, and in feeling their way from pool to pool through the midst of boulders and sand. Even the main streams are so low they may be easily forded, and their grand falls and cascades, now gentle and approachable, have waned to sheets and webs of embroidery, falling fold over fold in new and ever changing beauty.

Two of the most songful of the rivers, the Tuolumne and Merced, water nearly all the Park, spreading their branches far and wide, like broad-headed oaks; and the highest branches of each draw their sources from one and the same foundation on Mount Lyell, at an elevation of about thirteen thousand feet above the sea. The crest of the mountain, against which the head of the glacier rests, is worn to a thin blade full of joints, through which a part of the glacial water flows southward, giving rise to the highest trickling affluents of the Merced; while the main drainage, flowing northward, gives rise to those of the Tuolumne. After diverging for a distance of ten or twelve miles, these twin rivers flow in a general westerly direction, descending rapidly for the first thirty miles, and rushing in glorious apron cascades and falls from one Yosemite valley to another. Below the Yosemites they descend in gray rapids and swirling, swaying reaches, through the chaparral-clad cañons of the foothills and across the golden California plain, to their confluence with the San Joaquin, where, after all their long wanderings, they are only about ten miles apart.

The main cañons are from fifty to seventy miles long, and from two to four thousand feet deep, carved in the solid flank of the range. Though rough in some places and hard to travel, they are the most delightful of roads, leading through the grandest scenery, full of life and motion, and offering most telling lessons in earth sculpture. The walls, far from being unbroken, featureless cliffs, seem like ranges of separate mountains, so deep and varied is their sculpture; rising in lordly domes, towers, round-browed outstanding headlands, and clustering spires, with dark, shadowy side cañons between. But, however wonderful in height and mass and fineness of finish, no anomalous curiosities are presented, no "freaks of nature." All stand related in delicate rhythm, a grand glacial rock song.

Among the interesting and influential of the secondary features of cañon scenery are the great avalanche taluses, that lean against the walls at intervals of a mile or two. In the middle Yosemite region they are usually from three to five hundred feet high, and are made up of huge, angular, well-preserved, unshifting boulders, overgrown with gray lichens, trees shrubs, and delicate flowering plants. Some of the largest of the boulders are forty or fifty feet cube, weighing from five to ten thousand tons; and where the cleavage joints of the granite are exceptionally wide apart a few blocks may be found nearly a hundred feet in diameter. These wonderful boulder piles are distributed throughout all the cañons of the range, completely choking them in some of the narrower portions, and no mountaineer will be likely to forget the savage roughness of the roads they make. Even the swift, overbearing rivers, accustomed to sweep everything out of their way, are in some places bridled and held in check by them. Foaming, roaring, in glorious majesty of flood, rushing off long rumbling trains of ponderous blocks without apparent effort, they are not able to move the largest, which, withstanding all assaults for centuries, are left at rest in the channels like islands, with gardens on their tops, fringed with foam below, with flowers above.

On some points concerning the origin of these taluses I was long in doubt. Plainly enough they were derived from the cliffs above them, the size of each talus being approximately measured by a scar on the wall, the rough angular surface of which contrasts with the rounded, glaciated, unfractured parts. I saw also that, instead of being slowly accumulated material, weathered off, boulder by boulder, in the ordinary way, almost every talus had been formed suddenly, in a single avalanche, and had not been increased in size during the last three or four centuries; for trees three or four hundred years old were growing on them, some standing at the top close to the wall, without a bruise or broken branch, showing that scarcely a single boulder had fallen among them since they were planted. Furthermore, all the taluses throughout the range seemed, by the trees and lichens growing on them, to be of the same age. All the phenomena pointed straight to a grand ancient earthquake. But I left the question open for years, and went on from cañon to cañon, observing again and again; measuring the heights of taluses throughout the range on both flanks, and the variations in the angles of their surface slopes; studying the way their boulders were assorted and related and brought to rest, and the cleavage joints of the cliffs from whence they were derived, cautious about making up my mind. Only after I had seen one made did all doubt as to their formation vanish.

In Yosemite Valley, one morning about two o'clock, I was aroused by an earthquake; and though I had never before enjoyed a storm of this sort, the strange, wild thrilling motion and rumbling could not be mistaken, and I ran out of my cabin, near the Sentinel Rock, both glad and frightened, shouting, "A noble earthquake!" feeling sure I was going to learn something. The shocks were so violent and varied, and succeeded one another so closely, one had to balance in walking as if on the deck of a ship among the waves, and it seemed impossible the high cliffs should escape being shattered. In particular, I feared that the sheer-fronted Sentinel Rock, which rises to a height of three thousand feet, would be shaken down, and I took shelter back of a big pine, hoping I might be protected from outbounding boulders, should any come so far. I was now convinced that an earthquake had been the maker of the taluses, and positive proof soon came. It was a calm moonlight night, and no sound was heard for the first minute or two save a low muffled underground rumbling and a slight rustling of the agitated trees, as if, in wrestling with the mountains, Nature were holding her breath. Then, suddenly, out of the strange silence and strange motion there came a tremendous roar. The Eagle Rock, a short distance up the valley, had given way, and I saw it falling in thousands of the great boulders I had been studying so long, pouring to the valley floor in a free curve luminous from friction, making a terribly sublime and beautiful spectacle,—an arc of the fifteen hundred feet span, as true in form and as steady as a rainbow, in the midst of the stupendous roaring rock storm. The sound was inconceivably deep and broad and earnest, as if the whole earth, like a living creature, had at last found a voice and were calling to her sister planets. It seemed to me that if all the thunder I ever heard were condensed into one roar it would not equal this rock roar at the birth of a mountain talus. Think, then, of the roar that arose to heaven when all the thousands of ancient cañon taluses throughout the length and breadth of the range were simultaneously given birth.

The main storm was soon over, and, eager to see the new-born talus, I ran up the valley in the moonlight and climbed it before the huge blocks, after their wild fiery flight, had come to complete rest. They were slowly settling into their places, chafing, grating against one another, groaning, and whispering; but no motion was visible except in a stream of small fragments pattering down the face of the cliff at the head of the talus. A cloud of dust particles, the smallest of the boulders, floated out across the whole breadth of the valley and formed a ceiling that lasted until after sunrise; and the air was loaded with the odor of crushed Douglas spruces, from a grove that had been mowed down and mashed like weeds.

Sauntering about to see what other changes had been made, I found the Indians in the middle of the valley, terribly frightened, of course, fearing the angry spirits of the rocks were trying to kill them, The few whites wintering in the valley were assembled in front of the old Hutchings Hotel, comparing notes and meditating flight to steadier ground, seemingly as sorely frightened as the Indians. It is always interesting to see people in dead earnest, from whatever cause, and earthquakes make everybody earnest. Shortly after sunrise, a low blunt muffled rumbling, like distant thunder, was followed by another series of shocks, which, though not nearly so severe as the first, made the cliffs and domes tremble like jelly, and the big pines and oaks thrill and swish and wave their branches with startling effect. Then the groups of talkers were suddenly hushed, and the solemnity on their faces was sublime. One in particular of these winter neighbors, a rather thoughtful, speculative man, with whom I had often conversed, was a firm believer in the cataclysmic origin of the valley; and I now jokingly remarked that his wild tumble-down-and-engulfment hypothesis might soon be proved, since these underground rumblings and shakings might be the forerunners of another Yosemite-making cataclysm, which would perhaps double the depth of the valley by swallowing the floor, leaving the ends of the wagon roads and trails three or four thousand feet in the air. Just then came the second series of shocks, and it was fine to see how awfully silent and solemn he became. His belief in the existence of a mysterious abyss, into which the suspended floor of the valley and all the domes and battlements of the walls might at any moment go roaring down, mightily troubled him. To cheer and tease him into another view of the case, I said: "Come, cheer up; smile a little and clap your hands, now that kind Mother Earth is trotting us on her knee to amuse us and make us good." But the well-meant joke seemed irreverent and utterly failed, as if only prayerful terror could rightly belong to the wild beauty-making business. Even after all the heavier shocks were over, I could do nothing to reassure him. On the contrary, he handed me the keys of his little store, and, with a companion of like mind, fled to the lowlands. In about a month he returned; but a sharp shock occurred that very day, which sent him flying again.

The rocks trembled more or less every day for over two months, and I kept a bucket of water on my table to learn what I could of the movements. The blunt thunder-tones in the depths of the mountains were usually followed by sudden jarring, horizontal thrusts from the northward, often succeeded by twisting, upjolting movements. Judging by its effects, this Yosemite, or Inyo earthquake, as it is sometimes called, was gentle as compared with the one that gave rise to the grand talus system of the range and did so much for the cañon scenery. Nature, usually so deliberate in her operations, then created, as we have seen, a new set of features, simply by giving the mountains a shake,—changing not only the high peaks and cliffs, but the streams. As soon as these rock avalanches fell every stream began to sing new songs; for in many places thousands of boulders were hurled into their channels, roughening and half damming them, compelling the waters to surge and roar in rapids where before they were gliding smoothly. Some of the streams were completely dammed, driftwood, leaves, etc., filling the interstices between the boulders, thus giving rise to lakes and level reaches; and these, again, after being gradually filled in, to smooth meadows, through which the streams now silently meander; while at the same time some of the taluses took the places of old meadows and groves. Thus rough places were made smooth, and smooth places rough. But on the whole, by what at first sight seemed pure confusion and ruin, the landscapes were enriched; for gradually every talus, however big the boulders composing it, was covered with groves and gardens, and made a finely proportioned and ornamental base for the sheer cliffs. In this beauty work, every boulder is prepared and measured and put in its place more thoughtfully than are the stones of temples. If for a moment you are inclined to regard these taluses as mere draggled, chaotic dumps, climb to the top of one of them, tie your mountain shoes firmly over the instep, and with braced nerves run down without any haggling, puttering hesitation, boldly jumping from boulder to boulder with even speed. You will then find your feet playing a tune, and quickly discover the music and poetry of rock piles,—a fine lesson; and all nature's wildness tells the same story. Storms of every sort, torrents, earthquakes, cataclysms, "convulsions of nature," etc., however mysterious and lawless at first sight they may seem, are only harmonious notes in the song of creation, varied expressions of God's love.

CHAPTER IX

The Sequoia and General Grant National Parks

The Big Tree (Sequoia gigantea) is Nature's forest masterpiece, and, so far as I know, the greatest of living things. It belongs to an ancient stock, as its remains in old rocks show, and has a strange air of other days about it, a thoroughbred look inherited from the long ago—the auld lang syne of trees. Once the genus was common, and with many species flourished in the now desolate Arctic regions, in the interior of North America, and in Europe, but in long, eventful wanderings from climate to climate only two species have survived the hardships they had to encounter, the gigantea and sempervirens, the former now restricted to the western slopes of the Sierra, the other to the Coast Mountains, and both to California, excepting a few groves of Redwood which extend into Oregon. The Pacific Coast in general is the paradise of conifers. Here nearly all of them are giants, and display a beauty and magnificence unknown elsewhere. The climate is mild, the ground never freezes, and moisture and sunshine abound all the year. Nevertheless it is not easy to account for the colossal size of the Sequoias. The largest are about three hundred feet high and thirty feet in diameter. Who of all the dwellers of the plains and prairies and fertile home forests of round-headed oak and maple, hickory and elm, ever dreamed that earth could bear such growths,—trees that the familiar pines and firs seem to know nothing about, lonely, silent, serene, with a physiognomy almost godlike; and so old, thousands of them still living had already counted their years by tens of centuries when Columbus set sail from Spain and were in the vigor of youth or middle age when the star led the Chaldean sages to the infant Saviour's cradle! As far as man is concerned they are the same yesterday, to-day, and forever, emblems of permanence.

No description can give any adequate idea of their singular majesty, much less their beauty. Excepting the sugar-pine, most of their neighbors with pointed tops seem to be forever shouting Excelsior, while the Big Tree, though soaring above them all, seems satisfied, its rounded head, poised lightly as a cloud, giving no impression of trying to go higher. Only in youth does it show like other conifers a heavenward yearning, keenly aspiring with a long quick-growing top. Indeed the whole tree for the first century or two, or until a hundred to a hundred and fifty feet high, is arrowhead in form, and, compared with the solemn rigidity of age, is as sensitive to the wind as a squirrel tail. The lower branches are gradually dropped as it grows older, and the upper ones thinned out until comparatively few are left. These, however, are developed to great size, divide again and again, and terminate in bossy rounded masses of leafy branchlets, while the head becomes dome-shaped. Then poised in fullness of strength and beauty, stern and solemn in mien, it glows with eager, enthusiastic life, quivering to the tip of every leaf and branch and far-reaching root, calm as a granite dome, the first to feel the touch of the rosy beams of the morning, the last to bid the sun good-night.

Perfect specimens, unhurt by running fires or lightning, are singularly regular and symmetrical in general form, though not at all conventional, showing infinite variety in sure unity and harmony of plan. The immensely strong, stately shafts, with rich purplish brown bark, are free of limbs for a hundred and fifty feet or so, though dense tufts of sprays occur here and there, producing an ornamental effect, while long parallel furrows give a fluted columnar appearance. It shoots forth its limbs with equal boldness in every direction, showing no weather side. On the old trees the main branches are crooked and rugged, and strike rigidly outward mostly at right angles from the trunk, but there is always a certain measured restraint in their reach which keeps them within bounds. No other Sierra tree has foliage so densely massed or outline so finely, firmly drawn and so obediently subordinate to an ideal type. A particularly knotty, angular, ungovernable-looking branch, five to eight feet in diameter and perhaps a thousand years old, may occasionally be seen pushing out from the trunk as if determined to break across the bounds of the regular curve, but like all the others, as soon as the general outline is approached the huge limb dissolves into massy bosses of branchlets and sprays, as if the tree were growing beneath an invisible bell glass against the sides of which the branches were moulded, while many small, varied departures from the ideal form give the impression of freedom to grow as they like.

Except in picturesque old age, after being struck by lightning and broken by a thousand snowstorms, this regularity of form is one of the Big Tree's most distinguishing characteristics. Another is the simple sculptural beauty of the trunk and its great thickness as compared with its height and the width of the branches, many of them being from eight to ten feet in diameter at a height of two hundred feet from the ground, and seeming more like finely modeled and sculptured architectural columns than the stems of trees, while the great strong limbs are like rafters supporting the magnificent dome head.

The root system corresponds in magnitude with the other dimensions of the tree, forming a flat far-reaching spongy network two hundred feet or more in width without any taproot, and the instep is so grand and fine, so suggestive of endless strength, it is long ere the eye is released to look above it. The natural swell of the roots, though at first sight excessive, gives rise to buttresses no greater than are required for beauty as well as strength, as at once appears when you stand back far enough to see the whole tree in its true proportions. The fineness of the taper of the trunk is shown by its thickness at great heights—a diameter of ten feet at a height of two hundred being, as we have seen, not uncommon. Indeed the boles of but few trees hold their thickness as well as Sequoia. Resolute, consummate, determined in form, always beheld with wondering admiration, the Big Tree always seems unfamiliar, standing alone, unrelated, with peculiar physiognomy, awfully solemn and earnest. Nevertheless, there is nothing alien in its looks. The Madrona, clad in thin, smooth, red and yellow bark and big glossy leaves, seems, in the dark coniferous forests of Washington and Vancouver Island, like some lost wanderer from the magnolia groves of the South, while the Sequoia, with all its strangeness, seems more at home than any of its neighbors, holding the best right to the ground as the oldest, strongest inhabitant. One soon becomes acquainted with new species of pine and fir spruce as with friendly people, shaking their outstretched branches like shaking hands, and fondling their beautiful little ones; while the venerable aboriginal Sequoia, ancient of other days, keeps you at a distance, taking no notice of you, speaking only to the winds, thinking only of the sky, looking as strange in aspect and behavior among the neighboring trees as would the mastodon or hairy elephant among the homely bears and deer. Only the Sierra Juniper is at all like it, standing rigid and unconquerable on glacial pavements for thousands of years, grim, rusty, silent, uncommunicative, with an air of antiquity about as pronounced as that so characteristic of Sequoia.

The bark of full grown trees is from one to two feet thick, rich cinnamon brown, purplish on young trees and shady parts of the old, forming magnificent masses of color with the underbrush and beds of flowers. Toward the end of winter the trees themselves bloom while the snow is still eight or ten feet deep. The pistillate flowers are about three eighths of an inch long, pale green, and grow in countless thousands on the ends of the sprays. The staminate are still more abundant, pale yellow, a fourth of an inch long; and when the golden pollen is ripe they color the whole tree and dust the air and the ground far and near.

The cones are bright grass-green in color, about two and a half inches long, one and a half wide, and are made up of thirty or forty strong, closely packed, rhomboidal scales with four to eight seeds at the base of each. The seeds are extremely small and light, being only from an eighth to a fourth of an inch long and wide, including a filmy surrounding wing, which causes them to glint and waver in falling and enables the wind to carry them considerable distances from the tree.

The faint lisp of snowflakes as they alight is one of the smallest sounds mortal can hear. The sound of falling Sequoia seeds, even when they happen to strike on flat leaves or flakes of bark, is about as faint. Very different is the bumping and thudding of the falling cones. Most of them are cut off by the Douglas squirrel and stored for the sake of the seeds, small as they are. In the calm Indian summer these busy harvesters with ivory sickles go to work early in the morning, as soon as breakfast is over, and nearly all day the ripe cones fall in a steady pattering, bumping shower. Unless harvested in this way they discharge their seeds and remain on the trees for many years. In fruitful seasons the trees are fairly laden. On two small specimen branches one and a half and two inches in diameter I counted four hundred and eighty cones. No other California conifer produces nearly so many seeds, excepting perhaps its relative, the Redwood of the Coast Mountains. Millions are ripened annually by a single tree, and the product of one of the main groves in a fruitful year would suffice to plant all the mountain ranges of the world.

The dense tufted sprays make snug nesting places for birds, and in some of the loftiest, leafiest towers of verdure thousands of generations have been reared, the great solemn trees shedding off flocks of merry singers every year from nests, like the flocks of winged seeds from the cones.

The Big Trees keeps its youth far longer than any of its neighbors. Most silver firs are old in their second or third century, pines in their fourth or fifth, while the Big Tree growing beside them is still in the bloom of its youth, juvenile in every feature at the age of old pines, and cannot be said to attain anything like prime size and beauty before its fifteen hundredth year, or under favorable circumstances become old before its three thousandth. Many, no doubt, are much older than this. On one of the Kings River giants, thirty-five feet and eight inches in diameter exclusive of bark, I counted upwards of four thousand annual wood-rings, in which there was no trace of decay after all these centuries of mountain weather. There is no absolute limit to the existence of any tree. Their death is due to accidents, not, as of animals, to the wearing out of organs. Only the leaves die of old age, their fall is foretold in their structure; but the leaves are renewed every year and so also are the other essential organs—wood, roots, bark, buds. Most of the Sierra trees die of disease. Thus the magnificent silver firs are devoured by fungi, and comparatively few of them live to see their three hundredth birth year. But nothing hurts the Big Tree. I never saw one that was sick or showed the slightest sign of decay. It lives on through indefinite thousands of years until burned, blown down, undermined, or shattered by some tremendous lightning stroke. No ordinary bolt ever seriously hurts Sequoia. In all my walks I have seen only one that was thus killed outright. Lightning, though rare in the California lowlands, is common on the Sierra. Almost every day in June and July small thunderstorms refresh the main forest belt. Clouds like snowy mountains of marvelous beauty grow rapidly in the calm sky about midday and cast cooling shadows and showers that seldom last more than an hour. Nevertheless these brief, kind storms wound or kill a good many trees. I have seen silver firs two hundred feet high split into long peeled rails and slivers down to the roots, leaving not even a stump, the rails radiating like the spokes of a wheel from a hole in the ground where the tree stood. But the Sequoia, instead of being split and slivered, usually has forty or fifty feet of its brash knotty top smashed off in short chunks about the size of cord-wood, the beautiful rosy red ruins covering the ground in a circle a hundred feet wide or more. I never saw any that had been cut down to the ground or even to below the branches except one in the Stanislaus Grove, about twelve feet in diameter, the greater part of which was smashed to fragments, leaving only a leafless stump about seventy-five feet high. It is a curious fact that all the very old Sequoias have lost their heads by lightning. "All things come to him who waits." But of all living things Sequoia is perhaps the only one able to wait long enough to make sure of being struck by lightning. Thousands of years it stands ready and waiting, offering its head to every passing cloud as if inviting its fate, praying for heaven's fire as a blessing; and when at last the old head is off, another of the same shape immediately begins to grow on. Every bud and branch seems excited, like bees that have lost their queen, and tries hard to repair the damage. Branches that for many centuries have been growing out horizontally at once turn upward and all their branchlets arrange themselves with reference to a new top of the same peculiar curve as the old one. Even the small subordinate branches halfway down the trunk do their best to push up to the top and help in this curious head-making.

The great age of these noble trees is even more wonderful than their huge size, standing bravely up, millennium in, millennium out, to all that fortune may bring them, triumphant over tempest and fire and time, fruitful and beautiful, giving food and shelter to multitudes of small fleeting creatures dependent on their bounty. Other trees may claim to be about as large or as old: Australian Gums, Senegal Baobabs, Mexican Taxodiums, English Yews, and venerable Lebanon Cedars, trees of renown, some of which are from ten to thirty feet in diameter. We read of oaks that are supposed to have existed ever since the creation, but strange to say I can find no definite accounts of the age of any of these trees, but only estimates based on tradition and assumed average rates of growth. No other known tree approaches the Sequoia in grandeur, height and thickness being considered, and none as far as I know has looked down on so many centuries or opens such impressive and suggestive views into history. The majestic monument of the Kings River Forest is, as we have seen, fully four thousand years old, and measuring the rings of annual growth we find it was no less than twenty-seven feet in diameter at the beginning of the Christian era, while many observations lead me to expect the discovery of others ten or twenty centuries older. As to those of moderate age, there are thousands, mere youth as yet, that—

"Saw the light that shone

On Mahomet's uplifted crescent,

On many a royal gilded throne

And deed forgotten in the present,

. . . saw the age of sacred trees
And Druid groves and mystic larches,
And saw from forest domes like these
The builder bring his Gothic arches."

Great trees and groves used to be venerated as sacred monuments and halls of council and worship. But soon after the discovery of the Calaveras Grove one of the grandest trees was cut down for the sake of a stump! The laborious vandals had seen "the biggest tree in the world," then, forsooth, they must try to see the biggest stump and dance on it.

The growth in height for the first two centuries is usually at the rate of eight to ten inches a year. Of course all very large trees are old, but those equal in size may vary greatly in age on account of variations in soil, closeness or openness of growth, etc. Thus a tree about ten feet in diameter that grew on the side of a meadow was, according to my own count of the wood-rings, only two hundred and fifty-nine years old at the time it was felled, while another in the same grove, of almost exactly the same size but less favorably situated, was fourteen hundred and forty years old. The Calaveras tree cut for a dance floor was twenty-four feet in diameter and only thirteen hundred years old, another about the same size was a thousand years older.

The following Sequoia notes and measurements are copied from my notebooks:—

Diameter Feet	Diameter Inches	Height in Feet	Age Years
0	1 3-4	10	7
0	5	24	20
0	5	25	41
0	6	25	66
0	6	28 1-2	39
0	8	25	29
0	11	45	71
1	0	60	71
3	2	156	260
6	0	192	240

7	3	195	339
7	3	255	506
7	6	240	493
7	7	207	424
9	0	243	259
9	3	222	280
10	6		1440
12			1825[1]
15			2150[2]
24			1300
25			2300
35	8 inside bark		over 4000

[1] 6 feet in diameter at height of 200 feet.

[2] 7 feet in diameter at height of 200 feet.

Little, however, is to be learned in confused, hurried tourist trips, spending only a poor noisy hour in a branded grove with a guide. You should go looking and listening alone on long walks through the wild forests and groves in all the seasons of the year. In the spring the winds are balmy and sweet, blowing up and down over great beds of chaparral and through the woods now rich in softening balsam and rosin and the scent of steaming earth. The sky is mostly sunshine, oftentimes tempered by magnificent clouds, the breath of the sea built up into new mountain ranges, warm during the day, cool at night, good flower-opening weather. The young cones of the Big Trees are showing in clusters, their flower time already past, and here and there you may see the sprouting of their tiny seeds of the previous autumn, taking their first feeble hold of the ground and unpacking their tender whorls of cotyledon leaves. Then you will naturally be led on to consider their wonderful growth up and up through the mountain weather, now buried in snow bent and crinkled, now straightening in summer sunshine like uncoiling ferns, shooting eagerly aloft in youth's joyful prime, and towering serene and satisfied through countless years of calm and storm, the greatest of plants and all but immortal.

Under the huge trees up come the small plant people, putting forth fresh leaves and blossoming in such profusion that the hills and valleys would still seem gloriously rich and glad were all the grand trees away. By the side of melting snowbanks rise the crimson sarcodes, round-topped and massive as the Sequoias themselves, and beds of blue violets and larger yellow one with leaves curiously lobed; azalea and saxifrage, daisies and lilies on the mossy banks of the streams; and a little way back of them, beneath the trees and on sunny spots on the hills around the groves, wild rose and rubus, spiræa and ribes, mitella, tiarella, campanula, monardella, forget-me-not, etc., many of them as worthy of lore immortality as the famous Scotch daisy, wanting only a Burns to sing them home to all hearts.

In the midst of this glad plant work the birds are busy nesting, some singing at their work, some silent, others, especially the big pileated woodpeckers, about as noisy as backwoodsmen building their cabins. Then every bower in the groves is a bridal bower, the winds murmur softly overhead, the streams sing with the birds, while from far-off waterfalls and thunder-clouds come deep rolling organ notes.

In summer the days go by in almost constant brightness, cloudless sunshine pouring over the forest roof, while in the shady depths there is the subdued light of perpetual morning. The new leaves and cones are growing fast and make a grand show, seeds are ripening, young birds learning to fly, and with myriads of insects glad as birds keep the air whirling, joy in every wingbeat, their humming and singing blending with the gentle ah-ing of the winds; while at evening every thicket and grove is enchanted by the tranquil chirping of the blessed hylas, the sweetest and most peaceful of sounds, telling the very heart-joy of earth as it rolls through the heavens.

In the autumn the sighing of the winds is softer than ever, the gentle ah-ah-ing filling the sky with a fine universal mist of music, the birds have little to say, and there is no appreciable stir or rustling among the trees save that caused by the harvesting squirrels. Most of the seeds are ripe and away, those of the trees mottling the sunny air, glinting, glancing through the midst of the merry insect people, rocks and trees, everything alike drenched in gold light, heaven's colors coming down to the meadows and groves, making every leaf a romance, air, earth, and water in peace beyond thought, the great brooding days opening and closing in divine psalms of color.

Winter comes suddenly, arrayed in storms, though to mountaineers silky streamers on the peaks and the tones of the wind give sufficient warning. You hear strange whisperings among the tree-tops, as if the giants were taking counsel together. One after another, nodding and swaying, calling and replying, spreads the news, until at with one accord break forth into glorious song, welcoming the first grand snowstorm of the year, and looming up in the dim clouds and snowdrifts like lighthouse towers in flying scud and spray. Studying the behavior of the giants from some friendly shelter, you will see that even in the glow of their wildest enthusiasm, when the storm roars loudest, they never lose their god-like composure, never toss their arms or bow or wave like the pines, but only slowly, solemnly nod and sway, standing erect, making no sign of strife, none of rest, neither in alliance nor at war with the winds, too calmly, unconsciously noble and strong to strive with or bid defiance to anything. Owing to the density of the leafy branchlets and great breadth of head the Big Tree carries a much heavier load of snow than any of its neighbors, and after a storm, when the sky clears, the laden trees are a glorious spectacle, worth any amount of cold camping to see. Every bossy limb and crown is solid white, and the immense height of the giants becomes visible as the eye travels the white steps of the colossal tower, each relieved by a mass of blue shadow.

In midwinter the forest depths are as fresh and pure as the crevasses and caves of glaciers. Grouse, nuthatches, a few woodpeckers, and other hardy birds dwell in the groves all winter, and the squirrels may be seen every clear day frisking about, lively as ever, tunneling to their stores, never coming up empty-mouthed, dividing in the loose snow about as quickly as ducks in water, while storms and sunshine sing to each other.

One of the noblest and most beautiful of the late winter sights is the blossoming of the Big Tree like gigantic goldenrods and the sowing of their pollen over all the forest and the snow-covered ground—a most glorious view of Nature's immortal virility and flower-love.

One of my own best excursions among the Sequoias was made in the autumn of 1875, when I explored the then unknown or little known Sequoia region south of the Mariposa Grove for comprehensive views of the belt, and to learn what I could of the peculiar distribution of the species and its history in general. In particular I was anxious to try to find out whether it had ever been more widely distributed since the glacial period; what conditions favorable or otherwise were affecting it; what were its relations to climate, topography, soil, and the other trees growing with it, etc.; and whether, as was generally supposed, the species was nearing extinction. I was already acquainted in a general way with the northern groves, but excepting some passing glimpses gained on excursions into the high Sierra about the head-waters of Kings and Kern rivers I had seen nothing of the south end of the belt.

Nearly all my mountaineering has been done on foot, carrying as little as possible, depending on camp-fires for warmth, that so I might be light and free to go wherever my studies might lead. On this Sequoia trip, which promised to be long, I was persuaded to take a small wild mule with me to carry provisions and a pair of blankets. The friendly owner of the animal, having noticed that I sometimes looked tired when I came down from the peaks to replenish my bread sack, assured me that his "little Brownie mule" was just what I wanted, tough as a knot, perfectly untirable, low and narrow, just right for squeezing through brush, able to climb like a chipmunk, jump from boulder to boulder like a wild sheep, and go anywhere a man could go. But tough as he was and accomplished as a climber, many a time in the course of our journey when he was jaded and hungry, wedged fast in rocks or struggling in chaparral like a fly in a spiderweb, his troubles were sad to see, and I wished he would leave me and find his way home alone.

We set out from Yosemite about the end of August, and our first camp was made in the well-known Mariposa Grove. Here and in the adjacent pine woods I spent nearly a week, carefully examining the boundaries of the grove for traces of its greater extension without finding any. Then I struck out into the majestic trackless forest to the southeastward, hoping to find new groves or traces of old ones in the dense silver fir and pine woods about the head of Big Creek, where soil and climate seemed most favorable to their growth, but not a single tree or old monument of any sort came to light until I climbed the high rock called Wamellow by the Indians. Here I obtained telling views of the fertile forest-filled basin of the upper Fresno. Innumerable spires of the noble yellow pine were displayed rising above one another on the braided slopes, and yet nobler sugar pines with superb arms outstretched in the rich autumn light, while away toward the southwest, on the verge of the glowing horizon, I discovered the majestic dome-like crowns of Big Trees towering high over all, singly and in close grove congregations. There is something wonderfully attractive in this king tree, even when beheld from afar, that draws us to it with indescribable enthusiasm; its superior height and massive smoothly rounded outlines proclaiming its character in any company; and when one of the oldest attains full stature on some commanding ridge it seems the very god of the woods. I ran back to camp, packed Brownie, steered over the divide and down into the heart of the Fresno Grove. Then choosing a camp on the side of a brook where the grass was good, I made a cup of tea, and set off free among the brown giants, glorying in the abundance of new work about me. One of the first special things that caught my attention was an extensive landslip. The ground on the side of a stream had given way to a depth of about fifty feet and with all its trees had been launched into the bottom of the stream ravine. Most of the trees—pines, firs, incense cedar, and Sequoia—were still standing erect and uninjured, as if unconscious that anything out of the common had happened. Tracing the ravine alongside the avalanche, I saw many trees whose roots had been laid bare, and in one instance discovered a Sequoia about fifteen feet in diameter growing above an old prostrate trunk that seemed to belong to a former generation. This slip had occurred seven or eight years ago, and I was glad to find that not only were most of the Big Trees uninjured, but that many companies of hopeful seedlings and saplings were growing confidently on the fresh soil along the broken front of the avalanche. These young trees were already eight or ten feet high, and were shooting up vigorously, as if sure of eternal life, though young pines, firs, and libocedrus were runing a race with them for the sunshine with an even start. Farther down the ravine I counted five hundred and thirty-six promising young Sequoias on a bed of rough bouldery soil not exceeding two acres in extent.

The Fresno Big Trees covered an area of about four square miles, and while wandering about surveying the boundaries of the grove, anxious to see every tree, I came suddenly on a handsome log cabin, richly embowered and so fresh and unweathered it was still redolent of gum and balsam like a newly felled tree. Strolling forward, wondering who could have built it, I found an old, weary-eyed, speculative, gray-haired man on a bark stool by the door, reading a book. The discovery of his hermitage by a stranger seemed to surprise him, but when I explained that I was only a tree-lover sauntering along the mountains to study Sequoia, he bade me welcome, made me bring my mule down to a little slanting meadow before his door and camp with him, promising to show me his pet trees and many curious things bearing on my studies.

After supper, as the evening shadows were falling, the good hermit sketched his life in the mines, which in the main was like that of most other pioneer gold-hunters—a succession of intense experiences full of big ups and downs like the mountain topography. Since "'49" he had wandered over most of the Sierra, sinking innumerable prospect holes like a sailor making soundings, digging new channels for streams, sifting gold-sprinkled boulder and gravel beds with unquenchable energy, life's noon the meanwhile passing unnoticed into late afternoon shadows. Then, health and gold gone, the game played and lost, like a wounded deer creeping into this forest solitude, he awaits the sundown call. How sad the undertones of many a life here, now the noise of the first big gold battles has died away! How many interesting wrecks lie drifted and stranded in hidden nooks of the gold region! Perhaps no other range contains the remains of so many rare and interesting men. The name of my hermit friend is John A. Nelder, a fine kind man, who in going into the woods has at last gone home; for he loves nature truly, and realizes that these last shadowy days with scarce a glint of gold in them are the best of all. Birds, squirrels, plants get loving, natural recognition, and delightful it was to see how sensitively he responds to the silent influences of the woods. His eyes brightened as he gazed on the trees that stand guard around his little home; squirrels and mountain quail came to his call to be fed, and he tenderly stroked the little snowbent sapling Sequoias, hoping they yet might grow straight to the sky and rule the grove. One of the greatest of his trees stands a little way back of his cabin, and he proudly led me to it, bidding me admire its colossal proportions and measure it to see if in all the forest there could be another so grand. It proved to be only twenty-six feet in diameter, and he seemed distressed to learn that the Mariposa Grizzly Giant was larger. I tried to comfort him by observing that his was the taller, finer formed, and perhaps the more favorably situated. Then he led me to some noble ruins, remnants of gigantic trunks of trees that he supposed must have been larger than any now standing, and though they had lain on the damp ground exposed to fire and the weather for centuries, the wood was perfectly sound. Sequoia timber is not only beautiful in color, rose red when fresh, and as easily worked as pine, but it is almost absolutely unperishable. Build a house of Big Tree logs on granite and that house will last about as long as its foundation. Indeed fire seems to be the only agent that has any appreciable effect on it. From one of these ancient trunk remnants I cut a specimen of the wood, which neither in color, strength, nor soundness could be distinguished from specimens cut from living trees, although it had certainly lain on the damp forest floor for more than three hundred and eighty years, probably more than thrice as long. The time in this instance was determined as follows: When the tree from which the specimen was derived fell it sunk itself into the ground, making a ditch about two hundred feet long and five or six feet deep; and in the middle of this ditch, where a part of the fallen trunk had been burned, a silver fir four feet in diameter and three hundred and eighty years old was growing, showing that the Sequoia trunk had lain on the ground three hundred and eighty years plus the unknown time that it lay before the part whose place had been taken by the fir was burned out of the way, and that which had elapsed ere the seed from which the monumental fir sprang fell into the prepared soil and took root. Now because Sequoia trunks are never wholly consumed in one forest fire and these fires recur only at considerable intervals, and because Sequoia ditches, after being cleared, are often left unplanted for centuries, it becomes evident that the trunk remnant in question may have been on the ground a thousand years or more. Similar vestiges are common, and together with the root-bowls and long straight ditches of the fallen monarchs, throw a sure light back on the post-glacial history of the species, bearing on its distribution. One of the most interesting features of this grove is the apparent ease and strength and comfortable independence in which the trees occupy their place in the general forest. Seedlings, saplings, young and middle-aged trees are grouped promisingly around the old patriarchs, betraying no sign of approach to extinction. On the contrary, all seem to be saying, "Everything is to our mind and we mean to live forever." But, sad to tell, a lumber company was building a large mill and flume near by, assuring widespread destruction.

In the cones and sometimes in the lower portion of the trunk and roots there is a dark gritty substance which dissolves readily in water and yields a magnificent purple color. It is a strong astringent, and is said to be used by the Indians as a big medicine. Mr. Nelder showed me specimens of ink he had made from it, which I tried and found good, flowing freely and holding its color well. Indeed everything about the tree seems constant. With these interesting trees, forming the largest of the northern groves, I stopped only a week, for I had far to go before the fall of the snow. The hermit seemed to cling to me and tried to make me promise to winter with him after the season's work was done. Brownie had to be got home, however, and other work awaited me, therefore I could only promise to stop a day or two on my way back to Yosemite and give him the forest news.

The next two weeks were spent in the wide basin of the San Joaquin, climbing, innumerable ridges and surveying the far-extending sea of pines and firs. But not a single Sequoia crown appeared among them all, nor any trace of a fallen trunk, until I had crossed the south divide of the basin, opposite Dinky Creek, one of the northmost tributaries of Kings River. On this stream there is a small grove, said to have been discovered a few years before my visit by two hunters in pursuit of a wounded bear. Just as I was fording one of the branches of Dinky Creek I met a shepherd, and when I asked him whether he knew anything about the Big Trees of the neighborhood he replied, "I know all about them, for I visited them only a few days ago and pastured my sheep in the grove." He was fresh from the East, and as this was his first summer in the Sierra I was curious to learn what impression the Sequoias had made on him. When I asked whether it was true that the Big Trees were really so big as people say, he warmly replied, "Oh, yes sir, you bet. They're whales. I never used to believe half I heard about the awful size of California trees, but they're monsters and no mistake. One of them over here, they tell me, is the biggest tree in the whole world, and I guess it is, for it's forty foot through and as many good long paces around." He was very earnest, and in fullness of faith offered to guide me to the grove that I might not miss seeing this biggest tree. A fair measurement four feet from the ground, above the main swell of the roots, showed a diameter of only thirty-two feet, much to the young man's disgust. "Only thirty-two feet," he lamented, "only thirty-two, and I always thought it was forty!" Then with a sigh of relief, "No matter, that's a big tree, anyway; no fool of a tree, sir, that you can cut a plank out of thirty feet broad, straight-edged, no bark, all good wood, sound and solid. It would make the brag white pine planks from old Maine look like laths." A good many other fine specimens are distributed along three small branches of the creek, and I noticed several thrifty moderate-sized Sequoias growing on a granite ledge, apparently as independent of deep soil as the pines and firs, clinging to seams and fissures and sending their roots far abroad in search of moisture.

The creek is very clear and beautiful, gliding through tangles of shrubs and flower beds, gay bee and butterfly pastures, the grove's own stream, pure Sequoia water, flowing all the year, every drop filtered through moss and leaves and the myriad spongy rootlets of the giant trees. One of the most interesting features of the grove is a small waterfall with a flowery, ferny, clear brimming pool at the foot of it. How cheerily it sings the songs of the wilderness, and how sweet its tones! You seem to taste as well as hear them, while only the subdued roar of the river in the deep cañon reaches up into the grove, sounding like the sea and the winds. So charming a fall and pool in the heart of so glorious a forest food pagans would have consecrated to some lovely nymph.

Hence down into the main Kings River cañon, a mile deep, I led and dragged and shoved my patient, much-enduring mule through miles and miles and gardens and brush, fording innumerable streams, crossing savage rock slopes and taluses, scrambling, sliding through gulches and gorges, then up into the grand Sequoia forests of the south side, cheered by the royal crowns displayed on the narrow horizon. In a day and a half we reached the Sequoia woods in the neighborhood of the old Thomas Mill Flat. Thence striking off northeastward I found a magnificent forest nearly six miles long by two in width, composed mostly of Big Trees, with outlying groves as far east as Boulder Creek. Here five or six days were spent, and it was delightful to learn from countless trees, old and young, how comfortably they were settled down in concordance with climate and soil and their noble neighbors.

Imbedded in these majestic woods there are numerous meadows, around the sides of which the Big Trees press close together in beautiful lines, showing their grandeur openly from the ground to their domed heads in the sky. The young trees are still more numerous and exuberant than in the Fresno and Dinky groves, standing apart in beautiful family groups, or crowding around the old giants. For every venerable lightning-stricken tree, there is one or more in all the glory of prime, and for each of these, many young trees and crowds of saplings. The young trees express the grandeur of their race in a way indefinable by any words at my command. When they are five or six feet in diameter and a hundred and fifty feet high, they seem like mere baby saplings as many inches in diameter, their juvenile habit and gestures completely veiling their real size, even to those who, from long experience, are able to make fair approximation in their measurements of common trees. One morning I noticed three airy, spiry, quick-growing babies on the side of a meadow, the largest of which I took to be about eight inches in diameter. On measuring it, I found to any astonishment it was five feet six inches in diameter, and about a hundred and forty feet high.

On a bed of sandy ground fifteen yards square, which had been occupied by four sugar pines, I counted ninety-four promising seedlings, an instance of Sequoia gaining ground from its neighbors. Here also I noted eighty-six young Sequoias from one to fifty feet high on less than half an acre of ground that had been cleared and prepared for their reception by fire. This was a small bay burned into dense chaparral, showing that fire, the great destroyer of tree life, is sometimes followed by conditions favorable for new growths. Sufficient fresh soil, however, is furnished for the constant renewal of the forest by the fall of old trees without the help of any other agent,—burrowing animals, fire, flood, landslip, etc.,—for the ground is thus turned and stirred as well as cleared, and in every roomy, shady hollow beside the walls of upturned roots many hopeful seedlings spring up.

The largest, and as far as I know the oldest, of all the Kings River trees that I saw is the majestic stump, already referred to, about a hundred and forty feet high, which above then swell of the roots is thirty-five feet and eight inches inside the bark, and over four thousand years old. It was burned nearly half through at the base, and I spent a day in chopping off the charred surface, cutting into the heart, and counting the wood-rings with the aid of a lens. I made out a little over four thousand without difficulty or doubt, but I was unable to get a complete count, owing to confusion in the rings where wounds had been healed over. Judging by what is left of it, this was a fine, tall, symmetrical tree nearly forty feet in diameter before it lost its bark. In the last sixteen hundred and seventy-two years the increase in diameter was ten feet. A short distance south of this forest lies a beautiful grove, now mostly included in the General Grant National Park. I found many shake-makers at work in it, access to these magnificent woods having been made easy by the old mill wagon road. The Park is only two miles square, and the largest of its many fine trees is the General Grant, so named before the date of my first visit, twenty-eight years ago, and said to be the largest tree in the world, though above the craggy bulging base the diameter is less than thirty feet. The Sanger Lumber Company owns nearly all the Kings River groves outside the Park, and for many years the mills have been spreading desolation without any advantage.

One of the shake-makers directed me to an "old snag biggeren Grant." It proved to be a huge black charred stump thirty-two feet in diameter, the next in size to the grand monument mentioned above.

I found a scattered growth of Big Trees extending across the main divide to within a short distance of Hyde's Mill, on a tributary of Dry Creek. The mountain ridge on the south side of the stream was covered from base to summit with a most superb growth of Big Trees. What a picture it made! In all my wide forest wanderings I had seen none so sublime. Every tree of all the mighty host seemed perfect in beauty and strength, and their majestic domed heads, rising above one another on the mountain slope, were most imposingly displayed, like a range of bossy upswelling cumulus clouds on a calm sky.

In this glorious forest the mill was busy, forming a sore, sad centre of destruction, though small as yet, so immensely heavy was the growth. Only the smaller and most accessible of the trees were being cut. The logs, from three to ten or twelve feet in diameter, were dragged or rolled with long strings of oxen into a chute and sent flying down the steep mountain side to the mill flat, where the largest of them were blasted into manageable dimensions for the saws. And as the timber is very brash, by this blasting and careless felling on uneven ground, half or three fourths of the timber was wasted.

I spent several days exploring the ridge and counting the annual wood rings on a large number of stumps in the clearings, then replenished my bread sack and pushed on southward. All the way across the broad rough basins of the Kaweah and Tule rivers Sequoia ruled supreme, forming an almost continuous belt for sixty or seventy miles, waving up and down in huge massy mountain billows in compliance with the grand glacier-ploughed topography.

Day after day, from grove to grove, cañon to cañon, I made a long, wavering way, terribly rough in some places for Brownie, but cheery for me, for Big Trees were seldom out of sight. We crossed the rugged, picturesque basins of Redwood Creek, the North Fork of the Kaweah, and Marble Fork gloriously forested, and full of beautiful cascades and falls, sheer and slanting, infinitely varied with broad curly foam fleeces and strips of embroidery in which the sunbeams revel. Thence we climbed into the noble forest on the Marble and Middle Fork Divide. After a general exploration of the Kaweah basin, this part of the Sequoia belt seemed to me the finest, and I then named it "the Giant Forest." It extends, a magnificent growth of giants grouped in pure temple groves, ranged in colonnades along the sides of meadows, or scattered among the other trees, from the granite headlands overlooking the hot foothills and plains of the San Joaquin back to within a few miles of the old glacier fountains at an elevation of 5000 to 8400 feet above the sea.

When I entered this sublime wilderness the day was nearly done, the trees with rosy, glowing countenances seemed to be hushed and thoughtful, as if waiting in conscious religious dependence on the sun, and one naturally walked softly and awe-stricken among them. I wandered on, meeting nobler trees where all are noble, subdued in the general calm, as if in some vast hall pervaded by the deepest sanctities and solemnities that sway human souls. At sundown the trees seemed to cease their worship and breathe free. I heard the birds going home. I too sought a home for the night on the edge of a level meadow where there is a long, open view between the evenly ranked trees standing guard along its sides. Then after a good place was found for poor Brownie, who had had a hard, weary day sliding and scrambling across the Marble Cañon, I made my bed and supper and lay on my back looking up to the stars through pillared arches finer far than the pious heart of man, telling its love, ever reared. Then I took a walk up the meadow to see the trees in the pale light. They seemed still more marvelously massive and tall than by day, heaving their colossal heads into the depths of the sky, among the stars, some of which appeared to be sparkling on their branches like flowers. I built a big fire that vividly illumined the huge brown boles of the nearest trees and the little plants and cones and fallen leaves at their feet, keeping up the show until I fell asleep to dream of boundless forests and trail-building for Brownie.

Joyous birds welcomed the dawn; and the squirrels, now their food cones were ripe and had to be quickly gathered and stored for winter, began their work before sunrise. My tea-and-bread-crumb breakfast was soon done, and leaving jaded Brownie to feed and rest I sauntered forth to my studies. In every direction Sequoia ruled the woods. Most of the other big conifers were present here and there, but not as rivals or companions. They only served to thicken and enrich the general wilderness. Trees of every age cover craggy ridges as well as the deep moraine-soiled slopes, and plant their magnificent shafts along every brookside and meadow. Bogs and meadows are rare or entirely wanting in the isolated groves north of Kings River; here there is a beautiful series of them lying on the broad top of the main dividing ridge, imbedded in the very heart of the mammoth woods as if for ornament, their smooth, plushy bosoms kept bright and fertile by streams and sunshine.

Resting awhile on one of the most beautiful of them when the sun was high, it seemed impossible that any other forest picture in the world could rival it. There lay the grassy, flowery lawn, three fourths of a mile long, smoothly outspread, basking in mellow autumn light, colored brown and yellow and purple, streaked with lines of green along the streams, and ruffled here and there with patches of ledum and scarlet vaccinium. Around the margin there is first a fringe of azalea and willow bushes, colored orange yellow, enlivened with vivid dashes of red cornel, as if painted. Then up spring the mighty walls of verdure three hundred feet high, the brown fluted pillars so thick and tall and strong they seem fit to uphold the sky; the dense foliage, swelling forward in rounded bosses on the upper half, variously shaded and tinted, that of the young trees dark green, of the old yellowish. An aged lightning-smitten patriarch standing a little forward beyond the general line with knotty arms outspread was covered with gray and yellow lichens and surrounded by a group of saplings whose slender spires seemed to lack not a single leaf or spray in their wondrous perfection. Such was the Kaweah meadow picture that golden afternoon, and as I gazed every color seemed to deepen and glow as if the progress of the fresh sun-work were visible from hour to hour, while every tree seemed religious and conscious of the presence of God. A free man revels in a scene like this and time goes by unmeasured. I stood fixed in silent wonder or sauntered about shifting my points of view, studying the physiognomy of separate trees, and going out to the different color patches to see how they were put on and what they were made of, giving free expression to my joy, exulting in Nature's wild immortal vigor and beauty, never dreaming any other human being was near. Suddenly the spell was broken by dull bumping, thudding sounds, and a man and horse came in sight at the farther end of the meadow, where they seemed sadly out of place. A good big bear or mastodon or megatherium would have been more in keeping with the old mammoth forest. Nevertheless, it is always pleasant to meet one of our own species after solitary rambles, and I stepped out where I could be seen and shouted, when the rider reined in his galloping mustang and waited my approach. He seemed too much surprised to speak until, laughing in his puzzled face, I said I was glad to meet a fellow mountaineer in so lonely a place. Then he abruptly asked, "What are you doing? How did you get here?" I explained that I came across the cañons from Yosemite and was only looking at the trees. "Oh then, I know," he said, greatly to my surprise, "you must be John Muir." He was herding a band of horses that had been driven up a rough trail from the lowlands to feed on these forest meadows. A few handfuls of crumb detritus was all that was left in my bread sack, so I told him that I was nearly out of provision and asked whether he could spare me a little flour. "Oh yes, of course you can have anything I've got," he said. "Just take my track and it will lead you to my camp in a big hollow log on the side of a meadow two or three miles from here. I must ride after some strayed horses, but I'll be back before night; in the mean time make yourself at home." He galloped away to the northward, I returned to my own camp, saddled Brownie, and by the middle of the afternoon discovered his noble den in a fallen Sequoia hollowed by fire—a spacious loghouse of one log, carbon-lined, centuries old yet sweet and fresh, weather proof, earthquake proof, likely to outlast the most durable stone castle, and commanding views of garden and grove grander far than the richest king ever enjoyed. Brownie found plenty of grass and I found bread, which I ate with views from the big round, ever-open door. Soon the good Samaritan mountaineer came in, and I enjoyed a famous rest listening to his observations on trees, animals, adventures, etc., while he was busily preparing supper. In answer to inquiries concerning the distribution of the Big Trees he gave a good deal of particular information of the forest we were in, and he had heard that the species extended a long way south, he knew not now far. I wandered about for several days within a radius of six or seven miles of the camp, surveying boundaries, measuring trees, and climbing the highest points for general views. From the south side of the divide I saw telling ranks of Sequoia-crowned headlands stretching far into the hazy distance, and plunging vaguely down into profound cañon depths foreshadowing weeks of good work. I had now been out on the trip more than a month, and I began to fear my studies would be interrupted by snow, for winter was drawing nigh. "Where there isn't a way make a way," is easily said when no way at the time is needed, but to the Sierra explorer with a mule traveling across the cañon lines of drainage the brave old phrase becomes heavy with meaning. There are ways across the Sierra graded by glaciers, well marked, and followed by men and beasts and birds, and one of them even by locomotives; but none natural or artificial along the range, and the explorer who would thus travel at right angles to the glacial ways must traverse cañons and ridges extending side by side in endless succession, roughened by side gorges and gulches and stubborn chaparral, and defended by innumerable sheer-fronted precipices. My own ways are easily made in any direction, but Brownie, though one of the toughest and most skillful of his race, was oftentimes discouraged for want of hands, and caused endless work. Wild at first, he was tame enough now; and when turned loose he not only refused to run away, but as his troubles increased came to depend on me in such a pitiful, touching way, I became attached to him and helped him as if he were a good-natured boy in distress, and then the labor grew lighter. Bidding good-by to the kind Sequoia cave-dweller, we vanished again in the wilderness, drifting slowly southward, Sequoias on every ridge-top beckoning and pointing the way.

In the forest between the Middle and East forks of the Kaweah, I met a great fire, and as fire is the master scourge and controller of the distribution of trees, I stopped to watch it and learn what I could of its works and ways with the giants. It came racing up the steep chaparral-covered slopes of the East Fork cañon with passionate enthusiasm in a broad cataract of flames, now bending down low to feed on the green bushes, devouring acres of them at a breath, now towering high in the air as if looking abroad to choose a way, then stooping to feed again, the lurid flapping surges and the smoke and terrible rushing and roaring hiding all that is gentle and orderly in the work. But as soon as the deep forest was reached the ungovernable flood became calm like a torrent entering a lake, creeping and spreading beneath the trees where the ground was level or sloped gently, slowly nibbling the cake of compressed needles and scales with flames an inch high, rising here and there to a foot or two on dry twigs and clumps of small bushes and brome grass. Only at considerable intervals were fierce bonfires lighted, where heavy branches broken off by snow had accumulated, or around some venerable giant whose head had been stricken off by lightning.

I tethered Brownie on the edge of a little meadow beside a stream a good safe way off, and then cautiously chose a camp for myself in a big stout hollow trunk not likely to be crushed by the fall of burning trees, and made a bed of ferns and boughs in it. The night, however, and the strange wild fireworks were too beautiful and exciting to allow much sleep. There was no danger of being chased and hemmed in, for in the main forest belt of the Sierra, even when swift winds are blowing, fires seldom or never sweep over the trees in broad all-embracing sheets as they do in the dense Rocky Mountain woods and in those of the Cascade Mountains of Oregon and Washington. Here they creep from tree to tree with tranquil deliberation, allowing close observation, though caution is required in venturing around the burning giants to avoid falling limbs and knots and fragments from dead shattered tops. Though the day was best for study, I sauntered about night after night, learning what I could and admiring the wonderful show vividly displayed in the lonely darkness, the ground-fire advancing in long crooked lines gently grazing and smoking on the close-pressed leaves, springing up in thousands of little jets of pure flame on dry tassels and twigs, and tall spires and flat sheets with jagged flapping edges dancing here and there on grass tufts and bushes, big bonfires blazing in perfect storms of energy where heavy branches mixed with small ones lay smashed together in hundred cord piles, big red arches between spreading root-swells and trees growing close together, huge fire-mantled trunks on the hill slopes glowing like bars of hot iron, violet-colored fire running up the tall trees, tracing the furrows of the bark in quick quivering rills, and lighting magnificent torches on dry shattered tops, and ever and anon, with a tremendous roar and burst of light, young trees clad in low-descending feathery branches vanishing in one flame two or three hundred feet high.

One of the most impressive and beautiful sights was made by the great fallen trunks lying on the hillsides all red and glowing like colossal iron bars fresh from a furnace, two hundred feet long some of them, and ten to twenty feet thick. After repeated burnings have consumed the bark and sapwood, the sound charred surface, being full of cracks and sprinkled with leaves, is quickly overspread with a pure, rich, furred, ruby glow almost flameless and smokeless, producing a marvelous effect in the night. Another grand and interesting sight are the fires on the tops of the largest living trees flaming above the green branches at a height of perhaps two hundred feet, entirely cut off from the ground-fires, and looking like signal beacons on watch towers. From one standpoint I sometimes saw a dozen or more, those in the distance looking like great stars above the forest roof. At first I could not imagine how these Sequoia lamps were lighted, but the very first night, strolling about waiting and watching, I saw the thing done again and again. The thick, fibrous bark of old trees is divided by deep, nearly continuous furrows, the sides of which are bearded with the bristling ends of fibres broken by the growth swelling of the trunk, and when the fire comes creeping around the feet of the trees, it runs up these bristly furrows in lovely pale blue quivering, bickering rills of flame with a low, earnest whispering sound to the lightning-shattered top of the trunk, which, in the dry Indian summer, with perhaps leaves and twigs and squirrel-gnawed cone-scales and seed-wings lodged in it, is readily ignited. These lamp-lighting rills, the most beautiful fire streams I ever saw, last only a minute or two, but the big lamps burn with varying brightness for days and weeks, throwing off sparks like the spray of a fountain, while ever and anon a shower of red coals comes sifting down through the branches, followed at times with startling effect by a big burned-off chunk weighing perhaps half a ton.

The immense bonfires where fifty or a hundred cords of peeled, split, smashed wood has been piled around some old giant by a single stroke of lightning is another grand sight in the night. The light is so great I found I could read common print three hundred yards from them, and the illumination of the circle of onlooking trees is indescribably impressive. Other big fires, roaring and booming like waterfalls, were blazing on the upper sides of trees on hillslopes, against which limbs broken off by heavy snow had rolled, while branches high overhead, tossed and shaken by the ascending air current, seemed to be writhing in pain.

Perhaps the most starting phenomenon of all was the quick death of childlike Sequoias only a century or two of age. In the midst of the other comparatively slow and steady fire work one of these tall, beautiful saplings, leafy and branchy, would be seen blazing up suddenly, all in one heaving, booming, passionate flame reaching from the ground to the top of the tree and fifty to a hundred feet or more above it, with a smoke column bending forward and streaming away on the upper, free-flowing wind. To burn these green trees a strong fire of dry wood beneath them is required, to send up a current of air hot enough to distill inflammable gases from the leaves and sprays; then instead of the lower limbs gradually catching fire and igniting the next and next in succession, the whole tree seems to explode almost simultaneously, and with awful roaring and throbbing a round, tapering flame shoots up two or three hundred feet, and in a second or two is quenched, leaving the green spire a black, dead mast, bristled and roughened with down-curling boughs. Nearly all the trees that have been burned down are lying with their heads uphill, because they are burned far more deeply on the upper side, on account of broken limbs rolling down against them to make hot fires, while only leaves and twigs accumulate on the lower side and are quickly consumed without injury to the tree. But green, resinless Sequoia wood burns very slowly, and many successive fires are required to burn down a large tree. Fires can run only at intervals of several years, and when the ordinary amount of firewood that has rolled against the gigantic trunk is consumed, only a shallow scar is made, which is slowly deepened by recurring fires until far beyond the centre of gravity, and when at last the tree falls, it of course falls uphill. The healing folds of wood layers on some of the deeply burned trees show that centuries have elapsed since the last wounds were made.

When a great Sequoia falls, its head is smashed into fragments about as small as those made by lightning, which are mostly devoured by the first running, hunting fire that finds them, while the trunk is slowly wasted away by centuries of fire and weather. One of the most interesting fire actions on the trunk is the boring of those great tunnel-like hollows through which horsemen may gallop. All of these famous hollows are burned out of the solid wood, for no Sequoia is ever hollowed by decay. When the tree falls the brash trunk is often broken straight across into sections as if sawed; into these joints the fire creeps, and, on account of the great size of the broken ends, burns for weeks or even months without being much influenced by the weather. After the great glowing ends fronting each other have burned so far apart that their rims cease to burn, the fire continues to work on in the centres, and the ends become deeply concave. Then heat being radiated from side to side, the burning goes on in each section of the trunk independent of the other, until the diameter of the bore is so great that the heat radiated across from side to side is not sufficient to keep them burning. It appears, therefore, that only very large trees can receive the fire-auger and have any shell rim left.

Fire attacks the large trees only at the ground, consuming the fallen leaves and humus at their feet, doing them but little harm unless considerable quantities of fallen limbs happen to be piled about them, their thick mail of spongy, unpitchy, almost unburnable bark affording strong protection. Therefore the oldest and most perfect unscarred trees are found on ground that is nearly level, while those growing on hillsides, against which falling branches roll, are always deeply scarred on the upper side, and as we have seen are sometimes burned down. The saddest thing of all was to see the hopeful seedlings, many of them crinkled and bent with the pressure of winter snow, yet bravely aspiring at the top, helplessly perishing, and young trees, perfect spires of verdure and naturally immortal, suddenly changed to dead masts. Yet the sun looked cheerily down the openings in the forest roof, turning the black smoke to a beautiful brown, as if all was for the best.

Beneath the smoke-clouds of the suffering forest we again pushed southward, descending a side-george of the East Fork cañon and climbing another into new forests and groves not a whit less noble. Brownie, the meanwhile, had been resting, while I was weary and sleepy with almost ceaseless wanderings, giving only an hour or two each night or day to sleep in my log home. Way-making here seemed to become more and more difficult, "impossible," in common phrase, for four-legged travelers. Two or three miles was all the day's work as far as distance was concerned. Nevertheless, just before sundown we found a charming camp ground with plenty of grass, and a forest to study that had felt no fire for many a year. The camp hollow was evidently a favorite home of bears. On many of the trees, at a height of six or eight feet, their autographs were inscribed in strong, free, flowing strokes on the soft bark where they had stood up like cats to stretch their limbs. Using both hands, every claw a pen, the handsome curved lines of their writing take the form of remarkably regular interlacing pointed arches, producing a truly ornamental effect. I looked and listened, half expecting to see some of the writers alarmed and withdrawing from the unwonted disturbance. Brownie also looked and listened, for mules fear bears instinctively and have a very keen nose for them. When I turned him loose, instead of going to the best grass, he kept cautiously near the camp-fire for protection, but was careful not to step on me. The great starry night passed away in deep peace and the rosy morning sunbeams were searching the grove ere I woke from a long, blessed sleep.

The breadth of the Sequoia belt here is about the same as on the north side of the river, extending, rather thin and scattered in some places, among the noble pines from near the mains forest belt of the range well back towards the frosty peaks, where most of the trees are growing on moraines but little changed as yet.

Two days' scramble above Bear Hollow I enjoyed an interesting interview with deer. Soon after sunrise a little company of four came to my camp in a wild garden imbedded in chaparral, and after much cautious observation quietly began to eat breakfast with me. Keeping perfectly still I soon had their confidence, and they came so near I found no difficulty, while admiring their graceful manners and gestures, in determining what plants they were eating, thus gaining a far finer knowledge and sympathy than comes by killing and hunting.

Indian summer gold with scarce a whisper of winter in it was painting the glad wilderness in richer and yet richer colors as we scrambled across the South cañon into the basin of the Tule. Here the Big Tree forests are still more extensive, and furnished abundance of work in tracing boundaries and gloriously crowned ridges up and down, back and forth, exploring, studying, admiring, while the great measureless days passed on and away uncounted. But in the calm of the camp-fire the end of the season seemed near. Brownie too often brought snow-storms to mind. He became doubly jaded, though I never rode him, and always left him in camp to feed and rest while I explored. The invincible bread business also troubled me again; the last mealy crumbs were consumed, and grass was becoming scarce even in the roughest rock-piles naturally inaccessible to sheep. One afternoon, as I gazed over the rolling bossy Sequoia billows stretching interminably southward, seeking a way and counting how far I might go without food, a rifle shot rang out sharp and clear. Marking the direction I pushed gladly on, hoping to find some hunter who could spare a little food. Within a few hundred rods I struck the track of a shod horse, Which led to the camp of two Indian shepherds. One of them was cooking supper when I arrived. Glancing curiously at me he saw that I was hungry, and gave me some mutton and bread, and said encouragingly as he pointed to the west, "Putty soon Indian come, heap speak English." Toward sundown two thousand sheep beneath a cloud of dust came streaming through the grand Sequoias to a meadow below the camp, and presently the English-speaking shepherd came in, to whom I explained my wants and what I was doing. Like most white men, he could not conceive how anything other than gold could be the object of such rambles as mine, and asked repeatedly whether I had discovered any mines. I tried to make him talk about trees and the wild animals, but unfortunately he proved to be a tame Indian from the Tule Reservation, had been to school, claimed to be civilized, and spoke contemptuously of "wild Indians," and so of course his inherited instincts were blurred or lost. The Big Trees, he said, grew far south, for he had see them in crossing the mountains from Porterville to Lone Pine. In the morning he kindly gave me a few pounds of flour, and assured me that I would get plenty more at a sawmill on the South Fork if I reached it before it was shut down for the season.

Of all the Tule basin forest the section on the North Fork seemed the finest, surpassing, I think, even the Giant Forest of the Kaweah. Southward from here, though the width and general continuity of the belt is well sustained, I thought I could detect a slight falling off in the height of the trees and in closeness of growth. All the basin was swept by swarms of hoofed locusts, the southern part over and over again, until not a leaf within the reach was left on the wettest bogs, the outer edges of the thorniest chaparral beds, or even on the young conifers, which unless under the stress of dire famine, sheep never touch. Of course Brownie suffered, though I made diligent search for grassy sheep-proof spots. Turning him loose one evening on the side of a carex bog, he dolefully prospected the desolate neighborhood without finding anything that even a starving mule could eat. Then, utterly discouraged, he stole up behind me while I was bent over on my knees making a fire for tea, and in a pitiful mixture of bray and neigh, begged for help. It was a mighty touching prayer, and I answered it as well as I could with half of what was left of a cake made from the last of the flour given me by the Indians, hastily passing it over my shoulder, and saying, "Yes, poor fellow, I know, but soon you'll have plenty. To-morrow down we go to alfalfa and barley," speaking to him as if he were human, as through stress of trouble plainly he was. After eating his portion of bread he seemed content, for he said no more, but patiently turned away to gnaw leafless ceanothus stubs. Such clinging, confiding dependence after all our scrambles and adventures together was very touching, and I felt conscience-stricken for having led him so far in so rough and desolate a country. "Man," says Lord Bacon, "is the god of the dog." So, also, he is of the mule and many other dependent fellow mortals.

Next morning I turned westward, determined to force a way straight to pasture, letting Sequoia wait. Fortunately ere we had struggled down through half a mile of chaparral we heard a mill whistle, for which we gladly made a bee line. At the sawmill we both got a good meal, then taking the dusty lumber road pursued our way to the lowlands. The nearest good pasture I counted might be thirty or forty miles away. But scarcely had we gone ten when I noticed a little log cabin a hundred yards or so back from the road, and a tall man straight as a pine standing in front of it observing us as we came plodding down through the dust. Seeing no sign of grass or hay, I was going past without stopping, when he shouted, "Travelin'?" Then drawing nearer, "Where have you come from? I didn't notice you go up." I replied I had come through the woods from the north, looking at the trees. "Oh, then, you must be John Muir. Halt, you're tired; come and rest and I'll cook for you." Then I explained that I was tracing the Sequoia belt, that on account of sheep my mule was starving, and therefore must push on to the lowlands. "No, no," he said, "that corral over there is full of hay and grain. Turn your mule into it. I don't own it, but the fellow who does is hauling lumber, and it will be all right. He's a white man. Come and rest. How tired you must be! The Big Trees don't go much farther south, nohow. I know the country up there, have hunted all over it. Come and rest, and let your little doggone rat of a mule rest. How in heavens did you get him across the cañons—roll him? or carry him? He's poor, but he'll get fat, and I'll give you a horse and go with you up the mountains, and while you're looking at the trees I'll go hunting. It will be a short job, for the end of the Big Trees is not far." Of course I stopped. No true invitation is ever declined. He had been hungry and tired himself many a time in the Rocky Mountains as well as in the Sierra. Now he owned a band of cattle and lived alone. His cabin was about eight by ten feet, the door at one end, a fireplace at the other, and a bed on one side fastened to the logs. Leading me in without a word of mean apology, he made me lie down on the bed, then reached under it, brought forth a sack of apples and advised me to keep "chawing" at them until he got supper ready. Finer, braver hospitality I never found in all this good world so often called selfish.

Next day with hearty, easy alacrity the mountaineer procured horses, prepared and packed provisions, and got everything ready for an early start the following morning. Well mounted, we pushed rapidly upon the South Fork of the river and soon after noon were among the giants once more. On the divide between the Tule and Deer Creek a central camp was made, and the mountaineer spent his time in deer-hunting, while with provisions for two or three days I explored the woods, and in accordance with what I had been told soon reached the southern extremity of the belt on the South Fork of Deer Creek. To make sure, I searched the woods a considerable distance south of the last Deer Creek grove, passed over into the basin of the Kern, and climbed several high points commanding extensive views over the sugar-pine woods, without seeing a single Sequoia crown in all the wide expanse to the southward. On the way back to camp, however, I was greatly interested in a grove I discovered on the east side of the Kern River divide, opposite the North Fork of Deer Creek. The height of the pass where the species crossed over is about 7000 feet, and I heard of still another grove whose waters drain into the upper Kern opposite the Middle Fork of the Tule.

It appears, therefore, that though the Sequoia belt is two hundred and sixty miles long, most of the trees are on a section to the south of Kings River only about seventy miles in length. But though the area occupied by the species increases so much to the southward, there is but little difference in the size of the trees. A diameter of twenty feet and height of two hundred and seventy-five is perhaps about the average for anything like mature and favorably situated trees. Specimens twenty-five feet in diameter are not rare, and a good many approach a height of three hundred feet. Occasionally one meets a specimen thirty feet in diameter, and rarely one that is larger. The majestic stump on Kings River is the largest I saw and measured on the entire trip. Careful search around the boundaries of the forests and groves and in the gaps of the belt failed to discover any trace of the former existence of the species beyond its present limits. On the contrary, it seems to be slightly extending its boundaries; for the outstanding stragglers, occasionally met a mile or two from the main bodies, are young instead of old monumental trees. Ancient ruins and the ditches and root-bowls the big trunks make in falling were found in all the groves, but none outside of them. We may therefore conclude that the area covered by the species has not been diminished during the last eight or ten thousand years, and probably not at all in post-glacial times. For admitting that upon those areas supposed to have been once covered by Sequoia every tree may have fallen, and that fire and the weather had left not a vestige of them, many of the ditches made by the fall of the ponderous trunks, weighing five hundred to nearly a thousand tons, and the bowls made by their up-turned roots would remain visible for thousands of years after the last remnants of the trees had vanished. Some of these records would doubtless be effaced in a comparatively short time by the inwashing of sediments, but no inconsiderable part of them would remain enduringly engraved on flat ridge tops, almost wholly free from such action.

In the northern groves, the only ones that at first came under the observation of students, there are but few seedlings and young trees to take the places of the old ones. Therefore the species was regarded as doomed to speedy extinction, as being only an expiring remnant vanquished in the so-called struggle for life, and shoved into its last strongholds in moist glens where conditions are exceptionally favorable. But the majestic continuous forests of the south end of the belt create a very different impression. Here, as we have seen, no tree in the forest is more enduringly established. Nevertheless it is oftentimes vaguely said that the Sierra climate is drying out, and that this oncoming, constantly increasing drought will of itself surely extinguish King Sequoia, though sections of wood-rings show that there has been no appreciable change of climate during the last forty centuries. Furthermore, that Sequoia can grow and is growing on as dry ground as any of its neighbors or rivals, we have seen proved over and over again. "Why, then," it will be asked, "are the Big Tree groves always found on well-watered spots?" Simply because Big Trees give rise to streams. It is a mistake to suppose that the water is the cause of the groves being there. On the contrary, the groves are the cause of the water being there. The roots of this immense tree fill the ground, forming a sponge which hoards the bounty of the clouds and sends it forth in clear perennial streams instead of allowing it to rush headlong in short-lived destructive floods. Evaporation is also checked, and the air kept still in the shady Sequoia depths, while thirsty robber winds are shut out.

Since, then, it appears that Sequoia can and does grow on as dry ground as its neighbors and that the greater moisture found with it is an effect rather than a cause of its presence, the notions as to the former greater extension of the species and its near approach to extinction, based on its supposed dependence on greater moisture, are seen to be erroneous. Indeed, all my observations go to show that in case of prolonged drought the sugar pines and firs would die before Sequoia. Again, if the restricted and irregular distribution of the species be interpreted as the result of the desiccation of the range, then, instead of increasing in individuals toward the south, where the rainfall is less, it should diminish.

If, then, its peculiar distribution has not been governed by superior conditions of soil and moisture, by what has it been governed? Several years before I made this trip, I noticed that the northern groves were located on those parts of the Sierra soil-belt that were first laid bare and opened to preëmption when the ice-sheet began to break up into individual glaciers. And when I was examining the basin of the San Joaquin and trying to account for the absence of Sequoia, when every condition seemed favorable for its growth, it occurred to me that this remarkable gap in the belt is located in the channel of the great ancient glacier of the San Joaquin and Kings River basins, which poured its frozen floods to the plain, fed by the snows that fell on more than fifty miles of the Summit peaks of the range. Constantly brooding on the question, I next perceived that the great gap in the belt to the northward, forty miles wide, between the Stanislaus and Tuolumne groves, occurs in the channel of the great Stanislaus and Tuolumne glacier, and that the smaller gap between the Merced and Mariposa groves occurs in the channel of the smaller Merced glacier. The wider the ancient glacier, the wider the gap in the Sequoia belt, while the groves and forests attain their greatest development in the Kaweah and Tule River basins, just where, owing to topographical conditions, the region was first cleared and warmed, while protected from the main ice-rivers, that flowed past to right and left down the Kings and Kern valleys. In general, where the ground on the belt was first cleared of ice, there the Sequoia now is, and where at the same elevation and time the ancient glaciers lingered, there the Sequoia is not. What the other conditions may have been which enabled the Sequoia to establish itself upon these oldest and warmest parts of the main soil-belt I cannot say. I might venture to state, however, that since the Sequoia forests present a more and more ancient and long established aspect to the southward, the species was probably distributed from the south toward the close of the glacial period, before the arrival of other trees. About this branch of the question, however, there is at present much fog, but the general relationship we have pointed out between the distribution of the Big Tree and the ancient glacial system is clear. And when we bear in mind that all the existing forests of the Sierra are growing on comparatively fresh moraine soil, and that the range itself has been recently sculptured and brought to light from beneath the ice-mantle of the glacial winter, then many lawless mysteries vanish, and harmonies take their places.

But notwithstanding all the observed phenomena bearing on the post-glacial history of this colossal tree, point to the conclusion that it never was more widely distributed on the Sierra since the close of the glacial epoch; that its present forests are scarcely past prime; if, indeed, they have reached prime; that the post-glacial day of the species is probably not half done; yet, when from a wider outlook the vast antiquity of the genus is considered, and its ancient richness in species and individuals, comparing our Sierra giant and Sequoia sempervirens of the coast, the only other living species, with the many fossil species already discovered, and described by Heer and Lesquereux, some of which flourished over large areas around the Arctic Circle, and in Europe and our own territories, during tertiary and cretaceous times,—then, indeed, it becomes plain that our two surviving species, restricted to narrow belts within the limits of California, are mere remnants of the genus both as to species and individuals, and that they probably are verging to extinction. But the verge of a period beginning in cretaceous times may have a breadth of tens of thousands of years, not to mention the possible existence of conditions calculated to multiply and reëxtend both species and individuals. No unfavorable change of climate, so far as I can see, no disease, but only fire and the axe and the ravages of flocks and herds threaten the existence of these noblest of God's trees. In Nature's keeping they are safe, but through man's agency destruction is making rapid progress, while in the work of protection only a beginning has been made. The Mariposa Grove belongs to and is guarded by the State; the General Grant and Sequoia National Parks, established ten years ago, are efficiently guarded by a troop of cavalry under the direction of the Secretary of the Interior; so also are the small Tuolumne and Merced groves, which are included in the Yosemite National Park, while a few scattered patches and fringes, scarce at all protected, though belonging to the national government, are in the Sierra Forest Reservation.

Perhaps more than half of all the Big Trees have been sold, and are now in the hands of speculators and mill men. Even the beautiful little Calaveras Grove of ninety trees, so historically interesting from its being the first discovered, is now owned, together with the much larger South or Stanislaus Grove, by a lumber company.

Far the largest and most important section of protected Big Trees is in the grand Sequoia National Park, now easily accessible by stage from Visalia. It contains seven townships and extends across the whole breadth of the magnificent Kaweah basin. But large as it is, it should be made much larger. Its natural eastern boundary is the high Sierra, and the northern and southern boundaries, and the Kings and Kern rivers, and thus including the sublime scenery on the headwaters of these rivers and perhaps nine tenths of all the Big Trees in existence. Private claims cut and blotch both of the Sequoia parks as well as all the best of the forests, every one of which the government should gradually extinguish by purchase, as it readily may, for none of these holdings are of much value to their owners. Thus as far as possible the grand blunder of selling would be corrected. The value of these forests in storing and dispensing the bounty of the mountain clouds is infinitely greater than lumber or sheep. To the dwellers of the plain, dependent on irrigation, the Big Tree, leaving all its higher uses out of the count, is a tree of life, a never-failing spring, sending living water to the lowlands all through the hot, rainless summer. For every grove cut down a stream is dried up. Therefore, all California is crying, “Save the trees of the fountains,” nor, judging by the signs of the times, it is likely that the cry will cease until the salvation of all that is left of Sequoia gigantea is sure.

CHAPTER X

The American Forests

The forests of America, however slighted by man, must have been a great delight to God; for they were the best he ever planted. The whole continent was a garden, and from the beginning it seemed to be favored above all the other wild parks and gardens of the globe. To prepare the ground, it was rolled and sifted in seas with infinite loving deliberation and fore-thought, lifted into the light, submerged and warmed over and over again, pressed and crumpled into folds and ridges, mountains, and hills, subsoiled with heaving volcanic fires, ploughed and ground and sculptured into scenery and soil with glaciers and rivers,—every feature growing and changing from beauty to beauty, higher and higher. And in the fullness of time it was planted in groves, and belts, and broad, exuberant, mantling forests, with the largest, most varied, most fruitful, and most beautiful trees in the world. Bright seas made its border, with wave embroidery and icebergs; gray deserts were outspread in the middle of it, mossy tundras on the north, savannas on the south, and blooming prairies and plains; while lakes and rivers shone through all the vast forests and openings, and happy birds and beasts gave delightful animation. Everywhere, everywhere over all the blessed continent, there were beauty and melody and kindly, wholesome, foodful abundance.

These forests were composed of about five hundred species of trees, all of them in some way useful to man, ranging in size from twenty-five feet in height and less than one foot in diameter at the ground to four hundred feet in height and more than twenty feet in diameter,—lordly monarchs proclaiming the gospel of beauty like apostles. For many a century after the ice-ploughs were melted, nature fed them and dressed them every day,—working like a man, a loving, devoted, painstaking gardener; fingering every leaf and flower and mossy furrowed bole; bending, trimming, modeling, balancing; painting them with the loveliest colors; bringing over them now clouds with cooling shadows and showers, now sunshine; fanning them with gentle winds and rustling their leaves; exercising them in every fibre with storms, and pruning them; loading them with flowers and fruit, loading them with snow, and ever making them more beautiful as the years rolled by. Wide-branching oak and elm in endless variety, walnut and maple, chestnut and beech, ilex and locust, touching limb to limb, spread a leafy translucent canopy along the coast of the Atlantic over the wrinkled folds and ridges of the Alleghanies,—a green billowy sea in summer, golden and purple in autumn, pearly gray like a steadfast frozen mist of interlacing branches and sprays in leafless, restful winter.

To the southward stretched dark, level-topped cypresses in knobby, tangled swamps, grassy savannas in the midst of them like lakes of light, groves of gay, sparkling spice-trees, magnolias and palms, glossy-leaved and blooming and shining continually. To the northward, over Maine and Ottawa, rose hosts of spiry, rosiny evergreens,—white pine and spruce, hemlock and cedar, shoulder to shoulder, laden with purple cones, their myriad needles sparkling and shimmering, covering hills and swamps, rocky headlands and domes, ever bravely aspiring and seeking the sky; the ground in their shade now snow-clad and frozen, now mossy and flowery; beaver meadows here and there, full of lilies and grass; lakes gleaming like eyes, and a silvery embroidery of rivers and creeks watering and brightening all the vast glad wilderness.

Thence westward were oak and elm, hickory and tupelo, gum and liriodendron, sassafras and ash, linden and laurel, spreading on ever wider in glorious exuberance over the great fertile basin of the Mississippi, over damp level bottoms, low dimpling hollows, and round dotting hills, embosoming sunny prairies and cheery park openings, half sunshine, half shade; while a dark wilderness of pines covered the region around the Great Lakes. Thence still westward swept the forests to right and left around grassy plains and deserts a thousand miles wide: irrepressible hosts of spruce and pine, aspen and willow, nut-pine and juniper, cactus and yucca, caring nothing for drought, extending undaunted from mountain to mountain, over mesa and desert, to join the darkening multitudes of pines that covered the high Rocky ranges and the glorious forests along the coast of the moist and balmy Pacific, where new species of pine, giant cedars and spruces, silver firs and Sequoias, kings of their race, growing close together like grass in a meadow, poised their brave domes and spires in the sky, three hundred feet above the ferns and the lilies that enameled the ground; towering serene through the long centuries, preaching God's forestry fresh from heaven.

Here the forests reached their highest development. Hence they went wavering northward over icy Alaska, brave spruce and fir, poplar and birch, by the coasts and the rivers, to within sight of the Arctic Ocean. American forests! the glory of the world! Surveyed thus from the east to the west, from the north to the south, they are rich beyond thought, immortal, immeasurable, enough and to spare for every feeding, sheltering beast and bird, insect and son of Adam; and nobody need have cared had there been no pines in Norway, no cedars and deodars on Lebanon and the Himalayas, no vine-clad selvas in the basin of the Amazon. With such variety, harmony, and triumphant exuberance, even nature, it would seem, might have rested content with the forests of North America, and planted no more.

So they appeared a few centuries ago when they were rejoicing in wildness. The Indians with stone axes could do them no more harm than could gnawing beavers and browsing moose. Even the fires of the Indians and the fierce shattering lightning seemed to work together only for good in clearing spots here and there for smooth garden prairies, and openings for sunflowers seeking the light. But when the steel axe of the white man rang out on the startled air their doom was sealed. Every tree heard the bodeful sound, and pillars of smoke gave the sign in the sky.

I suppose we need not go mourning the buffaloes. In the nature of things they had to give place to better cattle, though the change might have been made without barbarous wickedness. Likewise many of nature's five hundred kinds of wild trees had to make way for orchards and cornfields. In the settlement and civilization of the country, bread more than timber or beauty was wanted; and in the blindness of hunger, the early settlers, claiming Heaven as their guide, regarded God's trees as only a larger kind of pernicious weeds, extremely hard to get rid of. Accordingly, with no eye to the future, these pious destroyers waged interminable forest wars; chips flew thick and fast; trees in their beauty fell crashing by millions, smashed to confusion, and the smoke of their burning has been rising to heaven more than two hundred years. After the Atlantic coast from Maine to Georgia had been mostly cleared and scorched into melancholy ruins, the overflowing multitude of bread and money seekers poured over the Alleghanies into the fertile middle West, spreading ruthless devastation ever wider and farther over the rich valley of the Mississippi and the vast shadowy pine region about the Great Lakes. Thence still westward, the invading horde of destroyers called settlers made its fiery way over the broad Rocky Mountains, felling and burning more fiercely than ever, until at last it has reached the wild side of the continent, and entered the last of the great aboriginal forests on the shores of the Pacific.

Surely, then, it should not be wondered at that lovers of their country, bewailing its baldness, are now crying aloud, "Save what is left of the forests!" Clearing has surely now gone far enough; soon timber will be scarce, and not a grove will be left to rest in or pray in. The remnant protected will yield plenty of timber, a perennial harvest for every right use, without further diminution of its area, and will continue to cover the springs of the rivers that rise in the mountains and give irrigating waters to the dry valleys at their feet, prevent wasting floods and be a blessing to everybody forever.

Every other civilized nation in the world has been compelled to care for its forests, and so must we if waste and destruction are not to go on to the bitter end, leaving America as barren as Palestine or Spain. In its calmer moments, in the midst of bewildering hunger and war and restless over-industry, Prussia has learned that the forest plays an important part in human progress, and that the advance in civilization only makes it more indispensable. It has, therefore, as shown by Mr. Pinchot, refused to deliver its forests to more or less speedy destruction by permitting them to pass into private ownership. But the state woodlands are not allowed to lie idle. On the contrary, they are made to produce as much timber as is possible without spoiling them. In the administration of its forests, the state righteously considers itself bound to treat them as a trust for the nation as a whole, and to keep in view the common good of the people for all time.

In France no government forests have been sold since 1870. On the other hand, about one half of the fifty million francs spent on forestry has been given to engineering works, to make the replanting of denuded areas possible. The disappearance of the forests in the first place, it is claimed, may be traced in most cases directly to mountain pasturage. The provisions of the Code concerning private woodlands are substantially these: no private owner may clear his woodlands without giving notice to the government at least four months in advance, and the forest service may forbid the clearing on the following grounds,—to maintain the soil on mountains, to defend the soil against erosion and flooding by rivers or torrents, to insure the existence of springs or watercourses, to protect the dunes and seashore, etc. A proprietor who has cleared his forest without permission is subject to heavy fine, and in addition may be made to replant the cleared area.

In Switzerland, after many laws like our own had been found wanting, the Swiss forest school was established in 1865, and soon after the federal forest law was enacted, which is binding over nearly two thirds of the country. Under its provisions, the cantons must appoint and pay the number of suitably educated foresters required for the fulfillment of the forest law; and in the organization of a normally stocked forest, the object of first importance must be the cutting each year of an amount of timber equal to the total annual increase, and no more.

The Russian government passed a law in 1888, declaring that clearing is forbidden in protected forests, and is allowed in others "only when its effects will not be to disturb the suitable relations which should exist between forest and agricultural lands."

Even Japan is ahead of us in the management of her forests. They cover an area of about twenty-nine million acres. The feudal lords valued the woodlands, and enacted vigorous protective laws; and when, in the latest civil war, the Mikado government destroyed the feudal system, it declared the forests that had belonged to the feudal lords to be the property of the state, promulgated a forest law binding on the whole kingdom, and founded a school of forestry in Tokio. The forest service does not rest satisfied with the present proportion of woodland, but looks to planting the best forest trees it can find in any country, if likely to be useful and to thrive in Japan.

In India systematic forest management was begun about forty years ago, under difficulties—presented by the character of the country, the prevalence of running fires, opposition from lumbermen, settlers, etc.—not unlike those which confront us now. Of the total area of government forests, perhaps seventy million acres, fifty-five million acres have been brought under the control of the forestry department,—a larger area than that of all our national parks and reservations. The chief aims of the administration are effective protection of the forests from fire, an efficient system of regeneration, and cheap transportation of the forest products; the results so far have been most beneficial and encouraging.

It seems, therefore, that almost every civilized nation can give us a lesson on the management and care of forests. So far our government has done nothing effective with its forests, though the best in the world, but is like a rich and foolish spendthrift who has inherited a magnificent estate in perfect order, and then has left his fields and meadows, forests and parks, to be sold and plundered and wasted at will, depending on their inexhaustible abundance. Now it is plain that the forests are not inexhaustible, and that quick measures must be taken if ruin is to be avoided. Year by year the remnant is growing smaller before the axe and fire, while the laws in existence provide neither for the protection of the timber from destruction nor for its use where it is most needed.

As is shown by Mr. E. A. Bowers, formerly Inspector of the Public Land Service, the foundation of our protective policy, which has never protected, is an act passed March 1, 1817, which authorized the Secretary of the Navy to reserve lands producing live-oak and cedar, for the sole purpose of supplying timber for the navy of the United States. An extension of this law by the passage of the act of March 2, 1831, provided that if any person should cut live-oak or red cedar trees or other timber from the lands of the United States for any other purpose than the construction of the navy, such person should pay a fine not less than triple the value of the timber cut, and be imprisoned for a period not exceeding twelve months. Upon this old law, as Mr. Bowers points out, having the construction of a wooden navy in view, the United States government has to-day chiefly to rely in protecting its timber throughout the arid regions of the West, where none of the naval timber which the law had in mind is to be found.

By the act of June 3, 1878, timber can be taken from public lands not subject to entry under any existing laws except for minerals, by bona fide residents of the Rocky Mountain states and territories and the Dakotas. Under the timber and stone act, of the same date, land in the Pacific States and Nevada, valuable mainly for timber, and unfit for cultivation if the timber is removed, can be purchased for two dollars and a half an acre, under certain restrictions. By the act of March 3, 1875, all land-grant and right-of-way railroads are authorized to take timber from the public lands adjacent to their lines for construction purposes; and they have taken it with a vengeance, destroying a hundred times more than they have used, mostly by allowing fires to run in the woods. The settlement laws, under which a settler may enter lands valuable for timber as well as for agriculture, furnish another means of obtaining title to public timber.

With the exception of the timber culture act, under which, in consideration of planting a few acres of seedlings, settlers on the treeless plains got 160 acres each, the above is the only legislation aiming to protect and promote the planting of forests. In no other way than under some one of these laws can a citizen of the United States make any use of the public forests. To show the results of the timber-planting act, it need only be stated that of the thirty-eight million acres entered under it, less than one million acres have been patented. This means that less than fifty thousand acres have been planted with stunted, woebegone, almost hopeless sprouts of trees, while at the same time the government has allowed millions of acres of the grandest forest trees to be stolen or destroyed, or sold for nothing. Under the act of June 3, 1878, settlers in Colorado and the Territories were allowed to cut timber for mining and educational purposes from mineral land, which in the practical West means both cutting and burning anywhere and everywhere, for any purpose, on any sort of public land. Thus, the prospector, the miner, and mining and railroad companies are allowed by law to take all the timber they like for their mines and roads, and the forbidden settler, if there are no mineral lands near his farm or stock-ranch, or none that he knows of, can hardly be expected to forbear taking what he needs wherever he can find it. Timber is as necessary as bread, and no scheme of management failing to recognize and properly provide for this want can possibly be maintained. In any case, it will be hard to teach the pioneers that it is wrong to steal government timber. Taking from the government is with them the same as taking from nature, and their consciences flinch no more in cutting timber from the wild forests than in drawing water from a lake or river. As for reservation and protection of forests, it seems as silly and needless to them as protection and reservation of the ocean would be, both appearing to be boundless and inexhaustible.

The special land agents employed by the General Land Office to protect the public domain from timber depredations are supposed to collect testimony to sustain prosecution and to superintend such prosecution on behalf of the government, which is represented by the district attorneys. But timber thieves of the Western class are seldom convicted, for the good reason that most of the jurors who try such cases are themselves as guilty as those on trial. The effect of the present confused, discriminating, and unjust system has been to place almost the whole population in opposition to the government; and as conclusive of its futility, as shown by Mr. Bowers, we need only state that during the seven years from 1881 to 1887 inclusive, the value of the timber reported stolen from the government lands was $36,719,935, and the amount recovered was $478,073, while the cost of the services of special agents alone was $455,000, to which must be added the expense of the trials. Thus for nearly thirty-seven million dollars worth of timber the government got less than nothing; and the value of that consumed by running fires during the same period, without benefit even to thieves, was probably over two hundred millions of dollars. Land commissioners and Secretaries of the Interior have repeatedly called attention to this ruinous state of affairs, and asked Congress to enact the requisite legislation for reasonable reform. But, busied with tariffs, etc., Congress has given no heed to these or other appeals, and our forests, the most valuable and the most destructible of all the natural resources of the country, are being robbed and burned more rapidly than ever. The annual appropriation for so-called "protection service" is hardly sufficient to keep twenty-five timber agents in the field, and as far as any efficient protection of timber is concerned these agents themselves might as well be timber.[7]

> [7] A change for the better, compelled by public opinion, is now going on,—1901.

That a change from robbery and ruin to a permanent rational policy is urgently needed nobody with the slightest knowledge of American forests will deny. In the East and along the northern Pacific coast, where the rainfall is abundant, comparatively few care keenly what becomes of the trees so long as fuel and lumber are not noticeably dear. But in the Rocky Mountains and California and Arizona, where the forests are inflammable, and where the fertility of the lowlands depends upon irrigation, public opinion is growing stronger every year in favor of permanent protection by the federal government of all the forests that cover the sources of the streams. Even lumbermen in these regions, long accustomed to steal, are now willing and anxious to buy lumber for their mills under cover of law: some possibly from a late second growth of honesty, but most, especially the small mill-owners, simply because it no longer pays to steal where all may not only steal, but also destroy, and in particular because it costs about as much to steal timber for one mill as for ten, and, therefore, the ordinary lumberman can no longer compete with the large corporations. Many of the miners find that timber is already becoming scarce and dear on the denuded hills around their mills, and they, too, are asking for protection of forests, at least against fire. The slow-going, unthrifty farmers, also, are beginning to realize that when the timber is stripped from the mountains the irrigating streams dry up in summer, and are destructive in winter; that soil, scenery, and everything slips off with the trees: so of course they are coming into the ranks of tree-friends.

Of all the magnificent coniferous forests around the Great Lakes, once the property of the United States, scarcely any belong to it now. They have disappeared in lumber and smoke, mostly smoke, and the government got not one cent for them; only the land they were growing on was considered valuable, and two and a half dollars an acre was charged for it. Here and there in the

Southern States there are still considerable areas of timbered government land, but these are comparatively unimportant. Only the forests of the West are significant in size and value, and these, although still great, are rapidly vanishing. Last summer, of the unrivaled red-wood forests of the Pacific Coast Range, the United States Forestry Commission could not find a single quarter-section that remained in the hands of the government.[8]

> [8] The State of California recently appropriated two hundred and fifty thousand dollars to buy a block of redwood land near Santa Cruz for a state park. A much larger national park should be made in Humboldt or Mendocino county.

Under the timber and stone act of 1878, which might well have been called the "dust and ashes act," any citizen of the United States could take up one hundred and sixty acres of timber land, and by paying two dollars and a half an acre for it obtain title. There was some virtuous effort made with a view to limit the operations of the act by requiring that the purchaser should make affidavit that he was entering the land exclusively for his own use, and by not allowing any association to enter more than one hundred and sixty acres. Nevertheless, under this act wealthy corporations have fraudulently obtained title to from ten thousand to twenty thousand acres or more. The plan was usually as follows: A mill company, desirous of getting title to a large body of redwood or sugar-pine land, first blurred the eyes and ears of the land agents, and then hired men to enter the land they wanted, and immediately deed it to the company after a nominal compliance with the law; false swearing in the wilderness against the government being held of no account. In one case which came under the observation of Mr. Bowers, it was the practice of a lumber company to hire the entire crew of every vessel which might happen to touch at any port in the red-wood belt, to enter one hundred and sixty acres each and immediately deed the land to the company, in consideration of the company's paying all expenses and giving the jolly sailors fifty dollars apiece for their trouble.

By such methods have our magnificent redwoods and much of the sugar-pine forests of the Sierra Nevada been absorbed by foreign and resident capitalists. Uncle Sam is not often called a fool in business matters, yet he has sold millions of acres of timber land at two dollars and a half an acre on which a single tree was worth more than a hundred dollars. But this priceless land has been patented, and nothing can be done now about the crazy bargain. According to the everlasting law of righteousness, even the fraudulent buyers at less than one per cent of its value are making little or nothing, on account of fierce competition. The trees are felled, and about half of each giant is left on the ground to be converted into smoke and ashes; the better half is sawed into choice lumber and sold to citizens of the United States or to foreigners: thus robbing the country of its glory and impoverishing it without right benefit to anybody,—a bad, black business from beginning to end.

The redwood is one of the few conifers that sprout from the stump and roots, and it declares itself willing to begin immediately to repair the damage of the lumberman and also that of the forest-burner. As soon as a redwood is cut down or burned it sends up a crowd of eager, hopeful shoots, which, if allowed to grow, would in a few decades attain a height of a hundred feet, and the strongest of them would finally become giants as great as the original tree. Gigantic second and third growth trees are found in the redwoods, forming magnificent temple-like circles around charred ruins more than a thousand years old. But not one denuded acre in a hundred is allowed to raise a new forest growth. On the contrary, all the brains, religion, and superstition of the neighborhood are brought into play to prevent a new growth. The sprouts from the roots and stumps are cut off again and again, with zealous concern as to the best time and method of making death sure. In the clearings of one of the largest mills on the coast we found thirty men at work, last summer, cutting off redwood shoots "in the dark of the moon," claiming that all the stumps and roots cleared at this auspicious time would send up no more shoots. Anyhow, these vigorous, almost immortal trees are killed at last, and black stumps are now their only monuments over most of the chopped and burned areas.

The redwood is the glory of the Coast Range. It extends along the western slope, in a nearly continuous belt about ten miles wide, from beyond the Oregon boundary to the south of Santa Cruz, a distance of nearly four hundred miles, and in massive, sustained grandeur and closeness of growth surpasses all the other timber woods of the world. Trees from ten to fifteen feet in diameter and three hundred feet high are not uncommon, and a few attain a height of three hundred and fifty feet or even four hundred, with a diameter at the base of fifteen to twenty feet or more, while the ground beneath them is a garden of fresh, exuberant ferns, lilies, gaultheria, and rhododendron. This grand tree, Sequoia sempervirens, is surpassed in size only by its near relative, Sequoia gigantea, or Big Tree, of the Sierra Nevada, if, indeed, it is surpassed. The sempervirens is certainly the taller of the two. The gigantea attains a greater girth, and is heavier, more noble in port, and more sublimely beautiful. These two Sequoia are all that are known to exist in the world, though in former geological times the genus was common and had many species. The redwood is restricted to the Coast Range, and the Big Tree to the Sierra.

As timber the redwood is too good to live. The largest sawmills ever built are busy along its seaward border, "with all the modern improvements," but so immense is the yield per acre it will be long ere the supply is exhausted. The Big Tree is also, to some extent, being made into lumber. It is far less abundant than the redwood, and is, fortunately, less accessible, extending along the western flank of the Sierra in a partially interrupted belt, about two hundred and fifty miles long, at a height of from four to eight thousand feet above the sea. The enormous logs, too heavy to handle, are blasted into manageable dimensions with gunpowder. A large portion of the best timber is thus shattered and destroyed, and, with the huge, knotty tops, is left in ruins for tremendous fires that kill every tree within their range, great and small. Still, the species is not in danger of extinction. It has been planted and is flourishing over a great part of Europe, and magnificent sections of the aboriginal forests have been reserved as national and State parks,—the Mariposa Sequoia Grove, near Yosemite, managed by the State of California, and the General Grant and Sequoia national parks on the Kings, Kaweah, and Tule rivers, efficiently guarded by a small troop of United States cavalry under the direction of the Secretary of the interior. But there is not a single specimen of the redwood in any national park. Only by gift or purchase, so far as I know, can the government get back into its possession a single acre of this wonderful forest.

The legitimate demands on the forests that have passed into private ownership, as well as those in the hands of the government, are increasing every year with the rapid settlement and up-building of the country, but the methods of lumbering are as yet grossly wasteful. In most mills only the best portions of the best trees are used, while the ruins are left on the ground to feed great fires, which kill much of what is left of the less desirable timber, together with the seedlings, on which the permanence of the forest depends. Thus every mill is a centre of destruction far more severe from waste and fire than from use. The same thing is true of the mines, which consume and destroy indirectly immense quantities of timber with their innumerable fires, accidental or set to make open ways, and often without regard to how far they run. The prospector deliberately sets fires to clear off the woods just where they are densest, to lay the rocks bare and make the discovery of mines easier. Sheep-owners and their shepherds also set fires everywhere through the woods in the fall to facilitate the march of their countless flocks the next summer, and perhaps in some places to improve the pasturage. The axe is not yet at the root of every tree, but the sheep is, or was before the national parks were established and guarded by the military, the only effective and reliable arm of the government free from the blight of politics. Not only do the shepherds, at the driest time of the year, set fire to everything that will burn, but the sheep consume every green leaf, not sparing even the young conifers, where they are in a starving condition from crowding, and they rake and dibble the loose soil of the mountain sides for the spring floods to wash away, and thus at last leave the ground barren.

Of all the destroyers that infest the woods, the shake-maker seems the happiest. Twenty or thirty years ago, shakes, a kind of long, board-like shingles split with a mallet and a frow, were in great demand for covering barns and sheds, and many are used still in preference to common shingles, especially those made from the sugar-pine, which do not warp or crack in the hottest sunshine. Drifting adventurers in California, after harvest and threshing are over, oftentimes meet to discuss their plans for the winter, and their talk is interesting. Once, in a company of this kind, I heard a man say, as he peacefully smoked his pipe: "Boys, as soon as this job's done I'm goin' into the duck business. There's big money in it, and your grub costs nothing. Tule Joe made five hundred dollars last winter on mallard and teal. Shot 'em on the Joaquin, tied 'em in dozens by the neck, and shipped 'em to San Francisco. And when he was tired wading in the sloughs and touched with rheumatiz, he just knocked off on ducks, and went to the Contra Costa hills for dove and quail. It's a mighty good business, and you're your own boss, and the whole thing's fun."

Another of the company, a bushy-bearded fellow, with a trace of brag in his voice, drawled out: "Bird business is well enough for some, but bear is my game, with a deer and a California lion thrown in now and then for change. There's always market for bear grease, and sometimes you can sell the hams. They're good as hog hams any day. And you are your own boss in my business, too, if the bears ain't too big and too many for you. Old grizzlies I despise,—they want cannon to kill 'em; but the blacks and browns are beauties for grease, and when once I get 'em just right, and draw a bead on 'em, I fetch 'em every time." Another said he was going to catch up a lot of mustangs as soon as the rains set in, hitch them to a gang-plough, and go to farming on the San Joaquin plains for wheat. But most preferred the shake business, until something more profitable and as sure could be found, with equal comfort and independence.

With a cheap mustang or mule to carry a pair of blankets, a sack of flour, a few pounds of coffee, and an axe, a frow, and a cross-cut saw, the shake-maker ascends the mountains to the pine belt where it is most accessible, usually by some mine or mill road. Then he strikes off into the virgin woods, where the sugar pine, king of all the hundred species of pines in the world in size and beauty, towers on the open sunny slopes of the Sierra in the fullness of its glory. Selecting a favorable spot for a cabin near a meadow with a stream, he unpacks his animal and stakes it out on the meadow. Then he chops into one after another of the pines, until he finds one that he feels sure will split freely, cuts this down, saws off a section four feet long, splits it, and from this first cut, perhaps seven feet in diameter, he gets shakes enough for a cabin and its furniture,—walls, roof, door, bedstead, table, and stool. Besides his labor, only a few pounds of nails are required. Sapling poles form the frame of the airy building, usually about six feet by eight in size, on which the shakes are nailed, with the edges overlapping. A few bolts from the same section that the shakes were made from are split into square sticks and built up to form a chimney, the inside and interspaces being plastered and filled in with mud. Thus, with abundance of fuel, shelter and comfort by his own fireside are secured. Then he goes to work sawing and splitting for the market, tying the shakes in bundles of fifty or a hundred. They are four feet long, four inches wide, and about one fourth of an inch thick. The first few thousands he sells or trades at the nearest mill or store, getting provisions in exchange. Then he advertises, in whatever way he can, that he has excellent sugar-pine shakes for sale, easy of access and cheap.

Only the lower, perfectly clear, free-splitting portions of the giant pines are used,—perhaps ten to twenty feet from a tree two hundred and fifty in height; all the rest is left a mass of ruins, to rot or to feed the forest fires, while thousands are hacked deeply and rejected in proving the grain. Over nearly all of the more accessible slopes of the Sierra and Cascade mountains in southern Oregon, at a height of from three to six thousand feet above the sea, and for a distance of about six hundred miles, this waste and confusion extends. Happy robbers! dwelling in the most beautiful woods, in the most salubrious climate, breathing delightful odors both day and night, drinking cool living water,—roses and lilies at their feet in the spring, shedding fragrance and ringing bells as if cheering them on in their desolating work. There is none to say them nay. They buy no land, pay no taxes, dwell in a paradise with no forbidding angel either from Washington or from heaven. Every one of the frail shake shanties is a centre of destruction, and the extent of the ravages wrought in this quiet way is in the aggregate enormous.

It is not generally known that, notwithstanding the immense quantities of timber cut every year for foreign and home markets and mines, from five to ten times as much is destroyed as is used, chiefly by running forest fires that only the federal government can stop. Travelers through the West in summer are not likely to forget the fire-work displayed along the various railway tracks. Thoreau, when contemplating the destruction of the forests on the east side of the continent, said that soon the country would be so bald that every man would have to grow whiskers to hide its nakedness, but he thanked God that at least the sky was safe. Had he gone West he would have found out that the sky was not safe; for all through the summer months, over most of the mountain regions, the smoke of mill and forest fires is so thick and black that no sunbeam can pierce it. The whole sky, with clouds, sun, moon, and stars, is simply blotted out. There is no real sky and no scenery. Not a mountain is left in the landscape. At least none is in sight from the lowlands, and they all might as well be on the moon, as far as scenery is concerned.

The half-dozen transcontinental railroad companies advertise the beauties of their lines in gorgeous many-colored folders, each claiming its as the "scenic route." "The route of superior desolation"—the smoke, dust, and ashes route—would be a more truthful description. Every train rolls on through dismal smoke and barbarous, melancholy ruins; and the companies might well cry in their advertisements: "Come! travel our way. Ours is the blackest. It is the only genuine Erebus route. The sky is black and the ground is black, and on either side there is a continuous border of black stumps and logs and blasted trees appealing to heaven for help as if still half alive, and their mute eloquence is most interestingly touching. The blackness is perfect. On account of the superior skill of our workmen, advantages of climate, and the kind of trees, the charring is generally deeper along our line, and the ashes are deeper, and the confusion and desolation displayed can never be rivaled. No other route on this continent so fully illustrates the abomination of desolation." Such a claim would be reasonable, as each seems the worst, whatever route you chance to take.

Of course a way had to be cleared through the woods. But the felled timber is not worked up into firewood for the engines and into lumber for the company's use; it is left lying in vulgar confusion, and is fired from time to time by sparks from locomotives or by the workmen camping along the line. The fires, whether accidental or set, are allowed to run into the woods as far as they may, thus assuring comprehensive destruction. The directors of a line that guarded against fires, and cleared a clean gap edged with living trees, and fringed and mantled with the grass and flowers and beautiful seedling that are ever ready and willing to spring up, might justly boast of the beauty of their road; for nature is always ready to heal every scar. But there is no such road on the western side of the continent. Last summer, in the Rocky Mountains, I saw six fires started by sparks from a locomotive within a distance of three miles, and nobody was in sight to prevent them from spreading. They might run into the adjacent forests and burn the timber from hundreds of square miles; not a man in the State would care to spend an hour in fighting them, as long as his own fences and buildings were not threatened.

Notwithstanding all the waste and use which have been going on unchecked like a storm for more than two centuries, it is not yet too late—though it is high time—for the government to begin a rational administration of its forests. About seventy million acres it still owns,—enough for all the country, if wisely used. These residual forests are generally on mountain slopes, just where they are doing the most good, and where their removal would be followed by the greatest number of evils; the lands they cover are too rocky and high for agriculture, and can never be made as valuable for any other crop as for the present crop of trees. It has been shown over and over again that if these mountains were to be stripped of their trees and underbrush, and kept bare and sodless by hordes of sheep and the innumerable fires the shepherds set, besides those of the millmen, prospectors shake-makers, and all sorts of adventurers, both lowlands and mountains would speedily become little better than desert, compared with their present beneficent fertility. During heavy rainfalls and while the winter accumulations of snow were melting, the large streams would swell into destructive torrents, cutting deep, rugged-edged gullies, carrying away the fertile humus and soil as well as sand

and rocks, filling up and overflowing their lower channels, and covering the lowland fields with raw detritus. Drought and barrenness would follow.

In their natural condition, or under wise management, keeping out destructive sheep, preventing fires, selecting the trees that should be cut for lumber, and preserving the young ones and the shrubs and sod of herbaceous vegetation, these forests would be a never failing fountain of wealth and beauty. The cool shades of the forest give rise to moist beds and currents of air, and the sod of grasses and the various flowering plants and shrubs thus fostered, together with the network and sponge of tree roots, absorb and hold back the rain and the waters from melting snow, compelling them to ooze and percolate and flow gently through the soil in streams that never dry. All the pine needles and rootlets and blades of grass, and the fallen, decaying trunks of trees, are dams, storing the bounty of the clouds and dispensing it in perennial life-giving streams, instead of allowing it to gather suddenly and rush headlong in short-lived devastating floods. Everybody on the dry side of the continent is beginning to find this out, and, in view of the waste going on, is growing more and more anxious for government protection. The outcries we hear against forest reservations come mostly from thieves who are wealthy and steal timber by wholesale. They have so long been allowed to steal and destroy in peace that any impediment to forest robbery is denounced as a cruel and irreligious interference with "vested rights," likely to endanger the repose of all ungodly welfare.

Gold, gold, gold! How strong a voice that metal has!

"O wae for the siller, it is sae preva'lin'!"

Even in Congress a sizable chunk of gold, carefully concealed, will outtalk and outfight all the nation on a subject like forestry, well smothered in ignorance, and in which the money interests of only a few are conspicuously involved. Under these circumstances, the bawling, blethering oratorical stuff drowns the voice of God himself. Yet the dawn of a new day in forestry is breaking. Honest citizens see that only the rights of the government are being trampled, not those of the settlers. Only what belongs to all alike is reserved, and every acre that is left should be held together under the federal government as a basis for a general policy of administration for the public good. The people will not always be deceived by selfish opposition, whether from lumber and mining corporations or from sheepmen and prospectors, however cunningly brought forward underneath fables and gold.

Emerson says that things refuse to be mismanaged long. An exception would seem to be found in the case of our forests, which have been mismanaged rather long, and now come desperately near being like smashed eggs and spilt milk. Still, in the long run the world does not move backward. The wonderful advance made in the last few years, in creating four national parks in the West, and thirty forest reservations, embracing nearly forty million acres; and in the planting of the borders of streets and highways and spacious parks in all the great cities, to satisfy the natural taste and hunger for landscape beauty and righteousness that God has put, in some measure, into every human being and animal, shows the trend of awakening public opinion. The making of the far-famed New York Central Park was opposed by even good men, with misguided pluck, perseverance, and ingenuity; but straight right won its way, and now that park is appreciated. So we confidently believe it will be with our great national parks and forest reservations. There will be a period of indifference on the part of the rich, sleepy with wealth, and of the toiling millions, sleepy with poverty, most of whom never saw a forest; a period of screaming protest and objection from the plunderers, who are as unconscionable and enterprising as Satan. But light is surely coming, and the friends of destruction will preach and bewail in vain.

The United States government has always been proud of the welcome it has extended to good men of every nation, seeking freedom and homes and bread. Let them be welcomed still as nature welcomes them, to the woods as well as to the prairies and plains. No place is too good for good men, and still there is room. They are invited to heaven, and may well be allowed in America. Every place is made better by them. Let them be as free to pick gold and gems from the hills, to cut and hew, dig and plant, for homes and bread, as the birds are to pick berries from the wild bushes, and moss and leaves for nests. The ground will be glad to feed them, and the pines will come down from the mountains for their homes as willingly as the cedars came from Lebanon for Solomon's temple. Nor will the woods be the worse for this use, or their benign influences be diminished any more than the sun is diminished by shining. Mere destroyers, however, tree-killers, wool and mutton men, spreading death and confusion in the fairest groves and gardens ever planted,—let the government hasten to cast them out and make an end of them. For it must be told again and again, and be burningly borne in mind, that just now, while protective measures are being deliberated languidly, destruction and use are speeding on faster and farther every day. The axe and saw are insanely busy, chips are flying thick as snowflakes, and every summer thousands of acres of priceless forests, with their underbrush, soil, springs, climate, scenery, and religion, are vanishing away in clouds of smoke, while, except in the national parks, not one forest guard is employed.

All sorts of local laws and regulations have been tried and found wanting, and the costly lessons of our own experience, as well as that of every civilized nation, show conclusively that the fate of the remnant of our forests is in the hands of the federal government, and that if the remnant is to be saved at all, it must be saved quickly.

Any fool can destroy trees. They cannot run away; and if they could, they would still be destroyed,—chased and hunted down as long as fun or a dollar could be got out of their bark hides, branching horns, or magnificent bole backbones. Few that fell trees plant them; nor would planting avail much towards getting back anything like the noble primeval forests. During a man's life only saplings can be grown, in the place of the old trees—tens of centuries old—that have been destroyed. It took more than three thousand years to make some of the trees in these Western woods,—trees that are still standing in perfect strength and beauty, waving and singing in the mighty forests of the Sierra. Through all the wonderful, eventful centuries since Christ's time—and long before that—God has cared for these trees, saved them from drought, disease, avalanches, and a thousand straining, leveling tempests and floods; but he cannot save them from fools,—only Uncle Sam can do that.

A THOUSAND-MILE WALK TO THE GULF

Introduction

"John Muir, Earth-planet, Universe."—These words are written on the inside cover of the notebook from which the contents of this volume have been taken. They reflect the mood in which the late author and explorer undertook his thousand-mile walk to the Gulf of Mexico a half-century ago. No less does this refreshingly cosmopolitan address, which might have startled any finder of the book, reveal the temper and the comprehensiveness of Mr. Muir's mind. He never was and never could be a parochial student of nature. Even at the early age of twenty-nine his eager interest in every aspect of the natural world had made him a citizen of the universe.

While this was by far the longest botanical excursion which Mr. Muir made in his earlier years, it was by no means the only one. He had botanized around the Great Lakes, in Ontario, and through parts of Wisconsin, Indiana, and Illinois. On these expeditions he had disciplined himself to endure hardship, for his notebooks disclose the fact that he often went hungry and slept in the woods, or on the open prairies, with no cover except the clothes he wore.

"Oftentimes," he writes in some unpublished biographical notes, "I had to sleep out without blankets, and also without supper or breakfast. But usually I had no great difficulty in finding a loaf of bread in the widely scattered clearings of the farmers. With one of these big backwoods loaves I was able to wander many a long, wild mile, free as the winds in the glorious forests and bogs, gathering plants and feeding on God's abounding, inexhaustible spiritual beauty bread. Only once in my long Canada wanderings was the deep peace of the wilderness savagely broken. It happened in the maple woods about midnight, when I was cold and my fire was low. I was awakened by the awfully dismal howling of the wolves, and got up in haste to replenish the fire."

It was not, therefore, a new species of adventure upon which Mr. Muir embarked when he started on his Southern foot-tour. It was only a new response to the lure of those favorite studies which he had already pursued over uncounted miles of virgin Western forests and prairies. Indeed, had it not been for the accidental injury to his right eye in the month of March, 1867, he probably would have started somewhat earlier than he did. In a letter written to Indianapolis friends on the day after the accident, he refers mournfully to the interruption of a long-cherished plan. "For weeks," he writes, "I have daily consulted maps in locating a route through the Southern States, the West Indies, South America, and Europe—a botanical journey studied for years. And so my mind has long been in a glow with visions of the glories of a tropical flora; but, alas, I am half blind. My right eye, trained to minute analysis, is lost and I have scarce heart to open the other. Had this journey been accomplished, the stock of varied beauty acquired would have made me willing to shrink into any corner of the world, however obscure and however remote."

The injury to his eye proved to be less serious than he had at first supposed. In June he was writing to a friend: "I have been reading and botanizing for some weeks, and find that for such work I am not very much disabled. I leave this city [Indianapolis] for home to-morrow, accompanied by Merrill Moores, a little friend of mine. We will go to Decatur, Illinois, thence northward through the wide prairies, botanizing a few weeks by the way. . . . I hope to go South towards the end of the summer, and as this will be a journey that I know very little about, I hope to profit by your counsel before setting out."

In an account written after the excursion he says: "I was eager to see Illinois prairies on my way home, so we went to Decatur, near the center of the State, thence north [to Portage] by Rockford and Janesville. I botanized one week on the prairie about seven miles southwest of Pecatonica. . . . To me all plants are more precious than before. My poor eye is not better, nor worse. A cloud is over it, but in gazing over the widest landscapes, I am not always sensible of its presence."

By the end of August Mr. Muir was back again in Indianapolis. He had found it convenient to spend a "botanical week" among his University friends in Madison. So keen was his interest in plants at this time that an interval of five hours spent in Chicago was promptly turned to account in a search for them. "I did not find many plants in her tumultuous streets," he complains; "only a few grassy plants of wheat, and two or three species of weeds,—amaranth, purslane, carpet-weed, etc.,—the weeds, I suppose, for man to walk upon, the wheat to feed him I saw some green algæ, but no mosses. Some of the latter I expected to see on wet walls, and in seams on the pavements. But I suppose that the manufacturers' smoke and the terrible noise are too great for the hardiest of them. I wish I knew where I was going. Doomed to be 'carried of the spirit into the wilderness,' I suppose. I wish I could be more moderate in my desires, but I cannot, and so there is no rest."

The letter noted above was written only two days before he started on his long walk to Florida. If the concluding sentences still reflect indecision, they also convey a hint of the overmastering impulse under which he was acting. The opening sentences of his journal, afterwards crossed out, witness to this sense of inward compulsion which he felt. "Few bodies," he wrote, "are inhabited by so satisfied a soul that they are allowed exemption from extraordinary exertion through a whole life." After reciting illustrations of nature's periodicity, of the ebbs and flows of tides, and the pulsation of other forces, visible and invisible, he observes that "so also there are tides not only in the affairs of men, but in the primal thing of life itself. In some persons the impulse, being slight, is easily obeyed or overcome. But in others it is constant and cumulative in action until its power is sufficient to overmaster all impediments, and to accomplish the full measure of its demands. For many a year I have been impelled toward the Lord's tropic gardens of the South. Many influences have tended to blunt or bury this constant longing, but it has out-lived and overpowered them all."

Muir's love of nature was so largely a part of his religion that he naturally chose Biblical phraseology when he sought a vehicle for his feelings. No prophet of old could have taken his call more seriously, or have entered upon his mission more fervently. During the long days of his confinement in a dark room he had opportunity for much reflection. He concluded that life was too brief and uncertain, and time too precious, to waste upon belts and saws; that while he was pottering in a wagon factory, God was making a world; and he determined that, if his eyesight was spared, he would devote the remainder of his life to a study of the process. Thus the previous bent of his habits and studies, and the sobering thoughts induced by one of the bitterest experiences of his life, combined to send him on the long journey recorded in these pages.

Some autobiographical notes found among his papers furnish interesting additional details about the period between his release from the dark room and his departure for the South. "As soon as I got out into heaven's light," he says, "I started on another long excursion, making haste with all my heart to store my mind with the Lord's beauty, and thus be ready for any fate, light or dark. And it was from this time that my long, continuous wanderings may be said to have fairly commenced. I bade adieu to mechanical inventions, determined to devote the rest of my life to the study of the inventions of God. I first went home to Wisconsin, botanizing by the way, to take leave of my father and mother, brothers and sisters, all of whom were still living near Portage. I also visited the neighbors I had known as a boy, renewed my acquaintance with them after an absence of several years, and bade each a formal good-bye. When they asked where I was going I said, 'Oh! I don't know—just anywhere in the wilderness, southward. I have already had glorious glimpses of the Wisconsin, Iowa, Michigan, Indiana, and Canada wildernesses; now I propose to go South and see something of the vegetation of the warm end of the country, and if possible to wander far enough into South America to see tropical vegetation in all its palmy glory.'

"The neighbors wished me well, advised me to be careful of my health, and reminded me that the swamps in the South were full of malaria. I stopped overnight at the home of an old Scotch lady who had long been my friend and was now particularly motherly in good wishes and advice. I told her that as I was sauntering along the road, just as the sun was going down, I heard a darling speckled-breast sparrow singing, 'The day's done, the day's done.' 'Wheel, John, my dear laddie,' she replied, 'your day will never be done. There is no end to the kind of studies you like so well, but there's an end to mortals' strength of body and mind, to all that mortals can accomplish. You are sure to go on and on, but I want you to remember the fate of Hugh Miller.' She was one of the finest examples I ever knew of a kind, generous, great-hearted Scotchwoman."

The formal leave-taking from family and neighbors indicates his belief that he was parting from home and friends for a long time. On Sunday, the 1st of September, 1867, Mr. Muir said good-bye also to his Indianapolis friends, and went by rail to Jeffersonville, where he spent the night. The next morning he crossed the river, walked through Louisville, and struck southward through the State of Kentucky. A letter written a week later "among the hills of Bear Creek, seven miles southeast of Burkesville, Kentucky," shows that he had covered about twenty-five miles a day. "I walked from Louisville," he says, "a distance of one hundred and seventy miles, and my feet are sore. But, oh! I am paid for all my toil a thousand times over. I am in the woods on a hilltop with my back against a moss-clad log. I wish you could see my last evenings bed-room. The sun has been among the tree-tops for more than an hour; the dew is nearly all taken back, and the shade in these hill basins is creeping away into the unbroken strongholds of the grand old forests.

"I have enjoyed the trees and scenery of Kentucky exceedingly. How shall I ever tell of the miles and miles of beauty that have been flowing into me in such measure? These lofty curving ranks of lobing, swelling hills, these concealed valleys of fathomless verdure, and these lordly trees with the nursing sunlight glancing in their leaves upon the outlines of the magnificent masses of shade embosomed among their wide branches—these are cut into my memory to go with me forever.

"I was a few miles south of Louisville when I planned my journey. I spread out my map under a tree and made up my mind to go through Kentucky, Tennessee, and Georgia to Florida, thence to Cuba, thence to some part of South America; but it will be only a hasty walk. I am thankful, however, for so much. My route will be through Kingston and Madisonville, Tennessee, and through Blairsville and Gainesville, Georgia. Please write me at Gainesville. I am terribly letter-hungry. I hardly dare to think of home and friends."

In editing the journal I have endeavored, by use of all the available evidence, to trail Mr. Muir as closely as possible on maps of the sixties as well as on the most recent state and topographical maps. The one used by him has not been found, and probably is no longer in existence. Only about twenty-two towns and cities are mentioned in his journal. This constitutes a very small number when one considers the distance he covered. Evidently he was so absorbed in the plant life of the region traversed that he paid no heed to towns, and perhaps avoided them wherever possible.

The sickness which overtook him in Florida was probably of a malarial kind, although he describes it under different names. It was, no doubt, a misfortune in itself, and a severe test for his vigorous constitution. But it was also a blessing in disguise, inasmuch as it prevented him from carrying out his foolhardy plan of penetrating the tropical jungles of South America along the Andes to a tributary of the Amazon, and then floating down the river on a raft to the Atlantic. As readers of the journal will perceive, he clung to this intention even during his convalescence at Cedar Keys and in Cuba. In a letter dated the 8th of November he describes himself as "just creeping about getting plants and strength after my fever." Then he asks his correspondent to direct letters to New Orleans, Louisiana. "I shall have to go there," he writes, "for a boat to South America. I do not yet know to which point in South America I had better go." His hope to find there a boat for South America explains an otherwise mystifying letter in which he requested his brother David to send him a certain sum of money by American Express order to New Orleans. As a matter of fact he did not go into Louisiana at all, either because he learned that no south-bound ship was available at the mouth of the Mississippi, or because the unexpected appearance of the Island Belle in the harbor of Cedar Keys caused him to change his plans.

In later years Mr. Muir himself strongly disparaged the wisdom of his plans with respect to South America, as may be seen in the chapter that deals with his Cuban sojourn. The judgment there expressed was lead-penciled into his journal during a reading of it long afterwards. Nevertheless the Andes and the South American forests continued to fascinate his imagination, as his letters show, for many years after he came to California. When the long deferred journey to South America was finally made in 1911, forty-four years after the first attempt, he whimsically spoke of it as the fulfillment of those youthful dreams that moved him to undertake his thousand-mile walk to the Gulf.

Mr. Muir always recalled with gratitude the Florida friends who nursed him through his long and serious illness. In 1898, while traveling through the South on a forest-inspection tour with his friend Charles Sprague Sargent, he took occasion to revisit the scenes of his early adventures. It may be of interest to quote some sentences from letters written at that time to his wife and to his sister Sarah. "I have been down the east side of the Florida peninsula along the Indian River," he writes, "through the palm and pine forests to Miami, and thence to Key West and the southmost keys stretching out towards Cuba. Returning, I crossed over to the west coast by Palatka to Cedar Keys, on my old track made thirty-one years ago, in search of the Hodgsons who nursed me through my long attack of fever. Mr. Hodgson died long ago, also the eldest son, with whom I used to go boating among the keys while slowly convalescing."

He then tells how he found Mrs. Hodgson and the rest of the family at Archer. They had long thought him dead and were naturally very much surprised to see him. Mrs. Hodgson was in her garden and he recognized her, though the years had altered her appearance. Let us give his own account of the meeting: "I asked her if she knew me. 'No, I don't,' she said; 'tell me your name.' 'Muir,' I replied. 'John Muir? My California John Muir?' she almost screamed. I said, 'Yes, John Muir; and you know I promised to return and visit you in about twenty-five years, and though I am a little late—six or seven years—I've done the best I could.' The eldest boy and girl remembered the stories I told them, and when they read about the Muir Glacier they felt sure it must have been named for me. I stopped at Archer about four hours, and the way we talked over old times you may imagine." From Savannah, on the same trip, he wrote: "Here is where I spent a hungry, weary, yet happy week camping in Bonaventure graveyard thirty-one years ago. Many changes, I am told, have been made in its graves and avenues of late, and how many in my life!"

In perusing this journal the reader will miss the literary finish which Mr. Muir was accustomed to give to his later writings. This fact calls for no excuse. Not only are we dealing here with the earliest product of his pen, but with impressions and observations written down hastily during pauses in his long march. He apparently intended to use this raw material at some time for another book. If the record, as it stands, lacks finish and adornment, it also possesses the immediacy and the freshness of first impressions.

The sources which I have used in preparing this volume are threefold: (1) the original journal, of which the first half contained many interlinear revisions and expansions, and a considerable number of rough pencil sketches of plants, trees, scenery, and notable adventures; (2) a wide-spaced, typewritten, rough copy of the journal, apparently in large part dictated to a stenographer; it is only slightly revised, and comparison with the original journal shows many significant omissions and additions: (3) two separate elaborations of his experiences in Savannah when he camped there for a week in the Bonaventure graveyard. Throughout my work upon the primary and secondary materials I was impressed with the scrupulous fidelity with which he adhered to the facts and impressions set down in the original journal.

Readers of Muir's writings need scarcely be told that this book, autobiographically, bridges the period between *The Story of my Boyhood and Youth* and *My First Summer in the Sierra*. However, one span of the bridge was lacking, for the journal ends with Mr. Muir's arrival in San Francisco about the first of April, 1868, while his first summer in the Sierra was that of 1869. By excerpting from a letter a summary account of his first visit to Yosemite, and including a description of Twenty Hill Hollow, where he spent a large part of his first year in California, the connection is made complete. The last chapter was first published as an article in the *Overland Monthly* of July, 1872. A revised copy of the printed article, found among Muir's literary effects, has been made the basis of the chapter on Twenty Hill Hollow as it appears in this volume.

WILLIAM FREDERIC BADÈ

Chapter I.

Kentucky Forests and Caves

I had long been looking from the wildwoods and gardens of the Northern States to those of the warm South, and at last, all draw-backs overcome, I set forth [from Indianapolis] on the first day of September, 1867, joyful and free, on a thousand-mile walk to the Gulf of Mexico. [The trip to Jeffersonville, on the banks of the Ohio, was made by rail.] Crossing the Ohio at Louisville [September 2], I steered through the big city by compass without speaking a word to any one. Beyond the city I found a road running southward, and after passing a scatterment of suburban cabins and cottages I reached the green woods and spread out my pocket map to rough-hew a plan for my journey.

My plan was simply to push on in a general southward direction by the wildest, leafiest, and least trodden way I could find, promising the greatest extent of virgin forest. Folding my map, I shouldered my little bag and plant press and strode away among the old Kentucky oaks, rejoicing in splendid visions of pines and palms and tropic flowers in glorious array, not, however, without a few cold shadows of loneliness, although the great oaks seemed to spread their arms in welcome.

I have seen oaks of many species in many kinds of exposure and soil, but those of Kentucky excel in grandeur all I had ever before beheld. They are broad and dense and bright green. In the leafy bowers and caves of their long branches dwell magnificent avenues of shade, and every tree seems to be blessed with a double portion of strong exulting life. Walked twenty miles, mostly on river bottom, and found shelter in a rickety tavern.

September 3. Escaped from the dust and squalor of my garret bedroom to the glorious forest. All the streams that I tasted hereabouts are salty and so are the wells. Salt River was nearly dry. Much of my way this forenoon was over naked limestone. After passing the level ground that extended twenty-five or thirty miles from the river I came to a region of rolling hills called Kentucky Knobs—hills of denudation covered with trees to the top. Some of them have a few pines. For a few hours I followed the farmers' paths, but soon wandered away from roads and encountered many a tribe of twisted vines difficult to pass.

Emerging about noon from a grove of giant sunflowers, I found myself on the brink of a tumbling rocky stream [Rolling Fork]. I did not expect to find bridges on my wild ways, and at once started to ford, when a negro woman on the opposite bank earnestly called on me to wait until she could tell the "men folks" to bring me a horse—that the river was too deep and rapid to wade and that I would “sartain be drowned” if I attempted to cross. I replied that my bag and plants would ballast me; that the water did not appear to be deep, and that if I were carried away, I was a good swimmer and would soon dry in the sunshine. But the cautious old soul replied that no one ever waded that river and set off for a horse, saying that it was no trouble at all.

In a few minutes the ferry horse came gingerly down the bank through vines and weeds. His long stilt legs proved him a natural wader. He was white and the little sable negro boy that rode him looked like a bug on his back. After many a tottering halt the outward voyage was safely made, and I mounted behind little Nig. He was a queer specimen, puffy and jet as an India rubber doll and his hair was matted in sections like the wool of a merino sheep. The old horse, overladen with his black and white burden, rocked and stumbled on his stilt legs with fair promises of a fall. But all ducking signs failed and we arrived in safety among the weeds and vines of the rugged bank. A salt bath would have done us no harm. I could swim and little Afric looked as if he might float like a bladder.

I called at the homestead where my ferryman informed me I would find “tollable” water. But, like all the water of this section that I have tasted, it was intolerable with salt. Everything about this old Kentucky home bespoke plenty, unpolished and unmeasured. The house was built in true Southern style, airy, large, and with a transverse central hall that looks like a railway tunnel, and heavy rough outside chimneys. The negro quarters and other buildings are enough in number for a village, altogether an interesting representative of a genuine old Kentucky home, embosomed in orchards, corn fields and green wooded hills.

Passed gangs of woodmen engaged and hewing the grand oaks for market. Fruit very abundant. Magnificent flowing hill scenery all afternoon. Walked southeast from Elizabethtown till wearied and lay down in the bushes by guess.

September 4. The sun was gilding the hill-tops when I was awakened by the alarm notes of birds whose dwelling in a hazel thicket I had disturbed. They flitted excitedly close to my head, as if scolding or asking angry questions, while several beautiful plants, strangers to me, were looking me full in the face. The first botanical discovery in bed! This was one of the most delightful camp grounds, though groped for in the dark, and I lingered about it enjoying its trees and soft lights and music.

Walked ten miles of forest. Met a strange oak with willow-looking leaves. Entered a sandy stretch of black oak called “Barrens,” many of which were sixty or seventy feet in height, and are said to have grown since the fires were kept off, forty years ago. The farmers hereabouts are tall, stout, happy fellows, fond of guns and horses. Enjoyed friendly chats with them. Arrived at dark in a village that seemed to be drawing its last breath. Was guided to the “tavern” by a negro who was extremely accommodating. “No trouble at all,” he said.

September 5. No bird or flower or friendly tree above me this morning; only squalid garret rubbish and dust. Escaped to the woods. Came to the region of caves. At the mouth of the first I discovered, I was surprised to find ferns which belonged to the coolest nooks of Wisconsin and northward, but soon observed that each cave rim has a zone of climate peculiar to itself, and it is always cool. This cave had an opening about ten feet in diameter, and twenty-five feet perpendicular depth. A strong cold wind issued from it and I could hear the sounds of running water. A long pole was set against its walls as if intended for a ladder, but in some places it was slippery and smooth as a mast and would test the climbing powers of a monkey. The walls and rim of this natural reservoir were finely carved and flowered. Bushes leaned over it with shading leaves, and beautiful ferns and mosses were in rows and sheets on its slopes and shelves. Lingered here a long happy while, pressing specimens and printing this beauty into memory.

Arrived about noon at Munfordville; was soon discovered and examined by Mr. Munford himself, a pioneer and father of the village. He is a surveyor—has held all country offices, and every seeker of roads and lands applies to him for information. He regards all the villagers as his children, and all strangers who enter Munfordville as his own visitors. Of course he inquired my business, destination, et cetera, and invited me to his house.

After refreshing me with "parrs" he complacently covered the table with bits of rocks, plants, et cetera, things new and old which he had gathered in his surveying walks and supposed to be full of scientific interest. He informed me that all scientific men applied to him for information, and as I was a botanist, he either possessed, or ought to possess, the knowledge I was seeking, and so I received long lessons concerning roots and herbs for every mortal ill. Thanking my benefactor for his kindness, I escaped to the fields and followed a railroad along the base of a grand hill ridge. As evening came on all the dwellings I found seemed to repel me, and I could not muster courage enough to ask entertainment at any of them. Took refuge in a log schoolhouse that stood on a hillside beneath stately oaks and slept on the softest looking of the benches.

September 6. Started at the earliest bird song in hopes of seeing the great Mammoth Cave before evening. Overtook an old negro driving an ox team. Rode with him a few miles and had some interesting chat concerning war, wild fruits of the woods, et cetera. "Right heah," said he, "is where the Rebs was a-tearin' up the track, and they all a sudden thought they seed the Yankees a-comin', obah dem big hills dar, and Lo'd, how dey run." I asked him if he would like a renewal of these sad war times, when his flexible face suddenly calmed, and he said with intense earnestness, "Oh, Lo'd, want no mo wa, Lo'd no." Many of these Kentucky negroes are shrewd and intelligent, and when warmed upon a subject that interests them, are eloquent in no mean degree.

Arrived at Horse Cave, about ten miles from the great cave. The entrance is by a long easy slope of several hundred yards. It seems like a noble gateway to the birthplace of springs and fountains and the dark treasuries of the mineral kingdom. This cave is in a village [of the same name] which it supplies with an abundance of cold water, and cold air that issues from its fern-clad lips. In hot weather crowds of people sit about it in the shade of the trees that guard it. This magnificent fan is capable of cooling everybody in the town at once.

Those who live near lofty mountains may climb to cool weather in a day or two, but the overheated Kentuckians can find a patch of cool climate in almost every glen in the State. The villager who accompanied me said that Horse Cave had never been fully explored, but that it was several miles in length at least. He told me that he had never been at Mammoth Cave—that it was not worth going ten miles to see, as it was nothing but a hole in the ground, and I found that his was no rare case. He was one of the useful, practical men—too wise to waste precious time with weeds, caves, fossils, or anything else that he could not eat.

Arrived at the great Mammoth Cave. I was surprised to find it in so complete naturalness. A large hotel with fine walks and gardens is near it. But fortunately the cave has been unimproved, and were it not for the narrow trail that leads down the glen to its door, one would not know that it had been visited. There are house-rooms and halls whose entrances give but slight hint of their grandeur. And so also this magnificent hall in the mineral kingdom of Kentucky has a door comparatively small and unpromising. One might pass within a few yards of it without noticing it. A strong cool breeze issues constantly from it, creating a northern climate for the ferns that adorn its rocky front.

I never before saw Nature's grandeur in so abrupt contrast with paltry artificial gardens. The fashionable hotel grounds are in exact parlor taste, with many a beautiful plant cultivated to deformity, and arranged in strict geometrical beds, the whole pretty affair a laborious failure side by side with Divine beauty. The trees around the mouth of the cave are smooth and tall and bent forward at the bottom, then straight upwards. Only a butternut seems, by its angular knotty branches, to sympathize with and belong to the cave, with a fine growth of *Cystopteris* and *Hypnum.*

Started for Glasgow Junction. Got belated in the hill woods. Inquired my way at a farm-house and was invited to stay overnight in a rare, hearty, hospitable manner. Engaged in familiar running talk on politics, war times, and theology. The old Kentuckian seemed to take a liking to me and advised me to stay in these hills until next spring, assuring me that I would find much to interest me in and about the Great Cave; also, that he was one of the school officials and was sure that I could obtain their school for the winter term. I sincerely thanked him for his kind plans, but pursued my own.

September 7. Left the hospitable Kentuckians with their sincere good wishes and bore away southward again through the deep green woods. In noble forests all day. Saw mistletoe for the first time. Part of the day I traveled with a Kentuckian from near Burkesville. He spoke to all the negroes he met with familiar kindly greetings, addressing them always as "Uncles" and "Aunts." All travelers one meets on these roads, white and black, male and female, travel on horseback. Glasgow is one of the few Southern towns that shows ordinary American life. At night with a well-to-do farmer.

September 8. Deep, green, bossy sea of waving, flowing hilltops. Corn and cotton and tobacco fields scattered here and there. I had imagined that a cotton field in flower was something magnificent. But cotton is a coarse, rough, straggling, unhappy looking plant, not half as good-looking as a field of Irish potatoes. Met a great many negroes going to meeting, dressed in their Sunday best. Fat, happy looking, and contented. The scenery on approaching the Cumberland River becomes still grander. Burkesville, in beautiful location, is embosomed in a glorious array of verdant flowing hills. The Cumberland must be a happy stream. I think I could enjoy traveling with it in the midst of such beauty all my life. This evening I could find none willing to take me in, and so lay down on a hillside and fell asleep muttering praises to the happy abounding beauty of Kentucky.

September 9. Another day in the most favored province of bird and flower. Many rapid streams, flowing in beautiful flower-bordered cañons embosomed in dense woods. Am seated on a grand hill-slope that leans back against the sky like a picture. Amid the wide waves of green wood there are spots of autumnal yellow and the atmosphere, too, has the dawnings of autumn in colors and sounds. The soft light of morning falls upon ripening forests of oak and elm, walnut and hickory and all Nature is thoughtful and calm. Kentucky is the greenest, leafiest State I have yet seen. The sea of soft temperate plant-green is deepest here. Comparing volumes of vegetable verdure in different countries to a wedge, the thick end would be in the forests of Kentucky, the other in the lichens and mosses of the North. This verdure wedge would not be perfect in its lines. From Kentucky it would maintain its thickness long and well in passing the level forests of Indiana and Canada. From the maples and pines of Canada it would slope rapidly to the bleak Arctic hills with dwarf birches and alders; thence it would thin out in a long edge among hardy lichens and liverworts and mosses to the dwelling-places of everlasting frost. Far the grandest of all Kentucky plants are her noble oaks. They are the master existences of her exuberant forests. Here is the Eden, the paradise of oaks. Passed the Kentucky line towards evening and obtained food and shelter from a thrifty Tennessee farmer, after he had made use of all the ordinary anti-hospitable arguments of cautious comfortable families.

September 10. Escaped from a heap of uncordial kindness to the generous bosom of the woods. After a few miles of level ground in luxuriant tangles of brooding vines, I began the ascent of the Cumberland Mountains, the first real mountains that my foot ever touched or eyes beheld. The ascent was by a nearly regular zigzag slope, mostly covered up like a tunnel by overarching oaks. But there were a few openings where the glorious forest road of Kentucky was grandly seen, stretching over hill and valley, adjusted to every slope and curve by the hands of Nature the most sublime and comprehensive picture that ever entered my eyes. Reached the summit in six or seven hours—a strangely long period of up-grade work to one accustomed only to the hillocky levels of Wisconsin and adjacent States.

Chapter II.

Crossing the Cumberland Mountains

I had climbed but a short distance when I was overtaken by a young man on horse-back, who soon showed that he intended to rob me if he should find the job worth while. After he had inquired where I came from, and where I was going, he offered to carry my bag. I told him that it was so light that I did not feel it at all a burden; but he insisted and coaxed until I allowed him to carry it. As soon as he had gained possession I noticed that he gradually increased his speed, evidently trying to get far enough ahead of me to examine the contents without being observed. But I was too good a walker and runner for him to get far. At a turn of the road, after trotting his horse for about half an hour, and when he thought he was out of sight, I caught him rummaging my poor bag. Finding there only a comb, brush, towel, soap, a change of underclothing, a copy of Burns's poems, Milton's Paradise Lost, and a small New Testament, he waited for me, handed back my bag, and returned down the hill, saying that he had forgotten something.

I found splendid growths of shining-leaved *Ericaceæ* (heathworts) for which the Alleghany Mountains are noted. Also ferns of which *Osmunda cinnamomea* [Cinnamon Fern] is the largest and perhaps the most abundant. *Osmunda regalis* [Flowering Fern] is also common here, but not large. In Wood's[1] and Gray's Botany *Osmunda cinnamomea* is said to be a much larger fern than *Osmunda claytoniana*. This I found to be true in Tennessee and southward, but in Indiana, part of Illinois, and Wisconsin the opposite is true. Found here the beautiful, sensitive *Schrankia*, or sensitive brier. It is a long, prickly, leguminous vine, with dense heads of small, yellow fragrant flowers.

> [1] Alphonso Wood, *Class-book of Botany, with a Flora of The United States and Canada.* The copy of this work, carried by Mr. Muir on his wanderings, is still extant. The edition is that of 1862.

Vines growing on roadsides receive many a tormenting blow, simply because they give evidence of feeling. Sensitive people are served in the same way. But the roadside vine soon becomes less sensitive, like people getting used to teasing—Nature, in this instance, making for the comfort of flower creatures the same benevolent arrangement as for man. Thus I found that the *Schrankia* vines growing along foot-paths leading to a backwoods schoolhouse were much less sensitive than those in the adjacent unfrequented woods, having learned to pay but slight attention to the tingling strokes they get from teasing scholars.

It is startling to see the pairs of pinnate leaves rising quickly out of the grass and folding themselves close in regular succession from the root to the end of the prostrate stems, ten to twenty feet in length. How little we know as yet of the life of plants—their hopes and fears, pains and enjoyments!

Traveled a few miles with an old Tennessee farmer who was much excited on account of the news he had just heard. "Three kingdoms, England, Ireland, and Russia, have declared war agin the United States. Oh, it's terrible, terrible," said he. "This big war comin' so quick after our own big fight. Well, it can't be helped, and all I have to say is, Amerricay forever, but I'd a heap rather they didn't fight."

"But are you sure the news is true?" I inquired. "Oh, yes, quite sure," he replied, "for me and some of my neighbors were down at the store last night, and Jim Smith can read, and he found out all about it in a newspaper."

Passed the poor, rickety, thrice-dead village of Jamestown, an incredibly dreary place. Toward the top of the Cumberland grade, about two hours before sundown I came to a log house, and as I had been warned that all the broad plateau of the range for forty or fifty miles was desolate, I began thus early to seek a lodging for the night. Knocking at the door, a motherly old lady replied to my request for supper and bed and breakfast, that I was welcome to the best she had, provided that I had the necessary change to pay my bill. When I told her that unfortunately I had nothing smaller than a five-dollar greenback, she said, "Well, I'm sorry, but cannot afford to keep you. Not long ago ten soldiers came across from North Carolina, and in the morning they offered a greenback that I couldn't change, and so I got nothing for keeping them, which I was ill able to afford." "Very well," I said, "I'm glad you spoke of this beforehand, for I would rather go hungry than impose on your hospitality."

As I turned to leave, after bidding her good-bye, she, evidently pitying me for my tired looks, called me back and asked me if I would like a drink of milk. This I gladly accepted, thinking that perhaps I might not be successful in getting any other nourishment for a day or two. Then I inquired whether there were any more houses on the road, nearer than North Carolina, forty or fifty miles away. "Yes," she said, "it's only two miles to the next house, but beyond that there are no houses that I know of except empty ones whose owners have been killed or driven away during the war."

Arriving at the last house, my knock at the door was answered by a bright, good-natured, good-looking little woman, who in reply to my request for a night's lodging and food, said, "Oh, I guess so. I think you can stay. Come in and I'll call my husband." "But I must first warn you," I said, "that I have nothing smaller to offer you than a five-dollar bill for my entertainment. I don't want you to think that I am trying to impose on your hospitality."

She then called her husband, a blacksmith, who was at work at his forge. He came out, hammer in hand, bare-breasted, sweaty, begrimed, and covered with shaggy black hair. In reply to his wife's statement, that this young man wished to stop over night, he quickly replied, "That's all right; tell him to go into the house." He was turning to go back to his shop, when his wife added, "But he says he hasn't any change to pay. He has nothing smaller than a five-dollar bill." Hesitating only a moment, he turned on his heel and said, "Tell him to go into the house. A man that comes right out like that beforehand is welcome to eat my bread."

When he came in after his hard day's work and sat down to dinner, he solemnly asked a blessing on the frugal meal, consisting solely of corn bread and bacon. Then, looking across the table at me, he said, "Young man, what are you doing down here?" I replied that I was looking at plants. "Plants? What kind of plants?" I said, "Oh, all kinds; grass, weeds, flowers, trees, mosses, ferns,—almost everything that grows is interesting to me."

"Well, young man," he queried, "you mean to say that you are not employed by the Government on some private business?" "No," I said, "I am not employed by any one except just myself. I love all kinds of plants, and I came down here to these Southern States to get acquainted with as many of them as possible." "You look like a strong-minded man," he replied, "and surely you are able to do something better than wander over the country and look at weeds and blossoms. These are hard times, and real work is required of every man that is able. Picking up blossoms doesn't seem to be a man's work at all in any kind of times."

To this I replied, "You are a believer in the Bible, are you not?" "Oh, yes." "Well, you know Solomon was a strong-minded man, and he is generally believed to have been the very wisest man the world ever saw, and yet he considered it was worth while to study plants; not only to go and pick them up as I am doing, but to study them; and you know we are told that he wrote a book about plants, not only of the great cedars of Lebanon, but of little bits of things growing in the cracks of the walls.[2]

> [2] The previously mentioned copy of Wood's Botany, used by John Muir, quotes on the title page 1 Kings iv, 33: "He spake of trees, from the cedar of Lebanon even unto the hyssop that springeth out of the wall."

"Therefore, you see that Solomon differed very much more from you than from me in this matter. I'll warrant you he had many a long ramble in the mountains of Judea, and had he been a Yankee he would likely have visited every weed in the land. And again, do you not remember that Christ told his disciples to 'consider the lilies how they grow,' and compared their beauty with Solomon in all his glory? Now, whose advice am I to take, yours or Christ's? Christ says,

'Consider the lilies.' You say, 'Don't consider them. It isn't worth while for any strong-minded man.'"

This evidently satisfied him, and he acknowledged that he had never thought of blossoms in that way before. He repeated again and again that I must be a very strong-minded man, and admitted that no doubt I was fully justified in picking up blossoms. He then told me that although the war was over, walking across the Cumberland Mountains still was far from safe on account of small bands of guerrillas who were in hiding along the roads, and earnestly entreated me to turn back and not to think of walking so far as the Gulf of Mexico until the country became quiet and orderly once more.

I replied that I had no fear, that I had but very little to lose, and that nobody was likely to think it worth while to rob me; that, anyhow, I always had good luck. In the morning he repeated the warning and entreated me to turn back, which never for a moment interfered with my resolution to pursue my glorious walk.

September 11. Long stretch of level sand-stone plateau, lightly furrowed and dimpled with shallow groove-like valleys and hills. The trees are mostly oaks, planted wide apart like those in the Wisconsin woods. A good many pine trees here and there, forty to eighty feet high, and most of the ground is covered with showy flowers. Polygalas [milkworts], solidagoes [goldenrods], and asters were especially abundant. I came to a cool clear brook every half mile or so, the banks planted with *Osmunda regalia, Osmunda cinnamomea*, and handsome sedges. The few larger streams were fringed with laurels and azaleas. Large areas beneath the trees are covered with formidable green briers and brambles, armed with hooked claws, and almost impenetrable. Houses are far apart and uninhabited, orchards and fences in ruins—sad marks of war.

About noon my road became dim and at last vanished among desolate fields. Lost and hungry, I knew my direction but could not keep it on account of the briers. My path was indeed strewn with flowers, but as thorny, also, as mortal ever trod. In trying to force a way through these cat-plants one is not simply clawed and pricked through all one's clothing, but caught and held fast. The toothed arching branches come down over and above you like cruel living arms, and the more you struggle the more desperately you are entangled, and your wounds deepened and multiplied. The South has plant fly-catchers. It also has plant man-catchers.

After a great deal of defensive fighting and struggling I escaped to a road and a house, but failed to find food or shelter. Towards sundown, as I was walking rapidly along a straight stretch in the road, I suddenly came in sight of ten mounted men riding abreast. They undoubtedly had seen me before I discovered them, for they had stopped their horses and were evidently watching me. I saw at once that it was useless to attempt to avoid them, for the ground thereabout was quite open. I knew that there was nothing for it but to face them fearlessly, without showing the slightest suspicion of foul play. Therefore, without halting even for a moment, I advanced rapidly with long strides as though I intended to walk through the midst of them. When I got within a rod or so I looked up in their faces and smilingly bade them "Howdy." Stopping never an instant, I turned to one side and walked around them to get on the road again, and kept on without venturing to look back or to betray the slightest fear of being robbed.

After I had gone about one hundred or one hundred and fifty yards, I ventured a quick glance back, without stopping, and saw in this flash of an eye that all the ten had turned their horses toward me and were evidently talking about me; supposedly, with reference to what my object was, where I was going, and whether it would be worth while to rob me. They all were mounted on rather scrawny horses, and all wore long hair hanging down on their shoulders. Evidently they belonged to the most irreclaimable of the guerrilla bands who, long accustomed to plunder, deplored the coming of peace. I was not followed, however, probably because the plants projecting from my plant press made them believe that I was a poor herb doctors a common occupation in these mountain regions.

About dark I discovered, a little off the road, another house, inhabited by negroes, where I succeeded in obtaining a much needed meal of string beans, buttermilk, and corn bread. At the table I was seated in a bottomless chair, and as I became sore and heavy, I sank deeper and deeper, pressing my knees against my breast, and my mouth settled to the level of my plate. But wild hunger cares for none of these things, and my curiously compressed position prevented the too free indulgence of boisterous appetite. Of course, I was compelled to sleep with the trees in the one great bedroom of the open night.

September 12. Awoke drenched with mountain mist, which made a grand show, as it moved away before the hot sun. Passed Montgomery, a shabby village at the head of the east slope of the Cumberland Mountains. Obtained breakfast in a clean house and began the descent of the mountains. Obtained fine views of a wide, open country, and distant flanking ridges and spurs. Crossed a wide cool stream [Emory River], a branch of the Clinch River. There is nothing more eloquent in Nature than a mountain stream, and this is the first I ever saw. Its banks are luxuriantly peopled with rare and lovely flowers and overarching trees, making one of Nature's coolest and most hospitable places. Every tree, every flower, every ripple and eddy of this lovely stream seemed solemnly to feel the presence of the great Creator. Lingered in this sanctuary a long time thanking the Lord with all my heart for his goodness in allowing me to enter and enjoy it.

Discovered two ferns, *Dicksonia* and a small matted polypod on trees, common farther South. Also a species of magnolia with very large leaves and scarlet conical fruit. Near this stream I spent some joyous time in a grand rock-dwelling full of mosses, birds, and flowers. Most heavenly place I ever entered. The long narrow valleys of the mountainside, all well watered and nobly adorned with oaks, magnolias, laurels, azaleas, asters, ferns, Hypnum mosses, Madotheca [Scale-mosses], etc. Also towering clumps of beautiful hemlocks. The hemlock, judging from the common species of Canada, I regarded as the least noble of the conifers. But those of the eastern valleys of the Cumberland Mountains are as perfect in form and regal in port as the pines themselves. The latter abundant. Obtained fine glimpses from open places as I descended to the great valley between these mountains and the Unaka Mountains on the state line. Forded the Clinch, a beautiful clear stream, that knows many of the dearest mountain retreats that ever heard the music of running water. Reached Kingston before dark. Sent back my plant collections by express to my brother in Wisconsin.

September 13. Walked all day across small parallel valleys that flute the surface of the one wide valley. These flutings appear to have been formed by lateral pressure, are fertile, and contain some fine forms, though the seal of war is on all things. The roads never seem to proceed with any fixed purpose, but wander as if lost. In seeking the way to Philadelphia [in Loudon County, Tennessee], I was told by a buxom Tennessee "gal" that over the hills was much the nearer way, that she always went that way, and that surely I could travel it.

I started over the flint-ridges, but soon reached a set of enchanted little valleys among which, no matter how or in what direction I traveled, I could not get a foot nearer to Philadelphia. At last, consulting my map and compass, I neglected all directions and finally reached the house of a negro driver, with whom I put up for the night. Received a good deal of knowledge which may be of use should I ever be a negro teamster.

September 14. Philadelphia is a very filthy village in a beautiful situation. More or less of pine. Black oak most abundant. *Polypodium hexagonopterum* and *Abspidium acrostichoides* [Christmas Fern] most abundant of ferns and most generally distributed. *Osmunda claytoniana* rare, not in fruit, small. *Dicksonia* abundant, after leaving the Cumberland Mountains. *Asplenium ebeneum* [Ebony Spleenwort] quite common in Tennessee and many parts of Kentucky. *Cystopteris* [Bladder Fern], and *Asplenium filix-fœmina* not common through the same range. *Pteris aquilina* [Common Brake] abundant, but small.

Walked through many a leafy valley, shady grove, and cool brooklet. Reached Madisonville, a brisk village. Came in full view of the Unaka Mountains, a magnificent sight. Stayed over night with a pleasant young farmer.

September 15. Most glorious billowy mountain scenery. Made many a halt at open places to take breath and to admire. The road, in many places cut into the rock, goes winding about among the knobs and gorges. Dense growth of asters, liatris[3], and grapevines.

[3] Wood's Botany, edition of 1862, furnishes the following interesting comment on *Liatris odoratissima* (Willd.), popularly known as Vanilla Plant or Deer's Tongue: "The fleshy leaves exhale a rich fragrance even for years after they are dry, and are therefore by the southern planters largely mixed with their cured tobacco, to impart its fragrance to that nauseous weed."

Reached a house before night, and asked leave to stop. "Well, you're welcome to stop," said the mountaineer, "if you think you can live till morning on what I have to live on all the time." Found the old gentleman very communicative. Was favored with long "bar" stories, deer hunts, etc., and in the morning was pressed to stay a day or two.

September 16. "I will take you," said he, "to the highest ridge in the country, where you can see both ways. You will have a view of all the world on one side of the mountains and all creation on the other. Besides, you, who are traveling for curiosity and wonder, ought to see our gold mines." I agreed to stay and went to the mines. Gold is found in small quantities throughout the Alleghanies, and many farmers work at mining a few weeks or months every year when their time is not more valuable for other pursuits. In this neighborhood miners are earning from half a dollar to two dollars a day. There are several large quartz mills not far from here. Common labor is worth ten dollars a month.

September 17. Spent the day in botanizing, blacksmithing and examining a grist mill. Grist mills, in the less settled parts of Tennessee and North Carolina, are remarkably simple affairs. A small stone, that a man might carry under his arm, is fastened to the vertical shaft of a little home-made, boyish-looking back-action water-wheel, which, with a hopper and a box to receive the meal, is the whole affair The walls of the mill are of undressed poles cut from seedling trees and there is no floor, as lumber is dear. No dam is built. The water is conveyed along some hillside until sufficient fall is obtained, a thing easily done in the mountains.

On Sundays you may see wild, unshorn, uncombed men coming out of the woods, each with a bag of corn on his back. From a peck to a bushel is a common grist. They go to the mill along verdant footpaths, winding up and down over hill and valley, and crossing many a rhododendron glen. The flowers and shining leaves brush against their shoulders and knees, occasionally knocking off their coon-skin caps. The first arrived throws his corn into the hopper, turns on the water, and goes to the house. After chatting and smoking he returns to see if his grist is done. Should the stones run empty for an hour or two, it does no harm.

This is a fair average in equipment and capacity of a score of mills that I saw in Tennessee. This one was built by John Vohn, who claimed that he could make it grind twenty bushels a day. But since it fell into other hands it can be made to grind only ten per day. All the machines of Kentucky and Tennessee are far behind the age. There is scarce a trace of that restless spirit of speculation and invention so characteristic of the North. But one way of doing things obtains here, as if laws had been passed making attempts at improvement a crime. Spinning and weaving are done in every one of these mountain cabins wherever the least pretensions are made to thrift and economy. The practice of these ancient arts they deem marks of advancement rather than of backwardness. "There's a place back heah," said my worthy entertainer, "whar there's a mill-house, an' a store-house, an' a still-house, an' a spring-house, an' a blacksmith shop—all in the same yard! Cows too, an' heaps of big gals a-milkin' them."

This is the most primitive country I have seen, primitive in everything. The remotest hidden parts of Wisconsin are far in advance of the mountain regions of Tennessee and North Carolina. But my host speaks of the "old-fashioned unenlightened times," like a philosopher in the best light of civilization. "I believe in Providence," said he. "Our fathers came into these valleys, got the richest of them, and skimmed off the cream of the soil. The worn-out ground won't yield no roastin' ears now. But the Lord foresaw this state of affairs, and prepared something else for us. And what is it? Why, He meant us to bust open these copper mines and gold mines, so that we may have money to buy the corn that we cannot raise." A most profound observation.

September 18. Up the mountain on the state line. The scenery is far grander than any I ever before beheld. The view extends from the Cumberland Mountains on the north far into Georgia and North Carolina to the south, an area of about five thousand square miles. Such an ocean of wooded, waving, swelling mountain beauty and grandeur is not to be described. Countless forest-clad hills, side by side in rows and groups, seemed to be enjoying the rich sunshine and remaining motionless only because they were so eagerly absorbing it. All were united by curves and slopes of inimitable softness and beauty. Oh, these forest gardens of our Father! What perfection, what divinity, in their architecture! What simplicity and mysterious complexity of detail! Who shall read the teaching of these sylvan pages, the glad brotherhood of rills that sing in the valleys, and all the happy creatures that dwell in them under the tender keeping of a Father's care?

September 19. Received another solemn warning of dangers on my way through the mountains. Was told by my worthy entertainer of a wondrous gap in the mountains which he advised me to see. "It is called Track Gap," said he, "from the great number of tracks in the rocks—bird tracks, bar tracks, hoss tracks, men tracks, all in the solid rock as if it had been mud." Bidding farewell to my worthy mountaineer and all his comfortable wonders, I pursued my way to the South.

As I was leaving, he repeated the warnings of danger ahead, saying that there were a good many people living like wild beasts on whatever they could steal, and that murders were sometimes committed for four or five dollars, and even less. While stopping with him I noticed that a man came regularly after dark to the house for his supper. He was armed with a gun, a pistol, and a long knife. My host told me that this man was at feud with one of his neighbors, and that they were prepared to shoot one another at sight. That neither of them could do any regular work or sleep in the same place two nights in succession. That they visited houses only for food, and as soon as the one that I saw had got his supper he went out and slept in the woods, without of course making a fire. His enemy did the same.

My entertainer told me that he was trying to make peace between these two men, because they both were good men, and if they would agree to stop their quarrel, they could then both go to work. Most of the food in this house was coffee without sugar, corn bread, and sometimes bacon. But the coffee was the greatest luxury which these people knew. The only way of obtaining it was by seizing skins, or, in particular, "sang," that is ginseng,[4] which found a market in far-off China.

> [4] Muir's journal contains the following additional note: "M. County produces $5000 worth a year of ginseng root, valued at seventy cents a pound. Under the law it is not allowed to be gathered until the first of September."

My path all to-day led me along the leafy banks of the Hiwassee,[5] a most impressive mountain river. Its channel is very rough, as it crosses the edges of upturned rock strata, some of them standing at right angles, or glancing off obliquely to right and left. Thus a multitude of short, resounding cataracts are produced, and the river is restrained from the headlong speed due to its volume and the inclination of its bed.

> [5] In his journal Muir spells the name "Hiawassee," a form which occurs on many of the older maps. The name probably is derived from the Cherokee Indian "Ayuhwasi," a name applied to several of their former settlements.

All the larger streams of uncultivated countries are mysteriously charming and beautiful, whether flowing in mountains or through swamps and plains. Their channels are interestingly sculptured, far more so than the grandest architectural works of man. The finest of the forests are usually found along their banks, and in the multitude of falls and rapids the wilderness finds a voice. Such a river is the Hiwassee, with its surface broken to a thousand sparkling gems, and its forest walls vine-draped and flowery as Eden. And how fine the songs it sings!

In Murphy [North Carolina] I was hailed by the sheriff who could not determine by my colors and rigging to what country or craft I belonged. Since the war, every other stranger in these lonely parts is supposed to be a criminal, and all are objects of curiosity or apprehensive concern. After a few minutes' conversation with this chief man of Murphy I was pronounced harmless, and invited to his house, where for the first time since leaving home I found a house decked with flowers and vines, clean within and without, and stamped with the comforts of culture and refinement in all its arrangements. Striking contrast to the uncouth transitionist establishments from the wigwams of savages to the clumsy but clean log castle of the thrifty pioneer.

September 20. All day among the groves and gorges of Murphy with Mr. Beale. Was shown the site of Camp Butler where General Scott had his headquarters when he removed the Cherokee Indians to a new home in the West. Found a number of rare and strange plants on the rocky banks of the river Hiwassee. In the afternoon, from the summit of a commanding ridge, I obtained a magnificent view of blue, softly curved mountain scenery. Among the trees I saw *Ilex* [Holly] for the first time. Mr. Beale informed me that the paleness of most of the women in his neighborhood, and the mountains in general hereabouts, was caused chiefly by smoking and by what is called "dipping." I had never even heard of dipping. The term simply describes the application of snuff to the gum by means of a small swab.

September 21. Most luxuriant forest. Many brooks running across the road. Blairsville [Georgia], which I passed in the forenoon, seems a shapeless and insignificant village, but grandly encircled with banded hills. At night I was cordially received by a farmer whose wife, though smart and neat in her appearance, was an inveterate smoker.

September 22. Hills becoming small, sparsely covered with soil. They are called "knob land" and are cultivated, or scratched, with a kind of one-tooth cultivator. Every rain robs them of their fertility, while the bottoms are of course correspondingly enriched. About noon I reached the last mountain summit on my way to the sea. It is called the Blue Ridge and before it lies a prospect very different from any I had passed, namely, a vast uniform expanse of dark pine woods, extending to the sea; an impressive view at any time and under any circumstances, but particularly so to one emerging from the mountains.

Traveled in the wake of three poor but merry mountaineers—an old woman, a young woman, and a young man—who sat, leaned, and lay in the box of a shackly wagon that seemed to be held together by spiritualism, and was kept in agitation by a very large and a very small mule. In going down hill the looseness of the harness and the joints of the wagon allowed the mules to back nearly out of sight beneath the box, and the three who occupied it were slid against the front boards in a heap over the mules' ears. Before they could unravel their limbs from this unmannerly and impolite disorder, a new ridge in the road frequently tilted them with a swish and a bump against the back boards in a mixing that was still more grotesque.

I expected to see man, women, and mules mingled in piebald ruin at the bottom of some rocky hollow, but they seemed to have full confidence in the back board and front board of the wagon-box. So they continued to slide comfortably up and down, from end to end, in slippery obedience to the law of gravitation, as the grades demanded. Where the jolting was moderate, they engaged in conversation on love, marriage, and camp-meeting, according to the custom of the country. The old lady, through all the vicissitudes of the transportation, held a bouquet of French marigolds.

The hillsides hereabouts were bearing a fine harvest of asters. Reached Mount Yonah in the evening. Had a long conversation with an old Methodist slaveholder and mine owner. Was hospitably refreshed with a drink of fine cider.

Chapter III.

Through the River Country of Georgia

September 23. Am now fairly out of the mountains. Thus far the climate has not changed in any marked degree, the decrease in latitude being balanced by the increase in altitude. These mountains are highways on which northern plants may extend their colonies southward. The plants of the North and of the South have many minor places of meeting along the way I have traveled; but it is here on the southern slope of the Alleghanies that the greatest number of hardy, enterprising representatives of the two climates are assembled.

Passed the comfortable, finely shaded little town of Gainesville. The Chattahoochee River is richly embanked with massive, bossy, dark green water oaks, and wreathed with a dense growth of muscadine grapevines, whose ornate foliage, so well adapted to bank embroidery was enriched with other interweaving species of vines and brightly colored flowers. This is the first truly southern stream I have met.

At night I reached the home of a young man with whom I had worked in Indiana, Mr. Prater. He was down here on a visit to his father and mother. This was a plain backwoods family, living out of sight among knobby timbered hillocks not far from the river. The evening was passed in mixed conversation on southern and northern generalities.

September 24. Spent this day with Mr. Prater sailing on the Chattahoochee, feasting on grapes that had dropped from the overhanging vines. This remarkable species of wild grape has a stout stem, sometimes five or six inches in diameter, smooth bark and hard wood, quite unlike any other wild or cultivated grapevine that I have seen. The grapes are very large, some of them nearly an inch in diameter, globular and fine flavored. Usually there are but three or four berries in a cluster, and when mature they drop off instead of decaying on the vine. Those which fall into the river are often found in large quantities in the eddies along the bank, where they are collected by men in boats and sometimes made into wine. I think another name for this grape is the Scuppernong[6], though called "muscadine" here.

[6] The old Indian name for the southern species of fox-grape, *Vitis rotundifolia*, which Muir describes here. Wood's Botany listed it as *Vitis vulpina* L. and remarks, "The variety called 'Scuppernong' is quite common in southern gardens."

Besides sailing on the river, we had a long walk among the plant bowers and tangles of the Chattahoochee bottom lands.

September 25. Bade good-bye to this friendly family. Mr. Prater accompanied me a short distance from the house and warned me over and over again to be on the outlook for rattlesnakes. They are now leaving the damp low-lands, he told me, so that the danger is much greater because they are on their travels. Thus warned, I set out for Savannah, but got lost in the vine-fenced hills and hollows of the river bottom. Was unable to find the ford to which I had been directed by Mr. Prater.

I then determined to push on southward regardless of roads and fords. After repeated failures I succeeded in finding a place on the river bank where I could force my way into the stream through the vine-tangles. I succeeded in crossing the river by wading and swimming, careless of wetting, knowing that I would soon dry in the hot sunshine.

Out near the middle of the river I found great difficulty in resisting the rapid current. Though I braced myself with a stout stick, I was at length carried away in spite of all my efforts. But I succeeded in swimming to the shallows on the farther side, luckily caught hold of a rock, and after a rest swam and waded ashore. Dragging myself up the steep bank by the overhanging vines, I spread out myself, my paper money, and my plants to dry.

Debated with myself whether to proceed down the river valley until I could buy a boat, or lumber to make one, for a sail instead of a march through Georgia. I was intoxicated with the beauty of these glorious river banks, which I fancied might increase in grandeur as I approached the sea. But I finally concluded that such a pleasure sail would be less profitable than a walk, and so sauntered on southward as soon as I was dry. Rattlesnakes abundant. Lodged at a farmhouse. Found a few tropical plants in the garden.

Cotton is the principal crop hereabouts, and picking is now going on merrily. Only the lower bolls are now ripe. Those higher on the plants are green and unopened. Higher still, there are buds and flowers, some of which, if the plants be thrifty and the season favorable, will continue to produce ripe bolls until January.

The negroes are easy-going and merry, making a great deal of noise and doing little work. One energetic white man, working with a will, would easily pick as much cotton as half a dozen Sambos and Sallies. The forest here is almost entirely made up of dim-green, knotty, sparsely planted pines. The soil is mostly white, fine-grained sand.

September 26. Reached Athens in the afternoon, a remarkably beautiful and aristocratic town, containing many classic and magnificent mansions of wealthy planters, who formerly owned large negro-stocked plantations in the best cotton and sugar regions farther south. Unmistakable marks of culture and refinement, as well as wealth, were everywhere apparent. This is the most beautiful town I have seen on the journey, so far, and the only one in the South that I would like to revisit.

The negroes here have been well trained and are extremely polite. When they come in sight of a white man on the road, off go their hats, even at a distance of forty or fifty yards, and they walk bare-headed until he is out of sight.

September 27. Long zigzag walk amid the old plantations, a few of which are still cultivated in the old way by the same negroes that worked them before the war, and who still occupy their former "quarters." They are now paid seven to ten dollars a month.

The weather is very hot on these sandy, lightly shaded, lowland levels. When very thirsty I discovered a beautiful spring in a sandstone basin overhung with shady bushes and vines, where I enjoyed to the utmost the blessing of pure cold water. Discovered here a fine southern fern, some new grasses, etc. Fancied that I might have been directed here by Providence, while fainting with thirst. It is not often hereabouts that the joys of cool water, cool shade, and rare plants are so delightfully combined.

Witnessed the most gorgeous sunset I ever enjoyed in this bright world of light. The sunny South is indeed sunny. Was directed by a very civil negro to lodgings for the night. Daily bread hereabouts means sweet potatoes and rusty bacon.

September 28. The water oak is abundant on stream banks and in damp hollows. Grasses are becoming tall and cane-like and do not cover the ground with their leaves as at the North. Strange plants are crowding about me now. Scarce a familiar face appears among all the flowers of the day's walk.

September 29. To-day I met a magnificent grass, ten or twelve feet in stature, with a superb panicle of glossy purple flowers. Its leaves, too, are of princely mould and dimensions. Its home is in sunny meadows and along the wet borders of slow streams and swamps. It seems to be fully aware of its high rank, and waves with the grace and solemn majesty of a mountain pine. I wish I could place one of these regal plants among the grass settlements of our Western prairies. Surely every panicle would wave and bow in joyous allegiance and acknowledge their king.

September 30. Between Thomson and Augusta I found many new and beautiful grasses, tall gerardias, liatris, club mosses, etc. Here, too, is the northern limit of the remarkable long-leafed pine, a tree from sixty to seventy feet in height, from twenty to thirty inches in diameter, with leaves ten to fifteen inches long, in dense radiant masses at the ends of the naked branches. The wood is strong, hard, and very resinous. It makes excellent ship spars, bridge timbers, and flooring. Much of it is shipped to the West India Islands, New York, and Galveston.

The seedlings, five or six years old, are very striking objects to one from the North, consisting, as they do, of the straight, leafless stem, surmounted by a crown of deep green leaves, arching and spreading like a palm. Children fancy that they resemble brooms, and use them as such in their picnic play-houses. *Pinus palustris* is most abundant in Georgia and Florida.

The sandy soil here is sparingly seamed with rolled quartz pebbles and clay. Denudation, going on slowly, allows the thorough removal of these clay seams, leaving only the sand. Notwithstanding the sandiness of the soil, much of the surface of the country is covered with standing water, which is easily accounted for by the presence of the above-mentioned impermeable seams.

Traveled to-day more than forty miles without dinner or supper. No family would receive me, so I had to push on to Augusta. Went hungry to bed and awoke with a sore stomach—sore, I suppose, from its walls rubbing on each other without anything to grind. A negro kindly directed me to the best hotel, called, I think, the Planter's. Got a good bed for a dollar.

October 1. Found a cheap breakfast in a market-place; then set off along the Savannah River to Savannah. Splendid grasses and rich, dense, vine-clad forests. Muscadine grapes in cart-loads. Asters and solidagoes becoming scarce. Carices [sedges] quite rare. Leguminous plants abundant. A species of passion flower is common, reaching back into Tennessee. It is here called "apricot vine," has a superb flower, and the most delicious fruit I have ever eaten.

The pomegranate is cultivated here. The fruit is about the size of an orange, has a thick, tough skin, and when opened resembles a many-chambered box full of translucent purple candies.

Toward evening I came to the country of one of the most striking of southern plants, the so-called "Long Moss" or Spanish Moss [Tillandsia], though it is a flowering plant and belongs to the same family as the pineapple [Bromelworts]. The trees hereabouts have all their branches draped with it, producing a remarkable effect.

Here, too, I found an impenetrable cypress swamp. This remarkable tree, called cypress, is a taxodium, grows large and high, and is remarkable for its flat crown. The whole forest seems almost level on the top, as if each tree had grown up against a ceiling, or had been rolled while growing. This taxodium is the only level-topped tree that I have seen. The branches, though spreading, are careful not to pass each other, and stop suddenly on reaching the general level, as if they had grown up against a ceiling.

The groves and thickets of smaller trees are full of blooming evergreen vines. These vines are not arranged in separate groups, or in delicate wreaths, but in bossy walls and heavy, mound-like heaps and banks. Am made to feel that I am now in a strange land. I know hardly any of the plants, but few of the birds, and I am unable to see the country for the solemn, dark, mysterious cypress woods which cover everything.

The winds are full of strange sounds, making one feel far from the people and plants and fruitful fields of home. Night is coming on and I am filled with indescribable loneliness. Felt feverish; bathed in a black, silent stream; nervously watchful for alligators. Obtained lodging in a planter's house among cotton fields. Although the family seemed to be pretty well-off, the only light in the house was bits of pitch-pine wood burned in the fireplace.

October 2. In the low bottom forest of the Savannah River. Very busy with new specimens. Most exquisitely planned wrecks of *Agrostis scabra* [Rough Hair Grass]. Pines in glorious array with open, welcoming, approachable plants.

Met a young African with whom I had a long talk. Was amused with his eloquent narrative of coon hunting, alligators, and many superstitions. He showed me a place where a railroad train had run off the track, and assured me that the ghosts of the killed may be seen every dark night.

Had a long walk after sundown. At last was received at the house of Dr. Perkins. Saw Cape Jasmine [*Gardenia florida*] in the garden. Heard long recitals of war happenings, discussion of the slave question, and Northern politics; a thoroughly characteristic Southern family, refined in manners and kind, but immovably prejudiced on everything connected with slavery.

The family table was unlike any I ever saw before. It was circular, and the central part of it revolved. When any one wished to be helped, he placed his plate on the revolving part, which was whirled around to the host, and then whirled back with its new load. Thus every plate was revolved into place, without the assistance of any of the family.

October 3. In "pine barrens" most of the day. Low, level, sandy tracts; the pines wide apart; the sunny spaces between full of beautiful abounding grasses, liatris, long, wand-like solidago, saw palmettos, etc., covering the ground in garden style. Here I sauntered in delightful freedom, meeting none of the cat-clawed vines, or shrubs, of the alluvial bottoms. Dwarf live-oaks common.

Toward evening I arrived at the home of Mr. Cameron, a wealthy planter, who had large bands of slaves at work in his cotton fields. They still call him "Massa." He tells me that labor costs him less now than it did before the emancipation of the negroes. When I arrived I found him busily engaged in scouring the rust off some cotton-gin saws which had been lying for months at the bottom of his mill-pond to prevent Sherman's "bummers" from destroying them. The most valuable parts of the grist-mill and cotton-press were hidden in the same way. "If Bill Sherman," he said, "should come down now without his army, he would never go back."

When I asked him if he could give me food and lodging for the night he said, "No, no, we have no accommodations for travelers." I said, "But I am traveling as a botanist and either have to find lodgings when night overtakes me or lie outdoors, which I often have had to do in my long walk from Indiana. But you see that the country here is very swampy; if you will at least sell me a piece of bread, and give me a drink at your well, I shall have to look around for a dry spot to lie down on."

Then, asking me a few questions, and narrowly examining me, he said, "Well, it is barely possible that we may find a place for you, and if you will come to the house I will ask my wife." Evidently he was cautious to get his wife's opinion of the kind of creature I was before committing himself to hospitality. He halted me at the door and called out his wife, a fine-looking woman, who also questioned me narrowly as to my object in coming so far down through the South, so soon after the war. She said to her husband that she thought they could, perhaps, give me a place to sleep.

After supper, as we sat by the fire talking on my favorite subject of botany, I described the country I had passed through, its botanical character, etc. Then, evidently, all doubt as to my being a decent man vanished, and they both said that they wouldn't for anything have turned me away; but I must excuse their caution, for perhaps fewer than one in a hundred, who passed through this unfrequented part of the country, were to be relied upon. "Only a short time ago we entertained a man who was well spoken and well dressed, and he vanished some time during the night with some valuable silverware."

Mr. Cameron told me that when I arrived he tried me for a Mason, and finding that I was not a Mason he wondered still more that I would venture into the country without being able to gain the assistance of brother Masons in these troublous times.

"Young man," he said, after hearing my talks on botany, "I see that your hobby is botany. My hobby is e-lec-tricity. I believe that the time is coming, though we may not live to see it, when that mysterious power or force, used now only for telegraphy, will eventually supply the power for running railroad trains and steamships, for lighting, and, in a word, electricity will do all the work of the world."

Many times since then I have thought of the wonderfully correct vision of this Georgia planter, so far in advance of almost everybody else in the world. Already nearly all that he foresaw has been accomplished, and the use of electricity is being extended more and more every year.

October 4. New plants constantly appearing. All day in dense, wet, dark, mysterious forest of flat-topped taxodiums.

October 5. Saw the stately banana for the first time, growing luxuriantly in the wayside gardens. At night with a very pleasant, intelligent Savannah family, but as usual was admitted only after I had undergone a severe course of questioning.

October 6. Immense swamps, still more completely fenced and darkened, that are never ruffled with winds or scorched with drought. Many of them seem to be thoroughly aquatic.

October 7. Impenetrable taxodium swamp, seemingly boundless. The silvery skeins of tillandsia becoming longer and more abundant. Passed the night with a very pleasant family of Georgians, after the usual questions and cross questions.

October 8. Found the first woody *compositæ*, a most notable discovery. Took them to be such at a considerable distance. Almost all trees and shrubs are evergreens here with thick polished leaves. *Magnolia grandiflora* becoming common. A magnificent tree in fruit and foliage as well as in flower. Near Savannah I found waste places covered with a dense growth of woody leguminous plants, eight or ten feet high, with pinnate leaves and suspended rattling nods.

Reached Savannah, but find no word from home, and the money that I had ordered to be sent by express from Portage [Wisconsin] by my brother had not yet arrived. Feel dreadfully lonesome and poor. Went to the meanest looking lodging-house that I could find, on account of its cheapness.

Chapter IV.

Camping among the Tombs

October 9. After going again to the express office and post office, and wandering about the streets, I found a road which led me to the Bonaventure graveyard. If that burying-ground across the Sea of Galilee, mentioned in Scripture, was half as beautiful as Bonaventure, I do not wonder that a man should dwell among the tombs. It is only three or four miles from Savannah, and is reached by a smooth white shell road.

There is but little to be seen on the way in land, water, or sky, that would lead one to hope for the glories of Bonaventure. The ragged desolate fields, on both sides of the road, are overrun with coarse rank weeds, and show scarce a trace of cultivation. But soon all is changed. Rickety log huts, broken fences, and the last patch of weedy rice-stubble are left behind. You come to beds of purple liatris and living wild-wood trees. You hear the song of birds, cross a small stream, and are with Nature in the grand old forest graveyard, so beautiful that almost any sensible person would choose to dwell here with the dead rather than with the lazy, disorderly living.

Part of the grounds was cultivated and planted with live-oak, about a hundred years ago, by a wealthy gentleman who had his country residence here. But much the greater part is undisturbed. Even those spots which are disordered by art, Nature is ever at work to reclaim, and to make them look as if the foot of man had never known them. Only a small plot of ground is occupied with graves and the old mansion is in ruins.

The most conspicuous glory of Bonaventure is its noble avenue of live-oaks. They are the most magnificent planted trees I have ever seen, about fifty feet high and perhaps three or four feet in diameter, with broad spreading leafy heads. The main branches reach out horizontally until they come together over the driveway, embowering it throughout its entire length, while each branch is adorned like a garden with ferns, flowers, grasses, and dwarf palmettos.

But of all the plants of these curious tree-gardens the most striking and characteristic is the so-called Long Moss (*Tillandsia usneoides*). It drapes all the branches from top to bottom, hanging in long silvery-gray skeins, reaching a length of not less than eight or ten feet, and when slowly waving in the wind they produce a solemn funereal effect singularly impressive.

There are also thousands of smaller trees and clustered bushes, covered almost from sight in the glorious brightness of their own light. The place is half surrounded by the salt marshes and islands of the river, their reeds and sedges making a delightful fringe. Many bald eagles roost among the trees along the side of the marsh. Their screams are heard every morning, joined with the noise of crows and the songs of countless warblers, hidden deep in their dwellings of leafy bowers. Large flocks of butterflies, flies, all kinds of happy insects, seem to be in a perfect fever of joy and sportive gladness. The whole place seems like a center of life. The dead do not reign there alone.

Bonaventure to me is one of the most impressive assemblages of animal and plant creatures I ever met. I was fresh from the Western prairies, the garden-like openings of Wisconsin, the beech and maple and oak woods of Indiana and Kentucky, the dark mysterious Savannah cypress forests; but never since I was allowed to walk the woods have I found so impressive a company of trees as the tillandsia-draped oaks of Bonaventure.

I gazed awe-stricken as one new-arrived from another world. Bonaventure is called a graveyard, a town of the dead, but the few graves are powerless in such a depth of life. The rippling of living waters, the song of birds, the joyous confidence of flowers, the calm, undisturbable grandeur of the oaks, mark this place of graves as one of the Lord's most favored abodes of life and light.

On no subject are our ideas more warped and pitiable than on death. Instead of the sympathy, the friendly union, of life and death so apparent in Nature, we are taught that death is an accident, a deplorable punishment for the oldest sin, the arch-enemy of life, etc. Town children, especially, are steeped in this death orthodoxy, for the natural beauties of death are seldom seen or taught in towns.

Of death among our own species, to say nothing of the thousand styles and modes of murder, our best memories, even among happy deaths, yield groans and tears, mingled with morbid exultation; burial companies, black in cloth and countenance; and, last of all, a black box burial in an ill-omened place, haunted by imaginary glooms and ghosts of every degree. Thus death becomes fearful, and the most notable and incredible thing heard around a death-bed is, "I fear not to die."

But let children walk with Nature, let them see the beautiful blendings and communions of death and life, their joyous inseparable unity, as taught in woods and meadows, plains and mountains and streams of our blessed star, and they will learn that death is stingless indeed, and as beautiful as life, and that the grave has no victory, for it never fights. All is divine harmony.

Most of the few graves of Bonaventure are planted with flowers. There is generally a magnolia at the head, near the strictly erect marble, a rose-bush or two at the foot, and some violets and showy exotics along the sides or on the tops. All is enclosed by a black iron railing, composed of rigid bars that might have been spears or bludgeons from a battlefield in Pandemonium.

It is interesting to observe how assiduously Nature seeks to remedy these labored art blunders. She corrodes the iron and marble, and gradually levels the hill which is always heaped up, as if a sufficiently heavy quantity of clods could not be laid on the dead. Arching grasses come one by one; seeds come flying on downy wings, silent as fate, to give life's dearest beauty for the ashes of art; and strong evergreen arms laden with ferns and tillandsia drapery are spread over all—Life at work everywhere, obliterating all memory of the confusion of man.

In Georgia many graves are covered with a common shingle roof, supported on four posts as the corner of a well, as if rain and sunshine were not regarded as blessings. Perhaps, in this hot and insalubrious climate, moisture and sun-heat are considered necessary evils to which they do not wish to expose their dead.

The money package that I was expecting did not arrive until the following week. After stopping the first night at the cheap, disreputable-looking hotel, I had only about a dollar and a half left in my purse, and so was compelled to camp out to make it last in buying only bread. I went out of the noisy town to seek a sleeping-place that was not marshy. After gaining the outskirts of the town toward the sea, I found some low sand dunes, yellow with flowering solidagoes.

I wandered wearily from dune to dune sinking ankle-deep in the sand, searching for a place to sleep beneath the tall flowers, free from insects and snakes, and above all from my fellow man. But idle negroes were prowling about everywhere, and I was afraid. The wind had strange sounds, waving the heavy panicles over my head, and I feared sickness from malaria so prevalent here, when I suddenly thought of the graveyard.

"There," thought I, "is an ideal place for a penniless wanderer. There no superstitious prowling mischief maker dares venture for fear of haunting ghosts, while for me there will be God's rest and peace. And then, if I am to be exposed to unhealthy vapors, I shall have capital compensation in seeing those grand oaks in the moonlight, with all the impressive and nameless influences of this lonely beautiful place."

By this time it was near sunset, and I hastened across the common to the road and set off for Bonaventure, delighted with my choice, and almost glad to find that necessity had furnished me with so good an excuse for doing what I knew my mother would censure; for she made me promise I would not lie out of doors if I could possibly avoid it. The sun was set ere I was past the negroes' huts and rice fields, and I arrived near the graves in the silent hour of the gloaming.

I was very thirsty after walking so long in the muggy heat, a distance of three or four miles from the city, to get to this graveyard. A dull, sluggish, coffee-colored stream flows under the road just outside the graveyard garden park, from which I managed to get a drink after breaking a way down to the water through a dense fringe of bushes, daring the snakes and alligators in the dark. Thus refreshed I entered the weird and beautiful abode of the dead.

All the avenue where I walked was in shadow, but an exposed tombstone frequently shone out in startling whiteness on either hand, and thickets of sparkleberry bushes gleamed like heaps of crystals. Not a breath of air moved the gray moss, and the great black arms of the trees met overhead and covered the avenue. But the canopy was fissured by many a netted seam and leafy-edged opening, through which the moonlight sifted in auroral rays, broidering the blackness in silvery light. Though tired, I sauntered a while enchanted, then lay down under one of the great oaks. I found a little mound that served for a pillow, placed my plant press and bag beside me and rested fairly well, though somewhat disturbed by large prickly-footed beetles creeping across my hands and face, and by a lot of hungry stinging mosquitoes.

When I awoke, the sun was up and all Nature was rejoicing. Some birds had discovered me as an intruder, and were making a great ado in interesting language and gestures. I heard the screaming of the bald eagles, and of some strange waders in the rushes. I heard the hum of Savannah with the long jarring hallos of negroes far away. On rising I found that my head had been resting on a grave, and though my sleep had not been quite so sound as that of the person below, I arose refreshed, and looking about me, the morning sunbeams pouring through the oaks and gardens dripping with dew, the beauty displayed was so glorious and exhilarating that hunger and care seemed only a dream.

Eating a breakfast cracker or two and watching for a few hours the beautiful light, birds, squirrels, and insects, I returned to Savannah, to find that my money package had not yet arrived. I then decided to go early to the graveyard and make a nest with a roof to keep off the dew, as there was no way of finding out how long I might have to stay. I chose a hidden spot in a dense thicket of sparkleberry bushes, near the right bank of the Savannah River, where the bald eagles and a multitude of singing birds roosted. It was so well hidden that I had to carefully fix its compass bearing in my mind from a mark I made on the side of the main avenue, that I might be able to find it at bedtime.

I used four of the bushes as corner posts for my little hut, which was about four or five feet long by about three or four in width, tied little branches across from forks in the bushes to support a roof of rushes, and spread a thick mattress of Long Moss over the floor for a bed. My whole establishment was on so small a scale that I could have taken up, not only my bed, but my whole house, and walked. There I lay that night, eating a few crackers.

Next day I returned to the town and was disappointed as usual in obtaining money. So after spending the day looking at the plants in the gardens of the fine residences and town squares, I returned to my graveyard home. That I might not be observed and suspected of hiding, as if I had committed a crime, I always went home after dark, and one night, as I lay down in my moss nest, I felt some cold-blooded creature in it; whether a snake or simply a frog or toad I do not know, but instinctively, instead of drawing back my hand, I grasped the poor creature and threw it over the tops of the bushes. That was the only significant disturbance or fright that I got.

In the morning everything seemed divine. Only squirrels, sunbeams, and birds came about me. I was awakened every morning by these little singers after they discovered my nest. Instead of serenely singing their morning songs they at first came within two or three feet of the hut, and, looking in at me through the leaves, chattered and scolded in half-angry, half-wondering tones. The crowd constantly increased, attracted by the disturbance. Thus I began to get acquainted with my bird neighbors in this blessed wilderness, and after they learned that I meant them no ill they scolded less and sang more.

After five days of this graveyard life I saw that even with living on three or four cents a day my last twenty-five cents would soon be spent, and after trying again and again unsuccessfully to find some employment began to think that I must strike farther out into the country, but still within reach of town, until I came to some grain or rice field that had not yet been harvested, trusting that I could live indefinitely on toasted or raw corn, or rice.

By this time I was becoming faint, and in making the journey to the town was alarmed to find myself growing staggery and giddy. The ground ahead seemed to be rising up in front of me, and the little streams in the ditches on the sides of the road seemed to be flowing up hill. Then I realized that I was becoming dangerously hungry and became more than ever anxious to receive that money package.

To my delight this fifth or sixth morning, when I inquired if the money package had come, the clerk replied that it had, but that he could not deliver it without my being identified. I said, "Well, here! read my brother's letter," handing it to him. "It states the amount in the package, where it came from, the day it was put into the office at Portage City, and I should think that would be enough." He said, "No, that is not enough. How do I know that this letter is yours? You may have stolen it. How do I know that you are John Muir?"

I said, "Well, don't you see that this letter indicates that I am a botanist? For in it my brother says, 'I hope you are having a good time and finding many new plants.' Now, you say that I might have stolen this letter from John Muir, and in that way have become aware of there being a money package to arrive from

Portage for him. But the letter proves that John Muir must be a botanist, and though, as you say, his letter might have been stolen, it would hardly be likely that the robber would be able to steal John Muir's knowledge of botany. Now I suppose, of course, that you have been to school and know something of botany. Examine me and see if I know anything about it."

At this he laughed good-naturedly, evidently feeling the force of my argument, and, perhaps, pitying me on account of looking pale and hungry, he turned and rapped at the door of a private office—probably the Manager's—called him out and said, "Mr. So and so, here is a man who has inquired every day for the last week or so for a money package from Portage, Wisconsin. He is a stranger in the city with no one to identify him. He states correctly the amount and the name of the sender. He has shown me a letter which indicates that Mr. Muir is a botanist, and that although a traveling companion may have stolen Mr. Muir's letter, he could not have stolen his botany, and requests us to examine him."

The head official smiled, took a good stare into my face, waved his hand, and said, "Let him have it." Gladly I pocketed my money, and had not gone along the street more than a few rods before I met a very large negro woman with a tray of gingerbread, in which I immediately invested some of my new wealth, and walked rejoicingly, munching along the street, making no attempt to conceal the pleasure I had in eating. Then, still hunting for more food, I found a sort of eating-place in a market and had a large regular meal on top of the gingerbread! Thus my "marching through Georgia" terminated handsomely in a jubilee of bread.

Chapter V.

Through Florida Swamps and Forests

Of the people of the States that I have now passed, I best like the Georgians. They have charming manners, and their dwellings are mostly larger and better than those of adjacent States. However costly or ornamental their homes or their manners, they do not, like those of the New Englander, appear as the fruits of intense and painful sacrifice and training, but are entirely divested of artificial weights and measures, and seem to pervade and twine about their characters as spontaneous growths with the durability and charm of living nature.

In particular, Georgians, even the commonest, have a most charmingly cordial way of saying to strangers, as they proceed on their journey, "I wish you well, sir." The negroes of Georgia, too, are extremely mannerly and polite, and appear always to be delighted to find opportunity for obliging anybody.

Athens contains many beautiful residences. I never before saw so much about a home that was so evidently done for beauty only, although this is by no means a universal characteristic of Georgian homes. Nearly all well-to-do farmers' families in Georgia and Tennessee spin and weave their own cloth. This work is almost all done by the mothers and daughters and consumes much of their time.

The traces of war are not only apparent on the broken fields, burnt fences, mills, and woods ruthlessly slaughtered, but also on the countenances of the people. A few years after a forest has been burned another generation of bright and happy trees arises, in purest, freshest vigor; only the old trees, wholly or half dead, bear marks of the calamity. So with the people of this war-field. Happy, unscarred, and unclouded youth is growing up around the aged, half-consumed, and fallen parents, who bear in sad measure the ineffaceable marks of the farthest-reaching and most infernal of all civilized calamities.

Since the commencement of my floral pilgrimage I have seen much that is not only new, but altogether unallied, unacquainted with the plants of my former life. I have seen magnolias, tupelo, live-oak, Kentucky oak, tillandsia, long-leafed pine, palmetto, schrankia, and whole forests of strange trees and vine-tied thickets of blooming shrubs; whole meadowfuls of magnificent bamboo and lakefuls of lilies, all new to me; yet I still press eagerly on to Florida as the special home of the tropical plants I am looking for, and I feel sure I shall not be disappointed.

The same day on which the money arrived I took passage on the steamship Sylvan Shore for Fernandina, Florida. The daylight part of this sail along the coast of Florida was full of novelty, and by association awakened memories of my Scottish days at Dunbar on the Firth of Forth.

On board I had civilized conversation with a Southern planter on topics that are found floating in the mind of every white man down here who has a single thought. I also met a brother Scotchman, who was especially interesting and had some ideas outside of Southern politics. Altogether my half-day and night on board the steamer were pleasant, and carried me past a very sickly, entangled, overflowed, and unwalkable piece of forest.

It is pretty well known that a short geological time ago the ocean covered the sandy level margin, extending from the foot of the Alleghanies to the present coast-line, and in receding left many basins for lakes and swamps. The land is still encroaching on the sea, and it does so not evenly, in a regular line, but in fringing lagoons and inlets and dotlike coral islands.

It is on the coast strip of isles and peninsulas that sea-island cotton is grown. Some of these small islands are afloat, anchored only by the roots of mangroves and rushes. For a few hours our steamer sailed in the open sea, exposed to its waves, but most of the time she threaded her way among the lagoons, the home of alligators and countless ducks and waders.

October 15. To-day, at last, I reached Florida, the so-called "Land of Flowers," that I had so long waited for, wondering if after all my longings and prayers would be in vain, and I should die without a glimpse of the flowery Canaan. But here it is, at the distance of a few yards!—a flat, watery, reedy coast, with clumps of mangrove and forests of moss-dressed, strange trees appearing low in the distance. The steamer finds her way among the reedy islands like a duck, and I step on a rickety wharf. A few steps more take me to a rickety town, Fernandina. I discover a baker, buy some bread, and without asking a single question, make for the shady, gloomy groves.

In visiting Florida in dreams, of either day or night, I always came suddenly on a close forest of trees, every one in flower, and bent down and entangled to network by luxuriant, bright-blooming vines, and over all a flood of bright sunlight. But such was not the gate by which I entered the promised land. Salt marshes, belonging more to the sea than to the land; with groves here and there, green and unflowered, sunk to the shoulders in sedges and rushes; with trees farther back, ill defined in their boundary, and instead of rising in hilly waves and swellings, stretching inland in low water-like levels.

We were all discharged by the captain of the steamer without breakfast, and, after meeting and examining the new plants that crowded about me, I threw down my press and little bag beneath a thicket, where there was a dry spot on some broken heaps of grass and roots, something like a deserted muskrat house, and applied myself to my bread breakfast. Everything in earth and sky had an impression of strangeness; not a mark of friendly recognition, not a breath, not a spirit whisper of sympathy came from anything about me, and of course I was lonely. I lay on my elbow eating my bread, gazing, and listening to the profound strangeness.

While thus engaged I was startled from these gatherings of melancholy by a rustling sound in the rushes behind me. Had my mind been in health, and my body not starved, I should only have turned calmly to the noise. But in this half-starved, unfriended condition I could have no healthy thought, and I at once believed that the sound came from an alligator. I fancied I could feel the stroke of his long notched tail and could see his big jaws and rows of teeth, closing with a springy snap on me, as I had seen in pictures.

Well, I don't know the exact measure of my fright either in time or pain, but when I did come to a knowledge of the truth, my man-eating alligator became a tall white crane, handsome as a minister from spirit land—"only that." I was ashamed and tried to excuse myself on account of Bonaventure anxiety and hunger.

Florida is so watery and vine-tied that pathless wanderings are not easily possible in any direction. I started to cross the State by a gap hewn for the locomotive, walking sometimes between the rails, stepping from tie to tie, or walking on the strip of sand at the sides, gazing into the mysterious forest, Nature's own. It is impossible to write the dimmest picture of plant grandeur so redundant, unfathomable.

Short was the measure of my walk to-day. A new, canelike grass, or big lily, or gorgeous flower belonging to tree or vine, would catch my attention, and I would throw down my bag and press and splash through the coffee-brown water for specimens. Frequently I sank deeper and deeper until compelled to turn back and make the attempt in another and still another place. Oftentimes I was tangled in a labyrinth of armed vines like a fly in a spider-web. At all times, whether wading or climbing a tree for specimens of fruit, I was overwhelmed with the vastness and unapproachableness of the great guarded sea of sunny plants.

Magnolia grandiflora I had seen in Georgia; but its home, its better land, is here. Its large dark-green leaves, glossy bright above and rusty brown beneath, gleam and mirror the sunbeams most gloriously among countless flower-heaps of the climbing, smothering vines. It is bright also in fruit and more tropical in form and expression than the orange. It speaks itself a prince among its fellows.

Occasionally, I came to a little strip of open sand, planted with pine (*Pinus palustris* or *Cubensis*). Even these spots were mostly wet, though lighted with free sunshine, and adorned with purple liatris, and orange-colored *Osmunda cinnamomea*. But the grandest discovery of this great wild day was the palmetto.

I was meeting so many strange plants that I was much excited, making many stops to get specimens. But I could not force my way far through the swampy forest, although so tempting and full of promise. Regardless of water snakes or insects, I endeavored repeatedly to force a way through the tough vine-tangles, but seldom succeeded in getting farther than a few hundred yards.

It was while feeling sad to think that I was only walking on the edge of the vast wood, that I caught sight of the first palmetto in a grassy place, standing almost alone. A few magnolias were near it, and bald cypresses, but it was not shaded by them. They tell us that plants are perishable, soulless creatures, that only man is immortal, etc.; but this, I think, is something that we know very nearly nothing about. Anyhow, this palm was indescribably impressive and told me grander things than I ever got from human priest.

This vegetable has a plain gray shaft, round as a broom-handle, and a crown of varnished channeled leaves. It is a plainer plant than the humblest of Wisconsin oaks, but, whether rocking and rustling in the wind or poised thoughtful and calm in the sunshine, it has a power of expression not excelled by any plant high or low that I have met in my whole walk thus far.

This, my first specimen, was not very tall, only about twenty-five feet high, with fifteen or twenty leaves, arching equally and evenly all around. Each leaf was about ten feet in length, the blade four feet, the stalk six. The leaves are channeled like half-open clams and are highly polished, so that they reflect the sunlight like glass. The undeveloped leaves on the top stand erect, closely folded, all together forming an oval crown over which the tropic light is poured and reflected from its slanting mirrors in sparks and splinters and long-rayed stars.

I am now in the hot gardens of the sun, where the palm meets the pine, longed and prayed for and often visited in dreams, and, though lonely to-night amid this multitude of strangers, strange plants, strange winds blowing gently, whispering, cooing, in a language I never learned, and strange birds also, everything solid or spiritual full of influences that I never before felt, yet I thank the Lord with all my heart for his goodness in granting me admission to this magnificent realm.

October 16. Last evening when I was in the trackless woods, the great mysterious night becoming more mysterious in the thickening darkness, I gave up hope of finding food or a house bed, and searched only for a dry spot on which to sleep safely hidden from wild, runaway negroes. I walked rapidly for hours in the wet, level woods, but not a foot of dry ground could I find. Hollow-voiced owls were calling without intermission. All manner of night sounds came from strange insects and beasts, one by one, or crowded together. All had a home but I. Jacob on the dry plains of Padanaram, with a stone pillow, must have been comparatively happy.

When I came to an open place where pines grew, it was about ten o'clock, and I thought that now at last I would find dry ground. But even the sandy barren was wet, and I had to grope in the dark a long time, feeling the ground with my hands when my feet ceased to plash, before I at last discovered a little hillock dry enough to lie down on. I ate a piece of bread that I fortunately had in my bag, drank some of the brown water about my precious hillock, and lay down. The noisiest of the unseen witnesses around me were the owls, who pronounced their gloomy speeches with profound emphasis, but did not prevent the coming of sleep to heal weariness.

In the morning I was cold and wet with dew, and I set out breakfastless. Flowers and beauty I had in abundance, but no bread. A serious matter is this bread which perishes, and, could it be dispensed with, I doubt if civilization would ever see me again. I walked briskly, watching for a house, as well as the grand assemblies of novel plants.

Near the middle of the forenoon I came to a shanty where a party of loggers were getting out long pines for ship spars. They were the wildest of all the white savages I have met. The long-haired ex-guerrillas of the mountains of Tennessee and North Carolina are uncivilized fellows; but for downright barbarism these Florida loggers excel. Nevertheless, they gave me a portion of their yellow pork and hominy without either apparent hospitality or a grudge, and I was glad to escape to the forest again.

A few hours later I dined with three men and three dogs. I was viciously attacked by the latter, who undertook to undress me with their teeth. I was nearly dragged down backward, but escaped unbitten. Liver pie, mixed with sweet potatoes and fat duff, was set before me, and after I had finished a moderate portion, one of the men, turning to his companion, remarked: "Wall, I guess that man quit eatin' 'cause he had nothin' more to eat. I'll get him more potato."

Arrived at a place on the margin of a stagnant pool where an alligator had been rolling and sunning himself. "See," said a man who lived here, "see, what a track that is! He must have been a mighty big fellow. Alligators wallow like hogs and like to lie in the sun. I'd like a shot at that fellow." Here followed a long recital of bloody combats with the scaly enemy, in many of which he had, of course, taken an important part. Alligators are said to be extremely fond of negroes and dogs, and naturally the dogs and negroes are afraid of them.

Another man that I met to-day pointed to a shallow, grassy pond before his door. "There," said he, "I once had a tough fight with an alligator. He caught my dog. I heard him howling, and as he was one of my best hunters I tried hard to save him. The water was only about knee-deep and I ran up to the alligator. It was only a small one about four feet long, and was having trouble in its efforts to drown the dog in the shallow water. I scared him and made him let go his hold, but before the poor crippled dog could reach the shore, he was caught again, and when I went at the alligator with a knife, it seized my arm. If it had been a little stronger it might have eaten me instead of my dog."

I never in all my travels saw more than one, though they are said to be abundant in most of the swamps, and frequently attain a length of nine or ten feet. It is reported, also, that they are very savage, oftentimes attacking men in boats. These independent inhabitants of the sluggish waters of this low coast cannot be called the friends of man, though I heard of one big fellow that was caught young and was partially civilized and made to work in harness.

Many good people believe that alligators were created by the Devil, thus accounting for their all-consuming appetite and ugliness. But doubtless these creatures are happy and fill the place assigned them by the great Creator of us all. Fierce and cruel they appear to us, but beautiful in the eyes of God. They, also, are his children, for He hears their cries, cares for them tenderly, and provides their daily bread.

The antipathies existing in the Lord's great animal family must be wisely planned, like balanced repulsion and attraction in the mineral kingdom. How narrow we selfish, conceited creatures are in our sympathies! how blind to the rights of all the rest of creation! With what dismal irreverence we speak of our fellow mortals! Though alligators, snakes, etc., naturally repel us, they are not mysterious evils. They dwell happily in these flowery wilds, are part of God's family, unfallen, undepraved, and cared for with the same species of tenderness and love as is bestowed on angels in heaven or saints on earth.

I think that most of the antipathies which haunt and terrify us are morbid productions of ignorance and weakness. I have better thoughts of those alligators now that I have seen them at home. Honorable representatives of the great saurians of an older creation, may you long enjoy your lilies and rushes, and be blessed now and then with a mouthful of terror-stricken man by way of dainty!

Found a beautiful lycopodium to-day, and many grasses in the dry sunlit places called "barrens," "hummocks," "savannas," etc. Ferns also are abundant. What a flood of heat and light is daily poured out on these beautiful openings and intertangled woods! "The land of the sunny South," we say, but no part of our diversified country is more shaded and covered from sunshine. Many a sunny sheet of plain and prairie break the continuity of the forests of the North and West, and the forests themselves are mostly lighted also, pierced with direct ray lances, or [the sunlight] passing to the earth and the lowly plants in filtered softness through translucent leaves. But in the dense Florida forests sunlight cannot enter. It falls on the evergreen roof and rebounds in long silvery lances and flashy spray. In many places there is not light sufficient to feed a single green leaf on these dark forest floors. All that the eye can reach is just a maze of tree stems and crooked leafless vine strings. All the flowers, all the verdure, all the glory is up in the light.

The streams of Florida are still young, and in many places are untraceable. I expected to find these streams a little discolored from the vegetable matter that I knew they must contain, and I was sure that in so flat a country I should not find any considerable falls or long rapids. The streams of upper Georgia are almost unapproachable in some places on account of luxuriant bordering marines, but the banks are nevertheless high and well defined. Florida streams are not yet possessed of banks and braes and definite channels. Their waters in deep places are black as ink, perfectly opaque, and glossy on the surface as if varnished. It often is difficult to ascertain which way they are flowing or creeping, so slowly and so widely do they circulate through the tree-tangles and swamps of the woods. The flowers here are strangers to me, but not more so than the rivers and lakes. Most streams appear to travel through a country with thoughts and plans for something beyond. But those of Florida are at home, do not appear to be traveling at all, and seem to know nothing of the sea.

October 17. Found a small, silvery-leafed magnolia, a bush ten feet high. Passed through a good many miles of open level pine barrens, as bounteously lighted as the "openings" of Wisconsin. The pines are rather small, are planted sparsely and pretty evenly on these sandy flats not long risen from the sea. Scarcely a specimen of any other tree is to be found associated with the pine. But there are some thickets of the little saw palmettos and a magnificent assemblage of tall grasses, their splendid panicles waving grandly in the warm wind, and making low tuneful changes in the glistening light that is flashed from their bent stems.

Not a pine, not a palm, in all this garden excels these stately grass plants in beauty of wind-waving gestures. Here are panicles that are one mass of refined purple; others that have flowers as yellow as ripe oranges, and stems polished and shining like steel wire. Some of the species are grouped in groves and thickets like trees, while others may be seen waving without any companions in sight. Some of them have wide-branching panicles like Kentucky oaks, others with a few tassels of spikelets drooping from a tall, leafless stem. But all of them are beautiful beyond the reach of language. I rejoice that God has "so clothed the grass of the field." How strangely we are blinded to beauty and color, form and motion, by comparative size! For example, we measure grasses by our own stature and by the height and bulkiness of trees. But what is the size of the greatest man, or the tallest tree that ever overtopped a grass! Compared with other things in God's creation the difference is nothing. We all are only microscopic animalcula.

October 18. Am walking on land that is almost dry. The dead levels are interrupted here and there by sandy waves a few feet in height. It is said that not a point in all Florida is more than three hundred feet above sea-level—a country where but little grading is required for roads, but much bridging and boring of many tunnels through forests.

Before reaching this open ground, in a lonely, swampy place in the woods, I met a large, muscular, brawny young negro, who eyed me with glaring, wistful curiosity. I was very thirsty at the time, and inquired of the man if there were any houses or springs near by where I could get a drink. "Oh, yes," he replied, still eagerly searching me with his wild eyes. Then he inquired where I came from, where I was going, and what brought me to such a wild country, where I was liable to be robbed, and perhaps killed.

"Oh, I am not afraid of any one robbing me," I said, "for I don't carry anything worth stealing." "Yes," said he, "but you can't travel without money." I started to walk on, but he blocked my way. Then I noticed that he was trembling, and it flashed upon me all at once that he was thinking of knocking me down in order to rob me. After glaring at my pockets as if searching for weapons, he stammered in a quavering voice, "Do you carry shooting-irons?" His motives, which I ought to have noted sooner, now were apparent to me. Though I had no pistol, I instinctively threw my hand back to my pistol pocket and, with my eyes fled on his, I marched up close to him and said, "I allow people to find out if I am armed or not." Then he quailed, stepped aside, and allowed me to pass, for fear of being shot. This was evidently a narrow escape.

A few miles farther on I came to a cotton-field, to patches of sugar cane carefully fenced, and some respectable-looking houses with gardens. These little fenced fields look as if they were intended to be for plants what cages are for birds. Discovered a large, treelike cactus in a dooryard; a small species was abundant on the sand-hillocks. Reached Gainesville late in the night.

When within three or four miles of the town I noticed a light off in the pine woods. As I was very thirsty, I thought I would venture toward it with the hope of obtaining water. In creeping cautiously and noiselessly through the grass to discover whether or no it was a camp of robber negroes, I came suddenly in full view of the best-lighted and most primitive of all the domestic establishments I have yet seen in town or grove. There was, first of all, a big, glowing log fire, illuminating the overleaning bushes and trees, bringing out leaf and spray with more than noonday distinctness, and making still darker the surrounding wood. In the center of this globe of light sat two negroes. I could see their ivory gleaming from the great lips, and their smooth cheeks flashing off light as if made of glass. Seen anywhere but in the South, the glossy pair would have been taken for twin devils, but here it was only a negro and his wife at their supper.

I ventured forward to the radiant presence of the black pair, and, after being stared at with that desperate fixedness which is said to subdue the lion, I was handed water in a gourd from somewhere out of the darkness. I was standing for a moment beside the big fire, looking at the unsurpassable simplicity of the establishment, and asking questions about the road to Gainesville, when my attention was called to a black lump of something lying in the ashes of the fire. It seemed to be made of rubber; but ere I had time for much speculation, the woman bent wooingly over the black object and said with motherly kindness, "Come, honey, eat yo' hominy."

At the sound of "hominy" the rubber gave strong manifestations of vitality and proved to be a burly little negro boy, rising from the earth naked as to the earth he came. Had he emerged from the black muck of a marsh, we might easily have believed that the Lord had manufactured him like Adam direct from the earth.

Surely, thought I, as I started for Gainesville, surely I am now coming to the tropics, where the inhabitants wear nothing but their own skins. This fashion is sufficiently simple, "no troublesome disguises," as Milton calls clothing,—but it certainly is not quite in harmony with Nature. Birds make nests and nearly all beasts make some kind of bed for their young; but these negroes allow their younglings to lie nestless and naked in the dirt.

Gainesville is rather attractive—an oasis in the desert, compared with other villages. It gets its life from the few plantations located about it on dry ground that rises islandlike a few feet above the swamps. Obtained food and lodging at a sort of tavern.

October 19. Dry land nearly all day. Encountered limestone, flint, coral, shells, etc. Passed several thrifty cotton plantations with comfortable residences, contrasting sharply with the squalid hovels of my first days in Florida. Found a single specimen of a handsome little plant, which at once, in some mysterious way, brought to mind a young friend in Indiana. How wonderfully our thoughts and impressions are stored! There is that in the glance of a flower which may at times control the greatest of creation's braggart lords.

The magnolia is much more abundant here. It forms groves and almost exclusively forests the edges of ponds and the banks of streams. The easy, dignified simplicity of this noble tree, its plain leaf endowed with superb richness of color and form, its open branches festooned with graceful vines and tillandsia, its showy crimson fruit, and its magnificent fragrant white flowers make *Magnolia grandiflora* the most lovable of Florida trees.

Discovered a great many beautiful polygonums, petalostemons, and yellow leguminous vines. Passed over fine sunny areas of the long-leafed and Cuban pines, which were everywhere accompanied by fine grasses and solidagoes. Wild orange groves are said to be rather common here, but I have seen only limes growing wild in the woods.

Came to a hut about noon, and, being weary and hungry, asked if I could have dinner. After serious consultation I was told to wait, that dinner would soon be ready. I saw only the man and his wife. If they had children, they may have been hidden in the weeds on account of nakedness. Both were suffering from malarial fever, and were very dirty. But they did not appear to have any realizing sense of discomfort from either the one or the other of these misfortunes. The dirt which encircled the countenances of these people did not, like the common dirt of the North, stick on the skin in bold union like plaster or paint, but appeared to stand out a little on contact like a hazy, misty, half-aerial mud envelope, the most diseased and incurable dirt that I ever saw, evidently desperately chronic and hereditary.

It seems impossible that children from such parents could ever be clean. Dirt and disease are dreadful enough when separate, but combined are inconceivably horrible. The neat cottage with a fragrant circumference of thyme and honeysuckle is almost unknown here. I have seen dirt on garments regularly stratified, the various strata no doubt indicating different periods of life. Some of them, perhaps, were annual layers, furnishing, like those of trees, a means of determining the age. Man and other civilized animals are the only creatures that ever become dirty.

Slept in the barrens at the side of a log. Suffered from cold and was drenched with dew. What a comfort a companion would be in the dark loneliness of such nights! Did not dare to make a fire for fear of discovery by robber negroes, who, I was warned, would kill a man for a dollar or two. Had a long walk after nightfall, hoping to discover a house. Became very thirsty and often was compelled to drink from slimy pools groped for in the grass, with the fear of alligators before my eyes.

October 20. Swamp very dense during this day's journey. Almost one continuous sheet of water covered with aquatic trees and vines. No stream that I crossed to-day appeared to have the least idea where it was going. Saw an alligator plash into the sedgy brown water by the roadside from an old log.

Arrived at night at the house of Captain Simmons, one of the very few scholarly, intelligent men that I have met in Florida. He had been an officer in the Confederate army in the war and was, of course, prejudiced against the North, but polite and kind to me, nevertheless. Our conversation, as we sat by the light of the fire, was on the one great question, slavery and its concomitants. I managed, however, to switch off to something more congenial occasionally—the birds of the neighborhood, the animals, the climate, and what spring, summer, and winter are like in these parts.

About the climate, I could not get much information, as he had always lived in the South and, of course, saw nothing extraordinary in weather to which he had always been accustomed. But in speaking of animals, he at once became enthusiastic and told many stories of hairbreadth escapes, in the woods about his house, from bears, hungry alligators, wounded deer, etc. "And now," said he, forgetting in his kindness that I was from the hated North, "you must stay with me a few days. Deer are abundant. I will lend you a rifle and we'll go hunting. I hunt whenever I wish venison, and I can get it about as easily from the woods near by as a shepherd can get mutton out of his flock. And perhaps we will see a bear, for they are far from scarce here, and there are some big gray wolves, too."

I expressed a wish to see some large alligators. "Oh, well," said he, "I can take you where you will see plenty of those fellows, but they are not much to look at. I once got a good look at an alligator that was lying at the bottom of still, transparent water, and I think that his eyes were the most impressively cold and cruel of any animal I have seen. Many alligators go out to sea among the keys. These sea alligators are the largest and most ferocious, and sometimes attack people by trying to strike them with their tails when they are out fishing in boats.

"Another thing I wish you to see," he continued, "is a palmetto grove on a rich hummock a few miles from here. The grove is about seven miles in length by three in breadth. The ground is covered with long grass, uninterrupted with bushes or other trees. It is the finest grove of palmettos I have ever seen and I have oftentimes thought that it would make a fine subject for an artist."

I concluded to stop—more to see this wonderful palmetto hummock than to hunt. Besides, I was weary and the prospect of getting a little rest was a tempting consideration after so many restless nights and long, hard walks by day.

October 21. Having outlived the sanguinary hunters' tales of my loquacious host, and breakfasted sumptuously on fresh venison and "caller" fish from the sea, I set out for the grand palm grove. I had seen these dazzling sun-children in every day of my walk through Florida, but they were usually standing solitary, or in groups of three or four; but to-day I was to see them by the mile. The captain led me a short distance through his corn field and showed me a trail which would conduct me to the palmy hummock. He pointed out the general direction, which I noted upon my compass.

"Now," said he, "at the other side of my farthest field you will come to a jungle of cat-briers, but will be able to pass them if you manage to keep the trail. You will find that the way is not by any means well marked, for in passing through a broad swamp, the trail makes a good many abrupt turns to avoid deep water, fallen trees, or impenetrable thickets. You will have to wade a good deal, and in passing the water-covered places you will have to watch for the point where the trail comes out on the opposite side."

I made my way through the briers, which in strength and ferocity equaled those of Tennessee, followed the path through all of its dim waverings, waded the many opposing pools, and, emerging suddenly from the leafy darkness of the swamp forest, at last stood free and unshaded on the border of the sun-drenched palm garden. It was a level area of grasses and sedges, smooth as a prairie, well starred with flowers, and bounded like a clearing by a wall of vine-laden trees.

The palms had full possession and appeared to enjoy their sunny home. There was no jostling, no apparent effort to outgrow each other. Abundance of sunlight was there for every crown, and plenty to fall between. I walked enchanted in their midst. What a landscape! Only palms as far as the eye could reach! Smooth pillars rising from the grass, each capped with a sphere of leaves, shining in the sun as bright as a star. The silence and calm were as deep as ever I found in the dark, solemn pine woods of Canada, and that contentment which is an attribute of the best of God's plant people was as impressively felt in this alligator wilderness as in the homes of the happy, healthy people of the North.

The admirable Linnaeus calls palms "the princes of the vegetable world." I know that there is grandeur and nobility in their character, and that there are palms nobler far than these. But in rank they appear to me to stand below both the oak and the pine. The motions of the palms, their gestures, are not very graceful. They appear to best advantage when perfectly motionless in the noontide calm and intensity of light. But they rustle and rock in the evening wind. I have seen grasses waving with far more dignity. And when our northern pines are waving and blowing in sign of worship with the winter storm-winds where is the prince of palms that could have the conscience to demand their homage!

Members of this palm congregation were of all sizes with respect to their stems; but their glorious crowns were all alike. In development there is only the terminal bud to consider. The young pawn of this species emerges from the ground in full strength, one cluster of leaves arched every way, making a sphere about ten or twelve feet in diameter. The outside lower leaves gradually become yellow, wither, and break off, the petiole snapping squarely across, a few inches from the stem. New leaves develop with wonderful rapidity. They stand erect at first, but gradually arch outward as they expand their blades and lengthen their petioles.

New leaves arise constantly from the center of the grand bud, while old ones break away from the outside. The splendid crowns are thus kept about the same size, perhaps a little larger than in youth while they are yet on the ground. As the development of the central axis goes on, the crown is gradually raised on a stem of about six to twelve inches in diameter. This stem is of equal thickness at the top and at the bottom and when young is roughened with the broken petioles. But these petiole-stumps fall off and disappear as they become old, and the trunk becomes smooth as if turned in a lathe.

After some hours in this charming forest I started on the return journey before night, on account of the difficulties of the swamp and the brier patch. On leaving the palmettos and entering the vine-tangled, half-submerged forest I sought long and carefully, but in vain, for the trail, for I had drifted about too incautiously in search of plants. But, recollecting the direction that I had followed in the morning, I took a compass bearing and started to penetrate the swamp in a direct line.

Of course I had a sore weary time, pushing through the tanglement of falling, standing, and half-fallen trees and bushes, to say nothing of knotted vines as remarkable for their efficient army of interlocking and lancing prickers as for their length and the number of their blossoms. But these were not my greatest obstacles, nor yet the pools and lagoons full of dead leaves and alligators. It was the army of cat-briers that I most dreaded. I knew that I would have to find the narrow slit of a lane before dark or spend the night with mosquitoes and alligators, without food or fire. The entire distance was not great, but a traveler in open woods can form no idea of the crooked and strange difficulties of pathless locomotion in these thorny, watery Southern tangles, especially in pitch darkness. I struggled hard and kept my course, leaving the general direction only when drawn aside by a plant of extraordinary promise, that I wanted for a specimen, or when I had to make the half-circuit of a pile of trees, or of a deep lagoon or pond.

In wading I never attempted to keep my clothes dry, because the water was too deep, and the necessary care would consume too much time. Had the water that I was forced to wade been transparent it would have lost much of its difficulty. But as it was, I constantly expected to plant my feet on an alligator, and therefore proceeded with strained caution. The opacity of the water caused uneasiness also on account of my inability to determine its depth. In many places I was compelled to turn back, after wading forty or fifty yards, and to try again a score of times before I succeeded in getting across a single lagoon.

At length, after miles of wading and wallowing, I arrived at the grand cat-brier encampment which guarded the whole forest in solid phalanx, unmeasured miles up and down across my way. Alas! the trail by which I had crossed in the morning was not to be found, and night was near. In vain I scrambled back and forth in search of an opening. There was not even a strip of dry ground on which to rest. Everywhere the long briers arched over to the vines and bushes of the watery swamp, leaving no standing-ground between them. I began to think of building some sort of a scaffold in a tree to rest on through the night, but concluded to make one more desperate effort to find the narrow track.

After calm, concentrated recollection of my course, I made a long exploration toward the left down the brier line, and after scrambling a mile or so, perspiring and bleeding, I discovered the blessed trail and escaped to dry land and the light. Reached the captain at sun-down. Dined on milk and johnny-cake and fresh venison. Was congratulated on my singular good fortune and woodcraft, and soon after supper was sleeping the deep sleep of the weary and the safe.

October 22. This morning I was easily prevailed upon by the captain and an ex-judge, who was rusticating here, to join in a deer hunt. Had a delightful ramble in the long grass and flowery barrens. Started one deer but did not draw a single shot. The captain, the judge, and myself stood at different stations where the deer was expected to pass, while a brother of the captain entered the woods to arouse the game from cover. The one deer that he started took a direction different from any which this particular old buck had ever been known to take in times past, and in so doing was cordially cursed as being the "d——dest deer that ever ran unshot." To me it appeared as "d——dest" work to slaughter God's cattle for sport. "They were made for us," say these self-approving preachers; "for our food, our recreation, or other uses not yet discovered." As truthfully we might say on behalf of a bear, when he deals successfully with an unfortunate hunter, "Men and other bipeds were made for bears, and thanks be to God for claws and teeth so long."

Let a Christian hunter go to the Lord's woods and kill his well-kept beasts, or wild Indians, and it is well; but let an enterprising specimen of these proper, predestined victims go to houses and fields and kill the most worthless person of the vertical godlike killers,—oh! that is horribly unorthodox, and on the part of the Indians atrocious murder! Well, I have precious little sympathy for the selfish propriety of civilized man, and if a war of races should occur between the wild beasts and Lord Man, I would be tempted to sympathize with the bears.

Chapter VI.

Cedar Keys

October 23. To-day I reached the sea. While I was yet many miles back in the palmy woods, I caught the scent of the salt sea breeze which, although I had so many years lived far from sea breezes, suddenly conjured up Dunbar, its rocky coast, winds and waves; and my whole childhood, that seemed to have utterly vanished in the New World, was now restored amid the Florida woods by that one breath from the sea. Forgotten were the palms and magnolias and the thousand flowers that enclosed me. I could see only dulse and tangle, long winged gulls, the Bass Rock in the Firth of Forth, and the old castle, schools, churches, and long country rambles in search of birds' nests. I do not wonder that the weary camels coming from the scorching African deserts should be able to scent the Nile.

How imperishable are all the impressions that ever vibrate one's life! We cannot forget anything. Memories may escape the action of will, may sleep a long time, but when stirred by the right influence, though that influence be light as a shadow, they flash into full stature and life with everything in place. For nineteen years my vision was bounded by forests, but to-day, emerging from a multitude of tropical plants, I beheld the Gulf of Mexico stretching away unbounded, except by the sky. What dreams and speculative matter for thought arose as I stood on the strand, gazing out on the burnished, treeless plain!

But now at the seaside I was in difficulty. I had reached a point that I could not ford, and Cedar Keys had an empty harbor. Would I proceed down the peninsula to Tampa and Key West, where I would be sure to find a vessel for Cuba, or would I wait here, like Crusoe, and pray for a ship. Full of these thoughts, I stepped into a little store which had a considerable trade in quinine and alligator and rattlesnake skins, and inquired about shipping, means of travel, etc.

The proprietor informed me that one of several sawmills near the village was running, and that a schooner chartered to carry a load of lumber to Galveston, Texas, was expected at the mills for a load. This mill was situated on a tongue of land a few miles along the coast from Cedar Keys, and I determined to see Mr. Hodgson, the owner, to find out particulars about the expected schooner, the time she would take to load, whether I would be likely to obtain passage on her, etc.

Found Mr. Hodgson at his mill. Stated my case, and was kindly furnished the desired information. I determined to wait the two weeks likely to elapse before she sailed, and go on her to the flowery plains of Texas, from any of whose ports, I fancied, I could easily find passage to the West Indies. I agreed to work for Mr.

Hodgson in the mill until I sailed, as I had but little money. He invited me to his spacious house, which occupied a shell hillock and commanded a fine view of the Gulf and many gems of palmy islets, called "keys," that fringe the shore like huge bouquets not too big, however, for the spacious waters. Mr. Hodgson's family welcomed me with that open, unconstrained cordiality which is characteristic of the better class of Southern people.

At the sawmill a new cover had been put on the main driving pulley, which, made of rough plank, had to be turned off and smoothed. He asked me if I was able to do this job and I told him that I could. Fixing a rest and making a tool out of an old file, I directed the engineer to start the engine and run slow. After turning down the pulley and getting it true, I put a keen edge on a common carpenter's plane, quickly finished the job, and was assigned a bunk in one of the employees' lodging-houses.

The next day I felt a strange dullness and headache while I was botanizing along the coast. Thinking that a bath in the salt water might refresh me, I plunged in and swam a little distance, but this seemed only to make me feel worse. I felt anxious for something sour, and walked back to the village to buy lemons.

Thus and here my long walk was interrupted. I thought that a few days' sail would land me among the famous flower-beds of Texas. But the expected ship came and went while I was helpless with fever. The very day after reaching the sea I began to be weighed down by inexorable leaden numbness, which I resisted and tried to shake off for three days, by bathing in the Gulf, by dragging myself about among the palms, plants, and strange shells of the shore, and by doing a little mill work. I did not fear any serious illness, for I never was sick before, and was unwilling to pay attention to my feelings.

But yet heavier and more remorselessly pressed the growing fever, rapidly gaining on my strength. On the third day after my arrival I could not take any nourishment, but craved acid. Cedar Keys was only a mile or two distant, and I managed to walk there to buy lemons. On returning, about the middle of the afternoon, the fever broke on me like a storm, and before I had staggered halfway to the mill I fell down unconscious on the narrow trail among dwarf palmettos.

When I awoke from the hot fever sleep, the stars were shining, and I was at a loss to know which end of the trail to take, but fortunately, as it afterwards proved, I guessed right. Subsequently, as I fell again and again after walking only a hundred yards or so, I was careful to lie with my head in the direction in which I thought the mill was. I rose, staggered, and fell, I know not how many times, in delirious bewilderment, gasping and throbbing with only moments of consciousness. Thus passed the hours till after midnight, when I reached the mill lodging-house.

The watchman on his rounds found me lying on a heap of sawdust at the foot of the stairs. I asked him to assist me up the steps to bed, but he thought my difficulty was only intoxication and refused to help me. The mill hands, especially on Saturday nights, often returned from the village drunk. This was the cause of the watchman's refusal. Feeling that I must get to bed, I made out to reach it on hands and knees, tumbled in after a desperate struggle, and immediately became oblivious to everything.

I awoke at a strange hour on a strange day to hear Mr. Hodgson ask a watcher beside me whether I had yet spoken, and when he replied that I had not, he said: "Well, you must keep on pouring in quinine. That's all we can do." How long I lay unconscious I never found out, but it must have been many days. Some time or other I was moved on a horse from the mill quarters to Mr. Hodgson's house, where I was nursed about three months with unfailing kindness, and to the skill and care of Mr. and Mrs. Hodgson I doubtless owe my life. Through quinine and calomel—in sorry abundance—with other milder medicines, my malarial fever became typhoid. I had night sweats, and my legs became like posts of the temper and consistency of clay on account of dropsy. So on until January, a weary time.

As soon as I was able to get out of bed, I crept away to the edge of the wood, and sat day after day beneath a moss-draped live-oak, watching birds feeding on the shore when the tide was out. Later, as I gathered some strength, I sailed in a little skiff from one key to another. Nearly all the shrubs and trees here are ever-green, and a few of the smaller plants are in flower all winter. The principal trees on this Cedar Key are the juniper, long-leafed pine, and live-oak. All of the latter, living and dead, are heavily draped with tillandsia, like those of Bonaventure. The leaf is oval, about two inches long, three fourths of an inch wide, glossy and dark green above, pale beneath. The trunk is usually much divided, and is extremely unwedgeable. The specimen on the opposite page[7] is growing in the dooryard of Mr. Hodgson's house. It is a grand old king, whose crown gleamed in the bright sky long ere the Spanish shipbuilders felled a single tree of this noble species.

[7] Of the original journal.

The live-oaks of these keys divide empire with the long-leafed pine and palmetto, but in many places on the mainland there are large tracts exclusively occupied by them. Like the Bonaventure oaks they have the upper side of their main spreading branches thickly planted with ferns, grasses, small saw palmettos, etc. There is also a dwarf oak here, which forms dense thickets. The oaks of this key are not, like those of the Wisconsin openings, growing on grassy slopes, but stand, sunk to the shoulders, in flowering magnolias, heathworts, etc.

During my long sojourn here as a convalescent I used to lie on my back for whole days beneath the ample arms of these great trees, listening to the winds and the birds. There is an extensive shallow on the coast, close by, which the receding tide exposes daily. This is the feeding-ground of thousands of waders of all sizes, plumage, and language, and they make a lively picture and noise when they gather at the great family board to eat their daily bread, so bountifully provided for them.

Their leisure in time of high tide they spend in various ways and places. Some go in large flocks to reedy margins about the islands and wade and stand about quarrelling or making sport, occasionally finding a stray mouthful to eat. Some stand on the mangroves of the solitary shore, now and then plunging into the water after a fish. Some go long journeys in-land, up creeks and inlets. A few lonely old herons of solemn look and wing retire to favorite oaks. It was my delight to watch those old white sages of immaculate feather as they stood erect drowsing away the dull hours between tides, curtained by long skeins of tillandsia. White-bearded hermits gazing dreamily from dark caves could not appear more solemn or more becomingly shrouded from the rest of their fellow beings.

One of the characteristic plants of these keys is the Spanish bayonet, a species of yucca, about eight or ten feet in height, and with a trunk three or four inches in diameter when full grown. It belongs to the lily family and develops palmlike from terminal buds. The stout leaves are very rigid, sharp-pointed and bayonet-like. By one of these leaves a man might be as seriously stabbed as by an army bayonet, and woe to the luckless wanderer who dares to urge his way through these armed gardens after dark. Vegetable cats of many species will rob him of his clothes and claw his flesh, while dwarf palmettos will saw his bones, and the bayonets will glide to his joints and marrow without the smallest consideration for Lord Man.

The climate of these precious islets is simply warm summer and warmer summer, corresponding in time with winter and summer in the North. The weather goes smoothly over the points of union betwixt the twin summers. Few of the storms are very loud or variable. The average temperature during the day, in December, was about sixty-five degrees in the shade, but on one day a little damp snow fell. Cedar Key is two and one half or three miles in diameter and its highest point is forty-four feet above mean tide-water. It is surrounded by scores of other keys, many of them looking like a clump of palms, arranged like a tasteful bouquet, and placed in the sea to be kept fresh. Others have quite a sprinkling of oaks and junipers, beautifully united with vines. Still others consist of shells, with a few grasses and mangroves circled with a rim of rushes. Those which have sedgy margins furnish a favorite retreat for countless waders and divers, especially for the pelicans that frequently whiten the shore like a ring of foam.

It is delightful to observe the assembling of these feathered people from the woods and reedy isles; herons white as wave-tops, or blue as the sky, winnowing the warm air on wide quiet wing; pelicans coming with baskets to fill, and the multitude of smaller sailors of the air, swift as swallows, gracefully taking their places at Nature's family table for their daily bread. Happy birds!

The mockingbird is graceful in form and a fine singer, plainly dressed, rather familiar in habits, frequently coming like robins to door-sills for crumbs—a noble fellow, beloved by everybody. Wild geese are abundant in winter, associated with brant, some species of which I have never seen in the North. Also great flocks of robins, mourning doves, bluebirds, and the delightful brown thrashers. A large number of the smaller birds are fine singers. Crows, too, are here, some of them cawing with a foreign accent. The common bob-white quail I observed as far south as middle Georgia.

Lime Key, sketched on the opposite page, is a fair specimen of the Florida keys on this part of the coast. A fragment of cactus, *Opuntia*, sketched on another page,[8] is from the above-named key, and is abundant there. The fruit, an inch in length, is gathered, and made into a sauce, of which some people are fond. This species forms thorny, impenetrable thickets. One joint that I measured was fifteen inches long.

[8] Of the original journal.

The mainland of Florida is less salubrious than the islands, but no portion of this coast, nor of the flat border which sweeps from Maryland to Texas, is quite free from malaria. All the inhabitants of this region, whether black or white, are liable to be prostrated by the ever-present fever and ague, to say nothing of the plagues of cholera and yellow fever that come and go suddenly like storms, prostrating the population and cutting gaps in it like hurricanes in woods.

The world, we are told, was made especially for man—a presumption not supported by all the facts. A numerous class of men are painfully astonished whenever they find anything, living or dead, in all God's universe, which they cannot eat or render in some way what they call useful to themselves. They have precise dogmatic insight of the intentions of the Creator, and it is hardly possible to be guilty of irreverence in speaking of *their* God any more than of heathen idols. He is regarded as a civilized, law-abiding gentleman in favor either of a republican form of government or of a limited monarchy; believes in the literature and language of England; is a warm supporter of the English constitution and Sunday schools and missionary societies; and is as purely a manufactured article as any puppet of a half-penny theater.

With such views of the Creator it is, of course, not surprising that erroneous views should be entertained of the creation. To such properly trimmed people, the sheep, for example, is an easy problem—food and clothing "for us," eating grass and daisies white by divine appointment for this predestined purpose, on perceiving the demand for wool that would be occasioned by the eating of the apple in the Garden of Eden.

In the same pleasant plan, whales are store-houses of oil for us, to help out the stars in lighting our dark ways until the discovery of the Pennsylvania oil wells. Among plants, hemp, to say nothing of the cereals, is a case of evident destination for ships' rigging, wrapping packages, and hanging the wicked. Cotton is another other plain case of clothing. Iron was made for hammers and ploughs, and lead for bullets all intended for us. And so of other small handfuls of insignificant things.

But if we should ask these profound expositors of God's intentions, How about those man-eating animals—lions, tigers, alligators—which smack their lips over raw man? Or about those myriads of noxious insects that destroy labor and drink his blood? Doubtless man was intended for food and drink for all these? Oh, no! Not at all! These are unresolvable difficulties connected with Eden's apple and the Devil. Why does water drown its lord? Why do so many minerals poison him? Why are so many plants and fishes deadly enemies? Why is the lord of creation subjected to the same laws of life as his subjects? Oh, all these things are satanic, or in some way connected with the first garden.

Now, it never seems to occur to these far-seeing teachers that Nature's object in making animals and plants might possibly be first of all the happiness of each one of them, not the creation of all for the happiness of one. Why should man value himself as more than a small part of the one great unit of creation? And what creature of all that the Lord has taken the pains to make is not essential to the completeness of that unit—the cosmos? The universe would be incomplete without man; but it would also be incomplete without the smallest transmicroscopic creature that dwells beyond our conceitful eyes and knowledge.

From the dust of the earth, from the common elementary fund, the Creator has made *Homo Sapiens*. From the same material he has made every other creature, however noxious and insignificant to us. They are earth-born companions and our fellow mortals. The fearfully good, the orthodox, of this laborious patch-work of modern civilization cry "Heresy" on every one whose sympathies reach a single hair's breadth beyond the boundary epidermis of our own species. Not content with taking all of earth, they also claim the celestial country as the only ones who possess the kind of souls for which that imponderable empire was planned.

This star, our own good earth, made many a successful journey around the heavens ere man was made, and whole kingdoms of creatures enjoyed existence and returned to dust ere man appeared to claim them. After human beings have also played their part in Creation's plan, they too may disappear without any general burning or extraordinary commotion whatever.

Plants are credited with but dim and uncertain sensation, and minerals with positively none at all. But why may not even a mineral arrangement of matter be endowed with sensation of a kind that we in our blind exclusive perfection can have no manner of communication with?

But I have wandered from my object. I stated a page or two back that man claimed the earth was made for him, and I was going to say that venomous beasts, thorny plants, and deadly diseases of certain parts of the earth prove that the whole world was not made for him. When an animal from a tropical climate is taken to high latitudes, it may perish of cold, and we say that such an animal was never intended for so severe a climate. But when man betakes himself to sickly parts of the tropics and perishes, he cannot see that he was never intended for such deadly climates. No, he will rather accuse the first mother of the cause of the difficulty, though she may never have seen a fever district; or will consider it a providential chastisement for some self-invented form of sin.

Furthermore, all uneatable and uncivilizable animals, and all plants which carry prickles, are deplorable evils which, according to closet researches of clergy, require the cleansing chemistry of universal planetary combustion. But more than aught else mankind requires burning, as being in great part wicked, and if that transmundane furnace can be so applied and regulated as to smelt and purify us into conformity with the rest of the terrestrial creation, then the tophetization of the erratic genus Homo were a consummation devoutly to be prayed for. But, glad to leave these ecclesiastical fires and blunders, I joyfully return to the immortal truth and immortal beauty of Nature.

Chapter VII.

A Sojourn in Cuba

One day in January I climbed to the housetop to get a view of another of the fine sunsets of this land of flowers. The landscape was a strip of clear Gulf water, a strip of sylvan coast, a tranquil company of shell and coral keys, and a gloriously colored sky without a threatening cloud. All the winds were hushed and the calm of the heavens was as profound as that of the palmy islands and their encircling waters. As I gazed from one to another of the palm-crowned keys enclosed by the sunset-colored dome, my eyes chanced to rest upon the fluttering sails of a Yankee schooner that was threading the tortuous channel in the coral reef leading to the harbor of Cedar Keys. "There," thought I, "perhaps I may sail in that pretty white moth." She proved to be the schooner Island Belle.

One day soon after her arrival I went over the key to the harbor, for I was now strong enough to walk. Some of her crew were ashore after water. I waited until their casks were filled, and went with them to the vessel in their boat. Ascertained that she was ready to sail with her cargo of lumber for Cuba. I engaged passage on her for twenty-five dollars, and asked her sharp-visaged captain when he would sail. "Just as soon," said he, "as we get a north wind. We have had northers enough when we did not want them, and now we have this dying breath from the south."

Hurrying back to the house, I gathered my plants, took leave of my kind friends, and went aboard, and soon, as if to calm the captain's complaints, Boreas came foaming loud and strong. The little craft was quickly trimmed and snugged, her inviting sails spread open, and away she dashed to her ocean home like an exulting war-horse to the battle. Islet after islet speedily grew dim and sank beneath the horizon. Deeper became the blue of the water, and in a few hours all of Florida vanished.

This excursion on the sea, the first one after twenty years in the woods, was of course exceedingly interesting, and I was full of hope, glad to be once more on my journey to the South. Boreas increased in power and the Island Belle appeared to glory in her speed and managed her full-spread wings as gracefully as a sea-bird. In less than a day our norther increased in strength to the storm point. Deeper and wider became the valleys, and yet higher the hills of the round plain of water. The flying jib and gaff topsails were lowered and mainsails close-reefed, and our deck was white with broken wave-tops.

"You had better go below," said the captain. "The Gulf Stream, opposed by this wind, is raising a heavy sea and you will be sick. No landsman can stand this long." I replied that I hoped the storm would be as violent as his ship could bear, that I enjoyed the scenery of such a sea so much that it was impossible to be sick, that I had long waited in the woods for just such a storm, and that, now that the precious thing had come, I would remain on deck and enjoy it. "Well," said he, "if you can stand this, you are the first landsman I ever saw that could."

I remained on deck, holding on by a rope to keep from being washed overboard, and watched the behavior of the Belle as she dared nobly on; but my attention was mostly directed among the glorious fields of foam-topped waves. The wind had a mysterious voice and carried nothing now of the songs of birds or of the rustling of palms and fragrant vines. Its burden was gathered from a stormy expanse of crested waves and briny tangles. I could see no striving in those magnificent wave-motions, no raging; all the storm was apparently inspired with nature's beauty and harmony. Every wave was obedient and harmonious as the smoothest ripple of a forest lake, and after dark all the water was phosphorescent like silver fire, a glorious sight.

Our luminous storm was all too short for me. Cuba's rock-waves loomed above the white waters early in the morning. The sailors, accustomed to detect the faintest land line, pointed out well-known guiding harbor-marks back of the Morro Castle long before I could see them through the flying spray. We sailed landward for several hours, the misty shore becoming gradually more earthlike. A flock of white-plumaged ships was departing from the Havana harbor, or, like us, seeking to enter it. No sooner had our little schooner flapped her sails in the lee of the Castle than she was boarded by a swarm of daintily dressed officials who were good-naturedly and good-gesturedly making all sorts of inquiries, while our busy captain, paying little attention to them, was giving orders to his crew.

The neck of the harbor is narrow and it is seldom possible to sail in to appointed anchorage without the aid of a steam tug. Our captain wished to save his money, but after much profitless tacking was compelled to take the proffered aid of steam, when we soon reached our quiet mid-harbor quarters and dropped anchor among ships of every size from every sea.

I was still four or five hundred yards from land and could determine no plant in sight excepting the long arched leaf banners of the banana and the palm, which made a brave show on the Morro Hill. When we were approaching the land, I observed that in some places it was distinctly yellow and I wondered while we were yet some miles distant whether the color belonged to the ground or to sheets of flowers. From our harbor home I could now see that the color was plant-gold. On one side of the harbor was a city of these yellow plants; on the other, a city of yellow stucco houses, narrowly and confusedly congregated.

"Do you want to go ashore?" said the captain to me. "Yes," I replied, "but I wish to go to the plant side of the harbor." "Oh, well," he said, "come with me now. There are some fine squares and gardens in the city, full of all sorts of trees and flowers. Enjoy these to-day, and some other day we will all go over the Morro Hill with you and gather shells. All kinds of shells are over there; but these yellow slopes that you see are covered only with weeds."

We jumped into the boat and a couple of sailors pulled us to the thronged, noisy wharf. It was Sunday afternoon,[9] the noisiest day of a Havana week. Cathedral bells and prayers in the forenoon, theaters and bull-fight bells and bellowings in the afternoon! Lowly whispered prayers to the saints and the Virgin, followed by shouts of praise or reproach to bulls and matadors! I made free with fine oranges and bananas and many other fruits. Pineapple I had never seen before. Wandered about the narrow streets, stunned with the babel of strange sounds and sights; went gazing, also, among the gorgeously flowered garden squares, and then waited among some boxed merchandise until our captain, detained by business, arrived. Was glad to escape to our little schooner Belle again, weary and heavy laden with excitement and tempting fruits.

[9] Doubtless January 12, 1868.

As night came on, a thousand lights starred the great town. I was now in one of my happy dreamlands, the fairest of West India islands. But how, I wondered, shall I be able to escape from this great city confusion? How shall I reach nature in this delectable land? Consulting my map, I longed to climb the central mountain range of the island and trace it through all its forests and valleys and over its summit peaks, a distance of seven or eight hundred miles. But alas! though out of Florida swamps, fever was yet weighing me down, and a mile of city walking was quite exhausting. The weather too was oppressively warm and sultry.

January 16. During the few days since our arrival the sun usually has risen unclouded, pouring down pure gold, rich and dense, for one or two hours. Then islandlike masses of white-edged cumuli suddenly appeared, grew to storm size, and in a few minutes discharged rain in tepid plashing bucketfuls, accompanied with high wind. This was followed by a short space of calm, half-cloudy sky, delightfully fragrant with flowers, and again the air would become hot, thick, and sultry.

This weather, as may readily be perceived, was severe to one so weak and feverish, and after a dozen trials of strength over the Morro Hill and along the coast northward for shells and flowers, I was sadly compelled to see that no enthusiasm could enable me to walk to the interior. So I was obliged to limit my researches to within ten or twelve miles of Havana. Captain Parsons offered his ship as my headquarters and my weakness prevented me from spending a single night ashore.

The daily programme for nearly all the month that I spent here was about as follows: After breakfast a sailor rowed me ashore on the north side of the harbor. A few minutes' walk took me past the Morro Castle and out of sight of the town on a broad cactus common, about as solitary and untrodden as the tangles of Florida. Here I zigzagged and gathered prizes among unnumbered plants and shells along the shore, stopping to press the plant specimens and to rest in the shade of vine-heaps and bushes until sundown. The happy hours stole away until I had to return to the schooner. Either I was seen by the sailors who usually came for me, or I hired a boat to take me back. Arrived, I reached up my press and a big handful of flowers, and with a little help climbed up the side of my floating home.

Refreshed with supper and rest, I recounted my adventures in the vine tangles, cactus thickets, sunflower swamps and along the shore among the breakers. My flower specimens, also, and pocketfuls of shells and corals had to be reviewed. Next followed a cool, dreamy hour on deck amid the lights of the town and the various vessels coming and departing.

Many strange sounds were heard: the vociferous, unsmotherable bells, the heavy thundering of cannon from the Castle, and the shouts of the sentinels in measured time. Combined they made the most incessant sharp-angled mass of noise that I ever was doomed to hear. Nine or ten o'clock found me in a small bunk with the harbor wavelets tinkling outside close to my ear. The hours of sleep were filled with dreams of heavy heat, of fruitless efforts for the disentanglement of vines, or of running from curling breakers back to the Morro, etc. Thus my days and nights went on.

Occasionally I was persuaded by the captain to go ashore in the evening on his side of the harbor, accompanied perhaps by two or three other captains. After landing and telling the sailors when to call for us, we hired a carriage and drove to the upper end of the city, to a fine public square adorned with shady walks and magnificent plants. A brass band in imposing uniform played the characteristic lance-noted martial airs of the Spanish. Evening is the fashionable hour for aristocratic drives about the streets and squares, the only time that is delightfully cool. I never saw elsewhere people so neatly and becomingly dressed. The proud best-family Cubans may fairly be called beautiful, are under- rather than over-sized, with features exquisitely moulded, and set off with silks and broadcloth in excellent taste. Strange that their amusements should be so coarse. Bull-fighting, brain-splitting bell-ringing, and the most piercing artificial music appeal to their taste.

The rank and wealth of Havana nobility, when out driving, seems to be indicated by the distance of their horses from the body of the carriage. The higher the rank, the longer the shafts of the carriage, and the clumsier and more ponderous are the wheels, which are not unlike those of a cannon-cart. A few of these carriages have shafts twenty-five feet in length, and the brilliant-liveried negro driver on the lead horse, twenty or thirty feet in advance of the horse in the shafts, is beyond calling distance of his master.

Havana abounds in public squares, which in all my random strolls throughout the big town I found to be well watered, well cared for, well planted, and full of exceedingly showy and interesting plants, rare even amid the exhaustless luxuriance of Cuba. These squares also contained fine marble statuary and were furnished with seats in the shadiest places. Many of the walks were paved instead of graveled.

The streets of Havana are crooked, labyrinthic, and exceedingly narrow. The sidewalks are only about a foot wide. A traveler experiences delightful relief when, heated and wearied by rains through the breadth of the dingy yellow town, dodging a way through crowds of men and mules and lumbering carts and carriages, he at length finds shelter in the spacious, dustless, cool, flowery squares; still more when, emerging from all the din and darkness of these lanelike streets, he suddenly finds himself out in the middle of the harbor, inhaling full-drawn breaths of the sea breezes.

The interior of the better houses which came under my observation struck me with the profusion of dumpy, ill-proportioned pillars at the entrances and in the halls, and with the spacious open-fielded appearance of their enclosed square house-gardens or courts. Cubans in general appear to me superfinely polished, polite, and agreeable in society, but in their treatment of animals they are cruel. I saw more downright brutal cruelty to mules and horses during the few weeks I stayed there than in my whole life elsewhere. Live chickens and hogs are tied in bunches by the legs and carried to market thus, slung on a mule. In their general treatment of all sorts of animals they seem to have no thought for them beyond cold-blooded, selfish interest.

In tropical regions it is easy to build towns, but it is difficult to subdue their armed and united plant inhabitants, and to clear fields and make them blossom with breadstuff. The plant people of temperate regions, feeble, unarmed, unallied, disappear under the trampling feet of flocks, herds, and man, leaving their homes to enslavable plants which follow the will of man and furnish him with food. But the armed and united plants of the tropics hold their rightful kingdom plantfully, nor, since the first appearance of Lord Man, have they ever suffered defeat.

A large number of Cuba's wild plants circle closely about Havana. In five minutes' walk from the wharf I could reach the undisturbed settlements of

Nature. The field of the greater portion of my rambling researches was a strip of rocky common, silent and unfrequented by anybody save an occasional beggar at Nature's door asking a few roots and seeds. This natural strip extended ten miles along the coast northward, with but few large-sized trees and bushes, but rich in magnificent vines, cacti-composites, leguminous plants, grasses, etc. The wild flowers of this seaside field are a happy band, closely joined in splendid array. The trees shine with blossoms and with light reflected from the leaves. The individuality of the vines is lost in trackless, interlacing, twisting, overheaping union.

Our American "South" is rich in flowery vines. In some districts almost every tree is crowned with them, aiding each other in grace and beauty. Indiana, Kentucky, and Tennessee have the grapevine in predominant numbers and development. Farther south dwell the greenbriers and countless leguminous vines. A vine common among the Florida islets, perhaps belonging to the dogbane family, over-runs live-oaks and palmettos, with frequently more than a hundred stems twisted into one cable. Yet in no section of the South are there such complicated and such gorgeously flowered vine-tangles as flourish in armed safety in the hot and humid wild gardens of Cuba.

The longest and the shortest vine that I found in Cuba were both leguminous. I have said that the harbor side of the Morro Hill is clothed with tall yellow-flowered composites through which it is difficult to pass. But there are smooth, velvety, lawnlike patches in these *Compositæ* forests. Coming suddenly upon one of these open places, I stopped to admire its greenness and smoothness, when I observed a sprinkling of large papilionaceous blossoms among the short green grass. The long composites that bordered this little lawn were entwined and almost smothered with vines which bore similar corollas in tropic abundance.

I at once decided that these sprinkled flowers had been blown off the encompassing tangles and had been kept fresh by dew and by spray from the sea. But, on stooping to pick one of them up, I was surprised to find that it was attached to Mother Earth by a short, prostrate, slender hair of a vine stem, bearing, besides the one large blossom, a pair or two of linear leaves. The flower weighed more than stem, root, and leaves combined. Thus, in a land of creeping and twining giants, we find also this charming, diminutive simplicity—the vine reduced to its lowest terms.

The longest vine, prostrate and untwined like its little neighbor, covers patches of several hundred square yards with its countless branches and close growth of upright, trifoliate, smooth green leaves. The flowers are as plain and unshowy in size and color as those of the sweet peas of gardens. The seeds are large and satiny. The whole plant is noble in its motions and features, covering the ground with a depth of unconfused leafage which I have never seen equaled by any other plant. The extent of leaf-surface is greater, I think, than that of a large Kentucky oak. It grows, as far as my observation has reached, only upon shores, in a soil composed of broken shells and corals, and extends exactly to the water-line of the highest-reaching waves. The same plant is abundant in Florida.

The cacti form an important part of the plant population of my ramble ground. They are various as the vines, consisting now of a diminutive joint or two hid in the weeds, now rising into bushy trees, wide-topped, with trunks a foot in diameter, and with glossy, dark-green joints that reflect light like the silex-varnished palms. They are planted for fences, together with the Spanish bayonet and agave.

In one of my first walks I was laboriously scrambling among some low rocks gathering ferns and vines, when I was startled by finding my face close to a great snake, whose body was disposed carelessly like a castaway rope among the weeds and stones. After escaping and coming to my senses, I discovered that the snake was a member of the vegetable kingdom, capable of no dangerous amount of locomotion, but possessed of many a fang, and prostrate as though under the curse of Eden, "Upon thy belly shalt thou go and dust shalt thou eat."

One day, after luxuriating in the riches of my Morro pasture, and pressing many new specimens, I went down to the bank of brilliant wave-washed shells to rest awhile in their beauty, and to watch the breakers that a powerful norther was heaving in splendid rank along the coral boundary. I gathered pocketfuls of shells, mostly small but fine in color and form, and bits of rosy coral. Then I amused myself by noting the varying colors of the waves and the different forms of their curved and blossoming crests. While thus alone and free it was interesting to learn the richly varied songs, or what we mortals call the roar, of expiring breakers. I compared their variation with the different distances to which the broken wave-water reached landward in its farthest-flung foam-wreaths, and endeavored to form some idea of the one great song sounding forever all around the white-blooming shores of the world.

Rising from my shell seat, I watched a wave leaping from the deep and coming far up the beveled strand to bloom and die in a mass of white. Then I followed the spent waters in their return to the blue deep, wading in their spangled, decaying fragments until chased back up the bank by the coming of another wave. While thus playing half studiously, I discovered in the rough, beaten deathbed of the wave a little plant with closed flowers. It was crouching in a hollow of the brown wave-washed rock, and one by one the chanting, dying waves rolled over it. The tips of its delicate pink petals peered above the clasping green calyx. "Surely," said I, as I stooped over it for a moment, before the oncoming of another wave, "surely you cannot be living here! You must have been blown from some warm bank, and rolled into this little hollow crack like a dead shell." But, running back after every retiring wave, I found that its roots were wedged into a shallow wrinkle of the coral rock, and that this wave-beaten chink was indeed its dwelling-place.

I had oftentimes admired the adaptation displayed in the structure of the stately dulse and other seaweeds, but never thought to find a highbred flowering plant dwelling amid waves in the stormy, roaring domain of the sea. This little plant has smooth globular leaves, fleshy and translucent like beads, but green like those of other land plants. The flower is about five eighths of an inch in diameter, rose-purple, opening in calm weather, when deserted by the waves. In general appearance it is like a small portulaca. The strand, as far as I walked it, was luxuriantly fringed with woody *Compositæ*, two or three feet in height, their tops purple and golden with a profusion of flowers. Among these I discovered a small bush whose yellow flowers were ideal; all the parts were present regularly alternate and in fives, and all separate, a plain harmony.

When a page is written over but once it may be easily read; but if it be written over and over with characters of every size and style, it soon becomes unreadable, although not a single confused meaningless mark or thought may occur among all the written characters to mar its perfection. Our limited powers are similarly perplexed and overtaxed in reading the inexhaustible pages of nature, for they are written over and over uncountable times, written in characters of every size and color, sentences composed of sentences, every part of a character a sentence. There is not a fragment in all nature, for every relative fragment of one thing is a full harmonious unit in itself. All together form the one grand palimpsest of the world.

One of the most common plants of my pasture was the agave. It is sometimes used for fencing. One day, in looking back from the top of the Morro Hill, as I was returning to the Island Belle, I chanced to observe two poplar-like trees about twenty-five feet in height. They were growing in a dense patch of cactus and vine-knotted sunflowers. I was anxious to see anything so homelike as a poplar, and so made haste towards the two strange trees, making a way through the cactus and sunflower jungle that protected them. I was surprised to find that what I took to be poplars were agaves in flower, the first I had seen. They were almost out of flower, and fast becoming wilted at the approach of death. Bulbs were scattered about, and a good many still remained on the branches, which gave it a fruited appearance.

The stem of the agave seems enormous in size when one considers that it is the growth of a few weeks. This plant is said to make a mighty effort to flower and mature its seeds and then to die of exhaustion. Now there is not, so far as I have seen, a mighty effort or the need of one, in wild Nature. She accomplishes her ends without unquiet effort, and perhaps there is nothing more mighty in the development of the flower-stem of the agave than in the development of a grass panicle.

Havana has a fine botanical garden. I spent pleasant hours in its magnificent flowery arbors and around its shady fountains. There is a palm avenue which is considered wonderfully stately and beautiful, fifty palms in two straight lines, each rigidly perpendicular. The smooth round shafts, slightly thicker in the middle, appear to be productions of the lathe, rather than vegetable stems. The fifty arched crowns, inimitably balanced, blaze in the sunshine like heaps of stars that have fallen from the skies. The stems were about sixty or seventy feet in height, the crowns about fifteen feet in diameter.

Along a stream-bank were tall, waving bamboos, leafy as willows, and infinitely graceful in wind gestures. There was one species of palm, with immense bipinnate leaves and leaflets fringed, jagged, and one-sided, like those of *Adiantum*. Hundreds of the most gorgeous-flowered plants, some of them large trees, belonging to the *Leguminosae*. Compared with what I have before seen in artificial flower-gardens, this is past comparison the grandest. It is a perfect metropolis of the brightest and most exuberant of garden plants, watered by handsome fountains, while graveled and finely bordered walks slant and curve in all directions, and in all kinds of fanciful playground styles, more like the fairy gardens of the Arabian Nights than any ordinary man-made pleasure-ground.

In Havana I saw the strongest and the ugliest negroes that I have met in my whole walk. The stevedores of the Havana wharf are muscled in true giant style, enabling them to tumble and toss ponderous casks and boxes of sugar weighing hundreds of pounds as if they were empty. I heard our own brawny sailors, after watching them at work a few minutes, express unbounded admiration of their strength, and wish that their hard outbulging muscles were for sale. The countenances of some of the negro orange-selling dames express a devout good-natured ugliness that I never could have conceived any arrangement of flesh and blood to be capable of. Besides oranges they sold pineapples, bananas, and lottery tickets.

Chapter VIII.

By a Crooked Route to California

After passing a month in this magnificent island, and finding that my health was not improving, I made up my mind to push on to South America while my stock of strength, such as it was, lasted. But fortunately I could not find passage for any South American port. I had long wished to visit the Orinoco basin and in particular the basin of the Amazon. My plan was to get ashore anywhere on the north end of the continent, push on southward through the wilderness around the headwaters of the Orinoco, until I reached a tributary of the Amazon, and float down on a raft or skiff the whole length of the great river to its mouth. It seems strange that such a trip should ever have entered the dreams of any person, however enthusiastic and full of youthful daring, particularly under the disadvantages of poor health, of funds less than a hundred dollars, and of the insalubrity of the Amazon Valley.

Fortunately, as I said, after visiting all the shipping agencies, I could not find a vessel of any sort bound for South America, and so made up a plan to go North, to the longed-for cold weather of New York, and thence to the forests and mountains of California. There, I thought, I shall find health and new plants and mountains, and after a year spent in that interesting country I can carry out my Amazon plans.

It seemed hard to leave Cuba thus unseen and unwalked, but illness forbade my stay and I had to comfort myself with the hope of returning to its waiting treasures in full health. In the mean time I prepared for immediate departure. When I was resting in one of the Havana gardens, I noticed in a New York paper an advertisement of cheap fares to California. I consulted Captain Parsons concerning a passage to New York, where I could find a ship for California. At this time none of the California ships touched at Cuba.

"Well," said he, pointing toward the middle of the harbor, "there is a trim little schooner loaded with oranges for New York, and these little fruiters are fast sailers. You had better see her captain about a passage, for she must be about ready to sail." So I jumped into the dinghy and a sailor rowed me over to the fruiter. Going aboard, I inquired for the captain, who soon appeared on deck and readily agreed to carry me to New York for twenty-five dollars. Inquiring when he would sail, "To-morrow morning at daylight," he replied, "if this norther slacks a little; but my papers are made out, and you will have to see the American consul to get permission to leave on my ship."

I immediately went to the city, but was unable to find the consul, whereupon I determined to sail for New York without any formal leave. Early next morning, after leaving the Island Belle and bidding Captain Parsons good-bye, I was rowed to the fruiter and got aboard. Notwithstanding the north wind was still as boisterous as ever, our Dutch captain was resolved to face it, confident in the strength of his all-oak little schooner.

Vessels leaving the harbor are stopped at the Morro Castle to have their clearance papers examined; in particular, to see that no runaway slaves were being carried away. The officials came alongside our little ship, but did not come aboard. They were satisfied by a glance at the consul's clearance paper, and with the declaration of the captain, when asked whether he had any negroes, that he had "not a d——d one." "All right, then," shouted the officials, "farewell! A pleasant voyage to you!" As my name was not on the ship's papers, I stayed below, out of sight, until I felt the heaving of the waves and knew that we were fairly out on the open sea. The Castle towers, the hills, the palms, and the wave-white strand, all faded in the distance, and our mimic sea-bird was at home in the open stormy gulf, curtsying to every wave and facing bravely to the wind.

Two thousand years ago our Saviour told Nicodemus that he did not know where the winds came from, nor where they were going. And now in this Golden Age, though we Gentiles know the birthplace of many a wind and also "whither it is going," yet we know about as little of winds in general as those Palestinian Jews, and our ignorance, despite the powers of science, can never be much less profound than it is at present.

The substance of the winds is too thin for human eyes, their written language is too difficult for human minds, and their spoken language mostly too faint for the ears. A mechanism is said to have been invented whereby the human organs of speech are made to write their own utterances. But without any extra mechanical contrivance, every speaker also writes as he speaks. All things in the creation of God register their own acts. The poet was mistaken when he said, "From the wing no scar the sky sustains." His eyes were simply too dim to see the scar. In sailing past Cuba I could see a fringe of foam along the coast, but could hear no sound of waves, simply because my ears could not hear wave-dashing at that distance. Yet every bit of spray was sounding in my ears.

The subject brings to mind a few recollections of the winds I heard in my late journey. In my walk from Indiana to the Gulf, earth and sky, plants and people, and all things changeable were constantly changing. Even in Kentucky nature and art have many a characteristic shibboleth. The people differ in language and in customs. Their architecture is generically different from that of their immediate neighbors on the north, not only in planters' mansions, but in barns and granaries and the cabins of the poor. But thousands of familiar flower faces looked from every hill and valley. I noted no difference in the sky, and the winds spoke the same things. I did not feel myself in a strange land.

In Tennessee my eyes rested upon the first mountain scenery I ever beheld. I was rising higher than ever before; strange trees were beginning to appear; alpine flowers and shrubs were meeting me at every step. But these Cumberland Mountains were timbered with oak, and were not unlike Wisconsin hills piled upon each other, and the strange plants were like those that were not strange. The sky was changed only a little, and the winds not by a single detectible note. Therefore, neither was Tennessee a strange land.

But soon came changes thick and fast. After passing the mountainous corner of North Carolina and a little way into Georgia, I beheld from one of the last ridge-summits of the Alleghanies that vast, smooth, sandy slope that reaches from the mountains to the sea. It is wooded with dark, branchy pines which were all strangers to me. Here the grasses, which are an earth-covering at the North, grow wide apart in tall clumps and tufts like saplings. My known flower companions were leaving me now, not one by one as in Kentucky and Tennessee, but in whole tribes and genera, and companies of shining strangers came trooping upon me in countless ranks. The sky, too, was changed, and I could detect strange sounds in the winds. Now I began to feel myself "a stranger in a strange land."

But in Florida came the greatest change of all, for here grows the palmetto, and here blow the winds so strangely toned by them. These palms and these winds severed the last strands of the cord that united me with home. Now I was a stranger, indeed. I was delighted, astonished, confounded, and gazed in wonderment blank and overwhelming as if I had fallen upon another star. But in all of this long, complex series of changes, one of the greatest, and the last of all, was the change I found in the tone and language of the winds. They no longer came with the old home music gathered from open prairies and waving fields of oak, but they passed over many a strange string. The leaves of magnolia, smooth like polished steel, the immense inverted forests of tillandsia banks, and the princely crowns of palms—upon these the winds made strange music, and at the coming-on of night had overwhelming power to present the distance from friends and home, and the completeness of my isolation from all things familiar.

Elsewhere I have already noted that when I was a day's journey from the Gulf, a wind blew upon me from the sea—the first sea breeze that had touched me in twenty years. I was plodding alone with my satchel and plants, leaning wearily forward, a little sore from approaching fever, when suddenly I felt the salt air, and before I had time to think, a whole flood of long-dormant associations rolled in upon me. The Firth of Forth, the Bass Rock, Dunbar Castle, and the winds and rocks and hills came upon the wings of that wind, and stood in as clear and sudden light as a landscape flashed upon the view by a blaze of lightning in a dark night.

I like to cling to a small chip of a ship like ours when the sea is rough, and long, comet-tailed streamers are blowing from the curled top of every wave. A big vessel responds awkwardly with mixed gestures to several waves at once, lumbering along like a loose floating island. But our little schooner, buoyant as a gull, glides up one side and down the other of each wave hill in delightful rhythm. As we advanced the scenery increased in grandeur and beauty. The waves heaved higher and grew wider, with corresponding motion. It was delightful to ride over this unsullied country of ever-changing water, and when looking upward from the shallow vales, or abroad over the round expanse from the tops of the wave hills, I almost forgot at times that the glassy, treeless country was forbidden to walkers. How delightful it would be to ramble over it on foot, enjoying the transparent crystal ground, and the music of its rising and falling hillocks, unmarred by the ropes and spars of a ship; to study the plants of these waving plains and their stream-currents; to sleep in wild weather in a bed of phosphorescent wave-foam, or briny scented seaweeds; to see the fishes by night in pathways of phosphorescent light; to walk the glassy plain in calm, with birds and flocks of glittering flying fishes here and there, or by night with every star pictured in its bosom!

But even of the land only a small portion is free to man, and if he, among other journeys on forbidden paths, ventures among the ice lands and hot lands, or up in the air in balloon bubbles, or on the ocean in ships, or down into it a little way in smothering diving-bells—in all such small adventures man is admonished and often punished in ways which clearly show him that he is in places for which, to use an approved phrase, he was never designed. However, in view of the rapid advancement of our time, no one can tell how far our star may finally be subdued to man's will. At all events I enjoyed this drifting locomotion to some extent.

The tar-scented community of a ship is a study in itself—a despotism on the small territory of a few drifting planks pinned together. But as our crew consisted only of four sailors, a mate, and the captain, there were no signs of despotism. We all dined at one table, enjoying our fine store of salt mackerel and plum duff, with endless abundance of oranges. Not only was the hold of our little ship filled with loose, unboxed oranges, but the deck also was filled up level with the rails, and we had to walk over the top of the golden fruit on boards.

Flocks of flying fishes often flew across the ship, one or two occasionally falling among the oranges. These the sailors were glad to capture to sell in New York as curiosities, or to give away to friends. But the captain had a large Newfoundland dog who got the largest share of these unfortunate fishes. He used to jump from a dozing sleep as soon as he heard the fluttering of their wings, then pounce and feast leisurely on them before the sailors could reach the spot where they fell.

In passing through the Straits of Florida the winds died away and the sea was smoothed to unruffled calm. The water here is very transparent and of delightfully pure pale-blue color, as different from ordinary dull-colored water as town smoke from mountain air. I could see the bottom as distinctly as one sees the ground when riding over it. It seemed strange that our ship should be upborne in such an ethereal liquid as this, and that we did not run aground where the bottom seemed so near.

One morning, while among the Bahama dots of islands, we had calm sky and calm sea. The sun had risen in cloudless glory, when I observed a large flock of flying fish, a short distance from us, closely pursued by a dolphin. These fish-swallows rose in pretty good order, skimmed swiftly ahead for fifty or a hundred yards in a low arc, then dipped below the surface. Dripping and sparkling, they rose again in a few seconds and glanced back into the lucid brine with wonderful speed, but without apparent terror.

At length the dolphin, gaining on the flock, dashed into the midst of them, and now all order was at an end. They rose in scattering disorder, in all directions, like a flock of birds charged by a hawk. The pursuing dolphin also leaped into the air, showing his splendid colors and wonderful speed. After the first scattering flight all steady pursuit was useless, and the dolphin had but to pounce about in the broken mob of its weary prey until satisfied with his meal.

We are apt to look out on the great ocean and regard it as but a half-blank part of our globe—a sort of desert, "a waste of water." But, land animals though we be, land is about as unknown to us as the sea, for the turbid glances we gain of the ocean in general through commercial eyes are comparatively worthless. Now that science is making comprehensive surveys of the life of the sea, and the forms of its basins, and similar surveys are being made into the land deserts, hot and cold, we may at length discover that the sea is as full of life as the land. None can tell how far man's knowledge may yet reach.

After passing the Straits and sailing up the coast, when about opposite the south end of the Carolina coast, we had stiff head winds all the way to New York and our able little vessel was drenched all day long. Of course our load of oranges suffered, and since they were boarded over level with the rail, we had difficulty in walking and had many chances of being washed overboard. The flying fishes off Cape Hatteras appeared to take pleasure in shooting across from wave-top to wave-top. They avoided the ship during the day, but frequently fell among the oranges at night. The sailors caught many, but our big Newfoundland dog jumped for them faster than the sailors, and so almost monopolized the game.

When dark night fell on the stormy sea, the breaking waves of phosphorescent light were a glorious sight. On such nights I stood on the bowsprit holding on by a rope for hours in order to enjoy this phenomenon. How wonderful this light is! Developed in the sea by myriads of organized beings, it gloriously illuminates the pathways of the fishes, and every breaking wave, and in some places glows over large areas like sheet lightning. We sailed through large fields of seaweed, of which I procured specimens. I thoroughly enjoyed life in this novel little tar-and-oakum home, and, as the end of our voyage drew nigh, I was sorry at the thought of leaving it.

We were now, on the twelfth day, approaching New York, the big ship metropolis. We were in sight of the coast all day. The leafless trees and the snow appeared wonderfully strange. It was now about the end of February and snow covered the ground nearly to the water's edge. Arriving, as we did, in this rough winter weather from the intense heat and general tropical luxuriance of Cuba, the leafless, snow-white woods of New York struck us with all the novelty and impressiveness of a new world. A frosty blast was sweeping seaward from Sandy Hook. The sailors explored their wardrobes for their long-cast-off woolens, and pulled the ropes and managed the sails while muffled in clothing to the rotundity of Eskimos. For myself, long burdened with fever, the frosty wind, as it sifted through my loosened bones, was more delicious and grateful than ever was a spring-scented breeze.

We now had plenty of company; fleets of vessels were on the wing from all countries. Our taut little racer outwinded without exception all who, like her, were going to the port. Toward evening we were grinding and wedging our way through the ice-field of the river delta, which we passed with difficulty. Arrived in port at nine o'clock. The ship was deposited, like a cart at market, in a proper slip, and next morning we and our load of oranges, one third rotten, were landed. Thus all the purposes of our voyage were accomplished.

On our arrival the captain, knowing something of the lightness of my purse, told me that I could continue to occupy my bed on the ship until I sailed for California, getting my meals at a near-by restaurant. "This is the way we are all doing," he said. Consulting the newspapers, I found that the first ship, the Nebraska, sailed for Aspinwall in about ten days, and that the steerage passage to San Francisco by way of the Isthmus was only forty dollars.

In the mean time I wandered about the city without knowing a single person in it. My walks extended but little beyond sight of my little schooner home. I saw the name Central Park on some of the street-cars and thought I would like to visit it, but, fearing that I might not be able to find my way back, I dared not make the adventure. I felt completely lost in the vast throngs of people, the noise of the streets, and the immense size of the buildings. Often I thought I would like to explore the city if, like a lot of wild hills and valleys, it was clear of inhabitants.

The day before the sailing of the Panama ship I bought a pocket map of California and allowed myself to be persuaded to buy a dozen large maps, mounted on rollers, with a map of the world on one side and the United States on the other. In vain I said I had no use for them. "But surely you want to make money in California, don't you? Everything out there is very dear. We'll sell you a dozen of these fine maps for two dollars each and you can easily sell them in California for ten dollars apiece." I foolishly allowed myself to be persuaded. The maps made a very large, awkward bundle, but fortunately it was the only baggage I had except my little plant press and a small bag. I laid them in my berth in the steerage, for they were too large to be stolen and concealed.

There was a savage contrast between life in the steerage and my fine home on the little ship fruiter. Never before had I seen such a barbarous mob, especially at meals. Arrived at Aspinwall-Colon, we had half a day to ramble about before starting across the Isthmus. Never shall I forget the glorious flora, especially for the first fifteen or twenty miles along the Chagres River. The riotous exuberance of great forest trees, glowing in purple, red, and yellow flowers, far surpassed anything I had ever seen, especially of flowering trees, either in Florida or Cuba. I gazed from the car-platform enchanted. I fairly cried for joy and hoped that sometime I should be able to return and enjoy and study this most glorious of forests to my heart's content. We reached San Francisco about the first of April, and I remained there only one day, before starting for Yosemite Valley[10].

[10] At this point the journal ends. The remainder of this chapter is taken from a letter written to Mrs. Ezra S. Carr from the neighborhood of Twenty Hill Hollow in July, 1868.

I followed the Diablo foothills along the San José Valley to Gilroy, thence over the Diablo Mountains to the valley of the San Joaquin by the Pacheco Pass, thence down the valley opposite the mouth of the Merced River, thence across the San Joaquin, and up into the Sierra Nevada to the mammoth trees of Mariposa, and the glorious Yosemite, and thence down the Merced to this place.[11] The goodness of the weather as I journeyed toward Pacheco was beyond all praise and description—fragrant, mellow, and bright. The sky was perfectly delicious, sweet enough for the breath of angels; every draught of it gave a separate and distinct piece of pleasure. I do not believe that Adam and Eve ever tasted better in their balmiest nook.

[11] Near Snelling, Merced County, California.

The last of the Coast Range foothills were in near view all the way to Gilroy. Their union with the valley is by curves and slopes of inimitable beauty. They were robed with the greenest grass and richest light I ever beheld, and were colored and shaded with myriads of flowers of every hue, chiefly of purple and golden yellow. Hundreds of crystal rills joined song with the larks, filling all the valley with music like a sea, making it Eden from end to end.

The scenery, too, and all of nature in the Pass is fairly enchanting. Strange and beautiful mountain ferns are there, low in the dark cañons and high upon the rocky sunlit peaks; banks of blooming shrubs, and sprinklings and gatherings of garment flowers, precious and pure as ever enjoyed the sweets of a mountain home. And oh! what streams are there! beaming, glancing, each with music of its own, singing as they go, in shadow and light, onward upon their lovely, changing pathways to the sea. And hills rise over hills, and mountains over mountains, heaving, waving, swelling, in most glorious, overpowering, unreadable majesty.

When at last, stricken and faint like a crushed insect, you hope to escape from all the terrible grandeur of these mountain powers, other fountains, other scenes break forth before you; for there, in clear view, over heaps and rows of foothills, is laid a grand, smooth, outspread plain, watered by a river, and another range of peaky, snow-capped mountains a hundred miles in the distance. That plain is the valley of the San Joaquin, and those mountains are the great Sierra Nevada. The valley of the San Joaquin is the floweriest piece of world I ever walked, one vast, level, even flower-bed, a sheet of flowers, a smooth sea, ruffled a little in the middle by the tree fringing of the river and of smaller cross-streams here and there, from the mountains.

Florida is indeed a "land of flowers," but for every flower creature that dwells in its most delightsome places more than a hundred are living here. Here, here is Florida! Here they are not sprinkled apart with grass between as on our prairies, but grasses are sprinkled among the flowers; not as in Cuba, flowers piled upon flowers, heaped and gathered into deep, glowing masses, but side by side, flower to flower, petal to petal, touching but not entwined, branches weaving past and past each other, yet free and separate—one smooth garment, mosses next the ground, grasses above, petaled flowers between.

Before studying the flowers of this valley and their sky, and all of the furniture and sounds and adornments of their home, one can scarce believe that their vast assemblies are permanent; but rather that, actuated by some plant purpose, they had convened from every plain and mountain and meadow of their kingdom, and that the different coloring of patches, acres, and miles marks the bounds of the various tribes and family encampments.

Chapter IX.

Twenty Hill Hollow[12]

[12] This is the hub of the region where Mr. Muir spent the greater part of the summer of 1868 and the spring of 1869.

Were we to cross-cut the Sierra Nevada into blocks a dozen miles or so in thickness, each section would contain a Yosemite Valley and a river, together with a bright array of lakes and meadows, rocks and forests. The grandeur and inexhaustible beauty of each block would be so vast and over-satisfying that to choose among them would be like selecting slices of bread cut from the same loaf. One bread-slice might have burnt spots, answering to craters; another would be more browned; another, more crusted or raggedly cut; but all essentially the same. In no greater degree would the Sierra slices differ in general character. Nevertheless, we all would choose the Merced slice, because, being easier of access, it has been nibbled and tasted, and pronounced very good; and because of the concentrated form of its Yosemite, caused by certain conditions of baking, yeasting, and glacier-frosting of this portion of the great Sierra loaf. In like manner, we readily perceive that the great central plain is one batch of bread—one golden cake—and we are loath to leave these magnificent loaves for crumbs, however good.

After our smoky sky has been washed in the rains of winter, the whole complex row of Sierras appears from the plain as a simple wall, slightly beveled, and colored in horizontal bands laid one above another, as if entirely composed of partially straightened rainbows. So, also, the plain seen from the mountains has the same simplicity of smooth surface, colored purple and yellow, like a patchwork of irised clouds. But when we descend to this smooth-furred sheet, we discover complexity in its physical conditions equal to that of the mountains, though less strongly marked. In particular, that portion of the plain lying between the Merced and the Tuolumne, within ten miles of the slaty foothills, is most elaborately carved into valleys, hollows, and smooth undulations, and among them is laid the Merced Yosemite of the plain—Twenty Hill Hollow.

This delightful Hollow is less than a mile in length, and of just sufficient width to form a well-proportioned oval. It is situated about midway between the two rivers, and five miles from the Sierra foothills. Its banks are formed of twenty hemispherical hills; hence its name. They surround and enclose it on all sides, leaving only one narrow opening toward the southwest for the escape of its waters. The bottom of the Hollow is about two hundred feet below the level of the surrounding plain, and the tops of its hills are slightly below the general level.

Here is no towering dome, no Tissiack, to mark its place; and one may ramble close upon its rim before he is made aware of its existence. Its twenty hills are as wonder-fully regular in size and position as in form. They are like big marbles half buried in the ground, each poised and settled daintily into its place at a regular distance from its fellows, making a charming fairy-land of hills, with small, grassy valleys between, each valley having a tiny stream of its own, which leaps and sparkles out into the open hollow, uniting to form Hollow Creek.

Like all others in the immediate neighborhood, these twenty hills are composed of stratified lavas mixed with mountain drift in varying proportions. Some strata are almost wholly made up of volcanic matter lava and cinders—thoroughly ground and mixed by the waters that deposited them; others are largely composed of slate and quartz boulders of all degrees of coarseness, forming conglomerates. A few clear, open sections occur, exposing an elaborate history of seas, and glaciers, and volcanic floods—chapters of cinders and ashes that picture dark days when these bright snowy mountains were clouded in smoke and rivered and laked with living fire. A fearful age, say mortals, when these Sierras flowed lava to the sea. What horizons of flame! What atmospheres of ashes and smoke!

The conglomerates and lavas of this region are readily denuded by water. In the time when their parent sea was removed to form this golden plain, their regular surface, in great part covered with shallow lakes, showed little variation from motionless level until torrents of rain and floods from the mountains gradually sculptured the simple page to the present diversity of bank and brae, creating, in the section between the Merced and the Tuolumne, Twenty Hill Hollow, Lily Hollow, and the lovely valleys of Cascade and Castle Creeks, with many others nameless and unknown, seen only by hunters and shepherds, sunk in the wide bosom of the plain, like undiscovered gold. Twenty Hill Hollow is a fine illustration of a valley created by erosion of water. Here are no Washington columns, no angular El Capitans. The hollow cañons, cut in soft lavas, are not so deep as to require a single earthquake at the hands of science, much less a baker's dozen of those convenient tools demanded for the making of mountain Yosemites, and our moderate arithmetical standards are not outraged by a single magnitude of this simple, comprehensible hollow.

The present rate of denudation of this portion of the plain seems to be about one tenth of an inch per year. This approximation is based upon observations made upon stream-banks and perennial plants. Rains and winds remove mountains without disturbing their plant or animal inhabitants. Hovering petrels, the fishes and floating plants of ocean, sink and rise in beautiful rhythm with its waves; and, in like manner, the birds and plants of the plain sink and rise with these waves of land, the only difference being that the fluctuations are more rapid in the one case than in the other.

In March and April the bottom of the Hollow and every one of its hills are smoothly covered and plushed with yellow and purple flowers, the yellow predominating. They are mostly social *Compositæ*, with a few claytonias, gilias, eschscholtzias, white and yellow violets, blue and yellow lilies, dodecatheons, and eriogonums set in a half-floating maze of purple grasses. There is but one vine in the Hollow—the *Megarrhiza* [*Echinocystis* T. & D.] or "Big Root." The only bush within a mile of it, about four feet in height, forms so remark-able an object upon the universal smoothness that my dog barks furiously around it, at a cautious distance, as if it were a bear. Some of the hills have rock ribs that are brightly colored with red and yellow lichens, and in moist nooks there are luxuriant mosses—*Bartramia*, *Dicranum*, *Funaria*, and several *Hypnums*. In cool, sunless coves the mosses are companioned with ferns—a *Cystopteris* and the little gold-dusted rock fern, *Gymnogramma triangularis*.

The Hollow is not rich in birds. The meadow-lark homes there, and the little burrowing owl, the killdeer, and a species of sparrow. Occasionally a few ducks pay a visit to its waters, and a few tall herons—the blue and the white—may at times be seen stalking along the creek; and the sparrow hawk and gray eagle[13] come to hunt. The lark, who does nearly all the singing for the Hollow, is not identical in species with the meadowlark of the East, though closely resembling it; richer flowers and skies have inspired him with a better song than was ever known to the Atlantic lark.

[13] Mr. Muir doubtless meant the golden eagle (*Aquila chrysaëtos*).

I have noted three distinct lark-songs here. The words of the first, which I committed to memory at one of their special meetings, spelled as sung, are, "Wee-ro spee-ro wee-o weer-ly wee-it." On the 20th of January, 1869, they sang "Queed-lix boodle," repeating it with great regularity, for hours together, to music sweet as the sky that gave it. On the 22d of the same month, they sang "Chee chool cheedildy choodildy." An inspiration is this song of the blessed lark, and universally absorbable by human souls. It seems to be the only bird-song of these hills that has been created with any direct reference to us. Music is one of the attributes of matter, into whatever forms it may be organized. Drops and sprays of air are specialized, and made to plash and churn in the bosom of a lark, as infinitesimal portions of air plash and sing about the angles and hollows of sand-grains, as perfectly composed and predestined as the rejoicing anthems of worlds; but our senses are not fine enough to catch the tones. Fancy the waving, pulsing melody of the vast flower-congregations of the Hollow flowing from myriad voices of tuned petal and pistil, and heaps of sculptured pollen. Scarce one note is for us; nevertheless, God be thanked for this blessed instrument hid beneath the feathers of a lark.

The eagle does not dwell in the Hollow; he only floats there to hunt the long-eared hare. One day I saw a fine specimen alight upon a hillside. I was at first puzzled to know what power could fetch the sky-king down into the grass with the larks. Watching him attentively, I soon discovered the cause of his earthiness. He was hungry and stood watching a long-eared hare, which stood erect at the door of his burrow, staring his winged fellow mortal full in the face. They were about ten feet apart. Should the eagle attempt to snatch the hare, he would instantly disappear in the ground. Should long-ears, tired of inaction, venture to skim the hill to some neighboring burrow, the eagle would swoop above him and strike him dead with a blow of his pinions, bear him to some favorite rock table, satisfy his hunger, wipe off all marks of grossness, and go again to the sky.

Since antelopes have been driven away, the hare is the swiftest animal of the Hollow. When chased by a dog he will not seek a burrow, as when the eagle wings in sight, but skims wavily from hill to hill across connecting curves, swift and effortless as a bird-shadow. One that I measured was twelve inches in height at the shoulders. His body was eighteen inches, from nose-tip to tail. His great ears measured six and a half inches in length and two in width. His ears which, notwithstanding their great size, he wears gracefully and becomingly—have procured for him the homely nickname, by which he is commonly known, of "Jackass rabbit." Hares are very abundant over all the plain and up in the sunny, lightly wooded foothills, but their range does not extend into the close pine forests.

Coyotes, or California wolves, are occasionally seen gliding about the Hollow, but they are not numerous, vast numbers having been slain by the traps and poisons of sheep-raisers. The coyote is about the size of a small shepherd-dog, beautiful and graceful in motion, with erect ears, and a bushy tail, like a fox. Inasmuch as he is fond of mutton, he is cordially detested by "sheep-men" and nearly all cultured people.

The ground-squirrel is the most common animal of the Hollow. In several hills there is a soft stratum in which they have tunneled their homes. It is interesting to observe these rodent towns in time of alarm. Their one circular street resounds with sharp, lancing outcries of "Seekit, seek, seek, seekit!" Near neighbors, peeping cautiously half out of doors, engage in low, purring chat. Others, bolt upright on the doorsill or on the rock above, shout excitedly as if calling attention to the motions and aspects of the enemy. Like the wolf, this little animal is accursed, because of his relish for grain. What a pity that Nature should have made so many small mouths palated like our own!

All the seasons of the Hollow are warm and bright, and flowers bloom through the whole year. But the grand commencement of the annual genesis of plant and insect life is governed by the setting-in of the rains, in December or January. The air, hot and opaque, is then washed and cooled. Plant seeds, which for six months have lain on the ground dry as if garnered in a farmer's bin, at once unfold their treasured life. Flies hum their delicate tunes. Butterflies come from their coffins, like cotyledons from their husks. The network of dry water-courses, spread over valleys and hollows, suddenly gushes with bright waters, sparkling and pouring from pool to pool, like dusty mummies risen from the dead and set living and laughing with color and blood. The weather grows in beauty, like a flower. Its roots in the ground develop day-clusters a week or two in size, divided by and shaded in foliage of clouds; or round hours of ripe sunshine wave and spray in sky-shadows, like racemes of berries half hidden in leaves.

These months of so-called rainy season are not filled with rain. Nowhere else in North America, perhaps in the world, are Januarys so balmed and glowed with vital sunlight. Referring to my notes of 1868 and 1869, I find that the first heavy general rain of the season fell on the 18th of December. January yielded to the Hollow, during the day, only twenty hours of rain, which was divided among six rainy days. February had only three days on which rain fell, amounting to eighteen and one-half hours in all. March had five rainy days. April had three, yielding seven hours of rain. May also had three wet days, yielding nine hours of rain, and completed the so-called "rainy season" for that year, which is probably about an average one. It must be remembered that this rain record has nothing to do with what fell in the night.

The ordinary rainstorm of this region has little of that outward pomp and sublimity of structure so characteristic of the storms of the Mississippi Valley. Nevertheless, we have experienced rainstorms out on these treeless plains, in nights of solid darkness, as impressively sublime as the noblest storms of the mountains. The wind, which in settled weather blows from the northwest, veers to the southeast; the sky curdles gradually and evenly to a grainless, seamless, homogeneous cloud; and then comes the rain, pouring steadily and often driven aslant by strong winds. In 1869, more than three fourths of the winter rains came from the southeast. One magnificent storm from the northwest occurred on the 21st of March; an immense, round-browed cloud came sailing over the flowery hills in most imposing majesty, bestowing water as from a sea. The passionate rain-gush lasted only about one minute, but was nevertheless the most magnificent cataract of the sky mountains that I ever beheld. A portion of calm sky toward the Sierras was brushed with thin, white cloud-tissue, upon which the rain-torrent showed to a great height a cloud waterfall, which, like those of Yosemite, was neither spray, rain, nor solid water. In the same year the cloudiness of January, omitting rainy days, averaged 0.32; February, 0.13; March, 0.20; April, 0.10; May, 0.08. The greater portion of this cloudiness was gathered into a few days, leaving the others blocks of solid, universal sunshine in every chink and pore.

At the end of January, four plants were in flower: a small white cress, growing in large patches; a low-set, umbeled plant, with yellow flowers; an eriogonum, with flowers in leafless spangles; and a small boragewort. Five or six mosses had adjusted their hoods, and were in the prime of life. In February, squirrels, hares, and flowers were in springtime joy. Bright plant-constellations shone everywhere about the Hollow. Ants were getting ready for work, rubbing and sunning their limbs upon the husk-piles around their doors; fat, pollen-dusted, "burly, dozing humble-bees" were rumbling among the flowers; and spiders were busy mending up old webs, or weaving new ones. Flowers were born every day, and came gushing from the ground like gayly dressed children from a church. The bright air became daily more songful with fly-wings, and sweeter with breath of plants.

In March, plant-life is more than doubled. The little pioneer cress, by this time, goes to seed, wearing daintily embroidered silicles. Several claytonias appear; also, a large white leptosiphon[?], and two nemophilas. A small plantago becomes tall enough to wave and show silky ripples of shade. Toward the end of this month or the beginning of April, plant-life is at its greatest height. Few have any just conception of its amazing richness. Count the flowers of any portion of these twenty hills, or of the bottom of the Hollow, among the streams: you will find that there are from one to ten thousand upon every square yard, counting the heads of *Compositæ* as single flowers. Yellow *Compositæ* form by far the greater portion of this goldy-way. Well may the sun feed them with his richest light, for these shining sunlets are his very children—rays of his ray, beams of his beam! One would fancy that these California days receive more gold from the ground than they give to it. The earth has indeed become a sky; and the two cloudless skies, raying toward each other flower-beams and sun-beams, are fused and congolded into one glowing heaven. By the end of April most of the Hollow plants have ripened their seeds and died; but, undecayed, still assist the landscape with color from persistent involucres and corolla-like heads of chaffy scales.

In May, only a few deep-set lilies and eriogonums are left alive. June, July, August, and September are the season of plant rest, followed, in October, by a most extraordinary out-gush of plant-life, at the very driest time of the whole year. A small, unobtrusive plant, *Hemizonia virgata*, from six inches to three feet in height, with pale, glandular leaves, suddenly bursts into bloom, in patches miles in extent, like a resurrection of the gold of April. I have counted upward of three thousand heads upon one plant. Both leaves and pedicles are so small as to be nearly invisible among so vast a number of daisy golden-heads that seem to keep their places unsupported, like stars in the sky. The heads are about five eighths of an inch in diameter; rays and disk-flowers, yellow; stamens, purple. The rays have a rich, furred appearance, like the petals of garden pansies. The prevailing summer wind makes all the heads turn to the southeast. The waxy secretion of its leaves and involucres has suggested its grim name of "tarweed," by which it is generally known. In our estimation, it is the most delightful member of the whole Composite Family of the plain. It remains in flower until November, uniting with an eriogonum that continues the floral chain across December to the spring plants of January. Thus, although nearly all of the year's plant-life is crowded into February, March, and April, the flower circle around the Twenty Hill Hollow is never broken.

The Hollow may easily be visited by tourists *en route* for Yosemite, as it is distant only about six miles from Snelling's. It is at all seasons interesting to the naturalist; but it has little that would interest the majority of tourists earlier than January or later than April. If you wish to see how much of light, life, and joy can be got into a January, go to this blessed Hollow. If you wish to see a plant-resurrection,—myriads of bright flowers crowding from the ground, like souls to a judgment,—go to Twenty Hills in February. If you are traveling for health, play truant to doctors and friends, fill your pocket with biscuits, and hide in the hills of the Hollow, lave in its waters, tan in its golds, bask in its flower-shine, and your baptisms will make you a new creature indeed. Or, choked in the sediments of society, so tired of the world, here will your hard doubts disappear, your carnal incrustations melt off, and your soul breathe deep and free in God's shoreless atmosphere of beauty and love.

Never shall I forget my baptism in this font. It happened in January, a resurrection day for many a plant and for me. I suddenly found myself on one of its hills; the Hollow overflowed with light, as a fountain, and only small, sunless nooks were kept for mosseries and ferneries. Hollow Creek spangled and mazed like a river. The ground steamed with fragrance. Light, of unspeakable richness, was brooding the flowers. Truly, said I, is California the Golden State—in metallic gold, in sun gold, and in plant gold. The sunshine for a whole summer seemed condensed into the chambers of that one glowing day. Every trace of dimness had been washed from the sky; the mountains were dusted and wiped clean with clouds—Pacheco Peak and Mount Diablo, and the waved blue wall between; the grand Sierra stood along the plain, colored in four horizontal bands:—the lowest, rose purple; the next higher, dark purple; the next, blue; and, above all, the white row of summits pointing to the heavens.

It may be asked, What have mountains fifty or a hundred miles away to do with Twenty Hill Hollow? To lovers of the wild, these mountains are not a hundred miles away. Their spiritual power and the goodness of the sky make them near, as a circle of friends. They rise as a portion of the hilled walls of the Hollow. You cannot feel yourself out of doors; plain, sky, and mountains ray beauty which you feel. You bathe in these spirit-beams, turning round and round, as if warming at a camp-fire. Presently you lose consciousness of your own separate existence: you blend with the landscape, and become part and parcel of nature.

Printed at Repro India Ltd.